D1466289

THE
WRITER'S
MANUAL

THE WRITER'S MANUAL

Roy E. Porter

Arthur F. Gould

Arthur Gould, Sr.

Jack C. Dierks

Boyd B. Burnside

William R. Burnside

Madden Cassidy

Fred Hahn

Carole Fitzgerald Hayes

Lynda Hungerford

Dale Miller

Michael Springer

AN ETC PUBLICATION

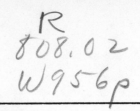

C | P

Library of Congress Cataloging in Publication Data

Main entry under title:

The Writer's Manual.

Bibliography: p.
Includes index.

1.   Authorship — Handbooks, manuals, etc.

I.   Cassidy, Madden.   II. Porter, Gould & Dierks.

PN145.W75   808'.02   75—43588
ISBN   0—88280—044—2 lib. bdg.
ISBN   0—88280—045—0 pbk.

Copyright © 1977 by ETC Publications
Palm Springs — California 92262

CONTENTS

INTRODUCTION

In the preparation of *The Writer's Manual,* it quickly became evident some duplication would be mandatory. For instance, Carole Hayes could not ignore some discussion of style in the writing of academic writing and university presses. A treatment of this area was essential to the over-all subject. Similarly, style is necessary in the writing concerned with the juvenile field, the novel, historical fiction, in fact, any of the general subject areas. Of course, style had to be treated more definitively in Jack Dierks'section by that name, nor could it go uncovered in Boyd and William Burnside's section on composition.

The decision was finally made in terms of the user: to make the general subject area meaningful, as an individual unit of the writing craft, but not necessarily definitive. Other reference works are constantly cited by the individual contributors, as sources that are useful for those who require exhaustive coverage. Our concern, therefore, was to cover the needs of the writer, without subjecting him to references that appear in other sections of the manual. We depend on the index to alert the reader to other sections where a particular point may be covered, sometimes in a way that has bearing on another particular problem, sometimes in a more exhaustive treatment.

No effort was made to bring all contributors into agreement on the use of his/hers in the text. However, we were all mindful of the footnote in Fred Hahn's section, "Throughout this text, 'he' and 'his' are used as neuter pronouns. When sex is indeterminate, the masculine embraces the feminine ——
Mrs. Woolf, 6th-grade teacher."

Although the major portion of *The Writer's Manual* was written during 1973 and 1974, much of what the reader will find here is the product of a wide range of experience in all aspects of the writing field. The authors have published features, poetry, scripts, short stories, novellas, reviews, books, and both professional and popular articles. Additionally, they have worked in publishing, as editors, as newspaper staff writers, editors of journals, readers and consultants. Five of the writers have had experience in author's agency work at the partnership level. Three others have served as agency manuscript readers or, as we prefer to think of them, as agency consultants. Six of the contributors have taught at the college or university level for long periods of time and others lecture or appear as speakers to various groups in writing and publishing. The writing of *The Writer's Manual,* therefore, is drawn from a wide range of agenting, writing, teaching and publishing experience.

Upon examining the existing literature which deals with the writing process one is struck by the fact that it has almost all been done by practicing writers. As a result we are left with a good deal of advice on what goes into print which is unfortunately once removed from the selection process itself. There are a fair number of books written by publishers and editors, but inevitably these tend to reflect the experience of time spent with a particular publishing house, or, perhaps two or three at most. Even the largest and best of publishers, no matter how general the book list may be, reflects a particular image, and the editor or publisher coming out of such a background is limited to that experience. The number of books written by authors' agents is thin indeed. For that reason, *The Writer's Manual* was conceived, a comprehensive book on all the major areas of writing, by people who work widely with all areas of writing and publishing in the United States and abroad.

There is a second purpose that has guided the creation of *The Writer's Manual.* The emphasis, at all times, is to offer advice and direction for the new writer while keeping in mind the established writer's needs. The writer who has managed to publish a half dozen major magazine pieces, perhaps a book or two, begins to get attention at the editor level that the new writer cannot command. Yet, it is the new writer that requires the most help and guidance if acceptance of a manuscript is to follow. As Madden Cassidy poses the problem in his section, "The British Apprentice," how many of today's Kafkas, Joyces or Katherine Mansfields or Faulkners are overlooked simply because the author's name isn't known or because the selection process of manuscripts is badly handled? We will never know. Emily Dickinson represented the writer's fragile ego in the extreme, yet, she wrote her fey cries for help to Thomas Wentworth Higginson, hoping for encouragement, hoping he would use his contacts at *The Atlantic Monthly* to test what she was writing and prove that she was worthy. She never knew that satisfaction during her lifetime. Other such examples have been told and retold in writing and publishing. Recently, several books have been published detailing the anguish and rebuff writers can encounter as they work at their craft. No matter how self-serving such books may be, they deserve attention and people in publishing who are responsible for changes should be grateful these ideas are being presented. (See Bruce Cook's "Wide Wide World of Books," *National Observer*, Jan. 20, 1975).

Of course the economics of publishing must be considered. Publishing is a business and even the subsidized University Press that has failed to show profit has learned the harsh reality of that fact in the recent economic crunch. Hopefully, we are done with that, but, at this writing, it still is a matter for hope as we enter the new year, 1977. As a result, vanity presses have taken to radio and newspaper advertising, preying on the weakness of the market condition. Increasingly, smallish printers honestly, or dishonestly, encourage private publication where little happens when the author becomes published. Smaller publishers ask for financial contributions to publication, and not infrequently succeed in getting such subsidies. Large publishers announce they will no longer accept supplemental books in the professional fields, and some announce indefinite moratoriums on certain types of new manuscripts because of the uncertainty of market conditions. Novel writers begin to develop cooperative publishing efforts where their books are published at their expense, but where the profits, if any, are shared in larger returns than normal royalty brings.

Some of these developments will surely make contributions to publishing. Others will languish and disappear. Old hands continue to berate vanity publishing while such outlets continue to prosper, ever writing glowing reports on manuscripts which, for the most part, cannot survive in the commercial side of publishing. Private publishing, ranging from scholarly works with very limited marketability to family genealogies and histories continue to pour off the presses and, in many instances, make the scholarly field richer and the family record more permanent. Private publishing always has had its place and, for a variety of reasons, continues to flourish — marking the contribution of people who live out their lives and prefer to pay a printer to set the record down rather than a psychiatrist's counseling fees.

All such authorship can benefit from studying *The Writer's Manual.* Fred Hahn, who writes "Promoting the Book," offers some frank advice on how books are brought to the public's attention. But, it is the writer who is thinking of commercial publication that we are mainly addressing, the writer who dares to test their mettle against that elusive element, public taste.

Any writer of a novel, a biography or historical fiction will find Dale Miller's and Michael Springer's script writing section far more than instruction in that process. Although this section is basically intended to teach how scripts should be written and serves that purpose well, it also is included to provide the writer with some idea of how conception, at the writing level, frequently determines whether a movie sale is possible.

No editor or agent is more disappointed than after he has spent limited and valuable reading time on a manuscript which employs competent writing ability only to realize the writer has failed to handle plot or characterization adequately. Some patience in learning those skills, first, makes all the difference. Yet, writers, by some improvident urge, turn the paper into the typewriter and begin writing, convinced they can ignore mechanics and still make the best seller lists. An established writer may well get away with that approach; the beginner needs all the assistance he can muster.

Anyone considering the writing of a novel will do well to study Arthur F. Gould's section on the short story and the novel. They are entirely different forms and being able to work in one does not assure you can write in the other. Many a novel is conceived when, at best, it is but a short story stretched beyond its limits. Similarly, his section on poetry will raise awareness of how concentrated word choice is used in the writing of poetry and, in that awareness, focus attention on economy of word use in the writing of good prose or give the writer some idea of lyrical expression that can heighten style and contribute elegance in expression.

No one can divine a precise path to follow in the learning of good writing. It is too personal, too much dependent on the inner wellsprings of personality, experience and ability. However, granting the presence of some degree of ability to perceive and communicate ideas, there is no question that the learning of writing techniques will enhance a writer's publication prospects. In that respect, any writer will find merit in studying *The Writer's Manual.* The sections on professional writing by Carole Hayes and that on term papers, theses and dissertations by Lynda Hungerford are valuable for their basic intent. At the same time, they serve to point out that writing aimed at professional publication has its special place and need, but it does not follow that it will serve the needs of the popular markets. Many a manuscript has been conceived to serve both markets. It is one thing to be read because the material is assigned reading; it is quite another to be read by reader choice which dominates the popular markets.

Roy Porter's section on juvenile publishing will make it clear that the writing of books for children is not the simple task many writers consider it to be. More carefully selected and edited at the editorial level, juvenile writing is one of the most demanding forms of writing.

Jack Dierks' non-fiction section and Carole Hayes' historical fiction are interesting to compare, back to back, for any writer. Both are rich in instruction, in practical, analytical terms that differentiate between the two genres.

Arthur Gould Sr.'s shorts and articles section is the product of a writer who has published widely in this area as well as in the novella and short story form. He also has taught tens of thousands at Northwestern University's Medill School of Journalism where he has served as a professor.

Lastly, but significantly, there is Jack Dierks' style section and Boyd and William Burnside composition section. Anyone who intends to write, anyone who is writing, will find them useful areas to study and re-study from time to time and as a constant source to turn to during the writing process.

Good writing is an art. It is understandable why many writers compare their work to that of the musician for just as it is the unity of purpose that makes for effective musical composition, it is no less the case in writing. Some of us are given to hearing the seven notes of the scale. Others listen and hear a variety of tonal qualities the seven primary notes suggest. It is in the latter talent that the difference occurs, in the construction of elegant, well structured writing that communicates and touches the reader so that he responds to an inner reaction that guides and activates his own insights and emotional responses. It is a case of John Keats' observation in "Ode On A Grecian Urn" which Arthur F. Gould uses in his poetry section: "Heard melodies are sweet, but those unheard are sweeter."

Roy E. Porter

Arthur F. Gould

Jack C. Dierks

Boyd B. Burnside

William Burnside

The Writer's Manual
Book 1

The Mechanics
of
Writing and
Getting
Published

By
Roy E. Porter

ABOUT THE AUTHOR

Roy E. Porter
writes out of a wide background in the publishing field.
After study at the University of Chicago,
he worked for twenty years with Rand McNally & Company
in a variety of administrative capacities,
organized and headed an institutional trade book department
in which all company products were represented,
including maps, globes, and atlases.
Eventually he headed the adult trade book department
as senior editor,
a position he held until becoming a partner
in Chicago's largest authors' agency, Max Siegel and Associates.
At the founder's death, he reorganized the agency as
Porter, Gould & Dierks and serves as president of the firm.

CONTENTS

        Publisher's Information Sheet
        Author's Information Form
        Publisher's Book Contracts
        Preparing the Index
        Proofreading the Manuscript
        Release Form
        All About Copyright

ACKNOWLEDGEMENTS

Use of Dorothy Aldis' acknowledgement section

from *Miss Quinn's Secret;*

a portion of the text from *Miss Quinn's Secret;*

the poems "Wasp" and "I'm Hiding";

and the quotes from *Ride the Wild Waves*

are reprinted here with the permission

of the copyright holder, Mary Cornelia Aldis Porter.

INTRODUCTION

If anyone could divine where writing begins, and be accurate, the world would beat a path to his door, so quickly, so overwhelmingly, the poor creature would have no time to eat or sleep. An idea for a manuscript can crop up from almost any incident or suggestion and go on to become number one of next year's best seller list. How it is nurtured and eventually developed into the written word is as imprecise a process as can be imagined. But, once it settles into the author's thinking, a complicated sequence of events is unleashed, and if the author stays the course, does the spade work well, acceptance, and even success, is sure to follow.

Perhaps the worst problem for the new author is impatience. It takes more than desire to write well. It takes more than conviction and will power, too. However, without all three -- desire, conviction and will power -- each playing its part, and each in proper balance, not much can happen at the writing stage. In addition, there is a matter of ability to write, the insights and perceptions of the writer, whether the subject matter is timely and a catalog of other talents and considerations that is, perhaps, indefinable in the final analysis. What works for one author will not work for anyone else. And this is the fascination of it all, for no one has all the answers.

Good writing must be self-taught. Nothing happens on paper until some-one rubs the right combination of words together about an idea that interests other people. When this happens, little can stem the tide and something quite personal and individualistic takes over to guide the effort. It can happen under the most tragic of circumstances, or at the pinnacle of joy; to someone unexposed to formal education or to someone that has rarely ventured far beyond the ivory towers. Mechanics can be taught, of course, and new authors profit from attending writers' conferences or writers' workshops, but, in the final analysis, nothing will happen until all this is assimilated and used to the proper end.

It is easy to understand why impatience often develops. The working author must cut himself off from all that tempts other people, face the typewriter, alone and, largely, unaided. The drive to accomplish is no less in the author than in anyone else. He works toward the moment when the manuscript is finished, whether it is the first or the thirty-first, to get it off to an editor who will confirm, hopefully, what the author believes -- that what he has been creating is good and publishable.

If you are just beginning to write, merely thinking about the prospect, or trying to improve your writing ability, "The Mechanics of Writing and Getting Published" is intended to help you. Read it through, quickly. As points that apply to you are read, make notes of them so you can probe deeper, later. After the first reading, go over your notes and add to them while the material is fresh in your mind. Give the material your best time -- the first thing in the morning, if that is when you function best, or during the early part of the evening if you are a P.M. person. Don't read the book in bits and pieces, and don't read it when you have had an exhausting day. Perhaps, for the first exposure, that will be enough. If you are seriously committed to writing, you will find ideas banging around in your thinking as you sit in a P.T.A. meeting, swab the floor, mow the lawn, weed the garden flower beds, or play nine holes of golf. A bit of "think-time" always helps. If you are a verbal type, discuss it with interested acquaintances, keeping the mind open to suggestion and tentative conclusions. However, if you do consult with anyone else, be certain you know when to listen and discard, as well as when to appropriate. There is a great difference in these two positions and many authors tend to turn to someone with whom they are comfortable, where a bit of discomfort is really what is needed. No one can really direct you in this pursuit, but it is essential that you search out competence, of the calibre you need.

When you feel you have absorbed this first quick reading period, choose a span of time when you can go back to the book and *study* it. Linger over points that apply most to you, and be sure you understand the text clearly. Use the notes you have on hand, and amplify them, as you proceed with your study work. Some sections will interest you less at this reading, but don't ignore them entirely, even if you think you are already proficient in that area. During this period, you should begin to evolve an approach to your writing that best fits you. You may have devised solutions that work well for you, but you should pick and discard, as you lay down the basics for writing the manuscript you have in mind.

If you feel unsure about your approaches at this point, perhaps a third study session is in order. Should that be the case, tackle it again, until you know how you want to begin. We all know the story of the opera diva who settled in Rome after achieving fame. Not infrequently, she appeared in roles at the Rome Opera, but she had grown callous with the assurance of success and her voice began to show it. She didn't practice as regularly as she once did, didn't keep in schedule, luxuriated in her acceptance and forgot how hard she had once worked to achieve it. The Italians love their opera and are exuberant about their approval, and disapproval. One night, when she was singing a very difficult aria, she reached up for the climatic note and sang it sharp. None the less, the audience went wild with applause and cried for an encore. The diva obliged, repeating a chorus of the same selection, and once again, she sang the last note sharp. The audience again went wild, but when the tumult was over, a voice from the top gallery cried out, "Sing it again. Sing it again and again, until you know it."

When that moment comes where you feel sure of your approach, that is the time to begin writing, and not before. Many authors have quivering egos, contrary to romantic notions about author arrogance. You are not alone in your insecurities, but if you can avoid arrogance, all the better -- for the agents and editors that you will have to deal with some day, not to mention those who have to live around you.

CHAPTER ONE

TOOLS AND WRITING HINTS

There are few preoccupations that compare with the act of writing when it comes to the question of demand on the individual and personal involvement. Such total commitment as writing requires, perhaps, brings the writer to a confrontation of self more keenly than most human acts and, therefore, it is no wonder that this personal involvement also spawns notions about the proper approach to writing, the use of tools of the trade, and, of course, devices and attitudes as to how all this is carried out. Personality and temperament compound the process, and creativity also adds its dimension of complication.

The purpose of "The Mechanics of Writing and Getting Published" is to provide a check-list of accepted approaches that have evolved in order for the writer to present written material in a form that will elicit the most favorable reaction to it on the part of an editor.

A harried University of Chicago humanities teacher who had assigned a four page theme stalked into the classroom and plunked the class effort down on her desk. Then, with all the venom she could muster, turned to the class and laid down the law. "Whether you write with a nub of a # 2 pencil wrapped in your toes, sitting in a filled bath-tub, using lined, legal sized note pads, is of no concern to me. If you have devised such a solution to writing, so be it. But, I want an assigned theme typed on unlined, 8½ x 11 inch, white paper, in nothing less than a 20 # stock. I want it typed in a good, bold print, and I don't want the e's and the a's to be such blobs of ink that you can't tell one from the other. A typewriter brush is cheap. Get one, and use it, often. I want the title of the theme centered on a title page, with your name three spaces below it. The text should begin on the second page, but is numbered page one, and the first paragraph should be sunk to one third of the depth of the page. The margin on the left should measure an inch and a quarter and the right hand margin should match it. Allow the same margin at the foot of the page. Paper is cheap. Use a good stick eraser and make any corrections neatly. If you must make an editing change after you have typed the theme in final form, re-do the page — don't mark up a line with diagonals and squeeze in a new phrase and expect me to be impressed. I won't be. Number all the pages in the upper right hand corner. Double space the text. Use a dictionary for proper word use and correct spelling. If you can't organize your thoughts in your mind, outline everything you write and then follow it. When a theme is due, it is your responsibility to turn it in on time. I have no time to listen to excuses, unless they are legitimate and extenuating. I have had the points I have just made mimeographed. You may have a copy of them, as you pick up your paper at the end of the class. Most are ungraded. If yours is one of them, have it corrected according to these instructions and return it to me when the second theme is due, next week. If you think I am being harsh, think for a moment that your class is but one of many I teach, that I have been teaching humanities classes for over fifteen years, that I read each and every one of your papers and must assign a fair grade to it. All this must be done within the work day, and I have but one brain and two eyes to help me get it done". With that, she launched into class work.

In many respects, the humanities teacher was reacting like an editor. Editors have invested perhaps years of preparation before being appointed to such a position. They have spent time in evaluating manuscripts, not only for literary merit, but for marketability. Most of their day, surely their evenings and week ends, are spent in reading manuscripts. And, they do this with "one brain and two eyes." How then can the writer improve the odds, so that a particular manuscript will be received under the most favorable circumstances? The answer lies in the tools used and the mechanical approaches for manuscript preparation. Let's begin then with *supplies and tools.*

Let's assume literary merit, that you have something worthwhile to write and that you are either learning how to accomplish that or have sufficient training to begin writing. Any good stationery store will have a variety of paper choices to offer. Choose a good, white bond, with 25% rag content. Avoid crinkled papers, except for onion skin or seconds. Consider your own eyes and feelings about reading a carbon as you make this investment. A smooth, second sheet, you'll find, is easier to handle, to file, and takes carbon well. The answer does not rest in paying for expensive paper. Good bond, or seconds, can be of an inexpensive grade, particularly when you are working out first drafts. Finished drafts, which you expect to offer for publication, may require something higher priced.

Most writers believe in what they are doing or they would not have begun writing. Don't be naive about this. It is pleasing to offer a manuscript for sale and make it on the first exposure. But, in the practical world of publishing, such sales are often the exception. You can submit your manuscript to four or five editors, perhaps even more, and still not get a sale. At the end of five submissions, a manuscript begins to show signs of circulation or exposure. An editor is mindful of this evidence, and often subjectively conditioned by it. Give your work the best possible break. Present it in the best possible way, so that it looks fresh and inviting. Using a good, white bond, with a 25% rag content is a prudent investment. It will stand up to several submissions and not look circulated.

No editor, unlike the humanities teacher, insists on paper of a particular weight. Some writers, erroneously cost conscious, will use 13 and 16 pound paper stock, and some can even get away with 9 #. A brilliantly written manuscript would, with the right editor, be willingly read if it were typed on brown, commercial paper toweling. But, are you certain your talents lie in those rather heady regions? Be practical about how you are using your time, and improve your opportunity of getting an editor's time and best attention. Place in the editor's hands the best possible effort you can devise. A 16 # paper stock will do; a 20 # stock will do even better.

If you do not know how to type, begin to learn. Writing in longhand, on yellow, legal pads is time consuming. Eventually you have to face up to getting it all put in type and getting a good typist to work with longhand only compounds the expense. Most good typists will charge by the hour to type from longhand, and many add a premium to their normal costs, or even refuse such typing assignments. Furthermore, it adds to the chance for error even if your handwriting is clear and legible. A typist, wanting to make time, can easily misread a word that may not be caught even in careful proofing.

If you do not own a typewriter, be cautious about making that investment. Perhaps, practically, it would be wise to pick up a second hand model, when you are first learning to type, then make a change to a more expensive model once you have developed the skill. Newspapers often list them for sale in the want-ad section and if you live in or around a college or university, stationery stores often run special sales of second hand equipment when the fall term begins. Take your time in making your choice. Try a portable, but don't over-look a good standard. Choose a bold faced type. Small type may allow you to get more words to the line, but it is a false economy in the long run. Think of the editor who will have to read your manuscript. Editors prefer large, clean type when reading manuscript. Small type is tiring to the eye, distracting to the mind. Think selfishly about this and you will probably make better choices in what you buy. Be careful in buying an electric, if you do not possess good manual dexterity. They do, however, provide a clear, easy to read manuscript page, if the type face is sufficiently large.

Typewriter maintenance is simple, for the most part. Learn to keep your typewriter covered. A clean cloth will do in the absence of a commercial cover. Stationery stores carry a range of plastic covers for this purpose. If you use a portable, it will usually come with a removable top, at the hinge; get in the habit of using it when you finish typing. It will save maintenance costs, protect your machine from dust, and also keep your ribbon from drying out prematurely.

Watch your typing for proper type alignment. If you develop such difficulty, don't try to correct it yourself. Take it to a good typewriter repairman. Your stationery store usually knows who can service typewriters. Depending on the volume you type, and the degree to which you make corrections, bits of the eraser fall into the machine and you will have to have the typewriter cleaned from time to time. Always keep your typewriter in top condition. It controls a great deal of the effect you are trying to create — a neatly presented product.

Buy a stick eraser and choose one that can be used for both carbon and ink; one end used for carbon (a softer, conventional looking brick color) and typewriter ink on the other, (a harder type, and white) each end being sharpened in a pencil sharpener. A piece of art gum is useful in removing smudges that may occur, and, unless you are unusually neat in making corrections, a plastic guard for making erasures is a helpful tool. They come with a variety of hole sizes so that you can lay the guard on the typewriter paper and avoid erasing anything but that which is intended. You will need a stiff typewriter brush to keep the keys clean. Use it often. If you watch the condition of the small letters e and a, you will soon know when the brush must come into action. A hat-pin or beaded head pin, such as is used for pinning on a corsage, is a good implement to have handy in cleaning those keys that clog up with ribbon ink most. A brush can then be used to dispense with the accumulation. There are a number of plastic type cleaners on the market, a block of gummy material that can be stretched and pushed into shapes. They are helpful in cleaning typewriter keys, once the ink on the keys has been loosened up by brushing. This material is also a great boon in making corrections. Simply press it over the type on the page, once or twice, and the ink disappears. Fluid type cleaners tend to deposit a gummy residue on the type faces adding to rather than removing the problem.

Note pad paper is necessary in making corrections in carbons. A piece should be slipped between the carbon during erasing, to avoid a messy carbon copy. Considering the amount of fourth class mail that pours into the average household these days, you might want to consider collecting the 8 x 11 inch size, when one side is unprinted, in the lid of a box from typewriter paper. An inexpensive paper cutter will reduce it to a size that can be kept on the desk without adding to clutter.

If you ask for midnight black carbon paper in your stationery store, you may be confronted with a variety of choices. Some types are more durable than others and you will have to experiment with what suits you most. Bear in mind, a good bold carbon can be a great time saver. Should the original of your manuscript get lost in the mails or in making a submission, a good carbon can be used, in these days of copying machines, to provide you with a good substitute for the original. Editors prefer to read an original, typed manuscript as they feel it is not active to other publishing sources at the same time, but they increasingly accept a clear copy made on a copying machine.

Carbon paper is expensive, but it is a false economy to use a sheet until it no longer provides a good, readable copy. Buy the smallest package you can, until you are satisfied that you have found the right brand. Larger packages, not adequately wrapped to preserve freshness, can dry out and will wear out quicker.

It is essential that any author must have a good dictionary available. Be sure it is the latest edition. Technology, medicine and finance, to name but a few, have contributed substantially to the language, but slang and dialect have also had their influence. For desk use *Webster's Collegiate* is a good selection. Follow it, consistently, for spelling, capitalization and usage. It is not amiss to own an unabridged dictionary, although it need not be an initial investment. The back-matter of either is very helpful to the author, containing a wealth of information in accessible, concise form. It can also be used for synonyms and antonyms and idiomatic phrases.

Use of a good thesaurus is almost inescapable for a good stylist. In using a dictionary, you begin by looking up a word and its meaning. In using a thesaurus, you look up the idea in the index. There you will find listed the closest synonyms and a numerical designation. Turn to the numerical reference and you will find listed many other synonyms and associated words. Work to enrich your writing style, constantly. Using a dictionary and a thesaurus is one way to assure this. Elizabeth Bowen, known for a fine sense of writing style had a remarkable grasp of the language. Howard Moss, writing about her in a *New York Times Book Review* section speculates her vocabulary developed out of a need to overcome a stutter. She learned synonyms in order to choose words that were less difficult to pronounce and in so doing, enriched her command of vocabulary so marked in her writing.

With some of these problems settled, you are better prepared to set to work on writing the manuscript itself.

CHAPTER TWO

TYPING THE MANUSCRIPT

Publishers increasingly ask for two copies of a full length book manuscript upon acceptance. A standard typewriter will give you an original and two bold copies without any difficulty, if you use a good carbon paper. Articles and short stories can be typed in an original and one copy.

Get in the habit of making a file copy of any manuscript, and be sure you keep it in a safe place. Should you ever produce a manuscript without making a copy, make a duplicate by using a copy machine before making any submission. Even then, it is risky and can result in time squandered needlessly if a portion gets lost or misplaced. No publishing source is responsible for the loss of a manuscript while it is in their possession. They do, in every reasonable manner, take precautions to avoid loss of a manuscript, but in the case of accidental loss, through fire or some other uncontrollable factor, the writer is expected to have a copy of his work in his possession.

Do not begin typing the final draft until you are sure you have worked out all the writing problems. There may come a time when you will not have to revise manuscripts as extensively as when you first begin writing, but this usually comes after some seasoning or experience. Concentrate on re-work and revising before you begin to type the final draft, then put all your energies into the typing. If you simply have to make additional changes at this point, it will be wiser to put additional time into the writing and set the typing aside until that has been worked out. To be sure, minor changes are likely to come to you every time you work with or read a manuscript. Nothing is ever in a pure state and improvement in writing is always possible. Working out major changes in the final draft may prove distracting enough that the typing will show it.

The first page of the short story or article manuscript should carry the author's name and address in the upper left corner. Establish all margins at this point and carry them over to all other pages of the manuscript. An example appears in illustrated form.

Rancid Slob   3,500 words
8257 Central Blvd.
Skokie, Illinois 60680

The Man With The Mop of Grey Hair

By

Geoffrey Older

Begin typing the text some five or six spaces below the author's name. Indent the first line not less than five spaces and not more than ten, and maintain the same form in typing all other pages. Typing must be double spaced. Never use both sides of the sheet for typing a manuscript.

In book manuscript typing, the procedure is more elaborate. It is customary, and expected, to use a title page and a Table of Contents. Other preliminary pages, such as dedication, foreword and/or preface, and acknowledgements can be supplied later, and as needed. Footnotes, where required, should accompany the original manuscript and should appear on a separate page following the page to which they relate. Although footnotes are essential to manuscript assessment, illustrations or tables may not be and, for the author's own protection, originals should not be included in seeking publisher interest. Supplying illustrations and tables, often a costly and time consuming undertaking, while soliciting publisher interest may result in loss or damage that will later require duplication. In the case of text that depends heavily on the use of illustration, where proper manuscript appraisal cannot be made except in supplying them, it is wise to handle and package them in a way that will insure easy care when they are being handled at the publisher level. Although editorial personnel are mindful that a manuscript is a costly investment on the author's part, often a matter of hundreds of dollars in typing costs and material, there is no assurance anyone else will treat your creation with the tender care that you may provide. Editors and publishers' readers are human, and they represent all the short-comings common to any other segment of people. Like the clinician in a hospital admitting office, they sometimes become insensitive to the author's investment for no conscious reasons except that familiarity breeds contempt. Plan your handling of a manuscript in such a way that you can avoid improper handling whenever possible.

Some authors, mindful of their time investment, type their full name, on the upper left hand corner of each manuscript page, and some even include the title of the manuscript. Although not required for manuscript submission, you may want to consider it. Should you decide to use the title on each page, it should appear in the upper right hand corner, at least two spaces below the page number. Three or four spaces below this, the text should begin.

When illustrations or photography are submitted with a manuscript, each piece should be identified and your name should appear on the back-side. Since a photograph can be marred to such an extent that it cannot be used for reproduction without being touched up if you write on the back of it -- for instance, using a ballpoint pen which causes an impression beyond the ink deposited -- it is always wise to type such information on a separate sheet of paper and attach it to the back with a piece of masking tape. An example of handling might be:

Garden illustration, chapter 1, ms. page 10
The Man With the Mop of Grey Hair
By
Geoffrey Older

As you complete each typed page, place it in the lid of the box from which your typing paper came or in a clean letter-size file box. Cover the manuscript with a clean cloth when you are not typing or working in order to protect it. You will also find it an organized way to refer to a previous page or to some portion of the manuscript. Picking the box up in the right hand, you can turn the contents out on the palm of the left hand, simply by turning it over in a flipping motion.

The manuscript is primarily the author's responsibility. It should be the final draft of what he intends to communicate and through it he pleads his case with all the support, reason and ability he can command. The publishing of a book is a long and complicated process. Proper planning at the typing of the manuscript stage can determine how smoothly the book moves into production and avoid exasperating delays or future difficulties.

Although few authors ever become involved in the production and manufacturing aspect of publication, a general knowledge of these procedures will help avoid pitfalls that might unknowingly be created in the manner in which a manuscript is handled. You will also find treatment of technicalities commonly used in publishing in other sections in *The Writer's Manual.*

If your manuscript carries an introduction, it may well have been the last portion of the manuscript to be written. Authors vary in how they approach the introduction. A good introduction, well worked out, can be the keel from which you work. In other instances, it is only generally formed in the author's mind and he will go back and revise it, completing it once he has marshalled all his persuasion in the writing of the manuscript. Whatever your approach, it does follow the table of contents page and is a part of the text for purposes of numbering the manuscript pages. The introduction, when used, should establish the main subject or over-all thrust of the discourse. Publishing house style sometimes dictates fine lines between what is considered an introduction or a preface, and sometimes the terms are used interchangeably. Where the editor differentiates, acknowledgements usually are expected to be part of the preface. Acknowledgements can, however, also be considered as a separate section, again, depending on publishing house style, as a portion of the preliminaries. On the other hand, a foreword should never be confused with the term preface. A foreword is always part of the preliminaries, short and introductory in tone, but written by a person other than the author.

Bibliography or references are always considered back matter and should appear in that order in preparing the manuscript, and numbered in proper page sequence.

The index can be the responsibility of the author and, in such a case, is expressly cited as such in the publisher's contract. Good indexing is a specialized talent and might better be left to the specialist. Depending on your temperament, you may find it intriguing work and not want to chance it to someone else. Again, *The Writer's Manual,* provides guidance in index preparation.

Sometimes a publisher establishes index contacts and prefers to have the work done under the publisher's supervision. Since indexing takes place at the stage when page proofs become available, it must be done promptly if a production schedule is to be maintained. Therefore, for the novice, it is probably unwise to attempt his own index, even though the publisher will either expect the author to pay such costs out of pocket, as is the case in some instances, or have the work commissioned by the publisher, paid for and charged back to the author's royalty income.

A book that requires intensive research, such as some books of non-fiction, provides the author with, or develops the author's ability for handling minutiae. If you prefer to do your own index, it will be wise to begin setting up file cards containing index material you will want to include, working from the copy of your manuscript, once a publisher indicates interest in publishing your manuscript, and assuming no extensive revisions are required. When page proofs arrive, it will then be a matter of working with your cards and adding the proper page, or pages, that apply. In the interest of proper use of your time investment, it is not wise to invest in such preliminary work, until publication is assured.

Running heads and copyright information are supplied by the publisher. Caption legends are prepared by the author. They should be typed on separate sheets of paper and placed in an envelope with the illustration to which they pertain. Do not tape them to the illustration. They are set in type in the print shop while the illustrations are converted into plates for printing. Never use paper clips in attaching legends to illustrations, particularly photographs, as they cause damage in shipping and handling.

The condition of any manuscript is important to its acceptance. Editors naturally think about "their list" or "their books." A critical review, referring to some aspect of publication that could have been avoided in handling does not sit well with an editor, nor add to his status. Most publishers will have a manuscript proofed to avoid errors. However, editors also expect the author to read galleys for the very same reason. A meticulously typed manuscript suggests a proof reading capability on the part of an author and if an editor believes he can expect this ability in working with a manuscript, it does make a difference in what is chosen for publication. Similarly, a publisher's reader will take this dimension into consideration in favorably recommending a manuscript. Beyond this point, a neat manuscript makes its way through handling with much less difficulty, in editing, and type setting, in particular, but also influences design and proofreading. Badly prepared copy compounds the problem of handling and may result in a pricing that will work to the finished book's disadvantage.

All manuscript text, both front matter or back matter, must be typed in double space form. Avoid using erasable bonds of any kind. Margins and double spacing are intended for editing needs. A manuscript passes through many hands before it reaches the buyer's book shelf. Erasable bonds soon smear and smudge making handling more than risky.

In a day when numerous copying devices are available, it is well to keep in mind the quality of the copy produced. Machine copies, such as xerox, are often preferred for duplicate manuscript copies. Be sure the machine is operating properly and produces a copy that is reasonably close to the original. Light reproduction or production on a machine type that uses paper other than regular bond is difficult to handle in the publishing process and should be avoided. Sensitized paper does not stack readily and it is difficult to get it to remain in squared or trim edges. It also tends to adhere and is difficult to separate one sheet from another. Some papers carry a lingering odor for months before it is dissipated. Finally, the paper tends to be brittle, shreds at the edges and can cause paper cuts. Some editors will overlook such impositions, but why chance it that you may be read by one who won't?

In using quotations, the quoted material must appear within the quotes. Short quotations constitute no problem. Longer quotes, that may run to several paragraphs, should be preceded by quotation marks before the first word quoted, as well as in the first word of each paragraph quoted, and again at the end of the last word quoted. Do not use quotation marks at the end of each paragraph quoted, except for the last one. An example follows:

Notice the author's freshness exhibited in the acknowledgements section when she writes,
"I just cannot imagine what I would have done without the companionship and generosity of Mrs. Flora W. Humphrey and Mrs. Belle D. Stepleton, who works at the Vevay library, but left their labors long enough to go up into the hills with me and find the Wright's log cabin. Miss Annette Danglade and Miss Knox came along on that exciting trip.

"Captain and Mrs. Leon Ash not only gave me all the information about boats in this book, but certainly one of the nicest times I ever had.

"Miss Mary Lamb and Uncle Billy Patton told me wonderful stories."

Quotations may be omitted in book print, if the quoted material is indented and run as a block of print and set off from the remainder of the text. However, in manuscript preparation, quotations are always used

All quoted material should receive the utmost care in presenting it in the manuscript. It is always wise to use primary rather than secondary sources so that possible printing errors can be avoided. A writer has every right to be quoted accurately and as your writing finds its way into printed form, you will begin to appreciate how keenly a writer feels about this point.

Quotations also beg the question of copyright questions and permissions. Another writer's work, appearing in print without the proper use of copyright, may cause the material to fall into the public domain. In that event, it is a proper basis for a suit against the offending writer who is liable for securing proper copyright citation for any writing protected by copyright. The copyright law is ambiguous, perhaps rightly so. For instance, use of quoted material in a book review is considered "fair use," without securing permission to quote. Where the book critic is permitted use of copyrighted material in this sense, it does not follow that another writer can without securing proper publisher permission. As a rule of thumb, fifty words or less is generally considered fair use of copyrighted material, without paying a permission fee. However, if you wish to avoid problems later -- and it is a matter of courtesy to the writer you quote -- secure a written permission. A particularly cogent passage of writing may constitute the substance of a writer's point and even one short sentence then has to be considered in a totally different light. The only sure protection the user has is to secure a permission to quote from the source holding the copyright. In the event the material is copyrighted in the name of the author, the publisher may refer you to that source. If the copyright holder is not agented, the delay may be endless, and perfectly within the right of the copyright holder. There are some authors who refuse to have their material quoted in other printed sources and they can justifiably refuse, or ignore permission to quote requests.

The cost of the permission is determined by the holder of the copyright and is usually in line with the going rate common to publishing at a given time. It can be based on the status the writer may enjoy and it often varies in terms of how prestigious the publisher chances to be. For instance, permission fees obtained from *The New Yorker* magazine are likely to be higher than those obtained from a small literary magazine which may not charge any fee. A line of poetry may well require a permission fee whereas the same number of words in quoting prose may be considered fair use. A line from a popular song, or the use of the title of a popular song should always be cleared with the copyright source. Where permission clearances are concerned, it is prudent to have the clearance in hand, if you want to avoid problems later. Clearance of permissions may well be demanded — should be — by any responsible publisher, but failure to secure such permissions ultimately rests with the author.

The publisher ordinarily provides you with a copy of the permission clearance form preferred. You may be required to identify the quote; tell how much it constitutes in relation to the word count of your manuscript;

what the pricing of the book is expected to be; when and by whom published; whether hardback or paperback; whether you will be using it for U.S. distribution solely (world rights generally require a higher permission fee, as do complete volume rights -- both hard and paperback rights); and will be advised that payment is expected to be made on publication.

Publisher's procedures on handling permission requests vary. Some obtain the permission themselves, simply to make certain it is handled legally and properly. Such costs may be considered as a portion of the advance the publisher will pay and ultimately charged against the income for the book which the author earns. In some cases, the publisher may share the permission costs. It is really a matter of what is concluded when the offer to publish is made and the author has to be governed accordingly.

When a publisher grants an author permission to quote another author, they will also provide the proper copyright citation to be carried in the new publication.

The permission to quote form that follows is more comprehensive than many publishers use, somewhat more strident in tone, on the punitive side, but represents an extreme with which you may have to cope. However, even a simplified, more congenially written form will cover most points cited in this example, with, perhaps the question of additional payment where book club sale results.

Heartland Press

Request for Permission to Reprint

Date:

Note: 1) Complete application in duplicate.
          2) Sign both copies and return them to the publisher.

The undersigned requests permission to reprint a selection, or selections. (Provide all details, including page numbers, number of words if prose is involved, and the book title under which the selection appeared. Use other side if additional space is required.)

From the publication:

This material is to be used in a volume entitled:

by: to be published by:

on or about: selling for:
            (date of publication)   (probable price)

The undersigned agrees: to give full credit to_____,
in the form specified below; to restrict use of the material to the work
named above; to make no changes, adaptions, or cuts in the material; to
forward two copies of the work, upon publication, to the publisher; to pay
the fee specified below, upon publication.

It is understood that permission to reprint listed in this application refers
only to the specific edition of the book named in this application and shall
not apply to any special, reprint, or cheaper edition. If this specific edition is
allowed to go out of print, this permission is automatically canceled, and all
rights revert to the copyright holder.

It is further understood that the applicant will not authorize any other party
to use the material, except that it may authorize a book club to distribute
the volume described, either as a monthly selection or a dividend or
premium, in which case the undersigned will pay the publisher, in addition
to the fee specified in this permission, a sum equal to that proportion of
one-fourth of the sums paid by the book club as the above material is to the
entire contents of the book.

                                            _____
                                            Signature of Applicant

                                            _____
                                            Applicant's Address

APPROVAL OF REQUEST

                                            Date_____

Fee for Reproduction:

Form of Credit

                        Approved by:_____
                                    for the Copyright holder

N.B. This permission, unless otherwise stated, is good only for circulation in
the United States and its dependencies.

Publishers sometimes offer the option of carrying the copyright in the name of the publisher publishing the work. In almost all instances, it is to the author's advantage to have the copyright in the name of the publisher. Authors tend to move about, and even if they live in the family home and never change their address, that address is less likely to be known compared to the address of a publisher. Furthermore, publishers have established procedures for protecting copyright. If copyright is carried in the publisher's name, it will more than likely be renewed, automatically, when renewal date comes due. If the publisher does not wish to renew the copyright, they will advise the author, or his heirs, so that a determination can be made as to whether the copyright should be dropped or remain in force. Few authors are equipped to police such matters for themselves. Consequently, it is best left in the hands of the publisher.

Although most countries of the world now subscribe to the rules governing international copyright, countries in the Communist block have only recently joined this community of nations. The chance of an unauthorized foreign edition appearing when copyright is carried in the name of the author is far more likely than if carried in the name of the publisher.

Authors often misunderstand what copyright constitutes. It protects writing from being used without proper recompense. It is the publishing contract which determines what income the author will receive and detail what rights are split with the author or reserved by the author. According to the contract signed, the author may speak to these rights or have assigned handling of them to the publisher. Once a contract is signed with a publisher, the author's rights are finally determined. It rarely changes after that point, and may be altered for subsequent books published, but not otherwise.

Although many authors block out a piece of writing so that they work within certain word count limitations, both in structuring chapters and in over-all word length, many others do not. Although no author should confine his writing too rigidly to word count, it often can save time-consuming revision later if he works within some consideration of length. Such a consideration assumes, of course, some organization or planning, before you begin to block out a writing project. In a day of high printing costs, length of a manuscript should be kept in mind. If you are shooting for an eighty thousand word manuscript, you can quickly break up chapters into ten eight thousand word sections, assuming you will require ten chapters to complete the manuscript. If you tend to run long on one, you can accommodate in another and trim it back. Keep in mind, any editor must work within a creative budget. If he must commit a large portion of that budget to accept your manuscript, he must also curtail what he will accept in word length for another manuscript. Therefore, an editor will look at word length, almost as soon as a manuscript comes to his desk and form some intuitive conclusions about it, before he reads too deeply. Naturally, if he concludes the writing is excellent, and the subject matter well handled, he may well decide to proceed with the manuscript, despite size, but he is always keeping a subjective consideration in the back of his mind: "If I recommend a hundred and twenty thousand word manuscript for publication, I will not be able to do those two sixty thousand word novels that I have put so much time into, unless I can get the creative budget increased." And, he knows it is very difficult to secure an increase in creative budget, unless his past books have been producing income at such a level to make an exception. No editor is above bad judgment on a certain portion of the books he recommends for publication and they are the books that will be most considered when he asks for an increase in creative budget.

Determining word count is easily done. Select three pages that constitute ordinary examples of the typed manuscript. Count the words on each page and divide by three for a figure that will establish the average word count by page. Multiply that figure by the total number of manuscript pages for the total manuscript word count. This provides a rough count, or casting, for the purposes of manuscript assessment. Another simple method is to count the number of words in five or six typed lines that represent average line length in the manuscript. Should you end up with an average of 10 words per line, next count the number of typed lines per page to obtain an average number of lines per page. If you have adhered to proper margins and page layout, it will be consistent. Assuming you get twenty eight lines to the page, at ten words per line, the rough count of the word length of the manuscript will be ten multiplied by twenty eight, or two hundred and eighty words to the page. Multiply this by the total number of manuscript pages for the final figure.

The decision to query an editor or write the manuscript may not even be considered if you are new at writing. For someone who has had some degree of success, a query to an editor evolves as a practical consideration. If you have been publishing in local publications, the editor may know something about your work. A good query, based on an idea that is within the editor's interest, may well meet with an assignment. However, if you are just beginning to write, with no publishing to your credit, it is more difficult to get a foot in the door. Your query letters may be ignored, take a long time before they receive any attention, and may come back with form rejections. It is a bleak time for a writer, and at a time when any publishing success is what is most needed. Don't despair. You are not the first writer to plod that path. Be persistent and learn to live with this time period. A self addressed, stamped envelope enclosed is absolutely necessary to reasonably assure a response from an editor.

Until you break into print, your best bet is to get to know a variety of publications in which you find your writing talent and interest areas fit. Sunday supplements use a good deal of article material. True, the name author gets a better break, but editors of such publications like to support the local writer, too. And, they are particularly interested in ideas that fit into their editorial interests. Although they tend to stick to local subject matter, they will take a flyer at a subject that has broad regional interest and even national interest if it is well researched and well written.

Study the make-up of the articles being published in the publication and begin to zero in on what interests the editor. Develop an article idea in that general area and your query will have a far more likely chance of getting the green light. Nothing displeases an editor more than to be queried about an article which lies wholly outside of the editorial interest of the publication he edits. You can't blame him. He may have two or three hours to consider hundreds of submissions. He naturally wants his time to be spent productively. Perhaps an editor's most common complaint, and the basis for many rejections, lies in the phrase "not suitable for our publication."

Know the publication you query. Know what has appeared recently. Obviously, no matter how well written, an editor will not run an article on a subject he printed three or four months ago and his response is likely to be, "we have already covered this idea." You can avoid such rejections if you have done your home-work well.

A good query letter can be developed in two pages or less. Make it as specific as possible. If the idea is too timely, the editor may find it impossible to schedule for publication. It should be fresh in concept. The writing level should be the best you can produce. Don't apologize for inadequacies; eliminate them before you write your query. Give grammar and spelling your very best attention. Make the query look professional. Allow generous margins all around. Never edit it without retyping it. The typing should be clean and the pages free of any smudges, coffee stains, cigarette burns or any other distraction. Never write a query letter in longhand. Finally, always enclose a self-addressed envelope with *sufficient* postage for return. Some editors will discard manuscripts submitted without return postage rather than run up the postage bill. It is a matter of courtesy on the writer's part. You are expecting a busy editor to give his time to your manuscript in evaluating it, without charge; don't impose further.

Let's assume that you want to query an editor of a conservation magazine. You have studied the magazine and notice they have been running articles rather consistently on re-forestration. You have learned the requirements of the magazine and know they want articles that run three to four thousand in word length, that they use photographs of high quality. Never address your query to the editor with a Dear Sir/Madam. Use the editor's name at all times. You will find it listed in directories published for writers' use such as *Writer's Market* or *Literary Market Place*, and other such sources. Your query might be as follows:

> 135 East Deerpath Ave.
> Lake Forest, Ill. 60045
> Date:

Dear Miss Perkins:

One cause in the rising price of lumber lies in the fact that we now depend on importing over half of our annual consumption, largely from Canada. At the same time, housing starts are headed for an all time high now that interest rates have fallen. Clearly, we are headed for disaster, unless we begin to plan some solutions as soon as possible.

During the thirties, I was active in the Civilian Conservation Corps. The National Park system got most of the attention, but we also did work in land reclamation and the tag end of the Corps' work was reforestation. Although there was a good, strong element of foresight and vision in the program, the C.C.C. often was the basis for newspaper and magazine cartoons, showing three men standing around holding up a shovel, while the substantive work of the program was ignored. Forty years later, we have enjoyed State and National Parks that first got their start from the C.C.C. We also have postponed the day of reckoning for lumber supplies.

From time to time, we hear proposals for the establishment of a National

Youth Corps. I would like to suggest that approach, placing emphasis on reforestration this time around, with refurbishing of the park system and land reclamation as secondary considerations. A by-product of this suggestion would spill over into social conservation as well. There are many advantages in directing the energies of the nation's youth as a means of creating purpose and commitment among them at a time when they are having difficulty in establishing social values.

Excellent photography is available covering the period of the thirties as well as recent examples pointing up the need for action.

The article is researched and would run about 3,500 words. I could complete the writing within six weeks following an approval. A self-addressed envelope is enclosed.

A list of my credits and a biog sheet is also enclosed. May I please have your reaction?

Sincerely,
R.E. Parker

Miss Jennine Perkins
Articles Editor
Heartland Magazine
1236 Sherman Ave.
Evanston, Ill. 60202

A very perceptive officer of a publishing company often when interrupted in reading manuscripts, used to raise his head and begin his conversation with, "Another writer who has a love affair with the typewriter and not much else." In some form or other, anyone who works in assessing manuscripts has known the same frustration. It is up to the writer to control that reaction. This chapter has attempted to point up some of the ways of avoiding this charge. Mechanics are very important, and within the control of any writer. If you expect to succeed, begin here and make certain your efforts are presented with eye-catching appeal. That is where is all begins. You will, of course, have to have content and contribution in what you write, but it will help if you work toward giving yourself half a break, by offering your writing in the best possible handling.

CHAPTER THREE

REVISING THE MANUSCRIPT

To write also means to rewrite. Before you turn to the final draft, whether you expect to type it yourself or turn it over to a professional typist, you will want to check the manuscript for style. It is really a matter of how you can juggle a variety of considerations in your work approach that determines how you do this. You will want to give attention to spelling, punctuation, capitalization, grammar, and expression. If you use a professional typist, you will have a second check on spelling and capitalization and, perhaps, punctuation to some extent. However, in expression, and since punctuation often influences expression, these are two areas that really fall to you. If you decide to handle all these areas, it surely is practical to read through the manuscript, carefully, concentrating on each of these areas. If this is your decision, it is best to begin with expression, first.

It is natural enough in the first draft to write in a straight-forward, direct sentence construction. You are, at this point, concentrating on clarity of statement and that means moving from beginning to the end of each sentence in the most economical way you can devise. But, if you hope to introduce an element of grace and elegance in your writing, this often comes with polishing the manuscript. You must be careful to not simply expand the manuscript. There are times when a short sentence can make a point very effectively. There are other times when you want the sentence structure to open up, to be expansive, and create a mood. There are times when the pace must be fast and there are times when you must allow the reader a breather, to assimilate what you have led him through. It really is a matter of what emotional response you have tried to evoke. If you have crawled into the hide of the creature you are spawning, if you know your material and the conclusions they point to, if you have organized them well so that you have an opening, a middle section of development and an end, you will soon become aware of how best to take advantage of these elements and use them to the most promising end.

Take, for example, the Twenty-third Psalm. If the psalmist had begun with, "I shall not want, because the Lord is my shepherd;" it not only offends the ear because we are so familiar with the psalm, but it places self above the help of the Lord, for He is the shepherd; He knows when the flock needs rest and finds the green pastures where they can lie down; He finds the still waters to refresh and, in doing so, "restores the soul." The stress of the thought must fall on "The Lord is my shepherd,..." It has to come right up front or the whole emphasis is lost.

This is the point where you have to make final decisions — ought to, at any rate. To many writers, the most demanding aspect of writing is polishing the script. To others, it is the very meat of writing, for it is, after all, the right coupling of words that creates the final effect.

There are a number of ways you can learn to assess the effect your writing creates. Turning to another piece of writing will force you into a new mood and if you have good absorption in your working habits, you will learn to shift gears from one project to another, letting go of the former and submerging yourself in the new work. This can wipe the slate clean and allow you to go back to the earlier work with fresh eyes. It may be agonizing to do this, but it will also pop up work that needs further attention.

Some authors, aware of a passage that has not come off with the right effect, read the passage aloud, concentrating on how it sounds, as though they were someone else hearing it for the first time. Placing the tip of your finger over your dominant ear -- the one that you use when listening to the phone -- can add a dimension that helps you to hear how a section sounds when read aloud. With the availability of tape recorders, sections spoken into a tape and played back sometimes set the "inner ear" in motion. You will soon find you can re-write without using such devices.

Good, creatively written non-fiction, at the re-write level, draws on many of the skills of the novelist, or the poet. True, the material being factual, you have to keep imagination in bounds or you will end up with fictionalized non-fiction, much in the way Truman Capote handled his *In Cold Blood*. Although he wrote an eminently successful book, many article editors are not prepared to have authors experiment with the article form in quite the same way, unless you can match the skill of Truman Capote. There is, however, an area in articles where tone and vitality add considerably to readability, if it is kept in balance. There is a great skill required in differentiating between what constitutes a "gee—whiz" quality in writing and what contributes freshness. It is a very subjective determination that many editors can't articulate, but they know it when they read such writing, and so do readers.

Dorothy Aldis came by the quality, almost innately, both in her writing and public speaking. Somewhere along the career of publishing thirty books, among them adults, young adults, juveniles, and both adult and children's poetry, she acquired the ability as her own. She also had great economy of language. In a public speaking engagement, she began with:

> When your program chairman, Jean Barr, phoned and asked me to speak to The Children's Reading Roundtable of Chicago, I asked her what she would like me to cover. "Tell us something of where you live, how you write, and out of what you write," she said.

> I live in a house, in Lake Forest that's almost a hundred years old. It used to have a swimming pool; now it is a rose garden. It used to have four children streaming through the house; now they are married with families of their own. It used to have a dog named Snoopy that lived long enough to see all the children move away; now there are only squirrels in the trees and chipmunks on the grounds.

With forty-three words, she named and acknowledged the program chairman's invitation, the organization, to which she was speaking, and blocked out her subject matter. In the next eighty-three words, she explains she is a mother and a grandmother, that a dog and great activity had been part of the four children's growing up, and that the house had retreated to what it had been, before the children arrived.

She could have said, I live in a house in Lake Forest. I've had four children. They are married and have children of their own. We had a dog named Snoopy that lived a very long time; much as many speakers might well have ticked off the biographical side. Instead, she works to evoke image – a hundred year old house in the North Shore suburb of Lake Forest. Her audience all knew something of that suburb and could visualize a Victorian, white clapboard, big house, set well back from the road, with acres of grass surrounding it, and huge trees and firs dotting the lawn, all circled with dense shrubbery that affords privacy to the occupants. Then she used quick, short strokes, a swimming pool that was converted to a rose garden; four active children that grew up and married; a dog that played at their heels and grew old in the process; and the house, quiet and sedate in old age, with nothing but squirrels and chipmunks to cause a stir.

Dorothy Aldis carried this over into her prose. Her first paycheck was earned writing in the newspaper world of *The Chicago Tribune.* She was a columnist there and learned to write with brevity and speed. In her work at the newspaper she learned to write the clipped phrase, how to trim excess verbiage from writing, how to pace writing and keep a breathless, fresh quality in the expression. To illustrate the point further, an example of a passage from her book, *Miss Quinn's Secret,* can be considered:

"You said you were going to show me something." But it didn't need to be seen now after all, said Miss Quinn. What she had to show Nora could easily wait.

Nora put her book down on the table. "No. Please now."

"Well, all right, come along then."

While she was still speaking, Miss Quinn had left the children's room and now she was streaking off toward the stacks, which were reached through a door behind her desk. With Nora following, she hurried along a narrow passageway lined almost to the ceiling on either side with books by author's names beginning with A through H. Having reached the end of this, she whisked round a corner and in doing likewise, Nora bumped into her. Almost fell on top of her in fact, but Miss Quinn seemed not to have noticed this painful meeting.

"Here, help me with this," she said.

"With what?"

"Why this trap door naturally." Miss Quinn was enjoying Nora's surprise as Nora quickly knelt beside her to help lift and then stood peering down into a square of blackness made by the folding back of the door. Steps descended into the blackness. Nora could count as many as five and was straining to see more when Miss Quinn started down them, saying, "Careful now."

"But what are we going to find?" asked Nora, close behind her.

"Don't get so excited. You may not think it exciting at all."

"Do you?"

"Indeed I do."

"Then tell me because I can't wait. Ouch."

"Too bad. I told you to be careful. Just one more minute, though, and we'll have a light."

"Do you come down here often?" Nora asked of Miss Quinn's invisible back. Her own voice sounded strange to her. She was feeling very carefully for each twisting step. She couldn't see a single thing.

"No. That is not very often. Because it makes me rather sad. Ah, at last! Now where's that switch?"

Nora was on ground level now, too, and glad to be.

"Sad?" she asked.

"Yes, Oh, dear, I should have brought some matches I guess. Now where in the world--"

Sad and exciting? Sad and exciting? Nora didn't have to puzzle over this much longer, though, because with a sudden click, light flooded.

For our purposes, expression should be construed to include grammar, composition, and tone. This is the point where you must consider smoothness in construction so that what you have written achieves the greatest degree of effectiveness. New writers are often strongly influenced by particular writers they admire and, quite unconsciously, at times, ape such styles. When an error of construction is pointed out to them, they, in turn, point to what they consider their authority -- the example of a writer who has long since achieved his mark. An editor may forgive an error in construction in dealing with an established name, but not always. We all know the thoroughness of editors at the *New Yorker,* who insist on the highest standards in all they publish. Your writing may well meet with such editorial standards at other publications. You must earn your eccentricities when it comes to writing.

The section on style, in *The Writer's Manual* series, treats this subject exhaustively. For our purposes, we will cite a number of common errors to help you think in such terms. If you need more detailed help in this area, it will be well to study the style section before proceeding further. In writing, it is always well to understand the term style involves two considerations to an editor and, ordinarily one to the writer. The editor is not only concerned with expression, but is equally concerned about a house style that insists on a certain use of capitalization, punctuation, handling of proper names and other such mechanics that a particular publisher sets. The writer usually considers style in literary terms, the way in which he writes or expresses himself.

Avoid an over-use of the subordinating conjunction in sentence construction. It tends to create a formal or dated sense in writing. Although it is proper construction to write

> I did not know that the sun was up.

it is equally proper to write

> I did not know the sun was up.

Any time you can do with one less word, you have improved expression. Take care in avoiding the common error of using a plural verb with a singular subject. For example,

> A group of students are protesting tuition costs. Group is the noun in

the sentence and is singular. The verb, are, is plural. The sentence should read

> A group of students is protesting tuition costs.

Watch for improper use of adverbs. Misuse often occurs when a writer must choose between a linking verb or an adverb. It is correct to write

> She always acts wise.

It would be incorrect to write

> She always acts wisely.

The difference lies in the use of the word, acts. In this sentence, it means to use one's powers so as to bring about a particular effect, but not in the sense of performing. The sentence

> She plays very meticulously when she practices.

illustrates the tendency to over-statement common to many writers who are evolving a style. It might be constructed to better advantage by

> She plays meticulously when she practices.

The word meticulously conveys all that is needed; the use of very is unnecessary.

For many years Billy Graham concluded his Sunday evening programs with "God bless you, real good." God might well forgive the evangelist for such a misuse, but grammarians will not, nor will editors. There is a wide-spread use of real for good and vice versa. What is real is genuine or corresponding to true; good means a sufficiency for the purpose. They are not interchangeable.

Another common misuse is the substitution of real for very. Real implies substantive existence. Very qualifies adjectives and adverbs.

> It is very hot.

It should never be

> It is real hot.

Other examples of such common misuse is let and leave, and bring and brought. In archaic usage, let did mean to leave or abandon. It is still used properly when accompanied by alone or be -- let alone or let be. But, the word is more commonly used, today, in the sense to permit or allow -- let me show you to your room. On the other hand, leave is most often used to connote departure -- I leave today for Boston.

A high school teacher of English once pounced on her freshman English class with, "If you can't remember that brought is the past participle of bring, think of them as a marriage. Marry *bring* to the preposition *to,* and *brought* to the preposition, *from,* in eternal, inseparable bliss, where one never appears without the other in your thinking."

Be mindful of double negatives. "I Ain't Got Nobody" might do well in a popular song, but has no place in properly written prose. To be sure, it would never have made it cleaned up as "I Do Not Have Anybody", but good construction does not allow any other choice.

Be mindful of how you use the four types of sentences, simple, compound, complex, and compound-complex. Writing which tends to fall into an abundance of one form to the absence of others soon grows tedious and repetitious. Strive for a balanced mixture, being careful of clause structure so that it is always clear. A weak complex sentence can almost always be cleaned up by looking at the order of the clauses or the connectives, and often by good punctuation.

A judicious use of the introductory clause helps to give variety to sentence structure and, consequently, adds to the readability of any writing. At the same time, they should not be over-used.

Check the manuscript for clear word choice, being careful to consider the use of abstract words as opposed to concrete words and how they are employed. Examples of abstract nouns are humanity, love, terror, and era. They fit when discussing ideas, but are not precise, or forceful as concrete words. Spoon is an example of a concrete word. To give it greater specificity, it can become a silver spoon, a dessert spoon, a wooden spoon, or a demitasse spoon, but for general purposes, the word spoon connotes a specific mental image.

Adjectives are best when used sparingly. An over-use tends to create a feeling of suspicion and tends to destroy objectivity or credibility.

Check case, tense, person, and number for these are areas where errors can creep in. An example of improper case might be

Us writers enrolled in the Midwest Writer's Conference. Clearly, broken down, you would not write "Us enrolled..." The sentence should be:

We writers enrolled in the Midwest Writer's Conference. In checking tense, make certain all verbs are in agreement. Improper tense use largely comes from mixing or shifting from one tense to another within the same sentence. A more common error lies in a shift in number. An example is:

> The wild chestnut is more intense in taste and their shell color is white.

Chestnut is singular; their is plural. The sentence should read

> The wild chestnut is more intense in taste and its shell color is white.

The new writer often tends to use complex words rather than a simpler choice. Avoid this pitfall. Effective writing communicates best when it is cast in ordinary usage. Anyone struggling with this problem will do well to study how Ernest Hemingway puts together his first chapter of *A Farewell to Arms.* Ford Madox Ford, in his introduction to the first Modern Library edition of the book, explains his reaction when he first read the opening of this chapter. He considers Hemingway as one of three impeccable writers, ranking him with Joseph Conrad and W.H. Hudson (Ford wrote this introduction in the early thirties, it should be remembered, but there is no question, Hemingway remains as a great craftsman in writing.) It is worth any writer's time to look at Ford's Introduction, and not only read the first chapter of *A Farewell to Arms,* but the entire book.

The English language is rich in possibilities where expression is concerned. It is also full of exceptions to the rule. Working out a style often raises a temptation to be innovative, naturally enough. Be cautious about this. Good style depends on expression, the combination of particular words, and the sequence in which they are used.

If you have been to London and suddenly discover British usage, resist using *colour* simply because you read it in the London *Times.* Preferred spelling is listed in any dictionary and you consistently find *color* listed first. Always use preferred spelling. The British use the term courier for a messenger, often a young girl who delivers or picks up urgent messages or small packets between two offices who do business with each other. In the United States, courier conjures up diplomatic pouches that are personally delivered from one embassy office to another while a messenger is often the office boy. It is difficult enough to convey exact images in using the English language. Don't compound it by using terms in a confusing manner. It is also a bit pretentious to the seasoned traveler who reads you, who may well be an editor, and who might be in the habit of popping over to London for a fling of winter theater every winter season. Always strive for precise meaning and that means paying close attention to word meaning for the market to which you are addressing yourself.

It is wise to avoid slang use, except in dialogue, and sparingly in that exception. Trend usage, such as the language of the counter culture, is so unstable as to date writing within the short period of a year's time. Of course, if you are aiming for a particular publication where such expression is encouraged or expected, by all means, it's a question of "right on," but that is, again, an exception to the rule.

Don't tilt at windmills in working out a style. New writers often convince themselves of what they are doing with "But, that's the only way I can write." Nonsense! Style is acquired through learning and anyone who wishes to improve in writing, can. Another frequent ploy is, "But, that's the way it really happened." Perhaps it did, but that does not necessarily mean it is the best use of material. A wife, commenting about her gregarious, Irish husband, who was known for his sense of humor and story telling ability, once said: "You have to be careful about Jim's facts when he is telling a story, but he sure knows how to use them interestingly." Jim, rising to his defense countered with, "Now, Peg, there is no reason why facts should ever get in the way of a good story."

Contractions are also permissible in dialogue, but not in exposition or particularly in formal writing. In fact, spoken language often employs a great number of contraction usage -- can't, don't, aren't, haven't -- making it difficult to create realistic dialogue without the use of contractions.

How to handle the use of numbers in a manuscript varies with particular house style. Generally speaking, the use of two or three figures should be spelled out -- His profit was twenty-five percent. -- while a greater number should remain in numerals -- $18.95. However, if a sentence begins with a number, it is always spelled out --

Eighteen dollars and ninety-five cents was the firm's retail price
for men's shoes in 1960.

Perhaps the most important consideration is consistency of handling throughout a manuscript. Make a decision about this, then make sure you follow it throughout the balance of the manuscript.

The use of capitals is again a matter of following your dictionary. Titles of books are always capitalized, except for minor words, unless they

appear as the first word of the title -- *My Life and Hard Times.* Proper names
are always capitalized as well as titles or commissions -- President Franklin
Roosevelt or General Terry Allen. The first word in a line of poetry usually
is capitalized, as well as the titles of poetry:

> Wasps
> Wasps like coffee
> Syrup
> Tea
> Coca-Cola
> Butter
> Me

In technical writing, figures are used throughout a manuscript, except
where they appear as the beginning of a sentence. In preparing such a
manuscript, it is always wise to query an editor about house style in advance.

From the purist's point of view, abbreviations should be avoided in
literary writing. State names and cities, days of the week, foreign countries
are often abbreviated in letter writing and in addressing mail, but Br. Is.,
Tues., or So. Dak. have no place in good manuscript preparation.

Punctuation is a most important point to consider. A single comma can
alter the whole meaning of a sentence, or make it clear. It also permits
variety in sentence make-up that would otherwise be impossible. Consider:

> He flew into Chicago on Friday afternoon phoned his family discovered
> they were at the family summer home in Wisconsin and renting a car
> drove to Door County to spend the week-end with them.

There is no way to write this thought, and make it clear to a reader,
unless it is chopped up into a series of short sentences. With the use of the
comma, you can dispense with a series of necessary facts, quickly handled
and move your character over a lot of geography at the same time.

> He flew into Chicago on Friday afternoon, phoned his family,
> discovered they were at the family summer home in Wisconsin and,
> renting a car, drove to Door County to spend the week-end with them.

A lack of understanding in the use of the comma might well result in,

> He flew into Chicago on Friday afternoon. From the airport he phoned
> his family. The housekeeper told him the family was in Door County at
> the family summer home. He rented a car and drove to Door County to
> spend the week-end with them.

The net effect is the addition of nine additional words to the writing, bringing in that unnecessary housekeeper, and ending up with a series of choppy sentences that do little to contribute flow or create effect.

Perhaps no two elements of punctuation are more ignored than the colon and semicolon. There are compelling reasons to master their usage, if you are concerned with making writing easier to read and more acceptable to the cultivated reader. All punctuation is ultimately involved with sentence structure and, therefore, meaning. As ignorance of the law is no substitute for innocence, a lack of understanding is no reason for ignoring the colon or semicolon - or any other forms of punctuation. If you think about punctuation, you begin to realize that it serves the basic purpose to indicate visual guidance to the reader that cannot be expressed in any other way. Tone can depend on how a sentence is constructed and expressed, but it can often be heightened by punctuation. The suggestion of pause, however, is almost wholly dependent on proper punctuation. Like the comma, the semicolon separates sentence elements. The comma suggests a slight separation; the semicolon a more positive one, but not as definite as a period. If you keep this in mind, you will have no hesitation to use the semicolon again. At the same time, it will focus attention on sentence structure, make you far more aware of expression and, in so doing, drastically affect your writing style. On the other hand, the colon is used to suggest anticipation; to precede a formal quotation; to introduce a series of detailed explanations or enumerations; after introductory clauses within a sentence; If you will examine this last sentence, the meaning should be clear for it illustrates the point being discussed, for both the colon and semicolon. Other used are covered in detail in the "Style" and "Composition" books of *The Writer's Manual*.

The period comes at the end of a declarative sentence, but is also used at the end of an imperative sentence that does not require an exclamation mark or in an interrogative sentence that makes a request.

Declarative: The moon was reflected in the lake.

Exclamation: Close that window immediately.

Interrogative: Will you please come in.

The exclamation point follows words, phrases, and sentences that convey strong or sudden emotion, and after entreaty or invocation.

Get out of my sight!
Hear me, Lord!

The question mark is used after a direct question, but never after an indirect question.

>How often does Harry write you?

>She asked how often Harry wrote.

A discussion of the use of the quotation marks, the dash, parentheses, the apostrophe, the hyphen and ellipsis are covered in detail in the "Style", and "Composition" books of *The Writer's Manual.*

CHAPTER FOUR

MARKET SLANT
— WRITE AND REWRITE

Whoever thinks a faultless piece to see,
Thinks what ne'er was, nor is, nor e're shall be.

Alexander Pope, *Essay on Criticism*

For the most part, we all read rewritten writing when we read anything in print. There are writers who, in a creative thrust or burst of energy, can catch effective expression in a first draft, but they are rare indeed. In Eunice Tietjens' *The World at My Shoulder,* she reminisces about the early days of *Poetry Magazine.* She recalls her contacts with Edgar Lee Masters, before and after he wrote *Spoon River Anthology.* She explains Masters wrote *Spoon River* out of rage when he was unable to convince a St. Louis newspaper editor to publish his poetry. The editor, well respected for his literary judgment, explained that Masters' subject matter was too ethereal and suggested Masters concentrate on what he knew best: people. Masters went home, crushed, and mad. He began to write and he poured out all his hurt against the editor as he wrote each contribution that eventually was published as *The Spoon River Anthology.* Tietjens knew his earlier work and she relates that she searched and searched for some glimpse of promise in what Masters had already written, unable to find anything that pointed to the capability that was to take the country once *Spoon River* made print. Nor did Masters ever hit this stride in subsequent work. *Spoon River* poured out of him, the product of his rage, and it came fast and furiously, almost full-bloom. It doesn't come that way to most writers.

A writer, confronted with rewriting, often stares at the manuscript, convinced it is his best effort and can't see where anything can be changed that will improve the effort. If you find yourself in this circumstance, let the material "cool" for a few days, longer if possible, then have another look at it. If you still agree it is good writing, and can stand as it, the next step is to get it to market and see what an editor has to say about it. If your assessment is wrong, you will learn that soon enough.

A writer, like a musician, should first understand mechanics before he can set them aside to write. He may have acquired his knowledge from formal study, practice or training, but he was not born knowing the mechanics of writing. He had to acquire that.

Few good writers can get by without reading widely, and few do. Verbal communication is also an acquired ability and it comes from exposure to other verbal communication, for the most part -- good conversation with people who have developed the capability of relating an incident well; others who have refined their art through years of trial and error, and polish. It is also true of good writing. What better way, then, than to read a writer who has passed the test and has already made it into print. Do not make the mistake of reading only in your interest area. Read, not for entertainment, but for analysis -- how other writers construct their sentences; how they develop paragraphs; how they mold a chapter. Learn to focus on word use and choice. Look for devices the writer uses to develop a point, to effectively put it across, and drive it home, to the reader.

One of the principle problems of many writers is to ignore readership. Learn to write with the reader in mind. What will it take to make the reader respond to your persuasion, your reasoning, your logic? How can you take the reader into your own experience, and keep him interested in your world? Often, this can be improved by revising sentences, by altering word groupings, by choosing stronger words that serve your purpose better -- all of this aimed at reader's expectation. The English language is very fluid, almost limitless in its capacity to express an idea in a wide variety of choices. Your object must be to choose the best solution, the one that best suits your purpose, the one that will convert mundane writing into publishable prose.

What follows will point up some of these problems: two versions of an article aimed at the Sunday newspaper magazine supplement. One version includes the editing used for the final draft. You will find a page of the draft appears on the left and final draft on the opposite right hand page. Insertions were added to expand and elaborate on various points making it impossible to keep similar text close together. However, it is printed in sequence, as it was written, and is reasonably easy to follow in that form.

MARY, THE
RAG-BAG LADY

- She lived in a small, Pennsylvania coal town, a town so small map makers didn't think it worth mention. She was a large, barrel-like woman, with an open face over which emotion rioted on almost any provocation – a child playing on the sidewalk, a robin nesting in a mock-orange bush, a summer sunset. (Insert A added in revision) [Her eyes grew wide, little crowsfeet wrinkles appeared at the corners, above the cheekbones, and she'd bite her lower lip, her large, over-worked hands touching her bosom almost in protection from the keenness she felt, raised in supplication.] Few people knew her full name was Mary Yolanski. They knew her as Mary, and, more commonly, "The Rag-bag Lady." She was a warm, expressive woman, always dressed in a drab gingham dress and an apron, a babushka tied over her head. Nothing ever matched, but they were always neatly washed and ironed.

- Her warm weather work was as a peddler of notions, sewing needles, thread of every weight and color, safety and straight pins, thimbles, embroidery threads, small sewing shears, sewing machine needles, bobbins and shuttles, but most of all, lace she had crocheted, handkerchiefs she embroidered, scarfs she knitted.

- She came to the kitchen door on her calls, her merchandise carried in the center of a large shawl which she carried slung over her shoulder, one hand grasping the ends of the shawl. Her large, square face broke into a toothless smile when you responded to her knock.

- "Hello, Mrs." she'd begin, "I have some t'hings today." That was as much sales pitch as Mary ever offered. Her customers knew what she sold and were always curious about what she might have in sewn or embroidery "t'hings," often wondering if she'd sold out before she called on them.

- She would come in the kitchen and lay her shawl on the kitchen table, a couch or chair, and sometimes on the kitchen floor if nothing else was clear. Then she'd lay the four corners open and go through her wares. Small talk was not Mary's forte. As she spread her array out, you reached for this or that and Mary would tell you the price. If you didn't select anything, she'd arrange her stock in the center of the shawl, pull the four corners together and sling the pack over her shoulders with, "Next time, Mrs." and off she'd go to the house next door.

- Mary was a very private person to most people, but the old father at St. Patrick's Catholic Church knew better. Over the years, Father Burns had

THE
RAG-BAG LADY

She lived in a Pennsylvania coal town, a town so small map makers didn't think it worth mention. She was a large, keg-shaped woman, with a round, open face over which emotion rioted on almost any provocation—a child playing on the sidewalk, a robin nesting in a mock-orange bush, a summer sunset. Her eyes grew wide with expression, little crow's-feet wrinkles appeared above the cheek-bones and she'd bite her lower lip in an attempt to contain the emotion. Her large, over-worked hands touched her bosom, almost in protection from the keenness of the moment; sometimes the huge hands were held, slightly in front of her, in supplication.

Few people knew her full name. They called her Mary or, more often, "The Rag-bag Lady." Always dressed in a drab gingham house-dress and an apron, with nothing ever matching, her clothes were freshly washed and ironed.

Her warm weather work was a peddler of notions—sewing needles, thread of every weight and color, safety and straight pins, thimbles, embroidery yarns, small sewing shears, sewing machine needles, bobbins and shuttles -- but, most of all, lace she had crocheted, handkerchiefs she had embroidered, scarfs and sweaters she knitted. They were magnificent craft-work and each one of a kind.

She came to the kitchen door on her calls, her merchandise carried in a large shawl slung over her shoulder, one hand grasping the four corners. Her robust face broke into a toothless smile to whomever responded to her knock.

"Hello, Mrs." she'd begin, "I have some t'hings today." That was as much sales pitch as she ever offered. Her customers knew what she sold in the notions line. What they were most curious about was her sewing or embroidery "t'hings," wondering what she might have sold before she called on them - what they might have missed, it the stock was light.

Mary would lumber into the kitchen, place her shawl on the table, a couch, a chair, on the kitchen floor if nothing else was clear. Then she'd lay back the four corners of the shawl and go through her wares. There was never much small talk. As she spread her array out, you reached for this or that and she would tell you the price. If you didn't select anything, she'd put her stock back in the center of the shawl, pull the four corners together, sling the pack over her shoulder with, "Next time, Mrs." and off she'd go to the house next door.

picked up many languages in ministering to his parishioners and he had a fair grasp of Polish, too. Mary talked a great deal to Father Burns. She enjoyed talking to Father Burns because she could express herself in Polish and not have to feel ashamed of her English.

■   Mary was like many emigrants. She came to the United States full of hope, but her roots were in "da ol' cuntry." She told Father Burns about the rich lady who paid her steerage passage to "dis cuntry" when Mary was fifteen. (Insert B) [That was in the 1880's.] Her mother died in childbirth and her father was happy to have her off his hands. She couldn't work in the Polish mines like her brothers. She was another mouth to feed and her older sister could do all the cooking and housework a miner and his sons needed. Mary was excess baggage.

■   She worked for the rich lady "long time, by Philadelphia." She cooked for the family, did housework and cared for the three children. She earned twenty-five cents a day plus room and board. The rich lady said the rest of her salary went to pay off the costs of bringing her from Poland. Mary had no idea how much that cost. (Insert C)[The rich lady never told her that.]

■   Eventually, she got to St. Procopius Church -- "You know St. Procopius Church, Fadder?" Mary's face would lite up. "Beeg!" Mary would explain, gesturing with raised arms in the shape of a gothic window. "Some people dere tell me go coal towns, by Pennsylvania."

■   After working for the rich lady for two years Mary had saved a hundred dollars. One night, she packed up all her possessions and placed them in the center of a shawl. It wasn't much and Mary slung the shawl over her shoulder and left for the train station. She waited for the green grocer that called in the neighborhood, sitting in the local park until nine o'clock the next morning. "Green grocer goot man, Fadder," she explained. "For two dollar, he take me by station." There Mary bought a ticket. She didn't know where the coal towns of Pennsylvania might be, but she saw a train with a coal tender behind the engine and concluded the train had to go to coal towns to get all that coal. The conductor sent her to the station to buy "ticket" and Mary managed that. When the train stopped, she was in another city, but she didn't know its name. She walked and walked until she found herself outside a hotel. She couldn't make anyone understand what she wanted and they sent her to the employment office, thinking she wanted a job.

■   They put her to work polishing the brass that ornamented the lobby,

To most people, she appeared to be a warm, quiet, private person, but the old father at St. Patrick's Catholic Church knew better. Over the years Father Burns had picked up many languages in ministering to parishioners and he had a good grasp of Mary's native tongue. She literally chattered when she was with Father Burns. She sould speak in Polish and not have to feel any shame about her English.

Like many emigrants she came to the United States full of hope for a better life, but her roots were still in "da ol' cuntry." She told Father Burns about the rich lady who paid her steerage passage to "dis cuntry" when she was fifteen. That was in the 1880's. Her mother died in childbirth and her father was happy to have Mary off his hands. She couldn't work in the Polish mines like her brothers. She was another mouth to feed and there already was an older sister who could do all the cooking and housework a miner and his sons needed. Mary was excess baggage, expendable.

She worked for the "rich lady, long time, by Philadelphia." She cooked, did the housework and cared for their three children. She earned twenty-five cents a day plus room and board. The rich lady said the rest of her salary went to pay the cost of bringing her over from Poland. Mary had no idea how much that cost. The rich lady never told her that.

Eventually she found St. Procopius Church -- "You know St. Procopius, Fadder?" Mary's face lit up. "Beeg!" she explained, gesturing with raised arms in the shape of a gothic arch. "Some people dere tell me go coal towns, by Pennsylvania."

After working for the rich lady for two years, she had saved a hundred dollars. One night she collected her possessions and placed them in the center of a shawl. It wasn't much, but she slung the shawl over her shoulder and left. She sat in the local park the rest of the night until nine the next morning when the green grocer that called in the neighborhood arrived. "Green grocer goot man, Fadder," she explained. "For two dollar, he take me by station." There Mary bought a ticket. She didn't know where the coal towns of Pennsylvania might be, but she had seen a coal tender behind a train and thought the train had to go to the coal towns to get all that coal. She rode the train for hours. When it stopped, she was in another city, but she didn't know its name. She walked "long time, Fadder," until she found herself outside a hotel. She couldn't make anyone understand what she wanted and they sent her to the employment office thinking she wanted a job.

They put her to work polishing the brass that ornamented the lobby with lots of it on the massive doors of the entrance. When she wasn't polishing brass, she swept up cigar and cigarette butts from the floor with a small dust broom and a brass dust pan that had a long handle on it so she could simply sweep debris into the pan as she walked around the lobby. She got her room and board and fifty cents a day. She had ended up in Baltimore, further away from the Pennsylvania coal towns than she had been when she was living in Philadelphia. When another two years slipped by, Mary had saved three hundred dollars. She told the "Fadder" at St. Mary's "I rich, like the lady by Philadelphia." and she decided to do something about it.

■ Mary had watched the people get on trains that ran in the streets. Her English was improved and she knew something about United States currency, but little about its geography. One morning, on her Sunday off, she again collected her possessions in the shawl and got on a train. She rode and rode, all day, and when it was dark, she decided she surely was close to the coal towns. When she got off, she looked around. "Mudder of Jesus, Fadder, Bal-ti-moore!" Mary had ridden a street car all day, all within the city of Baltimore.

■ Eventually she made friends at the Catholic Church. She learned about a lady who was going to visit her sister in Waverly, Pennsylvania. "They dig coal dere?" Mary asked, her eyes wide in anticipation. Her friend explained that was all you could do in Waverly. "You know how go dere?" Her friend said you took the Pennsylvania Railroad to Hazelton, the interurban to Freeland where you hired a livery to drive the four miles to Waverly. "I have dollars. You take me?" Mary asked. Her friend agreed and after four years Mary was ready to do something she wanted to do.

■ Waverly was like the coal towns in Poland, run-down miners shacks stretched on either side of the main street, unpaved roads, no sidewalks, dirty, dingy and uninviting, but it looked like home.

■ She got work in a boarding house. The boarders were immigrants who worked in the mines and Mary cooked for them and kept house. The owner, John Parkowski, worked in the mines. Mrs. Parkowski was sick. "She had the dropsy." Mary explained.

■ A year after Mary arrived, Mrs. Parkowski died and Mary took over the house. It was no more work. She had been doing it all by herself and Mr. Parkowski paid her a dollar a day. By that time, Mary's savings had grown to just under five hundred dollars, all of it in cash. Mary hid it under the edge of the rug in her bedroom.

■ Mr. Parkowski, twenty years older than Mary, eyed her efficiency and the massive doors of the entrance. When she wasn't polishing brass she swept up cigar and cigarette butts from the floor using a small broom and a brass dust pan that had a long wooden handle attached to it so she could sweep debris into the pan without stooping. She got her room and board and fifty cents a day. She had ended up in Baltimore, further away from the Pennsylvania coal towns than she had been when she lived in Philadelphia.

By the time another two years had passed, Mary had saved three hundred dollars. She told Father Burns, "I rich, like the lady by Philadelphia," jokingly. She decided to do something about it.

She had seen people get on trains that ran in the streets. Her English had improved and she knew something about United States currency, but little about its geography. One morning, on her Sunday off, she again collected her possessions in the shawl and got on a train. She stayed on the train all day. By the time it was dark, she decided she surely was close to the coal towns. When she got off, she looked around. "Mudder of Jesus, Fadder, Bal-ti-moore!" She had ridden all day, on a street car, all within the city of Baltimore.

She made friends at the Catholic church, among them a lady who had a sister in Waverly, Pennsylvania. "They dig coal dere?" Mary asked, her eyes wide in anticipation. The friend explained that was all you could do in Waverly. "You know how go dere?" The friend explained you took the train to Hazleton, the inter-urban to Freeland then either walked the four miles to Waverly or hired a livery. Mary became very excited. "I have dollars," she explained, "You take me?" The friend agreed and after four years Mary was ready to do something she wanted to do.

Waverly was like the coal towns in Poland, run-down miners shacks stretched on either side of a single street. The street was unpaved, had no sidewalks. It was dirty, dingy and uninviting, but to Mary, it looked like home.

She got work in a boarding house. The boarders were immigrants who worked in the mines. Mary cooked for them and kept house. The owner, John Parkowski, worked in the mines, too. Mrs. Parkowski was sick, "She had the dropsy." Mary explained. -

A year after Mary arrived, Mrs. Parkowski died and Mary took over the house. It was no more work. She had been doing it all by herself. Mr. Parkowski paid her a dollar a day and Mary managed everything. Her savings had grown to just under five hundred dollars, all of it in cash hidden under the edge of the run in her bedroom.

approvingly. Mary could get the board money out of the miners before they drank up their pay on paydays, and keep them happy, too. She could keep everything on a fine keel, watched the food bills and handle the men, even when they came home so drunk they couldn't navigate the stairsteps. Mary wasn't beautiful, but she was just about to turn thirty and Mr. Parkowski needed someone to keep his bed warm at night. When he proposed marriage, Mary accepted. Father Burns married them in St. Pat's Catholic Church and all the boarders were guests at the wedding.

▪ (Insert D) [It was a good enough marriage, except that John made all the decisions. Dealing with his wife who needed almost constant care made him very protective. He had no children by the first marriage and felt he was too old to start a family with Mary. He taught her "da trix" so she didn't become pregnant.]

▪ As John became more assertive, Mary withdrew from decision making. She spent more and more time sewing and less time on the boarding house operations. She didn't know why, but increasingly she drew into herself. John paid all the bills, kept track of all the money, took in new boarders and asked others to leave when they grew too troublesome. Mary resented all this, but "John was husband" and there was little she could do to change her circumstances.

▪ By the end of two years, Mary had no taste for anything but staying in her bedroom, most of the time in bed, embroidering, tatting, crocheting, and sewing. She did beautiful work, but she didn't want to have contact with the outside world. They hired a housekeeper, a widow whose husband had also been killed in the mines ... and things jiggled along.

▪ One spring bumped into the next and five years after Mary married, they brought Mr. Parkowski home from the mines for the last time. He had been killed in a fall of coal. Mary was a widow and owned the boarding house.

▪ The housekeeper was good to Mary, but almost as protective as John. She didn't tell her John had been killed. She thought Mary would not be able to stand the shock. So, John was buried in St. Anne's Cemetery, attended only by the boarders.

▪ Four days after John was buried, the housekeeper took Mary's breakfast to her bedroom as she did each morning after the boarders had left for the mines. Mary appeared to be sleeping. She suddenly sat up in the bed and asked, "John die?"

▪ The housekeeper, caught off guard, blurted out, "Yes, he's dead."

Mr. Parkowski, twenty years older than Mary, eyed her efficiency approvingly. She managed to get the board money out of the boarders before they drank up their pay checks and kept them happy, too. She watched the food bills and kept everything on a good, even keel, even when the boarders came home so drunk they couldn't climb the stairway to go to bed.

Mary wasn't beautiful, but she was about to turn thirty and John Parkowski needed someone to keep his bed warm at night. When he proposed marriage, she accepted. Father Burns married them in St. Pat's and all the boarders were guests at the celebration that followed.

To Mary, it was a good enough marriage, but John began to be suspicious of his new wife. More and more he began to make decisions that had once been left to Mary. Dealing with his sick wife, Mary reasoned, who needed almost total care at the end, had made him very protective. He had no children by the first marriage and felt he was too old to start a family with Mary. He did, however, teach her "da trix" so she didn't become pregnant.

As John became more assertive, Mary withdrew from decision making. She began spending more time sewing and less time on the boarding house operations. She didn't know why, but increasingly she drew into herself. John began paying all the bills, kept track of all the money, even took in new boarders when he asked others to leave because he thought they had become bothersome. Mary resented this, but "John was husband" and there was little she could do to change that or her circumstances.

By the end of their second wedding anniversary, Mary had no taste for anything but staying in her bedroom, most of the time in bed, embroidering, tatting, crocheting, and sewing. She did exquisite work and that seemed to be satisfaction enough. Meantime, she didn't want any contact with the outside world. John hired a housekeeper, a widow whose husband had been killed in the mines and everything jiggled along reasonably well.

One spring bumped into the next and five years after Mary was married they brought John Parkowski home from the mines for the last time. He had been killed by a fall of coal.

The housekeeper had been good to Mary, but almost as protective as John. She didn't tell Mary John had been killed. She thought she might not be able to stand the shock. John was buried in St. Anne's Cemetery, next to his first wife, attended only by the boarders and some mining buddies.

▪   "Well," Mary said, "to hell with him. We'll run the boarding house ourselves."

▪   She got out of bed, dressed herself and began to take stock of her years of sewing. The closet was full to overflowing, so were dressers and bureau drawers. Boxes of it were stuffed and stacked everywhere, under furniture, under the bed, any place it could be stored. Mary wondered what she should do with it all and she decided she would sell it. She'd crocheted a beautiful shawl and she decided to use it to bundle up her work and she'd walk over to Freeland and peddle it, door to door.

▪   The peddling went well. People liked her work and asked for items they needed, table cloths, runners, doilies, chair coverings. By trial and error, Mary worked out her prices and soon she was making more money than the boarding house brought in.

▪   When a letter arrived from the First National Bank of Freeland, Mary took it to Father Burns. John had money in the bank and Mary was the sole heir. She went to the bank and discovered John had almost seventy thousand dollars in his account.

▪   She had no idea what to do with it. She had her own savings under the edge of the rug, but had no idea how much it totaled, but she liked the "banker man" and she told him about the savings, wondering if she should put it in the bank. He explained about interest, and investments. He pointed out that John kept all his money in a safe deposit box and he thought that was wrong. He suggested Mary talk to Mr. Herbert Johnson, a lawyer and see if he couldn't make some suggestions.

▪   Mr. Johnson agreed, it was not wise to let all that money in the safe deposit box, or under the rug. He suggested she put some in stocks, but what stocks? Mary had watched the appearance of automobiles in Freeland streets. A few had even come to Waverly, bought by the younger miners. "Who makes automobiles?" she asked the attorney and he explained about the formation of General Motors and other car manufacturers. Mary thought General Motors sounded best and she decided to "buy some."

▪   Mr. Johnson referred her back to the bank and they advised Mary to put $10,000 in savings and buy stock with the rest. They could not persuade Mary to diversify. That was alien to her. General Motors was good enough for her.

▪   She blossomed with these new interests. Color came back to her cheeks and she enjoyed the exercise and walking she did, even carrying the pack on her back the four miles from Waverly to Freeland, knowing full well

Four days after John was buried, the housekeeper took Mary's breakfast to her bedroom as she did each morning after the boarders left for the mines. Mary appeared to be sleeping, but suddenly sat up in the bed and asked, "John die?"

The housekeeper, caught off guard, fumbled and said, "Yes, he's dead."

"Well, Mary said, "to hell with him. We'll run the boarding house ourselves."

With that, she got out of bed, dressed herself and began to take stock of her years of sewing. The closet was full to over-flowing, so were the dressers and bureau drawers. Boxes of it were stuffed and stacked everywhere, under furniture, under the bed, in any place it could be tucked away. Mary wondered what she could do with it and decided she would sell it. She had crocheted a magnificent shawl and she decided to use it to bundle up her work. She'd walk the four miles to Freeland and peddle it, door to door.

The peddling went well. People liked her work and asked her for other items, table cloths, runners, doilies, chair coverings. By trial and error, Mary worked out her prices and soon she was making more money peddling than the boarding house brought in.

When a letter finally arrived from the Freeland bank, Mary took it to Father Burns. John had a safe deposit box at the bank and since Mary was his sole heir, the bank wanted her present when the box was opened. At Father Burns' suggestion, she went to the bank and discovered John had almost seventy thousand dollars in cash between his checking account and the safe deposit box.

Mary had no idea what to do with the money. She had her own savings under the rug, had no idea how much it totaled. but she liked the "banker man" and she told him about her savings. He explained about interest, and investments. He pointed out that keeping money in a safe deposit box, or large amounts in a checking account, was not wise. He suggested Mary talk to Herb Johnson, a lawyer, and see if he couldn't make some suggestions.

Herb Johnson agreed, it was not sensible to allow money to lay idle. She should buy some stocks. But, what stocks? Mary had seen the appearance of automobiles in Freeland streets. A few had even arrived in Waverly, bought by the younger miners. "Who makes auto?" she asked the

the return trip would be lighter, with only the money from her sales wadded in a handkerchief and carried in her apron pocket as she walked home.

- The inheritance money came out of the safe deposit box and nice, crisp stock certificates went in. When dividend checks began to arrive, Mary asked that they be sent to the bank, instead, and placed in her savings account.

- As Mary proved her ability to sell her sewing, she added other items to her stock - needles and thread, first, then expanded to other notions as she found need for them. Meanwhile, the boarding house prospered and the widow ran it as efficiently as Mary once had.

- Life was good for Mary as the new decade of the twenties arrived. She knew hundreds of families from her peddling route. Years ago she had begun stopping at Reese's Candy Store and buying a bag of white and a bag of pink peppermints at the penny candy counter. It was the first thing she did when she got to Freeland. They went into the "candy pocket" of her apron and wherever she saw children in the homes of her customers or walking along the street, she allowed the children to select either a white or a pink mint. Wherever Mary went, hoards of children followed her, waiting for the Rag-bag Lady to give them candy.

- The safe deposit box at the bank filled up with General Motors stock certificates and finally she had to take out a second box. Stock splits arrived and more and more dividend checks arrived, always in larger and larger accounts.

- One morning she looked into the bureau mirror before she left her bedroom and noticed her hair was almost entirely white. She was edging on toward her sixties and she began to wonder what would happen to those boxes of stock certificates. Father Burns had died and she had begun talking to a new priest at St. Pat's, Father Small. She confided in him and he suggested she talk to Mr. Johnson about a will.

- Mr. Johnson told Mary her money would go to her heirs, if she didn't have a will when she died, but it would be hard to track them down. Mary knew nothing about them. Maybe they were all dead by this time. Mary thought about her early life in the United States, about St. Procopius when she met the lady who brought her to Waverly and about her other church contacts over the years. Why not leave it to the church she asked Mr. Johnson.

- Mary died quietly in her sleep one spring night in April. She was attorney and he explained about the formation of General Motors and other car manufacturers. Mary thought General Motors sounded best and she decided to "get" some.

Mr. Johnson referred her back to the "banker man" and he advised putting $10,000 in savings, buying stock with the rest. They could not, however, persuade Mary to diversify. That was beyond her. General Motors was good enough for her.

She blossomed with these new interests. Color came back to her face and the old spirit returned. She enjoyed the new activity, even all that walking she did to become known as The Rag-bag Lady. She didn't mind carrying the pack on her back the four miles from Waverly to Freeland. She knew the return trip would be lighter with the money from her sales wadded in a handkerchief and carried in her apron pocket, her "money pocket," as she called it.

The inheritance money came out of the safe deposit box and crisp stock certificates went in. When dividend checks began to arrive, she used them to buy more shares of General Motors.

As she proved her ability to sell her sewing, she added other items to her stock - needles and thread, first, then expanded to other notions. Meanwhile, the boarding house prospered for the widow ran it as efficiently as Mary once had.

Life was good for Mary as the new decade of the twenties arrived. She knew hundreds of families from her peddling route. She had always stopped at Reese's Candy Store as soon as she arrived in Freeland. She'd buy a bag of white and one of pink peppermints at the penny candy counter. They went into the "candy pocket" of her apron. Wherever she saw children, in the homes of customers or playing along the street, she offered them a selection of a white or a pink mint. No matter where Mary went, hoards of children followed her, waiting for the Rag-bag Lady to give them candy.

As the safe deposit box at the bank filled up with stock certificates, she took out a second box. Stock splits arrived and more and more dividend checks arrived, always in larger and larger amounts.

One morning she looked into the bureau mirror before she left her bedroom and noticed her hair was almost entirely white. She was edging on toward her sixties and she began to wonder what would happen to those boxes of stock certificates. Father Burns had died and she had found a new confidant in a young priest at St. Pat's, Father Small. She talked to him and buried in St. Anne's Cemetery, alongside of John. When her will was probated, Mr. Johnson, the executor, wrote a letter to The Propogation of the Faith office in Baltimore advising them they had been willed two millions in General Motors common stock shares by one Mary Yolanski Parkowski. He also wrote a letter to the boarding house housekeeper that all personal belongings, including the boarding house was willed to her.

■   Mary's journey from "da ol' cuntry" was over. One day a stone mason set a headstone on Mary's grave. It read, Mary Yolanski, Born July 27, 1865; died April 13, 1928. People knew her as "The Rag-bag Lady." The epitaph was stipulated in Mary's will.

he sent her to see Herb Johnson about a will.

Herb Johnson told Mary her money would go to her heirs if she didn't have a will when she died, but it would be hard to trace them if their names were not known. Mary knew nothing about them; perhaps they were all dead. She thought about her early life in the United States, about St. Procopius where she met the lady who took her to Waverly, about her other church contacts then and since. She decided to leave her money to the church.

Mary died quietly in her sleep one April night in 1928. She was buried in St. Anne's Cemetery with John's first wife on one side of him and Mary on the other. When her will was probated, Herb Johnson, the executor, wrote a letter to the Propagation of the Faith office in Baltimore advising them they had been willed two millions in General Motors common stock by one Mary Yolanski Parkowski. He also wrote a letter to the housekeeper that all Mary's personal possessions, including the boarding house, had been willed to her.

Mary's journey from "da ol' cuntry" was ended. One day a stone mason set a headstone on Mary's grave. It read: Mary Yolanski, born July 27, 1865; died April 13, 1928. People knew her as, "The Rag-bag Lady." The epitaph was stipulated in Mary's will.

An aside that may be of interest is the fact that this material is all factual. There was a Rag-bag lady, a Polish immigrant at 13, brought to the United States by a Philadelphia family and she eventually did find her way to Freeland, Pennsylvania. Her name was Mary and she did peddle notions and handi-crafts of her own creation. However, it was another immigrant, from China, who ran a family operated restaurant, a smallish, carefully run establishment. His name was Harry Ching and he did invest in General Motors common, and only that stock, with his savings over the years and for many years. When Madame Chiang Kai-shek made a trip to Chicago while she was visiting Washington D.C. to get support for her husband's ailing regime, she did so to accept a million dollar contribution from the restaurant owner, ironically, who felt he owed his native country support. Therefore, the piece is a weaving together of fact, and intended to point up the immigrant's lot, particularly the women. Most immigrant women that settled in the anthracite coal region of Pennsylvania were a pitiable lot. They brought the conventions and mores of their native countries with them and no matter how strong a matriarchial figure they appeared to be to outsiders, they were fundamentally commited to their husband's point of view, subverting personal desires to the male world, even when it was woefully misguided.

As an example of how material can be slanted, "The Case for the Common Sense Investor" follows. It is intended for a source such as a Sunday newspaper financial section or a Sunday supplement of a major metropolitan paper.

It draws on the basic material of "The Rag-bag Lady" piece, but supplements it with sufficient investment trappings to shift the emphasis. Note how this version niggles at smallish changes which stresses Mary's warmth; her ingenuity as a shrewd investor who saw the implications of the automobile; the town of Waverly developed as an unattractive "coal town" as many towns of this period were. Parenthetically, when the film, *The Molly Maguires* was filmed, Waverly, Pennsylvania was used for the town in which the miners lived and worked. It is hardly changed from the turn of the century, still without paved streets or sidewalks, and outhouses are still in use. Stranger still, people continue to live there.

The Case for the
Common Sense Investor

With the state of the stock market approaching something like the disaster of 'twenty-nine, investors begin to ponder where it all went wrong.

One significant reason may well be when money managers and financial advisors became the answer for many investors during the sixties. It seemed such a logical, reasonable step. These specialists were the new breed in investing. They had come out of pension funds, trust departments and mutual funds, rich in experience and full of professional jargon. They spoke of scientific balance in investing; street trends; the Fed's position; liquidity; P&E ratio. If that didn't bring the right response, they heaped on a second battery of financial sophistication such as cyclical swings; long term debt as opposed to current assets and kept hammering away until the dazed look of submission appeared on the potential investor's face.

What went wrong with the common sense investor? Why did he willingly accept discretionary management as his best solution? The answer lies in the same quality that has always caused financial losses: greed. Mr. John Q. Public had more money available to invest than he ever expected possible. If he got his feet wet for the first time in the 1967-1968 period, he suddenly became convinced he had been missing, for most of his life, the quickest way to make money. During that period, he could buy almost anything and make a few points in four or five months and, if he made a bad choice, he could always write the loss off on taxes. He was ripe for the professional money manager to take over, convinced the market would go up, long term, and he could spend retirement years paying capital gains taxes, gladly and willingly.

For three decades following the twenty-nine crash, banks and their trust departments cautioned customers that a sophisticated investor was anyone who bought stocks of good value, paid for them and collected dividends. By exercising their thrifty instincts, they bought into sound businesses in good times, bad times and indifferent times. If they bought a stock and were happy with the performance, they were urged to buy more. It was the in—and—outers, the smart guys with inside information, the followers of tips who were unsophisticated.

As long as most people's contact with the financial community didn't extend beyond banks, the system worked. Over the long haul the investor profited and if he was patient, more than satisfactorily. But, the seeds of destruction were part of the structure and did not allow for that basic element of greed that is part of mankind's lot. The more aggressive money manager found his clients by decrying the conservative posture of bank managed funds. He fast-talked and confounded a type of investor whose anxiety ratio is upset if the milkman's delivery alters to the extent that the milk bottle is left on the second rather than the first step outside the kitchen door. That kind of investor is only comfortable when dividend income arrives regularly and price appreciation means a steady, upward movement over the years.

It is amazing how well people make equity investment decisions when they trust their own instincts and many a family fortune has been built in that way. An instance to illustrate this involved a fifteen year old immigrant from a small mining town in Poland around the turn of the century.

She was brought to this country by a wealthy Philadelphia family when the lady traveled to Europe and learned about the au pair method of getting inexpensive domestic help. In Europe, still the case today, the au pair often substitutes for a governess or Nanny in exchange for room and board.

The immigrant's name was Yolanski. Her mother died in childbirth. She lived until she was fifteen with her father and a large family of brothers and her older sister. She was expendable as far as the father was concerned. She was another mouth to feed, another body to clothe. Mary's older sister could do all the cooking and cleaning a miner and his sons required and when a rich American lady offered to pay Mary's passage to the United States, the father willingly waved farewell and sent her off with a sigh of relief. Mary couldn't work in the mines like the sons and maybe she would come down in the valley of delight and make her fortune in the new country.

Mary traveled across the Atlantic in steerage. In Philadelphia, she earned her room and board and twenty-five cents a day. For that, she cooked for the family, cleaned the large house and cared for their three children. Within two years she had saved a hundred dollars.

Like many Polish immigrants, Mary gravitated to the Catholic Church. There she met other immigrants. She could reminisce about "da ol' cuntry" in her native tongue and not feel ashamed that she could neither read nor write English. The Church identity made the new world life bearable as it did for many immigrants.

On her own, cut off from all family support, she developed a good degree of independence. She wasn't exactly certain what a hundred dollars in savings meant, but it was more money than she had ever seen, despite the long, hard hours she worked to earn it.

At the church friends urged her to go to the coal towns of Pennsylvania where miners were making fortunes, according to her displaced friends. If nothing else, she could marry a rich miner.

When she got to one of the coal towns she again turned to the Church, St. Pat's, in Freeland, four miles away from Waverly where Mary lived. There, too, she got to know Father Burns, an Irish priest who had learned to speak Polish and many other languages in ministering to his flock. Mary told her saga to Father Burns, openly, almost proudly.

While she was living in Philadelphia, she had no idea where the Pennsylvania coal towns were, but she had decided to go there. One day, after working for "da rich lady by Philadelphia" for two years, she laid her personal possessions in the center of a shawl, a pitiable hoard, pulled the corners together and slung the pack over her back. She had become friends with the green grocer that called on the family and persuaded him to take her to the train station. "Green grocer goot man, Fadder," she told Father Burns. "He take me by station for two dollar."

Mary had no idea of U.S. geography, but when she saw all that coal in the tender behind a railroad locomotive she was sure she had found the right solution. The train had to go to the coal towns to get all that coal. She managed to buy a ticket and get on a train.

When the train stopped, she didn't know where she was, but she had traveled so long she was convinced she must be close to the Pennsylvania coal towns. Actually, she had ended up in Baltimore, further away from the coal towns than when she was living in Philadelphia.

She wandered into a hotel and since her English was poor, they thought she wanted a job and set her to work polishing lobby brass that ornamented the hotel and particularly the entrance doors. She got room and board and fifty cents a day.

Mary worked at the hotel for two years. She went to the Catholic church and friends she made there again urged her to get out of the cities and go to the coal towns where, they thought, all the money was being made.

Mary's savings were almost three hundred dollars when she decided to do something about her lot. She had noticed people getting on the trains that ran in the street. Again she packed her belongings in a shawl and one day she boarded a train. She rode all day and by the time it was dark, she figured she surely had to be close to the coal towns.

When she got off the train, she told Father Burns, "Mudder of Jesus, Fadder, Bal-ti-moore!" She had spent the day riding on a Baltimore street car.

Finally she met a friend at St. Procopius Church who occasionally visited a sister in Waverly, Pennsylvania. "They dig coal dere?" Mary asked her. Her friend explained that's all you could do in Waverly. "You know how go here?" Her friend told her how you took the Pennsy Railroad to Hazleton, the inter-urban to Freeland then walked or hired a livery to take you the four miles to Waverly. "I have dollars. You take me?" Mary asked. The friend agreed and after four years Mary was finally going to do something she wanted to do.

Waverly was the worst example of the coal towns, the drab company houses that eventually were sold to the miners that lived in them, each were identical to the other. It had one street and the houses, all attached, two family dwellings with exactly the same room layout, stretched on either side of the unpaved road. There were no sidewalks. Each two-family dwelling had a hand pump located centrally on the un-enclosed back porch. There was no inside plumbing. Even the outhouses were built back to back to service two families. It was dirty, dingy and uninviting. To Mary, it looked like the home she had known as a girl and that pleased her.

She found work in a boarding house. The owner, John Parkowski, also worked in the mines. His wife was mostly bedfast, "She had the dropsy." Mary told the Father. She was paid room and board and a dollar a day. For that, she cooked and did all the house cleaning for the boarders. After a year, Mary's savings totaled just under five hundred dollars, all of it in cash, hidden under the edge of her bedroom rug.

When Mrs. Parkowski died, Mary assumed charge of the boarding house. She had just turned thirty and Mr. Parkowski eyed her efficiency approvingly. She watched the food bills, yet her food was appetizing. She handled the boarders well, getting the board money out of them before they drank up their pay on paydays, and kept them happy, too. She even managed them well when they came home so drunk they couldn't climb the steps to get to bed.

Mr. Parkowski needed someone to keep his bed warm and when he proposed, Mary accepted. Father Burns married them in St. Pat's and all the boarders were guests at the wedding.

It was a good enough marriage except John began to impose himself more on the management of the boarding house. He had no children by his first marriage and felt he was too old to start a family with Mary. He taught her "da trix" so she wouldn't become pregnant.

As John became more assertive in managing the boarding house, Mary withdrew from all decision making. She spent more and more time sewing. She didn't know why, but increasingly she drew into herself. John paid the bills, kept track of all the money, asked boarders who he thought were too troublesome to leave and took in new ones. Mary didn't like this new trend but she reasoned it had come from all those years when he took care of his invalid wife. It had made him protective Mary explained to Father Burns. Furthermore, "John was husband" and to Mary there was nothing she could do to change her circumstances.

By the end of the first two years she had been Mrs. John Parkowski, she had no inclinations for anything but staying in her bedroom, most of the time in bed, sewing, embroidering, tatting, crocheting and knitting. Change for Mary became working on a new crafts project. All of her work was exquisite as she was a perfectionist. John hired a housekeeper, a widow whose husband had been killed in the mines and everything jiggled along.

One spring bumped into the next and five years after Mary was married, they brought John home from the mines for the last time. He had been killed in a fall of coal.

The housekeeper was good to Mary, but almost as protective as John. She didn't think she could stand the shock of John's death and didn't tell her the news. John was buried in St. Anne's Cemetery, attended only by the boarders and mine buddies.

Mary sensed the change in the house, but had learned to lose herself in her needle work. Four days after John was buried, the housekeeper took Mary's breakfast to her bedroom as she did each morning after the boarders left for the mines. Mary appeared to be sleeping, but suddenly she sat bolt-upright in bed and asked, "John die?"

The housekeeper, caught off guard, blurted out. "Yes, he's dead."

"Well," Mary replied, "to hell wid him. We'll run boarding house ourselves."

With that, she flung the covers back, got out of bed, dressed and began to take stock of her years of sewing. It was everywhere: under the bed, dressers, and bureau drawers were full of it. The closet was filled to overflowing. Mary began to wonder what she could do with it and decided to sell it. She had crocheted a magnificent shawl and she decided to bundle up her work in it, walk over to Freeland and peddle it, door to door.

The peddling went well. People liked her work and asked for other items they wanted, table cloths, runners, doilies, chair coverings. By trial and error, Mary worked our her prices and soon she was making more money than the boarding house brought in.

Finally, a letter arrived from the bank. John had made Mary his only heir. There was a safe deposit box and they wanted Mary to be present when it was opened. Mary went to the bank and they discovered that between a savings account and the box, Mary had been willed almost seventy thousand dollars.

Mary didn't know what to do with all that money. She talked to Father Burns and he suggested she talk to the only lawyer in town, Herb Johnson. He pointed out it wasn't wise to allow money to lay idle in a safe deposit box, or under the edge of a bedroom rug. He suggested she keep $10,000 in a savings account and put the rest in stocks. But, what stocks?

Mary had watched automobiles appear on the streets of Freeland. There were even a few in Waverly, bought by the younger miners. "Who makes auto?" she asked the lawyer. He explained about the formation of General Motors and other car manufacturers. Mary thought General Motors sounded best and she decided to "get some."

The lawyer referred her back to "the banker man." He tried to persuade Mary to diversify, but Mary would have none of it. The money all went into G.M. common.

She blossomed with this new interest. Her old, ruddy coloring returned and her zest for living bounced back. She didn't mind that four mile walk to

Freeland during the warm weather. She knew the load would be much lighter on her return with the money wadded on her handkerchief and stuffed in her apron pocket.

When dividend checks began to arrive, they went into her savings and eventually more shares of G.M.

As she gained confidence in selling her sewing, she added more items to her stock — needles and thread, first, then other notions — yarns, skeins of embroidery silk, thimbles, small sewing shears, buttons, even shoe laces.

Mary was never one for small talk when she was peddling. It was time consuming and she was embarrassed when she had to use her meager English. She could talk to Father Burns in Polish and she told him all and used him as a counselor in all her decisions.

In making her rounds, she always came knocking at the back door. When anyone responded, her robust face broke into a toothless smile and she'd lumber into the kitchen with her pack. "Hello, Mrs." she'd say, "I have some t'hings." Then she'd find a chair, a couch, the table, sometimes the floor if nothing else was clear, and lay out her wares. You picked this or that and Mary told you the price. Nothing was marked, but Mary always was correct about her prices. If you didn't buy anything, she'd place her array in the middle of the shawl, pull the four corners together and sling the pack over her shoulder with, "Next time, Mrs." and off she'd go to the house next door.

People bought notions from her, but it was the needle work they wanted to see most. They were all one of a kind, beautifully and pains-takingly done.

Mary found life good. She knew hundreds of families and all the children along her route. On her first day of peddling, she had stopped in Reese's Candy Store and bought a bag of white and one of pink peppermints. She put them in what would become known as "Da candy pocket" of her apron. The other was her "money pocket." Visiting Reese's penny candy counter became the first act of the day when she went to Freeland to peddle. Wherever she saw children, in the homes of her customers or along the sidewalk playing, she held out the bags so they could select a white or a pink mint. Hoards of children followed her wherever she went, waiting for The Rag-bag Lady to give them candy.

When the safe deposit box at the bank filled up with G.M. shares she rented a second. Stock splits and year-end bonuses arrived and more dividend checks appeared regularly, always in larger and larger amounts. All of the income went into more shares of G.M. common.

One morning Mary looked in her bedroom mirror and noticed her hair was almost wholly white. She began to think about what would happen to all that G.M. stock. Father Burns had died and she began talking to a new priest at St. Pat's, Father Small. She talked to Father Small about her problem and he sent her to Herb Johnson to talk about a will.

The lawyer explained about family heirs, but Mary did not know anything about her brothers or sisters; maybe they had all died. She thought about when she was new to this country and about St. Procopius where she had made friends, of the lady who had taken her to Waverly. She decided to leave her money to the Church.

Mary died one April night in 1928, in her sleep. She was buried in St. Anne's Cemetery on one side of John, his first wife on the other. When her will was probated, Herb Johnson wrote a letter to the Baltimore office of The Propogation of the Faith advising them one Mary Yolanski Parkowski had willed them two millions in General Motors common stock. He also wrote a letter to the boarding house housekeeper that all Mary's personal possessions, including the boarding house, had been willed to her.

Mary's saga from "da ol' cuntry" to the new was about over. One day a stone mason set a headstone on Mary's grave. It was a block of inscribed granite. The inscription had been stipulated in Mary's will and read: "Mary Yolanski, Born July 27, 1865; died April 13, 1928. People knew her as 'The Rag-bag lady'."

There is a strong case to be made for Mary Yolanski Parkowski's common sense instincts. She resisted the "banker man's" suggestion to diversify her investments simply because the idea was alien to her. She used religion and law contacts for her financial advisors, to guide her decision making, but actually made her moves out of her own convictions. Her advisors merely confirmed her judgments and kept them properly channeled. She obviously knew more about handling money than the man she married and when it came time to use that knowledge, she exercised it, well. Income came to her and she kept control over what went into the safe deposit boxes. She did not look for easy solutions in having the bank handle paper details or give it discretionary supervision over her investments. When she needed advice, she sought it. Mary bought the right stock, at the right time. Satisfied with the performance, she bought more, plowing back the income in additional shares. She was willing to delegate the running of her boarding house to a proven housekeeper and go out and develop a business of her own, expanding as she sensed a new market in notions. And, she was able to make friends of her customers, but most of all, the children with whom she came in contact.

The Rag-bag Lady was a remarkable example of ingenuity, sound financial judgment, and humanness. She was also a prime example of the common sense investor at the very best. We all can learn a good deal from this parable, even today.

CHAPTER FIVE

SUBMISSION

If you have followed the general discussion of "The Mechanics of Writing and Publishing," your manuscript will be in shape for submission. If it is of a technical nature, a publisher may have specific procedures for submission, as pointed out earlier and, in that case, you should adhere to what the editor advises in answer to your query. The problem with a letter of query for the new writer is a natural reluctance for an editor to respond to it with any real degree of positiveness. If the writer has special expertise in the subject area, the chance for encouragement is greater. For instance, if you are writing about private health insurance as opposed to nationalized medical care - a subject that has, by the way, been over-written - and you are the personnel officer of Blue Cross/Blue Shield, your query will be of greater interest to an editor. With this as an example, your query letter might be:

Mr. William Mudd
Editor
Today's Health
1236 Sherman Ave.
Evanston, Ill. 60202

Dear Mr. Mudd:

I have been Personnel Officer of Blue Cross/Blue Shield for five years. As such, I am familiar with medical insurance programs throughout the world and in particular, national programs in England and the Scandinavian countries of Europe. I have also had experience in Banker's Life, both in sales and managerial capacities, another firm that covers health insurance. I am a graduate of XYZ University. I have a degree in business and took a number of courses in the humanities and one in creative writing in the expectation that would sharpen my skills in the writing field.

I expect to objectively evaluate national health programs such as operate in other countries, but my article will not be a "put-down" of them. I will concentrate on the fact that people in the United States possess a character that is not well served in national programs where medical care is concerned. True, under our present Social Security Administration, medical care is available to the segment of the population that is over the age of sixty-five, and I expect to admit that we should consider that care a solution for the increasingly large group of people who live longer and who have a right to good medical coverage.

Something of the individualism of the frontier is still in the American character and this is not likely to diminish under our federal system of government. We are a large, widely sdiffering population, less cohesive than the smaller, more homogenous, Danish or Swedish countries. It is this very diversity that has made it possible for American medicine to develop a health care service that is unparalleled in the world, the inter-actions of the private and public sectors, each cooperating toward the fight against disease and improvement of medical services.

I have read your magazine and notice your audience is the informed layman, that your word length runs in the area of 3,500 words and that you tend to stress the use of personal examples in the kind of article you print.

I would appreciate having your reaction to this query and, if you are receptive to it, I would welcome any editorial suggestions or guidance you might wish to send me. I could have a finished manuscript in your hands six weeks after hearing from you with an affirmative interest.

Yours truly,

If you must rely on your research into health insurance, with no previous publishing experience, you will also have to turn out the manuscript before an editor is going to give it serious attention. In that event, make it the best that is in you. Once it is ready to submit, draw on all the background you can honestly muster in your cover letter. Such an example might be:

Mr. William Mudd
Editor
Today's Health
1236 Sherman Ave.
Evanston, Ill. 60202

Dear Mr. Mudd,

My interest in national health insurance was perked when I traveled in England and had cause to visit a clinic there when the touring bus I was traveling in collided with a passenger car. I had a first hand opportunity to compare English medical service with that received as a U.S. citizen dependent on private insurance programs. I was impressed with the English service, the consideration and humanness with which I was treated. When I returned home, I obtained recent material, through the consular offices in my city, on other national health programs and have researched the state of medical services in the United States, both from the American Medical Association and a number of services that operate under university auspices (both private and state) that are representative of medical care provided in any state of the country.

I have a B.A. from XYZ University and have studied writing for three semesters in night courses offered by Emerson University in its night school program. I worked on the University paper when I was in school, and published both poetry and features in it. I am currently employed in the public relations department of Ace Advertising, a firm that services a large number of national corporations in their advertising and public relation needs. As such, I am responsible for researching and developing manuscript assignments.

I hope you will find this article of interest and that you can find a place for it in your publication.

Yours truly,

In a book length manuscript, it is a matter of knowing what publisher is most likely to risk investment in an unpublished author, particularly if the work is a novel. From the publisher's viewpoint, there is something to be said for this caution. It is, after all, a matter of risking thousands of dollars in an effort to build a base for a book that possibly won't sell. Nothing is more uncertain than the life of a first book, either fiction or non-fiction. The risk is somewhat less in the case of non-fiction, only because the market is more certain for this writing form. Libraries, which form a large portion of the sales base for any book, are more likely to buy a non-fiction book, if it happens to be in an area where the published literature is sparse. But, in fiction, the library market is about as responsive as the public demand: they will buy, if the public demands the book.

An editor is as mindful of his budget as the most parsimonious housewife. The editor's position is dependent on how wisely he invests his creative budget, or that portion that is allotted to him. The creative budget is the number of dollars an editor has at his disposal for new books to be published. Ordinarily, the figure does not include manufacturing costs, but this is determined in how the publisher costs out its book product. Manufacturing costs are usually considered costs to create the product, in the same sense as reprint costs. Manufacturing cost consumes a large portion of the money required to remain in business. Once a product is placed in production, a business practice that pertains as much to the manufacture of canned beans as it does to books, such costs are considered investment in inventory or stock on hand. For our purposes, we will consider creative cost as that cost invested to bring the book to the point where it moves into production. Such costs cover the whole cost of the editorial segment of the company and is annually set on the basis of salaries and time invested in processing manuscripts (another term commonly used is, editorial overhead); the cost of buying art, providing design and layout; and the cost of creating plates for printing. Such costs vary, widely, depending on the kind of book involved. Naturally, an art book, where a good deal of four color artwork is employed, will cost more than a book of straight type, and no illustration except for jacket art.

How an editor commits this creative budget determines how profitable his books are to the firm. If his books sell well, all is well; if his books sell modestly or poorly, that too will show up in the sales totals, quickly. Therefore, each editor works to select what he believes will be most marketable. An author with a proven track record is not as speculative as someone who has not yet built up a readership or reader acceptance. Of course, now and then a *Kon Tiki*, a *Gone With the Wind*, or a *Jonathan Livingston Seagull* comes along and that keeps everyone on his toes in order to avoid missing the "big" book that just happens.

All of these factors are considered in whether an editor will respond favorably to a worthwhile manuscript. This is what editors mean when they respond with comment such as, "I like it, but I could not get it through the editorial board;" or, "I like it, but feel uncertain about its market;" or "It is capable enough, but I can't work up any conviction for it." Selecting for market acceptance is a tenuous process, and often very subjective.

On the practical side, do not think it is necessary for you to make an appointment and fly off to have lunch with the executive editor, simply because you have written a manuscript. Well over thirty thousand manuscripts now find their way into print each year, an astronomical number when you consider that half that number was likely to be published prior to federal funding that resulted when the Russians put their first Sputnik into orbit. No one knows the total number of manuscripts that are reviewed before the final selection of that 30,000 plus is made, but, conservatively, the ratio is one to a hundred in what a publisher accepts for publication. It no doubt is a much larger total than 300,000 manuscripts that are in the pipeline each year, all competing for editorial acceptance.

Manuscript screening is a very time consuming process, and also, very expensive. It is complicated and definite procedures must be followed if error is to be avoided. It is natural that you will feel a need to talk about your work. Yet, the editor who will grant such appointments, for whatever reasons, also knows that ten minutes of his time to "drop off my manuscript" will soon evolve into an hour, and forty or fifty dollars of overhead time will go into the manuscript even before the editor makes any decision about whether he will or will not be interested in publishing it. It is totally unfair to expect this on the part of any editor. No lawyer, dentist, or doctor would hold still for it, and no editor should be considered less than such a professional man.

A manuscript coming into a publisher is first cleared through files. This not only tells the publisher whether it has been active with the publisher at an earlier date but it also is set up as an active work under consideration. With literally thousands of manuscripts processed within any one year, no one can keep track of a manuscript without records. This handling varies from publisher to publisher. Some records indicate to whom it was active if it is a second submission — either for the same manuscript or a new manuscript. The record will indicate if it had multiple readings, and what that reaction was. It will indicate whether it was accepted or rejected, and any other pertinent data of value to the publisher. Editors sometimes have great facility for recalling such information; some do not. Neither editor necessarily is better for the memory or lack of it. The editor is mainly interested in the work at hand, but not mindful of what past contact might have been.

The most common means for submitting a manuscript is by mail. Most publishers will automatically acknowledge receiving it, usually by postal card.

A standard postal card is as follows:

> Heartland Press gratefully acknowledges receipt of _____(title)_____ on _____. If appropriate postage was not included, please send this separately. Every effort is made to protect the manuscript while it is in our possession, but we cannot be responsible for its safe-keeping. We will advise you of our decision concerning its possible interest to our publishing program as soon as possible.

Many manuscripts move in the mails by manuscript rate. If you include a transmittal letter, an additional amount of first class postage is charged. Both may be sent in the same package. Some writers prefer to send the letter separately. In case of loss in the mails, one or the other is more likely to get through and, therefore, possibly save time. However, if the transmittal letter is sent separately, it does mean the manuscript and letter have to be matched up by the publisher and that increases handling. Actually, the United States Post Office has an excellent record of handling parcels. If the manuscript is well wrapped, as it should be, with protective cardboard cut to size, and then wrapped in a double layer of good kraft paper, well sealed with a sturdy gummed tape, then tied tightly with stout cord or twine, there is little chance of loss in sending your work manuscript rate. It is always wise to include your return address inside the package, perhaps within the envelope that also includes proper return postage. Do not ask a publisher to return the manuscript by certified or insured mail, even if you include the appropriate postal cost. In many publishing houses, this means a messenger must be sent to the nearest postal station and that is time consuming and costly. Generally, publishers are careful about how they return manuscripts. However, a corrugated shipping box, obtainable through any good stationery store, will probably be used again in returning the manuscript, unless it has received unusually harsh handling in the mails. Writers soon realize what publishers handle manuscripts well, and what publishers handle them poorly. No matter how you caution some publishers, do not be surprised if your several hundred dollar investment in typing costs alone is stuffed into a manila envelope and returned to you, if rejected. You have no recourse, under such circumstances, other than avoid that publisher in subsequent submissions.

Good packing of a manuscript does suggest concern on your part. If you make it easier for handling at the editorial level, it usually is handled in kind. It is not unwise to include a self addressed, stamped post card for acknowledgment. Some publishers do not acknowledge manuscripts unless requested to do so. Certified mail, or return receipt requested is also a precaution to consider, if you are unduly anxious about the manuscript being properly received. You can send it that way; do not ask for it to be returned that way, should the manuscript be rejected.

Assessment time varies widely, in both the magazine and the book fields. It does not always follow that a delay in advising of publisher intent should be taken as a favorable indication, unless you know a good bit about the habits of the publisher or editor to whom you have made your submission. It is true, many editors will hold a manuscript longer when they find interest in it. That may mean they have asked for additional readings from other members of the editorial staff and that, of course, does compound the time required for assessment. It may also simply mean an unusually heavy schedule of reading of manuscripts. Larger publishers tend to maintain an editorial staff of a secondary level, to screen submissions. A busy editor may turn to such "readers" when the volume is too great, at least for a preliminary reading. Some publishers depend on outside readers for such purposes. Such readers know the publishers interest area and the assessment will fall in line with what the publisher accepts. The senior editor will know the capability of the reader and be influenced by the recommendation, but only to the extent that he will read a manuscript that has been favorably recommended. If the reader's report is critical, the editor may "dip" into the manuscript, for confirmation, or may react on the comments of the reader and pass them along as his own.

No publisher can operate inefficiently in manuscript assessment for very long. If the editorial department does not do a thorough job of handling manuscripts submitted, it surely will show up in the published list and reflect poor editorial processing. Although the writer may feel that his manuscript is worthy of top attention at the publisher level, in direct submissions some variation of the handling described is likely to be the case. In time, when a publishing record is established, increasing attention will come, but it is really a case of earning it.

As an average, it takes anything from three to six weeks for an article to be considered and five to eight weeks for a full book length manuscript. In the case of book manuscripts, editors are not unaccustomed to advising a writer they are impressed with a manuscript and ask for additional time to consider it. Depending on what editorial reaction has been, that could extend the process for another two to three weeks more. If the editor is uncertain about the writer's capability to follow editorial suggestion for revision, he may write an editorial letter, incorporating the body of reaction received, and ask to see it again, without offering a contract. If the manuscript indicates a capability of revision work, he may offer a contract with a cautious advance and, if less convinced, might pay a small option to see it again once revision work is completed.

If the contacts have been prompt and encouraging, it is sensible to consider working along with the editor, particularly if you agree with the editorial suggestions. But, here again, it is a matter of knowing something about the calibre of the publisher and the particular editorial capability. If the publisher's imprint is well established, you can get some idea of the acceptance of their books from Book Review Digest, available in most public libraries. It may be more difficult to learn what books he personally handled and it is awkward to ask for his credentials, under the circumstances. On the whole, the general tenor of the contacts you have had will by your best basis for making your decision. Generally speaking, both editor and author should have the same end in mind: to make the book the best work possible.

The magazine field works more quickly. The older, more established magazines, make an offer to buy a submitted manuscript. The price quoted is not really negotiable on a first sale. Generally the offer will come by mail and that will give you a chance to check out the price quoted against the prices listed in *Writer's Market* on literary directories that are available in libraries. If it is consistent with published prices, it is up to you to agree. Many magazines buy first North American rights, and some of the older, more established ones buy world rights. Whether this matters or not depends on your ability to judge manuscripts sales possibilities. If it is American oriented, it is of small value to argue about selling world rights as it may not be marketable in any other market than North America. Most magazines published in the United States do have both Canadian and some Latin American distribution. It is a matter of uniformity to buy such rights, making the future permissions problems simpler. Most reputable magazines will, upon request, reassign rights to the author, ranging from three months to a year following publication. If you are thinking of compiling a collection, later, this will present no complications. Magazines are usually pleased to grant such assignments. It also means mention of their name in hard cover publication or paperback publication - an extension of their image. If the magazine purchases world rights, whether they sell them or not is really dependent on how aggressive their rights department is. Generally, they depend on their circulation to bring this material to the attention of foreign editors. Sales can result from that exposure, of course, but it is not a very satisfactory way of selling foreign rights. If the Rights department does succeed in selling the piece, income is usually split, 50% to the magazine and 50% to the author, but payment is not made until the income is received and processed through the magazine accounts.

An offer from a book publisher is far more complicated. For the most part, publishers' contracts have evolved from those devised in England. The contract is usually worded in legal terminology, but, if you are persistent, you can master it. It is often the writer's first urge to turn to a lawyer. Publishing law is a special area in itself and few lawyers understand much about it. In fact, most lawyers will throw up their hands at the usual publisher's contract form. Consequently, you will end up paying a legal fee for advice that the publisher is likely to disregard. If the publisher has been in business for some time, it is safe to assume the contract will fairly cover the standard terms of publishing practices — that the publisher covenants to manufacture and sell your work, at his expense; that you guarantee the material to be original and in no way libelous. In signing, you assent to the terms of the contract as the publisher does in executing the contract at his end. The sections to watch with some care are those that relate to any discussed terms, such as the rate of royalty offered, the advance and how it is to be paid, and any other terms that might have been expressly raised in your negotiations. More than likely, all book club and paperback income will be split evenly with you. On a first book, other rights income, including foreign editions, may be handled similarly. It is this area that can become negotiable, once you establish some record of sales performance. If the book sells moderately well, a second contract may be on the same terms, and remain so until you break through with a book that proves highly salable. When activity of that kind results, it is time to choose an agent. It will save you money.

The well established companies that you recall as names that were on the spines of books you have read over the years, or were on the textbooks you used in school, long understood that a dollar of rights income can add more to the profit column than a dollar earned in a bookstore sale. A dollar which the publisher received from any rights sale in which the publisher shares is almost pure profit. Ordinarily, he has to sell four or five books to earn a dollar in profit. If you are fortunate enough to be dealing with a publisher with a well developed rights department, your first book sale might well be regarded as a learning process. Following the performance of the publisher in any rights sales will teach you what their performance is worth and give you some basis to make intrusions in that area with subsequent books, assuming your sales continue to advance.

Publishing is a business. Not unlike other businesses, it is wise to buy low and sell high. It Isn't so much a case of anyone taking advantage of the other as it is a case of how such terms can be negotiated. Many publishers do their level best to be fair to the author they publish, a truism that pertains more to publishing than to many other business areas. That is not to say you can't get "skinned" under the right circumstances, and with a publisher whose business sense dominates his relations with the authors he publishes. It is all a matter of learning what is fair to both parties and making your decisions accordingly.

The contract will raise the question of under whose name the work should be copyrighted.

Publishers control a great deal of rights areas for backlist that they have published. They are organized to be concerned about copyright expiration or changes in the copyright law which may influence rights questions. Individuals are rarely set up to handle such matters, and handle them effectively. Consequently, it is just as sensible to allow the copyright to be carried in the publisher's name rather than that of the author. Where foreign editions are involved, this is doubly true.

Author's rights will be spelled out in the publisher's contract form. What rights remain the author's are the only areas that the author can speak to. In first books, submitted directly by an author, the publisher usually handles all rights.

Publishers' contracts, among the older publishing houses, do not change materially from year to year. A new development can alter them, in some sections, such as when television, cassette, and audio visual material began to appear. Changes in law can also influence changes in contracts, but these usually mean revising the section of the contract affected, and that is about all that gets revised. In working with literary estates during research, authors are often struck with how little has been altered in the contract form of an older publishing house over fifty or even a hundred years. A publisher's contract evolves from the publishing practices of the whole industry and they tend to be somewhat standardized. New publishers sometimes devise poorly drawn contract forms, but this is generally a learning process and you will find them more likely to be revised over the years until a form is established that serves all parties well.

Costs can sometimes affect contracts and some publishers will write exceptions in the royalty section which, under certain circumstances, negate the agreed upon terms that may be mentioned in the editor's letter offer.

For instance, some publishers amend royalty escalations, if the reprint quantity is less than a certain size, perhaps, 2,500 or less. Prior to this habit, publishers simply raised the list price of small reprints in order to accommodate to the terms of the contract. As an example, 10% of a book that lists at $6.00 means a royalty payment of $.60 will eventually be paid to the author. If the original printing was for 10,000 books, the cost run will be smaller and the royalty payment of $.60 to the author can be absorbed in the inventory price to the publisher. With a printing of 2,500 copies or less, a fixed cost of $.60 royalty is almost impossible to absorb and, an increase in list price, to accommodate it may well dry-up the remaining sales that may be realized. Increasing the price is not always possible since the publisher may have contracted with boards of education or other sources serviced by contractual agreement and it is, therefore, impossible to pass on an increase in list price. This also applied to book wholesalers who also service contractual accounts.

A careful consideration of any publisher's contract will quickly convince you that it is a tenuous agreement as far as publication is concerned. Anything can happen before a book reaches print and is on sale in book supply sources. It is well, therefore, to remember this and never consider you have published any book successfully until the royalty checks begin to come in regularly. The loopholes are all in the publishers' favor and under a number of instances, the publisher can abandon publication, if the right circumstances develop. Fire, for instance, is sufficient reason for a publisher to back out on a book contractual agreement, as is labor disputes and, sometimes purely economic reasons. Editorial changes can often bring about closing out whole areas of publishing interest. An editor who possesses very specialized knowledge in certain areas, be it cookbooks or public affairs, who is wooed away by another offer and leaves his old firm without competent editorial help to handle what is already under contract can create havoc.

Royalty payments usually are made twice a year. Increasingly, newer and smaller firms tend toward an annual payment. You will find the contract specifies how royalty is paid and how long after the close of a period the payment can be expected. This period varies from publisher to publisher, but generally, is paid sixty to ninety days after the close of the royalty period. Royalties often tend to be higher for the period covering the last half of the year. In many publishing lists, as much as 60% of income can come in during the last three months of the year. Such lists are heavily in bookstore business and the big sale to bookstores always comes during the fall and year- end holiday period. Textbooks are also bought heavily just before the beginning of the school year, accounting for peaks in publisher income, and, conversely, royalty payout. Publishers who appeal to the school library markets tend to spread income more evenly over the year since library needs are more uniform and, therefore, buying continues as books are published, no matter when the publication dates break.

In considering royalty payment it is important to differentiate between payment on *list* price or *net* received by the publisher. Traditionally, trade books — those sold through bookstores — carry a list price, the price at which the customer buys the book. Ten percent of a five dollar list price is $.50, the amount of royalty the publisher will pay to the author on each book sold. However, if the price is based on *net* amount received by the publisher, that may average out as high as 43% off the list price. In essence, then, the royalty to the author is about cut in half. Based on a five dollar list, a loss of $.285 (10% of $2.85, the net amount received by the publisher or a payout of $.285 per book sold). Contracts for textbook material — books that are adopted for classroom use — and even supplementary material that is aimed at the school market, frequently are written in terms of the net amount received by the publisher where royalty payment is concerned.

These two areas, text and trade books, are long established book areas. Although the two major book associations have recently merged into the Association of American Publishers, the older associations, The American Book-Sellers Association and The American Textbook Association will continue to work in their separate areas, perhaps always, as far as discounts and royalties are concerned. The Association of University and College Bookstores, stores that handle the majority of textbooks ordered from publishers everywhere, fought long and hard to obtain discount from publishers. On average, the same discount originally obtained, 20% off the text price, prevails, although there is some signs of this being increased, recently. On the other hand, bookstores have always expected 40% off list price for books which they purchase for sale. In both text and trade books, the buyer pays cartage costs, usually as much as four to five percent of the invoice total. Although the cartage cost is uniform in both instances, the difference in discounts offered the bookstore buyer can make a great deal of difference in the profit column.

Large amounts of books are sold through book wholesale sources, particularly where library purchases are concerned. Consequently, the wholesaler receives additional discount, sometimes as high as 46% off list, where trade books are involved, and text discount plus a variable allowance where textbook material is concerned. Some publishers of text material will, for instance, allow a wholesaler 20%, plus an additional 10% as a functional discount for handling book orders.

All those circumstances create the basis for a variance in how publishers pay royalty, basing it on the use to which the book is aimed or the channel of purchase.

A logical question, often asked, is what will be earned, once a publishing contract is signed. In the magazine sale, it can either be North American rights or world rights. In some instances a simple letter of agreement is drawn up and if the author signs the payment check, that in itself becomes binding. Sometimes a simple contract is signed, expressly outlining the terms, which the publisher and author sign and each retains a copy. If the sale involves world rights, the publisher will be responsible for any reprint use and the terms of agreement will detail how that income is split. Ordinarily, it is shared on a fifty-fifty split. Before a writer establishes a reputation, such terms are rarely negotiable. Magazines are notorious for their lack of any aggressive reprint sales effort, depending on wide distribution of the magazine to secure such sales. On the other hand, they are loath to make any exceptions, if only because exceptions are harder to police when income is received. It is simpler to operate under a uniform policy that applies to all of the reprint income and they take the path of least resistance. Income, therefore, from magazine sales is fairly cut and dried and the author will know what income is produced at the time of sale, with the possibility of additional, but nominal income, if the material is sufficiently universal in interest to encourage reprint use.

Where book income is involved, amounts are even harder to determine. Any advance paid will be clear enough at the time a contract is offered. If the book earns income over and above the advance, it will be paid out in royalty income as specified under the royalty section of the contract. There is no way to judge what that income over advance paid might be for it is determined by the acceptance of the book. If it is well reviewed and distributed, and if it sells in the book markets, the income will be in proportion to that sale. Editors are likely to offer general comment about sales, when made at all — it is selling up to expectations; sales says the advance sale has been good; it seems to be holding up; or some such. Editors have long since learned that quoting advance sales figures to an author can result in future misunderstanding. There is reason for this, and valid reason. A publisher's books are sold to bookstores, but where new books are concerned, the sale is not final until the book itself is sold. True, the bookstore may order books and pay the invoice when due, usually thirty days after receipt, but the book is protected by the publisher and will be accepted for full credit, if returned under the publisher's return plan. Such plans may allow as much as a six month period after shipment or as much as nine months. Publishers have used such plans to get preferential treatment at the bookstore level and may make exceptions to the regular plan, if they wish to push a particular book more aggressively. They may also offer pre-publication offers — one free for every ten books ordered by a certain date; a price below list on which sales are computed for a specified period of time; or cooperative advertising, where the publisher agrees to pay a percentage of newspaper advertising costs or the cost of making folders available for mailing purposes, and not infrequently, even the cost of mailing, or a percentage of it. All of this cumbersome process can lift a book's sale, but it also stretches out the period when returns are made to the publisher. Only when return shipments come in is the publisher able to determine what the net sale has been. For that reason, a percentage of the sale of books shipped is held in reserve on many publishers' first royalty statement. If the book continues to sell, the reserve is released to the author on the second royalty statement or used to make adjustments in returns, if the returns exceed sales.

Perhaps the best advice to any author, in considering what the income from a book sale might be in advance of receiving the royalty might well be, don't borrow against it and plan to use it only after it is in hand.

Some income will be fixed. For instance, a dramatic sale or paperback sale. That figure is agreed upon, and the publisher writes a separate contract for it at the time of sale. The contract will be negotiated between the publisher and the buyer in accordance with the terms of the contract held with the author. The split of such income will be spelled out in the rights income of the author's contract. Most publishers do not pay out such income until the next royalty period arrives, unless the author has enough promise to negotiate that at the time a contract is signed or prevail upon the publisher to pay it at the time the income is received.

As is evident from this short discussion of a publisher's contract, there are many imponderables and few clear-cut answers. Once signed, a serious writer should regard a publisher's contract as sufficient reason to begin writing on another project, absorbing energies in the most positive sense, rather than become too preoccupied with sales or performance. Most professional writers do.

CHAPTER SIX

DEVELOPING THE

PUBLISHER—AUTHOR RELATIONSHIP

Publishing is a difficult, highly speculative business; so is writing. Both are dependent on the vagaries of that unknown, public taste. It is wise to remember, however, that both publishing and writing *is* a business, but unlike any other commercial pursuit.

Before dealing specifically with the subject of publisher/author relationship, it will be well to examine some areas of the writer's lot that have important bearing on how the publisher/author relation evolves.

At most publishing association meetings, a fair smattering of aspiring writers can be found in attendance. They ply the display booths and go to panels and discussion groups to observe and absorb whatever might be helpful. It is unfortunate more writers don't participate in these meetings for it is a chance to see how a wide range of publishers conduct themselves and how they do business. True, you will find them on their best behavior when they are comporting with their colleagues and customers, but you will see some seams showing that aren't intended for public viewing, too. You also get a chance to study handling, how a display booth is used, what promotion devices are employed, the calibre of manufacturing, the way jackets are executed, the catalogues and brochures that are used. All of these will help form a base of objective opinion and tell you a good bit about how a particular publisher functions. Registration fees are generally nominal and well worth the outlay.

Writers are more likely to find educational and library meetings more meaningful than the American Booksellers Association meetings. The A.B.A. is concerned with the bookseller's activities and is, generally, more commercially oriented. At A.B.A. meetings you will find publishers talking among themselves in terms of what business has been written, how booth attendance is running, what the convention registration is -- all the factors that may underwrite the cost of attending the convention. Such concern cannot be wholly discounted at the education and library meetings. At such conventions you will also find a wide range of professional meetings offered, in addition to the purely business meetings. A panel discussion on book selection, for instance, will bring together a group of experts who candidly discuss what books they select, how they select them and why some books are not bought. In fact, the American Library Association annual meeting, or the National Education Association annual meeting will provide such richness in meetings offered it really becomes a question of which one to choose so you won't miss a meeting that is more important.

When professional educators and librarians get together, they can be very objective about the wares of publishers and an alert writer can learn a great deal about what publishers to approach with a manuscript and what ones to avoid.

Professional review services are another means of establishing this awareness. For instance, among the American Library Association publications you will find in any public Library, *Booklist* is sure to be one of them. It is intended to provide librarians with book reviews written by librarians who are specialists on the subject. *Booklist* publishes reviews which recommend books libraries should consider buying.It does not publish reviews of books that are not recommended for purchase. On the other hand, *Library Journal* and *Publishers Weekly* may roast a book in the review and even list it as "not recommended for purchase." *School Library Journal* uses a star system, weighting the degree of recommendation.

If it is inconvenient to attend association meetings, these review sources are a worthy substitute to learn what books specialists are choosing, and why. You can also subscribe to these organization's official publications where the activities of the organization are covered and reports on organization meetings are regularly offered. Many institutional meetings are also organized on a regional or state level making participation in the organization more accessible to members and attendants.

You will find librarians ready to help you in guiding you through this labyrinth of professional organizations and often will be very helpful in discussing the merits of publishers in a general sense, in particular if you have established a good relationship at the local public library.

If all this begins to sound forbidding, you'll begin to understand why the literary agent came into being. It is the agent's business to know publishers and publishing. The agent must know who can best exploit a manuscript; what list it will fit; what publisher will possess the capability of handling the writing, in terms of editing as well as manufacture, advertising, promotion, and distribution.

Publishers increasingly rely on agents as a means of screening and supplying manuscripts for publication. Some publishers will not accept direct submission of manuscripts by writers while others build a list wholly out of agents' submissions. As a result, agents increasingly assume more of the traditional role of the editor, guiding the writer through the intricate process of developing or shaping manuscript work, discussing book ideas with writers, as well as handling the business aspects of a writer's career.

This shift of roles, where the publisher traditionally screened manuscripts and nurtured the writing progress, places an increased burden on the agent. Responding to this shift, agents have established procedures to keep from being inundated by aspiring writers. Some agents accept no new clients and leave the novice to sort out solutions in whatever way is possible. Others have established registration fees before they will discuss their services with a potential client. Still others charge reading fees to assess a manuscript.

The agent is a professional, a specialist, no less so than a doctor, a lawyer or a counselor. His time is just as valuable as other professionals and he has invested no less time and cost in preparing himself for the career in which he functions. It seems odd that the agent should be expected to perform professional services without compensation when a lawyer, a doctor, a psychiatrist most certainly will not, but the old myth that an agent should not charge for his services persists. Consequently, many agents simply refuse their services to new writers until such time as they can prove an income level where they are productive enough to handle at a reasonable profit-income. This solution may seem harsh to the struggling neophyte, especially at a time when they require more help and direction than the established writer. The only solution for them is to work with those agents who offer their services for a registration fee or charge a reading fee to assess manuscript capability.

Increasingly, editorial service offices have sprung up about the country, some of them having provided such services for a long period of time and with varying degrees of success. If you avail yourself of such services, it really becomes a question of convincing yourself that the contribution is worth the outlay. Sometimes it is possible to judge the service by offering a small manuscript, an article or short story, perhaps a chapter or two of a book length manuscript, as an indication of the calibre of work you can expect, deciding for yourself if you wish to proceed with something more ambitious. Agents, as well as publishers, can sometimes make suggestions as to what offices, or individuals, can provide competent editorial work. It is wise to proceed with caution in this area. It does not follow that the local teacher of English is necessarily able to provide solid editorial manuscript direction. If this were so, publishing would not have to worry about finding good editors who not only can judge editorial competence, but at the same time have a well established market sense in selecting manuscripts that will sell later as books.

As publishers tend to grow in size, merge or are bought up by conglomerates, personal identity inevitably suffers. It is axiomatic, the president of any firm can, and usually does, speak with more authority than a sub-editor who is working for position within the firm. But, it is also impossible to expect any president of any firm to make all the decisions. As soon as a publisher develops a degree of reputation, the president must assume wider responsibilities for the success of the business and play less of a role in manuscript selection. There are some publishers whose top officers, even the president, continue to maintain an active part in manuscript selection, but such positions tend to be concerned with administrative decisions important to the functions of the firm. Therefore, it is more than likely that your contacts will begin with an associate or sub-editor.

Editors are human beings subject to the same foibles as any other segment of people. If you have written a novel and select an editor's name out of *Literary Market Place* or *Writer's Market*, and make your submission to that individual, there is no way of telling in advance if that particular editor happens to be in a heavy reading period or one that is relatively slack. Depending on the editor's work schedule, he or she will read your manuscript, or have it read by other staff members, and react accordingly. If the editor depends on a reader's opinion, you can be sure the editor has looked into the manuscript sufficiently to confirm the reader's opinion. If the reader recommends publication, the editor will surely read the manuscript before the book is finally recommended for publication.

Some editors are unusually cautious with a new author, making suggestions for revision before they will present it to the publication committee where a decision will be made as to whether a contract offer is to be made. If this happens, you may have a considerable exchange of letters out of which you begin to evolve a working relationship. If the editor seems sympathetic to your work, making suggestions that you accept, ones that you agree with and can use, you may be on the way to a continuing association in subsequent manuscripts you write.

It is well to remember, any editor is almost always over-worked. Manuscript selection is only one aspect of the work load. Attending company and professional meetings is part of the game, all of which take time away from the desk. Supervising a book through copy editing, getting it into production, checking the work as it proceeds, working with promotion and advertising is enormously demanding and time consuming. No matter how the firm is organized, all these areas are important to the success of any book, and the editor has an interest in them, and sometimes plays a key role in shepherding a book through the publishing process.

Your book is but one that the editor handles. The editor may have six to ten others, at any given time, all of which demand the same attention.

In the sense that you use your time wisely in writing, the successful editor uses his or her time in the same sense, to another end. Both activities are aimed at the same result, to make the book the best possible and get it sold.

It may come as a shock that anything as personal as a written manuscript is treated as an object of production and manufacture, but nothing much will happen until these functions are handled well. If you allow yourself to become anxious about how the work is proceeding at the publisher level, you may only serve to compound the work of the editor by writing needless letters or answering phone calls. An editor will provide specifics that affect the publishing of the book, when the book will go into copy editing or production, and when it is expected the book will be finished and ready for shipping. Depending on the publisher, this may take anywhere from nine to eighteen months. Smaller publishers tend to have more flexibility and often move quickly in moving a book through production and manufacture, sometimes as quickly as six to nine months. Whatever the case, the editor will keep you advised.

As in all areas of contact, maintaining a degree of civility and trust in your relationship is the best way to conduct your contacts with an editor. The contract will spell out your rights and what the publisher will do. The editor will guide you through any possible revision work, put in motion requests for author biographical information, author promotion suggestions, see that copies of reviews are sent to you (in most firms) and bring to your attention anything else that has bearing on the book's handling through the production and manufacturing process.

Many authors become very restive during this waiting period and that often unreasonably creeps into the contacts. It is senseless to allow this to happen. It is time consuming for all concerned, and, for the most part, counter-productive.

If you are a serious writer, there are innumerable ways to employ your time profitably. There is the next writing project to consider. Your time will be better spent in new research or planning toward the next writing project. Learn to submerge yourself in such productive work once a contract is signed and in hand.

Writers naturally are interested in other writers' contacts with publishers. They feel the need to talk to other writers and read what us happening to other authors. This may provide balm to you and build your assurance. It may also consume a great deal of your time and energies. If you find the association necessary, relax with it and take out of it what you need. If you find it non-productive, get back to the library or at the typewriter as quickly as possible.

Agents can be helpful during this period, interpreting and advising you in the publishing process. But, it is no less positive to use the agent unwisely than to impose on an editor's time. In the final analysis, a writer should write and leave the mechanics of publishing and selling to the publisher. When the balance is right, author/agent/publisher all working in concert, with the common end of getting the book the widest exposure, the ultimate question comes back to how well the writer has done the job. No one can make a success of a book that squeaks through the publishing process, no matter how well it is manufactured and distributed. Nor can anyone accurately predict sales success until the book finds itself in the market place and public taste comes into play.

Every book presents a new and unique challenge. In addition, there is an element of timing and pure luck often involved which will have to be counted on. A book, by a widely read author, in the same subject area as yours, may dominate the market. A shift in public concern can affect the success of a book. An enormous publishing success that happens to break with your publisher at the same time your book is announced can take precedence over your book and detract from the attention your book might otherwise receive. None of these factors are predictable. Some of them are unfortunate to the writer who reaps the disadvantage, but all of them are operative elements that may be your lot, for good or bad.

A writer is also at the mercy of reviewers. Hopefully your book will receive consistently good reviews, but it is not likely. At best, you can hope for a body of reaction that will be favorable to recommending the book. Even the established author is not always consistently reviewed without qualification.

When Iris Murdock's *The Black Prince* was reviewed in the *New York Times* book section, the reviewer, Lawrence Graver, quoted the author's statement, "Art has got to have form whereas life need not." Yet, Graver points out, she has been consistently criticized in reviews that her "reality is subjective and relative," while at the same time, praised for her "narrative energy and intellectual weight." Critics will sometimes delve in such literary quagmires about writing. There is little purpose in flying to your own defense as writers sometimes do. If the battle gets heated enough, other critics will do the job better. Otherwise, it is best to take note of such comment and use it in a positive sense, if you agree that it is worthwhile.

If your publisher suggests promotion appearances, do your best to handle them well. There are authors who feed on this contact and find it valuable to their writing. There are others who cringe at the very prospect of speaking before a local writers group. There are others who simply will not use their time to "hawk" their wares.

It does not follow that any author can be used effectively to promote the sale of a book. If you have the inclination, and the ability, relax with such work and let it run. Don't anguish over it unduly if it makes you uncomfortable or if you simply cannot find it in yourself to do it at all.

It is difficult to be objective about a book you have written that doesn't end up on the best seller list or doesn't get to be a selection of the Book of the Month Club. It is easy to blame the publisher, the critics, the level of public taste, and any number of imagined reasons. If you can honestly blame the publisher, justifiably blame the publisher, charge the venture to experience and look for another publisher. The least amount of time you can devote to such personal anguishing should be — your prime concern so that you can get back to writing as soon as possible.

For good or for worse, we are all in the business together. Recriminations are a form of self-indulgence that are, in the end, debilitating. Some authors are avaricious; so are some publishers and agents. Some authors are perpetually disgruntled; so are some editors. Some authors allow their temperament to dominate their relationships; so do some editors. Some authors are constantly disappointed, (even when their book is selling well and a movie is flooding the movie screens of the country,) stalking the talk-shows and pouring out their venom on the airwaves. Yet, by and large, the preponderance of writers do find fruitful and rewarding relationships with their agents and publishers and they systematically practice their craft, working to produce the best manuscript that is in them. It all begins at that point -- always has, always will.

A P P E N D I X

Although book form consigns the material which follows to an appendix

it surely does not qualify, as Webster would have us believe,

as "matter added to a book,

but not essential to its completeness."

You will find here examples of forms and procedures

which are requisite to successful publication.

They appear in the order in which they arrive

in your experience as an author.

Publisher's
Information Sheets

Publisher's information sheets vary widely. They are generally quite restrained in tone and can range from terse to complete. Some publishers do not supply them at all. Some send you small, bound publications that not only cover the publisher's requirements and expectations, but also provide some history of the firm. Whatever the case may be, the following is the essence of information you will be asked to supply. It is a composite of a number of publishers' forms that are sent automatically at the time a contract offer is made.

A typical publisher's information sheet supplied by a publisher:

Length and preparation of MS:

Type the MS double-spaced on 8½ x 11 paper. Corrections, if any, must be legible and clean. Submit the original, but keep a copy for yourself at all times. Number all pages consecutively. Length may vary greatly, but the average is between 50,000 and 100,000 words, depending on subject and handling.

Subject Area:

We publish both fiction and non-fiction, virtually all categories of the latter. If the subject is specialized or technical, a query letter should be sent first. Generally, we do not publish poetry, plays, or short stories.

Submitting of MS:

Most manuscripts are submitted by mail. If you deliver your manuscript to the office, do not expect to talk to an editor, unless you have arranged a prior appointment. In either case, author's name, address and zip code should appear on the *first page* of the MS as well as on the outside of the package. In either case, instructions for return should be included, *and* return postage. In mailing, wrap the package with heavy wrapping paper and protect it with a sturdy cardboard box or corrugated wrap. You will receive an acknowledgement of receipt within a few days after it arrives.

Reading the MS:

It runs from two to five weeks before readings are completed because of the large number of manuscripts received. A MS that requires considerable consultation may be kept longer. In such a case, you will be notified. Do no request or expect a detailed evaluation of your MS if rejected. Time does not permit this.

Suggestions:

To expedite a decision in less time, a one or two page summary or a chapter-by-chapter outline of the MS, with the first 75-100 pages of the text will help. Your cover letter should include any information that is helpful to reading of the MS and any information about yourself that you feel will be beneficial. If the sample section of the MS meets with interest, you will be invited to send in the balance of the work.

Rejected MS:

A letter will be sent to the author advising the MS has been rejected and will be returned separately by Fourth Class Manuscript rate.

Accepted MS:

If a MS is accepted, terms of publication will be discussed and these will be incorporated in the publishing contract and sent to the author. The publisher will bear all costs of producing the MS in book form. Most authors are paid a royalty which is detailed in the contract and in accord with payment dates listed in the contract.

Copyright:

No book can be copyrighted until it has been published. The publisher applies for the contract, either in the name of the author or the publisher, as agreed upon in the contract.

The Heartland Press
1236 Sherman Ave
Evanston, Ill. 60201

Author

Information Form

In the exhilaration of having a book published, many authors do not complete the author's information form that usually arrives after a contract is signed with any degree of care. If the publisher is well organized on the promotion and publicity level, nothing could be more damaging to a book's success. The form will be consulted in a variety of ways by the publisher. It will be used when the jacket copy is written to provide author information. It will be used by the advertising department in placing advertising in publications that circulate in the area where the author is known. It will be used for author biographical information that is sent to review sources and critics, to schools that inquire for information about an author, by the promotion department in sending out review copies, by the rights department in supplying information in placing whatever rights the publisher exercises control.

It deserves care, objectivity, a nose for promotion and sales, and, above all, time.

A typical Author's Information form:

Please give this form careful thought and return it, once completed, to

Heartland Press
1236 Sherman Avenue
Evanston, Ill. 60201

This information will be helpful in promotion, catalogue and advertising preparation. Give it your best attention and don't be modest. You may find it best to "rough" it out on paper before continuing with this form. Author's biographical requests will be drawn from this form. A well handled Author's Information form will help the Publisher develop a thorough promotional program while the manuscript is being processed through the publishing stages, allowing maximum time for a good sales program to be devised.

Name: _____
         First   Middle   Last

If you write under a pen name, what is your legal Name:

_____
         First   Middle   Last

Address: _____
         Street and number   City, State, and Zip Code

All phone numbers where you can be reached:

_____
      Residence: Business: Other:

Born: _____ Where? _____
         Day   Month   Year   City   State

If not residing at place of birth, when did you leave? Do members of your family still reside at your birth place? If so, provide names and addresses. What other cities and towns have you lived in, including dates, please?

_____

_____

_____

If you are married, complete the following:

Full name of spouse: _____

Spouse's occupation: _____

Your children, and their ages: _____

_____

Please supply a brief biographical resume in three hundred words or less. Describe early writing experiences, particularly if they include accolades.

Draw heavily on anecdotes about yourself, and family, that relate to your writing interest. Be sure to include any interest in hobbies, bits about your professional life, your education, travels and any other experiences that could have interest to the press, radio and television audiences.

If immediately available, include a good glossy of a recent photograph of reproduction quality. If none is available, return the form and arrange to have a photograph taken. Send it along as soon as it becomes available. If satisfactory, it will be used on the jacket flap of your book as well as in other promotion programs.

On a separate sheet, in no more than 300 words, summarize your manuscript, pointing out the purpose, general theme and scope of your manuscript. This will be considered in writing both catalog and jacket copy.

If writing has not been your principal occupation, supply a description of other employment:

- Religious affiliation, if any. Religious publications often give attention to writing of one of their members.

- Citations, prizes, awards, etc. Be sure to give dates.

- List all organizations to which you belong. Provide full name of the organization, its purpose or intent; include offices you may have held with dates served.

- Previous publishing. List title, publisher, age level, date of publication.

- Attach separate sheet to complete, if necessary.

- Have you had any experience in being interviewed on radio or television or in public speaking? If not, would you be willing to work in developing such a program?

- Briefly describe your experience if above question was answered affirmatively:

- List names of publications, including personnel with whom you have had contact, who may be interested in featuring you, reviewing or promoting your book.

- Do you have any other suggestions as to how your book might be promoted?

Publishers'

Book Contracts

Although there is wide variety in the way publishers handle their contracts, the greatest difference is in expression. They all cover the same fundamental considerations although the order is a matter of publisher preference.

By and large, the publisher's contract is derivative, borrowing heavily on the older publishing practices of Europe and particularly from those of Great Britain. To read some English contracts is like reading a legal document that might have been devised and written in the seventeenth century. They are full of rigid, legal statement, but once you plow through them, they can be reduced to the identical points covered in the U.S. publisher's contracts and no more.

Since the contract form of publishers can send a chill down the spine of the average author once it is finally obtained, it is well to remember that it is nothing more than a covenant that is binding, once signed by both parties, and it commits both parties to terms that have been agreed upon. Terms, discussed in a publisher's letter do not sound so forbidding. The royalty, the advance, the rights areas, and a due date for final manuscript may be all that are offered in the initial discussion. If the author agrees to the offer, the contract follows. It may be a document of seven or eight pages or as simple as two or three pages long. But, in either case, it will be full of legal formality and richly sprinkled with terms such as whereas; hereby; warrants and guarantees; assigns; and many more.

Some publishers, realizing the disquiet many authors experience in reading a publisher's contract have done their best to present the contract in layman's expression. Nonetheless, it will cover the basic agreement on terms the most forbidding contracts cover.

Publishing law is a narrow field. The average lawyer who is asked to review many publishers' contracts is likely to consider it a throwback to the Dark Ages. That reaction is largely the result of unfamiliarity with publishing as a business and a lack of understanding about its functions. Few lawyers ever have a great deal of contact with publishing and those who do largely are consulted for reasons other than guidance in executing a publishing contract. Publisher contact with lawyers generally falls into the area of acquisitions, mergers, and other administrative needs. A good agent knows more than most lawyers when it comes to publisher contract provisions and is better at negotiating terms because of a knowledge of the practices that exist in publishing circles.

If you take the time to read the contract, you will find it far less disturbing than the initial impact may suggest. It is simply an agreement of what you can expect in the publication of a book. If you have confidence in the publisher's capability, respect the editorial contacts you have developed, the signing of the contract is a confirmation of that and ought not to be cause for anything other than celebration, as long as it faithfully represents the terms agreed upon.

Regardless of the arrangement or expression, the contract is the publishing agreement and it is not that difficult to understand. A discussion of contract provisions follows.

Grant:

This should be the first provision. It states that the author agrees to assign to the publisher the right to print, publish, and sell the book. If unagented, these rights will be exclusive English language rights, including United States territories and possessions. If the book has foreign edition possibilities, an agent will want to retain such rights and place them directly with overseas publishers. Since publishers in the United States have all established Canadian distribution in one form or another, Canadian book rights are assigned to the U.S. publisher and, consequently, excluded from the rights an agent will retain on foreign edition sales.

Most unagented books assign all volume rights to the publisher. There is little point for an author to retain such rights, even when they have overseas contacts that may facilitate placing foreign edition rights. Even a poor publisher's rights department, on average, is a far better solution to selling overseas rights than any author's effort directed to the same end. The grant area may also allow the U.S. publisher non-exclusive English language rights for orders received for the U.S. edition from other countries commonly handled by Great Britain. This is generally referred to as the *open market.*

The Warranty:

This section guarantees to the publisher that the author is the sole owner of the work and possesses the authority to enter into agreement with the publisher. It also states the author has the right to copyright the work, that it is not scandalous or libelous, and that it does not infringe on any work already copyrighted in any language.

If the book is published and the author has knowingly or unknowingly beoken the law, any law suit that results becomes the author's liability. The author holds the publisher blameless from any such decree or judgment that is sustained against the publisher on the ground that (1) the work violates copyright or the ownership rights of any other party; (2) that the work contains actionable, libelous or scandalous material or invades the personal rights of any other person.

The author is expected to defend himself in such legal action, promptly, and at his own expense, *if* the publisher notifies him of the action. In the event the author fails to respond to such a notification, he agrees to grant the publisher the right to proceed with such a defense, but the costs will be assumed by the author.

Some contracts cover other legal actions, such as appeal if the first judgment runs against the author. It may also specify the time an author has, after having been notified by the publisher that a case has been brought against him, to prepare changes or deletions that the publisher feels is necessary to make the work acceptable for publication. If the author does not respond in the time specified, *nor* authorize the publisher to make such changes, the contract may be terminated and all money advanced by the publisher to the author must be repaid.

Copyright:

The author authorizes the publisher to copyright the work in his name, or in the name of the publisher, whichever the author elects, and to make renewals of copyright as may become necessary.

Frequently the expression *the author, his heirs, executors, and administrators* will appear. It simply means that you, as author, agree to speak for yourself and in the event of your death, for your heirs and any other official who may administer your estate. Mentioned in this section, it means you and your assigns are liable for providing any clearance on copyrighted material that might be needed for the publisher to proceed in publishing the work. This may mean permissions from other authors or publishers that pertain to your use in the work in question.

Manuscript:

This section will mention manuscript length and the date on which final manuscript is due. It will explain that the manuscript must be submitted ready to go to press and that all illustrative material will accompany it. If the author is not responsible for such illustration, the contract will indicate that. However, if you are responsible for the illustrations and fail to meet the deadline, you automatically authorize the publisher to obtain illustrations with the cost charged against the author.

It must be remembered, the manuscript *must* be acceptable to the publisher. Once in hand, the publisher will consider the work "in character, content, and form." If the manuscript is not acceptable to the publisher, requiring additional work, the publisher will notify the author. This section may specify how many days the publisher will allow for such work to be completed and may be as little as fifteen days. If the author does not respond in time, the publisher may have the work done and charge the cost against the author's income. If the publisher considers the author has failed to comply with the provisions of the contract, and since content, character, length, and form are considered provisions of the contract, the publisher may notify the author of this decision and terminate the agreement. In that event, the author or his agent is expected to place the work with another publisher and to repay all money advanced under the terminated contract out of the payments made to the author after another publisher accepts the work. However, if the publisher's scheduling allows more extensive time for revision work, this section may place a limit on the time allowed — for instance, three months — and if the author does not respond within that time, the agreement may be terminated at the option of the publisher.

Publication:

This section explains the publisher will publish the work at his own expense, that he has the right to publish the work in a form that will bring about the best sale. This includes book design, manufacturing, and pricing. The expected retail price of the book may be stated and the amount of time the publisher has to publish the book. If serial rights are sold, the publisher has the right to delay publication date for the book, but a maximum time may be mentioned. If the publisher fails to publish the book as agreed upon, except for circumstances beyond his control such as material shortages, labor disputes, etc., the author may request the agreement be terminated and retain any money paid in advances or other agreed expenses.

Proofs:

Alterations in excess of a permissible amount—usually stated as 10% of the whole work — are paid for by the author, excluding printer's errors, if made after the type has been set. The author will also pay for any changes or corrections made which are necessary to correct actual errors once plates have been made or the book has been printed, if the printed work conforms to final and corrected proof.

Royalties and Income:

The royalty section is a crucial section. It can be one of the most complicated of the contract. It will specify the amount of royalty paid on the number of copies sold. It may escalate in rate paid after a given number of copies are sold and all this will be established once the contract is signed and executed. Exceptions to the usual sales are itemized here. Canadian and foreign sales are paid at a reduced rate in almost all instances. Foreign sales are costly to ship and handle and income is slow to be received by the publisher; loss is higher and theft often occurs. Royalty is set to allow for these problems.

Sheet sales, either in folded and gathered or sewn forms, sold to pre-binders, reading circles, sometimes to other publishers abroad or book clubs are all considered outside the normal book-selling area and are treated as exceptions to normal shipping and selling.

Editions that are sold at prices less than the publisher's original list price, either in hardback or paperback, but not at conventional paperback prices—usually known as cheaper editions—are usually paid for at a flat rate.

Income from a licensed use granted to another publishing source who will issue a cheap edition, including educational, audio or visual use is generally split evenly between author and publisher.

Book club income is split evenly, but if the publisher has to agree on assuming unusual costs for the edition to be accepted, such costs are usually shared by author and publisher.

When the publisher grants permission to reprint extracts or portions from the work, the income is split equally with the author.

Overstock adjustments or the remaindering of publisher's stock is paid for on the net amount received. If sold at, or below, the publisher's cost of manufacture, no royalty is paid.

Smaller than ordinary printings, perhaps 2,500 copies or less, may cause the royalty to revert to a lower royalty rate, usually set at 10% of list.

Wholesale shipments or large bookstore orders that fall beyond normal discounting procedures are paid for at a reduced rate, as well as books that are provided to bookstores in payment for advertising or promotion costs incurred by the book seller.

No royalty is paid on copies supplied for reviews or promotion or copies handled at "no charge" for publicity, sampling purposes, desk copies for instructors who have adopted the book as a required classroom text, or for copies destroyed by fire or water damage.

Inspection of Account:

An author has the right to examine accounts of the publisher to the extent they relate to his work, but the author bears the cost.

Sales by Contract with others:

Any substantial contract, often stated as involving $100.00 or more, will be brought to the attention of the author in writing. This may include such sales as foreign translation rights or an article for a periodical. It is not customary to consult the author in such negotiations, but he may inspect the contract at the publisher's offices or request a copy by written request.

Payments:

This will detail when the publisher will make royalty payments. Where royalty is paid twice a year, for example, at December 31 and June 30, payment is made at a date following the close of the royalty period, customarily, ninety days, but it can vary from publisher to publisher. Some publishers may pay once a year, with a similar period taken after the royalty period closes. A statement detailing how the income is derived will accompany the payment. Any other exceptions to ordinary payment will be explained, such as non-payment for income that is lower than a minimum amount, for example, under ten dollars.

Overpayment:

Should an author have several books with a publisher and royalty has been paid on a book for which there are substantial returns, later, it is possible the publisher may carry a debit balance in their favor. Some publishers consider this an overpayment and place provisions in their contracts which permit them to lump income from all book sales and make adjustments in royalty income accordingly.

If the publisher deems it advisable to revise a work and the author does not assume the responsibility, the publisher may secure the services of another party to make the revisions and charge that cost against future income for the revised edition.

Author Copies:

The number of free, author copies supplied will be stated here. An author may purchase additional copies from the publisher at a stated discount — usually forty percent for trade books and 20% for textbooks—for personal use.

Termination of Contract and Rights Reversion:

Should the book go out of print and the publisher does not notify the author of plans to re-issue it, the author can request termination of the contract with all rights reverting to the author. (An author will know when a book goes out of print as royalty income will stop being paid.) If the publisher's edition is discontinued, but another cheaper edition remains in print, the book will be considered by the publisher as in print and the publisher will continue to exercise his rights under the contract. He may, for instance, continue to process permission requests for extracts from the work outlined in the royalty section.

Under this section publishers often include a statement that covers the author's rights in the protection of his interests. Usually the contract cites the possibility of the publisher defaulting in paying royalty. If this should happen and the author notifies the publisher, in writing, the contract may be considered terminated within a stated number of days, without prejudice to any monies due the author.

At the termination of the agreement, the author usually has the right to purchase the publisher's plates as well as unbound and bound stock. The plate cost is usually stated as a percentage of the publisher's cost and the book stock is sold at the manufactured cost. In many instances, the author must exercise this right within a specified period of time, otherwise the publisher is free to dispose of both plates and stocks in the most profitable or practical way. (See Note 1 below)

Works that are Competitive:

As long as the contract is in force, the author must agree not to publish, or permit to be published, any work that will compromise or infringe on the sale of the work covered by the contract.

Notices:

This provision states where publisher notices or statements are to be addressed or directed, for both author and publisher.

Waivers:

No waiver concerning a breach of the agreement will be considered valid unless it is in writing and signed by the party exercising the right to the contract.

Assignment:

The contract is binding on the assigns, heirs, executors, and administrators of the author, as well as on the assigns or successors of the publisher. The agreement can be assigned by either party, in whole, but no portion of interest may be assigned by either party without the consent of the other. This provision does not restrict assignment or transfer of any monies due.

Option on the Next Work:

Many contracts write an option for the next manuscript — sometimes the next two — in a contract. Usually, the publisher does not have to exercise the option until a given number of months after publication of the work in question. If a publisher rejects a manuscript submitted because of an option clause, the author is free and clear of the option responsibility. (See Note 2 below)

The Understanding:

This affirms that the contract states the complete understanding of both parties, that it supersedes all other oral or written agreements, and that it may not be modified, except in writing, and agreed to by the publisher.

Subsidiary Rights:

Unagented authors will find in this section how the income from foreign editions will be split. Foreign editions on agented books are handled through agent's contacts, at the customary agent's rate. As a result, many publishers now expect less than the old fifty-fifty split. The amount retained by the publisher on unagented book varies, but can be as low as 25% of income.

Second serialization is almost always handled by the publisher at a fifty-fifty split. First serial, reprints, or condensations may preclude second serial rights sales, if they are obtained before publication date of the work. Hence the name, second serial, meaning it is secured after publication date.

On unagented books, it is generally wise to give first serialization, motion picture, dramatization, television and radio, mechanization (including renditions, reproduction or recordations, graphic or plastic use) to the publisher. This section will detail how such income is split.

Additional provisions:

The final section contains agreements that are not covered elsewhere in the contract. It may be the section where the agent's clause appears if the book is represented by an agent, can cover the manner in which the advance is paid out — so much on signing, so much on acceptance — any special allowances the publisher might have agreed to — such as a photography allowance or payment of subsidiary rights income as it is received rather than retained for payment within the royalty period in which it falls, and other such matters.

Agent's Clause:

Although some agents sign contracts with the authors they represent, others do not, assuming the relationship they maintain with their clients is most satisfactory when it is mutual, and are willing to have it dissolved if either party considers that action best. In either case, an agency clause will appear in the contract as follows:

The author hereby authorizes his Agent, Porter, Gould & Dierks, 1236 Sherman Avenue, Evanston, Ill. 60202, to collect and receive all sums of money payable to the author under the terms of this Agreement, and declares that the receipt of such sums by the said Porter, Gould & Dierks shall be a good and valid discharge in respect thereof, and the said Porter, Gould & Dierks is hereby empowered to act in the Author's behalf in all matters arising out of this agreement.

Interpretation:

The contract will be interpreted under a particular state's laws of the United States of America, regardless of the place where it is physically executed. This is usually the state in which the publisher's principal office is located.

Witness:

This is the portion where the author signs as well as the authorized official for the publisher. The signatures are usually witnessed by a second party who also signs as witness for the author. Most publishers request an author to sign a contract, have it returned to them for their signature, and will pay out the first advance payment as provided.

Notes

(1.)   There are few circumstances where it is practical for an author to buy the publisher's plates. In almost all instances, it would be less expensive to consider using photo-offset to re-issue another edition.

(2.)   Although many authors have no objection to an option clause in a contract, there is little valid reason for it to be part of the contract. If both parties are pleased with the results and handling of a previous book, the basis for publishing the next work with the same publisher is better established than all the options ever written. It is, perhaps, best to leave it to that possibility rather than a clause in the contract.

Preparing the

Index

From all practical considerations, no one is in a better position to compile an index for a book than the author. The author best knows the purpose and subject matter of the book and any good index must start with those considerations. An index, properly prepared, makes it possible for a reader to quickly locate significant statements in the book — all of them. On the other hand, it should not be concerned with incidental information. It is not a table of contents, which is part of the front matter of any book, nor is it an alphabetical listing of all the principal words in the book. An index, therefore, is determined by the range of the work, aimed at the readership of the book and anticipating reader needs, bearing in mind that the book as a whole is made up of individual parts, each contributing to the total result. Obviously, the indexer must have background in the subject matter and be able to appreciate subtleties of the text. Clearly, then, the author is the most ideal indexer.

To turn out a good index, the first requisite is objectivity. You must be analytical about the text, familiar with what an editor expects the index should be, clearly understand accepted publishing practices in the preparation of indexes, organized, and prepared to complete it in the least amount of time.

The completion of any manuscript often brings with it a period of restiveness. The writing has been demanding, taking all the creative energy that can be brought to bear. Many authors become very personal about their writing, hesitant to let go of a manuscript and send it out into the world. If you follow this pattern, it may be difficult to be objective enough about the work to prepare your own index. Some authors immediately lose themselves in a new work and haven't time to devote to indexing. Others develop a detached attitude toward work completed and aren't anxious to work with it further. If you react in this way, there are, fortunately, professional indexers available to do the work.

Every work of non-fiction deserves an index. If it is a book of value and will contribute to other research, it must be indexed to be of any real use to others. By the time your book is under contract, the editor will have decided if it should be indexed. That is the time for you to make a decision. Either you will prepare the index, arrange for it to be prepared, or the editor will agree to have the index prepared and charge the cost against income.

There is no good reason why you, as author of the work, cannot turn out a good index and it will be assumed you are prepared to make a choice of your capability. You have done the research, know the material better than anyone else, and if you bring patience to the project, you will also have the satisfaction of knowing it is done accurately and well.

First be sure that you have plenty of work space. For the most part, you will not have to begin until page proof is received. Some authors prefer to begin work from unpaged galleys. If the copy of your manuscript is an exact duplicate of the original from which the galleys have been set, it is possible to work from it in a preliminary way. If it is the first index you have ever prepared, it may remove some of the pressure to begin setting up your index cards from either the manuscript copy or the galleys. It is a matter of personal choice, how accurate you are in working with detail, time, and how you work under pressure.

At the time the index is prepared, everything hangs on the indexing. The book is already in type and waiting for the index which has to be set as the last step before the book goes to press. Binding time has already been arranged. The book is already in the publisher's printed catalog. Promotion and advertising budgets have been allocated. The sales department is waiting for finished books to sell. Everything centers on getting the index done.

If you work from manuscript or galley proofs, it will also mean you have to read the index against page proof when that arrives. It is this extra step that may lead you to the decision to wait for page proof. If you have already done the basic work before the galleys arrive, you may find reading your cards against page proof less demanding. The decision is up to the individual.

Types of indexes

For the most part indexes include all proper names and subject entries. If the work is very long and complex, two indexes may be necessary, one for proper names of persons and the other of subjects and proper names other than persons. Some works may require further breakdowns. For instance, a book on "The Story of the Armory Show" would logically index the artist entries, perhaps include the sales made and to whom. Poetry often includes an index of first lines.

Entries and subentries

Each entry is a major subdivision and constitutes a heading and the page on which it appears. It should be a precise statement of the subject treated. If the subject runs more than one page, the page reference must reflect that. The term *passim* sometimes appears in indexes when references run more than a single page. It is a matter of house style as to whether this term is used and tends to be omitted except in scholarly works and Press books. Subentries are included to help a reader locate aspects of the entry that are discussed in other pages of the book. Subheadings are constructed in such a way as to be grammatically dependent on the heading. Care should always be taken to avoid the use of any word that can be used in two or more senses within any entry. It is permissible to depart from keeping subheadings grammatically dependent on the heading in instances where the subdivisions are part of a larger category, listing them as they appear in proper page sequence, as:

> Army, U.S.
> Ordinance, 28-34; Infantry,
> 198-204; Artillery, 230-235;
> Quartermaster, 250-254

Cross-references

Cross-references are used to call attention to additional information that pertains to the heading in question. For example:

> Baptist Church, See Southern Baptist Church
> Greece. See Athens

The Work of Indexing

The primary point to keep in mind while indexing is that it must reflect the text as it is set. If the indexer comes across obvious errors, a list of these should be kept and discussed with the editor as to whether further delay is wise to correct them or whether they can be corrected in subsequent editions. Actually, such errors should have been caught in proofing the galleys, but human beings are fallible and you may find errors that have been overlooked. However, this is no time to change the text and that should be avoided at all costs if scheduling in manufacturing the book is maintained. Therefore, the index must be consistent with the text at hand, in all aspects, spelling, capitalization and all other mechanics.

Don't trust your memory. It is wise to first read through the complete text so that it is fresh in your thinking. If the proofs are in long galley form, it might be wise to cut them to page size or at least mark each page boldly with a felt tip pen, drawing lines under each folio so that it can be quickly and accurately spotted.

File cards of the three-by-five inch variety are used for each entry. Secure a set of alphabetic cards available at any stationery store and either purchase a file box or make one to size out of cut cardboard reinforced with gummed kraft tape, about two inches deep. You will find such a construction easier to work with as you proceed and have need to work with cards already filed. The greater height of the stationery store file box is awkward to use for quick access to the cards.

You are now ready to begin.

It is best to type the cards rather than make the entries in longhand, even if you do your own typing later in putting the card entries into manuscript form. If someone else is going to do the typing for you, double reason why your cards should be typed to avoid any errors. Stationery stores will be able to supply perforated index card stock that comes in a continuous form for easy typing and which permits you to tear each completed card free for filing.

As you make a choice for a card entry, underline it on the proof page so it will be simple to locate later as you proofread the cards. It also helps you realize that you have caught the essential subjects of the text for index purposes.

At this point, an over-zealous attitude toward making card entries is preferable than making too few. It is easier to eliminate marginal entries later and more difficult to locate subjects that you may have overlooked while you are proofing your work.

Ordinarily, preliminary material, nor any of the back matter is indexed. If there are any exceptions to this rule, the editor will offer you guidance. Footnotes and notes printed as back matter are indexed when they contain text that amplifies the main body of the work. This also holds true of graphs, charts or tables, as well as other illustrative material the book may contain, if they have particular significance to discussion covered by the entry in question.

The index card information will cover a subject sufficiently important to warrant being an index heading, and, if you are working from page proof, the page number. Do not make any more than one entry per card at this stage. A concise statement about the subject should also be typed on the card and the reference should, of course, contain the page number. For example:

Keeley, James
as reporter on *Kansas City Journal*, 32

As you proceed in working with the page proofs, use the margins to make note of suggested headings as they occur to you. Later, you can make the decision as to what constitutes a final choice for a heading or whether it best fits as a subheading. Although you may abbreviate as you work with the index cards, all abbreviations should be kept to a minimum in the final index manuscript.

Keep the expression in the index consistent with the tone and usage in the text. If the text uses terms interchangeably, the index should list them under one entry only.

A good indexer is able to visualize the reader of the text. How will the reader expect to look up a given subject? How can the word choice make the entry meaningful to the reader? Is my choice clear, concise, too full? Finally, constantly remind yourself that you must remain controlled by the text in both its dimension and limitations.

Although all proper names are included in an index, it should be kept in mind that the subject of the text also determines the choice. For instance, in the statement; "Chicago, unlike New York and San Francisco, is an inland port city." You will, of course, index "Chicago", but not the other cities mentioned as they are incidental to the point being made. Should either of these cities be mentioned later in the text and used as subject matter, they would be indexed for that page and any other entries for which this would hold true. The crucial question to remember is that the thrust of the text must be kept in mind at all times. The index should provide the tool to use the text in the easiest possible way.

The largest element of most indexes falls to proper names. The indexer can easily remedy some of the problems of possible confusion by a well prepared index. For example, a woman who plays a significant part in the text and first appears under her single name, but later marries and appears under her married name. The index entry will read:

Small, Gertrude, 52-71
　　education of, 53
　　marriage to James Keeley 52-62
　　see Gertrude Keeley

Identical names that can be readily confused can be clarified in the index.

Aldis, Arthur T., 82-94
　　see Arthur Aldis

or, handled as entries, can be listed:

> Aldis, Arthur T. (father)
> Aldis, Graham (son)
> Aldis, Owen F. (grandson)

Women, also known by their married names should be:

> Aldis, Dorothy (Mrs. Graham)

Names that can be confused should be listed:

> Portland (Oregon)
> Ohio (river)

or

The reference	*Index*
"the Windy City"	Chicago
"the tri-cities"	Davenport, Rock Island, Moline

In great measure,(a sad note on indexing,) the page proof restricts the work of indexing. By that time, the publisher has approved whatever the author's usage happens to be and the index is determined by that fact. The examples listed here are those with which the average author comes into contact. The most definitive, and most universally used, source of authority on indexing can be found in *A Manual of Style,* published by The University of Chicago Press. An editor that accepts a manuscript might be well advised in cautioning the author to consider the manuscript in one final reading, correcting it against the style according to the standards the publisher follows, which is not infrequently, the above book. This would allow the author to correct the text, taking into consideration that many of the accepted standards of good indexing will require changes that will allow for a more perfect index to be prepared when that time comes, not to mention benefit of such adjustments in the text itself.

Working with the index cards

Many indexers file their card entries by page number as they complete the cards. It has the advantage of being easier to proof and verify all page entries once this step of the work is completed. Some professional indexers work this way. Others alphabetize as they go, preferring to rely on memory for the ability to verify that you already have a given heading set up, making it possible to simply add another page number to an existing card. It also makes it easier to change or alter headings, as you work, if this comes up, as is often the case.

Cards should be alphabetized letter by letter up to the first mark of punctuation, much the preferred method. In the word by word approach, you stop alphabetizing at the end of the first word, but may draw on the second word when two or more headings begin with the same word.

Numerals and dates are alphabetized as they are pronounced and introductory articles, prepositions, and conjunctions are ignored.

Since personal names often present several choices, perhaps the best solution is to pick a standard authority such as an unabridged dictionary or a biographical dictionary and consistently follow that direction. This particularly applies to foreign names. Names beginning with articles, such as La Courneuve, are filed under the article spelling. A standard atlas will help provide answers in handling geographic names as they follow standard procedures.

Editing the cards

After compiling the index up to this point, it is wise to read the page proof again, checking your galley notes as you do to insure that all is in perfect order and that nothing has been omitted. It is a time to make final determinations that all subjects worthy of indexing are covered. It is also a time to double check that the index cards contain all the information they should.

This is the point where the index will take shape. Unnecessary entries can be dropped; headings that will stay in the final manuscript will be determined. Subheading groupings will be decided. The number of cross references will come into balance.

If main headings contain too many page numbers, make them more manageable by adding subheadings so that the index is more usable for a reader. Consider all such decisions in terms of the reader. How can you make the listings more meaningful? It is the only way to make such choices, for there is no rule that establishes how many page entries can follow a heading.

Subheadings should be arranged according to the appearance in the text, although it is also acceptable to arrange them alphabetically. Practically speaking, any reader interested in a particular entry conditioned to think of them in book page sequence, will expect to look them up in that order, despite other argument to the contrary.

A guide to accepted punctuation is clear in the index examples used in this section and is further amplified by the index that appears in this book.

After you have settled on the final choice of entries and subentries, consider the cross-references and make certain they are consistent with those choices.

Typing the manuscript

It is a wise indexer who checks the cards to make certain they are in perfect alphabetical order, before beginning typing. It can save scrapping pages of partially typed manuscript later. The manuscript is typed on 8½ x 11 inch paper. You will need to know something about width of type used in the printing to set your limitations. If you know something of the process the editor will have to solve, you should be able to help.

Normally, two columns of type are used to set the index. It also is usually set in a reduced type face than will appear in the text, quite often two sizes smaller. In the ordinary book, the subentries follow one another, without break. This is known as a run-in style. The indented style is often employed, as well, where each sub-entry begins a new line, always indented from the left. Problems in type setting cannot be anticipated completely and may require allowing more or less space in each line, sometimes dropping a line in a column to balance the other column, all depending on how the copy breaks. Such matters rightly belong to production specialists and are less the concern of the indexer, but it is well to know that someone else has to fret over whether an index comes out well or not.

The length of an index varies with the kind of material being indexed. A page of two column index generally consumes one hundred lines. If the index cards run about five entries per type page, the index will run about one-fiftieth the length of the text. Indexes can run longer, depending on the subject matter and the number of entries per text page, but, generally such longer indexes fall into the scholarly book area.

This section on indexing is aimed at the usual trade book demands. If your book is aimed at the scholarly market, a professional list or University press, it will be well to consult some of the more advanced literature available in most libraries, or turn to the more definitive publication, The University of Chicago's *Manual of Style.*

Proofreading
the Manuscript

Proofreading a book manuscript has compensations other than offering tangible proof that publication date is drawing very close. Months have elapsed since the manuscript was accepted for publication, sometimes as much as a year, or more. As a result, the author can look at the galleys with fresh eyes. That advantage should make it possible to catch printer's errors more readily. It is not, however, a time to make text changes and that temptation must be resisted, no matter how strongly it surfaces.

Some publishers send extensive instructions on what they expect in proofing galleys; some assume you have the capability and offer no direction at all. The proofing marks listed in this section are not exhaustive, but they do include those symbols that are universally accepted, and which are likely to be needed.

The basic point to keep in mind is to make all corrections clearly and precisely. Use an ink pen; never use a felt tip variety. In lining out any word, a line drawn through it in the text indicates it is to be deleted. Do not obliterate the word; the printer has to see what has to be removed. Use the caret (that small, inverted v shaped symbol listed in Proofreaders' Marks) at the point in any line where a change is to be made. Support that with a marginal reference of what you want changed, using the left hand margin for the left hand portion of the page and the right margin in the same sense. Some symbols can, and should be used directly in the line of print, such as those for caps, close up, delete, transpose; others, such as *ital, spell out, stet* should be written in the margin and the reference carried over to that portion of the printed line to which it refers. For example, a word or phrase that should appear in italics that falls in the left hand side of the page: place the symbol, *ital,* in the left hand margin next to the line in question and underline the words in question, or you may mark it also with a series of dots under the passage in question.

In most listings of proofreading marks the effort is to be exhaustive and the writer gets more than he or she needs to know. Don't be disturbed by this. Many of the marks included in such lists are applicable to a proofreader who is reading for corrections with more background in production than the average author ever will possess. The printer's or publisher's proof readings must mesh, eventually, and they have to use a universal set of symbols to convey each other's instructions. Such proofing as the printer and publisher do will have to be concerned with crooked lines, poorly leaded lines, widows and other technicalities that are important to the appearance of the text. Editors will not depend on authors for such knowledge, if they have any regard for excellence in the books they publish. Such changes will appear on the master set of page proofs in the publisher's hands. It is also that set to which your corrections, as author, will ultimately be transferred and turned over to the printer.

Proofreaders' Marks

≡ put in caps

⌒ close up

space

9 invert letter

℘ ⌒ take out letter
   and close up

℘ delete

tr. transpose

lc. lower case

⊙ add period

⋏ add comma

⊻ add colon

;/ add semicolon

⌄ add apostrophe

= add hyphen

⌄⌄ add quotation mark

] carry further
   to right

⊏ carry further
   to left

⋎ close up –
   no space

stet ignore correction

⊓ elevate a letter
   or word

⊔ depress a letter
   or word

ital put in italic type

less # less space

⋀ insert at this point

wf used when a letter
   is the wrong face

bf⌇⌇⌇ print in bold face type

rom roman

Ⓢ spell out

X broken type

¶ paragraph

Rowena Fry

Manuscript Copy Illustrating Use of Proofreaders' Marks

≡/⌒/# she⋏ lived in a Pennsylvania coal town⋏ a town ⁊

⅃ so∅ small map⹀makers didn't think it worht ⌣

⊙ mention⋏ She Was a large, ⌐keg-shaped Wo- lc./⌐

⌒ man,⌒ with a round, |open| ⌐Face⌐ over which ⌐ ⌐/⅃

tr./⌣ emotion on rioted, almost any provocation — rom.

on/ a a child playing⋏ the sidewalk, a robin robin ⅃

tr./⌣/⊗ nesting a in mock orange bush, a summer

less #/⌒ sun set. Her⋏ eyes grew wide with expression⋏ ⁊

=/⁊ —/ little crow's feet wrinkles appeared⋏above the #

cheek-bones and she'd bite her lower⋏ lip less #

⌣ in an atempt to contain theᵍ emotion. ⅃

Same Copy After Corrections Have Been Made

She lived in a Pennsylvania coal town, a town
so small map makers didn't think it worth
mention. She was a large, keg-shaped woman,
with a round, open face over which emotion
rioted on almost any provocation — a child
playing on the sidewalk, a robin nesting in a
mock-orange bush, a summer sunset. Her eyes
grew wide with expression, little crow's-feet
wrinkles appeared above the cheek-bones and
she'd bite her lower lip in an attempt to contain
the emotion.

Rowena Fry

A Royalty

Statement

    They can range from simple to very complex computerized forms. No matter what form the publisher chooses, they cover the same information contained in the following:

Heartland Press, 1236 Sherman Ave., Evanston, Illinois 60202

Boyd B. Byside Agent	ROYALTY STATEMENT
545 Post St.	from 1-1 To 6-30-74
San Francisco, Calif. 94102	

Title of Book: Ride the Wild Waves   Author: Dorothy Aldis

Price	Number Sold & Description of Sales		Rate of Royalty		
$5.50	633	Domestic - Trade	12½%	.6875	$435.19
		Domestic - Library	%		
	2	Foreign	10 %		.77
	50	Domestic Special	10 %		9.63
		Foreign Special	%		
	685				$445.59

Deductions:

Advance:

Charges to Author:

Reserve for returns:

Unearned balance brought forward
from previous statement:. . . . .

                     Unearned balance carried forward:

                     Total Royalties due: $445.59

                     (Parentheses indicate Net Returns)

Obtaining a Release

for Publication

In signing a contract for publication you become responsible for offering to the publisher text and, in some cases, illustrations, which are cleared or released for publication. If the illustration is a photograph, you will be expected to have a signed release on file for any individual that appears prominently in the photo. Similarly, interview material you may have taken down in notes or with a recorder can return to plague you, if a release for publication is not obtained.

The following release form may be used for such purposes.

RELEASE

For good and valuable consideration, receipt whereof is hereby acknowledged, I give _____ , his successors and assigns and those acting under his permission or upon his authority, or those for whom he is acting, the right and permission to copyright and publish, in whole or in part (here describe the appropriate subject, such as "interview material taken in notes on July 14, 1976."). It is understood such right includes all volume rights for both domestic and world use and for any subsidiary purposes lawfully obtained in any other media.

I hereby waive any right to inspect or approve the finished product and warrant that I am of full age and have every right to contract in my own name in the above regard and hereby acknowledge that I have read this release, prior to signing it, and that I am fully familiar with its content and provisions.

In witness whereof, I have hereunto set my hand this day of _____ , 19_.

_____

Full name

_____

Street address

_____

City, State and zip-code

Consent by Guardian:

I am the parent, guardian or custodian of the minor named above and I have the legal authority to execute the above consent and release. I hereby approve and waive any rights to the material described herein.

Full name
_____

Street address
_____

City, State and zip-code

"Good and valuable consideration" is understood to mean an agreed sum of money, the cost of a lunch or dinner or a service rendered. For instance, a photographer may agree to supply a blow-up of the subject picked from contact sheets.

Where photographic reproduction is concerned, the first paragraph of the release should be altered where the parentheses begin, as follows:

. . . in whole or part, photographic portraits or pictures of me or in which I may be included in whole or part, or composite of distorted character, or form, in conjunction with my own or a fictitious name, or reproductions thereof in color or otherwise, reproduced in any media for art, advertising, trade, or any other lawful purpose whatsoever.

The balance of the text remains the same.

All About Copyright

In almost all cases it is the publisher who applies for copyright in both book and magazine publication.

Copyright is a form of protection provided under law to the authors of literary, musical, dramatic, artistic and other such creations of the mind. Under the law, the owner of a copyright has exclusive right in the work and can exercise the right to print; the right to reprint and to use the work in other writing. The *copyright owner* can sell or cause to be distributed any and all copies of the work, including the right to have the work dramatized, translated, arranged as a musical, used in audio or visual context (generally covered by the term recording) and in all other public uses.

You cannot copyright *unpublished works,* that is, a work that is not made available for public sale or distribution. There are, however, two other solutions available for such properties while they are being considered or offered for sale. *Common Law Literary Property* is covered under state law and is not handled in the Washington, D.C. Copyright Office. Many states, today, operate offices on a regional basis or in cities where density justifies such offices under the general heading of State Resource Offices. The writer can make application for Common Law Literary Property protection in accordance with procedures the resident state prescribes. Such protection generally lasts as long as the work is unpublished, and terminates once the work becomes published, or once statutory copyright is obtained. *Statutory copyright* is provided by federal law and also applies to works not yet published in the areas of all forms of drama, drawings, photographs, musical compositions, work offered in oral delivery, and sculptural works of a technical and scientific character. Although it is not required that such work be registered, such registration does constitute protection to the creator of the work. If you apply for *Statutory Copyright* of an unpublished work, the law requires a second copyright be secured once the work is published, and the proper copyright citation notice must appear in all copies made for any distribution. Conversely, books, short stories, poems and narrative outlines, maps, sound recordings, prints, periodicals and reproductions of works of art cannot be registered for *Statutory Copyright* in unpublished form. These works are copyrighted at the time of publication when proper notice of copyright is issued.

To secure copyright for an unpublished work you must file a claim with the Copyright Office in Washington, D.C. This requires an application form, a copy of the work in question, and the payment of a registration fee. A letter request, addressed to the Copyright Office, will be answered with the application form. The form contains instructions you must follow. For instance, in the case of a script or lecture, a copy of the manuscript must accompany the application and the payment of the applicable fee. Presently, the fee is $6.00 and cannot be sent in cash. Your check or money order must be made out to the *Register of Copyrights.*

To secure copyright for a published work the procedure is somewhat similar. In most all cases the publisher applies for copyright of a published work, often in the name of the author, although a copyright registered in the publisher's name is just as valid and is sometimes more practical especially where multiple authorship is involved as in periodicals or magazines. Privately printed works usually means the author must make copyright application.

To qualify for copyright protection the work must be 1) published; 2) all copies reproduced must carry the proper copyright notice in the form obtained and in the position copyright prescribes; 3) the claim must be registered in the *Copyright Office* promptly after publication.

The *Copyright Office* will provide the necessary application form free of charge. The form must be completed in all details that apply to the work in question. Two "best" copies (hard cover rather than soft cover when simultaneously published) of the finished work must accompany the application and payment of the $6.00 registration fee, in check or money order, must accompany the application. Obviously, when all three elements are submitted in one package the handling moves more efficiently.

Each work must be copyrighted separately. There is no provision, under law, for *blanket copyright* where an author can cover multiple or subsequent work. Only an author, or those to whom he has legally delegated the responsibility, can apply for copyright. Minors may copyright their work, but since state law varies as to what rights minors possess it is wise to know how the state of residency covers a minor's protection. Possession or ownership of a given manuscript does not constitute a basis for copyright application if the possessor or owner is not the author.

The form of the *Copyright Notice* involves three elements: the year of copyright; the appearance of the term Copyright in all copies produced; and the name of the copyright owner. The symbol, ®, is almost universally used since it facilitates coverage in countries that subscribe to the *Universal Copyright Convention.* An example of the proper notice of all three elements is as follows:

Copyright® 1976 by Cornelia Aldis Porter

If the work has been registered in unpublished form, both the year-date of the first registration and that of the published registration should appear in all copies produced, the earlier date preceding the year-date of publication.

The copyright notice for any publication printed in book form should appear on either the title page or the page following. The term of *Statutory Copyright* extends for twenty eight years and is counted from the date the work is published. In the case of unpublished works, the date is counted from the date of registration.

Copyright may be renewed for an additional twenty-eight-year period, if renewal is applied for during the last year in which the original copyright is in effect. A renewal application form may be obtained from the Copyright Office and once completed and filed with an additional payment of $4.00, the second term becomes effective.

The Copyright Office does not provide legal guidance in matters concerning copyright law. In the event of infringement or dispute, it is best to consult an attorney.

The address of the Copyright Office is:

> Register of Copyrights
> Library of Congress
> Washington, D.C. 20559

Writers frequently ask whether they should copyright a manuscript before publication. Since both an unpublished and published work are protected by common law, it is not necessary for a writer to secure copyright protection before submitting a work for publication. Among the wary, a *"poorman's copyright"* is sometimes used where the writer mails a copy of the work in question to himself through the United States' mails, certified mail, return receipt requested. The title of the manuscript is recorded on the registery form number provides proof to the writer that his manuscript is, indeed, his work and has passed, as such, through the United States' mails as a confirmation of that fact.

The Writer's Manual Book 2

How to Write Fiction

By
Arthur F. Gould

CONTENTS

ABOUT THE AUTHOR

Arthur F. Gould
holds a bachelor's and master's degree in English
and has done work at the doctoral level
in the field of literary criticism.
He wrote educational material for Borg-Warner's Systems 80,
researched the Chicago chapter for Vance Packard's
Nation of Strangers,
wrote forewords for Scholastic's High School Classics series,
was associate editor of Northwestern University's *Tri-Quarterly,*
and has worked as a newspaper reporter,
feature writer, and metro-editor for Newhouse Publications.
Since 1972
he has been a partner in the authors' agency,
Porter, Gould & Dierks.

ONE

INTRODUCTION

A story is a complete dramatic action creating life with words Flannery O'Connor said about writing fiction in her book *Mystery and Manners.*[1]. The emphasis should be placed on being *complete*, for a good story or novel is not a fragment, or a glimpse of life. It is not a reminiscence, an episode, an opinion, or an anecdote, Ms. O'Connor explains. A piece of fiction is a summation of experience with a beginning, middle, and end in which characters act and speak significantly according to the author's vision. A complete fictional work includes strong characters, conflict, plot, story line, action, drama, emotional impact, and considerations of time and place. Other elements are transitions, viewpoint, flashbacks, dialogue, motivation, and descriptions. A story is written for the sake of telling the truth, as experience is created with language. At the same time, a piece of fiction must be consistent with reality. If the author ignores concrete details and fails to anchor the story solidly in the world, the work will be unsold and unread. The writer will have failed to create life with words.

In this section we'll be discussing creation of life through the medium of words, but first a word of warning: you will not suddenly become a successful writer after reading what is written here, or by knowing what Flannery O'Connor, or any author, says about writing. There is only one way to learn to be a better writer: to write as much and as often as possible. As a young man, William Saroyan took a year out to improve himself as a short story writer. He practically lived on coffee and cigarettes and every morning he began a new short story. He worked all day on the story and in the evening, if the story was unfinished, he set it aside and the next day started work on another. The example Saroyan set is extreme, but the kind of discipline he imposed on himself goes into any successful writing and without it not much good writing is accomplished. If you are determined to be a good writer, if you have accepted the fact that you can write well only by working hard, experiencing some sacrifice and disappointment--even distress or pain--with your eyes wide open; and if you've set aside time each day to work on your writing, then what's written here will help you in a very difficult task.

Perhaps the greatest challenge a fiction writer faces is keeping straight the difference between a story and reality and, at the same time, maintaining a close relationship between the story and the real world. Any good writer knows that the one gives rise to the other. Without actual experience no author could write a story. But the writer's responsibility is to impose order on events so the truth, or significance, of a situation is made clear to the reader. Ultimately, the difference between a good story and reality is the amount of unnecessary, meaningless, time wasting details, events, and conversations to which the reader is exposed. A writer who understands this knows that a story exposes only what is necessary for the satisfactory outcome of a complete tale. In reality, our lives are over extended: we say too much; carry out too many unnecessary acts; let our minds dwell on insignificant thoughts, and our senses are occupied with countless trivial details. In a successful short story, or novel, experience is leaned-down so that only details that further the development of the story are included. Accordingly, it's often what the author leaves out--and therefore what he has selected to include--that makes the difference between success or failure.

Without a clear idea of what is significant, the writer will have an impossible time deciding what to include in his or her story. Significance is subjective, but essential, in the area of story idea selection. No authority or teacher of writing would pass judgment on whether an idea for a story was significant or not. Most ideas a writer comes up with for stories can be made significant, depending on the author's talent. But we're concerned with the general significance of details included in a story. You should take valuable space to describe a tree, a stormy sky, a man driving a horse and wagon *only* if they somehow influence characters and events in the story. Lightning strikes the tree, felling it as the wagon passes underneath, killing the driver whose death alters the life of the story's central character. However, if the sequence of events is merely an aside with no effect on the hero, or heroine, then the storm and the death are a waste of space, distracting the reader. A short story, or novel, is life created with words, but it is also very discriminating, limited in scope, concentrating on the evolution of a specific situation.

Limited in scope, yes, but not in meaning or depth. For another responsibility of the writer is to include universals in a story. No one approaches a story with the idea of reading a treatise in philosophy, but all good stories relate significantly to the human condition. The importance of what a story says is reflected in the action, dialogue, characters, and other elements the writer employs.

In all of this we are explaining the author's task of heightening reality. Put another way, a short story, or a novel, is a reflection of life in words, a significant creation that is complete in that it is true to the real world without imposing too much of the baggage of reality on the reader. The author heightens reality through the story to lift it from the hodgepodge of daily life and in the process the vision of truth becomes clearer.

Theoretically, this heightening process is the life giving energy of the story, *the nature of the beast.* Specifically, you will want to know about the nuts and bolts of fiction writing: characterization, conflict, dialogue, plot, action, description, situation, theme, time and timing, transitions, flashbacks, beginning-middle-end structure, length, motivation, language, order, point-counterpoint, rise and fall, crisis, climax, resolution, judgment and vision, voice and viewpoint, depth and meaning.

Good fiction writing involves understandings between the author and his or her story, and, as significantly, the relationship between the reader and the story. The better a character is understood, the more effective he or she will be in a story and the closer the reader will come to realize the author's intentions. Understanding is reached when we know what motivates a character. A writer should carefully plan the forces of thought and desire that move a person to action. Knowing what's going on in a story is knowledge of plot, too. Plot is the necessity of a structure, with built-in conflicts and resolutions within which characters function and the story evolves. Once the writer has made his or her characters' motivations clear, the plot falls into place. The story, itself, is what's told about the characters, the result of the actions of certain persons; while the plot is the structure within which the story unfolds. In other words, the story is the substance of what the writer wants to show the reader. While there may be a limited number of plot structures--only eight common ones, according to the critic and teacher F.A. Rockwell[2]--there are an almost infinite number of ways--story-lines--to illustrate them.

With plot, story and characters, theme and viewpoint are important elements, touchstones to the particular slant of a story. But no consideration, is important unless there is action to sustain reader interest. Successful action is plausible action: believable action within our expectations of the character's ability to function. For instance, Gods can act in ways that men cannot; certain men and women function better than others. The credibility of the writer is often judged on how well he or she is able to conceive justifiable action.

As the story evolves, attention must be paid to two kinds of time, one governing the characters in the story and the other, timing, that is the author's rhythm controlling the flow of events from beginning to end. Time which passes in a story may be an hour, a day, a week, a month, a year. Characters will be expected to function plausibly within a specific length of time. If the amount of time is a day, a character cannot be expected to journey from New York to California by car during the story. That is obvious. But in the same sense, a character cannot be expected to eat a meal in 15 seconds, or write a five page letter in a minute. The writer must make allowances for a character's actions relative to the total amount of time that will pass in a story. The writer must also pay attention to the order of events and how fast they take place. If the amount of time is one day, the climactic scenes should not happen in the morning of the day, with the afternoon and evening devoted to only excessive action. This handling is known as the author's timing. The climax of a story should coincide with the final minutes, hours, days of story-time. The rhythm of events should build toward that end.

Setting and historical time present other problems. A story may be set any place, at any time, as long as the characters function in accordance with time and place. The author should be familiar enough with the setting and the period in history to give a credible account, to create an effective illusion of reality.

Generally, there should be a recognizable order of events, a clear direction in which the story is moving, a natural flow of action, enough description to cause characters and setting to come alive for the reader, and an overall logic--even if an absurd logic--to the story. There should be no action without a reaction; no rise without a fall and no conversation without an answer, if an effective picture of life is to be created in words.

TWO

CHARACTERIZATION

Crashing The Ho-Hum Barrier

Good writers are masters of their craft--*entertainers* of the first rank. For instance, Shakespeare could well be pictured wearing a coxcomb and fools bells rather than the deadly serious expression of a *literary lion*. With every successful author, he shares the mastery of illusion that keeps readers and audiences coming back to his plays out of sheer joy, like patrons to a fascinating side show at a carnival. Whatever social, philosophical, or historical benefits are derived from the spectacle owe their hearing to the less ponderous delights of the performance. The responsibility for all the attention rests on the shoulders of the leering, laughing, crying characters, both male and female. Without these elements the author's magnificent fabrication of life in words is so much ink and paper signifying nothing.

Characterization is the writer's most important task. The illusion of reality a writer creates is as strong as the weakest character. It's true that all characters should not have the same depth of reality. You can imagine the hopelessness of *Hamlet* if each character displayed the depth of personality of the doomed prince. Yet two of the most obscure characters in *Hamlet* have inspired a modern play of their own, *Rosencrantz and Guildenstern Are Dead*. Successful characterization is a matter of degree, a variety of kin and kind who share the reality of the story without trespassing on each others responsibilities.

Depending on the critics' choices of labels, characters are simple, lacking complexity; complicated; flat, one dimensional; round, fully developed; or, background, undeveloped. In the hands of a master, the latter should be as insignificant as Shakespeare's two courtiers.

Simple characters manifest one dominant trait throughout the story. Such characters are easy to spot, though often more forgettable than memorable. Memorable ones include the pathetic Bob Cratchit in *A Christmas Carol* or the vindictive editor in Twain's *Journalism in Tennessee;* both difficult to create. They usually function as touchstones to other characters and represent extremes like the good but naive Maria in Joyce's story *Clay.* It is easy to lose interest in a simple character and a writer certainly should not use one as the hero of a novel. Even in a short story like *Clay* the reader's attention is almost entirely diverted from Maria, at the end, by the more complex Joe. If the story went any further, she would fade entirely as the central character. It's one sign of Joyce's story telling genius-- he knew when to stop.

But the writer should not confuse lack of complexity with shallowness. If a character you've created doesn't put a dent in the ho-hum barrier, don't rationalize by saying, "I *meant* her to be a simple character." You'd be confusing simplicity with ineffectiveness. A well drawn simple character is fully developed within the dominant trait of the character. He or she may embody some shading of good, evil, love or hate. The character will be definitive, with enough vitality to avoid lifeless stereotyping. Assertive Mrs. Barrows in *The Catbird Seat*, by James Thurber; the self sacrificing heroine of Maupassant's *The Necklace*; the sucker in *Swallowing An Oyster Alive*, by John S. Robb, and stubborn Flannery, the railway clerk in Ellis Parker Butler's delightful story *Pigs Is Pigs* are all memorably simple characters.

The point about such characters is an easy one in theory, but difficult in practice: keep the simple character alive but uncomplicated. The appearance of a second or third dominant trait will alter the character making him, or her, *complex,* another type altogether. As the number of traits increase, the character becomes less general and takes on greater individuality creating a more complex illusion of reality. Encountering complex characters, the reader is less called on to suspend his or her disbelief. Complicated characters are more real because they reflect the pluralism of real life. They excite great interest and attract the reader's attention more readily than a simple character.

The reason for this is the presence of two or more strong, contradictory or conflicting traits. In *Hamlet*, the ambitious but fearful King is a complex character. He murders to gain the throne, but he fears retribution and his anguish gives him away. If he were a simple character--strictly ambitious-- no self doubt would interfere with his sense of security. The trait of ambition is strong, but not of equal strength with the trait of fear. The latter finally causes the King's downfall.

A formula for a complex character might be as follows: there should be at least two strong traits vying for the upper hand, with the resulting conflict creating reader interest for the individual. Such characters are almost alive, but they lack the three dimensional quality of a fully developed, *round*, character.

This type is a central character wherever he or she appears in a story or novel, play, or poem. The depth of such a character should be nearly infathomable --a Hamlet, an Ahab, a Bloom. Claudius is life-like. Hamlet lives, his character traits strong and many. He is philosophical, loving, hateful, spiteful, comical, shrewd, jealous, scheming, ambitious, fearful, revengeful, doubting--the list could be extended to encompass all human characteristics. If such a character could achieve the ultimate step across the ho-hum barrier-if he was not, after all, an illusion of reality--he would walk off the stage and disappear into the audience.

In part, the symmetrical types gain life through contrast with the others, including flat characters with no dominant traits, and the most obscure coat-holders in the background.

How does a writer create life-like characters? The mechanics of characterization can be spelled out. For instance, since a character is a personification of human traits, the author can follow F.A. Rockwell's advice to express the traits in eight ways: background (birth, schooling, economics, social standing); emotions (feelings about persons, events, and situations); setting (clothes, etc.); thoughts and philosophy; speech (dialect, accent, a stutter); opinions of other characters; action; physical description.[3] Each point should illuminate the trait, explaining it to the reader, and creating a feeling of motivation that justifies the character's existence. If the character is ambitious, for instance, background will shed light on that trait. There should be emotional revelations and the setting should say something about the character's ambitions. The desires will be revealed by thoughts and attitudes toward life. A person may speak affectedly, or fain a street accent--whatever will help realize the ambition. The opinions of others are important.

CAE   . . . Yond Cassius has a lean and hungry look.
He thinks too much, such men are dangerous.

As Maren Elwood has pointed out, character may be expressed without action, too, through appearance, detail, age, gender, name, facial expression, posture, habitual expression, clothing, surroundings and occupations.[4]

Details of character should be presented in as natural a way as possible, to avoid cataloguing. Two examples will help make the point.

WRONG: Ms. Goodwoman, a tall, 35-year-old, redhead was the aggressive, annoying managing editor of a fashion magazine read by 25 million people a month. The sparse steel and leather furniture in her office, her expensive but simply designed clothes, and her cold expression conveyed her stern, practical, ambitious nature. Ms. Pleasant, the editor, who had been with the magazine 20 years, had no doubt Ms. Goodwoman was after her job. Worse, the older woman had half-convinced herself the magaging editor could do a better job.

RIGHT: Ms. Goodwoman entered the editor's office with a feeling of triumph.

"Jean, I have the solution for boosting the advertising revenue," she said.

"Sit down and tell me your idea," Jean Pleasant said to her managing editor. Together they ran the popular fashion magazine, *Update.*

"It's simple, really. I don't know why you haven't thought of it. The auto industry spends millions on magazine advertising. We can capture part of the market by running some first rate car articles for women."

"I don't know if that's right for us, Alice."

"Of course it is!" There was already an authoritative edge in Alice's voice. Her eyes flashed sternly. She was annoyed by Jean's hesitance at the suggestion of a new idea. 'When I'm editor . . . .' Alice caught herself thinking. She looked around the little office-- manuscripts, layout sheets, and back issues were piled on the stuffed chairs and on the heavy roll top desk. The chaos contrasted sharply with her own office, with sparse steel and leather furniture, orderly file cabinets and carefully indexed shelves of manuscripts. Ms. Pleasant had been running the magazine for 20 years. 'She looks tired,' Alice thought.

"I'll raise the question at Tuesday's meeting with the publisher. Thank you Alice." Jean watched the young woman leave. 'The tall redhead, with her gray suits, is after my job.' she thought. Jean was suddenly afraid, not because of a possible battle with Alice, but because Jean knew that the managing editor was right about the auto advertising. Jean was frightened that Alice could do a better job.

. The point of contrast between the two passages is the way the characterization flows naturally from a number of elements--dialogue, thoughts, observations, and descriptions--in the second example, while in the first, the author has written a paragraph of direct statements about the two women, telling the reader what to think about them, rather than showing them in action and let the reader draw his or her own conclusions. This is a key point in successful characterization. The reader should be able to draw the correct picture of a character without having to be told directly what to think.

Besides dialogue, which builds the story, gives information and shows emotion, other elements contribute to good characterization. A character's thoughts provide past, present, and future information. Action stimulates reaction and thus shows character. A list of figures of speech that show character includes: simile, metaphor, personification, sarcasm, irony, metonymy (replacing one word with a more pictorial word to intensify reader reaction), hyperbole (excessive exaggeration), paradox, and onomatopoeia (imitative and naturally suggestive words associated with its referent as cuckoo or boom). Such figures of speech can give punch to the language, if they are used correctly. If they are mis-used, however, they can make the material hopeless.

Characters must be well motivated to make strong impressions. The reader should understand why a character acts a certain way, or says something important. Part of effective characterization is establishing premises for behavior. In a well designed story, the central character has an all important problem to solve. There should be other problems, but they are only a part of the central issue.

Usually, a character wants something for himself, or herself, or wants to prevent something from happening. The more human and immediate the problem the better the story. Today, readers do not hold their breath over another story about a young person setting out to bring peace to the world, equality to the races, redistribution of wealth and education for all. They are worthy goals, but far too overwhelming for a character in a short story, or even a novel.

In general, the writer has successfully motivated the character when the reader understands the necessity for the character's action. If the reader must ask why a character is taking certain action, the author has failed to make the reader understand that figure. The reader's satisfaction is not discovering causes, but in understanding effects. A story of revenge must contain reasons for vengeance. Accidental, or coincidental acts of love or violance have no place in good fiction. There must be a feeling of necessity in whatever happens. It is the crucial difference between art and reality.

Motivation is the result of life-like characters with significant problems in logical situations. This framework is the source of action. Most critics agree with Ms. Elwood that there are five basic types of motivation: self-preservation, love, religion, power and society.[5] All five can be present in a story, although it is probably unwise to have more than two. In any case, one of them will dominate depending on the central character's most important trait. Of course, these elements are not self-sustaining. Action, dialogue, thoughts, author narration keep the story going after the initial crisis, the statement of the problem, through to the middle development and on to the end.

While the characters are being introduced, the problems stated, the motivations set forth, the illusion of reality is enhanced by emotions. Nature, machinery, and other inanimate objects are inherently emotionless. Personification is a reflection of the beholder's state of mind and characterizes the person creating the image. There is no original emotional value in a *laughing* brook, an *angry* sky or even an *impersonal* machine, because we know these things are incapable of self-generating feelings--that the brook never *cries*, the sky is never *happy* and the machine is never *personal*. The potential for expressing and feeling emotions in a man, or woman, is the primary source creating a sense-of-being-alive in a story. No storm really rages--it simply is. But a person may rage and we then have that wonderful sense of *intelligent* emotion. There are reasons why a storm exists --rage is not one of them. King Lear, for instance, may think he sees a sympathetic universe "cracking" on the heath at midnight, but what he really perceives is the breaking of his own heart. Emotions exist in men and women, not in wind and rain.

Generating an emotional response in a reader is essential to capturing interest in a story. The emotions of the characters help create conflict and, in turn, create emotional responses in readers. These feelings are the basis of sympathy--identification--for the characters. After the relationship between reader and characters has been established through emotional *contact*, there is a good chance the author's intentions will be understood.

Characterization is an on-going process, focusing on development of dominant traits. Although a person may change character in real life, a character should not change from the beginning to the end of a story. Structurally, it is unthinkable for a character to shift from good to evil, for instance. A character may possess a blend of traits, but one of them will decide the course of the action and it should remain constant to preserve order within the story. The most well developed villains will approach the character of good men without losing their essential evilness. Consider the humanity of Ahab when he discusses his love for his young wife near the conclusion of *Moby Dick*. At the same time, good characters will have elements that make us quake with fear. Consider Hamlet's blood-lust--the abandonment with which he kills Polonius, although he has no idea who is really behind the curtain in his mother's bedroom. Good, or well developed, characters reflect a wide range of traits within their roles. If characters are tailored to fit into a preconceived plot structure, they will be wooden. The characters must be allowed to come alive, so the reader has the illusion that they are controlled by internal motivations.

A writer should know his or her characters well before writing about them. The author's knowledge of a character must be strong. It is not unwise to write a history of each character including his or her life before and after the time in which the story takes place. Think of the character in a variety of circumstances. A character file is helpful, too, with name, general physical description, age, birth place, parents' backgrounds, interesting relatives, education, interests, dominant traits, flaws, and goals. Circumstances of death may be important too.

In a final analysis, good characterization is structural, mechanical, and magical . . . creating a seamless illusion of reality.

THREE

PLOT:
Creating Structural Necessity

A young man and woman meet and fall in love, but they are prevented from marrying because of a family feud. As a result, they commit suicide. The plot structure in *Romeo and Juliet* is a common one: *goal-unachieved*. We will discuss others in this chapter, but all of them share one point: they create a structural necessity for the action of the story-line.

While a story involves characterization, emotional responses, action, conflicts and other elements, plot is concerned with structuring those elements and directing them toward a preconceived goal. In a well plotted story there is nothing inconclusive about the structural goals. It is difficult to imagine a reader in doubt about the end of "The Cask of Amontillado," a story with a *goal achieved* plot in which Poe has set our sense of morality on edge. There is self-conscious mystery in character and theme, but the reader knows, with a sense of horror, that Fortunato's doom is sealed once the gormand decides he will have a taste of the rare sherry. The moments of calculated doubt are an important key to this plot.

Obstacles are often part of the plot structure that gets the action going. For instance, imagine the plight of Melville's narrator in "Bartleby The Scrivener", when he is confronted by a young copiest who "prefers" not to do as he is told. He refuses to be fired as well. Bartleby is a story of civil disobedience showing the diversity of human nature, subjects that fit the author's *style*. But the plot, and therefore the action, is concrete.

While the story of a man who defies assumptions stimulates the reader to a variety of philosophical speculations, the immediate suspense of this *come-to-realize* plot holds the reader firmly in this world. Into a well ordered universe, in which men are assumed to act correctly, enters a person who follows his preferences, instead. He dies as a result, but the narrator learns that men have preferences that must be respected: "The great point was, not whether I had assumed that he would quit me, but whether he would prefer so to do. He was more a man of preferences than assumptions." What makes the story especially worth reading is the simplicity with which Melville poses the conflict. After asking the scrivener to proof a legal brief, his employer states.

> Imagine my surprise, nay, my consternation, when without moving from his privacy, Bartleby in a singularly mild, firm voice replied, "I would prefer not to."

The lines of the conflict are drawn and it would take a person of singularly shallow curiosity to stop reading.

There are stories in which villains are the central characters, and they call for a special kind of plot. Since a successful writer directs where sympathies will fall, a way of stacking the deck, villians, truly evil characters, rarely triumph. Of course, the author relies on predictable responses from readers, and when the central character is a real villain the _goal-foiled_ plot calls for his or her downfall as a result of the character's own actions.

Pushkin used this kind of plot in "The Queen of Spades", a story of love, manners and gambling in 19th Century Russia. The central character violates the ethics of love and manners in his desire to win at cards. But he is a doomed man, and, as in watching a Greek tragedy, the pleasure is derived from seeing the author's style of fulfillment. The man's greed dooms him, because character flaw is essential to the _goal-foiled_ plot. Unless the character contains the seeds of his own undoing so that the fall is brought about from within, the whole course of events will appear as clumsy, contrived author imposition.

Obstacles in the path of the villain must be good elements in the story. His or her momentary triumph over them keeps the reader turning pages. In "The Queen Of Spades," the officer's greed is so intense that he murders to discover the secret that will bring a fortune at the game of faro. The same psychological force that drives him to murder causes him to dream a winning three card combination. He believes in the hallucination and plays the game, winning twice, but loses all on the last card. He goes mad and the girl he has used marries an obscure official and lives happily ever after. The plot of this rather complicated story-line is very simple: the central character's evil intentions are foiled by his own actions. Pushkin's genius created the story that brought the structure to life.

In a _decision plot_, the central character must choose between courses of action, where one is good and the other bad, within the context of the story.

The reader's interest is maintained as the character sways from one choice to another. The story will usually convey a moral and the action is linear, following a steady progression of events marked by the character's doubt. The *decision plot* is not complicated in structure. It is relatively easy to control the reader's reactions with respect to the characters' actions. The conflict of emotions, dialectical in nature, insures reader involvement. But such plot simplicity does not mean the writer can get away with one dimensional characters, uninteresting action, cliche ridden language, lack of motivation, or lack of conflict. The individual elements in the story are clearly visible to the reader. Since the danger is in being too mechanical, the writer must create strong characters and action, sound motivations. significant crisis and resolutions. Most important, the consequences of the central character's decision must be significant enough to justify his or her struggle.

"Young Goodman Brown", Hawthorne's tale about the depravity of the human heart, demonstrates the swaying rhythm of a *decision plot.* At issue in the story is the central character's choice between baptism by the devil and faith in the Puritan community of God. During the course of the story, the young man suffers a series of disillusionments as he sees *good* men and women go to the devil. At last his wife, Faith, appears evil too. In a final gesture of devotion, he admonishes her to look to Heaven and the scene of debauchery in the forest vanishes, leaving him alone with a vision of depravity. It is a bitter triumph, and Goodman Brown lives out his days in gloom and despair. However, he has made the right choice within the story's alternatives.

Hawthorne's success with the tale rests on the way each of Brown's nine confrontations with the devil seems to be the final one. A sense of crisis is generated and the reader feels relief when he rejects the devil and anguish when he follows him further into the forest. The suspense is a natural outgrowth of the Brown-devil conflicts: what will be Brown's final decision?

In this kind of plot, there must be at least one time when the hero or heroine opts for the wrong choice and appears headed for doom. In Hawthorne's story, the choice is clearly between good and evil. In any *decision plot,* the choice must be between right and wrong as the two concepts are defined within the story.

A *goal-abandoned* plot has a hero who gives up a goal because he or she sees it as evil or harmful. This kind of plot is different from *goal-unachieved.* In the latter, the central character does not *willingly* give up the goal. He or she is prevented from accomplishing it by outside forces. In a goal-abandoned plot, the central character must be sympathetic, someone capable of better actions than the one he or she is undertaking. But the reader must understand why the central character is set on accomplishing the negative goal, and that the character is justified in carrying it out. As a result, the abandonment will make the character a far better person.

In "The Long Exile," Tolstoy's story of a merchant convicted of a murder he did not commit, the central character, Aksionov, has a chance to avenge himself but in the end opts for a higher sense of humanity. After years of exile in Siberia, Aksionov encounters a man named Makor Semyovich who has been sent to the same prison camp for stealing a horse. Semyovich brags that he has managed to remain free for years even though he has committed a far more serious crime. Aksionov realizes that Semyovich is the murderer for whom he has been serving a life sentence. He is filled with rage and the reader sympathizes with his desire for revenge. But a fortnight later, when Aksionov has a chance to turn the real murderer in for trying to escape, he does not betray Semyovich. Filled with guilt because of Aksionov's generosity, the murderer confesses to Aksionov and begs for and receives his forgiveness. He is spiritually stronger and the reward for the reader is seeing Aksionov's character remain untainted. He gives up his plans of vengeance for unselfish reasons, reaping richer spiritual rewards.

The *rebuilt-character* plot involves an unsympathetic person who has his or her original humanity restored through an extraordinary involvement with another character, or as a result of some traumatic experience. Dickens' *A Christmas Carol* is an obvious example in which the central character rediscovers his humanity. It's important that the writer makes clear that the person was once admirable before going into a character decline. Dickens does this through the masterful use of flashbacks presented as visitations by the spirits.

The reverse of the *rebuilt-character* plot is *character-deteriotation.* In this plot structure an apparently good person reverts to his or her true state of being. Hopes for rehabilitation are raised at the crisis, but the character slips and is finally lost. The reader holds out for a better ending, but the central character is doomed. This is the plot structure at the center of Conrad's *Heart Of Darkness.* The apparently saintly reformer-missionary Kurtz goes up the Congo river where he finds the malignancy at the center of his own character.

In a *lost-goal* plot the character is sympathetic but life does not work out happily and an otherwise admirable goal is lost. John O'Hara's "Over The River And Through The Wood." Fitzgerald's *The Great Gatsby,* and Joyce's story "Eveline" in the *Dubliners* contain *lost-goal* plots.

Before an author begins to write a story involving any of these plots, his, or her, first task is to work out the technical design--the plot structure. The idea for a story may have been an inspiration, but the execution is painstaking. Writing is hard work, not wishful thinking.

Concerning structure, the writer must keep in mind that there is a difference between truth and reality in writing. Because something really happened to you, or someone you know, does not make the incident material for a story or novel. Reality itself is no excuse for the written word in fiction, because most lives are very dull. What the writer is after in a good story is the combination of truth and fiction. Reality is only a reference source for keeping the reader's attention. Fiction is a *planned* improvement over life, using a plot which has problem and solution plus crisis, as F.A. Rockwell points out.[6]

A random selection of incidents and characters does not make up a plot, but needless complication is not the answer, either. Keep the plot simple for a short story. A writer may intrigue more in a novel. And it is important to build the structure, whether simple or complex, toward the crisis by piling-on the incidents, using smooth transitions, so the reader cannot guess the ending. At the same time, avoid hackneyed or too extraordinary plots. They tend to create reader frustrations and little else.

There is, of course, a distinction between plot and story. A plot supplies the structure that gives shape to a story. A story is what a writer wants to show and plot offers a way to the reader. There is really very little a critic or teacher can tell a writer about choosing a story. Each author has countless tales worth telling, some more significant than others, but each with its own value. The crucial task is finding a way to show the significance of a story to readers. A plot is a way of ordering the events, the characters, the action, the emotions to create a successful story or novel.

FOUR

VIEWPOINT:

Outside Looking In

We experience life directly through our own senses or vicariously through someone else who relates experience for us to enjoy. Because we are immediately involved with only a small part of what happens in the world, most of us depend on others--newspeople, commentators, neighbors, friends, and relatives--to add dimension to our lives. Usually, we are discriminating in our sources--a favorite broadcaster, or newspaper, a trusted advisor, an honest friend, or a close relative. As a result, our lives are crowded with viewpoints that let us see a random of activities.

This chapter is about viewpoint in a short story, or novel, and the frames of reference an author may use for the reader on the outside looking in. Coleridge, in *Biographia Literaria,* discusses the author's responsibility to create "a semblance of truth sufficient to procure for these shadows of imagination that willing suspension of disbelief for the moment, which constitutes poetic faith." The reader should have no doubt in the illusion of reality. Using the correct point of view is a crucial part of that persuasion. There is a character in every story from whom the life of the story flows. He, or she, is the *viewpoint character,* the one who conveys experience from the story to the reader. Six viewpoints are often cited by critics and teachers of writing.

Internal third person is the most commonly used viewpoint. The reader follows the story through the mind of one central character. While the reader is kept at a distance, the character's thoughts, emotions, and feelings are revealed allowing subjective participation in the action. The author uses good control with this point of view, although the reader must sometimes make judgements concerning the character's true understanding of events. When inaccuracies in the character's judgment are clearly intentional, the author is saying something important about the person's sense of understanding. However, when mis-judgments are obviously unintentional as a result of the author's own confusion about the material, he or she has failed to control the viewpoint character and poor writing is the result. This problem is easy to spot by testing what the author has shown to be true about events and other characters and what the viewpoint character believes to be true about them. If he or she makes a mistake in judgment and *there is no motivation, or justification, later in the story for the mis-judgment,* the author may be unaware of the inconsistency, or unable to control the course of events. The reader must always ask how far can the subjective third person narrator be trusted to give a true impression of events. A good author signals the reader when the central character is not relating the events accurately. This is always done on purpose, for the sake of some aspect of the story. The danger for the beginning writer is unconscious mistakes of judgement that creep into the text as a result of telling a story entirely from the subjective viewpoint of a single character. An author may have the viewpoint character give an impression of an event one way on page 20 and give another impression of the same event on page 150, without realizing the error. Unless the error serves the purpose of the story, consistency of judgement by the viewpoint character is the key to a well written story. Masterful handling of shifting subjective third person point of view is to be found in John Barth's *The Sot-Weed Factor.* Naive Eben Cooke makes so many mis-judgements about the substance of reality that he ends up questioning his own existence.

Although depending too heavily on a single subjective third person point of view may strain that character's credibility, it is confusing to the reader to have many subjective third person viewpoint characters in a single story, or novel. Balance is desirable. An author may set the scene using omniscient viewpoint; then, introduce the viewpoint character through whom the reader experiences the rest of the story, with an occasional glimpse through the eyes of other minor characters.

Another reason to avoid undue shifting of viewpoint is the diluting effect it has on the emotional impact. The concentration of sympathy on a single character is the major strength of a good story. When two characters demand great, and equal, amounts of emotional reaction, the reader seldom has the strength to sustain that level of concentration. When two characters equally share the viewpoint role in a story, the emotional energy is not doubled--it is halved. In the subjective viewpoint, empathy is lost by shifting from inside one character to inside another.

Internal third person causes the reader to feel the way the character does, creating the necessary bond of sympathy that will keep the reader turning pages to find out the central character's fate. Although the viewpoint character cannot know the minds of others in the story--the way an omniscient narrator can--he, or she, passes judgements on to the reader, which may be right or wrong. When the subjective character is correct, it builds up trust, which contributes to reader sympathy.

With *external third person viewpoint* the reader is never inside the character's mind--that is the difference between the two third person viewpoints. Writing objectively the author shows the story from an exterior viewpoint and never from within the central character. The following two examples will make the point:

Objective:

> With a look of disdain, Harry shot the wounded enemy soldier between the eyes.

> "Go to hell," Harry shouted. Everyone he killed revenged the death of his buddy.

Subjective:

> After Harry's buddy was killed, he was possessed with an irrational desire for revenge. 'Go to hell,' Harry thought, looking at the wounded enemy soldier. With a feeling of disdain, Harry shot him between the eyes.

In the first example, we understand Harry by the way he looks, by what he says and does. This objectivity is characteristic of the *external third person* point of view. The second example is subjective because we are inside Harry's mind, which is possessed; the oath is thought; the disdain is felt.

Using the external viewpoint, the author cannot bring the reader in as close to the central character as in the internal viewpoint. Although it is possible to write a story with complete objectivity, most authors use a combination of the two viewpoints. They spell each other--external relieving the tensions of strong subjective passages, while internal brings the reader in close to the emotional center.

By itself, the external viewpoint presents the facts, laid out for the reader. There is less emotional involvement. Any newspaper provides daily examples of this technique. Many reporters who turn to fiction and fail to create a strong emotional bond between reader and characters have failed because they continue to use external viewpoint exclusively.

Internal first person is the most intimate point of view. The author is the narrating central character. This viewpoint offers the closest reader identification, because the author speaks directly to the reader baring every thought, feeling, and motivation. Poe was a master of the internal first person and used it with terrifying effect in "The Cask of Amontillado", "The Tell-Tale Heart," "The Pit And The Pendulum", and "The Black Cat." The stream-of-consciousness style evoked by the narrators of these stories shows the primary characteristic of this subjective technique. The illusion of reality is quickly created and there are few wasted words.

Controlling the *internal first person* is difficult and telling stories from this viewpoint requires great discipline. Vision is limited, because the *I* character can show only what he, or she, directly sees, hears, feels, and thinks. Since the illusion of reality depends on convincing the reader that the author and the narrator are one, the writer cannot shift to another viewpoint. The reader knows that Poe is not really the *I* character in "The Cask of Amontillado," but then who is telling the story? After wrestling with that critical question for a while, one begins to appreciate the complexity of this fictive style.

The more difficult it is for the reader to break through the illusion--to tell the difference between the author at work writing the story and the *I* character relating it--the greater control the writer has of the material. A momentary slip into another viewpoint is enough to ruin the illusion created by the *internal first person*. If a writer has to introduce details that can come from outside the *I* character's range of vision, dialogue is the most effective medium to use. The *I* character can always reproduce conversation to show the reader another viewpoint.

The greatest drawback of the *internal first person* is the risk of creating an egomaniac.

> I went without sleep 48 hours, working my way back from behind enemy lines, concentrating on one thought: 'I must keep moving.' I am sure no one else in the platoon could have endured the ordeal, and the realization of my own strength acted as a tonic on my nerves and tired muscles. I swam rivers; I climbed ravines and I crawled across open fields of wheat stubble to safety.

I. . .I. . .I. the repetition becomes monotonous. There is a high risk of melo-drama. Other characters remain undeveloped, and the reader is subjected to a long emotional strain with little chance of relief.

Although the *internal first person* firmly establishes viewpoint, the author must work to dramatize action, dialogue, and thoughts. From this point of view it is easier to tell the story, rather than show it. There is authority in the *I* character, as well as close contact with the reader. Since the narrator has survived to tell the tale, there is no doubt that he or she will escape any dangers. The question, therefore, is never, "did he or she make it?" But, rather, "how?"

With the *external first person,* the narrator plays a secondary role telling a story about someone else without consciously revealing very much personally. This is the technique in *Moby Dick, The Great Gatsby,* and *The Golden Bowl,* for instance. Interestingly, in *The Heart Of Darkness* Conrad uses both *external* and *internal first person.* The narrator sets the scene on board the Nellie and then Marlowe takes over as the internal *I* character.

Characteristically, the *external first person* gives enough objective information to capture the reader's interest, but he, or she, refrains from imposing a subjective judgement on characters or events. This creates an intimate but detached narrative viewpoint.

Second person viewpoint is rarely used, today, because asking the reader to project himself, or herself, as a character in the story seems awkward and affected to us. For example:

> You are aware of the dripping faucet. At first you ignore it, but the sound increases in volume in direct proportion to your efforts to shut it out. First one pillow, then another until your head is wrapped in a thick layer of feathers and linen, but, still, the water pounds into the sink. You pull the blankets over the mound of pillow with your head at the center. With a desperate leap you're out of bed, pillows and blankets flying. Over goes the bedside table, the lamp, the books, and the flowers. There is a cry in the night as someone in the boarding-house responds. Raging, you march into the bathroom and, with a mighty twist, wrench off the faucet handle. The hot water is running, full blast, and you hold the broken piece of plumbing. You are screaming and lights go on all over the house . . . .

Used to advantage, the *omniscient* viewpoint sets the general scene of the story, before the viewpoint of a central character takes over. Obviously, *omnisicient* can not be used with either internal or external first person.

When the omnisicient viewpoint is misused the author abuses his or her all-knowing, all-seeing advantage and the landscape of the story appears with even clarity as a blurr of perception. The reader is allowed to understand everything about all the characters, their motivations and the events surrounding them. Everything is revealed in a ponderous display of sympathy by the author for his or her creation. *Omniscience* is often the beginning writer's point of view. He or she wants to make the story everyone's story and, as a result, it is no one's. The reader is fatigued by maintaining a high emotional empathy for all the characters. In this way, the author loses control. Without a central character as a point of focus there is no way the author can be sure that the reader will appreciate the outcome of the story. For instance, at the end a reader may be sympathizing with the villian, against the author's intentions. Or, after getting to know the characters equally well, a reader may be unable to decide which ones are sympathetic. Consequently, a decisive resolution will be impossible.

There is a kind of story that demands the complete omniscient viewpoint. Francis L. Fugate sums up such a story in which all the principal characters are sympathetic to the reader, but on the outs with each other.[7]. The reader must want the characters to get together at the end. There is little depth, however, and the situation lends itself to less critical forms of comedy, such as farce or burlesque. Most situation, or family comedy shows on television are written from an omniscient point of view--our sympathies are shared equally by the characters in the "Beverly Hillbillies", "All In The Family", "Maud", or the older ones, "The Honeymooners", "I Love Lucy", and "Father Knows Best". We are satisfied at the conclusion of each episode when the characters fall into each others arms in a laughing embrace. No one would ever accuse these skits of having intellectial pretensions.

As a rule, consistency of viewpoint strengthens the effect of a story. Switching point of view will dilute the reader's interest, because empathy will be divided among a number of characters. If a writer uses more than one viewpoint to tell a story, he or she will sacrifice some emotional energy. The creative effects of viewpoint show a character's motivations, to a greater or lesser degree, the thoughts, feelings, and emotional levels. Viewpoint translates the world of the story for the reader, thus communicating the author's ideas. Unless a writer lives through the viewpoint, he, or she, can expect little vicarious participation by the reader.

FIVE

SUPER STRUCTURE

Beginning-Middle-End

Beginning

A Massachusetts newspaper reporter working the late police beat drove 40 miles to get home each morning, at 2 a.m., with a portable tape recorder running beside him on the front seat. He dictated the opening lines of short stories into the machine. After an evening of reporting crime in the city, his reservoir of experience was usually churning and story ideas flowed easily. Often an attention getting lead sentence that he had used as a *grabber* on a news story an hour earlier would be put on tape during the lonely drive. Later, the reporter would expand these beginnings into short stories, or novels. The taped conversations with himself were the seeds of fiction. In order to preserve the stimulation of the moment the ideas were recorded; he was careful that his verbal notes were intriguing *pops* of information; that they were immediate and concise; that they promised a story worth reading, and that a reader would become directly involved. He knew that these are the basic points a writer should keep in mind when he or she begins to write fiction.

In this chapter we will consider how a successful story ought to begin. There is a theoretical line starting someplace in actual experience and ending with the last words of a completed story. The crime reporter is a good example because he moved information of experience from reality to the tape where it became the idea for the opening of a story. Later he developed it into complete fiction. He started the story telling process when experience gave him an idea of fiction: soon afterwards he recorded the beginnings on tape. That was his way of doing it. You may keep notebooks, or run to a typewriter the moment you have an idea and begin writing. Flannery

O'Connor said, in a keen statement, "the fiction writer begins where human perception begins."[8].

Through a subjective process an author decides to create a story about characters reacting to one another, to events and to situations. There is little gained by speculating on how a writer comes up with a specific idea for a story, or why that particular ideas seems just right at a given moment for the author. The initial concept for the story is purely personal, so much so that the author may not fully understand the significance of the moment. However, a writer does come up with an idea for a story and the next step is getting it down on paper and that opens the process to scrutiny. When the typewriter keys hit the page, the writer is committed to an audience. He or she wants the story to sell, to be read and appreciated. We can, however, make some comments about how to capture the attention of editors and readers.

Eva Ibbotson, the author of hundreds of short stories, has indicated four *must* points in an ideal story opening.[9]: beguile and interest; direct and concise reference; promises which are kept; and reader involvement. They are similar to opening- elements stressed by Edward S. Fox in his book *How To Write Stories That Sell.*[10]. and F.A. Rockwell's excellent book, *Modern Fiction Techniques.*[11]. The newspaper reporter was concerned about the same points in his tapes. Let's look at some of his story openings.

> Frank Lash knelt beside the corpse. It was his first suicide story as a cub police reporter.
>
> "Who is it?" he asked the cop. The burly sergeant shrugged.
>
> "There's nothing in the apartment to identify the body," the policeman said.
>
> Frank raised the sheet covering the face.
>
> "My God, I know her," he said, staring at the face of his former roommate's sister. Suicide seemed impossible.
>
> "Sergeant, this is no suicide. It's murder.!"
>
> * * *
>
> If a funeral home other than C.E. Ransom Co. got the publicity and profit from moving the bishops out of their vault in the cathedral to Cloudrest Cemetery, it would be over Johnny Ransom's dead body.
>
> * * *

I was awakened early in the morning by the cat crying at the front door. She stretched at the threshold and blinked at the sun rising on the third day of our mid-February power failure. I had let the poor creature outside to get warm. I picked up the newspaper on the front step. "President of Evenshire Gas Company Missing," was the page one headline. I swore out loud and the cat jumped into the porch swing. As the newspaper's police reporter I'd have to find President Propaine for tomorrow's edition.

The author's style is a little clipped and he tends to be too dramatic, but each opening does grab the reader's attention. We want to read more. There is a compulsion to find out what happens next. Analyze them yourself: are there pops of information; are they immediate and concise; do they promise stories worth reading, and is the reader directly involved? You will find that the author has been stronger in some than others, and that you may be able to improve them, but before you try, consider a few story openings of the first rank.

In the beginning God created the heaven and the earth.

* * *

And the children of Israel did evil in the sight of the Lord, and served Baalim. And they forsook the Lord God of their fathers, which brought them out of the land of Egypt, and followed other gods, of the gods of the people that were round about them, and bowed themselves unto them and provoked the Lord to anger.

* * *

Now the word of the Lord came unto Jonah the son of Amittai saying, "Arise, go to Nineveh, that great city, and cry against it; for their wickedness is come up before me." But Jonah rose up to flee unto Tarshish from the presence of the Lord, and down to Joppa; and he found a ship going to Tarshish; so he paid the fare thereof, and went down into it to go with them unto Tarshish from the presence of the Lord.

* * *

Arms I sing, and the hero, who first, exiled by fate, came from the cost of Troy to Italy, and the Lavinian shore: much was he tossed both on sea and land, by the power of those above, on account of the unrelenting rage of cruel Juno: much too he suffered in war till he founded a city and brought his gods into Latium; from whence the Latin progeny, the Alban fathers, and the walls of lofty Rome.

> Virgil's *Aeneid*

* * *

In the eighteenth year, the two and twentieth day of the first month, there was talk in the house of Nabuchodonosor, king of the Assyrians, that he should, as he said, avenge himself of all the earth.

> Judith A Tale

* * *

Sing in me, Muse, and through me tell the story of that man skilled in all ways contending, the wanderer, harried for years on end, after he plundered the stronghold on the proud height of Troy.

> Homer The *Odyssey*

* * *

There was an old man that could not well see, who had a fair young wife, and with them dwelt a young man . . . .

> Elizabethan Tale

* * *

Taman is the nastiest little hole of all the seaports of Russia. I was all but starved there, to say nothing of having a narrow escape from being drowned.

> Mikhail Lermontov "Taman"

* * *

Once upon a time there were two officials. They were both empty-headed, and so they found themselves one day suddenly transported to an uninhabited isle, as if on a magic carpet.

> Mikhail Saltykov
> "How A Muzhik Fed Two Officials"

* * *

Oh, while she is still here, it is still alright; I get up and look at her every minute; but tomorrow they will take her away--and how shall I be left alone? Now she is on the table in the drawing-room, they put two card tables together, the coffin will be here

tomorrow--white pure white "gros de Naples"--but that's not it. . .
Dostoevsky "A Gentle Spirit"

* * *

During the whole of a dull, dark, and soundless day in the autumn of the year, when the clouds hung oppressively low in the heaven, I had been passing alone, on horseback, through a singularly dreary tract of country; and at length found myself as the shades of the evening drew on, within view of the melancholy House of Usher.
Poe "The Fall Of The House Of Usher"

Animals talk to each other, of course.
Twain "Barker's Blujay Yarn"

There was a commotion in Roaring Camp.
Bret Harte "The Luck Of Roaring Camp"

The Shakers is the strangest religious sex I ever Met.
Artemus Ward "The Shakers"

It looked like a good thing; but wait till I tell you.
We were down South, in Alabama--Bill Driscoll and myself--when this kidnapping idea struck us.
O. Henry "The Ransom Of Red Chief"

After the reader's attention is captured, all of the characters should be introduced, the scene set and the problems stated within the first few pages of a short story or the first few chapters of a novel. The amount of space devoted to a good beginning necessarily varies. Generally, a fifth of the length is about right, with three fifths for the middle and a fifth for the end. In a ten page short story, for instance, the ratio is 2:6:2. Edward S. Fox maintains, in short story writing, that by the end of page one there should be a narrative hook, setting, introduction of all central characters, (though sometimes this is not possible), a characterization of the protagonist, emotional tone set, and an apparent conflict and problem has been established.[12] .Fox emphasizes that the writer has to make every word count. This can work out but one page for all this is unnecessarily limited. In a novel, the space allowed may be a chapter or two for an introduction. Whether a reader is involved is the test for a good beginning.

F.A. Rockwell puts it this way: first plan the story, characters, incidents, then win the reader.[13] · Be sure to include only essentials and omit all non-essentials. The writer should stir suspense, arouse expectancy, promise more to come, and pose a problem. Ms. Rockwell sums up the ingredients of a good beginning with the newspaper reporter's formula: who what, when, where, and why.

There are types of openings of which to be aware in fiction writing. One such presents an intimate picture of the protagonist from whom all action will flow: another intends to give a certain unique or singular effect. There are rapid fire beginnings that lead immediately into action. A fourth type emphasises where and when; a fifth idea. There are openings that stress the problem and there are conversational beginnings that signal the reader that the story will emphasize character communication. These sum Ms. Rockwell's beginnings as character, emotion, action, atmosphere, philosophical intent, situation, and dialogue.[14].

A short story, or a novel, moves quickly from one point to another. To put it another way a story is *never* a point of stasis. Without action, any story will be ignored by editors and readers. A successful beginning says: keep reading because something significant is going to happen. In the successful story openings cited, the seeds of future action are planted. In a few lines, and in many cases in a single line, the author has promised to tell a tale worth reading. Without the promise of significant action, the reader is encouraged to put down the story. Phyllis A. Whitney contends that a piece of successful fiction should start with a state of crisis out of which future action grows.[15]. She goes on to establish some rules: crisis depends on the central character for action: the problem belongs to the main character; after the opening, every scene must contain a problem, a purpose and a goal, and the hero's path is strewn with problems and difficulties which contain conflict. The writer should keep a resolution of the story in mind and work toward it, with all secondary problems tied into the overriding issue. Ideally, the means of resolution to the central character's problem should be contained in the opening of the story.

Knowing where to begin presents a challenge. If you start too far in advance of significant crisis and action, the reader will stop long before he or she reaches a point of interest. The temptation of the beginning writer to "lay down" a great deal of background, or to "set" the story in time and place can be a deadly mistake. However, if you begin the story too late, then you will be put in the awkward position of summarizing action and crisis, depending too heavily on flashback, losing the reader in a "history" of events. Most writers and critics, including Fox, Rockwell, and Whitney, agree that a story should begin *in media res.* Place the reader in the middle of things, or just before a crisis, or just after one. Reread the examples given earlier. Even the neophyte newspaper reporter cut the reader in at the most exciting point in a preliminary crisis. Someone has died before Frank Lash goes to the apartment; there has been a decision to move the bishops before Johnny Ransom, the greedy undertaker, is faced with the possibility that he may not be the one to move them to the cemetery, and there has been a mid-winter power failure prior to the disappearance of the gas company president. A writer should keep in mind what has happened before a story begins, as well as what will take place in the future. A good attack is to write down what you think happened leading up to the point when you begin to show the story to a reader. You should keep in mind a history of characters and events in the story. The reader wants a sense of continuity with the past and future. A story is only a part of the characters' lives that we see, a complete part but in the end only a section of their lives. It will be a significant view of their lives, but they did *exist* before the story began and likely will continue to do so after the final words. There should be something of this in the story, especially at the beginning and at the end.

Although it may sound obvious that the main character should be introduced first, it is often a failing of many short stories and novels written by beginners. An otherwise promising piece will be greeted by editors with the comment that the central character appears too late in the writing, perhaps as late as the third or fourth page in a short story, or after many chapters in a novel, when the hero, or heroine steps in to resolve a crisis. Consequently, the author was forced to suspend the flow of action, at the crisis point, to fill in the hero's background, his or her character, how he or she felt toward the other characters, why the central character was in a position to resolve the situation and where he or she had been all this time. Clearly such a story is a failure. Let the reader see the central characters right away and show how they feel toward each other. The reader wants to know what to expect from each character and how they will act when they are together. If the reader is in a state of confusion, he or she won't take kindly to the writing.

One of the few rules in writing is never keep a character on stage by himself very long. There is nothing more fatal to a story than a single character contemplating the universe, struggling over his or her problem, taking to himself or herself about other characters and situations, staring off into the sky, or down into the ocean for page after page of lonely intimacy. If the writer finds a character alone for more than a few paragraphs, bring on another important person, involve the character in some form of action or conversation.

Plant information at the beginning. That's what the first few paragraphs or chapters, of the story or novel are for. If the writer fails to set the scene in the reader's mind, he or she will flounder along to the end trying to figure out what's going on. No one wants to be put in that position.

It is best to end the first scene with suspense, or mystery, or both. A guessing reader is one who is turning pages to find out more. If the author succeeds in making the reader want to know what happens next, the opening of the story is good. At the beginning the writer should keep up the pace, keep the reader alert, and all the time plan ahead to the ending.

Ernest Hemingway once said the best way to learn to write is to read everything you can get your hands on. He was right, of course, and there's no better way to learn than reading what other writers have to say about their vocation. The assimilation of ideas is the essence of education. This is as true of creative writing as it is of philosophy, science, history, or mathematics. The author is not writing in a void. There is a literary tradition as there is a historical tradition. What successful authors, agents, and editors say about writing is as important as the opinions of political scientists on politics, historians on history, and theologians on religion.

In a story, details will attract meaning from the story itself, Flannery O'Connor has said.[16] It's important, therefore, that the details included at the beginning remain significant through-out and that they grow in meaning. A writer will have to be selective in what he or she says. An author doesn't have time to waste on insignificant details, descriptions, characters, actions, or events. What is put forward at the beginning must have lasting importance all the way to the end.

A story comes out in the writing of it, Peggy Simson Curry contends.[17] That states as clearly as possible the importance of how to begin. It is not an easy task, and the real beginning is the discovery that you have something important to say. Then it is a matter of bringing together the elements. Evan S. Connell, Jr., points out, when the writer has a story in mind getting it down will be easy, especially for the middle and end. The crucial part if finding a beginning.[18] Samuel W. Taylor sums up the problem with: satisfy the reader by arousing interest as quickly as possible and by letting him or her in on the story.[19]

Middle

After introducing characters, stating problems, setting up conflicts, and establishing a setting, the author should move toward the major crisis of the story. The thrust toward crisis is the middle section of the story, which dramatizes material presented in the beginning. The momentum of action following the crisis builds to a climax and resolution at the end. It's important to keep in mind that the crisis, at the end of the middle section, is the opposite of the climax. For instance, if the hero or heroine is to triumph at the end of the story, the crisis represents the lowest point in his or her fortunes.

The middle is the largest section of the short story or novel including most of the suspense, tension, character development, conflict, action, and dialogue.

Consistency is an important element in working with the middle section. The central character's objectives laid out at the beginning should not change in the middle of the story. The hero or heroine should not alter character in any radical way. Minor characters should not be allowed to push themselves forward eclipsing central characters. In the same vein, the middle section is no place to introduce an important character for the first time. That will dilute suspense by distracting the reader's attention from the dramatic action.

The primary function of the middle is to develop the story as it was conceived at the beginning. This section should never be a retelling of the opening. It is the space in which characters act out the roles given them earlier, according to the plot structure. This is based on goals and conflicts. By the time of crisis, the momentum of the action should be carrying events at a strong pace toward the end.

End

A story ending has characteristics as clearly recognizable as the elements of the beginning and middle sections. For instance, the end should take the least amount of space. Here problems are solved, doubts dispelled, conflicts resolved and emotions purged. These things should take place in the least amount of time with the most effectiveness. If the end of the story doesn't work with the rest of the material, the writer should be prepared to go back and rewrite. Revision can be painful, but it is worthwhile if it means the difference between acceptance or an encouraging rejection.

To best judge a story ending, the writer should project himself or herself into the reader's position and ask: does the ending justify the time spent reading the story or novel? No one wants to read anything that falls apart at the end. It's like finishing a gourmet-style meal with a ball park hot dog. Many first effort endings are as cheap and unsatisfactory as that. Fiction editors will not buy a short story or novel with a bad ending, no matter how effective the start and the middle sections may be.

Many good endings include an unexpected element to give a *kick* to the conclusion. At the beginning, everything is a surprise. In the middle the basic frame work should not be upset, but at the end a twist can work. However, the climax must be true to the story material that has come before. The ending should be a part of the logical pattern of the story. If the author springs something on the reader, the elements for the surprise must be planted at the beginnning. The writer's ability to mask the end, to develop the climax through action and to successfully lift the curtain for the reader will determine how the writing will be received.

Unless the story comes full circle, it will not prove satisfactory. There is more than philosophical symmetry in James Joyce's novel, *Finnegan's Wake*, in which the last sentence is a continuation of the first. Joyce was saying something important about writing technique too. Any good ending is there at the beginning. What comes between the two is development. Unless the climax reflects everything put in at the start, the story will fall short of its greatest expectations. The reader must have sudden awareness at the end, but an awareness that realizes that the conclusion was in sight all the time, only it was very well hidden.

Of course, the element of surprise is important. Unless the writer can keep the details of the conclusion from the reader, why would anyone want to read the story? It is an extremely difficult task--getting to the end without letting the reader down, or giving it away too soon, but it is also a necessary requirement. No one has ever said being a good writer is easy.

Most writers and critics identify six kinds of endings that work well. The *uncomplicated ending* is the most definitive. The ending summarizes events in the most satisfactory way for the reader. The hero or heroine triumphs by solving the big problem. There are no questions left unanswered, no doubts about a resolution. The villian is dead, and James Bond has saved England, and the world. This kind of ending often is unsophisticated and lacks variety and realism. Less literary than you might enjoy, it is more profitable than you might expect. For instance, there are 400,000,000 copies of Agatha Christie's books in print. The uncomplicated ending is not limited to mysteries and suspense thrillers, however. A story can be constructed to end firmly and stand as first rate literature.

The *futuristic ending* points the reader's attention to something beyond the end of the story. The climax brings to an end a part of the central characters' lives. There will be other times, other faces, and the reader is asked to speculate about how life will go on for the people in the story. But if the author wants to give a convincing illusion of a *further* reality, it is best not to say too much about the future. Hint at more to come, but stop there, unless you want to lose the reader in speculation.

The *Great Gatsby* has a futuristic ending. Nick is infected with Gatsby's idea of quest. He sees that longing for success in all of us and there will be a future for Nick too. There is a feeling of continuation, although Fitzgerald did not force it down out throats.

The lady or the tiger ending asks the reader to decide for himself, or herself, how events will be resolved. It is a subjective kind of ending and may often be used in very *literary, or intellectual* stories in which the author's primary concern is a psychological study of character rather than a neat resolution to a well structured plot and story line. The end of such a story often raises moral and ethical questions that are left unanswered by the author. They are questions the reader must answer to decide how the hero or heroine triumphed or failed. The background for asking such questions should be spelled out in the story so the reader has some basis on which to make a correct decision. Such novels as *The Scarlet Letter, Moby Dick, The Brothers Karamozov,* and *Ulysses* readily come to mind. Of course these books have *mechanical* endings, the story lines come to a halt, but the authors have raised important issues that are not really resolved in the conclusions. For instance, is Captain Ahab really diabolical in his megalomania, or does he represent the summit of humanity struggling to understand his own nature and the mysterious nature of deity, which may or may not be represented by the white whale? The question is open for debate and it is the central problem of the book left unresolved.

The *kicker-ending* employs an anti-climax to jolt the reader just when he or she thinks the story is over. In *From Russia With Love,* James Bond, and the reader, believes the story is over in the hotel room, when Bond tells M that, "It will be routine from here on." We breathe a sigh of relief. Bond has captured the decoding machine, foiled Specter's nefarious plan, and saved the Russian beauty. A maid enters the room while Bond is on the telephone and we recognize her as Specter's Number Three. This is the kicker--literally so--as she tries a last time to kill Bond with a poison dagger held in the toe of her shoe. Of course 007 triumphs in the scuffle, but we have the pleasure of one last emotional wallop. The anti-climax improves the story because it accounts for an important character who has dropped out of sight. It settles the question of the Russian beauty's allegiance--she kills the Specter woman, thus bonding herself to the hero. And it re-emphasizes the premises that good triumphs over evil, an assumption in all the James Bond thrillers. Flemming is very obvious about what we are supposed to accept as good and evil.

The *antithetical ending* reverses the opening of the story. If the villain is in complete control at the beginning, at the end he or she will be in chains. *The Magnificent Seven* has this structure. The story opens with the outlaws enslaving a village of Mexican farmers. It ends with them defeating the bandits. This is routine and the flaw of such a story is its obviousness. In order to keep the reader's interest, the story must contain plenty of action and emotional impact with strong conflicts. In *The Magnificent Seven* our attention is held through a series of gripping battles between the outlaws and the villagers with their hired gunmen. Watching the seven gunmen being recruited and seeing them defeat the bandits really carries us through to the end.

The *trick ending* employs an unexpected character, device, or event at the end to resolve the problem of the story. The *deus ex machina* of classical Greek drama is the forerunner of the gimmick ending. It is the least desirable way to resolve a story because it has an obvious feeling of contrivance.

Short stories and novels must have the basic structure of a beginning-middle-end. In both writing forms, the beginning is the section of the story in which the main characters are introduced, the action is set in time and place, emotions are raised, the action is started, and the plot structure is established.

The middle section is the place for development, with events of great impact that carry through to the crisis, and then to the climax and resolution.

The end represents the natural resolution of the story--problems are solved, emotions are purged, characters triumph or are defeated, and a solution is offered.

SIX

CHRONOLOGY

Fiction depicts an ordered view of existence, one that is compressed and heightened to tell the truth about the characters in an entertaining way. Involvement with chronology is an important part of the author's concern for the story--the assimilation of time into a story and the task of getting the impression of time across to the reader. This chapter studies the uses of time in four forms: time passing, timing or rhythm, transitions, and flashbacks. They are crucial aspects of story telling and success or failure depends on an author's ability to handle them.

In blocking out a story the writer should decide how much time is going to elapse--an hour, a day, a week. This is the time-set, the chronological framework. The rhythm of the story--working from beginning to middle to end--will work out proportionately. According to the amount of time allowed, and the use of that time to build to a crisis, climax, and resolution, transitions should be tailored between scenes and flashbacks included when necessary, to relate past to present, to give vital information, and to heighten characterization.

The amount of time that passes in a story depends on the kind of tale an author is telling. Usually, limited time adds drama, excitement, and tension to the material. A definite time-set in which the characters must achieve their goals imposes pressure that stimulates action and gives a feeling of urgency to the events. A dull story can be saved by adding a time factor upon which depends the success or failure of the hero. If the plot structure calls for the central character to achieve his or her goal, time works in the person's favor. The opposite is true if it is a goal-unachieved plot. In either kind of story, time limits are set and the action is concluded according to plan. In a third type, time is dissipated without a decisive resolution of the central character's problem. He or she may or may not be successful depending on the implications the author established at the end. This ideological ending, as F.A. Rockwell calls it, is difficult to achieve so that the reader does not feel confused, or cheated out of a definite conclusion.[20] The writer must feel confident that the reader will agree with his, or her, conclusion that the ending is better left undecided. The primary point in all three types of stories is to what extent staying within a time-set, or missing it, affects the lives of the characters.

A consensus of critics and teachers of writing points up a list of story types that draw their basic energy from time limitations. There is the race against time in which the central character must achieve a goal before the clock runs down. There are stories in which nature imposes a time limit: a forest fire burning out of control towards a town, for instance. The two central characters may be locked in a chase, as in *Les Miserables*. A patient's life may depend on a medical breakthrough, due at any moment. A story may be decided by the duration of a person's love, or hatred. Whatever the pattern, the outcome of the story is tied directly to passage of time.

Of course, there are stories in which time limitations do not have a direct bearing on the resolution. However, every story must take place during some set period. The reader feels more comfortable if he, or she, is aware that a day, a week, or a year has passed by the time the tale is concluded. People are time oriented and the writer's consideration of time helps create a better illusion of reality. Time that passes in a story establishes a limiting pattern in which events may be understood. Used correctly, time is a controlling device that narrows the range and focus of a story.

Time is also an important means of keeping length under control. If the writer intends to have a great deal of time pass in the story, he, or she, must understand how to use transitions. All writing uses some transitions, from sentence to sentence, paragraph to paragraph. But there is another kind of transition that will indicate, without going into great detail, spatial and temporal movement.

Most often a transition connects two scenes and is used to carry the momentum of a story forward when a complete catalogue of events would stop the action. Transitions indicate change without spelling it out unnecessarily. The best transitions are unnoticed and the reader is into a new set of circumstances without being aware of how he got there. Transitional devices may be time references: In an hour . . . .: The clock had finished striking the hour of ten when she stepped outside; By the end of the day . . .

Senses may be used: It was a matter of minutes before her eyes grew accustomed to the dark. A whippoorwill singing in the copse told the blind man it was dark and time to get moving. The afternoon sun was hot on his face, by the time he reached the crest of the hill.

There are emotional transitions: After a night with her, his love had cooled. And transitions using weather: The monsoons had ended by the time he returned to Vietnam.

The choice of transitions depends on the context of the story, of course, but two general rules apply: a transition fills a void in the action, and it often gives a breather after tense, dramatic scenes.

Some other types of transitions that are useful are:
A)   A word that reflects the mood in the preceeding scene:
>   The guard's hatred of the black prisoner was increased by the arrogant way he disobeyed the silence orders.
>
>   Angrily, the guard pounded his baton against the cell door of the prisoner playing the harmonica.

B)   Sometimes a transition will jump a scene completely:
>   John and linda disappeared into the barn. The moon was setting when John slipped through the back gate and went upstairs to his room--his passion sated.

C)   Questions and answers may serve as transitions, too:
>   "Do you think we'll ever make it to the top?"she asked Mike.
>
>   "There's someone at the peak, now," Will said, handing the binoculars to his father.

D)   Omniscience is a form of transition:
>   Looking out the window, I saw the old woman go out, leaving the back door open.
>
>   When the police questioned me, I was able to identify her as the one who left the house open.

E)   A common transitional device is the association of something to connect two scenes:
>   The missing amulet had been a favorite of his murdered friend and he gave a start seeing it hanging around the neck of the suspect.

F)   Description is often used to bridge scenes:
>   The bonfire illuminated the faces of the mob about to lynch the three strangers.
>
>   Reaching a crest, the sheriff spurred his horse toward the glow in

in the sky above the next ridge,

G)   Contrasts can be used effectively:
By three o'clock in the afternoon, the heat of the desert sun had killed three more of the survivors of the crash.

Philip shivered and pulled the blanket tighter around his shoulders. The frigid desert night will kill more of us before morning, he thought.

H)   Memory can make a good transition:
"Joan is here," William said.

All through dinner, John waited for her special kind of verbal attack he remembered her using on him two years before on the train to Baltimore.

I)   A common transitional device is skipping. Rather than relating the whole scene, the author breaks up the action, going to the end, after establishing the situation:

After months of preparation, Charles stood before the examining committee. The first question was asked, and his mind went blank.

"That will be all," the committee chairman said, an hour later. The disappointment and, in a couple of cases outrage, in the eyes of the members of the committee told Charles he had done very poorly. His failure would mean two years of work wasted.

Sometimes an author may find that no transition suits the situation. Faulkner never liked transitions and usually stopped when it was convenient and picked up the action again without worrying too much about the reader's need to be led carefully from scene to scene.

The argument over when, and even whether, to use flashbacks has been debated for a long time. Any writer is sure to get caught up in it, too, the longer he or she writes. Flashbacks are a necessary part of a good story, we think, and they can work well if handled correctly. A poor writer will do little that is correct. A good writer knows how to temper and refine, when to hold back and when to add, and that is especially important when it comes to flashbacks. It is very easy to become dependent on them at the cost of good forward motion. Flashbacks are supposed to catch the reader up. Unavoidably, action is suspended and the thrust of the story blunted. The real danger is the degree of involvement in a flashback. It can distract the reader's attention from the main course of action. Or, it might stand so solidly between the reader and the story that there is no hope of getting back to the narrative line. A flashback should, as the name implies, refer back to an incident that tells the reader something vital to the present action. It is a flashback within the chronology of the story being told. Almost always, a flashback is placed at the beginning of the story, and certainly no later than the middle. Never at the end, where the author runs the risk of creating a false surprise ending. The function of the flashback is to relate the important details, concerning the present, not to tell another whole story. As Edward Fox puts it, a successful flashback is worked out in scenes, acted, nor narrated. [21] When the information is narrated, the passage is not a flashback but simply the author talking directly to the reader about the story.

Transitions are an essential part of successful flashbacks. The writer has to get the reader in and out smoothly, while keeping in mind the time involved and the length of the story. These three elements govern the use of a flashback. The author may want to cut directly to the past tense in handling the flashback, or use the pluperfect tense for a few paragraphs and for looking-backward. Likewise, the writer must indicate when he, or she, is returning to the ongoing action. The type of transition used depends on the context of the story.

This kind of flashback is called transitional, not only because it employs transitions to get the reader in and out but because it lends progress to an understanding of the story, while it interrupts the action. A reader's thoughts are thrust forward, for a successful transitional flashback supplies necessary information that keeps the momentum of the narrative line going towards the conclusion.

A second kind of flashback makes up the whole story. Rather than giving details for a story in progress, the flashback is the story. This is a posturing technique used by an author to give depth, mystery, and suspense. It is not surprising that many mystery and suspense stories are told this way. The structure is spatially similar to boxes, one within the other, each with its own time reference, but all related to the original structure. Part of the reader's sense of adventure comes from delving into the receding forms. Conrad used a flashback-story to tell *The Heart Of Darkness*, as Marlowe's reminiscense of Kurtz. Most readers have come across stories that open on a lonely road, or moor—to create mood—that, then, flashback to the story of a crime committed on that spot in the past.

The use of flashback-story structure gives dimension. A scene is set; characters introduced, and then following a transitional passage the flashlight-story is told. A structurally successful flashback-story will include a resolution for characters introduced as background at the beginning. Sometimes, however, the whole tale ends at the conclusion of the flashback.

In any case, the characters introduced at the beginning should not be made so important that they steal interest from the characters in the flashback. At the same time, we shouldn't have any lingering questions about the initial characters' fates. All characters, inside and outside the flashback, must be accounted for.

To put it another way, the characters who appear before the flashback-story begins are listeners--just as we are--to the tale. It is a matter of positioning the audience with those inside the story as other characters and those completely outside as readers. The author is simply adding another layer of illusion between the reader and the story in hopes of heightening the sense of reality. The paradox is a startling one: the more and better the illusion greater the sense of reality. Of course, a flashback story must be able to stand alone, without the elements that make it a flashback. For instance, the story of Kurtz' corruption is quite clear without need of Marlowe and the listeners on the ship in England. Without them, however, Conrad would have lost much of the feeling of psychological depth and mystery that characterizes the mood of the novella.

While the central story in a book such as *The Heart Of Darkness* is the flashback, itself, the crucial rule governing a transitional flashback is not to get caught in one. Therefore, the flashback must be made brief and highly charged with information. The writer should always ask, is the flashback absolutely necessary? If not, introduce the material in other ways--through dialogue, narration, a letter, diaries, or internal monologues. Flashbacks should not be used in stories that have plots which fall naturally into a linear, temporal sequence. There are stories, however, that require some reflection on prior events to make sense of present action. But the circumstances of the ongoing story should be set up first before flashing back. If the writer is unable to create such flashes spontaneously, he, or she, should find another solution. As a story-teller, the writer's first task is to entertain. If a flashback introduces dullness, it should be cut and other solutions found.

A problem any writer will have to face with a flashback is how it affects the rhythm of the story. Timing is always crucial and the writer should not have elements in a story that needlessly slow down the pace so that the action falters and then stumbles to the conclusion. Every story is fast, or slow, and the pace is set at the beginning. The rhythm will be determined by the amount of time that will pass, the length and complexity of transitions, and the number of flashbacks used. The greatest threat to the rhythm of the story is giving away the resolution early in the tale. Get the reader interested by starting during, or just after a crisis. Then present the characters' central problem and build scene by scene, making each one more interesting than the last until the climax and resolution are reached. If the pace seems too fast, add a transitional passage, or a flashback, to slow things down. Action can be written into dull scenes to quicken the pace. Primarily, rhythm should be invisible. The writer doesn't want the reader to realize: the author has gotten me out of breath and is giving me a chance to rest with this long, gossipy flashback.

The writer can avoid being obvious by developing a sense of proportion after blocking out the story. If one day is to pass during the story, the writer will not want to put all the crucial events into the waning hours. He or she knows the pace is going to be quick in a short story and time adjustments must be made. As a rule details slow down a story, while a sparse tale moves more quickly. The importance of economy of words is paramount. Language should be compressed and charged with meaning. Reading poetry is a good way to understand how words can convey the most meaning in the least amount of time and space. Prose has a definite rhythm, too, determined by transitions, flashbacks, and time passing in a story.

SEVEN

REVISION

Learning to write is learning to rewrite
Eloise Jarvis McGraw

When the last word of the story or novel is written, there is often a feeling of accomplishment, perhaps even relief! When the writing was begun, it might have seemed such a moment would never come. But, finally the story is finished; all that remains is typing a clean copy and mailing it off, with hopes of quick publication. If this sounds like it applies to you, you probably also know the disillusionment of rejection, too. If the editor had time--usually not the case--he or she may have jotted down a few suggestions on how the manuscript should be revised.

There is nothing more frustrating for an editor than reading a story that would meet publishing standards, if only the author had taken the time to polish the work after the first draft. The days when a Maxwell Perkins took time to carve out Thomas Wolf novels from thousands of raw manuscript pages are over. Each year about 30,000 books are published in the United States. Editors consider in excess of 300,000 manuscripts to find those books. Frankly, for most writers the burden to produce highly polished pieces of writing falls entirely on their own shoulders. One of the keys to submitting a manuscript that an editor can take seriously is the ability to rewrite the first, second, and perhaps even the third, or fourth, drafts.

This chapter is intended to help the writer through the painful, often traumatic, but hopefully rewarding period of manuscript revision.

Many authors say their most creative--productive--writing comes in the second or third draft of a manuscript. The T.S. Eliot-Ezra Pound revision of *The Wasteland* is probably the most famous 20th Century example of this. For some writers, however, rewriting is sheer torture. Polishing is a little of both: the writer should expect it to be painful, as well as inspiring. There is one constant in manuscript revision: the author is alone. The second draft is strictly a one man--woman--job and no time for consensus criticism. That may come later, but in the initial revision, the author is on his or her own. That means the writer must train himself, or herself, to approach the story with a detached point of view. The best way to do this is to set the manuscript aside for a time. Dorothy Aldis, the children's writer, always let a manuscript rest six months before going into revision work. Each writer will set a time limit, but a lapse between the completion of the first draft and the beginning of the second is important. It allows the writer's thoughts to settle in and gives time to discover better solutions for a character, a situation, or even a whole plot structure.

Short story writer Barbara Robinson has suggested that good revision starts by cutting to break up the rhythms of the first draft.[22] The initial rhythm may be too fast, or too slow, too jerky, or with no sense of timing, at all. This is because the first draft is usually very mechanical, as the author hurries to get down the idea of the story. The revision will transform the idea into a real story with form and part of the process is establishing the right pace (see the chapter on chronology). While the writer is cutting into the manuscript, he or she should watch out for passages that are special favorites. Make sure not to sacrifice the rest of the story to them. Unless a character, or event, contributes to the story in an important way, cut out that person, or piece of action. A good editor is ruthless with a blue pencil.

Descriptions are often overwritten in a first draft and this is another area where careful cutting is important. In describing anything, the desired effect is a clear image. The writer should be concise and make the language work for him or her. On the basic side, any place one word can take the place of two, make all such changes. To create a picture of a character in the reader's mind, it is not necessary to describe the person from hair color to length of toe nails. A writer must possess the power of suggestion and because most readers share a common set of experiences with the author, the author can draw on that reservoir to relate impressions of the world in as few words as possible.

In a short story, there are about 5000 words, maximum, to work with. There isn't room for a long passage on the details of a painting in the hero's bedroom, unless that painting is a key to the hero's problem. A novel offers more space for detail work, but there is a selection process in longer manuscripts, too. The writer has to decide what material is worth a few words and what is worth a few pages. Everything can not occupy the reader's attention in the same way, or for the same length of time.

The revision of dialogue presents the same problem. Conversation for its own sake has no place in a well written story. In editing, the writer must learn to recognize dialogue that conributes to the story by depicting character, furthering the action, or feeding information to the reader. Passages about rain, snow, or heat, when the weather plays no part in the story, are extraneous. As a rule, dialogue should be accurate within the framework of the story and consistent within the context of character.

Be aware of transitions that are not smooth or clear. Change names that are too similar and will confuse the reader. Keep times consistent. Remember when, and where, the story is taking place and watch out for geographic inconsistencies and anachronisms. If dialect is used, make sure that it is true to the regional setting.

A checklist for rewriting suggested by Eloise Jarvis McGraw is well to keep in mind. Watch out for: weak plot, wooden characters, poor style, faltering pace, an unclear story line that lacks direction, grammatical faults, tedious, or boring writing, ineffective writing, undisciplined writing, writing that is too sparse, or awkward, trite dialogue, and unclear action, character relationships, motivations, setting, timing, and resolution.[23] Usually persons who want to write are also good readers, who can recognize someone else's bad writing. It is a matter of discipline to apply the same high standards to your own material. If a writer is unable to recognize his, or her own mistakes, it is probably because the author is unwilling to admit that he or she has made a mistake. Often there is a great fear of having to *redo* the whole work, especially by the beginning writer. He or she is tempted to get by with a poorly written first draft rather than take on the hard work or rewriting. But an editor who sees many manuscripts a week will have no reservations about rejecting the badly written, or the inadequately revised story. As unappealing as rewriting may be for an author, some day he or she will find out, as James Michener has, that revision equals perfection.

EIGHT

WRITING THE NOVEL

*If God could tell the story of the universe,
the universe would become fiction.*
E.M. Forster

Preface
What we have dealt with in the first half of this section deals with
both short story and novel writing.
However, the demands for the novel are something apart--
they are all that has preceded, but more.
In the following pages of the section, which we have intentionally set-off
from the rest, we examine some of the problems of writing the novel.

Creating a separate but equal reality is the novelist's task--distilling a fiction from reality that tells a good story. While the novelist writes about life, he, or she, is creating an illusion of life. Because a novel is an illusion of reality, apart from the real world, the impact of the writing should be equal to the impact of life itself. Although a novel exists as a physical form, it is nothing more than words on pages between book covers, stimulating certain responses in readers. That is what novel writing is all about. It is not a dissertation or a treatise, a methodical discussion of facts and principles. Questions of philosophy, theology, or politics may be raised but the writer's primary task is to entertain. The novelist tells a good story about people.

People are the novelist's starting point and telling a specific story about certain characters is the writer's immediate problem.

Theme is often included as a starting point, along with character, and some writers like to have a strong story-line in mind before they begin. The important point is not to let ideas, or even plot, take attention away from characters. A novel is a self-contained universe with people at the center who are more in command of themselves than we could ever say of people in real life.

Although much of actual life does not require Man's presence for its self-contained significance, a novel without men, women, and children is a contradiction in terms. Characteristically, a novel must have human life at its center. There are very good animal stories, but they aren't novels, according to the history of the genre and the body of criticism that has grown up with it.

Writers first began experimenting with the novel form during the 16th Century, with the rise of Elizabethan prose fiction, which is a startling and self-assured mixture of disparate forms. Thomas Nashe's tour de force, *The Unfortunate Traveler,* included the four classical genres: lyric, epic, comedy, and tragedy. Nash added jests, outlandish chronicle and inverted medieval romance, the pornography of the day.[24] Today, there is still great interest for the professional and amateur writer, as well as the scholar, in looking up the works of such Elizabethan prose masters as Greene, Nashe, and Deloney. There is great vigor in their work, with mixing of forms, that is fresh three centuries later. There is the maverick, the unexpected and the unusual. Action is loosely structured and the comments of the narrator and the characters are openly didactic. Although the stories are rarely told from the subjective third person, and we do not experience the inner person of the characters, there is great faith in Man and our attention is focused on humanity.[25]

By the end of the 18th Century, the novel, as a specific genre, was firmly established and such writers as Defoe, Richardson, and Fielding in England, and Fureliere, Scarron, and Lesage in France, were putting the emphasis on realism. It meant that Moll Flanders was a thief, Pamela a hypocrite, and Tom Jones a fornicator.[26]. The 18th Century novelists were painfully aware of the new search for Truth that characterized their Age, when traditional universals of religious and political faith were being questioned and broken down into specifics. They came to the conclusion that truth was discovered through the senses and they strove to portray a great fandom of human experience, as realistically as possible. The path of sensuous involvement led to Truth and, as a result, the idea of novel writing as a process of holding-a-mirror-up-to-nature has come down to us.

If a critic says a novel is good because it reminds us most of real life, it is because that correspondence between life and literature runs deep in our literary tradition. The impact of literature is expected to equal the impact of life, for the sake of truth. That a novel and actual life are separate realities only adds to the author's challenge. The task of the writer is to recognize the difference between the two, because of the responsibility to impose order on life.

It's too pedantic for our purposes to trace the novel tradition through centuries of authors. Not only would it be a tedious aside in a manual on basic writing, but a surprisingly fruitless task. For novels have been written in much the same way since the end of the 18th Century. Thackeray is very much like Fielding, so far as technical developments in the novel are concerned--specifically the omniscient narrator--although nearly 100 years separate the two authors.[27] Novelists from De Cervantes to Barth have been concerned about the vagaries of language and communication. Truman Capote's *In Cold Blood* might have been guided by Defoe's Moll Flanders, who said, "I am giving an account of what was, not of what ought or ought not to be." The works of Joyce and Nabokov reflect George Eliot's statement that her strongest effort was to,

> give a faithful account of men and things as they have mirrored themselves in my mind. The mirror is doubtless defective: The outlines will sometimes be disturbed; the reflection faint or confused; but I feel as much bound to tell you as precisely as I can what that reflection is, as if I were in the witness-box, narrating my experience on oath.

For someone trying to understand how novels are written, how others have written them, and how he, or she, might write one, it is best to do as E.M. Forster says: to imagine all the novelists writing their novels at once.[28] Forster bases the idea in the assumption that "history develops and art stands still." He warns that he's sloganizing and that there is only partial truth in the statement, but enough truth to focus our vision on what's important in novel writing, the constants that any writer has had to deal with--story, character, plot, imagination, theme, structure, and pace. These are elements we've discussed earlier in this section on fiction writing and we'll examine them again as they apply to the novel.

At one point, Forster talks about literary tradition as the borderland lying between literature and history. There may be novels of "the times," but the tradition of the novel is not bound by history. What defines a novel is constant--the elements that create a separate but equal reality. This section will show how to use those elements. No one can guarantee a writer success at what he, or she, is doing, but if the writer does not have a good grasp on the fundamentals there is little chance for anything but failure.

NINE

GREAT IS THE ART
OF BEGINNING

Considering the mirror of the mind, Dorothy Van Ghent points out that ". . . it does not passively 'reflect' things-as-they-are, but creates things-as-they-are. [29.] The idea of creation comes first in novel writing. The writer does not reflect life; he, or she, creates it as an illusion. The characters and what happens to them allude to real life so that we understand and sympathize with what is going on. We recognize enough of our own world in theirs to appreciate the drama, but we're mistaken if we take their world for ours. The novel is a separate creation and not just a reflection. With this in mind, we can discuss aspects of beginning to write a novel.

Obviously, the would-be novelist must have a command of language. The reader, an editor or agent, has a right to expect that the author has a working knowledge of grammar, spelling, and composition. These areas of writing are covered in the section on English Composition in *The Writer's Manual.* But it's worth pointing out that without a grasp of the rules a writer will have a difficult, if not impossible time, getting an agent, or a publisher's reader, or an editor to consider his or her novel.

After the writer begins thinking of himself as a creator and assumes a knowledge of the mechanics of language, the next step is starting to write. Does an author start with character, idea, theme, plot, or story-line? Many writers and critics have argued for a specific one of these elements as the only correct place to begin. But it doesn't really matter which one a writer chooses, as long as it works for him, or her, to get the book going. The first draft of the novel is not something to show anyone and there will be plenty of time to work out the structure afterwards. The first draft is a statement of the writer's intentions for the novel, and it might be a collection of notes, character sketches, fragments of dialogue, scenes, events, conflicts, diagrams of plot structure, and a statement of the story-line. The first draft, itself, is the starting point for the novel. It is not the novel in any finished sense. The novel is a rewrite. There is no set number of drafts to write, either, but there certainly will be at least two.

Where the writer begins the first draft has to do with his, or her, sense of the world. There has to be a strong view of people, events, relationships, and ideas. A command of grammar isn't enough without a vision of characters in conflict. The language has to tell a story with events, feelings, atmosphere, emotions, and situations. There will be a theme, a plot, a beginning-middle-end, a point of crisis, a climax, and a resolution--all the elements to construct an illusion of reality. But the structure will signify nothing, if the author lacks insight, or does not understand the motivations and importance of people in the real world.

Begin with compassion for the human condition and sympathy for people in particular. All that emotional energy will drive a writer to record his, or her, feelings. Nearly all writers have gone through a period when they put down on paper a rush of feelings. That chaos of expression can clear the air, until the author discovers what he, or she, has to say. The epiphany may take shape as a character, a theme, a single scene, a story-line, or a way to use a plot structure. One point is certain, the chaos of momentary expression is not the novel. There has to be order.

Compassion for the human condition and then a craving for order are the first two steps in novel writing. They may come simultaneously, in a moment of *inspiration.* Some writers like to contend that they are inspired in their writing. What they mean is that the desire to write is inspired. The actual writing is methodical hard work. Sometimes it is dull, sometimes painful, and once in a while it feels good.

Feeling for a character may precede the desire to order the impression and it may be years before the novel takes shape. Whether the writing is inspired in a moment or delayed over years, the author must set a limited objective when he, or she, begins to write. Not everything can, or should, be told in what the author has to say. The first draft will say a lot more than what the author intends, as he, or she, lets thoughts run wild over the paper. Later, during the revision process, the story will be tightened and much may be eliminated.

Since this is a definitive study of writing, drawing on a wide range of critical opinion, there will not be a stand for one particular point of view. The only important consideration is what works best for the individual author. Christopher Derrick, in the *Writing of Novels*, says that the first necessity is a well contrived plot in the form of a summary or a synopsis. Thomas C. Turner, in his article "The Novelist and His Theme," says that characters come before theme and theme before structure. Author Robert Glynn Kelly, in the *Novelist's Dilemma,* tells the writer to never think that he, or she, is just writing a draft, but to go all out for a finished work. Seymour Epstein, in *The Personal Motif In Fiction,* says the writer should begin with a personal experience. Sue Grafton--*Where Does A Novel Begin--* contradicts this idea and says that a person should write about something interesting, not necessarily something he, or she, knows. Marion Montgomery, in *The Maturing Of Novel Ideas,* offers another suggestion: start with a situation, then character, then theme. E.M. Forster advocates beginning with a story-line. Another writer says to begin with setting: another advises to block out scenes; another theme and idea, and yet another says, just start. filling pages with words. As you can see there is a range of opinion, some of it contradictory, on how to begin.

Start with a story-line, Forster points out because this is the basic function of a novel--to tell a story.[30] In fact, story telling is the aspect, ". . .without which the novel could not exist," he says. A good story-line can be a fruitful place to start. It does not preclude other starting points, however. But a story-line is a very handy place to begin. A good story has only one requirement: it must make the reader want to know what happens next. The idea is a universal one, not unique to Forster, and one that every would-be writer has had to face, or live up to, or discover with great anguish that he, or she, has failed to develop in a novel. One reason many writers turn away from this starting point is because they find it impossible to coldly think out a story of very great interest. Sometimes it is better to approach the novel from character, or setting, and let the story grow of its own accord out of conflict and action.

A story can be defined as a narrative of events arranged in their time sequence.[31] For instance, the body was found in the library on Monday; the detective was baffled on Tuesday; he discovered a clue on Wednesday; he lost track of the suspect on Thursday; he found the trail again on Friday; the suspect was arrested on Saturday, and the unfortunate fellow was tried and hung on Sunday. Other elements--plot, character, theme, setting, action, conflict, climax, and resolution--then turn the story-line into a complete novel. But, as we see, first comes the story-tellers scene--a time, a place, and a character filling space.

But perhaps the place to begin is with that character. The argument in favor of starting with characters is a strong one: novels are about people, so the writer should begin with the most important element. A novel cannot exist without characters, although it can survive a weak story-line, no plot, or little action. From this point of view, the story takes shape out of the characters and the action is directed toward the resolution of what the characters are as people in conflict.[32.]

A writer should know everything about the characters before he, or she, begins to work, and the best way to acquire this knowledge is to write a biography of the people who will take major roles in the novel. It is impossible to know about all the characters who will pop up along the way, but the writer should have a firm idea about the central figures. Write about their lives before the novel opens and carry on their histories through the course of the book and afterwards, too. The writer should know more about them than he, or she, will write about in the novel. The sense of biography will allow for hints of events in the character's past that will add depth. A character is real in a novel only when the writer knows everything about it. For this reason, not surprisingly, many first novels are autobiographical because the beginning writer turns to himself, or herself, for a sense of past, present, and future. As the author develops, so will the ability to create fully developed, but completely fictional characters.

The writer has to be sure enough of his, or her, characters at the beginning to speculate about them--if he killed her, how would that fit in with his character biography? Her marriage late in life is going to have to be justified by elements in her life that came earlier, perhaps outside the time of the novel.

The important point, however, is to make sure that a story does evolve out of character. It's not enough to have a few people forever talking, traveling, eating, thinking, experiencing life in general, without a specific goal and significance to their actions. If you start with a character, Hannal Lees maintains, then personality, dialogue, events, actions, and reactions must produce plot and story-line.[33.] Begin with one character, then add others that relate to that choice. Start dramatically, Lees adds, but keep the plot simple and gradually a picture will evolve. The writer must have faith that all story-lines derive from character; that a novel equals, ". . .a character in collision with a truth," and out of that confrontation comes drama.[34.]

To start with plot imposes the greatest discipline; plot is the cause, the structural reason for action. Faced with the task of deciding a structural goal for the novel, the author will come up with ideas for a story and characters. A plot will suggest a story-line, and then come the characters to act out the drama. It is impossible to think of the few plots available to writers without story ideas coming to mind. Plots afford structure; a goal-foiled, a come-to-realize, a decision, a goal-abandoned, a rebuilt-character, a character-deterioration, or a lost-goal.

Plot is deterministic and it is a rigid task-master for the story, the characters, and the author. Plot dictates how the novel will end and that is very important because it is an essential that must be known. It means the writer will have to bring the characters into line to conform to a given structure. The author cannot go off on a tangent midway through the manuscript, unless the digression is carefully planned so that it will return to the central structure. That is what defines plot; a causitive support for the world the writer has created.

If the writer starts with story, or character, then he, or she, can worry about imposing plot structure later, after the first draft is written and the course of the book is apparent. But if the writer starts with a plot, then everything else must conform to its structural outcome. For instance, a goal-achieved plot will have the central character triumph, while a goal-lost plot will see the hero fail. Unless the writer is sure that he, or she, wants the central character to end up in a specific condition, don't start writing with a set plot in mind.

This doesn't mean that plot will play a minor part in a novel begun from the story of character point of view.   Plot will develop from these two conditions through the finished draft and the polishing later. Starting with plot is more structurally definitive, to be sure. It imposes strict order from the start, and the author won't have time to play around with the characters and the story-line to find out where they are going. With a plot, the author knows where the novel will end.

Understanding this special role of plot is important, because beginning writers tend to confuse story-line with plot, or to think that there is no difference between the two. The mistake can be fatal for a novel. The confusion invites such editorial comments as, "The work has no sense of form," or, "The novel is weak in its foundations." These are observations that mystify, while they intrigue because of their apparent complexity. All they mean is this: the story-line has gone outside the plot structure; and the plot makes unnecessary allowances for the story so that we end up at a different point than the plot indicated at the beginning. For instance, if the story-line gets out of control and the author has to switch from a goal-achieved plot to a lost-goal, we say the story-line has gone outside the plot structure forcing unwanted changes. Unless the author catches this and keeps the story within bounds of the plot, the novel will be confusing and lack direction.

Although plot guides the author to the story's finish, there must be elements of surprise and mystery for the reader. The outcome should not be readily apparent from the start. The masking of intent keeps the reader turning the pages, but when the story is over, events, characters, and actions should make sense within the plot structure.

Many writers and critics believe that the most expedient way to begin is with personal experience. A writer should know what he, or she, is talking about and most of us have had personal experiences that would make good stories. But facts alone are not a novel and just because something really happened doesn't mean that it would be effective as a novel. Experience is invaluable, but the writer has to avoid becoming a slave to reality. Begin with a real event, but then distill fiction from the reality. The writer should become immersed in the immediate present of the character and not his, or her, own past.[35.]

Facts have value because they serve the novel which must develop a life of its own. A news story is limited to the facts of an event. That's good journalism, but unacceptable novel writing. Facts limit the author and what he, or she, needs most is the freedom to create and to speculate about the most important elements of the creation--the characters. The author seeks truth--a valid cliche--rather than reality and facts. The impression of truth that a real incident generates is more important for developing the writer's perceptions than a faithful reproduction of the facts.

After plot and other structural elements are imposed, including character development, a real incident may be barely recognizable. For instance, Melville's novella, *Billy Budd*, is based on an experience of the author's cousin, who was an officer in the U.S. Navy. A seaman under his command tried to organize a chapter of a college fraternity on board his ship. The fraternity's secrets, written in code, were discovered and the young man refused to explain them to the captain. The boy was hung as a result. From that incident, Melville created the story of the angelic British seaman who is hung for killing an evil master-at-arms. In reality, the fraternity organizer was executed by Melville's cousin, but there is only the faintest resemblance between his experience and the story of *Billy Budd.* Melville had to expand on the facts of the situation aboard the American ship in order to speculate on the nature of good and evil, the great theme of the novella. The subjectivity of writing allowed Melville to create his own order, and his own special interests for the reader.

Theme is the idea of a novel. The issue may emerge as a novel is written, or the author may start with a set theme in mind and go on from there to illuminate the idea with characters, story, and plot. Theme is not a moral, nor is it an overview of the story or plot.

Moral is a lesson a reader learns from a written work. At the end of his essay, "Of Studies," Francis Bacon wrote, "So every defect of the mind may have a special receipt." That moral is Bacon's message spelled out so the reader won't miss it.

An overview of a story or plot says what happens in a few words.

Theme, on the other hand, is a specific idea that gives a general significance to the work. The theme of a novel may be one of alienation, decadence, survival, the generation gap, appearance-versus-reality, good-and-evil, racial prejudice, women's rights, political corruption. Theme may be more specific too: drug addiction in the suburbs, success or failure of a commune, unrest on college campuses, selling of a president. There may be more than one theme, major and minor cords, in the work, each with its corresponding characters and circumstances related to the central action through the plot structure and story-line.

In making a statement about life, theme is a generalization derived from the action of the novel.[36]   The generalization should come spontaneously from the reader, as he, or she, understands what the author is saying dramatically. The action must visualize the theme. If the writer takes time to state it too directly, at great length, with cosmic scope, he, or she, runs a high risk of boring the reader. The drama of characters in conflict keeps the reader interested and the themes grow out of the action. The writer must let the reader know what the issue is in the novel, so that he, or she, understands the significance of the book. But if a writer starts with theme, he, or she, should not concentrate too much on getting the point across. Write with a general idea in mind, but let the characters act out the issue. The writer can always go back during revision to build the impact of the ideas. In the first or second drafts the author should concentrate on telling the story.

Another way to begin is by blocking out the major scenes. An event may come to mind and is written down, and then another comes. They may not be in the right order, but don't worry about that. If the sap is up, keep working, as Heminway used to say. The last scene of the novel may be clear; therefore, get it down. As the work progresses, the scenes will begin to arrange themselves. This should be a spontaneous effort, however, and no one should begin with the last scene, or something in the middle, just for the sake of working that way. If the second to the last scene isn't going to come, start someplace else, or use another approach.

Setting is also a good way to get the story going. Describing the country-side, a house, a village, or a city street can stimulate ideas about characters, events, and other elements in the novel. The same is true of starting with a situation, or vignette involving some minor characters, or a point of crisis that leads into the major drift of the novel. Whatever it is, it should be interesting and capture the reader's attention.

However the writer begins, the first draft may have to be changed later. As Christopher Derrick points out, the initial opening may work for the author, to get going, but not the reader.[37] As work on the manuscript continues, what's written at the beginning may turn out to be all wrong for what follows and the writer will have to make adjustments in the opening. Whichever of the openings the writer uses--story, character, plot, personal experience, theme, blocked scenes, situation, or setting--he, or she, should remain flexible enough to rewrite, if that means strengthening the manuscript.

Great is the art of beginning, Longfellow said, and great is the author's success if he, or she, can keep the reader turning pages to the end.

TEN

A PAGE A DAY

FOR A YEAR

In writing a novel, getting started is most of the effort. After a point of view is established, the writer should be impatient to get on with the work. The words should flow as scenes take shape, characters develop, plot structure builds, and story unfolds. There should be no stopping as chapters roll through the typewriter. Sometimes novels are written in this promising way, but often the author will find a place to begin and then just stop.

At this point, writers need all the help they can get, or else their novels will never see the light of day as first drafts, let alone be published. At this time, all writers run up against what Christopher Derrick calls the technological fallacy.[38.] Translated that means there is no defined novel writing technique. A novel is not pieced together like a car, nor is it stamped from a die. When a writer is stuck the corpus of world literature will offer no patterns, rules or precedents telling him, or her, how to write the novel that's moving through the typewriter at that moment. Each novel is the *novel*, and it is a product of loneliness.

The writer works alone in a non-technical relationship to the manuscript. There is an emotional bond between the author and the writing. If the effort stops after the opening ideas, the writer must either give up completely, or else sit and stare at the empty page until he, or she, can start writing again. No one is forcing the author to write and, often, no one is paying for the effort, either. In most instances, novel writing is irrational, irresponsible, uneconomical, a waste of time for the author, the author's family, and the author's creditors. But novels are written, thousands of them every year, and the urge is a subjective one that's blind to the logical objectives of the world. That doesn't mean if you are irresponsible you will make a novelist. The spark, the desire to write, is irrational and will not be denied. The writing itself may need some coaxing and a great deal of discipline.

Write something every day, and do it in a set period of time. Without the most rigid discipline a novel will not be completed. When the writing is going well, the author won't have to worry about working every day for five hours. He, or she, will be writing every day for 10 hours, without thinking about it. But here we're concerned about the times that it's all going wrong.

There are ways a writer can *trick* himself into his work. Start writing a letter to a friend about the book in the works (of course, you won't mail the letter). Write biographical sketches of the characters. List all the possible endings. Write scenes. Sum up the idea for the book in a poem, using concrete images that may inspire further prose writing. Tell yourself that you really don't care about the manuscript and that attitude may relax you enough to start writing. Finally, suspend criticism of the work until the first or second draft is completed and accept the fact that even after seven drafts the novel may fail.

A great temptation for writers is to talk out a novel to a spouse, a friend, or a relative. No one knows how many books have been lost this way, but it's fatal to some degree to verbalize your problems about a work in progress. After such discussion, you'll feel emptied, wasted, with little desire to go over the material again to get it down on paper. Quality is often a spontaneous element in writing. The turn of a phrase, the mood, the flavor of a scene is set down in the fury of the moment. If it is a moment of speech, the excellence will be difficult to recapture, afterwards, when you sit down to write. What may have been a brilliant bit of characterization during cocktail conversation, may seem dull when you finally get to a typewriter. The writer should contain himself, or herself, keep a tight lip and save the brilliance for the writing.

Getting to the end is a thing in itself, Derrick points out.[39] For most writers the process of writing is more important than the finished novel. Becoming, rather than being, is what the author craves, in existential terms. The process includes keeping a card file on anything that stimulates the imagination. Creativity may come out of illness, exhaustion, unhappiness, drink, drugs, and disabuse. Or, it may be the product of hard work, plenty of rest, contentment, and sobriety. The elements of the author's life inescapably contribute to his, or her, creativity. They are often outside personal control and they may defy reason. Frederick Nietzsche, for instance, could not write unless his desk was cluttered with rotten apples. Heminway had to stand up to write, and so did Henry James. The list of eccentricities is endless. But they are not to be feared, avoided, or even discouraged, if they work to get the novel written. Whatever motivates the writing is the right way for the author. In perspective, the elements will fit into the process of getting to the end result.

The author has to be comfortable with the process and one of the things that contributes to a feeling of assurance is knowing that you are writing the novel that you want to write. There has to be total commitment to the subject, faith that the material will make a good novel. If a writer constantly questions the significance of the work, then something is wrong. True, many a novel has progressed on the basis of misguided intent, but we are concerned here with the possibility of publication. If the author has little interest in the material, or doesn't take the effort seriously, that doubt and cynicism will come across to the reader. It's painful to see someone making fun of himself, or herself, and if it happens in writing, the reader will give up in disgust. Apathy thrives in the medium of the written word and it is highly contagious, infecting the reader easily. It is deadly for a novel. If the writer is bored, the reader will be, too. But if the writer is enthusiastic about the work, if it is good writing, the novel will attract readers. Readers are interested in what an author finds important about human life. In order to communicate those elements, the author must structure his, or her, ideas about existence in a way that the reader will feel and understand.

A common failure, after a writer has decided on a starting point, is putting down a great deal of material related to that point and calling it a novel. The author's self-control and not self-expression creates a novel. Writing is not psychological therapy for the author (although it may help the writer's state of mind to create in this way). Writing is a craft and its primary purposes are to entertain and to instruct. The author should have the facility to do this. He, or she, should be a skilled entertainer and should not venture too far away from this idea, or else run the risk of presumptuous lecturing. Don't write for the sake of self-expression that can crush a novel. Many beginning novelists turn to James Joyce, or Thomas Wolfe for models. The novices mistakenly think that these two 20th Century masters of the stream-of-consciousness style wrote their novels by sitting back and running off at the mouth. That would be an easy way to write, but the truth is that Joyce was painfully calculated in his writing and Wolfe was exhaustively edited by Maxwell Perkins, the outstanding Scribner's editor. There may be an appearance of formlessness in their work, but the structures are there subtly supporting the seemingly chaotic impressions of life. It is up to the novice to understand this and improve on the masters, if that is the challenge. Their material is under emotional control, showing a balance of engagement and detachment. They distill fiction from reality by keeping their feelings about the material under control.

Compiling events, feelings, moods, emotions, and situations creates the material for novel writing. The author must find the exact words that will make the reader see, feel, and experience the illusions. And when the author does this, he or she should work as though there was a deadline. A sense of urgency can stimulate the writer to excite the reader. It's not a question of haste. The story must come naturally. But once the material is at hand--all the notes are completed and the point of view established--drawing out the writing process can stifle the creative energy.

As the author writes, he, or she, should keep close track of what's going on in the manuscript so that characters' names aren't duplicated or confused from chapter to chapter; or, there are inaccurate time changes: or, impossible geographic relocations. Watch out for anachronisms and keep the actions within the characters' abilities to function.

In writing the manuscript, keep to a daily time schedule: a daily word count; and, later, a daily rewrite schedule. Don't turn away from the task or it will never be completed. The writer has to depend on his, or her, own mind, desire, ability, and creativity. As Lolah Burford says, let no one read the manuscript who is not directly involved in the business of getting it published.[40] Don't solicit, or listen to the advice of friends, relatives or fellow writers concerning the book you are working on. For those of us in publishing, you would be amazed how many Aunt Tillies crop up--the local authority for all that is literary: the critic who has seen others struggling writers achieve success.

Writing itself is a learning process. It is selfinstructive and the lessons come as the novel is written. In the first draft, ordinarily, the last half should be better than the first, and in the rewrite the level of the manuscript should be brought up to the best passages in the book. Whatever else happens, finish the first draft, aim for about 80,000 words, between 300 and 400 pages-- about a page a day for a year, if you want to think of it that way. In order to learn, the author has to write those 400 pages; and in order to do that, he, or she must have the seat of the pants to the seat of the chair, everyday. There is no other solution. You might do it in less time, but that is the kind of flack that makes for good promotion copy, if it is true. More than likely, in a first novel, it is not true. A first novel, that becomes a success, is usually the result of a life time of living.

ELEVEN

NOVEL STRUCTURE

All novels are structured in the same general sense. There is a beginning, a middle, and an end. There are major and minor characters that are simple, lacking complexity, complicated, flat or one dimensional, round or fully developed, and many who serve as background figures. There is a goal for the characters--a plot structure--and each character is related to that goal according to its desires, motivations, and significance. There is a feeling of necessity--an importance of purpose. There are flashbacks. Drama is created through conflicts and action. Dialogue shows character, feeds information to the reader, and motivates action. Theme provides the idea behind a novel. There is crisis, climax, and resolution. Description lets the reader see the characters, the settings, and the props. Emotions are generated. But, all the elements are contained within the story of what happens.

Whichever element the writer focuses on as a starting point, the beginning of the novel should contain a crisis that captures the reader's attention. The opening may be a point of crisis, itself, or a point immediately following one. For instance, the opening crisis for Pip, in *Great Expectations*, is a matter of life and death, when he is confronted by Magwich in the graveyard. The meeting is the key to the book we find out later, but at the beginning its significance rests only in the terror it raises in Pip and the sympathy and interest it generates for the central character in the reader.

After the opening crisis, the beginning section of the novel introduces the characters, gives the goal/s, lays out the motivations, and creates interest for the story. Events prior to the opening are related through flashbacks, or other integrating devices. There is a danger in overuse of flashbacks that interrupt, or completely stop the forward motion of the narrative thrust. A poor flashback may distract the reader by carrying the reader off on impossible tangents that lose sight of the central story-line.

If the writer discovers himself, or herself, writing unrelated stories within the flashbacks, the novel has opened too late in the story. If pages and pages of the opening section of the novel are consumed by prior incidents, the author should reconsider the point at which he, or she, began. The author may find it impossible to work with flashbacks without getting completely distracted. In that case, there are other ways to get information to the reader--through dialogue, letters from one character to another, narrative, or omniscient asides. A flashback is such an obvious device that it can be laborious and mechanical, if it is handled badly.

A good flashback begins and ends with smooth transitions that subtly lead from the present action and returns to the mainstream of the story with no interruption of thought or continuity. Nabokov is a master of the flashback and his novels flow from the story's present to its past and even its future without disorienting the reader.

The middle section of the novel develops the elements introduced at the beginning. The conflicts become critical and the action should be intense, as the momentum of the story reaches a point of crisis. Generally, the major crisis of the book marks the end of the middle section. It is the point when the central character's fortunes are lowest and the major goal of the book is unlikely to be achieved. In a mystery novel, for instance, the crisis comes when the detective has no chance of solving the crime. He has run down all the leads and they prove false; the clues that seemed significant at the beginning are suddenly meaningless; the criminal is out of reach. The detective is in a state of hopelessness and confusion. For all appearances, the villain has triumphed. In an adventure novel, the crisis comes when the central character/s is/are beaten by nature, or other elements and circumstances that represent the counter-points to the hero/s. In less formal novels, in the psychological novel for instance, the pattern is not defined so clearly, but the idea of crisis is the same--it is the point at which the hero, or anti-hero, is furthest from a goal such as communication, understanding the human condition, attaining a semblance of sanity and order, discovering meaning, love, or some aspect of truth.

The end of a novel is made up of two elements: a climax and a resolution. In the detective novel, the climax is the point when the hero collars the criminal. In the adventure novel, it represents the moment the central character finds the treasure, reaches the top of the mountain, circumnavigates the globe, lands on the moon ... whatever the goal was at the beginning. In other novels, the pattern is the same: the nurse marries the doctor, the sheriff guns down the outlaws, the anti-hero achieves some degree of understanding.

The resolution finishes the story, accounting for characters, and other elements in a way that impresses the reader with a feeling of completeness. The end is the natural resolution of the story. Problems are solved; emotions purged, characters triumph or are defeated, and solutions are offered.

TWELVE

HACK WORK

There is a type of novel writing that always causes controversy and attracts criticism--the category novel, or formula writing. Generally, the category novel is called hack work because the author follows a relatively rigid pattern based on the success of other novels like the one he, or she, is writing. Formula writing is filled with stock characters, set structures, happy endings and special categories like a nurse-doctor. love struck men and women, the loner against the outlaws, gothic, science fiction, campus setting, and others. These novels are often considered shallow because of their slightly developed characters, cliche situations and predictable story-lines; their limited plot structures and their base, obvious emotional appeals. They are often cheap forms of wish-fulfillment for readers.

But it would be unprofessional for an author to think that a category novel is easy to write well. Even the least critical writing is difficult to accomplish so that readers enjoy it. It takes a special talent to write good pornography, or grade B novels. A novelist of great literary stature may scoff at writers of category novels and it's unlikely that a master would want to write a trite nurse romance; but it's also true that a writer of outstanding literature might find it extremely difficult, if not impossible, to write cheap fiction. F. Scott Fitzgerald, for instance, wrote many unproduced Hollywood film scripts that are collecting dust on the shelves of the movie companies that bought the original rights.

Category novels, as a genre, are the products of paperback publishers who set up certain categories and then decided how many of each one they will bring out each month.[41]· The genre is no longer limited to paperbacks, although the most obvious ones are usually not published as hardback books. Generally, three common plots define the category novel: ideals versus economic pressure, nurse-doctor, and love versus loyalty. Since other novels may also have one of these plots, there are other elements that make the category novel unique.

Most writers and critics agree with Isabel Moore that the characteristics include: chapters that open with conversation and introduce a new or different character. The novel itself opens with a life-style conflict. The emotional resolution is saved to the last. In romances, the man doesn't win the woman, or vice-versa, until the very end. Each chapter is titled to show the progress of the story. The background is always familiar and the characters, settings and events are never so unique that they have to be explained. Interesting details of the characters' occupations should be included, but not so much material that it prevents the story from moving steadily forward.

The two most important elements are theme and characters. The theme should be something that most readers will readily understand: love, success, honor, winning, overcoming loss. The characters that personify the ideas and act them out should not be too complex. They should have a single strong trait such as lovers, haters, idealists, workers, achievers, strivers, administrators. These characters are dedicated, resourceful, villainous, obsessed, fearful, romantic, or suspicious, according to what they represent. They are not concerned with philosophy, theology, or psychology in the abstract. In fact, nothing about them is abstract or complex. The characters function to evoke simple emotional responses in readers. Characters that do not directly advance the plot should be cut, until each character in the book plays a part of resolving the protagonist's basic conflict.

In the plot ideals versus economic pressure, a conflict between what a man, or woman, believes to be right and the negative pressure of monetary needs, or interests, must be resolved. For instance, a young woman from a wealthy family graduates from a college where she has become involved in trying to improve the living conditions of migrant workers. She has a boy friend who is equally concerned with the issue. Her anti-union father owns a large amount of land in California used for farming lettuce and grapes. To heighten the conflict, the girl goes to the aid of workers striking her father's farms. He threatens to cut her off, unless she gives up her union organizing. She is immediately caught in a dilemma: if she obeys her father, she will have to forsake her ideals and her boyfriend; but if she disobeys, her father will write her out of his will and she will not have the money to accomplish what she believes in. The resolution must fit the category with a happy ending. It might be this: father, who is a complete villain, is killed, or dies, so the girl, an only child, inherits the fortune and the farms. She and her boy friend marry and together, with the union workers, create a model farm. On the other hand, if fate is not to play such an important role, the girl must directly work-out a solution with her father that solves the dilemma in a favorable way for her. If the father triumphs, the novel may be more realistic, more interesting, more complex, more literary, but it will no longer be a category novel with an ideals-versus-economic pressure plot.

The nurse-doctor plot is a popular one for category novels. It involves romance between nurse and doctor and the background of a big city hospital contributes the tension, action, and exciting details that keep the story going. This situation is used by script writers as the basis for the most successful television soap operas. In order to write this kind of category novel, the author should have enough basic knowledge of medicine and how a hospital works to give the necessary authority to the work. At least, obvious medical language and technology should be mastered. At the end of the book, the nurse wins the doctor.

In the love-versus-loyalty story, the hero, or heroine, must choose between two potentially correct alternatives; love of spouse or dedication to job; love of country, or commitment to a higher ideal; love of nature, or the necessity to exploit it.

A current situation for a love-versus-loyalty plot would involve a Catholic priest torn between love for a woman he would like to marry and his loyalty to the Church and his priestly vows of obedience and celibacy. The strength of the story rests in the lack of room for compromise. The choice would be a definitive one: either the priest leaves the Church to marry the woman, or he forsakes his love for loyalty to the order. There must be anguish and, whatever the choice, a feeling of loss that must be balanced by happiness in the final decision.

THIRTEEN

THE MOST COMMON TYPES

OF NOVELS

Originality is the mark of any successful novel. It is a difficult element to define because it is the most subjective characteristic of a work. But generally, originality is the author's unique way of using common situations to tell the reader something new about life. It is the fresh use of language to offer insight and understanding. Emotions appear in all novels and when we read about people whose actions reveal fresh insight into emotions, we say the author's writing is original. The basic situation of a novel may have been used before--although a writer will find it difficult to avoid cliches completely--but the cliches sustain a level of originality when they are cast in the author's own vision. If it is a vision of truth, the novel can be successful.

A great many novels resemble each other to a point that their subjects become cliches. An author should be aware of these common types, not to avoid them, but to be sure to use the forms in a purist sense. Along with other critics, Christopher Derrick has identified the most common types of novels:

The novel of a distant past is based on the reconstruction of events through archaeology, anthropology, or comparative religion.

A cousin of this first type has the same basis, but includes sex, violence and religion.

The campus novel has become so popular that it is no longer just a fad, but has become a cliche that imitates such classics as *Lucky Jim, Getting Straight, Good-bye Columbus,* and *The Graduate.* Related to it are the academic novels, that try to model themselves on high themselves on high

English literature. A third type of campus novel is the bitter-and-disillusioned-professor-story.

There are politico-military thrillers like *Fail Safe, Seven Days In May.*

Ever since James Joyce wrote *Dubliners* and *Portrait Of The Artist As a Young Man,* writers have been after the Irish for subject matter. Recently, books such as *The Ginger Man* have continued the fad. All this effort has given rise to the Irish Novel, often written by young Americans who have spent little time in Ireland, as Derrick points out.

At the same time, there is the American novel, also written by young Americans trying to write like Nathanial West, John Steinbeck, William Faulkner, Herman Melville, or Kurt Vonnegut. Such novels include much suffering, absurdity, irony, and loss of innocence.

Holiday novels are common fare and usually fit into one of the romance categories.

The absurd, macabre, foolish, and debased aspects of society are common subjects for writers trying to imitate *Day Of The Locust, The Loved One, Man With The Golden Arm, Naked Lunch,* and others.

The rush of pornographic novels during the 1960s and 1970s helped generate the rise of dull, solemn pornography. Material that's intended to be sexually exciting should have no saving moral or social value. A writer shouldn't try to excite us with one hand and save our souls with the other. Anyone interested in writing good pornography should read the 19th Century masterpiece, *The Pearl,* a collection of stories and poems from the underground Victorian magazine by the same name.

Inevitably, beginning writers get around to penning the stories of how they did, or didn't get seduced during a summer vacation, tour of Europe, or next to the back fence.

There are the Catholic novels: birth-control, priests, nuns, and missionaries.

Novels about men mistreating women and women taking advantage of men fill the book sellers' shelves.

The greatest examples of the end—of—adolescence-novel, *Catcher In The Rye,* and its model *Huckleberry Finn,* have probably exhausted the field, but each year thousands of imitators come along more, or less, failing to equal their masters.

The identity novel is always popular, someone finding out who she, or he, really is.

Every war produces some outstanding fiction--from the *Odyssey* to *Naked and The Dead.* But the trash of war also includes bad fiction and the army novel is certainly a cliche.

A recent popular type is the psycho-clinical, case history non-fiction novel *(Sybil,* or *Ward Three,* both descended from Mary Jane Ward's classic *Snake Pit.*

Probably the most successfully written cliche novels are the vast family chronicles. They're good most of the time, because they're so hard to write. Only a professional has the ability and the time to stick with a book from conception to publication, one or two thousand pages long, with the results showing up five years later.

The last kind of cliche novel that Derrick cites is the one that plays games with the novel convention. The models are books like Joyce's *Finnegan's Wake,* Gertrude Stein's work, or the novels of Nabokov, particularly *Ada.*[42].

Generally, the writer is best advised to avoid fad and fashion. Draw on what is needed from the period that's being written about, but don't become a slave to what's popular. The writer should use his, or her, own character with its strengths and limitations as the boundaries for a book.

When a writer discovers what he, or she, *cannot* do, that is important, too. Hemingway did not write much poetry. T.S. Eliot never wrote a great novel. Shakespeare did nothing with the personal essay. Fitzgerald could not write a good film script. But each was a master in the area of writing that he could do best. It's up to each writer to find that area which is best for himself, or herself. If it's the novel, then the writer has to be prepared for a lot of hard work, and disappointment, but the rewards, in money and self-satisfaction, can be great.

FOOTNOTES

1   Flannery O'Connor, "Writing Short Stories," *The Writer* January 1970, p. 18.

2   F.A. Rockwell, *Modern Fiction Techniques,* Boston: The Writer, Inc., 1962, pp. 126-141.

3   Rockwell, *Fiction Techniques,* pp. 32-36.

4   Maren Elwood, *Characters Make Your Story,* Boston: The Writer, Inc., 1972, pp.20-28.

5   Ibid., p. 117.

6   Rockwell, *Fiction Techniques,* pp. 126-140.

7   Francis L. Fugate, *Viewpoint: Key to Fiction Writing,* Boston: The Writer, Inc. p.35.

8   O'Connor, "Short Stories," p. 18.

9   Eva Ibboston, "In The Beginning," *The Writer* August 1971, pp. 9-12.

10 Edward Fox, *How To Write Stories That Sell,* Boston: The Writer, Inc., 1969, pp. 12-21.

11 Rockwell, *Fiction Techniques,* pp. 161-172.

12 Fox, *Stories That Sell,* p.7.

13 Rockwell, *Fiction Techniques,* p. 161.

14 Ibid., pp. 160-166.

15 Phyllis A. Whitney, "I Couldn't Put It Down," *The Writer* April 1973, p. 12.

16 Flannery O'Connor, "The Nature and Aim of Fiction," *The Writer,* October 1969, p. 13.

17 Peggy Simson Curry, "Genisis of a Short Story," *The Writer* December 1972, p. 9.

18 Evan S. Connell, Jr., "Beginnings," *The Writer* September 1970, p.9.

19 Samuel W. Taylor, "Four Rules For The Short Story," *The Writer* February 1963, pp. 7-9.

20 Rockwell. *Fiction Techniques*, p. 176.

21 Fox, *Stories That Sell*, pp. 114-120.

22. Barbara Robinson, "Don't Lick the Stamp Yet," *The Writer* September. 1963, p. 11.

23 Eloise Jarvis McGraw, *Techniques of Fiction Writing*, Boston: The Writer, Inc., 1959, p. 173.

24 Merritt Lawlis, ed., *Elizabethan Prose Fiction*, New York: The Odyssey Press, 1967, p. 4.

25 Ibid., pp 1-12.

26 Ian Watt, *The Rise Of The Novel*, Berkeley: University Of California Press, 1964, p. 11.

27 Dorothy Van Ghent, *The English Novel: Form and Function*, New York: Harper Torchbooks, 1953, p. 139.

28 E.M. Forster, *Aspects Of The Novel*, New York: Harcourt, Brace World, Inc., 1954, p. 14.

29 Van Ghent, *English Novel, p.* 172.

30 Forster, *Aspects*, p. 26.

31 Ibid., p. 27.

32 Thomas C. Turner, "The Novelist and His Theme," *The Writer* December 1963, p. 12.

33 Hannah Lees, "Every Novel Is Like Another Planet," *The Writer* October 1972, pp. 12-15.

34 Borden Deal, "People and Characters," *The Writer* April 1971, p. 18.

35 Seymour Epstein, "The Personal Motif in Fiction," *The Writer* July 1967 p. 13.

36 Turner, *Theme*, p. 12.

37 Christopher Derrick, *The Writing Of Novels*, Boston: The Writer. Inc., 1969, pp. 50-65.

38 Ibid., pp. 41-42

39 Ibid., pp. 50-65.

40 Lolah Burford, "Writing A First Novel (Part II)." *The Writer* November 1971, p.20.

41 Isabel Moore, "The Category Novel," *The Writer* September 1964, p.10.

42 Derrick, *Novels,* pp. 91-94.

BIBLIOGRAPHY

Burack, A.S. *Techniques of Novel Writing.* Boston: The Writer, Inc., 1973

Burford, Lolah. "Writing A First Novel (Part II)". *The Writer* November 1971: 19-25;

Connell, Evan S., Jr. "Beginnings." *The Writer* September 1970: 9-11.

Curry, Peggy Simson.   "Genisis of a Short Story." *The Writer* December 1972: 7-10.

Daiches, David. *The Novel and The Modern World.* Chicago: University of Chicago Press, 1960.

Deal, Borden. "People and Characters." *The Writer* April 1971: 16-18.

Derrick, Christopher. *The Writing of Novels,.* Boston: *The Writer, Inc.,* 1969.

DeVoto, Bernard. *The World Of Fiction.* Boston: The Writer, Inc., 1950.

Elwood, Maren. *Characters Make Your Story.* Boston: *The* Writer, Inc., 1972.

Epstein, Seymour. "The Personal Motif in Fiction." *The Writer* July 1967: 11-14.

Forster, E.M. *Aspects Of The Novel.* New York: Harcourt, Brace, World, Inc., 1954.

Fox, Edward. *How To Write Stories That Sell.* Boston: The Writer, Inc. 1969.

Fugate, Francis L. *Viewpoint: Key To Fiction Writing.* Boston: The Writer, Inc., 1968.

Ibbotson, Eva. "In the Beginning." *The Writer* August 1971: 9-12.

Lawlis, Merritt, ed. Elizabethan Prose Fiction. New York: The Odyssey Press, Inc., 1967.

Lees, Hannah. "Every Novel Is Like Another Planet." *The Writer* October 1972: 12-15.

Mahl, Mary R., ed. *Seventeenth-Century English Prose.* New York: J.B. Lippincott Co., 1968.

McGraw, Eloise Jarvis. *Techniques Of Fiction Writing.* Boston: The Writer. Inc., 1959.

Moore, Isabel. "The Category Novel." *The Writer* September 1964: 9-13.

Novarr, David, *17th Century English Prose.* New York: Alfred A. Knopf. 1967.

O'Connor, Flannery. *"The Nature and Aim Of Fiction."* The Writer October, 1969: 11-14 & 43.

O'Connor, Flannery, "Writing Short Stories." *The Writer* January 1970: 17-19 & 27-30.

Robinson, Barbara. *"Don't Lick The Stamp Yet."* The Writer September 1963: 11-13 & 44.

Rockwell, F.A. *Modern Fiction Techniques.* Boston: The Writer, Inc. 1962.

Taylor, Samuel W. *"Four Rules For The Short Story."* The Writer February 1963: 7-9.

Turner, Thomas C. *"The Novelist and His Theme."* The Writer December 1963: 12-13 & 45.

Van Ghent, Dorothy, *The English Novel: Form and Function.* New York: Harper Torchbooks, 1961.

Watt, Ian. T*he Rise Of The Novel.* Berkeley: University Of California Press, 1964.

Whitney, Phyllis A. *"'I Couldn't Put It Down."* The Writer April 1973: 11-14 & 23.

The Writer's Manual
Book 3

How to
Write
Non-Fiction

By
Jack C. Dierks

ABOUT THE AUTHOR

Jack Dierks
is a partner of Porter, Gould & Dierks,
formerly Max Siegel & Associates,
literary agents representing authors both in the United States and abroad.
He received his BA from Beloit College
and an MS from Northwestern University's Medill School of Journalism.
After having served as a journalist in the U.S. Navy,
he worked in both the public relations and advertising fields
for three large corporations from 1957 to 1963,
and was an editor of *Food Business* magazine (1963-64).
He has been a free lance writer for several years,
with many articles and two books to his credit,
the most notable being *A Leap to Arms,*
a study of the Spanish-American War of 1898.

CONTENTS

ONE

NON-FICTION VERSUS FICTION

No one knows any better than the literary agent (with the possible exception of the fledgling author himself) just how hard it is to place a first novel with a publisher nowadays. The typical novelist's initial effort has always been well thought of in the publishing business if it broke even, instead of losing its sponsor's money. Traditionally a first novel has been contracted for because the editors involved saw some spark of talent and future promise in its creator and were counting on the fact that he would continue to turn out more (and hopefully better) books, thereby building a successful combination between the author and the house that publishes him.

The game hasn't changed at all in recent years, except for the fact that the dice seem to be loaded just a little more against the novel writer. And the reason for increasing caution on the part of publishers is the steady -- even accelerating -- trend toward non-fiction as time goes by. In a day of rocketing costs and murderous profit squeezes, non-fiction is considered definitely less risky from the financial standpoint. Though it's not the only point of view, profit-and-loss is usually the dominant one. A look at the facts will tell the story. A novel has earned the right to be included in the "best-seller" category if it sells 40,000 copies or so; a non-fiction book which clicks, on the other hand, will almost always soar to the 100,000 level or higher. The situation is spelled out clearly enough in the most recent *Publishers Weekly* statistics which list the total number of new books published for the year 1974 as 30,575, with 27,078 of these or 87 percent of the whole falling into the non-fiction category.

What's the cause of all this? Why have the great magazines that once made up the basic structure of the short story market -- *Collier's, Woman's Home Companion, The Saturday Evening Post (*in its original form, anyway) vanished, to be replaced by non-fiction periodicals catering to followers of tennis, psychology, motorcycling, the occult, and every other specialized interest under the sun? Why is non-fiction riding so high, both in the magazine and the book field?

To answer this, we must define (or try to, anyway, because the dividing lines are now always clearly cut) just what fiction and non-fiction attempt to do for the reader. It seems to make sense to class non-fiction as being basically *informative,* and fiction *entertaining* on its lower levels and *instructive* -- that is, transmitting insights into the basic human condition -- at its upper, or "quality" level. One thinks immediately of the convoluted interpersonal relationships found in the writing of Henry James, the panoramic sweep of a Tolstoy, mapping out an entire human cavalcade, or the introspective meanderings of a Proust, all of which are attempting to interpret to the reader the unchanging basics of human personality and action.

If fiction deals primarily with relationships -- between man and man, man and God, man and the inanimate -- non-fiction usually provides pretty solid and factual information on matters that the author feels the reader either knows something about already or wants to know more about. The novelist, though, faces a different problem. For his books to have any meaning, for his fictional characters to be able to transmit what used to be termed the "eternal verities," and communicate what the author wants to communicate, there must *be* eternal verities of some kind, a meeting ground upon which an author can count on a common response from his readers.

Nowadays, unfortunately, this is largely lacking. Society is not only shifting physically because of increased mobility, but standards and values which once were held universally sacred have been shifting at what many feel to be an alarming rate. Virtually every personal relationship one can name --- between men and women, parents and children, between employer and employee, between different races, even between humans and animals (and plants?) --- have all changed and are continuing to do so. The moral structure --- the basic concepts of what is right, wrong, fashionable, or acceptable --- has undergone the type of overhauling that makes a book like Alvin Toffler's *Future Shock* strike home so deeply at what seems to be troubling man in the eighth decade of the twentieth century. What it all means is that the successful novelist must have readers with some well-grounded and unchanging concept of the way life operates; of what's possible and what's plausible, at a time when emotional isolationism is the sickness of our age. The ability to identify with other people's and other groups' problems has never been more difficult.

Writer and reader must have a close communication; words must mean the same things to both, and they must adhere to the same rules. Yet with so much of the social, cultural, and emotional background people once had in common gone or going, an author finds it more and more difficult to count on any kind of predictable reaction to his work. One reader responds one way, someone else another. Moral judgments sway here and then there. Fiction no longer communicates in the same way to everyone, but instead becomes a way of speaking to the special groups it is aimed at. Recently this writer got into a discussion with a good friend of his, an educated and extremely well read man, on the subject of contemporary authors Kurt Vonnegut and Tom Wolfe. He could find nothing deep or lasting in either. The best thing he could say about Vonnegut's novel *Breakfast of Champions* was that it read like something out of a college humor magazine, and was about as profound. His characters were stereotypes, his situations all black and white, and the whole story lacked any kind of subtlety beyond the kind of hacking away at American institutions that might be expected of a piece of undergraduate satire. Wolfe he wrote off as being flamboyant and confused to the point of being incomprehensible.

Still Vonnegut and Wolfe are among the most widely read authors among young people today. Undoubtedly the reason for this is that they speak the language and appeal to the attitudes of a portion of the young adult population that reads its own books and goes to its own films; a portion that has veered off to the extent of adopting quite different forms of entertainment and intellectual stimulation. In this case anyway, reader response shows as much of a generational deviation as a cultural and emotional one.

The fact that the world has shrunk so drastically and communication has expanded to such a degree has not only stirred our interest in what is going on across the globe, but made us feel guilty if we don't stay informed about it. Much of it is sensational and much unpleasant, but that only seems to result in our gobbling up the pages of *Time* and *Newsweek* more avidly, and make us stare, more fascinated than ever, at scenes of crisis and calamity on the five o'clock news.

All this probably won't kill the novel at all, and that literary form is adjusting or trying to adjust to an audience which has long since accustomed itself to the graphic presentation of movie film and the video camera. We hope, for the sake of the civilized everywhere, it does so successfully. What we do emphasize is that because of the temper of the times, the opportunity has never been greater for the writer of non-fiction who now finds himself aiming at a reading audience whose appetite for well-laid-out history, biography, political and social commentary — even how-to-do-it books — seems insatiable. Better education, more awareness, and simply more curiosity than ever before have done their job in this respect.

TWO

TYPES OF BOOKS

Non-fiction books come in such a wide assortment of types, and there are so few hard and fast taboos in publishing today, that the author is lucky in the respect that there is less than ever before to keep in mind when he proceeds to start on his manuscript.

Some of the basics do remain, however. Though non-fiction books can run almost any length within reason, an author should probably try to get at least 60,000 words down on paper if he wants his work to be considered seriously. You will see books around of 30,000 words of course -- cookbooks, humor books, slim volumes of essays, expanded pamphlets -- but these are the exception rather than the rule. For most subject matter it would be better to try to hit that minimum of 200-300 double-spaced typed pages.

Some beginning writers get all the way through a manuscript and find it only comes out to 20,000 or 25,000 words. They are disconcerted when somebody finally tells them that they really don't have a book at all, that there wasn't enough vital material there for a successful book idea in the first place.

On the upper end of the scale the sky is virtually the limit -- up to a point -- and that point is probably somewhere around a half million words, where a single volume is concerned. William L. Shirer's *The Rise and Fall of the Third Reich* was about this size, but it was a very big book, in both heft and importance, and you won't see many around of this length. Multi-volumed books, of course, can run much longer. Winston Churchill's *History of the Second World War* came out in six volumes, one being published every couple of years or so, and Will and Ariel Durant's exhaustive *History of Civilization* in eleven volumes comes to mind as well, but these are massive and special projects — to be considered in every respect the *magnum opus* of a career.

Long, short or average-sized, your book must hang together -- that is, have a definite unity about it. Many beginning writers have a tendency to wander far afield in a book length manuscript -- something they wouldn't be guilty of in a magazine article -- simple because they are writing much more than they are accustomed to. It's something to be on guard against, because this kind of diffuseness can ruin an otherwise strong manuscript. Keep to one subject, or a number of closely related subjects. One of the best examples of a book with natural unity is the biography, but does a series of biographies collected in one volume have the same validity, for instance? It does if the subjects have something in common. A book like Churchill's *Great Contemporaries* meets this standard, since all the subjects of these short but incisive sketches were colleagues of the author -- political friends or adversaries -- or had intimate dealings with him in some other way. A book about the lives of several American women might or might not have this quality of unity we are looking for. If they shared some experience -- a common standard of success, a misfortune of some kind, a common lifestyle or place of residence — that would fill the requirement. Or, conversely, even if they had little in common at all, provided the treatment dealt with a "cross-section" of women, describing various types, levels, and stratification. There's no set of rules to refer to here; you must simply use your common sense. An editor won't be long in pointing it out if he thinks you're wrong.

Non-fiction of course covers the widest possible field, but generally speaking you might divide books of this type into five broad categories. These are books whose primary purpose is:

> to inform
> to persuade
> to interest and entertain
> to teach
> to arouse emotion

There are many book ideas which may fall into more than one of these broad types, depending on how the author handles his subject, or the book may legitimately embrace two or more simultaneously. Fashions change, too. Because the tendency in non-fiction nowadays is toward a more colorful, readable style directed toward as wide an audience as possible, the "interest and entertain" category is considerably wider than it used to be. Barbara Tuchman's fine history of the opening days of World War I, *The Guns of August* is certainly informative, but is laced with all the detail, insights, and color needed to make it personally engrossing as well. And just where does one place a book like "J's" *The Sensuous Woman?* It informs, certainly, tries to teach, is undoubtedly interesting and entertaining, and from all that one heard about it at the time of its publication, almost invariably aroused emotions in most people of one kind or another!

The *informative* book's basic job is to provide the reader with factual matter that he doesn't have and that the writer wants him to have. History and biography would have to be classed as informative first of all, as would most political and sociological studies, and even the expose-type of book. One rule to keep in mind in regard to the informative book is that it should deal with a subject important enough to warrant lengthy treatment. Don't make the mistake of thinking that a good magazine article idea would make a good book idea, and that all it needs is a little expansion. The two can be entirely different. Anyway, if you are wrong, there are plenty of editors around to tell you so, hopefully before you invest a lot of time and work. That's what they're there for.

The *persuasive* book is designed to get not only some kind of reaction out of the reader, but some action as well. The writer's aim here is arousal -- the awakening of sleeping dogs, perhaps. Here we may find a lot of exaggeration and just plain falsehood; the publicity and propaganda fields fall into the persuasive category, of course. It is not known whether Harriet Beecher Stowe meant her notorious *Uncle Tom's Cabin* to be a persuasive book, or merely an emotional one -- possibly both -- at any rate the misadventures of Little Nell eventually turned out to be among the potent factors in spreading a revulsion of slavery in the northern states and galvanizing abolitionist supporters into the attitudes and actions which ultimately brought on the Civil War.

The *interest-and-entertainment* category is a common one; much autobiography would be classed thus, particularly if it is light and humorous. It must contain curious and intriguing factual matter and keep the reader glued to its pages. Usually more successful if it isn't the "deepest" material in the world, a book of this type ought to give the reader a sense of progress -- of making him want to keep on to see what will happen next. Most true life adventure would have to be classed as having considerable interest and entertainment value. A travel book like Thor Heyerdahl's *Kon-Tiki*, for instance, disaster tales like *The Great Chicago Fire, A Night to Remember,* and *The Day Lincoln was Shot* lead the reader on skilfully page by exciting page. They represent high water marks in this rather distinctive type of non-fiction book. They are quite often excellent sellers.

Probably the most obvious variety of non-fiction book which purports to *teach* is the how-to-do-it book, and this covers a wide selection -- from raising chinchilla to macrame to brewing your own stout and making a fortune in the commodity markets -- that it shouldn't be necessary to go into examples here; they are obvious. These are popular books from the writer's standpoint; many a tyro author has looked at the sales figures for some overwhelming success of this genre and become convinced that a vast reading public is all out there, only waiting to be exposed to their particular hobby or brand of puttering. Well, possibly so; it's been known to happen. But before you start you'd better make sure that you have something new and interesting to say and that there is somebody to hear you say it. Sound out an editor first via query letter approach (see Part 4) and if you get shot down at this early point, you will have saved yourself a great deal of work. The first rule is to steer away from subjects that have a wealth of books written about them already. Unless it's something very special, the market needs another slim volume on woodworking, gardening, or cooking with wine like it needs the proverbial hole in the head.

The book written to arouse *emotion* must be astutely handled to be successful, since leading the reader's feelings along the channels the writer thinks they should be led is a difficult (and possible dangerous) thing to do. No one who has never tried it will realize how easy it is to become maudlin when you really want to be sentimental, disgusting when you are seriously trying to shock in a positive way, or laughable in the use of honest exaggeration to make a point. It's not really that difficult to sway the ignorant, the prejudiced, or the unstable with inflammatory material, but your book will probably never see print if that is the only audience you are aiming at. All but the most desperate, most sales-and-dollar-hungry publisher will turn you down unless you have more substance to offer than that. Trying to sustain an emotion throughout the length of a book is not easy, since you mustn't bore the reader, or saturate him to the point where your message begins to lose its impact after a time. You must sustain it, yet not lose the effect you want.

THREE

GETTING THE IDEA

One of the most exasperating things for the hard-working professional, and conversely one of the most encouraging things for the tyro, is the apparent ease with which so many relatively non-experienced writers seem to be able to turn out books that become sellers -- even "top-ten-of-the-best-sellers book list". Of course they are always written (or at least edited) well enough to be readable, and yet seemingly no more competently than some project an author with three or four solid books to his credit has spent a year and a half on.

How then is the rank beginner able to "hit the big time," on the first try? The answer of course lies in coming up with that catchy, attractive, compelling idea, that vital first step any writer must take before he even starts paragraph one, and which he must sell to a publisher before he'll get any commitment out of anybody. It's the idea and all that it suggests that will convince a book editor that he ought to read your manuscript in the first place, and if and when it finally gets into print will in turn convince the reader to pick your book off the shelf in the store where it sits in competition with a hundred others and buy it. Whether or not it will sell well is going to depend on the quality of your writing, and other factors too, but without a good initial idea your book will never get between the covers.

But, isn't the beginner terribly handicapped in this department? Doesn't the experienced writer who has hashed out book concepts in the past, shared talk and cups of coffee with editors, gone through innumerable tomes in his research and picked up a pretty good idea what has and what has not been done in a particular field already have a big head start when it comes to thinking up a new wrinkle? Well of course he has some advantage, but not all that much. You may be an individual with specialized knowledge and a one-in-a-million book idea within you that only needs to be nourished and brought to fruit. Or you may have been close to some great personage or great event and have a story to tell. Or you may be like "J." authoress of the smash best-seller *The Sensuous Woman*, who is neither a professional writer nor an expert in the subject matter, but simply has discovered how to present an old topic in a new and unusual way.

In his recently published work *Writing and Selling the Non-Fiction Book*, Max Gunther lists eight qualities what would seem to be essential ingredients of the good and salable book idea. They will make even better sense to you if you stop and think what you would be looking for as potential publishable material if you were on the other side of the desk -- if you were the editor, that is.

1.   In the first place a good book deals with a single idea -- one subject, in other words, which can be well-defined, rather than a loose accumulation of facts about one thing or another. It is important to start off and maintain a definite focus.

2.   You should not only concentrate on a single subject, but make sure as well that it has the potential of filling up the book with solid, viable material. It must "stand by itself" and be important enough to qualify for book status without extraneous padding.

3.   It must be a subject that the reader will be interested in. Gunther makes the important point that your book should not merely be "about" something, but also "for the purpose of" something. The story of your experiences as a reformed alcoholic should have some value to the reader; you are asking him to draw some conclusions, to absorb something usable or thought-provoking from the reading of it. You must be able to visualize just what you are going to be able to communicate to the reader that will benefit him before you ever start to write. To say that you're just doing it because you think it will be interesting is not really enough. If you can't visualize a more specific purpose your idea will be a nebulous one and will seem so to the publisher, too.

4.   In order to want to buy your book, an editor must be able to project what the potential readership must be. Before he will agree to invest his own time and the publishing house's money in your material he must know how many potential readers there are apt to be, how and to whom the advertising and promotion will be directed, and just what the results of such a business transaction with you are apt to be. You must be aware, too, of just what type of individual is likely to read your book, that is, who you will be writing to.

5.   Don't ever forget the vital quality of being topical in your idea. Though you may wince at another mention of that greatly overworked term, the word "relevance" is applicable here. What is there about your book that would make anyone want to publish it now? Would next year be just as good? If the answer is no, you must know why and be able to convey why to an editor within your basic book idea.

6.   You must have something new to say, too. What is going to make your book any different from those which may already be on the market and which deal with the same subject? If the subject itself is so new or unusual that it hasn't been done before at all, then, of course, you have no worries along that line. But if it's a history of the Second World War, a biography of Abraham Lincoln, a study of Renoir's painting, then you must be convinced and convince an editor that you are offering the reader something he hasn't been exposed to, bringing out some heretofore unexplored angle, treating the subject in a way that previous books have failed to do.

7.   You ought to know, before you start to write, how you feel about your subject matter and what kind of response you want to get from the reader. What tone will you take? How do you want him to feel as he reads your words? Reread the earlier section on types of books, and what their aims are. Remember that you've got to make these decisions at the idea stage.

8.   Lastly the book must be possible, that is, the idea must be capable of being done and you, as writer, must be capable of doing it. You are going to have to convince an editor that you are qualified to handle the work; that you have the ability to do the research and the writing, and that you have the *credibility* as well to write a book which the reader can accept as believable. Gunther stresses the point that the writer must have the necessary confidence in his ability to produce, and must convey this feeling to his editor.

Good book ideas may come as a flash out of the blue, that all too rare thunderbolt of inspiration, or through a lengthy process of cerebrating and mental selection to determine just what the book market needs and will contract for; or perhaps as the result of a series of experiences or a lifestyle that you think would be interesting enough to a sufficiently large audience to make a valid book.

Joy Adamson, the author of *Born Free, Living Free and Forever Free* got the notion of doing a book about her and her husband's experience in raising Elsa, the now-famous pet lion, as a result of her life in East Africa as a painter of flowers and of the tribes of people that lived there. Her husband brought three lion cubs home one day after having had to kill their mother in self-defense in the course of an expedition in search of a man-eater. The Adamsons raised and became very close to one of the cubs, whom they named Elsa. They took extensive notes and a good many photos and films of the whole succeeding animal-human relationship, and the result was a book which sold more than three million copies, was translated into more than twenty languages, and which later became a very popular motion picture. Mrs. Adamson had never done a book before, but there was something about the story itself that was immensely appealing. Elsa was so strong, and had so much to give, that even what she called her "utterly amateurish approach" made an impact. She feels that Elsa made us realize, consciously or unconsciously, how far we have come away from the basic things in life. The book's enormous sales -- its impact upon the entire world -- proved the hunger of people to return, in whatever way they can, to a world of genuine proportion, a world in which our balance and basic values have not been destroyed.

Ralph Moody is another author that looked to his own experiences -- those of his boyhood and early manhood in the West -- in his series of autobiographical books that began with *Little Britches*. Moody was a late starter, joining a University of California evening school class in short story writing when he was well past forty even though he had only gone through eighth grade in school. His initial effort was a story about his first job away from home, as a waterboy on a Colorado cattle ranch when he was ten years old, and it so impressed his professor that it was suggested he expand it into a full-length book. Moody promptly sat down and began to write the story of his boyhood from the age of eight to eleven, doing it as if he were ten years old and telling it verbally, since he didn't have such confidence in his talent for composition or even spelling. His theme embraced the principles that had governed his own life, and described a way of existence that produced self-reliant industrious citizens, but which he felt Americans were losing sight of in the midst of their tremendous scientific, economic, and social advancements.

Moody had intended to hire a professional writer to put it into acceptable shape, and to his surprise he was told it was ready for submission as it was. In no time he had a contract, and *Little Britches* became the first of a very popular series of autobiographical books on the West. Moody's advice to the aspiring writer? "Read, read the classics of anything that you'd be proud to have written yourself, but read from the viewpoint of the author." Though he hadn't been to college, he found little difficulty in writing because he'd been a constant reader and had had the best teachers there were --- the great authors of English literature. If you don't have a real compulsion about reading, Moody feels, you may find it almost impossible to write successfully, and while one really doesn't need any dramatic experiences to use as material, one does have to have a liking for people, the talent for understanding them, and the ability to see problems from someone else's point of view.

Bruce Catton is another man whose early interest in history prompted his initial decision to write. Catton more or less grew up in the memory of the Civil War, since the town he lived in as a boy was filled with Civil War veterans, and he remembers marching with all the other school children every Decoration Day down to the town hall where they'd listen to the old soldiers recall the battles of long ago. Afterwards they would all go out to the cemetery to lay bouquets of flowers on the graves of the fallen.

It was only in later years, after he'd spent a lot of time in the newspaper business and in government work, that he decided he wanted to do a book about the war that had fascinated him so much as a boy. He didn't realize at first that he was writing history as such; he just wanted to do something about the Army of the Potomac. His first book actually started out as a novel, since he felt that if he were going to write on the Civil War it would have to be in that form. He didn't think he was knowledgeable enough to attempt non-fiction. About half way through he realized it was a just plain bad novel, so he threw the whole thing away and started over. He said to himself, "I'm just going to sit down and write about this army," and that's what he did. The book was accepted by a publisher, so he wrote another to follow that. It finally became obvious that he was writing Civil War history, but at the beginning he had no plan to become a historian.

It's the history writer's business, of course, to describe the past; an equally fertile field for many authors is the complex phenomenon that makes up contemporary society. Margaret Halsey, for example, like so many others, has long been deeply concerned with the conduct, the ethics, and the morals of present day life in America. Her book *The Pseudo Ethic* came about as the result of a great deal of thought on the subject of what she felt to be the overweening twentieth century hypocrisy --- the broad chasm between what is passed off to young people as good and righteous and what is actually done; in other words, the business of "getting away with something" that seems to be so prevalent in our society.

The purpose of her idea is to convince the reader that the chances of our developing a new moral standard in America are slim, and so we must return to the old one; that it won't be our morality that must change but our behavior. She feels that there have always been elements in any culture that will do all they can to destroy moral standards, simply because people are self-indulgent by nature and don't like restrictions. And because of this there must always be at least a small segment of the people working to keep moral standards high.

Jerome Weidman's collection of essays, *Back Talk,* came about through the same need for self-expression on the subject of modern society, and specifically because of Weidman's urge, as a writer of fiction, to air some of his thoughts himself, rather than through a character he has invented. Weidman wasn't a total stranger to non-fiction --- he had done magazine articles, book introductions and so forth throughout the years --- but he was curious to see whether his basic beliefs and opinions had changed over the span of a long writing career. To his surprise and pleasure he found most of the opinions he had expressed years before on people, books, and so on hadn't changed much. He collected various pieces he had done, some about close literary friends like Somerset Maugham, or about public personalities like Eleanor Roosevelt; some which explored the problems of raising children, of living in the suburbs or the country, or the pleasure of returning to the city, put them all together "for whatever sense they made," and the result was *Back Talk.* The book, he claims, resurrected his favorite non-fiction work and his most firmly-held opinions. There are those who claim that the personal essay is a long lost art, but Weidman found there is a good market for those who have solid opinions and can express them well.

He believes that most writers start writing "inadvertently," that is, they don't set out to pursue a literary career, but just kind of fall into it. At a certain point in their lives the talented writer will begin to write, perhaps as the result of a strong emotional experience that he wants to share with others, or maybe just from economic necessity, "Every man," he believes, "sees life through his own peculiar lens. After all, the only thing a writer has to offer is his own personality as it emerges through his work."

A writer like Jessica Mitford happened to strike gold when she took one facet of American life, which had hitherto been not only unexplored, but virtually untalked about. What made her hit upon the idea of probing into the whole hushed-up area of American funeral practices -- to become interested in the material that resulted in *The American Way of Death?* Her husband, who was a lawyer, had long been concerned about the depletion of the estates of his smaller clients through what he deemed to be excessive funeral costs. He and Mrs. Mitford began to explore the matter in depth, and were astounded at the bitterness with which the undertaking "establishment" attacked clergymen and others who were attempted to simplify funerals. There was the whole elaborate American process for the burial of its dead, which contrasted so sharply to the simple English funerals to which she was accustomed. She and her husband traveled extensively, collecting data on a subject with which they had clearly become fascinated. In spite of rather vicious attacks from funeral organizations, and lobbies which brought considerable pressure to bear both before and after publication, the result was a book which exposes a world which many of us hardly realized existed. Clearly another first, and a case of a book which needed to be written.

Then there is an author like Leo Rosten, who claims he can't really tell where his ideas come from. "A writer lives and breathes and sees and hears. Perhaps he knows that all the facets of his life, his experiences are materials he can use." Rosten does explain how he got the notion to write *Religions of America,* however. He was out walking one day, and in the course of the stroll passed several churches, temples, and synagogues. It occurred to him that he didn't have any idea what went on in a Lutheran church, for example, or how an Episcopalian's beliefs differed from those of a Quaker. He knew virtually nothing about Christian Scientists or Mormons, though he had some rather vague general ideas, as almost everyone does.

He worked up a series of nineteen articles for *Look* magazine entitled "What is a Methodist?" "What is a Seventh Day Adventist?" etc., and the response was so encouraging he decided to put them all in book form. He wrote to Roper, Gallup, and all the other poll takers asking for everything they had collected over the years on religion in the United States. He compiled tables, charts, and statistics of all kinds. The result was a very complete study of virtually every faith professed by the American people. It's the one volume, Rosten says, that people can refer to if they want to know the Catholic position on baptizing and purgatory, on why Jews will eat one kind of meat and not another, or whether a Christian Scientist really believe that a practitioner can heal somebody who is hundreds of miles away, or what the real differences are between the Roman Catholic and Greek Orthodox faiths.

All this may explain how books in specialized fields and dealing with specific or topical subjects came to be written, but how about the biographical study? The decision to devote many months to interpreting the life of some historical figure surely doesn't come about as the result of a flash of insight one night in the wee hours -- a light bulb going on in the brain, so to speak, but rather in a more calculated, well-thought-out manner. Well,this is normally the way it comes about. Hesketh Pearson's biography of Henry of Navarre seemed a natural thing, given his interest in that monarch which Pearson said stemmed from the time he was twelve when he became engrossed in the fascinating romances of Alexandre Dumas. Much later, after he was married, he made a trip to France and his interest in Henry was reawakened. He reread all the books he had so enjoyed in his boyhood and many more as well, taking about nine months to do his preliminary research and about another year to write the book.

Pearson had decided to become a biographer originally because of an early interest in famous men in general. He started off with his own ancestor, Erasmus Darwin, because there were quite a few more or less private papers his mother and friends of the family could give him. Having finished *Doctor Darwin* he found himself so absorbed in this type of work that never again was there a question of his doing anything else.

Pearson found he formed definite likes and dislikes as far as the subjects of his books were concerned. He discovered that the personality of Sydney Smith, the English clergyman and wit, appealed to him about as much as any historical personage he knew of, but then he admits he is prejudiced toward those with quick brains and a good sense of humor. In Oscar Wilde's case he felt he was able to picture him as the unusual character that he was --- a great humorist and wit and a charming man. "His physical pecularities, rather, sexual peculiarities, made it difficult to tackle him when I did, because the prejudice against him then was so strong; a prejudice my book overcame."

Arthur H. Lewis came to write his biography of Hetty Green, too, because he had been intrigued by this peculiar woman, and by eccentrics in general since childhood. All his books, he claims, are about eccentrics. It all began when a lawyer who had read his previous book approached a friend of Lewis' with an idea for a new book he wanted to discuss with him. A meeting was arranged, and the attorney happened to have in his possession a great deal of fascinating material on Hetty Green, the "robber baroness."

The Day They Shook the Plum Tree turned out to be a best seller, which surprised both Lewis and the publisher. In fact Lewis takes a rather jaundiced view of "popular" books in general. "A majority are well-done, but there are an apalling number of best sellers that are drivel." He thinks that unless a writer is an O'Hara or a Shirer or a Cozzens, that is, in the bracket of those whose works make the best seller lists automatically, then he's usually surprised when a book goes over big.

Victor Lasky wrote his best-selling *J.F.K., the Man and the Myth* when President Kennedy was still alive and it met with immediate success. He first got the idea during the presidential campaign of 1960 when Norman Cousins, who was the editor of *The Saturday Review,* asked him to review the Arthur Schlesinger book, *Kennedy or Nixon, Does it Make Any Difference?* Lasky felt that Schlesinger had ignored many of the facts behind Kennedy's rise to power and his bid for the nomination. He also felt that he treated Nixon unfairly in questioning the Republican candidate's ability to change without being motivated by opportunism. As it seemed to him, Nixon couldn't change his position on anything without being labeled an opportunist by Schlesinger, but on the other hand Kennedy could change his own stance on almost any issue and have it attributed by Schlesinger to idealism. Schlesinger, it seemed to Lasky, found ambition a damnable trait in one man and a commendable one in the other. So then and there he wrote a rather strong review which appeared right at the height of the campaign, and which he later expanded to become the hit seller *J.F.K., the Man and the Myth.*

FOUR

THE QUERY LETTER

The biography or history or political science writer has one big advantage over his counterpart in the fiction field. Where the latter may spend months, and in some cases, a year or more sweating and putting his plot, his characters, and all the rest of it down on paper; revising, rewriting, and polishing it all, only to have a publisher turn the whole thing down at the end with a form letter or a few perfunctory and totally un-helpful comments of rejection, the non-fiction author may sell his book before he even writes it. He avoids the whole frustrating business, except in such rare cases when he is such an incompetent that he simply cannot produce something publishable in the end. It's not *quite* as easy as that, of course. Getting a contract out of a publisher early in the game won't come about just because you want it to; you have to work toward that end and go through some careful preliminary steps.

To pre-sell a book, an author must first approach a publisher with his idea, and the standard way of going about this is by means of the *query letter*, which is simply a piece of correspondence designed to tell an editor what you have to offer him. This initial step in communication doesn't always have to be handled by mail -- an author who is well known by the editor in question can spell out his idea almost as easily over the telephone -- but let's assume you are an unknown, a beginner. This initial query is a good way to find out how the wind blows right away, for if you can't interest any publisher in your book idea at this point, you can (and perhaps should) drop the whole thing then. No editor will commit himself all the way just on the strength of a query letter. But the kind of response you are looking for, and what you can expect if you've a good idea, is simply an expression of interest in the "this-sounds-good-I'd like-to-see-what-you do-with-it" vein, in which case the editor will logically expect you to proceed to step two.

At this point his interest has been aroused, and he will want you to provide something a little more concrete for him to look at -- in other words, an elaboration of your idea as you expect it to take shape in book form. The editor is curious to see how your book will look chapter by chapter; most of all he wants to see how you put words down on paper, and it's your job to satisfy him at this stage of the game. The thing to do, therefore, is to write and send him two or three chapters of your manuscript, along with an outline of the remainder of the book to give him an idea of what it will consist of. It won't do as well to just pick chapters at random; it's better to begin at the beginning and make at least two of the chapters the first two. He'll want to see how you approach your subject and whether you spark his (and the reader's) interest.

This much has been known to do the trick. If your idea is sound enough, and the samples of your writing are impressive enough, *and* if he has confidence that you'll be able to finish the job up to expectations, he may offer you a book contract there and then. Or he may continue to express interest and ask for some more sample chapters instead. Either way you have gone about it so far in the most sensible manner, gearing first your approach and then your work to the man who will ultimately (you hope) buy it. You've expended nothing but some effort, and have made no commitment as yet. If the reaction is too discouraging, you can quit at any point along the line or try another publisher. Until you have signed the contract, you're under no obligation to anyone.

It would be misleading to deny that there's something of a knack to writing a good query letter, and it frankly scares some people. For some reason many authors seem to choke up when it comes to putting their preliminary ideas down on paper. Some plead with their agents to do it for them, and they shouldn't. It's not an agent's job to begin with, and it defeats the whole purpose really, since one object of a query is to let a publisher familiarize himself with the author's personal thoughts on his book subject and how he expresses himself.

It's really not that difficult anyway, as long as you keep certain things in mind.

Number one is that editors are busy men and women — very busy — and though there will come a point in a future successful relationship where you will enjoy nothing more than a long and intimate chat over a Beefeater with a twist, that point has yet to come. You may be the most fascinating correspondent since Lord Chesterfield and Madame De Stael, but stow it all just for now. All he wants to begin with is an introduction from you, and a short rundown on an idea which hopefully is going to be profitable to you both. So be brief and to the point. If you are as good a writer as you think you are, you ought to be able to convey your enthusiasm in a paragraph or two. A surfeit of words won't convince him any more. The query letter isn't designed to describe your project in great detail -- that will come, later -- so a couple of single-spaced, typewritten pages are almost always enough to do the job. Editors appreciate someone who can be concise and succinct.

Take some pains in the way you express yourself. Remember that this is your only contact with your editor thus far. He's not aware of all that vast potential swelling within you; all he has in front of him is your letter, so be sure that it's an intelligent, lively, friendly, and informative one. Don't be stiff and unbending, with that "trusting-to-hear-from-you-I-remain" type of business-ese, but don't be slangy and overly familiar either -- just be natural.

Let us repeat that point about being informative, since it's an important one. Give the editor everything he is going to need to make a decision in your favor -- that is, convince him that he's interested in you and your work and wants to proceed further. Every editor is looking for this; after all he's in business to find best sellers, or at least profit makers, and you'd be surprised how seldom a real eye-opener of an idea comes across his desk. When it does his day is made, and he'll be just as happy as you are. A good query letter ought to contain all of the following points:

If you are a new or unknown author — or at least unknown to the publishing house you are writing to -- then be sure to identify yourself. Tell them who you are and why you should be considered worthy of joining their stable of authors. Something like:

> Dear Sir:
>
> I'm not a professional writer as yet, though I'd like to be, and I've had some unusual experiences during a fascinating career as a deep sea diver, which I think might be the subject of an engrossing book. Let me tell you about it.

After the editor has learned who you are, he wants to hear about your book idea. Put it down, as briefly as possible -- in one sentence if you can. Don't try to expand on it at this point or go into much detail; your object is to let the editor see the book concept in toto and get him mulling it over in his mind.

Hopefully your idea will be something new or unique, and if this is the case you must tell him why, since it will be the book's major selling point. Even when an editor has become sold on you and what you've written, he must in turn make his editorial selection board see what he sees in it -- so spell it out for him. "My book will take a fresh and unique look at the subject, in light of new material recently discovered," or "My own findings have turned up some surprisingly provocative material, which may open up a whole new area. This is the story behind it . . " Something on that order.

Don't forget to mention whom you think might be interested in reading the book. The editor will have his own notion about this, of course, but he must use material of this sort as a selling point once again. Your ideas will be welcome.

At this point in the letter you may provide some meat for the skeletonized one-sentence description of your basic book idea. Go a bit deeper into the structure and character of the proposed manuscript, let the editor know how you will put the pieces together and how it will look to the eye and sound to the ear. What you say here may draw some response from him in his reply, if he likes the initial idea. He may suggest changes in your angle or in your tone, but that shouldn't matter at all. There's hardly a non-fiction idea around that didn't change somewhat from initial concept to finished book, and some of them changed a great deal. The important thing at this stage is that you've convinced him that you have gone into your subject thoroughly enough to know what's involved, and that you have the interest and stick-to-it-iveness to do the proper job if he does give you the go-ahead.

Give him some idea of what your sources are, and where they are located -- just how you intend to go about obtaining your factual matter. He must be convinced that the material is available to you, and that you know how to dig it out. If you've done some preliminary research (and you should have by now), let him know about it. Spend two or three days in the library, or in an interview or two, enough to convince yourself the idea has a certain amount of authority. If you are writing a personal experience book, that is, if *you* are the authority, you should let him know just why you should be considered competent enough to handle the thing.

Lastly, offer to send him some sample chapters and an outline of the rest of the book with no obligation on his part. Show him that you have enough confidence in both your idea and your writing ability to invest some time and work on it for him. If you and your book idea "come over", well, he will offer encouragement in the form of a return letter. You would be foolish to expect a contract at this point. You won't get one -- not till you are a bit further along in the game. And that's what you should get busy on now.

FIVE

THE OUTLINE

There's no doubt that to some -- perhaps most -- authors, making up an outline can be both trying and somewhat unpleasant work. The whole process brings back memories of grammar school days when we were forever being asked to break something down into this type of form, keeping in mind that one must never use just a single subhead, but always two or more. It made sense, of course, but many times there only seemed to *be* one logical heading.

The material you will submit to a publisher to give him an idea of what the remainder of your book will consist of doesn't have to be formalized into the Point-A — Point-B standard -- the only requirement is that it be *informative*. Nevertheless, it can be difficult to put down, primarily because it requires a vision or concept of what the complete book will consist of and look like at a time when the whole thing may be pretty vague in your mind. You've hardly done any of the writing, at this point. You're not even sure that your research will provide you with all the material you expect it to. In fact the whole book may branch off and assume a different shape from what you originally anticipated.

Now editors know all this, of course, and happily are invariably pretty liberal when it comes to making any author stick to what he has set down in his outline -- something that was drawn up in most cases before the contract was even signed. So you needn't worry about being pinned down and held fast to every point in your outline -- nobody who deals with the creative process would dream of being *that* hard-nosed -- though you should stick closely enough to your basic theme so that you don't come up with some other book entirely! Neither you nor the editor could operate under that kind of confusion. Just remember that an outline is a promise of a sort, not a contract in its own, and in effect you are saying: "Here's how I plan to proceed with my book, but I can't guarantee it will turn out this way exactly." An editor will accept this, since he knows better than anyone that books must be allowed to grow and develop during the writing process and not be forced into preconceived and precommitted channels.

Well then, how do you proceed with your outline? As mentioned, the form it takes isn't that important. Most authors seem to do their outlines chapter-by-chapter, breaking their theme down into logical segments which lend themselves to chapter divisions and simply listing them in order this way. Others are not really point-by-point outlines at all, but simply a good description of the material the book will contain, and how their creator plans to approach it. If you feel you can't predict the course of your book accurately enough in this initial stage to divide it into chapters, or to set down what you plan to do in numerical or formal "outline" structure, then just dispense with it, and tell the editor what you plan to do in as complete and informative a manner as possible. He'll get your point all right. All an editor wants at this stage is the reinforcement of his opinion that the idea you spelled out in the query letter, the idea that intrigued him originally and caused him to give you the go-ahead on your manuscript, is still a sound one, and that you can handle it in the way he hopes and expects that you will.

As to length, there can be a lot of variation; the important thing is saying what you have to say. Some outlines are no more than five double-spaced pages, some are as many as fifteen. The average probably runs about ten. There's really no need to double-space at all, incidentally, since an editor won't be making any corrections on this material. Of course an overly short outline may give him the impression that you dashed it off hastily, or, worse, that you haven't thought your book idea out carefully either. On the other hand, editors normally have an enormous amount of reading to do in the course of their day-to-day work, and appreciate anybody who can get their point across concisely.

Remember that your outline must carry on the selling job that your query letter has begun. It must convince the editor, along with the sample chapters which will be discussed later, of your ability to produce a finished book -- one that he would want to publish. The concept of your book, its tone, and the way you intend to attack it all should come through. You should also include some further information on where you will obtain and how you plan to handle your research for the book. If you have reached this stage, you obviously persuaded him in your query letter that you had a good book idea, and one that was possible to put down on paper. Now you've got to dispel any lingering doubts in his mind that you, as a novice writer, or at least one whose work he is as yet unfamiliar with might not be able to deliver the goods. So make sure to give him a complete rundown again at this point on just how you are going to go about gathering your factual material, and convince him that there is enough of it available to you to produce a solid and informative book. You've said it once in the query letter; now say it again in more detail. If you do the job well, it may be enough to convince him to go to bat for you with his editorial selection people, provided you have also convinced him you know how to put down one sentence after another. The sample chapters will do that job for you.

Sample Chapters

After you have finished your outline you ought to pick a "pet" chapter -- one that you know the most about -- and write it out in full. Most publishers will want to see at least two sample chapters -- perhaps more -- to accompany the outline and give them some idea of your ability. In most cases the initial chapter of your book will be one that is the easiest to write, because it introduces your reader to the subject, and generally doesn't require all the research in depth that accompanies the writing of the later ones. If it does necessitate a lot of fact-finding, then go ahead and do it. But whatever you do, don't fake any material or "pad" it out to fill up space. An editor can spot such tactics right away, and you want to make this an example of the best writing you're capable of. Starting at the beginning is valuable from the editor's standpoint, too. You set the scene and tell him what your book is going to be about. Take a lot of pains with the sample chapters you send in. You've got time to polish, so do it, since they, along with your outline, serve as the final sales pitch for your book, your bid for a formal contract. If they fall short, a publisher will have a lot of doubts about proceeding further, even though the outline and overall possibilities may intrigue him.

Of all the obstacles to overcome in any literary project, those first few paragraphs of actual writing seem to be the toughest. That blank page with "Chapter I" at the top staring out of the typewriter often has the same effect as the empty stretch of white canvas to a novice painter -- it can be intimidation of the first degree. Many known and unknown authors think up every outlandish excuse in the world to postpone that moment. Well, even this is all right up to a point, provided the time is used to help ideas germinate within. After all, there's no rule that says you can't spend several days -- or several weeks, if it's a complicated subject -- in formulating the general shape of the book in your mind before you start in. Some people just sit down and begin when a moment of inspiration comes over them, and then sheer persistence carries them on step by step. Others have to have a book "cerebrally organized" before they put words down on paper. Some make a lot of notes beforehand, some just get their plan of attack organized, since "Chapter I" will represent their whole tone and attitude toward the subject matter.

When you finally do begin, keep in mind that your first chapter must fulfill certain obligations. Right off the bat you will have to:

1.   Let the reader know what the book is going to be about. Give him some general idea what he can expect to find in your material.

2.   Give him a clue as to the book's "personality." Borrow a technique from the novelist and the short story writer by setting the emotional tone right away, and letting the reader become aware of what his reaction should be. Are you going to be funny? Make him indignant? Enlighten him? Familiarize him with your own thoughts on the subject, and the style in which you are going to present them.

3.   Intrigue him and make him want to read more. He must care about the rest of the book, or he'll never read it, and neither, by the way, will the editor who is passing judgment on it at this stage.

SIX

STARTING TO PUT THE
PIECES TOGETHER

There's hardly an author that doesn't get to feeling a little queasy when he knows he has a book to write and a certain time in which to write it. There's something about a definite commitment -- and a deadline -- that can affect anyone, not only the tyro who's faced with the job of putting more than 7,000 words down on paper for the first time in his life, but the veteran typewriter-puncher with several books to his credit.

The reason, of course, is that it seems like such a *big* project when you think of the number of pages to be done and the seemingly vast amount of work destined to go into them. Well, it *is* big -- three hundred pages, or four hundred can look like the task of a lifetime to someone who has never turned out anything longer than a college term paper or a magazine article.

There's only one way to overcome this feeling, and that's the way you set about climbing a mountain -- step by step. You simply don't think of that four-inch thick final typescript at all -- you think about the two, or three, or five pages that you've made up your mind to do every day, fair weather or foul. Three pages daily for three months is well over 250 pages, (and that's with Sundays off.) Any publisher is going to allow you a lot more time than that to turn anything out -- probably more like a year for a finished and acceptable manuscript.

Of course, you ought to like and be interested in what you're doing or you shouldn't be doing it. So it really isn't work at all, they'll tell you. Well, it *is* work, and hard work, if you're going to do it right -- but it's nowhere near impossible, even for a rank beginner, and not all that onerous, either.

Where non-fiction is concerned, the job will logically divide up into two major work steps, the first involving the research and the second the writing of the book itself, with a certain amount of organization of material coming

in between. Now, if you want to you can research the book entirely --
straight through, from beginning to end – and then write it. This is the
approach many authors use who must gather their material in some foreign
locale or under conditions removed from their normal writing habitat and
milieu. You can either allot yourself a certain amount of time for digging up
facts and then a certain amount for putting them down, or you can just
research until it's all done and then use the time remaining (but be sure to
leave yourself enough!) for writing. You can even divide your manuscript up
for this purpose according to the difficulty of various portions, assigning a
greater amount of time for some particularly sticky problem; allotting less
time to the colorful bits you are familar with already and can put
down easily.

This is not necessarily the best approach. Both the researching and the
writing job can become tiresome if done day after day. Spending a Monday,
or a Monday through Wednesday looking up facts, and then a Thursday and
Friday in writing may be better for you. There are those days, or times of
the day when you'll feel particularly "on the ball" creatively, and you'll
want to sit right down at the typewriter then and there and take advantage
of it. Other days the words just won't come at all, and the time can best be
spent in the library, doing the more mechanical work of pouring over source
books and note-jotting. Sometimes you may want to go even one step
further. When in a writing mood, you'll not only get some first draft work
down, but may get so involved in that particular element of the book that
you'll want to do some polishing and final draft work on it. There's nothing
wrong with this approach, provided you don't spend so much time on a
favorite section that you lose your train of thought and the "flow" where
the book as a whole is concerned. Turning out a good passage and seeing
your words down on paper may give you satisfaction. It is therapeutic to
finish something well right in the middle of the work project. It makes the
whole task seem less plodding and impersonal, and helps you take advantage
of those times that come along periodically when you're really in the
working frame of mind and that flow comes easily. It seems silly to
submerge this feeling just because you're in the "research phase" and then
try to summon it up day after day when you're in the final, "smoothing"
stage. It won't work, because the creative flame or what have you tends to
come when it will come.

Publishers have had a lot of experience in determining just how long it
ought to take to finish one kind of book or another, and they will give you
enough so that you won't be rushed. If you are fortunate enough to be able
to write full time you may be astonished at how quickly the job will go. If

you really want to press, you *can* produce something acceptable in a couple of months, but nobody's going to ask you to unless you're a real proven pro of a work horse rushing to beat a couple of competitors with material that may become out of date -- like yesterday. It will probably take you from half a year to nine or ten months, if you put in full writing days; maybe three times as long on a part time basis. If it's a major book, you may wind up spending even longer than that on it, but if you set yourself a pace you can maintain, and stick to it every day, you ought not to have any trouble making your deadline. As for unavoidable emergencies that interfere -- well -- these have been known to happen before, and publishers can be surprisingly understanding.

SEVEN

THE PROBLEM OF RESEARCH

We can now assume that somehow -- through observation, reading, or conversation, plus the trial-and-error procedure of examining and discarding possible topics, you have come up with an idea that interests you, has interested a publisher, and will ultimately interest (both you and he hope) a wide reading audience. You are at that point where inspiration and that sudden flash of creative fire that can produce a winning short story or a moving magazine article or that perfect poem must join forces with something that will enable you to persist over the long pull. We are of course talking about research. It's a large subject, and really the most important one for the non-fiction writer to master, since it deals both with the basic step-by-step process of laying factual bricks on a foundation -- the "meat and potatoes" of non-fiction -- and the gingerbread, that provides the color, the technique, the choice tidbits of material which can turn a dry tome into a gripping and fascinating piece of prose.

You had to do some research in the initial stages of your book idea of course, simply to convince yourself, and in turn a publisher, that your idea was a new, or unique, or salable one. How many other writers have picked the same subject for a book? It was the first question you had to ask yourself, keeping in mind the highly competitive nature of the book business and the fact that no publisher is likely to dance for joy over a manuscript dealing with a subject that has recently been covered by more than one book. So the mere process of seeing what has been done on your subject, or subjects directly allied to it, and the decision that *your* approach will be new and different and fresh, or will treat some aspect that has not been covered, is research of the preliminary kind.

Looking Things Up

Now you are ready for the "nuts and bolts" of the job.

In his unique and valuable book, *The Modern Researcher*, Jacques Barzun has spent some time in spelling out what he calls "the searcher's virtues." These he defines as the impulses the fact-finding author must encourage (or curb) in himself, if he is to do a good job of digging out what he needs and marshalling the collected material into a viable and worthwhile book.

Accuracy is number one on the list. Anyone who has ever worked as a newspaper reporter, or been trained in reporting as preparation for a career dealing with some other aspect of the printed or spoken word, has this impressed upon him the day he sits in his first journalism class. You *must* copy down dates, names, and other facts correctly, and keep them all where you can find them when you want to refer to them. You must train yourself to catch small errors almost automatically. Everyone will make some mistakes; the important thing is not to let them get by. How often have you read a book and noticed a typographical error here and there, or a factual boo-boo that you caught on your own? If they are there, it's because they slipped by both the author's and the publisher's proofreading. Just before my last book was set in type I got a long letter of several pages from an editor at my publishing house who had been assigned the job of checking my facts and querying me about them. There were dozens of questions about dates, descriptions and some (what I considered) very minor points. I had to take each one and explain why I had said this or that just to make sure no mistake would slip through. I had an answer for almost everything I had included in the book, but in one or two instances I saw that I had slipped up a little. If someone hadn't gone over the manuscript as meticulously as they did, these minor blunders would have been printed as they stood. Perhaps not one reader in a thousand would have caught them even then, but they would have been there, nevertheless.

Barzun's second virtue is one he calls *love of order*. Perhaps "love" is rather a strong word here; but it is the ability to adhere to a certain system in one's work. Many writers don't particularly love order, but they know they have to live with it, since it's obvious that there must be a system of some kind in a task which includes reading, note-taking, verification, organization, and all the rest of it. It takes a certain type of person to consistently keep everything in actual or mental pigeon-holes, but if you have a tendency to lose your notes or get them mixed up, get the pages of your different drafts confused, let other lapses interfere with the momentum of your work, then you are making your job that much harder. Slow down, keep cool, and take an hour every once in a while to gather material together and put it somewhere, so that you can lay your hands on it when you want to.

Then there is the need to be logical -- logic, that is, as it applies to the practical application of researching in the library. Every library is a pretty systematized institution -- there is a place for everything and everything (well, almost everything) in its place. The librarian is there to help you, but you can't go running to him or her with every little difficulty you run into in looking something up. Learn to use your head, and figure out your own problems, and you'll soon find you develop into a much better fact-hunter because of it.

The good researcher must be honest, which links in closely with accuracy, but which goes a bit further. You must record what you find truthfully, and without distortion, and if you run across some unlooked-for and unexpected material which destroys or casts new doubts on some theme or theory of yours, you may have to do some painful re-examination, perhaps of your book as a whole, in light of the new information. This is a difficult thing to face, and it would be naive to assume that every writer does it -- he doesn't, but as the author of a non-fiction book you are, by definition, a seeker of the truth, an individual who has an obligation to his readers to be someone they can rely upon.

Many people are honest in their own minds, but are unrealistic in their view of themselves and the world, and lack the ability to judge things clearly and reasonably. Without a certain measure of *self-awareness* you run the danger of being dishonest without knowing it. It is necessary for the writer to keep his emotions and prejudices under control to the extent that he can be impartial when he must be, as when he runs up against standards and values differing from his own, or even from our own age and society. No one can be completely impartial -- it's just not in the human character, and all of us are influenced to a greater or lesser extent by our culture, background, and upbringing -- yet it is important for the writer to communicate to the reader in some way the standards he used to make value judgments . . . and just how he reflects and interprets the material he has employed in his book.

Imagination is Barzun's final virtue, and one of the most important.. Imagination in research is not exactly the same as imagination in writing, but the same principle is involved. Barzun's theory is that the researcher must picture in his mind's eye the kind of source he would like to be able to find before he can actually find it. Even if such an ideal source doesn't actually exist, the writer can proceed from what he knows and already possesses to what he must have in order to know more. The secret would seem to be not so much as to develop an active imagination (if that can be done) as to let loose that which we already possess, but don't always use. Conventional habits of thinking and plain, ordinary laziness often dampen down the inspired idea which would take the writer where he wants to go. It's his job to release the inhibitions of thought that keep him from it, by encouraging the mind to wander and run freely.

EIGHT

THE LIBRARY

There are an amazing number of bright and well informed persons occasionally called upon to do a paper, or even an article of some kind, and who simply don't know how to use the library. It's hard to imagine how this can be so, since the rudiments of the Dewey Decimal System should have been taught in school to conduct simple research for school class papers in the local branch of the public library. Yet many intelligent people don't really know what's in the libraries, or how to make use of what they have to offer.

For most it's probably never going to be a crippling ignorance -- the need to do any kind of research may arise rarely or never -- but if you are going to be a non-fiction writer it's an entirely different matter. There are occasions when you'll be spending so much time there that one library or another will seem like a second home to you, and if such a prospect seems discouraging, then you might just as well decide to go to Majorca or the Greek islands and write novels!

This type of work can be a time-consuming and at times lonely business, but it doesn't always have to be, since help is there for the asking, if you know where to seek it. One of the most valuable friends you can make in the course of researching a book is your public librarian. More often than not he or she is a walking repository of facts and information which is at your disposal if you need it. Too many people are unaware of what a librarian is there to provide, and some are just reluctant to make demands on their services. It's silly, of course, since helping you is his or her whole job. Since he or she knows what books are on his/her shelves, (and has perhaps, in fact, read many of them personally) he or she can save you a great deal of "browsing" time by making selective recommendations, as well as providing pamphlets, booklets, periodicals, and other allied material that you may not even be aware of at all.

Reference Books

The reference room, (or section if it is a small institution) of your library is one that you will want to become completely familiar with. The general collection of a small library may not give you much to work with, and if this is the case, you will have to dig up a bibliography that covers your subject and draw from it a list of books and articles that you can hunt up later. You will use the reference room, too, when you really don't know what you're looking for, that is when you are totally at a loss as to what titles are in existence, and also when you are seeking out information that isn't in books at all, but only found in magazines.

So you must acquaint yourself as soon and as completely as possible with just what the reference room contains. You must learn just what kind of book features which kind of facts. The following list will give you some idea of the different varieties of reference books, even though it is only a sort of general catalogue, since the scientific and industrial fields, as well as many other specialized areas of interest can boast many reference sources of their own. But this is a general breakdown:

First there are the *encyclopedias.* Probably you are already familiar with, or at least have seen standards like the *Encyclopedia Britannica,* the *Encyclopedia Americana,* the *World Book Encyclopedia, Funk & Wagnall's Encyclopedia* and *Colliers' Encyclopedia.* They will all be grouped together in the reference room or section. These are general reference works, but if you wish to dig deeper you will go to the specialized works. *Van Nostrand's Scientific Encyclopedia,* which provides information about basic and applied science in laymen's language, the *Encyclopedia of the Social Sciences,* for facts relating to politics, law, economics, psychology, and sociology; the *Catholic Encyclopedia* and the *Jewish Encyclopedia* for information on history, doctrine, and customs pertaining to those two faiths; *Grove's Dictionary of Music and Musicians* for a wealth of data on musical instruments, composers, and performers. For others check through the *Guide to Reference Books* and *Subject Guide to Reference Books.*

If you do much writing, by the way, you will soon find that one of the smaller one-volume encyclopedias can be immensely valuable and save untold steps. The *New Columbia Viking Desk Encyclopedia* is one of the best, and there are others. They won't provide information in the same kind of detail as the *Britannica,* of course, but they are invaluable for providing quick referral to names, dates, places, and the most important facts about virtually every subject contained in the larger, multi-volume reference works.

You will also find in the reference section general *dictionaries* of the type you have been accustomed to using all your life — — massive ones like the giant unabridged monsters and ranging all the way down to simple desk-sized works. There are *biographical* works, such as the *Dictionary of American Biography* and its British counterpart, the *Dictionary of National Biography*, both of which are historical in nature as all of the individuals listed in them are dead. These are multi-volume books, and very complete. To research a living personage you might want to check out *Who's Who in America*, or one of the regional editions like *Who's Who in the Midwest*, or those listed noted individuals in the more specialized areas, such as *Who's Who in Commerce and Industry*, *Who's Who in the American Theater*, etc. There is also a women's *Who's Who*, though many illustrious women can be found in the *America* edition.

There are many more dictionary types of works to be found among the reference materials. There will be *dictionaries of quotations*, of which *Bartlett's* is undoubtedly the best known; and *language dictionaries* of various kinds, which will enable you to translate, for example, German into English, English into German and so forth. You may not feel that you'll have use for these, until you find it necessary to determine the exact definition of a quote located somewhere in your readings. The situation arises more often than you would think.

You may also find *chronologies* or books of dates to be useful, and certainly the many *bibliographies*, broken down nationally and topically, which you ought to check with first of all if your situation is that of the writer who is unaware of the literature available on the subject of his potential book. One of your first steps anyway should be to "size up the competition." Ask the librarian where you can find *Books in Print*, listing all current books available, and the *Cumulative Book Index*, which lists all English-language books by author's name, book titles, and subject, going back to 1898. You will want to examine all books written on your particular subject. This is not nearly as difficult a job as it sounds; as you become familiar with your topic and with the process of research in general you will often find that a perfunctory glance will tell you that some previous competitor has fallen short, or is hopelessly out of date, or simply has nothing to contribute. Other authors can prove very valuable. You will discover angles which hadn't occurred to you, details you have omitted; facts, references, dates, and additional material mentioned by others which will be helpful to you later on.

The reference room will also contain *atlases* and *gazeteers*, both current and historical. An atlas is a collection of maps, charts, and tables, while a gazeteer is really a dictionary of geographical names – of the world, of a region, of certain classes. You'll find both to be helpful.

One of the most important elements of the reference section will be the *periodical indexes*. Of great value to you as a researcher is the *Reader's Guide to Periodical Literature*, which lists by subject matter and by author articles which have appeared in major magazines. The *Guide* goes all the way back to 1900, and you can obtain even earlier listings by looking through *Poole's Index to Periodical Literature*, which covers articles published throughout most of the nineteenth century. The *Reader's Guide* doesn't list minor magazines, and many specialized fields, such as engineering, education, and psychology are covered by periodical indexes of their own. Ask your librarian about these. Most magazines are glad to cooperate with writers in hunting down material they may have published. The custom is usually to write to them for an "index reading" and a list of dates and page numbers of the pertinent material. Then look it up on your own later.

The *New York Times Index* lists by subject all the stories that have appeared in that paper, and from that point on it is an easy matter to look up the microfilm record of the subject in question. If your library is a good sized one, it will have machines that you can use to view the film.

The *Almanacs* -- the *World Almanac* and similar volumes published by the large metropolitan newspapers -- can provide a wealth of factual matter in many areas. Libraries carry them, or they can be purchased in paperback form in most book stores for two or three dollars. In fact a good almanac is a handy home reference tool that a writer should never be without. The same type of material, in somewhat more detailed and specialized form, can be found in the voluminous *Statistical Abstract of the United States*, which has facts and figures on all aspects of the economic and commercial life of this country.

The Stacks

One of the first things a writer should find out when getting acquainted with an unfamiliar library is whether or not he or she will have access to the stacks. Many places just don't allow this, and insist instead that the borrower fill out a slip with the book's name and author that he wishes to check out. One of the library staff will then go get it for him. It's always very disappointing not to be allowed back in the stacks. The ability to roam around from shelf to shelf at will is such a necessary part of effective research. Anyone who's done much of this type of work can tell a great deal from reading a page or two of a book or just from its physical appearance;

the title alone may tell you relatively nothing, and you've then caused one of the librarians to make a trip for nothing.

The Card Catalogue

Needless to say, you will want to acquaint yourself thoroughly with the workings of the card catalogue. Most libraries now use the standard Library of Congress cards, which are kept in drawers in alphabetical order -- from A to Z -- and which contain the name of the author, the title of the book, the date and place of publication, and where the book can be found in the library.

If you know the name of the author you are looking for, your task may be relatively simple. Just go to the right alphabetical drawer and look him up. However, remembering the man's last name is not enough. You may discover some eight or ten authors with the same surname. You'd be amazed at the frequency with which even some very peculiar names will occur in a big card catalogue. Even on occasion the first and last names might not be enough; if you're dealing with a "Brown" or a "Peterson" you've got to have the middle initial as well. But then you'll find all this out for yourself.

If you don't know the name of the author, then you've got to start with the name of the book. The same volume will be catalogued under both the author's name and its own title, so you can find it either place. Of course you have to know the exact title, and it's surprising how easily that kind of thing can slip the mind. I remember the trouble I once had looking up some information on the life and times of King Edward VII. I thought I knew my book, only to find that there were three volumes in the library titled *The Edwardians*, and several others called *The Edwardian Age*, *Edwardian Lives* and titles similar enough to what I thought was mine to cause a lot of wasted time. All because I didn't bother to write it down originally. Librarians themselves tend to remember books by their authors rather than their titles and you should do the same.

If you are missing both author and title, then you will probably have to resort to the subject index. In most libraries this will be in a card catalogue of its own, and adjacent to the author and title index, and alphabetized the same way. You must have a pretty good idea, of course, just what it is you are after. You won't necessarily find it useful to look under "Civil War" if what you are seeking is information on General Grant's personal character. You may be interested in lighter-than-air craft and find yourself looking up "Aeronautics," "Flying," "Transport," Air," and finally "Dirigibles," which probably was what you were after in the first place. If you are looking up an individual, he can be found under his last name, and his birth and death date will be listed also to narrow down the possibilities for you, just in case there is more than one person with the same name in the catalogue.

There are times when your task will be harder, since the location of the desired books on the shelves will depend on the librarian's own method of alphabetizing and cataloguing, and this can vary from library to library. For example, doing research on the Spanish-American War, you will find information under "United States of America, History, Nineteenth Century" "Spain, History, Nineteenth Century," "United States Navy," "Cuba," and under several other headings. Not only that, the same books will be found under different headings in different libraries. You will often be referred to other sections of the catalogue (such as "see 'Santiago, Battle of')", and perhaps referred back again, but check them all out and you should find what you want in the end.

The cards in the catalogue carry a good deal of information, some of which will be useful, some of which you might not need. The publisher and publishing date will be listed, as will the number of pages the book contains, and whether it includes illustrations or maps. The book's size is even noted on the card. As mentioned earlier, it helps to examine a book personally. You can tell a good deal about whether it will be of any help just by glancing through it and reading a page or so. Because many large libraries do forbid access to the stacks, the card does provide some helpful clues as to what a book is like without seeing it.

Titles can convey a certain character once you get familiar with "reading" them. They will often give an indication as to whether a book is an academic work, or one written more for a popular or mass audience. You will find yourself using both types in your research, the academic study providing necessary factual matter than cannot be left out of any serious book, and the more popular account giving the necessary color and subsidiary information that can make an otherwise prosaic volume come to life.

Equally important to the researcher is the date of publication on the card. As you become more familiar with searching out facts in general, you will soon find that styles and the matter contained in books dealing with the same subject will vary considerably depending upon when the work was written. Let's assume that you are attempting a book on the causes of the First World War, for instance. Many books on the subject were published during the actual period of hostilities, of course, and there have been a more or less continual stream of them ever since. You will find many of these written during the war years to be patriotic to the point of ultra-jingoism, often inflammatory in their depiction of the enemy, and everything connected with him. On the other hand, books written from the perspective of fifty years are usually a good deal more reasoned and fair in their approach toward the whole "war guilt" question. Lies have largely been forgotten, passions have cooled, and historians can afford to be a good deal more objective. This does not mean that the contemporary accounts are valueless. In many cases they will be more detailed, and provide us with the on-the-spot color (this is assuming we can attest to its truthfulness) that we need, and that may have been lost in the intervening years. They may also be valuable purely as an example of the very wartime emotions we want to recall.

The same care must be taken in biographical matter. During the life of a great leader a good many laudatory accounts will be published, as the cult of virtual hero-worship overwhelms the faults and blemishes we might ordinarily see. Years later, we often find the opposite tendency taking place, as old loyalties and values die, and newer iconoclastic authors seem almost to take a perverse pleasure in debunking the idols of the past. Wartime heroes such as Churchill and MacArthur have undergone this process, and it will probably take the passage of even more time to put them in the proper perspective. Sometimes the situation is reversed, and men who were vilified or passed over lightly during their active lives begin to be taken seriously by the following generation. Harry Truman's reputation stands higher today than it did in the immediate post-war years, and the spate of Adolph Hitler books being published nowadays hints at an attempt, as if not to humanize, at least to understand a man who was simply dismissed as a monster thirty years ago.

The researcher, and primarily the historian, must educate himself enough in the area of human psychology to be able to "read" between the lines and arrive at a certain level of objectivity. Later information -- undiscovered facts and hitherto unrevealed matters -- may cast a different light on personalities and situations; on the other hand, if one is writing about something that happened in the past, one must be able to judge and reflect the "temper of the times" as well.

Once you have found what you are looking for in the card catalogue, mark down the call numbers that appear in the upper left hand corner of the card. If you do not have access to the stacks, you will have to fill out a call slip with this identifying information on it; if you are allowed to browse through the shelves, you will need it to refer to. It would be wise, too, to familiarize yourself to some extent with the way libraries shelve their books, which in most cases is according to the Dewey Decimal System. Under this method, various categories of material have been given numbers, from 000 to 1000. and each author has a letter, taken from the first letter of his last name. Every book has its own number, therefore. The advantage of the Dewey system is that with some exceptions you will know with reasonable certainty where any specific work can be found in the stacks, and that you will find similar books close by it that you can use for comparison. This will of course apply to any library who uses the system. Here is a listing of how the divisions are made under the Dewey Decimal System by a large university library:

000 - 099	General Works	800 - 809	Literature, General
100 - 199	Philosophy & Psychology	810 - 819	American Literature
200 - 299	Religion	820 - 829	English Literature
300 - 309	Sociology	830 - 839	German Literature
310 - 319	Statistics	840 - 849	French Literature
320 - 329	Political Science	850 - 859	Italian Literature
330 - 339	Economics	860 - 869	Spanish, Portugese Lit
340 - 349	Law	870 - 879	Latin Literature
350 - 359	Public Administration	880 - 889	Greek & Byzantine Lit
360 - 369	Social Welfare	900 - 909	General History
370 - 379	Education	910 - 919	Geography & Travel
380 - 389	Public Service & Util.	920 - 929	Biography
390 - 399	Customs & Folklore	930 - 939	Ancient History
400 - 499	Language	940 - 949	European History
500 - 599	Pure Science	950 - 959	Asian History
600 - 699	Technology	970 - 979	North American History
700 - 779.9	Art	980 - 989	South American History
M780-M789.9	Music	990 - 999	History of the Pacific
790 - 799	Theater, Games		

Decimals are used to subdivide these major categories into more detailed ones. Thus European History begins with 940, starting with general history and then proceeding country by country. American history begins with 970, and as in the case of European history, the first books in the category deal with earlier times, and the higher numbers with more recent events, in regular sequence. Biography is usually shelved separately. Sometimes you can find it under number 920, and sometimes it can be found under the related subject matter, or with his own works, if the subject is an a author. Oversized books often have an "L" preceding their regular numbers and can sometimes be found in a special section of the stacks. There are other variations in the shelving practices of libraries, too. In the particular example used for the above listing, there is a special library building for the music collection and special sections for art and government publications. There is also a special room set aside to house African and Asian books and periodicals.

A closing note about research in general: Being systematic about note-taking can save untold anguish later on. All that jotting down that you do as you track down the elusive name, date, and fact can get mislaid, and the sheer mass of paper you always seem to wind up with can become totally unmanageable if some system isn't employed. One way to minimize this problem is to keep all notes, paper, or cards of uniform size. Others prefer notebooks, and it doesn't really matter, just as long as you stick to one or the other. Somewhere along the line it's best to sort the whole thing into categories, too. This is easier to do as you go along. Learn to take complete notes. If you don't discipline yourself to the practice of writing down the author, the book title, and the page number each time you copy down a fact or quotation, you will lose hours later in attempting to track down the exact reference.

NINE

WRITING
FOR INFORMATION

The easiest way to do research for a non-fiction book project is in libraries, since you can go there when you like, work at your own speed, check books out and look them over at your leisure at home. To many people -- at least to those who have overcome initial nervousness or lack of confidence -- the most pleasant way to do it is by talking to people via the personal interview, with all the personality interplay, the skilful questioning, the exchange of views and ideas that can, as far as they're concerned, make up much of the fun part of writing.

There will be times, however, when you just won't be able to meet your subject face-to-face. Your potential subject will be three thousand miles away and the information he has won't be vital enough for you to come up with the plane fare to bring the two of you into that kind of contact. Or, he may be Howard Hughes, have a phobia about personal interviews. If you run across a set of circumstances such as these, you are going to have to use the mails and try to get the information you need by letter.

To begin with, you may be surprised at just how much you can obtain in this way. Let's face it, there are some people who are simply too suspicious or inhibited to really let themselves go in front of a stranger armed with a notebook or a tape recorder, no matter how diplomatically you have set the scene and go about the business of interviewing. They are just more comfortable when telling what they know by mail, where they can think out what they are going to say fully, check it when they are done, and make certain no embarrassing slips are down there for the world to see or hear.

There are some things you ought to keep in mind, though, when you sit down to compose the letter that will bring the kind of replies you want. Some of them are the simple businesslike considerations you would follow when corresponding with anyone who is, after all, a perfect stranger to you. Others have to do with the fact that you are formulating an approach which will hopefully gain for you, through a series of pertinent queries, the information you must have. First of all, address your letter to an individual, not simply to an organization. In a big company nobody will want to take the bother of replying to a letter marked "Dear Sir." Aim your letter to the public relations director. In some companies he may have a slightly different title, but at any rate it will go to the proper party. Begin by telling the recipient who you are. You're a writer, working on a book, and you are letting him know what the subject of it is. This is only sensible, since nobody is likely to reply to an unknown, who just drops him a line out of the blue with a "Can you give me a little dope on your activities with the CIA?" type of approach.

Take the first couple of sentences to explain why you want the data you are requesting of him and what you plan to do with it. He's never heard of you, remember; spell out politely and in detail just what you are after. This is a good chance, too, to tell him how he is important to your research; why you've picked him to provide the information you're asking for. If he isn't satisfied that you have some good reason for bothering him, the chances are he'll just skip answering altogether. Be friendly, stick to the point, and couch your letter in a way that will convince him that he can trust you -- that you won't -- deliberately or accidentally -- use what he is about to give you in a way that will hurt him in some manner.

Don't ask him to reply at great length. No one is going to sit down and write several pages for you, and you must couch judicious questions in a way that will allow him to answer in brief statements, if he wants to. Bearing in mind that you must get a complete store of information from him through your letter alone, your task is to draw him out -- make him want to answer more fully without feeling he has to. What we're looking for here is a "leading" question that will bring forth a voluntary but hopefully voluble response.

If your subject matter is a sensitive one, offer to let the recipient of your letter look over, and edit if he likes the section you write which deals with the material he has supplied. This is not, frankly, an especially good habit to get into. Editing by an outsider, especially one who is not closely involved in the book in its entirety, can be terribly trying, and cause no end of frustration. Don't just promise outright to send him a manuscript unless he asks for it. It is far better to say that you'll be glad to send it to him if he thinks it might help. He may (and you hope so) feel it's unnecessary, but you've made the gesture, anyway, and put him at ease.

When he has given you what you ask for; even if his answer has been somewhat disappointing or incomplete, always write him back and thank him for his efforts on your behalf. You go away leaving a good impression behind, and if you ever have to return to this individual (and if he's an important source and you intend to write more some day on his general field of interest) you will be remembered favorably. And it might pave the way for a more successful face-to-face interview at some later date.

TEN

PLANNING
THE INTERVIEW

The non-fiction book you write may turn out to be strictly a "library piece," that is, it may be possible to do the whole thing by taking already published reference material, rearranging it, putting it in your own words, toning it and coloring it up and coming out with what you hope, in the end, is an acceptable job.

Some writers specialize in this kind of thing, and some can skip through a whole career, of sorts, by just "winging it," and never turning out anything really good or original. So unless you are working on some historical subject, with all the people involved -- and the people who knew them -- dead and gone, then the chances are you are going to have to talk to individuals and ask questions as part of your research job.

By now you have found out at least a little bit about your subject, maybe even enough to give you some idea who the recognized "authorities" in that particular field might be who would be qualified to pass information on to you. Or perhaps you have an idea about what organizations are involved, but are still in the dark about which individual knows what. If so, remember that first of all telephone books can provide a great fund of information, and it might be wise to "let your fingers do the walking" through the yellow pages of one of the big metropolitan directories. Chambers of commerce and newspaper offices have lists of organizations that might be helpful, too. Of particular value is the *United States Government Organization Manual,* a paperbound book which is published annually by the Government Printing Office, and which lists all officers by name and title of every federal agency throughout the United States. This volume can be found in most public libraries.

Once you have located someone you feel will be of help to you, you're going to have to exercise a little push to arrange a meeting of some kind. Now, it is possible to use the telephone, if the subject is a long way off, but let's face it, this is conducting an interview the hard way. Time is limited, you must have all your questions right on hand, ready to fire off, you don't have the advantage of meeting your subject face to face, seeing "what makes him tick," and carrying out the leisurely conversation that can bring so many un-looked-for insights to a question and answer session.

The Interview

I'll never forget my own first interview. I was out after some material for a magazine article on pollution in the Great Lakes, and my subject was an authority in the Bureau of Fisheries. He certainly wasn't a celebrity or an important executive on the national scale, and yet I was pretty nervous about the whole thing. I somehow had the feeling I was making a nuisance of myself to someone who had better things to do; that I was imposing on his time, and that he was bound to resent it, and perhaps make things uncomfortable. Then, too, I was such a greenhorn at this interviewing business, I was afraid I wouldn't bring it off satisfactorily, that I would somehow forget to ask enough or the proper questions, or wouldn't be able to take his responses down fast enough. I was feeling what a lot of beginning writers feel, and a lot of seasoned research people as well who have gone along without having to get their information through personal contact.

Well, in about the first five minutes I learned some interesting things. This particular fellow wanted to be interviewed. He was rather flattered that he'd been singled out for the attention, and was in fact a little nervous himself. I've learned since that in nine times out of ten, and probably more, the whole thing will go off in a smooth, if not actually congenial way. If the subject is accustomed to being interviewed – a well-known figure of some kind -- the chances are he accepts being asked questions as a matter of course; on the other hand if it's new to him, he'll react pretty much as my Bureau of Fisheries man did.

Now as far as conducting a professional interview is concerned, competence comes with practice; if you do it very often you will soon pick up the knack. Here are a few suggestions to make it easier for you and help you secure a more successful interview, from your first communication with your subject until you say goodbye at the end of your session.

To begin with, always allow the interviewee some time to arrange his schedule and think about meeting with you, by either phoning or writing several days before the time when you want to get together. Ask the subject to set a date and time when it would be convenient for him to talk with you. This will give him time to prepare for what he wants to discuss, and apart from the matter of common courtesy will often insure much better results from your own standpoint than if you acted as though you had to have the material "yesterday." Unless you are a newspaper reporter with an extra-tight deadline to meet, don't telephone someone right out of the blue and expect them to drop everything and talk to you right at that moment. If anything has a tendency to rub a busy man the wrong way, this type of approach will do it. He may suggest (and none too politely) that you just forget the whole thing.

Always make sure you identify yourself fully when writing or calling for an appointment, and let the subject know just what you want from him and why you want it. Explain what your book is about and why you have chosen to talk with him. Tell him which publisher is interested in the book, tell him about other people in his business you have interviewed or plan to interview, and just how he can personally help you. Be relaxed and amiable. You really shouldn't have that much trouble in getting him to set a time and place for a personal meeting.

Always be on time. If you have an appointment with somebody at eleven o'clock, get there at a quarter to eleven if possible. Whomever you are going to talk with is probably setting aside time in his schedule to accommodate you and it's not your job to put him to any inconvenience. If something comes up and you can't make the scheduled meeting, phone him, apologize for your inability to see him, and ask for another appointment. And make sure you keep the second one. If the interviewee is agreeable to the idea, you might try to schedule a lunch or dinner date with him, since things have a way of going more smoothly when you can chat in some spot removed from the office atmosphere and the noise of phones and typewriters. Almost everybody relaxes better in a convivial atmosphere. Don't rush your own schedule, either. Allow plenty of time for the meeting -- well over an hour if possible. You can always leave early if it turns out to be totally unproductive, but sometimes an interviewee will take awhile to "warm up" and then begin talking volubly on his own, in which case you may wind up with more and better material than you ever bargained for. Don't ever begin the conversation with the statement that you only have forty-five minutes and must cover everything in that time, but on the other hand it's just as well not to spring on him the fact that you've allowed three hours either. He may wonder just what he's getting into. You want the whole thing to be as relaxed as possible -- nothing uptight at all.

If you have the time, you would be wise to do a little pre-meeting preparation; find out enough about the subject and his job or interests, so that you don't come across as a complete ignoramus. And also prepare a few questions that will require a more involved answer rather than just a simple "yes" or "no." Some controversial point or a pet interest of his may loosen things up and draw him out. Once an individual begins to talk, don't interrupt him continually with more questions. If someone has to stop and explain things to you every minute or so, it will break up the flow of his thought and he's liable to "dry up." Many people will tend to get off the subject, of course, and begin to ramble on about their families, hobbies, sports interests, even their ailments. In the beginning of an interview this type of chatter may be helpful since it puts you both at ease, but your time and his are limited, and there comes a point when you must tactfully and skilfully turn the conversation back to your primary purpose. On the other hand you don't want to miss out on the type of "side" material you need to bring some color to your book, to make it come to life. You're going to need quotes and stories, and you ought to make the interviewee's personality come through in your material. So instead of playing the Hollywood newspaper reporter with the typical machine gun interrogation, it's far better to relax and let the subject talk at his own pace, while you act as listener and recorder rather than questioner. If a subject leaves something out or doesn't cover it to your satisfaction, don't interrupt him at that point; make a note of it and after he has finished talking, bring up the matter and then let him satisfy you.

Don't make yourself too obtrusive, either, by the fact that you must get down, in some manner, the gist of what he is talking about. Taking notes is one big element of interviewing, of course, and it certainly helps to have the knack of determining just what is and what is not significant enough to record for your purposes. It's not really that difficult. College students quickly learn to judge the important points in a professor's lecture and the technique here is exactly the same. Even easier in fact, since an informal talk will naturally contain less "meat" than a prepared address. If you use a notebook and are writing in longhand, adopt the habit of taking down key words or abbreviations that will bring to mind the content of the conversation at some later date when you review your notes.

When your interviewee makes a statement that you feel would make a good quotation for your book, ask him whether he would mind if you quoted him, and if he agrees ask him to repeat the remark so that you can take it down verbatim to avoid any mistakes. If you plan to do much interviewing, you might want to learn shorthand or take a course in one of the speedwriting methods. There are people who rely totally on their memories, writing up the content of the meeting as soon as possible after the interview while it is still fresh in mind. Some can do this and others can't , and if your memory isn't exceptional (and even if it is) it's better to take notes of some kind on important points to avoid forgetting them. Above all, you must avoid inadvertently distorting quoted statements to the point where something the subject said is completely misconstrued. And this is easier to do than you would think.

Using a tape recorder is, of course, the best method in interviewing as far as sheer efficiency and accuracy is concerned. Every question and answer, every statement of any kind, every joke and comment and expletive is recorded verbatim. There are no loose pages of notes to be lost, there is no question of what he said or what you said, (even the voice inflections are down on tape to be considered for their significance, if any) and during the course of the interview you can sit back and concentrate on the conversation itself without having to take down the subject's statements. Tape recorders would be ideal, were it not for the fact that many people "freeze" when confronted by them, particularly when the topic dealt with is a controversial or an emotional one, simply because their innermost feelings, their mistakes, their "ums and ahs" and sudden outbursts are all captured impartially. There are some types of people who tend to clam up a bit when confronted with any type of note-taking. They will talk more freely in just a man-to-man type of interview over dinner or a cup of coffee. But unless you have that stellar memory, it won't do you much good.

While you're about it, you don't want to forget those little embellishments that can turn an ordinary question and answer session into a colorful (and therefore valuable) interview, that will serve your purposes as author. First of all there are the anecdotes, those juicy bits which not only give you the chance to use some dialogue, but also help to physically break up those gray, forbidding paragraphs which so many readers tend to skip over. A few anecdotes, some personal exchanges, a judicious and pithy quote inserted now and again, make a page more attractive visually and *seem* more interesting than one made up wholly of factual matter. Often questions like "Who was the most interesting (or disagreeable) person you've ever run across in your work?" or "What was your first day on the job like?" may cause your subject to open up with any amount of useful material. Anecdotes should be pertinent to the subject matter of your book, of course. If too far afield, resist using them, no matter how bright or engaging they are.

Most readers like a chuckle and if you know a good joke that can illustrate a point, or if your subject comes up with an apt one, by all means use it. Humor can add a light and attractive touch to material that can grow ponderous if unrelieved by a change of pace of some kind.

Lastly, don't be afraid to dig into the negative aspects of the relation between your interviewee and the subject matter of your book. People will almost always try to create a favorable impression of themselves and of their work, but there may be something beneath the surface that could be vital to your material. There are disgruntled types who might not open up to a complete stranger, but who can become astonishingly frank over dinner and a drink or two. Don't be afraid to ask people what they *don't* like about what they're doing. With no ax to grind, and with the knowledge that their words may appear in print, most people will prefer to stick only to the bright side of a question, but can often be drawn out. If so, it may open up entire new avenues of approach for you.

ELEVEN

WRITING YOUR BOOK

The process of writing is such a personal one; so tied up with the author's background, training, interests, and total outlook on life that I've always taken a somewhat dim view of people, schools and courses who profess to be able to turn the incipient and aspiring Mailer or Melville into the real thing overnight. Journalism schools do serve a purpose, since the field is a highly disciplined one, and the instilling of habits having to do with speed, accuracy, and other necessary reportorial techniques can be done successfully up to a point, given the proper teaching and the proper milieu in which to practice them.

However it seems that the longer the piece of writing in question, the less value this type of formalized instruction and training has, and the more the author must draw on the resources -- inborn or acquired over the experiences of a lifetime -- that he finds deep inside him. It may be said that all writing is a "craft", and there are some good arguments to support this. But many such proponents seem to be oversimplifying, especially when one is dealing with the full length non-fiction book which tends these days to use the "fiction" techniques of color, drama, and suspense and depends so much on the author's particular personality, his special view of life, and of the subject he is writing about.

Can the aspiring writer benefit, at all, then, from hints on how established and successful professionals think and work and approach the process of writing their own books? I think he can, not merely that he may learn that one best-selling author writes ten hours and turns out three thousand words a day and another only five hundred, but that he may experience the reassuring revelation that the best of them can suffer writer's block, stories that don't shape up, difficulties with editors and deadlines, and occasional disillusionment over an idea which seemed originally to have so much validity and to which he may have devoted much time and effort.

And if describing the pro's thought processes and feelings toward his or her work does no more than encourage the budding writer to *read* the individuals concerned, it will have accomplished much of its purpose. I've been influenced greatly by various writers in different periods of my life, all of which helped whet my interest in and (I hope) ability to deal with the printed word. A few years ago I recall finding myself greatly impressed by the writing of Barbara Tuchman, particularly her best-seller, *The Guns of August*, which was one of the most successfully handled and most interesting books of its type I could ever remember reading. I was prejudiced in her favor, to begin with, since I am a history buff of sorts, but there were, after all, other books on the subject of the First World War, and few of them seemed to have the color, impact and fascinating detail going for them that Mrs. Tuchman's did.

Of course this was no accident, since she had, and has, very definite ideas on the subject of writing history in general.

Mrs. Tuchman is a firm believer in the historian as artist, as a creative writer in the same bracket as the poet or novelist, with all the same obligations to apply the force of imagination to his work in order to make it not only understandable, but compelling to the reader and a force on his thinking.

To begin with she quarrels with the term "non-fiction" used to describe books dealing with factual matter, ("I do not feel like a non-something; I feel quite specific,") and thinks it has negative connotations that may let the writer off the hook as far as fully doing his job is concerned. She believes, along with George Trevelyan, former Cambridge professor of modern history, that the best historian is the one who combines complete knowledge of the facts with "the largest intellect, the warmest human sympathy and the highest imaginative powers." Both imagination and sympathy go to make up a large measure of the historian's creative equipment; the former working on the facts to supply the reason behind all that has happened in the past, and sympathy serving as the necessary ingredient to any understanding of the motive behind men's deeds.

Mrs. Tuchman thinks the creative process divides naturally into three elements. The first is the quality within the writer of perceiving a truth that needs to be communicated, the second is the medium -- typewriter and paper -- by which he expresses it, and lastly is the design or structure of the work itself. As far as historical writing is concerned her own method of expression is through the narrative or story-telling form, with an emphasis on clarity, interest, and aesthetic pleasure. This type of narrative writing is not easy to do, when dealing with a complex subject, but the end result can be worth all the trouble, a polished piece that can be very satisfying to the one who takes the time and effort to bring it to perfection. She is fond of comparing the process to the creation of a painting; both depend on arrangement, composition, and planning, as well as a considerable preliminary trial-and-error kind of work period.

The whole question of structure can be a problem. The author must stick to the discipline required of the historian, while at the same time making the past come to life for the reader of today. The difficulty lies in the selection, Mrs. Tuchman thinks, "an agonizing business," because there's always more material than one can use in a book. The problem is what to select out of all that happened in regard to the story without giving a false emphasis which distorts the truth. Obviously one can't put in everything; the result would be an unwieldy mess. The task is to keep the narrative going without leaving out any vital facts or altering the material to suit one's convenience. It's tempting to do this, she admits, but if you do you invariably get caught in the end. These, then, are the basic problems peculiar to writing this type of history --- how to fit the essential backgrounding in with an ever-moving narrative, and how to maintain suspense, drama, and anticipation in a story where everyone knows how it is going to come out in the end.

It may be comforting to learn that this problem of selection can temporarily stymie a professional like Mrs. Tuchman almost as readily as it can a less experienced writer. At any rate, while at work on a recent book, she admits to passing into the never-land of a typical "block." Her writing, she says, slowed down to a trickle until one terrible day when she sat in her study from nine till five "in a blank coma" and came out without having put down a single word. "Anybody who is a writer will know how frightening that was. You feel you have come to the end of your powers; you will not finish the book; you may never write again."

She did, of course, and the result was that masterful study of pre-1914 Western World, *The Proud Tower.*

Bruce Catton is another historian whose books on the Civil War published about the time of the centennial in the early sixties won him wide acclaim and a perennial place on the best seller lists. Catton's basic idea was virtually the same --- to bring the story of the war down to the personal level, to make the reader feel involved individually. He had always found himself more interested in the impact of the war on the ordinary soldier than in the broader scope of strategy and tactics. Catton has never claimed to be a military expert, but says that over the years he has learned a lot about the ordinary "G.I." who fought in the Civil War --- what his life was like, what he thought about, the food he ate, what kind of medical care he received. He feels that everything he's done in that area simply grew out of that interest in the common man. Apparently his readers were as fascinated as he was.

Catton believed that he had the same obligation as the newspaper reporter, which was to find out exactly what happened, and tell the story as well as he could to people who weren't there and would only know what happened by what he wrote.

The historian's job is really the reporter's job, he thinks, that is, to be guided by the facts as they stand. He must steer away from preconceived ideas, and has to start out with a thirst for knowledge, a desire to know what things were really like, and what actually took place. Then he's got to tell his story in as uncomplicated a way as he can.

Catton thinks that it's the task of the young writer to concentrate on what really interests him most; to pick an area that he really wants to learn and to write about, and then to study all he can about that particular field. Clarity is a very strong point with him, also, and he feels it's a great mistake to be condescending toward one's readers' intelligence; inaccuracies, half-truths, and prejudicies on the part of the author will always show through. The writer must be earnest and sincere, and be dedicated to the idea of expressing himself as clearly and completely as he can.

If he's just trying to take advantage of some popular fad --- if he's writing with an eye to being clever rather than deep --- then he isn't going to produce anything of consequence. He has to believe in what he's doing, Catton feels, that it's the most important thing there is, and pursue his work with that spirit.

In leaving the history field then, it would pay to take a look at an area that has always been closely allied to it --- that of biography. Biographies can do very well on publisher's lists --- a survey taken not long ago of successful men in many totally unrelated fields revealed that biography was an almost invariable choice when they considered reading matter --- but it can be very difficult and demanding to do well. Emphasis is extremely important, along with accuracy since the writer of biography is really taking it upon himself to hold up his subject to posterity's eye; how he treats Henry VIII or Theodore Roosevelt may determine to a large extent just what the world thinks of the man.

Hesketh Pearson, for example, is one biographer who is noted for being able to involve the reader completely in the character, color, and personality of the person, place, and time he is writing about. He has done Charles II, Henry of Navarre, Bernard Shaw, and Benjamin Disraeli in book form -- all very successfully -- and also combined several subjects into a book of brief biographies called *Lives of the Wits.*

Accuracy is the number one essential in this form of writing, according to Pearson. Yet, he insists, the author can only tell the truth as he sees it, and nearly everybody else will see the truth differently. His book on Oscar Wilde, for example, was written because he saw Wilde as a wonderful man, but shortly after it was published St. John Irvine wrote another biography of the playwright, and he obviously thought Wilde was a grotesque man. "He is no doubt as honest as I am," Pearson says, "but the points of view were so different we might easily have been writing about totally different people." To Pearson, the biographer's only purpose is to tell the truth, and while every reader will add his own interpretation, the writer has nevertheless fulfilled his obligation to his subject, to himself, and to his public.

Enthusiasm, Pearson claims, is the first requisite for the young biographer, since it brings out all the other necessary qualifications for doing the work. Beyond that he must have both the ability and the patience to study everything he can find which is pertinent to his subject. And in the event that he is dealing with a person whom people still remember, he should hunt up all of the subject's contemporaries he can find to learn what their thoughts and knowledge and reactions are. He should set himself the task of reading every book and every document on the subject, and to do this his enthusiasm has got to be so intense that it absorbs all of his time and thought. Pearson believes in a relatively short but intense work session --- about three or four hours of stick-to-it concentration in the mornings, after which he calls it a day.

Arthur H. Lewis shares the same feelings about honesty as the principal objective of the biographer, and the writer's duty to make a real effort not to let his own prejudices creep into his work. In certain instances, Lewis feels, one must skip over some things for the sake of good taste, and some-times the writer is tempted to introduce facts which don't contribute to the story but are interesting in themselves. He prefers to use the old-fashioned word "integrity," and along with it must go an intense intellectual curiosity about people and places. In preparing to write *The Day They Shook The Plum Tree*, the story of Hetty Green, Lewis not only had to go over the testimony of three trials which totalled over four million words, but had to track down, too, many witnesses who were still living (Hetty Green died in

1916) and find out everything he could about her character. He ransacked newspaper files and spent seven months talking to people.

Lewis defines the type of research he does as just a matter of endless hours of probing and then gaining the confidence of people. He never interviews anybody without telling them what he's doing -- yet they frequently claim that they've talked too much. "I always get them to okay their quotes."

His advice to the young biographer or writer in general is simply to sit down and produce something, and not wait for inspiration to come along. He practices what he preaches, and his own schedule is rigid and unchanging. He works from 8:30 in the morning until 12:30 every day, seven days a week, and finishes a book in about seven months.

The biography of a living man, especially a prominent one, can offer up different problems. Victor Lasky's book, *J.F.K., the Man and the Myth,* published the summer before the Kennedy assassination in Dallas, was an instant best-seller, but was received with very mixed reactions. It was a project that took three years to write, and was regarded in many quarters as a "king-sized hatchet job." This is understandable to an extent, since the biography of any political figure, not to say an American president, is bound, unless done in a totally bland way, to please some people and offend others. Lasky's work was not as laudatory as many supporters of this popular president would have hoped, but as might be expected, this didn't hurt sales any.

Lasky himself never felt that his book was a conservative hatchet-job, but felt his job was that of the reporter, reporting facts as best he could. He ransacked newspaper libraries and morgues in cities all over the country, and talked to many political figures. He thought that his responsibility in writing the book was first to seek out all the pertinent material on record, then to document every piece of evidence on a fact-by-fact, word-by-word basis. He did it, too. In the back of the book there are at least thirty to forty pages of solid documentation which his wife spent a month in compiling.

There are pitfalls, though, in writing about contemporary figures. One reporter spent three years doing a book on Prime Minister Kishi of Japan, and then Kishi resigned a month before publication date, and another turned out a study of the Indian political scene, only to find that it had changed almost completely by the time the book was nearing completion. At the time *J.F.K.* was published -- in the summer of 1963 -- Lasky himself was preparing a sequel to it -- an analysis of the New Frontier in operation. By November, of course everything had changed.

Such a situation can be terribly frustrating, and it is here that the ability to bounce back is of paramount importance. Then there is the difficulty of facing a whole new task next time. Ben Hecht once said that you never did learn, from writing four books, how to do the fifth, that each piece of work was a brand new task, that you made the same mistakes, had to do the same number of rewrites, and that the development of any kind of facile "technique" simply meant that you weren't expressing yourself honestly.

Leo Rosten has made quite a study of the whole problem of writer-reader communication. He feels that anything the writer puts on paper allows the reader a look at the world that exists within the author's mind and heart. However it has to be put down in terms of the reader's perspective and perhaps a reader who is alien to you or who doesn't like what you write. Rosten feels that people who communicate well with others -- either in speech or through the written word – also can communicate well with themselves.

It's too bad, Rosten thinks, that most people don't know what they mean, and don't really know what they want to say, either. He calls most verbal output -- whether it's conversation or writing -- little more than a "spraying out of words," which are ejaculated on the assumption that somehow they will all wind up fitting together in some sort of meaning, and will say something greater than their separate parts, and greater than the writer or speaker intends them to.

The able communicator, he says, segregates his material, organizing and apportioning it internally, trying it out on himself, seeing if it makes sense to him before he transmits it to others. He disagrees with Hecht on one point. Rosten has been a professional writer for thirty years and says each time he starts a new project he thinks it's going to be easier -- that he's learned his techniques, can master his content, and do a lot toward bridging the gap between himself and the reader.

Ilka Chase was asked not long ago about this whole question of communication, and she came up with a little more liberal viewpoint. The older she grows and the more she writes the more she strives for simplicity, precision, and clarity. However she thinks anyone who is telling something in a book -- in a book of non-fiction, anyway – is faced with a problem. Should he tell exactly what happened, or try to make it interesting? Sometimes by a small omission or a minor addition you can add some spice to what might actually have been in the dull side. "It is in moments like this that an author and his conscience are alone in a quiet room wrestling it out to the ultimate throw. Who comes up on the side of the angels?"

Miss Chase admits to being a big "truth addict," but in the circumstances mentioned feels that a very small manipulation of fact is permissible if it can make the story more vivid to the reader. "If it gives him more fun, go ahead, gussy it up a bit." However if fact and objectivity are the important thing, then this sort of tinkering is nothing short of criminal. A newspaper reporter or historian, for instance, mustn't even consider any sort of invention or shifting of emphasis. In these two areas one must be scrupulously honest, since with all the care in the world one is bound to make mistakes and errors in judgment. The important thing is to resist all temptation to do it deliberately. Then too, Miss Chase says, "not only is truth stranger than fiction, it is often more engrossing."

There is another area of writing that really doesn't get a lot of attention and yet is worth taking a look at. This is the travel book. Now plenty of people would like to do them; they seem like so much fun -- taking a lot of trips and then writing about them and all. It's not quite that simple -- one must be primarily a writer, with the travel involved being considered the necessary research for the book -- yet it can have great personal rewards.

To produce *A View of All the Russias,* South African author Laurens van der Post spent nearly three months touring the Soviet Union, from one end to the other, a tremendous job but a vastly enriching experience as well. The whole project reinforced deep feelings van der Post has always had of being a part of life and humanity in general, feelings which he believes every author must have to be successful. The writer needs a purpose, or mission, must strive for reality as opposed to unreality, for truth as opposed to untruth, for perspective instead of distortion. "If you are false," says van der Post, "you are a bad writer, technically, and an inept one, spiritually."

In writing as a whole, but in travel writing in particular, van der Post feels, the writer must be the total receptacle. "Everything is important -- color, smell, scenes, where life has taken you, whatever you've felt." Perhaps in no other area is the danger of letting preconceived opinions get in the way of objective reporting, especially in regard to the in-depth study which takes an entire nation and people and subjects them to the scrutiny of foreign eyes, as did van der Post's book. The greatest lesson he's learned from his extensive travel, he says, is that in his heart the modern man has a greater sense of brotherhood than he's ever had before and a greater potential for living in peace. This, and not simply information on the price of hotels in Majorca or a dinner at the Paris Ritz, is the type of significant feeling the writer of this type of book must convey to his reading audience.

Let's take up one final facet of non-fiction work, one that has always remained something of a mystery, since its practitioners have a tendency to remain incognito. After all, how many ghost writers do you know? And would you know it if you saw one?

They deal in autobiography of course, in most cases in the form of a collaboration with a celebrity of some sort who has a story to tell, would like to tell it in his own words, and yet needs the services of a professional writer to help him get it down on paper. Such a relationship can be a profitable one, too, depending on the financial arrangements made and the ultimate success of the book. Some "ghosts" or collaborators will simply do the job for a flat fee paid beforehand or in installments of some sort and calculated on the work involved and an estimation of the eventual sales of the book. Others will agree to do the work for a percentage of the royalties to come. The writer who agrees to this type of arrangement gives up the advantage of a "bird in the hand" but leaves himself the opportunity of making a financial killing if the book proves to be a smash hit. In the case of a collaboration, he may have his name linked with the subject on the cover of the book. ("Racquel Welch and Richard Brown" or "Racquel Welch as told to Richard Brown") or his name may be missing entirely. In the case of a "celebrity" book this is most often the case, since the reader seems to want the feeling of reading the famous person's own words, even though he suspects they were written by somebody else, anyway.

Gerold Frank is one of the more notable ghost writers, having done *I'll Cry Tomorrow; Too Much, Too Soon; Beloved Infidel* and *My Story*, bringing to the American public the lives of Lillian Roth, Diana Barrymore, Sheilah Graham and Zsa Zsa Gabor. The first three were made into successful motion pictures as well. Frank had his own special way of working and developed his own particular relationships with all of them. He talked with the ladies in question for about a year each, and gathered about three quarters of his research material through this type of personal contact. It all entailed a great amount of interviewing, day in and day out, a "psychoanalytical unfolding" he calls it, of their lives. The rest of his material was gained from outside fact-hunting -- interviewing everyone he could who knew them, from childhood associates up to contemporaries, reading their letters, diaries, and everything that had been written about them in newspapers, magazines, and books.

In working with Sheilah Graham, Frank of course did a lot of research on F. Scott Fitzgerald, talking with all the friends of his who were still living, including his New York psychiatrist. The interviews with Lillian Roth and Diana Barrymore turned out to be almost like one long continual session of analysis, with no secrets between them, as he delved into the innermost being of these two tragic women. Zsa Zsa Gabor he handled in a different, lighter vein. It entailed a different type of analysis -- the study of glamor and what makes the beautiful and desirable woman click.

Frank thinks of his obligation as a "ghost" type of biographer is to present the subject to the reader with as much factual honesty as possible, and at the same time to help the subject, as much as he can, to understand his own impulses, drives, and conflicts. He thinks both writer and subject are searching together in order to discover who and what the latter is, and what is leading and shaping the course of his life, and that because the writer is on the scene, yet removed from the subject, he may be able to correct distortions until the two of them achieve a result in the end that is as close to the truth as possible.

TWELVE

TIPS

ON WORK HABITS

By now you have learned, hopefully, something about selecting a topic for your writing project, pre-selling it to a publisher by means of a query letter and sample chapters, some tips on library researching for factual matter, and interviewing those who can provide additional valuable material. You have gathered a great many notes and at this point you may have a copy of a signed contract in your hands which sets down a specific deadline for you to provide the publisher with a complete and acceptable manuscript.

You now face the job of collecting it all together in your own mind and getting the whole thing down on paper. If you are like the majority of people, and this can include the most experienced and professional writers you can name, you will probably experience a powerful urge to postpone the actually beginning of the writing task. There is something menacing -- even terrifying -- about that initial blank sheet of paper in the typewriter, and all kinds of excuses for delaying the moment when you must confront it will leap to mind. Is there another source you suddenly feel must be checked into? A final rearrangement of notes, cards, and more chapter organization to be done? Or worse yet, some other job -- the car, the house, the lawn -- completely apart from writing that suddenly looms and demands your attention? If so, you are simply suffering the common variety put-off-syndrome, the irrational desire to escape the job at hand, that moment of truth and exposure of self that writing really is.

You'll probably never really get over this affliction. Experience and success with one finished product doesn't seem to dissipate it at all the next time, but there are things you can do to modify it, to keep the feeling from dragging your creative life down into a pit of inertia. In the first place, you ought to try and set yourself a regular work schedule. Most serious authors insist that regular hours at the typewriter are absolutely essential in order to do continuing productive work. It doesn't matter what time of day you make it -- suit your own schedule and temperament -- some authors are at their best early in the morning, working till noon or so, and then having the rest of the day to themselves to let the well "fill up" again. Others seem to feel the most productive later at night, when it's quiet, and they have no distractions. I have always found the afternoons better for me; it seems to take me till one o'clock or so to really get underway, and though I often come up with some good ideas during the evening hours, I find that a full work day late at night makes my mind so active it's impossible to get to sleep afterward.

The important thing is to sit down there and put in your hours regularly, whether you feel like working or not. It's silly to think you can write only when you feel "inspired," and still turn out any serious and steady work. You ought to stay at that typewriter for the three or four-hour period of time you've fitted into your schedule and turn out *something*, even if you are dissatisfied with it. You can always go over it later, (you'll have to anyway) and at least you will have something down in black and white. You must establish rhythm of work, and you must be able to lose yourself in your subject without being especially conscious of the time. Allow yourself a good long period where you won't have to keep one eye on the clock and try to find some place to write regularly where you will be free from distractions. If your home and kids are noisy, retreat to a remote attic. I know one author who lives in the country and who exiles himself in a tiny one-room cabin, situated just close enough to home and family so that he can hear the dinner bell. Another sneaks off to a houseboat tied up in the river nearby. Others rent small, unpretentious offices just for the purpose of giving them a place to concentrate undisturbed, but it's not a good idea to write in your regular business office if you are going to be bothered by the telephone and your co-workers.

The real cause of the reluctance to begin the actual writing of a book lies in the scrutiny it exposes us to. We have to marshal our thoughts and feelings and express them there on paper where the whole outside world can observe them and criticize. It's partly self-protection and partly timidity that makes us want to postpone this process. So start out some place where you can be alone and uninterrupted. I've learned that as soon as I get something down on paper, the rest will come in time, and I pass from a reluctance to an eagerness to get back to the job.

Here are some suggestions that may be helpful in overcoming some of the initial stumbling blocks every writer faces. I know they've helped me:

. . . Although there are writers who like to get all or most of their research taken care of before they start writing, most people are somewhat intimidated by a large mass of notes, and find it preferable to research some and then write some, as a particular topic seems to "jell."

. . . Don't be hesitant about committing something to paper, just because you feel it's not in finished form and may have to be polished up at a later date. Some first drafts are great and some are terrible; it's important to simply get the ideas down in the beginning. It's a lot easier to smooth something out working from a first draft than to write well from scratch.

. . . It's not necessary to begin at the beginning of your manuscript and work straight through to the end. Pick out sections that seem easiest or that you are most comfortable with, work on them and do the others later, even though the procedure may be out of sequence. I personally like to get the beginning down -- work it up really smooth – and then turn to some highlight within a certain section, such as a piece of description or a portion of biographical material and knock that out. Then I'd do the transitional parts when the whole was more familiar in my mind. This way of writing won't appeal to everybody; I just mention it to stress the fact that you have a lot of latitude in your work habits. The important thing is to get it all down in the end. Try to maintain your momentum while you are writing. The first half hour, or hour might come hard, but you'll reach a point when you're in the swing of it and are functioning more smoothly. Don't waste time looking things up or searching for words and ways of expressing things, but leave them blank and come back to them later. If you get stymied, go over what you've written and see if the flow will begin again. Hemingway used to start his writing day by reading everything he had done for the previous day or two. Then the thoughts were coming and he was ready to begin again.

. . . Many writers have a fondness for the beginning of a chapter; I know I do, since I feel it allows me to indulge in dramatic, or anecdotal, or some "higher level" writing than what may follow. I like to grab the reader's attention this way, and feel that if I've written a good page or two of a chapter beginning, half the battle is won. This is partly psychological, but not wholly, since beginnings can be hard going for many writers. As you collect and collate your research be on the lookout for themes, stories, sentences, dramatic incidents with which you can lead off a chapter or even the book itself.

. . . It won't take long for you to determine just how you work best -- whether you compose on the typewriter or write in longhand, typing the whole thing later; just how you use your notes and other research materials, where you like to work, and at what times of the day. None of these things matter, as long as you can do the job, and it doesn't hurt a bit to indulge yourself in what to others might be the most peculiar of work habits. In fact it's better this way, since it gives you no excuse to postpone or abandon the task at hand.

I find the first draft is by far the hardest. Many writers -- novelists especially -- feel the cutting and polishing in the revision stage to be sheer tedium, but I've always found this part of the job much more pleasant and satisfying. The bare bones of the project is down where you can see it, you know approximately how long the book will be, the elements are all, or mostly all, there. The only thing left is to make it all readable, and if a writer has the love of words and the pride in his craft that he ought to have, he shouldn't object to making what follows the first draft as professional as he possibly can.

Probably the best way to proceed is to do revisions as you go right through the manuscript, that is, smooth out the earlier chapters while the later ones are still in first draft form, or even still in the form of notes and not typed up at all. Revising and smoothing one section and then roughing a later one will enable you to see the process from beginning to end and you'll wind up writing a lot better.

THIRTEEN

TITLES

AND CHAPTER HEADINGS

Titles can be fun or they can be frustrating, depending on whether you are one of those people who have a knack for coming up with pithy ones, fraught with meaning; or one of those who can't string two or three words together at the top of a page to save their lives. I'm one of the latter. If you're with me, you shouldn't let yourself get too concerned about it, since nobody's going to depend on you to come up with a title if you just don't have it in you, and the publisher himself can always be relied upon to do the job if he has to. In fact relatively few titles remain unchanged en route from author to printed page. I know I had quite a time with my book on the Spanish-American War. Originally I had suggested *Thy Banners Made Tyranny Tremble*, taken from the song "Columbia, the Gem of the Ocean." The answer on this one was that it was a little too long, so I tried two or three more, but only seemed to come up with increasingly far-fetched offerings. At last I ran across a book of contemporary Spanish-American War poetry in the patriotic vein, and sat down to read it, feeling there had to be a juicy quote somewhere. I finally copied out a stanza or two of a poem by Richard Hovey which began:

Bugles! and a great nation thrills and leaps to arms . . . I suggested two or three possibilities, the publishers liked one of them and it became the title of the book -- *A Leap to Arms.*

More often than not titles have their origin through this trial and error process, rather than the sudden flash of inspiration that people assume gives birth to them. Many editors are excellent when it comes to hitting the nail on the head effectively, simply because it is good business -- the title is a reader's first introduction to the book.

It's usually a good idea, though, for a writer to at least make an attempt, since a working title -- which is the name for the tentative choice -- while the book is in progress will help center your efforts on the subject at hand during those periods when you are tempted to become diffuse (and we all do, at times). It's best if you can have a working title right off the bat, and though a good one doesn't always come to you, try to have *something* to call your book by the time you send in your outline and sample chapters. After all, those at the publishing house have to refer to it in some way, and if it has a name that intrigues editors, it will go a lot further toward selling the book to the editorial selection people than if everyone gets in the habit of calling it "that Middle East war thing" or "that book about seaweed and how it prolongs life."

There really aren't any hard and fast rules for what goes to make a good title; any look at the best selling books of any given year will provide examples of titles that are pretty far out and unorthodox, but unless you have that talent for hitting on just the right thing, you are probably safer in sticking to generally accepted practices in your selection.

The editors thought my own first choice for a title too lengthy, and it's true that most say what they have to say in half a dozen words or less. The best-seller lists are a good example of this kind of brevity, and the reason is that both editors and readers seem more attracted to short titles. One word for example, can be very punchy and effective if it's the right one. Take *Rape!* for example, the documented case history of the victim of an assault and the aftermath of her ordeal; *Jaws*, the rather frightening name of a novel about a huge shark that terrorizes a seaside resort; *Babe*, the biography of Babe Ruth. There are quite a few one-word examples that say all they have to say in the bare minimum. What would be a better name for columnist Mike Royko's book on Chicago's Mayor Daley than simply *Boss?* Or what more effective way to describe the horrifying ordeal of a soccer team stranded in the Andes by a plane crash which caused them to resort to cannibalism to survive than just *Alive?*

These all describe what the book contains which once upon a time was considered a title's primary function. There's certainly no question of what *You Can Profit From a Monetary Crisis* is about, or *The Sherlock Holmes Scrapbook* either. But I've always had something of a weakness for the clever or somewhat obscure name that intrigues and draws the reader's eye. It might have a connection with the subject that the knowledgeable will be able to divine right away, like *Ah-One, Ah-Two!* the Lawrence Welk autobiography, which means everything to those who have listened to Welk, but probably very little to those who haven't. Or *Everybody Loves*

Somebody Sometime -- Especially Himself, the story of Dean Martin and Jerry Lewis, which is derived from Dean's theme song. (This, by the way, technically makes the six word limit, but they sure are long words!) Or Grace Lichtenstein's treatise on women's pro tennis, *A Long Way Baby,* which might seem obscure to anyone unfamiliar with Virginia Slims' cigarette advertising, or the fact that the product was the sponsor of the major women's winter tennis tour.

Titles should have life, jump out at you, and make you think. Often humor will do this or even more cleverness, *Some Call it Kitsch,* a picture book on once popular Victorian and Edwardian painting is eye-catching, and *Zen and the Art of Motorcycle Maintenance* ought to be enough to make anyone open the book, anyway, just to see what the author's talking about. A book name like *Bets Wishes Doc* would seem to be just funny, at first, until one discovers the story is about children with perceptual handicaps, and then it becomes astonishingly poignant. And one like Kurt Vonnegut's *Wampeters, Foma and Granfaloons,* is merely incredible.

It's not easy; you have to turn the words over in your mind, reject innumerable possibilities, try them this way and that, sometimes abandon the whole idea to another tack entirely. The Bible, Shakespeare, and the classics have always been fair game. Consider *The Little Foxes, The Voice of the Turtle, The Sun Also Rises* and *If Thine Eye Offend Thee* from the Scriptures; *For Whom the Bell Tolls,* from John Donne, *This Hallowed Ground* from the Gettysburg Address. Consider the titles that have been gleaned from the verses of "The Battle Hymn of the Republic," which must have set some kind of record: *Mine Eyes Have Seen the Glory, The Grapes of Wrath* (Biblical, as well) *Terrible Swift Sword, Never Call Retreat.*

The possibilities are endless. If you aren't thinking on the same level as the examples mentioned here, don't worry about it. Just go on writing, and the chances are it will come to you, either in a flash, if you're lucky, or through the slower process of refinement, as you proceed. And if you really are stumped, chances are your publisher will have somebody tucked away in a small office somewhere whose sole job it may be to come up with the inspiration everyone will give *you* credit for someday.

Chapter Heads

One area of writing that receives almost no attention is the matter of chapter headings. Not all non-fiction books have them, of course; in some the chapters will simply be numbered, and there are even those who consider flashy and imaginative chapter headings to be little more than the expression of an author's desire to show off. (See how witty, how provocative I am!)

As far as my own feelings are concerned, I couldn't disagree more. Chapter heads break the book up into useful sections (and some books certainly need this) and relieve the monotony of the printed page. They also give the reader some idea of the content. I can't tell you how many times I've picked up a volume in a book store, opened it up to the table of contents, and been either turned off then and there or intrigued enough to browse further or even buy the book. And all simply by how the headings strike me. I've found it to be an almost infallible guide to whether a book will wind up being tedius or colorful and interesting, or perhaps overly cute or just inconsequential.

In *A Leap to Arms,* my history of the Spanish-American War, I used the following headings which I hoped would strike a fine line between subtlety and direct reference to incidents in the text which would spark the reader's interest:

I   "An Idea Who's Time Has Come" — (Pertaining to the "ripeness" of the late nineteenth century United States for expansion on an international scale.)
II   "The Game in Progress: The Queen's Knight Gambit Accepted." (The war begins and the Spanish Admiral Cervera makes a risky sortie to the West Indies with his naval squadron.)
III   "Courage and Confusion" — (America's unreadiness for war, and her involved lotistic mixup as she prepared to raise an army and land an expedntionary force on the coast of Cuba.)
IV   "The Battle That Fought Itself" — (A chapter on the land battle of Santiago, with the use of a quote from Colonel Theodore Roosevelt, who fought with the Rough Riders.)
V   "Signal 250" — (A chapter about the naval battle off Santiago, with the heading derived from the signal hoisted by the ships about to go into action.)
VI   "Tell Your Bullies They're Doing Great Work" — (Another battle chapter, with a quote from the commander, Admiral Schley, regarding the flagship's fighting men.)
VII   "Fallen Idols Leave Clear Horizons" — (A plan on words of a sort, referring to the emergence of the United States after the defeat of Spain and the old European order she represented.)

These may not be the best examples in the world, but I included them to show how I attempted to make my chapter headings of interest and provoke the reader. It's certainly worth the time and effort to give them some thought.

FOURTEEN

ILLUSTRATIONS

Whether or not your book will contain illustrations will probably depend on several factors. One is cost. Pictures in a book cost money, and if the budget doesn't warrant it, you may have to do without. Most budgets will allow something for illustration, and the question of whether to provide it will depend on whether the subject matter requires or would be helped by it. If you're writing in a historical vein, or if you're doing any kind of biography, it will usually be enhanced by illustration of some type, and of course any kind of a how-to-do-it book will need them. A travel book may have a good many. However, if you are doing a work of philosophical, psychological, or sociological nature, it may not require them at all. Most illustrations will be photographs, which generally appear in black and white (exceptions would be the whole "art book" or "coffee table" category of display pieces which sell in the $12 and $14 and up range. Not all illustration depends on the camera, however. It may also include line drawings and maps and charts that are reproduced in the finished book as well.

Keep in mind that it will be your responsibility, and not your publisher's, to obtain photographs. Some you may be able to get free of charge, some you may have to pay for, but anything you supply to the publisher should be of good quality, be of the "glossy" type and of 8 x 10 inch size. (In some cases 5 x 7 may suffice, but certainly nothing smaller.) And when you submit pictures, send in enough of them so that the editors can make a good selection from the bunch.

Sometimes digging up photos to illustrate a book can be easy and sometimes a chore, depending on just what you are looking for. Businesses usually maintain extensive photo files of their own personnel, products, and activities, and most companies are only too happy to cooperate in the matter of supplying both facts and photos requested. Requests for material of this type should normally be made to the head of the firm's public relations department. The title may be Public Relations Director, Director of Public

Information, or of Community Relations, or something else, but that is the person to contact.

Agencies of the federal and state governments can also provide both photos and factual matter through their public relations divisions, and the armed forces public information departments maintain extensive files of pictures of both personnel and military material. When I worked in the public information office of U.S. Navy Atlantic fleet headquarters, there were continual requests for photos of ships and aircraft of every type, and our office maintained file cabinets filled with them.

The easiest thing to do is simply write for what you want to the appropriate company or government agency that might have some connection with the subject matter of your book. Describe the product, item, or individual you need a picture of and more likely than not they will be only too pleased to give it to you. In most cases it's a simple matter of smart P.R.

You may be allowed to keep photos you receive from such sources or you may be requested to return some of them, when you are finished. Your publisher will make his selection from among those you send him at the time you give him your completed manuscript, and will return those which he doesn't plan to use to you. After your book has been published he will send all of them back, so don't forget to return those prints which the suppliers have asked you to mail back to them.

There are one or two important things to keep in mind when selecting photos to send in with your manuscript. Make sure the shots are clear and show considerable detail since they will almost always be reduced for publication and may lose some of the fine points. Look for contrast, too, since any kind of an overall gray quality can cause a serious toning down of detail in the reproductive process.

The chances are that you won't be able to get all your photos just for the asking; you'll have to use other means. Many writers simply buy them outright. Almost every historian I know, for instance, makes a practice of going straight to the Library of Congress when he's in need of American illustrative material. Here we have a vast collection of photographs of every type -- they have literally millions on hand -- including illustrations from books and manuscripts going back hundreds of years. If the library has a negative on hand, it will sell you an 8 x 10 glossy print for under a dollar. If you write to them -- to the Division of Prints and Photographs, Library of Congress, Washington, D.C. -- they will send you a catalogue which is published by the department and which describes the collection. These photos from the library can be published without fear of copyright infringement, because copyrights have all expired.

The National Archives also boasts a large assortment of pictures, being especially strong in history and in the activities of the American government, past and present. Send any requests you may have to the Still Pictures Branch, Audio-Visual Records Division, National Archives, Ninth Street and Constitution Avenue, N.W., Washington, D.C. Don't overlook the Smithsonian Institution, either. Though not a photo repository on the scale of the Library of Congress or the National Archives, the Smithsonian has a large collection of pictures on hand of its exhibits. You may want to explore the possibility of commercial firms which will sell news and historical photographs, too, the best known of which is probably Bettmann Archive, Inc., 136 E. 57th St., New York, N.Y.; Harris & Ewing, 1304 G. St. N.W., Washington, D.C., and Underwood & Underwood, 3 W. 46th St., New York, N.Y. are also prominent in the field.

The newspaper wire services will often be willing to sell you prints of pictures taken by their staff photographers. Send your request along to the editors and include the following information: the date and page number of the newspaper in which the photo you are interested in appears, the name of the photographer if it is listed, the caption as it appears beneath the photo, and a description of the picture.

You may be working on a non-fiction book which requires a series of specific illustrations that must be taken for just that purpose, and you might want to hire a professional photographer to do this. If so, and you don't know one personally, look through the yellow pages of the telephone directory under "Photographers." A word of warning at this point: Be sure you have an understanding with any commercial photographer before you tell him to go ahead with the job. First explain to him carefully just what you need, and find out how we will charge, and just what the whole job will cost you. Some photographers work on a flat fee basis for the job, others charge so much per picture, and still others at a daily rate plus the cost of prints. Find out all about costs beforehand.

At this point you may ask, why hire a professional photographer when I can take my own shots just as well? By all means go ahead if you are good with a camera and if you want to take the time and effort to do your own work. There are one or two things to keep in mind, however, if you do. First of all, remember that the resulting print must be reproduced, and to assure that it will come out well, you ought to allow for a greater amount of contrast than the ordinary photograph. A print suitable for reproduction in your book will probably seem overly harsh to you, but ideally that's the way it ought to be. Don't pose your subject against cluttered backgrounds;

you want a clear illustration of your topic, and extraneous details will just have to be airbrushed out later by the publisher's production people. Keep in mind that your 8 x 10 print will be reduced considerably when it finally appears in your book, and what you want is a simple, direct photo that says what it's supposed to about your text material. Unless you are doing a travel book, or art, or natural history book, don't bother shooting in color. Color reproduction sends a publisher's costs way up and almost all book illustrations are in black and white. Finally, a word here about cropping. Cropping is simply the cutting out of the photo of unnecessary material you feel should be eliminated. An additional border is simply cut off the top, bottom, or either of the sides to get rid of people or objects within the photo that you don't feel add anything to what you are trying to show. It's probably just as well if you don't do this yourself; it's a job that ought to be handled by an experienced production man. If you feel one of your pictures should be cropped, you may indicate just where on the shiny side of the photo with a red grease pencil.

In some cases you will want to use drawings or paintings as illustrative material, and your book may require certain maps or charts. Original art work may be arranged for by the publisher, if he thinks he knows someone suitable for the job, or by yourself, if you are acquainted with an artist, and you feel he can fill the bill. Such an arrangement between author and artist can be an informal one -- you may just pay him a stipulated fee for the work he does -- or a contract may be drawn up, giving him a share of the author's royalties. The figure will be arrived at through mutual agreement between the two of you, the illustrator's percentage being dependent upon what type of book it is, the number of illustrations and how important they are to the material, and the amount of work he has put in. On the one extreme we might have a book for six-year olds in which the story is told largely through pictures, and at the other the case of an artist who does a simple pen and ink line drawing or two to illustrate the chapter headings.

Once again, it you are a competent artist yourself, you might be capable of doing your own illustration, and if you are good enough to want to attempt such a job, you probably are sufficiently aware of the technical processes to make sure that you use black India ink on a substantial white paper stock in order that they will reproduce well. And of course simple sketches on your part can always be used just for the purpose of explaining to an artist what you are looking for from him.

Maps, charts, and diagrams can pose a little different problem. Many books -- historical and military ones in particular -- need them, and it is really the author's responsibility to come up with the original material. You may want to reproduce old maps, provided they are not protected by copyrights, or have new ones drawn. Once again, the publisher may have someone on hand who can do this, or you may know of an artist yourself who will want to tackle it. In my own case I have simply Xeroxed older maps and sent them in with my manuscript to the publisher, who had the maps redrawn by his own artist in a slightly different style which he felt suited the book better. The same situation applies to diagrams which are more specifically tailored to a book's content. Colin Simpson's recent book, *Lusitania*, featured cross-sections of the doomed liner's decks and cargo spaces to illustrate her construction and the position of contraband material she was carrying. It's just a matter of accumulating the proper information and having it drawn to meet the best iillustrative requirements.

FIFTEEN

PROOFING

After your manuscript has first been set in type, it will be run off by the printer on *galley proofs,* which are long, narrow sheets of paper on which your text will appear much as it will in finished book form. You will now be confronted with a task that many authors abhor -- namely the careful reading and checking of the galley proof pages and the notation of any mistakes or matter to be corrected which you find there. It's no use complaining about this somewhat demanding task -- you must do it -- because no publisher will take the risk of allowing anything to reach the final printing until the author has made a final check of the material as it appears in type. The galley proof stage is, after all, the last one before the book is made up into pages.

The purpose of galley proofing is to make sure that the printer has followed your typescript copy correctly and that there are no mispellings, errors in punctuation or mistakes of any kind. Wide margins are provided on the sheets for the purpose of making corrections, and there are standard proofreader's marks which you will be expected to use to make it easy for the printer in handling any corrections necessary. You don't have to learn them; just have a proofreader's sheet in front of you when you do the work and follow that.

Now one word of warning: *Resist* with all the determination you have the temptation to make revisions in the proof at this stage. Most contracts specify that any alterations that the author makes beyond a certain amount will be charged to him, and believe me, printing costs are high! Any kind of stylistic changes should be made in the manuscript stage -- not now. Costs are what they are partly because most books are set by the linotype process, which means that every line in your book is set on a single piece of metal cast by the linotype machine. Any time a change is made, no matter how minor, the entire slug of type must be recast. And to make it worse, if you change the first line in a paragraph of type, all the succeeding lines in that paragraph must be reset as well unless you can compensate by adding or subtracting another word of similar length in that line or one near to it. All this is very expensive as is the new phototype process -- labor costs for printing keep rising all the time — and this is why the publisher will insist you share them if alterations go beyond a certain point.

When you send back the corrected galley proofs the publisher ; will pass them on to the printer to make the necessary changes, and you will then get another and final set of page proofs. These will be on the same long narrow sheets, but the textual matter will have been divided up into pages, just as they will appear in your book, with one page per sheet. You may still make final corrections on these, but this will be your last change before your material appears in book form. Just as any changes in the text should have been made in the manuscript before it went into type setting, so it is at the page proof stage: the step should only be used to catch printer errors. Other changes made at this point will affect printing schedules, possibly causing your book to be late or even postponed. Nothing can be more disastrous to launching a book for either to happen. Don't you be the cause for it.

SELECTED
BIBLIOGRAPHY

Barzun, Jacques, and Graff, Henry F. *The Modern Researcher.* New York: Harcourt, Brace and Co., 1957.

Gunther, Max. *Writing and Selling a Non-Fiction Book.* Boston: The Writer, Inc., 1973.

Writing the Modern Magazine Article. Boston: The Writer, Inc., 1968.

Jacobs, Hayes E. *A Complete Guide to Writing and Selling Non-Fiction.* Cincinnati: Writer's Digest, 1967.

MacCampbell, Donald. *Writing for Publication.* Cleveland and New York: World Publishing Co., 1966.

Newquist, Roy. *Counterpoint.* Chicago: Rand McNally and Co., 1964.

Reynolds, Paul R. *The Writing and Selling of Non-Fiction.* New York: Doubleday and Co., Inc., 1963.

Weeks, Edward. *Breaking into Print.* Boston: The Writer, Inc., 1966.

**The Writer's Manual
Book 4**

How to
Write
Historical
Fiction

By
Carole Fitzgerald Hayes

ABOUT THE AUTHOR

Carole Fitzgerald Hayes
has taught creative writing, freshman composition,
nineteenth century poetry and prose,
a two year program in world literature,
and conducted a seminar in detective fiction during her teaching career.
She has also
published book reviews and written advertising copy.
In addition to serving as a consultant to the authors' agency,
Porter, Gould and Dierks,
for the past six years,
she has also worked as a publisher's proofreader of scholarly books.
Ms. Hayes is married and the mother of two young daughters
in addition to her professional life.

TABLE OF CONTENTS

INTRODUCTION

Historical Fiction

". . . anything but history,
for that is bound to be false"

Robert Walpole

All historical writing, according to Paul Murray Kendall, is essentially an exercise of the human faculty that combines and associates — the imagination. To isolate a segment of time is to deal in metaphor, not truth. In Kendall's view, the novelist works from the data of personal experience, the historian from evidence that has survived time. Both writers work imaginatively, rubbing facts together in order to see their meaning.

Historical novels are fiction. Fiction is a narrative form in which a story is dynamically told. No matter how vivid the illusion of action occurring *now* a novel may give -- must give -- that action is past tense. In a sense, then, all novels are historical since their actions are related by the writer to the reader. And yet . . .

When a friend asks, "Have you read this? A first rate historical novel," the prospective reader's expectations do differ from those he might bring to the "non-historical" novel. Historical novels make more conscious use of the past, of the fact that a story is being told, than does fiction in general; however, the historical novel compensates for being in the past by giving a strong illusion of the present. If the past does not live, the novel dies.

No writer wants to sit on the ground and tell sad stories of the death of a novel, particularly one's own novel. How is the historical novel given life? Success here, as in any novel, comes through technique and vision. If a manual cannot provide vision, it can make certain suggestions about technique and offer examples from historical novels with comments from their authors on the nature of their art. (Incidentally, the field offers equal opportunity for employment: Sigrid Undset, H.F.M. Prescott, Zoe Oldenbourg, Marguerite Yourcenar, Helen C. White, Mary Renault, Cecilia Holland are among the names that spring to mind in any serious discussion of historical fiction.)

A novel can be divided into source, setting, plot, and character only for purposes of analysis, and even then the elements resist separation. One reads that somewhere long ago something happened, or is happening, and someone reacts; that is the story, or the beginning of a story. Still, this manual on historical fiction is arranged according to source, setting, plot, and character. Overlapping occurs. So does greater emphasis on sources and setting than would happen in a general commentary on the novel. Plot and character, it is probably safe to day, are more important than sources and setting in any novel, even the historical novel. But the historical novelist must make sources and setting part of plot and character; otherwise, the result may be dull narrative in which the research notes show, or a moody costume drama is what emerges.

Sources and setting in historical novels may be dustier than those used in other novels. Let the potential historical novelist who wonders whether his work will be dismissed as a mere period piece be consoled by one whose works were once incredibly classified as Gothic — Flannery O'Connor: "Fiction is about everything human, and we are made out of dust, and if you scorn getting yourself dusty, then you shouldn't try to write fiction. It's not a grand enough job for you."

"In some old magazine or newspaper I recollect a story, told as truth..."
Hawthorne begins one of his tales, "Wakefield." In alluding to "some old"
source, Hawthorne, who cannot even remember the name or nature of the
periodical, suggests a truth about writers of historical fiction: they can be
irritatingly vague about the roots of their work. To the historian, brooding
on the vast abyss of collective human experience, the historical novelist may
seem weightless. To the general reader the historical novelist, particularly the
one whose work is documented by charts, maps, and family trees, may seem
too heavily pulled down by actuality.The writer of historical fiction, then, is
caught between readers who insist on more facts and those who want
fewer. The distinction between things as they are and things as they are said
or thought to be is older than Aristotle, who spoke also of things as they
ought to be according to probability or necessity. The theoretical basis of
historical fiction rests here in this ground or air of "ought"; yet, the novelist
deals, too, with things as they are in historical reality and with things as they
are said or thought to be in legend or speculation.

Unlike Matthew Arnold's ideal critic who stands and sees life steadily
and sees it whole, the historical novelist moves by trial and error through
the maze at Hampton Court, the archives of the Vatican, the labyrinth
at Crete. The potential writer will search in vain for an infallible guide, but
saving hints may come through observing how various historical novelists
have worked with their sources. The authors to be discussed differ in their
methods of research and use of historical sources. Taken as a group, these
writers offer no "sense of the meeting," but are yoked together rather
strongly by their mutual faith (in varying degrees) in actual events. To any
question the reader might raise about historical or imaginary sources, the
poet's now maddening, now illuminating answer might be given: "I learn
by going where I have to go."

How important then are sources to the historical novelist? The question leads to other questions: How does the writer look upon sources? How much time is spent in actual research? How is the research transformed into fiction?

In *The Heirs of the Kingdom* (trans. Ann Carter, Pantheon, 1971) Zoe Oldenbourg says in her prefatory note: "This is not a historical novel." The author goes on to say what else the book is not — history disguised as fiction, historical pageant, scholarly work. After declaring any novel to be a portrayal of the human condition, Oldenbourg says "students of history may take comfort; the events described in their book are true." The work begins to sound very like historical fiction, in spite of the author's introduction. In commenting on what she thinks is the novel's accurate picture of the Medieval poor, the author points out that historians tend to give little information about these people. Besides having their source in the historical Crusades, the novel's main characters and "heirs of the kingdom" derive from the biblical version in James's description of the divine choice of the poor of the world as heirs "rich in faith."

Novelist Joan Sanders ("Getting into Historical Fiction," *The Writer*, August 1966) believes a good subject is one about which the general history is known — with gaps. But mere loss of records or lack of documentation except through archaeology cannot account for the success of novelists of ancient history such as Mary Renault, Marguerite Yourcenar, Thornton Wilder, or Robert Graves. In any case, for some of their works considerable research material was available, and the authors might be justly offended by the suggestion that they had failed to do their homework. When the sources are in fact scarce, a writer succeeds because of a general knowledge of a period and because of intuition, control, and craft.

In describing her approach to sources, Joan Sanders lists her necessities: a reliable general history, geneological sheets to keep characters straight, maps, diagrams of battles, charts of dates, appropriate pictures of all kinds, colored marking pencils, a loose leaf binder with dividers for places and things, a bibliography, a card file with a card for each character indicating other sources in which that character is mentioned.

R. F. Delderfield begins his novels by drawing a treasure island map ("Birth of a Saga," *The Writer*, November 1969). For *A Horseman Riding By* the author drew in and named every hill, valley, and family in a particular corner of the English west country before working on character and time span. Admitting that a novelist cannot check every line against actuality, Delderfield comments on the reception of "I enjoyed your novel but" letters from knowing readers who offer evidence that his research has been inadequate. Historical novelists should find such letters a source of consolation, realizing their readers enjoy the immense satisfaction of knowing something the novelist did not know.

In his prefatory note to *Julian* (Little, Brown, 1964), Gore Vidal cites Robert Graves' long bibliography in *Claudius, the God*, an answer to reviewers who seemed to think Graves had glibly made his previous novel *I, Claudius* out of the gossip of Suetonius. Vidal, although he modestly says he has not read all the relevant texts extant, includes a bibliography for his novel of the fourth century emperor Julian and the times to which we are heir. The author warns readers looking for Julian's famous last words that they will search in vain, for "Thou hast conquered, Galilean" is the fine rhetoric of Theodoret, whose church history was written a century after the emperor's death.

Historical novelists sometimes give detailed descriptions of source material. Before the first page of *The Kings in Winter* (Atheneum, 1968), Cecilia Holland presents three pages of background for her novel set in the times of Brian Boru. The sources begin in 999, the year of victory for Brian, king of Munster, over Danish invaders and Irish rebels led by Maelmordha, king of Leinster. According to the chronicles, Maelmordha, who hid in a yew tree during the massacre, had given bad military advice to the Danes. Maelsechlainn, king of Tara and head of the O'Niall clan, then surrendered the high throne to Brian Boru. The sources further tell of tribute brought in 1011 by Brian's old enemy Maelmordha, of the exchange of insults, and of another war. This time not only the Danes of Ireland fought on Maelmordha's side; they were reinforced by North Sea Vikings. Before the invasion the Danes were called to assemble in Dublin on Easter of 1014; Brian called his men to meet near the city by Palm Sunday. All these historic incidents form the plot of the novel, right? Not exactly, for Cecilia Holland uses the chronicles as background for the story of her invention of the character Muirtagh, his family and his feud.

In a note to *Until the Sun Falls* (Atheneum, 1969), Cecilia Holland gives the reader helpful information, in this case about the Mongols of the thirteenth century and the division of their empire among the heirs of Tenujin, Genghis Khan, whose holdings extended from the Volga to the Yellow Sea. Each heir ruled his own territory but was subject to the elected Kha Khan in foreign policy. The Mongol armies moved with the usual speed of nomads but with more than usual discipline and communication. A Mongol column could, and did during the European war, cover 270 miles in three days, since each man had a string of led horses to replace tired mounts.

Communication between separated columns was effective, even with one group in Poland, the other in Hungary, and a wintry mountain range in between. Mongol couriers carried messages along various waystations, averaging up to two hundred miles per day and making possible communications with the Kha Khan six thousand miles away.

After further details about Mongol warriors and their generals, clearly presented and supportive to the actual plot, the author notes that Psin and his family are her own creations, and that she altered the character of one Altun Uruk, a historical figure. Since "sometimes it's better to be understood than right," Cecilia Holland tells the reader she has used modern place names and familiar forms of Mongol words — e.g. *Ghenghis* instead of the more accurate English spelling *Chingis.* Quotations in the novel, except for those from the letters of Frederick II, are from the *Secret History of the Mongols;* neither source is used for its own sake but adds authenticity to the story and suggests the feeling of the novel. From Frederick, "Hence fear and trembling have risen among us, owing to the fury of these impetuous invaders." From Tenujin, "If heaven grants a way, you will embark in wars beyond the sea....Beyond the mountain rocks you will launch campaigns...Send back news on wings."

Going back to her first successful novel, *The Firedrake,* Cecilia Holland ("Writing Historical Fiction," *The Writer,* April 1968), says that she knew she would write a novel, probably Medieval, then decided to link the Norman conquest with an imaginary character riding through her mind, Laeghaire of the Long Road. Historical novels set around 1066 were already in existence, particularly Hope Muntz's *Golden Warrior* and Bryher's *Fourteenth of October,* as the young author was no doubt aware. With her own new character in whom to center the novel's perception, Cecilia Holland went on with her research and found several accounts and chronicles in disagreement as to what really had happened. She concluded that what happened was irrelevant and that most of the "facts" were assumptions. In the main faithful to the few undisputed facts, the author notes points of departure for the sake of her narrative. By the time of her novel *Rakossy* Cecilia Holland was working "all fiction but the bare bones," the Turkish invasion of Hungary in 1526.

Mary Renault, whose novels *The King Must Die* (Pantheon, 1958) and *The Bull from the Sea* (Pantheon, 1962) are based on the legends surrounding Theseus, explains her interpretation of the original material and which versions she followed — for example, the generally accepted view that the tribute youths sent from Athens to Crete were compelled to participate in the dangerous sport of bull leaping. The author is clear about what incidents she invented, such as the revelation of Phaedra's guilt by her son Akamas. The constant factors in the various stories are Phaedra's attempt to seduce Hippolytus, his silence in spite of her slander, Theseus' prayer to Poseidon, and the bull from the sea which kills Hippolytus. The Renault version differs from that of Euripides, whose Phaedra hangs herself, having left a note falsely accusing Hippolytus of rape.

The novelist does not accept those scholarly efforts which have "explained away in religious terms as the suppression of goddesses' shrines" Theseus' pursuits of women. A more likely and simpler explanation is to be found in the old aristocratic practice of piracy. Mary Renault does subscribe, however, to the scholarly assumption of two forms of divine kingship in ancient Greece; that of the Shore Folk and Minoans who worshipped the Earth Mother, and that of the people represented by Theseus, who worshipped the male Sky Gods. In the first or matriarchal religion, the king was an expendable consort sacrificed yearly that his potency might be renewed; in the second or patriarchal version, the king was a much stronger ruler who could nobly volunteer his life if the auguries required it. Thus, in some accounts, Theseus among the tribute victims through the casting of lots; in others, by his own choice. Mary Renault sees in Theseus' life the struggle between conflicting forces in Mycenean Greece, but he is primarily a character who in his own right interests the reader. Plutarch's epitaph is a source of the sympathetic treatment of Theseus: "His tomb is a sanctuary and refuge for fleeing slaves, and all men of low estate who fear the mighty, in memory that Theseus while he lived defended the oppressed, and heard the suppliant's prayer with kindness."

Because she uses her sources imaginatively and creates such highly readable fiction, Mary Renault has earned the praise of both general and scholarly readers. A reviewer in *Classical Outlook* suggest that her *Fire from Heaven*, a novel about the young Alexander, belongs in every classicist's library, and that even those who know well what will happen in the last twenty pages will read with bated breath to the end. Writers of historical friction, whether or not their period is classical antiquity, might profit from reading Mary Renault's novels and her clear explanatory notes on sources.

Also profitable would be the perusal of Maurice Druon's *Iron King* (trans. Humphrey Hare, Scribners 1956), at the end of which appears a set of numbered notes giving background. Included is information about the Knights Templar, the Cathari, various members of the French court of Philip IV, and the discrepancies arising from lack of international standards in dating the beginning of a calendar year. Had this sort of detail been provided in the text, the plot would have been interrupted. Coming as they do at the novel's end, the notes can be skipped by the casual reader and enjoyed by the curious who want to know more about Druon's use of sources.

Margaret Barnes, whose *My Lady of Cleves* (Macrae-Smith, 1946) offers a sympathetic view of the heroine and may strike some readers as costume romance, also cites her sources. From three visual records — Holbein's three-quarter portrait now at the Louvre, his miniature at the Victoria and Albert, and a portrait by an unknown German artist at St. John's, Oxford, the author concludes that Anne was not, as popular tradition has it, fat. That the miniature was sent to Henry VIII so he could have a look at his prospective bride, and that the Holbein of the novel falls in love with Anne diminishes the force of the author's argument. Although the reader appreciates Margaret Barnes's citation of Anne's letters, the Losely manuscripts, and the queen's "human and endearing" will, it is perhaps too much to hope that "most of the remarks made about Anne by characters in this book were in fact made by people who knew and saw her," unless the reader allows for loss in translation to contemporary idiom.

A successful historical novelist working in a period closer in time and space is James Sherburne. In an endnote to his *Way To Fort Pillow,* *(Houghton Mifflin, 1972)* the author says that his greatest debt for this novel about his character Hacey Miller is William Townsend's *Lincoln and the Bluegrass.* Sherburne also cites John Rogers' *Birth of Berea College,* Eastham Tarrant's *Wild Riders of the First Kentucky Cavalry,* Margaret Leech's *Reveille in Washington,* Otto Eisenschiml's *Celebrated Case of Fitz John Porter,* the Wade subcommittee's report on the Fort Pillow massacre, John Allen Wyeth's *Life of General Nathan Bedford Forrest,* C.M. Clay's *Memoirs,* and T.W. Higginson's *Army Life in a Black Regiment.*

Sherburne further notes that J. Winston Colema drew him a detailed map of antebellum Lexington through which he could imagine he was walking the town's streets. The late Cassius Clay provided facts on the poisoning of his great-uncle. The novelist had access to a collection which included old bowie knives and hospitality at several libraries, among them Chicago's Newberry. After examining so much conflicting evidence on Fort Pillow, Sherburne concludes: "I can't swear it did happen this way, only that it *could have."*

Not that a thing is recorded to have happened in such a way, but that with due consideration of all the evidence, it could have, such is the imaginative approach taken by Hugh Ross Williamson in his *Historical Whodunits* (Macmillan, 1956). Williamson, a historian whose field of concentration is the first half of the seventeenth century in England, is also the author of historical novels and plays. *Historical Whodunits* resists classification, having elements of both straight history and detective fiction. Potential writers of historical novels will find in this book how recorded facts may be used as the bases for various theories which may explain those facts or fill in the gaps in evidence. Considered in his work are such baffling, unsolved cases as the death of William Rufus, the princes in the Tower, Perkin Warbeck's identity, Amy Robsart's death, Kirk O'Field, the Gowrie conspiracy, the Gunpowder Plot, the murder of Sir Thomas Overbury, the assassination of Colonel Rainsborough, the Campden Wonder, the mystery of James de la Cloche, the murder of Sir Edmund Berry Godfrey, and the Appin murder. Like a detective, Williamson examines all the clues — and when more than one plausible theory arises — he offers all the possibilities, showing which solution is most likely and why. The method is hardly mere speculation but a cross between the observations of Sherlock Holmes and the application of Aristotelian probability.

In an introductory chapter on the relationship between history and the writer, Williamson raises several questions, many of which spring from the difficulty if not impossibility of determining the significance of recorded facts and their significance in relation to the recorder. Even one day in a person's life poses problems. Does one know the meaning of facts he may record on a given day? And are these the significant facts? Can these facts be evaluated in their relationship to other people? Williamson argues that when an observer is part of the process he is observing, no "science is possible, and that academic history is a combination of myth, propaganda and guess work." As an example the author considers the period 1485-1688, citing the propaganda furnished by Tudor against Plantagenet, Protestant against Catholic, Parliament against the Stuarts. In the eighteenth century, Robert Walpole, whose political career covered almost fifty years and placed him in a position to know the difference between what in fact happened and what was said to have happened, lay dying. When he asked to be read to and was in turn asked his preferences, he said, "Anything but history, for that is bound to be false."

Beyond propaganda, pure or diluted or even accompanied by antidote, Williamson contends that there remains in history the strong element of myth, which grows out of the human desire for meaning. Some historians believe in the myth of progress; others in the missing acorn myth, in which the observer looks at an institution not as it is today but as it was or ought to have been in its embryonic state. Both progress and acorn myths are attempts to find a pattern in a multitude of events. The Judeo-Christian myth or that of Marxism, on the other hand, do not attempt to construct a philosophy of history but instead see history as part of philosophy. The Jew or Christian sees history as God's dealings with the world, the Marxist, as the class struggle for power.

Yet another myth, that of the Great Person, sees history as a form of fiction and as such requires good guesswork as well as sound research. In Williamson's view, the "higher forms of history [are] the historical novel and the historical play," since these forms allow scope for the imagination, while academic history forbids the invention of thoughts and speeches not a matter of record. Still, the novelist must do the research of the academic historian lest his work be costume stuff. The writer must find out or create the general and particular circumstances of a character, his circle of people, family, economic status, temperament, religion, politics, health, appearance, clothes. The writer comes to know his characters as well as his own family, with a knowledge that can come through the sensitive exploring of letters, diaries, public documents and other primary sources when available.

The challenge of the historical novelist Williamson compares to that of the classical dramatist whose audience knew in advance how the play would end. What can the novelist do with the old and hard facts? Approach them through a fresh interpretation of what is known rather than through an invention that will not fool the reader. The historical novelist makes the reader see and feel that the ending of his book is inevitable, not in terms of history, but of the novel itself.

In dealing with historical mysteries the writer must begin at the climax and work backwards — asking, like any good detective, questions about people and motives. In discovering the motive the writer may realize in some cases that there is no mystery, only facts hidden by myth or propaganda. Of the death of the princes in the Tower Williamson says, "The interesting question for the historian is not, Did Richard III murder the Princes? but, When did Henry VII order their death?" The novelist seeking to clear up historical mysteries needs not only a comprehensive knowledge of a period but the ability to state a problem without distortion in the simplest possible terms.

Readers of Josephine Tey's *Daughter of Time* (Macmillan, 1951) or Jeremy Potter's *Trail of Blood* (McCall, 1970), novels not based on Tudor propaganda, may already have exonerated Shakespeare's foul bunch-backed toad Richard, but they will still benefit from Williamson's version in *Historical Whodunits.* Television viewers who may remember the Earl of Leicester's wife, Amy Robsart, from the series on Elizabeth I, may be in for a surprise in Williamson's conclusions about the case. Students who recall reading Overbury's "Characters" in seventeenth century literature classes will be interested in the account of his murder. Williamson here provides an example of his own detective methods and willingness to change his mind should his latest theory contradict statements in his own previous books. Another historical whodunit, "The Death of William Rufus," fascinates the reader while linking the king's death with three forms of dualism in the period — Catharism in the church, philosophic paganism outside it, and witchcraft and fertility worship. The best thing about a work like Williamson's is that a reader is never compelled to accept the author's interpretations but is shown how to go about interpreting sources.

At the end of H.F.M. Prescott's *Man on a Donkey* (Macmillan, 1954) a graphic source is reproduced from *Collectanea Topographia et Genealogica,* 1838. The plan is of Marrick Priory, as it was probably fifty years after its dissolution. The novelist says in an endnote that most of the episodes in which well known historical figures appear — Henry VIII, Katherine of Aragon, Anne Boleyn, Wolsey, Cromwell, Princess Mary, Thomas More, Cranmer — are grounded in documentary evidence. For example, Queen Katherine's words to Montfalconnet and to nobles and clergy in 1531 were reported to the emperor by his ambassador, Anne Boleyn's conversation with Kingston upon her arrival at the Tower in 1536 was repeated by him to the king. Although the nuns of Marrick are the novelist's inventions, she did draw their names from a list of those pensioned at the dissolution. Evidence as to the character of the prioress may have been scant, but Prescott found what evidence there was suggestive. Documentation exists for Lord Darcy, while Julian Savage and Gilbert Dawe are fictitious. Robert Aske's early life is fabricated, as is his association with Margaret Cheyne, but both characters are based on historical persons. The incidents in the Pilgrimage of Grace have their factual counterparts in massive evidence found in records and letters of which Prescott made extensive use, although the war prevented her getting to the original manuscripts and forced her reliance upon printed versions.

Because it is a novel, *The Man on a Donkey* is a work of the imagination; yet, the author was careful to adhere to known facts with two minor exceptions cited. Prescott further notes that her account of the death of Robert Aske differs from those of other writers; her authority is Writhosley's detailed report of the execution.

Sometimes historical novelists luckily find sources close to home. Zoe Oldenbourg was born into a family of scholars; Sigrid Undset was the daughter of archaeologist Ingvald Undset. Working and talking with her father led to her knowledge of the Viking and Medieval periods in Scandinavian history. The depth of Sigrid Undset's knowledge is barely suggested by the few explanatory notes which accompany *Kristin Lavransdatter* (Knopf, 1923) and give the factual background for some of the incidents in that great novel.

In *Sword at Sunset* (Coward McCann, 1963), Rosemary Sutcliff attempts to recreate from fragments of known facts, from likelihoods, deductions, and "guesswork pure and simple" the man and war leader Arthur — or what he may have been. The novelist has kept some elements of the traditional Arthurian matter because of their "atmosphere of truth." The original double framework is preserved; sin carries its own retribution, and brotherhood is broken by love between the leader's wife and his best friend. Also followed are the theme of the sacred king's divine right to die for his people; the earliest named Arthurian companions, Bedwyr, Cei, Gwalchmai (with the difference that Bedwyr is Guenhumara's (Guenever's) lover instead of the later French addition, Lancelot); the presence of the king's hound and white horse. Rosemary Sutcliff discovered some factual basis for a connection between Medraut and Cerdic, the half legendary founder of the kingdom of Wessex, and she offers her own interpretation of the archaeological find at the Roman fort Tremontium, the bones of a dwarf girl and nine horses.

The author acknowledges other authors from Gildas to Geoffrey Ashe as well as personal sources. A Canadian friend sent a poem "Hic Jacet Arthurus Rex Quondam Rexque Futures," whose origins were traced by an intelligence corps sergeant and his wife. A major in an east Anglian regiment spent three afternoons helping the novelist plan Arthur's campaigns in Scotland and work out a tri-color staff map of the victorious battle of Badon. Rosemary Sutcliff's open attitude toward all possible sources may inspire potential historical novelists to seek information wherever it is available.

To an even greater degree than *Sword at Sunset,* T.H. White's *Once and Future King* (Dell, 1960) shows how worthwhile it can be to rework old sources like the Arthurian matter. As Robert Graves has said, the legends themselves form a strange web of history, saga, and religious myth, made still stranger after the Norman Conquest and the resulting Breton additions to the early Welsh stories. The historical Arthur was not a king but a British cavalry general who won a decisive battle against the Saxons at Mount Badon in 517 and lost another battle and his life near Glastonbury. The scene of death was a place sacred to an ancient pagan cult as well as the site of Christian shrine connected with Joseph of Arimathea. Although the members of the Round Table are Christians fighting under the cross, and although there are elements of communion, an apostleship of twelve, and a leader whose return is prophesied, Arthur's sponsor is Merlin, son of the devil and a nun. According to the scholar Loomis, Corbonek, the grail castle, derives its name from a magic cornucopia belonging to Arthur's double, Bran. A Welsh bardic tale identifies Arthur with Bran called Arddu, or Arthu, the Dark One, whose return is prophesied. Giraldus Cambrensis and Edward I are said to have seen Arthur's coffin, but another Welsh legend says the grave will never be discovered.

The immediate sources of Thomas Malory's *Morte d'Arthur* were Norman French romances and the English alliterative epic, *Morte Arthur.* Although Malory's tales are uneven, he does give some coherence by concentrating on certain episodes. Little time is spent on physical detail; Malory's reader knows only that Arthur's eyes are gray. By modern standards the storyline is uncomplicated. By Robert Graves' reckoning, four-fifths of Malory's minor plots spring from chivalrous incognito practiced by Arthur and Accolan, Gawain and Uwayne, Balan and Balin, Tristram and Lancelot, Palomides and Lamorok — whose disguises are shed at a crucial moment to reveal not an enemy but a friend, perhaps a relative.

Fascinating in its confusion, the Arthurian matter has attracted writers through the ages. Milton had considered Arthur as a poetic hero but changed his mind in favor of a biblical source. Tennyson's *Idylls of the King,* if its characters do resemble Victorian ladies and gentlemen, shows further evidence of abiding interest in ancient sources. Contemporary writers such as Rosemary Sutcliff, Anya Seton, Dorothy Roberts, Arthur Quiller-Couch, Mary Stewart, and Henry Treece, have reworked the material. But it is White's *Once and Future King* which Orville Prescott in *The New York Times* called "a glorious dream of the Middle Ages as they never were but as they should have been." White's novel begins with Arthur as a boy nicknamed "Wart" and shows Merlin as an absent minded magnician. The characters are all there -- Guenever, Lancelot, pure Galahad, and evil Mordred. The sources of character and plot, or their suggestion in the sources, may be generally available, but White's imagination remains the primary source of *The Once and Future King.*

The Arthurian sources are numerous and hard to trace specifically in a contemporary historical novel set in an ancient times. Easier to see and closer to the times is the way in which Hawthorne used historical sources. Readers will think immediately of *The Scarlet Letter,* but a look at some of the author's shorter fiction is equally revealing. In his story "My Kinsman Major Molineux," Hawthorne begins by citing the annals of the Massachusetts Bay Colony which record that of six governors during a period of forty years after the surrender of the old charter under James II, only two men enjoyed occasional peace. Two were imprisoned because of popular insurrection, one was probably driven out by a musket ball, another harassed by bickering with the house of representatives. Lesser officials suffered, too — but the reader, says Hawthorne, should avoid "a long and dry detail of colonial affairs" and dispense with an account of the circumstances which caused "much temporary inflammation of the popular mind." Actually, the only reason the reader dispenses with such an account is that Hawthorne does so. It is solely in the first paragraph that the historical setting is clearly given. The second paragraph introduces Robin on a moonlit evening, away from home for the first time, searching for his kinsman. The search and discovery of Molineux as a leader in disgrace, tarred and feathered, is a further indication of the historical period described and dismissed at the beginning of the tale.

Similarly, "Roger Malvin's Burial" begins with the historical setting and the presence of moonlight, this time in a figurative sense: "One of the few incidents of Indian warfare naturally susceptible of the moonlight of romance was that expedition undertaken for the defense of the frontiers in the year 1725, which resulted in the well-remembered 'Lovell's Fight.' " A paradox appears, for while "Imagination, by casting certain circumstances judiciously into the shade may see much to admire in the heroism of a little band...," on the other hand, "history and tradition are unusually minute in their memorials of the affair." What then is imagined and what recorded? Hawthorne concludes the introductory paragraph by pointing out that in spite of his use of fictitious names, some of the incidents will be recognized.

David Lovejoy in "Lovewell's Fight and Hawthorne's 'Roger Malvin's Burial' " (*New England Quarterly,* December 1954, reprinted in Agnes McNeill Donohue's excellent *Casebook on the Hawthorne Question,* Crowell, 1963) argues that Hawthorne in his extensive reading would have seen numerous accounts of the battle between the Massachusetts farmers, led by Captain John Lovewell, and the Indians of Pigwacket. In Lovejoy's view, historical sources are apparent not only in Hawthorne's first paragraph but throughout the entire first half of the story. In a contemporary report by Rev. Thomas Symmes, in a ballad "Lovewell's Fight," and in an article on the Indian troubles by "J.B.H.," Hawthorne had access to material for his plot. Historical incidents include wounded men left in the forest when the soldiers retreated and the use of a handkerchief tied to a bush to mark the place in which a soldier awaited rescue. Lovejoy admits that although Hawthorne relied on historical sources for the first half of "Roger Melvin's Burial," the second part is a psychological study and product of the author's imagination. The reader might conclude, then, that the true source of the story lies less in the facts and more in what the facts suggested to Hawthorne.

A book that is not quite a historical novel — perhaps not quite a novel at all — is the lighthearted biography of an author's friend whose history and background span almost four centuries. The book is Virginia Woolf's remarkable *Orlando, a* philosophical life of Victoria Sackville-West. The central figure in *Orlando* changes in time, behavior, style, and even sex, according to social and literary periods. Although, as David Daiches says in *Virginia Woolf* (New Directions paperback, 1963), most readers will miss many points in the novelist's attempt to cover her friend's physical and literary ancestry, the book succeeds because of several memorable passages and its revelation of character creating and created by history. In her preface, Virginia Woolf acknowledges friends who helped her with her work -- Defoe, Browne, Sterne, Scott, Macaulay, Emily Bronte, De Quincey— literary sources signifying the direction often taken in modern prose. In Virginia Woolf's imagination a recorded fact becomes a springboard. Daiches particularly admires the lively descriptive passage on the great frost of 1604 with its images of flounder trapped under the clear ice of the Thames, an ice so thick bonfires will not melt it. A thaw eventually occurred, of course, and with it a climactic moment in the book.

Jose Maria Gironella describes his sources for *One Million Dead* (trans. Joan MacLean, Doubleday, 1963), written fifteen years after the end of the Spanish civil war and much of it away from Spain. The author cites his personal experience of life in both war zones and his preconceived attitude corrected by the painful facing of facts and by charity. Gironella questioned several eyewitnesses, Spanish and foreign, reviewed periodicals, photographic archives, and pamphlets. His reading included almost a thousand post-war books, monographs, and diaries. Aware that one's own testimony and that of others may suffer from exaggerations and omissions, Gironella came to lean heavily on daily newspapers and pictures. After the massive work of informing himself of the facts, the author says that nevertheless his aim was to write fiction, not history, and that he has always reserved the novelist's recourse to imagination: "What has always been important to me, all my life, is primarily the psychological rigor, the circumambient atmosphere."

That John Steinbeck's use of sources in *The Grapes of Wrath* struck some readers as uncomfortably accurate is shown by the negative reaction, to the point of suppression in certain regions, when the novel first appeared. Among sympathetic critics there were those who could not decide whether the work was primarily literature or social document. As late as 1974 a speaker for the United Farm Workers told an audience that if they wanted to grasp the plight of the migrant workers, they ought to reread a chapter from *The Grapes of Wrath.*

The struggles and triumphs of another group — the Swedish farmers of Minnesota in the mid-nineteenth century — are presented through characters in Wilhelm Moberg's *Unto a Good Land.* Readers unfamiliar with Moberg's work may have seen the movies based on it, *The Emigrants* and its sequel *The New Land.*

Documentary or literary sources can be used as points of departure in the manner of revisionist history or of plain fun. To enjoy such a novel the reader must have at least a general idea of the background which the author distorts. The range of these serious romps is wide -- John Gardner's *Grendel.* Thomas Pynchon's *Gravity's Rainbow,* Gabriel Garcia Marques' *One Hundred Years of Solitude,* John Barth's version of the John Smith and Pocahontas story in *The Sot Weed Factor,* Charles Portis's cornspun spoof of the Western, *True Grit,* George Fraser's Flashman series which takes as hero the villian of *Tom Brown's School Days,* Anthony Burgess's *Napoleon Symphony,* or his *Vision of Battlements,* which gives a view of military life on twentieth century Gibraltar in a framework of Vergil's *Aeneid.* Sources can be mined for suggestions of detective fiction plots, as in the case of Jeremy Potter's *Trail of Blood,* Josephine Tey's *Daughter of Time,* Michael Innes' *Hamlet, Revenge!,* and John Dickson Carr's *Captain Cut-throat.* In 1974 a novel on the creation of Scotland Yard was published: John Creasey's *Masters of Bow Street.*

Eloise Jarvis McGraw, in advising would-be historical novelists to immerse themselves in the past, says that for six years she lived in ancient Egypt during which time she wrote two novels (The Writer, 1959): *Mara, Daughter of the Nile* and *Pharaoh.* For writers who cannot reach primary sources or eyewitness accounts (which may be unreliable, anyway), McGraw recommends extensive reading of non-fictional works on a given period. Her own notes represent only a ninth of what is in her head, but some notes are necessary; how many and their style of organization differs according to author.

What is most important about the use of sources is how they are used.

Writers of historical novels should avoid putting in everything they know, lest the background overshadow the plot. In reworking five dozen times a passage in *Mara, Daughter of the Nile* which was to give the reader necessary information, the author wrestled with the problem of how to make the reader think he wanted that information. The final device was to endow the information with secrecy, to make one character (and the reader with her) worm the secret out of another.

In *The World of Fiction (The Writer,* 1956), Bernard DeVoto stresses the principle that the novel must keep moving through time, space, or emotion. While definition, differentiation, and analysis are sometimes necessary, these elements in the modern novel are disguised or made part of the action. A historical novelist would profit from reading a passage (beginning on page 257) in which DeVoto contrasts the approaches of Fenimore Cooper and Mary Johnston in works separated by some seventy-five years. Cooper's *Pioneers* contains essays crammed with information on frontier life; *The Long Roll* by Mary Johnston dramatizes historical material through the actions of several characters, military and civilian, some of whom exist only to make information part of the novel. The contemporary reader is not likely to accept the presence of a character who is there obviously to dramatize a phase of Stonewall Jackson's Shenandoah Valley campaign. Neither Cooper's straight expository method nor Johnston's dramatic sweep of characters, however, is a good plan for the modern historical novelist. A successful book may contain astonishing amounts of factual material, but it must be integrated with character in action. That action is not limited to battle scenes but covers quiet moments as well.

Another possible source for the writer lies in the history of ideas. The potential historical novelist may be intent on illustrating ideas through his characters, a feat which can be achieved if the writing is specific and concrete. DeVoto praises Arthur Koestler's *Darkness at Noon,* in which integrity, imprisonment, the breaking point, destruction of personality, and death all pivot on the ideas at issue — but ideas absorbed into characters.

Almost any first rate historical novel has sources in ideas and events. Such sources play not before the reader at all times but in the underground. To the historical novelist whose work in progress has led into a labyrinth, the only way out is by following any thread that leads not to the realm of essays but to the place where fiction lives. "No ideas but in things."

TWO

SETTING

Setting is vital to any work of fiction, if only for the homely reason that "nothing happens nowhere." In historical fiction setting needs to be developed to the point that makes the past vividly present. That point lies midway between the line of too few details, which makes the reader feel amnesiac, and the line of too many details, which makes him feel he is wandering through a wax museum.

False details in time, place or person may be tolerated. Vergil used anachronisms in *The Aeneid*, and Shakespeare gets away with his seacoast in Bohemia. Keats has even earned praise for naming Cortez as discoverer of the Pacific Ocean. Such errors seem almost charming, in keeping with the truth in which all fiction is grounded. To err in a physical fact is not necessarily to destroy what Jung called psychic reality. But there are details which are false both physically and psychically. Unless the historical novelist deletes errors of this sort, he risks spoiling the reader's illusion. An electric blanket on a Victorian bed, a Mississippi River running west to east, a Henry VIII celebrating his golden wedding anniversary — any one may stop a reader dead. Good fiction preserves illusion, keeping the reader's disbelief in a state of willing suspension. As Wallace Stegner says, it is not faking in fiction that is bad, but faking badly.

No formula exists for the correct proportion of details in historical fiction, or for how such details should be presented. Some touches are light enough to lose the reader but hold him sufficiently captive until his attention is bound to the plot. One may here think of Sigrid Undset's classic *Kristin Lavransdatter*, on which a friend once remarked: "Great! Just stick out those fifty pages of life in a fourteenth century Norwegian manor." Informing the reader about such life is necessary, as it turns out, not only to the right feeling of the period but to the whole story. The characters Lavrans, Kristin, and Erlend cannot be fully understood apart from their environment. Nor could the characters' struggle, essential to any plot, be fully developed in another time and place. It is necessary that Lavrans be a wealthy landowner, from a family of builders, loyal to the king, that he romanticize the monastic and conventual life lived by those set apart to pray for outsiders burdened by the darkness of worldly affairs, that he have feelings both of love and ownership for his family, that he be an observer of traditions almost without thought about them.

Daughter Kristin does not favor her father's choice of a husband for her, although she admits to herself marriage to Simon would be better than life in a convent. To that convent in Oslo she goes — to stay for a year before being formally betrothed to Simon. For Kristin, removed from the familiar setting of home, the convent proves not to be what her father saw as a place of refuge from the world, but her gateway to it, and to a character opposed to Lavrans, Erlend Nikulaussen, a rebel against his time and place. The similarities and differences between Kristin's childhood home and the household over which she presides as wife of Erlend and "Mistress of Husaby" are intrinsic to the story. Sigrid Undset has earned critical acclaim not so much for her knowledge of the architecture of the period as for her insights into the daily lives of people in their time and place in history. The author's other vast novel of the period, *The Master of Hestviken,* is not what a reader once called it, "another *Kristin Lavransdatter,* only male." Similarities between the novels are outnumbered by differences — one of which occurs in the setting — dark, neglected Hestviken and its effect on the general atmosphere of the book. A novel set earlier in Scandinavian history, *Gunnarsdatter,* devotes less space to physical detail, mostly because plot and characters call for a simpler setting.

In *The Man on a Donkey* (Macmillan, 1952), H.F.M. Prescott begins her chronicle of the prioress Christabel with a description of her father's house in Yorkshire at the end of the fifteenth century. Built by her grandfather, the stone house is solid but not so large as the warehouse in which wool is stored. The Cowper house is a place where gold is hidden and silver cups are displayed, and where the reader is almost immediately introduced by swift narration to the dying grandfather making his will with the aid of an old monk who had been his childhood friend. Instead of dwelling on the deathbed scene, Prescott shows Brother William writing the will, sighing, relaxing his toes which had been cramped upward with the effort of composing in Latin, and switching to English. Not only is attention diverted from the dying to the living man, the reader learns painlessly of the eventual death of one language and its replacement by another in official documents.

V.S. Pritchett once described poor historical fiction as "faked up costume stuff." Readers dismiss as frivolous a novelist who is too anxious about what his characters are to put on, but the right degree of attention to clothing helps sustain the illusion of historical fiction. Remember the masks of classical drama? An author need not be inspired to a philosophical discussion of the meaning of clothes in the fashion of Carlyle's *Sartor Resartus,* nor convey a theme through imagery like Macbeth's "borrow'd robes." When the historical novelist uses clothing as part of the setting, he should keep in mind the characters. What is to be avoided is an excess of detail which results in the reader's feeling that the characters are dolls dressed and paraded or stiff figures in a tableau. Clothing can be used as a means of identification; or. as Congreve and writers of detective fiction prove, naked is the best disguise. Used selectively, references to clothing can distinguish people — even animals, as in Prescott's allusion to the "nuns' neat black-stockinged Swaledale sheep."

The author's homework in the history of costume should not be obvious but should support the total effect. Henry James's celebrated principle of being "one on whom nothing is lost" is hardly an injunction to spare the reader no details of a character's dress. The realistic use of detail is as psychological as it is physical: it is only in moments of extreme boredom that one person notices everything another is wearing. Even then, with the possible exception of police workers and private investigators, most observers notice only a few physical elements which contribute to a total impression. The reader as observer can take in only so much; he will not be induced to *see* a woman who is 5'6", weighs 123 pounds, is wearing a three piece print pants suit rather badly matched in the inseam of the left leg, of floral print of white, green, red, and lavender on a navy background, carrying (not, incidentally, a dangling participle, that, for it is still the character being described, although the reader may have lost sight of her by now) a large sisal handbag woven in Yucatan on an afternoon in the rainy season when....

If a reader is exasperated by such attention to contemporary dress, he will be no less annoyed by a character from the past whose costume is rendered in similar excruciating detail. The reader needs a few details; he must see something but not everything, lest the plot run like a fashion show commentary. How to keep a description moving by making it into an incident is shown in a scene in *The Man on a Donkey.* Taking delight in disorder, Henry in the presence of a few intimate members of his court unravels a ribbon from Katherine's underskirts. The incident is not so much about clothing as about the differences between characters — husband and wife, king and queen, England and Spain.

In *A Watch in the Night,* Helen C. White uses clothing to reveal character in a dramatic moment. The hero's young wife, a spectator at a tournament, is seriously injured in an accident. Examination of her unconscious body reveals that underneath the costly gold dress her husband had given her she wears a hair shirt. Set in any other time and place, the incident would not work; in this novel of Medieval Italy the young woman's hidden asceticism and her husband's recognition of some hard and life changing truths are elemental to the plot.

In *Kristin Lavransdatter* Sigrid Undset takes a young girl's interest in clothes, typical of a character her age, as an opportunity to provide cultural information on Medieval Norway. A detail such as Kristin's fine linen hosen shows that her family has means sufficient to make her fashionable. More significantly, the clothing gives the author a chance to show the reader Kristin's youthful vanity and prepares for the impressionable state in which she surrenders to Erlend and the exciting life he represents.

Another young girl interested in clothing, more as a sign of status, is Christabel in *The Man on a Donkey.* When her parents tell her at the age of eleven that she is to be a nun, she decides after her older sister's lying in that the convent will be better than marriage — even if nuns' clothing is not so fine as her sister's grey velvet nightgown with white fur. In any case, Christabel has noticed that a prioress who attended the baby's christening wore silk and that her open skirt showed a damask petticoat, rich if black. When she is a nun, Christabel tells herself, she will wear silk and have a gold pin. Later, when Christabel's parents deliver her to Marrick Priory, she gives a sharp cry. Although the prioress interprets this as a pang of separation, the reader sees that Christabel's concern is for the bundle of clothing and possessions she has brought from home on which a dog is threatening to urinate. Still later, when Christabel has become cellaress and treasurer, she receives gifts willed her by her father. Included are the wall hangings she remembers from her childhood with which she can dress her chamber. Instead of stirring up filial memories, however, the old hangings arouse her suspicions that her brother may have cheated her out of the fine new Arras hangings of which she has heard but never seen. All these touches are clues to the character development of the prioress Christabel is to be. The reader knows, of course, what that character is to be like as early as the second page, for H.F.M. Prescott actually begins her novel with its ending and flashes back through chronicles of the main characters. The reader knows, then, that Christabel in the end is an angry woman -- angry not with the king for suppressing abbeys and priories, but with God for tricking her into thirty years of conventual life only to take away the temporal power she has gained during that life.

A similar passage of time marks Kristin Lavransdatter in different fashion. From the young girl interested in clothes, to whose costume Sigrid Undset devoted considerable detail, Kristin is transformed into the older wiser woman who one morning almost objectively contemplates her shrunken breasts that have nursed seven sons. (She is to bear and lose an eighth.) Naked *is* the best disguise; the scene reduces the character's sense of individual identity and increases the feeling of universal mortality.

Clothing conveys not only individual characteristics and cultural information but a means of providing the author's value judgments. In David Stacton's *Signal Victory* (Pantheon, 1960), a novel set in Central America, the white *huipils* or smocks worn by the women are signs that in spite of the scarcity of water, the people have high standards of cleanliness, a fact which the writer uses to gain the reader's sympathy for the "primitive" and antipathy toward the scruffy conquistadors.

Mary Renault's Theseus in *The Bull from the Sea* looks at his team of Athenian bull dancers with whom he has returned from Crete. He realizes why the homecoming seems strange: there is nothing except his light hair recognizably Hellene about him. He still wears the foreign costume of the Cretan bull ring — the gilded cinch belt, the peacock-eyed embroidery, the silk kilt, eyes shadowed with kohl, and the costly gauds given him by Cretan fans instead of the "grave jewels of a kingly house."

Writers of historical fiction are not the only authors who use clothes and furnishings. Tolstoi was not above such details as Natasha in lilac or Anna Karenina in a white dress with black ribbons. Flannery O'Connor has praised Flaubert for remembering to put list slippers on the villager listening to Emma Bovary playing the piano. (The reader who has forgotten that passage might remember the more intimate setting of Emma and her lover and a reference to her "our slippers," an image of their whole passion.) The contemporary novelist Thomas Pynchon, whose *Gravity's Rainbow* is set in World War II, makes much of uniforms, outlandish suits, a pig costume, nylon repair kits. Of a more serious mien, there is Hawthorne's scarlet letter emblematic against Hester's somber dress, or his minister's black veil. The list could go on, for, in Oscar Wilde's words: "It is only shallow people who do not judge by appearances. The mystery of the world is in the visible, not the invisible."

A practical rule for any writer, but especially for writers of historical fiction, is never to throw in any image of which one is not quite sure. Atmosphere does not require a catalogue of concrete details. A slavish devotion to facts in the hope of being realistic may destroy the sense of reality the author was trying to create in the first place. Wallace Stegner once told the story on himself of how, through the unnecessary and inaccurate use of information on the process of threshing, he alienated the wheat farmers of Saskatchewan who knew better than he and for whom his mistake spoiled the illusion vital to any novel.

The historical novelist can look at a history of costume or an ancient cookbook not so much for the facts as for the implications of those facts. The heavy keys worn by the chatelaine may show her control in the absence of her warrior husband over the estate. Less glamorously, the predominance of soft over chewy foods, or tough foods reduced to mushy consistency, in Medieval recipes suggests something about utensils and cooking methods and more about the dental health of the diners. According to one author, most people by the time they were teenagers had suffered such tooth loss as to render the eating of fibrous foods virtually impossible. But wait — the inclusion of that sort of detail might spoil a scene; the reader does not want to see the Medieval chatelaine at the high table gumming her way through a feast. The reader of Prescott's *Man on a Donkey* is spared the sight of Julian's husband Laurence at table (a kindly man who never intentionally offends anyone but who is afflicted with blackened teeth and foul breath), but Julian does cook for him. In one scene she plans a menu, recites a charming rhymed recipe for flawnes which gives ingredients but not amounts, and confesses she has trouble with her pie crusts. The passage could have sounded like a treat from Betty Crocker, but H.F.M. Prescott writes with the art that conceals art and through a few selected details finds the poetry of the domestic setting in sixteenth century England. Or, more accurately, since she is a novelist and not a lyricist, she finds the right prose.

In another scene Prescott shows Lord Darcy interrupted in his writing of a list of items for his steward to buy in London. On the list are sixty Spanish onions, nutmeg, citron, a butt of malmsey — an entry the reader, remembering how Shakespeare and possibly Richard III drowned the Duke of Clarence, will accept as authentic. Another incident in *The Man on a Donkey* reveals Dame Christabel, in her usual pragmatic style which the reader has come by then to know and dislike, ordering the gardener to plant gooseberry bushes, raspberry canes, and strawberries.

In culinary matters a *few* details satisfy the historical fiction fan. The author should recall the eighteenth century poet's just condemnation of epical celebrations of custards. A full menu is superfluous, but the right touches can give an earthy sense of the times. One has only to think of Herodotus reporting the quantity of garlic and onions consumed by the slaves building the pyramids. Or of Dickens' Abel Magwitch in *Great Expectations* and his vivid primal memory of eating carrots in a field. Or the gardens of Alan Watts in his *In My Own Way.* Or Keats's midnight banquet scene with its delicacies "soother than the creamy curd." Or Pynchon's food romps in *Gravity's Rainbow:* a quick one on candies with wildly incongruous soft centers and a longer, disgusting food fantasy that breaks up a formal dinner.

These instances are brought up not to encourage writers to flesh out thin plots with well researched culinary allusions but as evidence that the mundane things of life do enter serious literature and help shape it — as surely as spices influenced the crusades and a famous potent beverage is immortalized in the meadhalls of our earliest literature.

Wallace Stegner once said writers should spend no more than two hours checking on background material for a novel. The historical novelist cannot get by so easily, for he deals with a greater number of actual people or events whose accuracy must be verified. In historical fiction the violation of a well known fact can destroy the illusion necessary to the reader. The contradiction of a little known fact may pass unnoticed, which makes actual characters about whom little or nothing is known attractive subjects to many authors in the field. What is most important is getting the right feeling of the times. Whether taken from legend or chronicle, a character who emerges as psychologically incredible cannot be defended by the writer on the grounds that "legend has it" or that an event is actually true. The reader of historical novels, like any other reader of serious fiction, demands psychological rightness over absolute fidelity to the facts. The facts cannot be ignored but should be interpreted with care.

The historical novelist has the same source of settings as any other writer in his own store of sensory impressions. This source, although it may not be the whole collective unconsciousness of the race, may be the author's private share of universal human experience. Good settings come about through giving sufficiently vivid impressions to the reader — impressions the author has had in his own experience, an experience which of course includes reading.

Several writers stress early impressions stored away almost out of memory. Babs Deal explains her southern towns as settings which grew out of what was too good to waste, eighteen years of life lived and breathed in a certain atmosphere and region. Willa Cather once claimed that the novelist was formed before the age of nine. Flannery O'Connor felt that anyone who survived childhood had more than enough sensory experience out of which to write.

Childhood impressions may remain so clear that the author draws on them over and over, perhaps in a way of which he is not fully aware. What works for the novelist in general works for the historical novelist in particular: setting is rendered through direct or indirect appeal to the reader's senses. Purists might insist that the sense that is really functioning as one understands a work of art is the aesthetic sense rather than the usual five or six; even so, the other senses of author and reader do come into play. The sights, sounds, smells, tastes, and feelings of a writer's summer morning fuse with the reader's own impressions to make a new summer morning that has a life of its own, existing in its own right, going on forever. In spite of meteorological evidence for climactic changes over the centuries, the historical novelist can count on the timeless quality of a summer day, if only a slight thaw in a frigid zone.

The historical novelist gives enough details to let the reader know it is the past that is being made present; yet, no matter how remote the landscape or the time, some signs of the familiar must be provided. The familiar is the measure of experience: "This is just like home," says the weary traveler. In novelist Heimeto von Doderer's opinion, "A man steps out in Sydney no differently from the way he steps out in Dubrovnik." Or, to state the case negatively, in terms of unfamiliarity, there is the Victorian theatre goer whose response to *Antony and Cleopatra* was, "How strangely unlike the life of our dear Queen."

According to the *Preface to the Lyrical Ballads*, a work planned as a joint venture, Wordsworth and Coleridge divided their labors: one was to make the familiar unfamiliar, the other to make the unfamiliar familiar. It sounds like a game, a game most novelists probably play both ways.

Eloise Jarvis McGraw in *Techniques of Fiction Writing* offers her own experience in familiarizing a contemporary reader with a house in ancient Babylon. To avoid an architectural digression that would have lost the reader, she built on the fact gleaned from her research that the Babylonians kept pet dogs. While a dog in a house is familiar to a reader, the custom of keeping water jars cool in recesses in the floor is unfamiliar. That dogs in hot weather seek cool places to sleep is well known; that this Babylonian dog sleeps near the coolness of the water jars links the known with the unknown. The story is not interrupted, then, when the character Thoth enters the room and drinks from the water jar. The reader is not distracted by having to be told something like "It was customary among the Babylonians to keep water jars cool by means of..." The story keeps moving, or the reader's illusion of movement is preserved.

As the convenience of the water jars is a sign of the comfort of things, so the reader can be counted on for familiarity with the orneriness of things. A failure of power steering is not the same as a broken rein, but the irritation of characters when things break down is universal. If the exact cause of a character's irritation involves things unfamiliar to the reader, he will at least understand the way the character feels. Effective settings are made possible through the selective use of specific and typical details, presented almost accidentally, as things appear at any given moment to the characters in the foreground.

Rendering the familiar is the stock in trade of some of the best writers of stories of horror or suspense. The everyday world seems to change before the reader's eyes, as the good things of the day begin to droop and drowse. A lovely, calm scene provides just the place for sinister deeds. In this connection one thinks of the "pleasant air" of Macbeth's castle, or of the house in "The Jolly Corner," a ghost story by Henry James.

It might seem that the challenge of the historical novelist is to make the reader familiar with what is strange, but another approach exists. The writer may take a character or event the student of history knows by heart and show him something he did not know. In this method the reader is given what Frost called the surprise of poetry, remembering something that one didn't know that he knew.

Any school boy knows about the Wars of the Roses, the white rose of York and the red of Lancaster. In reality, as Paul Murray Kendall says in *The Yorkist Age* (Norton, 1962), there was only one rose, the white of York. The red rose was a Tudor, not a Lancastrian, device. A novelist setting his work in the Yorkist period might surprise his readers by creating peaceful scenes. After all, what about the Wars of the Roses? Where are the violent events remembered from an evening in the Shakespearean theater? As Kendall sees matters, the Yorkist period was a time of comparative peace in contrast to those grim days of Tudor land enclosure, debasement of the coin, misery among the lower classes. As for the Wars of the Roses, there were none -- in any modern sense. Tudor propaganda was inventive in elaborating on whatever strife existed in the previous era in order to show the greatness of strong Tudor rule.

Enough on symbolic wars; now on to literal roses. The historical novelist can create a garden with its sights and smells from his own gardens — roses, honeysuckle, rosemary, sweet basil. Modern hybrids must be weeded out, or the sense of the past will be broken for the reader who knows anything about horticulture — and a number of readers probably do. But violets and primroses are as good then as now. The scent of a dark root cellar is timeless, as is that of wet leaves. What the historical novelist must keep from his reader's nose is the odor of mothballs, or whatever devices make the story sound dated and good only for storage in some forgotten corner. The successful novelist may work in dusty corners, but the work should give signs of life in the present in the light of past experience.

People who have a lively sense of the past — and who else would be writing or reading historical novels — experience it as present. An author might be inspired just by living near Stonehenge or the Coliseum or the field of Gettysburg. But lots of people who live near monuments of the past never write historical novels. Most of us cannot see the past without the help of someone who sees it first and more deeply. Any novelist is concerned about his readers' seeing: above all, said Conrad, he wanted to make his readers *see*.

Although television offers hardly the sort of seeing Conrad had in mind, that medium has nevertheless opened some magic casements to the past. In the Masterpiece Theatre series on Henry VIII and Elizabeth I, viewers saw a regal past; a domesticated and more recent past was revealed in the episodic *Forsyte Saga* and in *Upstairs, Downstairs.* Nostalgia and escapism cannot explain all the reasons viewers go to Walton's mountain, any more than costumes and furniture can sustain the interest of an audience.

How might the historical novelist heighten sensitivity to the past and what it has to say to the present? Settings which are authentic but not distracting are part of the process. Libraries are time machines to the historical novelist who needs old newspapers, letters, diaries. Antonia Fraser, whose biographies of Mary Stuart and Cromwell have received critical acclaim, says she never begins her work without looking first at any letters her subject has written that may be available, Of course, she has access to the British Museum. Writers living great distances from primary sources and without means of traveling to them must rely on material closer at hand. The local library may lack a rare book room yet have on its shelves books like *Warwick the Kingmaker, Richard III,* or *The Yorkist Age* by Paul Murray Kendall, which clearly show the author's use of primary sources and which provide background for novelists working in the last decades of the fifteenth century.

When possible, actual visits to a scene may help — if the writer is not put off by candy bar wrappers floating on Walden Pond or distracted by crowds bustling by an archaeological treasure hidden in plain sight in a Mexico City subway station. Probably it helps to wander lonely as a cloud over such scenes, but solitude cannot always be arranged. The writer gifted with a sense of the living past is able to feel its presence beneath the hum of tourists or the noise of traffic. The rest of us may feel the spell of the past only when walking alone over a path in the jungle to a small ruined Mayan temple. One may wonder then about the relationship of the present setting to the past. How has the landscape changed? Was the foliage once more dense? Does the iguana now darting across the stone wall resemble its ancestor here when the ancient civilization flourished? Given the ubiquitous sacred rattlesnake on the temple frieze, what can be said about the rattlesnake population of the past? Of today? — but here the charm is broken, for if in spite of the guide-book's assurance that snakes are found here only in the rainy season one recalls having seen a henequen worker wearing high protective boots ... Practical considerations about safety call the researcher away from fantasies about how this landscape looked in the deeper past. And yet, the experience of that remote age is as real as the immediate practical reason, escape from a possibly present rattler, which sends one back over the tangled path and rather quickly at that. Perhaps the moment of the sense of the past can be relived later, an experience recollected in tranquillity. The stillness of that hot noontime will return to the writer who will create out of it a scene in which a Mayan Indian boy seven centuries ago is fatally bitten by a snake. Must the novelist have visited Yucatan before he can create a realistic setting? Of course not. Although such a trip might help, so would a journey through Thomas Hardy's chapter in *The Return of the Native* in which a middle aged woman is stung by an adder. There are topographical differences between jungle and moor, but the essential experience suffered by both characters is a bite from a poisonous reptile. The various elements of each setting must be made part of each character's experience. The Mayan boy and Mrs. Yeobright are separated by an ocean and several hundred years; however, either setting can be made familiar to the reader, and both places have in common the external details of a day of oppressive heat in a somnolent landscape and the internal feature of growing apprehension about the characters meeting a snake.

The geography of the setting is one challenge of the historical novelist; chronology presents another. What is the best way for the author to answer the reader's question of what time it is? No absolute rule exists. In some novels the reader is expected to enjoy wandering about for a few pages, catching the flavor of the setting, eventually arriving at the approximate date of the work. Or, a novel could begin: "It was 1503 in the village of Chislehurst . . ." A better beginning would be: "John was born in 1503 in the village of Chislehurst . . ." Such a start is rather unexciting; yet it has the merit of not gearing the reader to demand any event from the year other than the birth of John. Had the year been 1066 or 1492, the reader would have had his expectations of the obvious aroused — and such expectations would probably lead to some measure of disappointment. These years are too specific and heavy with historical events. If a date must be mentioned at the outset, it ought to be at least a little before or after a watershed year in history. On the other hand, introductions such as "In seventeenth century England," or "The scene was America in the nineteenth century," are too general. The whole problem could be avoided if the author rids himself of any compulsion to tell the date at once. When dates are intrinsic to the plot, one approach is to cast the novel in the form of chronicles or make use of devices that would normally be dated, such as letters or diaries (actual or fabricated); the years may then be unobtrusively given as they go by. Even when the year appears at the top of each page to indicate a section of a chronicle instead of a chapter title, the reader will not object. He may not even notice, but if he does, he may welcome what is literally a sign of the times. Mentioned dates in a historical novel are like the wrinkles of age; they come as no surprise, but no one wants to emphasize them unduly. The writer who harps on the dates and how long ago his story was is in danger of killing off the lively sense of the past he hopes to sustain until the last page.

Although chronology and geography are not one and the same thing, in the historical novel these elements cannot be separated for long. The reader wonders almost simultaneously when and where he is, and if he wonders this way too often, chances are the writer has failed to create for his characters and plot a sufficiently local habitation and a time. The historical fiction fan does not expect a travel guide or a time line, but he does want some satisfaction of the geographic and chronological senses. Alfred Duggan in *The Right Line of Cerdic* (Pantheon, 1961) does not announce the date on the first page, but he plunges the reader immediately into the group of chamberlains and chaplains standing outside the Lateran palace in Rome. The reader already knows from the dust jacket and the map of England inside the cover that this historical novel has something to do with the life and times of Alfred the Great. Rosemary Sutcliff is less specific at the beginning of *Sword at Sunset.* She begins with some timeless sense impressions of a full moon, the branch of an apple tree, shadows on the wall during a windy night, before she moves to the shadow of that branch the harpers sing of, the claiming of whose nine silver apples can make clear the way into the web of the novel. Such is the right mood for the author to evoke in a novel springing from the Arthurian matter.

The historical novelist thinks about his reader and what knowledge he brings to his reading of this particular book. Perhaps the reader can be counted on for at least general knowledge about American life at the turn of the century but would need more background for Poland in the same period. If the setting is exotic or remote in time and place, the author does not need to dump an avalanche of information in the first few paragraphs. The reader would prefer to get his own bearings from the evidence the author provides. Sometimes it is fun to move over a landscape for a time as a stranger, feeling the uncertainty summed up by L. Frank Baum's Dorothy when she announced to Toto that she did not think they were in Kansas anymore. Oz, like any other foreign place, takes time to assimilate. In the best historical fiction the reader's sense of time and place deepens as the story develops, because setting is part of the story. Sometimes in the midst of a scene sudden recognition occurs; for example, the reader may realize he is seeing a forgotten phrase from a history text if an incident like the Defenestration of Prague is made into an episode in the plot. One reader of Mary Renault's *Last of the Wine* remarked about a young character, "So *this* is Plato!" In retrospect the same reader was grateful to the novelist for her fresh interpretation of the philosopher as he might have been in his youth. Character is developed partly through setting, whether in the place where the games and sports of antiquity are played or in the backgrounds for quiet dialogues. An austere and rocky stretch of beach provides the setting for a fiercely compelling love scene which conveys without explanatory or moral comment the Greek attitude toward homosexuality; the setting itself seems to be part of the characters.

Time and place in the historical novel can be suggested, then filled out to expand the original impression. An obsidian blade in the first paragraph suggests a setting in pre-Columbian Central America. A pack of Barbary apes indicates that Gibraltar is the scene. The location in the first instance could be a museum; in the second, a zoo — but these are only possibilities. Readers have always preferred probabilities to possibilities. Still, more details than a weapon or a group of animals will be needed before the setting will fully emerge.

Readers often expect a historical novel to have several settings. In satisfying this expectation, the author should avoid giving the impression that the characters are being ruthlessly transferred around for the sake of a change of scenery. The various settings can be strengthened when they represent more than geographic facts. One thinks of Kristin Lavransdatter and the early security of her father's house, of her growing rebellion at the thought of marrying Simon and moving "just down to Formo," of her own household at Husaby from which her husband Erlend absents himself for long periods, of a scene of difficult travel by ship with Kristin trying to get one of their young sons to make water between the boards, of the rustic farm house in which husband and wife meet after a period of estrangement, or of the scene in which Kristin rushes through the dark but numinous woods because her nephew is near death and she would propitiate the forces of the old religion as well as St. Olav, the Virgin, and the God of the Christianity to which she adheres during the other ninety-nine percent of the novel.

Like Sigrid Undset, H.F.M. Prescott uses a variety of settings to keep the story moving in *The Man on a Donkey.* Marrick Priory on the day of its dissolution is seen deserted and illumined by the winter sun, surrounded by oak, beech, and ash trees except for the patch grazed by the sheep. The scene is changed in time not place by a reference to the fine weather of other days when the nuns embroidered and spread the convent laundry to bleach against the greenery of that clearing, a memory in sharp contrast with the priory's current emptiness. The details of the setting are homelier than Shakespeare's image of "Bare, ruined choirs where late the sweet birds sang," but the sense of desolation is very similar.

In a different Prescott scene, a lord's "closet" is suggested by the presence of "butter yellow parchments," evidence of land and office grants to ancestors, and "newer, larger, more floridly written in the present style of the Chancery" documents, more recent grants to Lord Darcy. The estate of the Askes, of whom Robin is to figure so largely in the uprising called the Pilgrimage of Grace, is set in the north marshy country, with pools and twisting channels, green ings for cattle grazing — a country whose low lands are seasonally washed when the Derwent rises. Fishing is good in such a place, a fact which provides the natural background of the incident which occurs during one of the many quarrels between young Robert Aske and his older brother Kit. When Kit charges at his brother, his fishing pole enters Robin's eye. The accident results in the loss of the eye and other significant changes in Robin.

[The word Prescott uses to denote the Aske meadows is *ings;* consequently when she writes of "green ings," readers may falsely assume a printer's error. Although an extant song celebrates the rain in Spain, composers have traditionally neglected the ing in spring. Perhaps Prescott meant "greenings," as in the "greening of America." But readers whose consciousness has been raised either by residence in northern England or by possession of a hefty unabridged dictionary will recognize an ing when they see one. Webster's *New International Dictionary* (2nd ed.). for example, defines *ing:* "ON *eng*, a low pasture or meadow. Chiefly N of England." Curiously, the cross reference for the previous entry *Ing*, see *Frey*, indicates the same origin as the *Ing* of Anglo Saxon sources. A coincidence is thereby revealed, for *Frey* is related to fertility — a likely condition of low pasture-land subject to seasonal floods, as illustrated in ancient agricultural practices along the Nile and in the homely wisdom of the saying, "Greedy folks build by the river," attributed to a grim observer whose identity cannot be traced. Such a statement casts aspersions neither on Egyptian farmers of the Old Kingdom nor on the Askes in the reign of Henry VIII. The Aske family lived in the backwaters of English history until son Robert, during the Pilgrimage of Grace, took arms against what he considered to be a sea of troubles.

As for contemporary usage, no person interviewed, American or English, regarded *ing* as anything but a suffix. This note, it is modestly hoped, will increase the vocabulary of readers anxious for a substitute for *gin* in anagrammatical games. Doers of crossword puzzles, ever alert to the possibility of short and tricky words, are advised to watch out for *ings.* The editor of the present manual, acting on a hunch that he would find an ing or two in a book set in Beatrix Potter country, has conducted a recent and unsuccessful search through the volume in question; however, he remains confident that ings did in fact exist in the rough draft of the original manuscript. Meanwhile, among modern novelists, the field — or the ing — is undivided. The term appears to be the exclusive preserve of H.F.M. Prescott.]

Settings can also be made to exert direct influence on the action. An army can be most dangerous in late autumn, as in Duggan's *Right Line of Cerdic,* when it moves easily over stubble and short grass and finds food from the harvest stored all around. Ships crossing during a stormy season are more likely to be scattered than in calmer weather--which means that if a writer knows generally what months are stormy he will not have to whip up a special storm. Not that a writer has to be scrupulous about an almanac: Wallace Stegner knew a writer who kept records of lunar phases so that a full moon on a given date in a novel had its basis in fact, but that kind of zeal eats up time that could be spent writing. Although full moons can play a role in stories other than romances or tales of werewolves, only the most fanatical reader of historical novels might insist that every fictional moon have its factual counterpart. Possibly an author needs to check in case of a total eclipse on record which is also part of his plot. Probably in most cases the reader would be none the wiser, having no access to ancient weather reports or records of the moon, and the author need not worry about such details.

In historical novels, particularly those by contemporary writers, setting is often identified closely with character and plot. Besides giving time and place, a single introductory sentence can reveal the speaker, as in Mary Renault's *Bull from the Sea*: "It was dolphin weather when I sailed into Piraeus with my comrades of the Cretan bull ring. Knossos had fallen, which time out of mind had ruled the seas...The smoke of the burning Labyrinth still clung to our clothes and hair." The speaker is Theseus, whose youth was the subject of Renault's earlier book, *The King Must Die.* Her *Bull from the Sea* is divided into four sections, designated by place names: Marathon, Pontos, Epidauros, Skyros. The author is counting on at least some vague associations from the reader, but each section fills in what he does not know or has forgotten about the history and legends born in these places. Reminiscent of the Pindaric "Water is the best thing there is," each section begins with some reference to the sea. The first has already been quoted; the second, "Half Athens saw us off at Piraeus when we had sacrificed to the Lady of the Winds." Theseus alludes to the threat of piracy and says that in defense of their own shores kings "sometimes sailed out to take vengeance." (The statement also prepares the reader to be sympathetic to Theseus should he engage in any acts of piracy.) The third section of the novel begins, "I have sailed all the seas since then." For Theseus, seeing new things "is better than wine or poppy and fitter for a man." He briefly rehearses his passing between Scylla and Charybdis and his catching a siren and living to tell about it. In Skyros, the fourth section, Theseus says that his memories of the remote past are strong but that he has forgotten exactly when in the proximate past the god's hand struck him: "I know I was at sea with Pirithoos...and seeing Melean pirates sailing hull-down with loot." On windy Skyros, an island shaped like a bull's head, Theseus, now an exile and guest of King Lykomedes, dreams of the past glories of Marathon. Waking, he dreams beside the swelling sea of swimming under the moon, plunging with the dolphins.

The sea is more than a source of images in the novel; from its waters comes the bull of Poseidon which causes the death of Theseus' son Hippolytus. Mary Renault assumes some familiarity between reader and legend. This familiarity is increased by details of the setting which strengthen the story: the scent of Crete in Phaedra's clothes, the sight of blood when

Hippolytus' wounded horses must be slain, and the priest-doctors who vainly minister to the dying youth, warming him as his corpse grew cold, even trying some old forbidden magic of the Shore Folk. For this violation the priestly leader is soon struck down by the swift death of Apollo, angry over this attempt to raise the dead. Here setting, character, and plot carry the idea of the Greek religious struggle between earth-mother and sky-father cults.

In quite another sort of setting, that of James Sherburne's *Way to Fort Pillow*, the reader perceives the miseries of wartime through the sense impressions of the narrator. With Hacey Miller, the reader feels the damp night along the Kentucky River, when the dew falls from the trees like rain, making uniforms sodden, and "The opaque gray mist that rose from the river was simply a rarified kind of water. Every breath of air we drew into our lungs brought drops of water trickling down our windpipes. Very soon the men started coughing..." Yet Hacey bears up cheerfully, "if Morgan had come down that road he would have heard the sound of our massed bronchial discomfort two miles away."

In a happier setting, Hacey recuperates from a battle wound at home in an October when "tobacco plants turned from green to gold, and the ears hung heavy on the cornstalks, and the walnuts and hedge apples fell unexpectedly from their branches and soon lay on the ground like oversized marbles."

John Gardner's *Grendel* (Knopf, 1971) contains this delicate setting for remembered violence: "The tender grasses peek up, innocent yellow, through the ground, the children of the dead. (It was just here, this shocking green, that once when the moon was tombed in clouds I tore off sly old Athelgard's head.)" And later, "Such are the tiresome memories of a shadow-shooter, earth-rim-roamer, walker of the world's weird wall." In some of his insights Grendel seems more man than monster; in fact, Grendel says that men, along with deer, rabbits, and bears, are incapable of making fine distinctions, because "(That is their happiness): they all see life without observing it."

Setting is part of the tone of a passage. In Heimeto von Doderer's *Waterfalls of Slunj* (trans. Eithne Wilkins and Ernst Kaiser, Harcourt, Brace & World, 1963), the opening paragraph subordinates scenery to character and the novel's past to its present. The hill in southwestern England, lovely as it is, serves mainly as "the spot where Robert Clayton — he was twenty-seven at the time — first saw the girl who was to become his wife (and for that matter still is)..." A different tone is set in a much later passage beginning,

"Late autumn and winter were the best time of year from the business point of view taken by Finy and Feverl .... In a damp and misty season the male sex, or that section of it that is given to prowling on the loose, is more susceptible than ever to the appeal of receptive cavities where one can huddle away." The first setting seems distant in time, place and tone when compared to the intimacy of the second scene.

A novel which is technically not historical fiction but which nevertheless gives a sense of the sweep of time and place is Willa Cather's *My Antonia*. Consider the narrator, who first heard of Antonia when he was ten and on what seemed "an interminable journey across the great midland plain of North America." Later, at his grandparents' place in Nebraska, he feels the motion of the earth "as if the shaggy grass were a sort of loose hide, and underneath it herds of wild buffalo were galloping, galloping..." (The passage may appeal scientifically as well as aesthetically to the reader familiar with the excavations at Nebraska's Hudson-Meng bison kill site.)

In her prologue to her historical novel, *Death Comes for the Archbishop* (Knopf, 1959) Willa Cather begins on a summer evening in 1848 with three cardinals and a missionary bishop from America who dine in villa gardens in the Sabine hills overlooking Rome. The book's next time setting is 1851 when a lone horseman is seen with a pack mule somewhere in central New Mexico. Like the journey at the beginning of *My Antonia* this trip and its setting play tricks with the character's sense of time. In the Southwest the sameness of the country makes the rider feel he has been standing still, although he knows he must have gone through thirty winding miles among the conical red hills, shaped like Mexican ovens. The similar shape of the juniper trees of yellowish green gives the traveler (and the reader who perceives through the traveler) a sense of "geometrical nightmare" from which he is suddenly awakened by a single, different juniper, the "cruciform tree" which gives its name to the first chapter. Later, in a more specific setting — the low plain between Laguna and Acoma —the traveler-bishop sees rising from the flat sea of red sand, rock mesas whose general Gothic shape reminds him of cathedrals. The very topography suggests the remains of an ancient city. Here, as in the description of the great buffalo herds imagined under the earth in *My Antonia,* the setting acquires a layer of scientific authenticity for the reader familiar with recent discoveries about the mesa country of the Southwest.

Such settings, although they seem to exist both horizontally in space and vertically in time, are simple in their immediate effect upon the reader. Willa Cather through a few selected details gives the reader the joy of recognition, but she does not intrude upon her story.

Some writers, especially among contemporary historical novelists, choose to give fewer details than Willa Cather. Cecilia Holland prefers in *Until the Sun Falls* to suggest the scene through dialogue, moving the reader immediately into the action. On the other hand, Zoe Oldenbourg in her *Cities of the Flesh* (Pantheon, 1963) writes a more detailed introduction: "One warm, flushed evening, on a feast day, hawks were soaring and swooping like arrows in a fiery red sky while magpies and wood pigeons fluttered in terrified circles and the air rained blood." At first glance the people appear incidental to the setting: "The ladies on their palfreys were strung out like a necklace of bright colored gems against the brown and russet trees..." Yet among the women watching their hawks one soon emerges clearly, and the hero Roger de Montbrun finds her as beautiful as she is devoted to the Catharist cause. The passage, which may strike some readers as a shade too purple, does not exist for its own sake; actually, the scene is blood red and prepares for the story set in the times of the Albigensian crusade, as that deep conflict and eventual civil war in twelfth century France was called.

In Zoe Oldenbourg's *Heirs of the Kingdom* considerable space is given to the setting of the walled city of Antioch, with emphasis on its strong fortification which includes a moat on two sides formed by deflecting a river. Within a week the crusaders' zeal has changed the landscape: the hills "lost their dark verdure and were transformed into timber yards." The joy with which the crusaders hack down cedars, oaks, and pines makes up for their lack of skill. Amid fallen tree trunks, wood chips, and strips of bark, "They had never dreamed of such freedom: these rich forests all to themselves, the trees of these ancient forests falling one by one beneath the ax, to be stripped of their great branches the way an animal is skinned." The destruction of the trees around Antioch foreshadows a later scene when Jerusalem has been invaded and the crusaders walk barefoot "over the bodies of the dead, by now so thoroughly trampled that they lay like a deep red litter in the gateway, heads and ribs smashed, bones protruding through the flesh, a tangle of blue entrails mixed with scraps of clothing." Still later, the Christian Greeks, who had rejoiced in the crusaders' victory, now look upon the soldiers looting bodies and find it "hard to believe that these wild men could be inspired by feelings of piety." Zoe Oldenbourg can play a descriptive passage for all it is worth, but she is equally capable of devastating understatement. If the passages from Oldenbourg's novel suggest a grim truth about historical fiction fans, that they expect a bit of gore, the writer should remember that *The Heirs of the Kingdom* is a long novel, that only a few passages have been isolated, and that the work as a whole is most significant for its scenes of the everyday life of the poor.

Cecilia Holland in an article in *The Writer* (October 1969) points out that sieges are boring and may bore the reader. Although she included a siege in her longest novel to date, *Until the Sun Falls*, she exercised care lest it drag out and lose the reader. Many historical novels end rather too conveniently with a battle; the author decided to resolve her plot through the Mongols' withdrawal from a battle. The cause of their retreat was not military weakness but an accident thousands of miles from the battle scene.

James Sherbune's *Way to Fort Pillow* belongs to that group of historical novels which do end with a battle. The device works well here, and there is an epilogue whose setting is several years after the Civil War. During the war and well into the novel, the hero and narrator, Hacey Miller, a white officer with black troops, arrives at the fort to be told by a sentry that the place is a stagnant backwater. Later — in the understatement of the novel — the guard admits there is a little current. The action, toward which all the previous actions of the novel have been rising, is the massacre at Fort Pillow. Sherburne devotes seven short paragraphs to the description of this "ugly but impressive installation." The physical details of river, bluff, and steep ravine are to figure in the climatic battle scene and need to be at least generally fixed in the reader's mind. The actual battle does not happen until the next chapter, but Sherburne wisely spends time — what seems to be almost leisure time — on the topography and the characters who are to be in the battle. The men are shown at ease: a few are concentrated upon while most are background figures (Miller's command is forty troops). Although the setting is presented in the straight description of Hacey Miller's narrative, the characters are reported by him in action and dialogue. The entire novel, of course, and the reader's perception are lodged in Hacey's memory.

Because the groundwork has been laid, the novel's last chapter is free to begin without being slowed down by detailed physical description of the fort. Now there is only the atmosphere of "wet fog and quiet cursing and a sense of fear" when the troops wake to the sound of rifle fire. Although the massacre seems bad enough, the narrator recalls that "the real horror of Fort Pillow" began after sunset. Once the Confederates had penetrated the walls, the fighting had lasted only fifteen minutes. The ultimate horror comes when the bushwhackers search the bodies for valuables. Wounded and playing dead, Hacey feels filthy hands search his mouth for gold fillings. Luckily he has none. Hacey, unlike his tortured black friend Star, survives. Eventually, in the peaceful setting of the epilogue, Hacey looks south to the blue mass of the mountains, toward Wildcat and Lebanon, toward Beaufort and the Sea Islands, toward Fort Pillow. In spite of the pain and the blood and the dying associated with that last place, Hacey Miller's final judgment is that he has lived in a good time. In a more recently published book by James Sherburne, *Rivers Run Together* (Houghton Mifflin, 1974) civil strife is given a different setting in time and place: Chicago and the 1960's.

The author who uses a famous place for his setting knows the reader will have his own picture in mind. The challenge here is for the novelist to give a few touches that will seem right, to let the reader feel good about his knowledge of a place but also to suggest things about it that the reader may not have known. Consider the successful and lively setting in which an important event is about to occur, the sentencing of four Knights Templar by an ecclesiastical court. The chapter is "At the Great Door of Notre-Dame" in Maurice Druon's *Iron King.* A cordon of archers keeps the crowd away from the space in front of the cathedral, but curious heads appear in every window. At seventy years old, Notre Dame is a work in progress, its white stone illumined by the pale sunlight that has dissolved the mist. The light pierces the lacework of the rosewindow, giving rose shadows to the statues. If Druon were to continue with the physical description of such a well known landmark, even if the view of Notre Dame is what it must have looked like early in the fourteenth century, the narrative would fall into the style of a guide book. To save the scene from turning into a picture postcard, the author turns the reader's attention from the architectural wonder to the chicken sellers who usually did business mornings in front of the church and who are now forced back. A cock crows, not symbolically, and feathers float "head high in the air." Later, when sentence has been pronounced and two of the convicted men protest their innocence and are supported by the crowd, the chickens are most lustily heard from again. With the birds screeching in the background, the Tribunal itself "like a flock of terrified guinea-fowl hurried into Notre-Dame and had the door quickly shut behind them." In this case, sanctuary is incongruously sought by the alleged dispensers of justice.

A far different kind of time and place is found in Delderfield's *Theirs Was the Kingdom* (Simon and Schuster, 1970). This long novel begins with "A View of the River" in 1878 and concludes with "Another View in 1889. In the earlier setting the reader is introduced to a noontime world, a sprawl of sheds and warehouses where carters and stablemen munch bread, cheese, and penny pies, and London sparrows look for crumbs of pastry. The scene is different at dawn or dusk, when only a pair of robins come, hoping to be fed by Adam Swann, ruler over this transport kingdom, whose office is in an old belfrey. The odor of the Thames in summer is a sour whiff, "a compound of bilges, decaying flotsam, spoiled vegetables, drowned cats, and half-starved, ownerless dogs." Debris is spread along a twenty foot margin of "hard packed bluish mud that was the permanent residue of Plantagenet, Tudor, Stuart, and Georgian sewage." In midwinter, when the novel actually begins, the river smell takes fourth place behind the odors of a nearby soap factory, a tannery, and horsedroppings. Having spent twenty years of business life with an office in this location, Adam Swann is used to the smells and would not abandon his peak in Darien from which he can feel England's pulse. Swann does travel the distance to his home, of course, and he takes frequent business trips throughout the country, but his heart is in his London office. Yet, elevem years later he retires from "this octagonal remnant of a Medieval nunnery" where more than files and mementoes have been stored: "The place was full of ghosts and he was already one of them."

I   In "Change of Landscape," Adam's wife Henrietta awakens in what seems in her husband's absence to be "about an acre of bed." A storm has apparently brought down a great three-hundred year old oak. Any storm makes the house seem to Henrietta to be a ship, with its structure creaking, groaning, stirring, whispering. As the mother of a large family and mistress of many servants in this large old place, she has learned to enjoy calm periods in the midst of a "domestic turmoil that less experienced women would have mistaken for anarchy." Sometimes Henrietta Swann accompanied her husband on business trips, leaving her "shore problems behind," but not this time, and the storm outside resembles her uncharacteristic inner disquiet. Through this storm, almost as the fulfillment of her intuition and restlessness comes a young man from a neighboring farm with the startling news that . . .

But this discussion is concerned for now only with the middle-aged woman in her present setting, "Tryst," who as a young girl had felt that reapers in a field were part of a grand design, controlled by an unseen master. Now Henrietta is working out, or trying to, the design of her children's lives, their advance on the horizon.

How unlike her old house of Tryst the Swanns' eldest daughter, Stella, finds "the value like stillness" of her bridegroom's house. Although Tryst was old, its surfaces gleamed and smelled of lavender and resin, while Courtlands is in bad repair, its metal trimmings dull or broken, its smell of mildew and dry rot. It is in this anonymous and dreary place that Stella discovers her husband is a homosexual and her father-in-law a lecher. On the night of the storm that awakened Henrietta, Stella escapes. One of the reasons the plot does not fall into the suds of soap opera is Delderfield's careful use of setting to illustrate character. His people are revealed in harmony with their environment sometimes; in sharp contrast to other times, as is the case with Stella, who struggles against the environment of Courtlands and its characters.

Later in the novel, the Swanns' scholar gypsy son, Giles, is shown in a happier setting in Wales. Giles meets the girl Romayne when he gives her help she does not really need in getting out of a river. Easily persuading himself that he is hopelessly in love with her, he sees Romayne as the personification of the landscape in its wild beauty and quickly changing moods.

The Swanns' eldest son, Alex, is seen in yet a different place: he is a young soldier in Africa, under a cloudless blue sky, wide and empty as an ocean, and again, on a "wide and dusty plain under an incredibly tall sky, where the mind made a compound of past, present, and future..." with the sun "a ball of bedstead brass." The troops Alex commands are Basutos, good natured tribesmen who are unequal to a Zulu attack. It is only when the first Basuto screams— clowning, Alex thinks —and falls that Alex looks out over the scorched landscape and sees what he cannot readily identify but which reminds him of plum jam or a wilderness of berries or of tarpaulins advancing. Then he realizes what it is that is moving toward him and the Basutos, "a mass of men, crouching and advancing behind an oxhide shield, moving on the double."

After the defeat at Isandlwana, Alex escapes, crossing a river in spate. In the shallows he splashes past a Zulu removing his assegai from the throat of a dead Kaffir, but there is no time for a horrified reaction. All are running as if they were killing rabbits for sport on the riverbanks near Tryst. But, unlike home, the waters here are icy and the current swift. Delderfield's insertion of a familiar home scene heightens the contrast between the old familiar place and the frantic present scene.

On the homefront, Delderfield spends less space on actual settings to illustrate life beneath the shining surface of Victorian England; however, he does present the world of poverty and degradation through the perceptions of Swann's ward, Deborah Avery, who devotes herself to bringing social injustice to light. Instead of coming in actual scenes, much information is given through such devices as newspaper reports and the responses they elicit from some of the major characters in the novel.

Any discussion of setting in historical fiction keeps turning to matters of plot and character. Remoteness of time and place cannot make the historical novel; yet, the writer must work carefully on the setting. The reader of novels asks, "Who? What's happening?" The reader of historical novels adds, "When? Where?" The successful historical novelist answers all the questions simultaneously, by rendering time and place as part — and a very substantial part — of plot and character.

THREE

PLOT

Arguments over whether it is plot or character that is primary are like speculations about who came out, the lady or the tiger? Or which came first, the chicken or the egg? Literary theories shift back and forth, but in practice plot and character resist separation. Aristotle's ideas about the primacy of plot have been invoked to explain the fascination of detective fiction with its "sheer plots." In these stories character does seem to take second place. It may even be true that the popularity of detective fiction in certain academic circles proves beyond the shadow of doubt that teachers of literature need a break from in depth characters and their streams of consciousness. Yet the term *whodunit* suggests strongly that at least two characters must have been involved in the plot, even if one of them is dead from the outset.

Northrop Frye, finding the Aristotelian concept of tragedy applicable to all fiction and commenting on the primacy of plot, holds that while plot is necessary in a work, it is difficult for a reader, once he has read that work, to recapture the plot. In retrospect, the plot tends to have disappeared or given way to the reader's more vivid memories of character or scenes or images. Frye praises the *Oxford Companion to English Literature* because it summarizes so many of the plots one has forgotten; Frye does not really blame the author who in that work apparently forgot the plot of Shakespeare's *King John* but persevered in summarizing it.

To the reader *reading* a novel, plot is what makes him turn the pages. Critics sometimes sound embarrassed for writers who say old fashioned things about the importance of telling stories. What is a story? In terms of craft, a story is a combination of plot and characters, the interaction of events and people. What does the story mean? That is a fair question which has unfortunately led to the belief that a novel can or must have a single theme. The novel is too complex a form to be so circumscribed. Fully understood, the story is the meaning, whatever themes and ideas may be dropped along the way.

Potential historical novelists who feel they have a workable hunch or character may be put off by the techniques of plotting. For reassurance and practical guidance, one can turn to authors who have shared their methods. Writers vary considerably in their approaches to plotting. Mari Sandoz once told an audience that she did most of her preparation mentally. Her plans were in her head when she sat down to write, so that the actual writing did not require extensive outlining. Eloise Jarvis McGraw, on the other hand, says that for her it is necessary to make a blueprint *(Techniques of Fiction Writing, The Writer,* 1959). In her chapter, "Plotting without Pain," the author advises starting with a character, asking what he wants, what interferes, what he does then, what results from his action, what show downs occur, and finally whether he gets what he wants or not. When she has answered all these questions of plot, Eloise McGraw asks, "Now — exactly what have I *said?"*

A look at the chapter titles in a historical novel can be revelatory. Consider these from Alfred Duggan's *Right Line of Cerdic:* "A Child of Rome," "The Lady Osburn," "Travels with Father," "Brothers United," "Heathen Men in Britain," "Mercian Alliances," "The Battle Winter" (three chapters — "Reading," "Ashdown," "King Ethelred)", "Wessex Pays Tribute," "The End of Mercia," "A King Forsaken," "Edington," "Christian Kings," "The Obligations of Duty," "The End of the Wars," "The Lawgiver."

The plot announced in the chapter titles suggests an orderly progression from Alfred as young atheling to old king, a man who has brought civilization and peace to his people. The historical Alfred did achieve peace, but Duggan's epilogue, taken from the Anglo-Saxon Chronicles, describes the period after 900, the year of Alfred's death. Then new wars broke out, this time between Ethelwold, son of Ethelred, Alfred's brother who had died in Easter week of the battle winter, and King Edward, Alfred's son. The plot of *The Right Line of Cerdic* does not cover this period, but the reader familiar with events as they occurred after the death of Alfred is in a position to appreciate the irony of a dialogue in chapter nine between Alfred and his brother, then King Ethelred, who swear an oath of friendship for their children. Ethelred's plan is to have Alfred succeed him, should he die, and to have Alfred eventually retire and pass the crown to Ethelwold: "It's all quite simple. We have nothing to worry about." Alfred with greater foresight and concern for his own son Edward points out, "Brothers trust one another, cousins don't," a remark which could start the plot of another book.

The oath of friendship sworn between Ethelred and Alfred for their sons makes the brothers feel better about the future. For now they must continue their battle plans against the Danes. The reader knows from history what will happen: Ethelred will die from the strain of warfare and the coughing sickness which plagues the Cerdinga line; Alfred will become king. Beyond the plot of this novel, the cousins will fight — Ethelwold against Edward, whose name Alfred had chosen to remind him he would never be king. These struggles and Edward's kingship lie in the future; now Alfred praises his brother for his conduct in the battle winter. Alfred tells Ethelred how tiresome it is that Edmund, king of the East English, should be invoked as a saint when he fought only once against the heathen and in a losing battle at that, while the king of the West Saxons, Ethelred, has fought all winter and actually beat the heathen forces once.

Historical fiction is no escape from reality but a plunge into it. The potential historical novelist ought to cultivate the ability to see different levels of reality in a single image or situation; symbols should operate on the surface as well as in the depths. According to Flannery O'Connor, "The larger and more complex the personal view, the easier it is to compress it into fiction."

Although fiction is a narrative form, the novel relies on dramatic techniques. In the novel an experience is contemplated, a story told; yet, the reader expects a sense of scenes unfolding around him. This expectation is especially strong in the novel after Henry James. Unlike Fielding and the Victorians, the modern author--even in historical fiction--is counted on to disappear or to control unseen a self-contained dramatic unit.

The contemporary reader may not welcome the author's essay comments which intrude on the story, and the author must work around the reader. When information and background cannot be presented in the dramatic context of the novel, there are several alternatives. External solutions include such methods as separating the material from the text by putting it in prefatory or end notes, geneological charts, chronological charts, maps, and diagrams. Moderation is necessary, or the reader may be put off the story entirely by having to flip through too many pages. Internal methods keep the plot moving; the author can add information by shifting the point of view as H.F.M. Prescott does in the various chronicles of *The Man on a Donkey.* Or, if the primary focus is on one character, that character can be shown over a sufficiently long period of time, changing locations and attitudes, meeting new characters of different backgrounds. Such is the case with Kristin Lavransdatter, Sigrid Undset's character whom the reader comes to know and love. The ordinary incidents of life fall naturally into the plot of *Kristin Lavransdatter:* church services, wedding celebrations, household management, childbirth, and other events in the novel absorb the reader while giving him information about customs and ceremonies in fourteenth century Norway.

Dialogue in which one character informs another is another means the author has of working within the novel to convey historical knowledge to the reader. The dialogue between Mr. Brain and Hacey Miller in *The Way to Fort Pillow* is an example of the successful use of this technique.

If the writer can bring it off, the reader takes special pleasure in being caught up in a scene and discovering midway that he is experiencing a living historical event. Finally, although the modern reader may not expect essay comments, there are occasions on which he will tolerate them. A short paragraph or two in an otherwise action packed historical novel may become an intermission and not a serious interruption. The writer should remember, however, that many readers tend to skip what looks like a page of description and go on to what appear to be dialogue. Bernard DeVoto may have been right: few readers not compelled to do so would stay on Hardy's famous *Egdon Heath* for long.

Does dialogue belong to character or plot? Given that absolute separation of plot and character is impossible even for purposes of analysis, the question may lead nowhere. What does dialogue do in a novel? It keeps the reader, particularly the reader who is inclined to skim expository or descriptive passages. More positively (although there is nothing negative about the idea of keeping readers), dialogue reveals character by adding to, changing, or destroying the reader's previous impressions. Dialogue also advances the plot, keeps the novel going when a summary would kill it. Dialogue can be action, but it can be narrative, too, giving a report on the physical or psychological action. What dialogue cannot do is exist for its own sake or resemble too closely what Bernard DeVoto calls the "agreeable pointlessness" of actual speech.

The speeches of characters are the most revised sections in almost any novel. The challenge is to keep proper balance between what is said and what is implied. Historical novelists need to guard against writing dialogue which is thinly disguised exposition or discussion of Great Ideas or Events. A lively dialogue is the one previously mentioned which occurs in Sherburne's *Way to Fort Pillow*. The reader's perception comes through Hacey, to whom the astute and rather windy old lawyer, Brain, imparts his political insights. The "Dominoes" of the second chapter's title refers to Lincoln's question to Stephen Douglas at Freeport as to whether he believed the territories could exclude slavery before they were admitted as states. According to Brain,

Douglas leaped for the question like a trout, giving "the answer the Illinois apple-knockers wanted to hear." Meanwhile, "nobody notices Lincoln watching from the wings like some slab-sided prairie Iago." Brain is impressed by what he considers Lincoln's sacrifice of a senatorial election to drive a political wedge by which "the Democratic Party will split down the middle as cute as a baby's butt." In Brain's irreverent opinion, all along the South has been "bristling like a constipated porcupine." The old lawyer predicts a Republican victory, possibly by Lincoln himself, secession, war — all of which Hacey has no choice but to endure. Because Brain is both shrewd and garrulous, the reader accepts from him a greater quantity of speech then he might from a laconic character; besides, his speech is colorful and has non-partisan tones of "a plague on both your houses."

The distinctive nature of Brain's speech illustrates another principle of good dialogue: avoid having characters all talk alike. Verbal tags or mannerisms to denote a character's speech can be overdone; contemporary loyal readers of Dorothy Sayers' detective stories may be annoyed by the missing g's, not charmin', of Lord Peter Wimsey. Still, some means of distinguishing characters by speech must be found. A little dialect or slang, unless the writer is extremely skilled in this area, goes a long way toward distracting the reader. The safest approach for the author is to get to know his character so well that he will be able to recognize that character's voice. Another helpful hint to the writer of dialogue: shun the treasury of synonyms for *said* and *asked*. Bits of speech followed by "she queried jubilantly" or "he declared significantly" are as silly as they look on the page. And, since reading aloud is not quite a lost art, some reader may discover the words sound silly, too. A writer scanning his work and finding a multitude of "he said's" and "she said's" might drop the phrases to see whether the speakers can be distinguished by their speech alone. Henry James is a master of this art, but even he sometimes confuses the reader. Probably a few designations by "he said" or "she said" are needed. Like any other novelist, the writer of historical fiction must pay scrupulous attention to dialogue, working and reworking the speeches which move the plot and reveal the characters. The historical novelist strives in addition for dialogue that will sound right for the time and place. The speech should not sound archaic or dated lest it spoil the illusion that it is spoken by characters now living in the novel. Some tricks would obviously be irritating; for example, changing final -ed to 'd to show the novel is plac'd in Shakespeare's time. Some readers, notably Cecilia Holland, who admits *Kristin Lavransdatter* is a great book, may even be bothered by Sigrid Undset's archaisms; most readers probably do not mind such things as her use of *deem* for *think* or *flit* for *move*. As an excess of archaic words and phrases will distract the reader, so will the intrusion of anachronistic speech in the form of contemporary idiom or slang. In doubt, an author should try to be straightforward and clear in dialogue. Perhaps no writer archieves the perfect dialogue, the authentic illusion of human speech. As he writes and rewrites the characters' speeches, let the historical novelist avoid spoiling the reader's illusion either through faddish phrases and slang or through what Josephine Tey once called "writing forsoothly."

Good plotting of historical fiction requires control of the incidents. With this requirement in mind, historical novelists might benefit from reading the first chapter in Erich Auerbach's *Mimesis* in which the styles of Homer and the Old Testament are compared and contrasted. Auerbach's comments on the relationship between legend and history are particularly valuable, as is his detailed account of the two different methods of managing characters and incidents in a recognition scene in *The Odyssey* and in the Old Testament story of Abraham and Isaac.

In the Homeric style events are externalized; everything is in the foreground, whether an episode or a digression. When Euryclea at a climatic moment recognizes from his scar on his leg that the stranger she is bathing is Odysseus, the narrative takes up immediately the matter of the scar and how it resulted from a wound years ago in a boar hunt. After the full development of this story within the story (although *within* is inadequate to describe a story which is simply here), Euryclea drops Odysseus' foot back in the water. Fortunately, Penelope has all this while been distracted by Athene; otherwise, she too might have noticed the scar and recognized her husband by it. The Homeric style, concludes Auerbach, can be analyzed but not interpreted.

In contrast, the biblical story of Abraham and Isaac cries out for interpretation, since so much of what happens and why it does is in shadow. God speaks to Abraham, the reader does not know where nor from whence God has come, but, says Auerbach, surely not from a feast on Olympus. The details of the journey of Abraham and his son are not given; the characters are not described. Whereas Homer's details and digressions prevent the build up of suspense, the lack of these elements in this biblical story creates overwhelming suspense. In Homer, speech externalizes thoughts; with Abraham and Isaac, what is said makes the reader wonder about what is unsaid.

The Homeric and Old Testament approaches are both valid, and, although they are ancient, the modern writer might learn from either method, perhaps deciding that one approach is more congenial to his talent than the other. Consider how different the works of Mary Renault are from those of Hawthorne, or H.F.M. Prescott's *Man on a Donkey* from Ford Madox Ford's impressionistic *Fifth Queen.*

The relationship of plot and character is so close no analysis can keep them apart for long. It is this character who wants something or someone, who is thwarted, who struggles and keeps the reader in suspense, who may or may not get what he wants. Suspense comes more easily in some situations than in others: will the murderer strike again tonight? But there are authors who can create suspense out of the most unlikely material. Rex Stout, hardly a stranger to the techniques of suspense, recently praised Jane Austen for keeping us on the edge of our chairs wondering whether Mr. Woodhouse will remember to put on "his goddamned shawl."

Anthony Burgess, in a wild epistle to the reader following his *Napoleon Symphony* ((Knopf, 1974) says his original idea was to have a Mozartian clash between Jane Austen and the Marquis de Sade, but he ended up with, "A novel on Napoleon Bonaparte that followed Ludwig von, and not Mozart." The novel itself is plotted in four movements, including an overture to Josephine and a coda to the "quizzical gaze of World History." Various Napoleonic themes are his love for his Creole bride, his roles as cuckold in a French farce, as war leader, as great general, as tyrant, as Promethean figure seeing his life in ruins. The whole story, says Burgess, was written in "elephantine fun" to show the impossibility of the task of giving symphonic form to verbal narrative, *Point Counter Point* and *The Four Quartets* notwithstanding.

In the historical novel, as in all fiction, whatever works, works, whether in the vein of Burgess's *Napoleon Symphony or* Anthony Powell's "music of the times" series of novels. What makes a good story? Almost any meaningful encounter of people, events, things. These elements of the story must be transformed and concentrated; the substance of fiction must be brought into form. In the process, according to DeVoto, the author must be concealed and the means of concealment and of illusion hidden. How does a writer know when and how to begin? "Unless you feel delirious with excitement over the prospect of telling a story," says Delderfield, "don't tell it."

In the story of *Death Comes for the Archbishop,* Willa Cather is selective in her choice of incidents for the plot. She begins with a prologue in Rome, a device which works to get young Father Latour to his new assignment, from Cincinnati to New Mexico, as bishop. Latour is actually introduced in New Mexico on his way from Santa Fe to Old Mexico for his credentials. The previous journey, from Ohio to the Southwest, is rehearsed and information about the difficulties of travel in the period is briefly given. The railway from New York ends in Ohio; merchants there know only two routes to New Mexico, one the dangerous Santa Fe Trail from St. Louis, the other by river to New Orleans, then to Galveston, then across Texas. Latour's misadventures on the year long trip are swiftly enumerated: his steamer sunk in Galveston Harbor, a leg injured when he traveled in a traders' caravan across Texas. That he had saved his books from shipwreck at the risk of his life, and that he had hurt his leg while jumping from an over-turning wagon suggest that he is an active man, quick to respond, if not always wisely, in situations of personal danger.

The closing incident of book one is a visit to Latour by an old priest, Padre Escalastico, who has recently achieved the pious wish of this lifetime—to see the shrine of Guadalupe. Before Escalastico comes, Latour and his fellow Frenchman, Father Joseph Vaillant, have been discussing a bell whose fine tone Latour attributes to the presence of silver. The Spanish, who taught the Indians silver working, had learned that art from the Moors. Joseph cannot understand Latour's scholarly interest in the bell; he turns Latour's attention to the practical business of the day — the meeting with Padre Escalastico. Both priests listen carefully to the third priest's story, and both are impressed but respond differently. To Joseph, who wants to make a similar pilgrimage, who believes in the superiority of miracle to doctrine, and whose sincerity and zeal endear him to the bishop, Latour answers that where there is great love there are always miracles, that an apparition is but human vision corrected by divine love.

The incidents of book two occur on Latour's missionary journeys, in one of which he encounters the outlaw Buck Scales. In following sections, events are sometimes clutstered about a character such as Dona Isabella, who with her husband is Latour's friend and benefactor, or Padre Martinez, who used to enjoy lording over the priests of northern New Mexico but who now seems to Latour a "left over from the past." Other sections of the novel link place names with incidents: "The Mass at Acoma" or "Gold under Pike's Peak." In the fortress like church at Acoma, Latour passes through a crisis of faith. The discovery of gold in Colorado is the incident which separates Latour and Vaillant, who wants to save souls in the mining camps. In their parting, Latour gives his old friend a pair of mules, recalling the comic incident early in the novel in which Vaillant managed to gain the animals as a reluctant gift from a wealthy ranchero. Up to this point the plot has included several temporary separations for the two missionaries; Latour points out that one of these partings will be the last. In the final section, death comes for the archbishop. The incidents of the plot have been so arranged as to seem more than the events of a single lifetime. The archbishop Latour is said to have accomplished, not simply lived through, an historic period.

The historical novelist must decide to what degree actual historical events are to determine his plot — or, more accurately, how strong the illusion of these events should be. In Sherburne's *Way to Fort Pillow*, the main character is caught up in the Civil War. The character Hacey Miller is created in response to forces beyond his control. That he is shown to be a likable, decisive, and brave young man does not render the war a subordinate element in the plot. The reader cannot imagine Hacey Miller and his circle of characters apart from the war, any more than he can think of Crane's *Red Badge of Courage* without considering the effects of great external struggle on the inner conflicts of a character. Even a chapter title like "School's Out". a phrase which calls up joyous children on a holiday takes on a different meaning when the school is Berea College, where Hacey teaches and which is closed by a pro-slavery mob. From "School's Out" to "Hell at Fort Pillow," Sherburne follows the struggles of Hacey Miller, whose own family is as divided as the country on the issues in the Civil War. Hacey's own inner conflict between truth and loyalty is universal, but the particular form that struggle takes in his life is influenced by the war between North and South. The previously discussed dislogue between Brain and Hacey is one of the author's lively ways of giving the reader background on the issues. Brain had ended their talk by advising Hacey to marry Ellie. The war gives starting a family an urgency beyond personal desire and need.

In contrast, the plot of Delderfield's *Theirs Was the Kingdom* is concentrated upon the members of the Swann family. The setting is Victorian England, and the plot follows the various characters to the continent and, in the case of Alex, to Africa with incidents at Isandlwana, Rorke's Drift, and Khartoum; however, the main line of the plot is a family saga. Larger historic events are subordinate to personal destinies, as a glance at the chapter titles, "To Kill a Zulu," "The Gladstonisation of Giles," and "Adam in a Holly Bush," reveals. Nevertheless, the reader does come away with a heightened sense of the social history of the period. While Delderfield's method of plotting differs from Sherburne's in emphasis, both novelists succeed in creating memorable characters and a lively sense of the past.

One way to control the plot is to write from a limited point of view, as Mary Renault does with Theseus or John Gardner with Grendel. This approach differs according to artist: consider Ford Madox Ford's impressionistic fictional biography of Katherine Howard in *The Fifth Queen* or Norah Lofts' *Crown of Aloes* in which the perception comes through Isabella of Spain. Still another example is Hilda Lewis's *I Am Mary Tudor.* What the plot gains by being concentrated in such a work, it stands to lose in larger historical events, or in the attempt to cover material inaccessible to the narrator — the speaker's infancy, for example. Hilda Lewis says in her foreword that part of the difficulty is resolved by Mary's being a royal child whose early life was a matter of record; moreover, Mary could rely on the credibility as witnesses of her lady-governor the countess of Salisbury and her nurse Lady Bryan. (The reader could but probably will not question the accuracy of these good women, one of whom is a Plantagenet and so might provide an anti-Tudor view of events.) The reader is likely to accept Mary Tudor's account of her father's words at her birth and her baptism at the age of three days, even the description of the chapel as given by Lady Salisbury, who adds that Wolsey, holding his baby godchild, had hard eyes. Mary sets out to tell the truth from her perspective. Instead of "Bloody Mary," Lewis presents in the narrative voice of the queen a woman "sick of the burnings". Later she is revealed as a lenient character in the merciful act of pardoning Jame Grey. The novel may change the reader's idea of Mary Tudor, but Hilda Lewis has no intention of distorting history. While she says she would not alter the lives of her historical characters by a single act, she believes in searching documentary evidence for clues about her characters' motivation and behavior. The author describes her work as "a detective story in reverse. I know what they did; I must find out *why.* " That *why* is a strong element in any plot presented through the first person narrative of a known historical figure. As Mary Tudor says in the novel, "Above all the thoughts of my heart I must search out, for none knows them but me." The queen also speaks of the need to study "not only the things that happened to me but myself that let them happen."

Readers sometimes assume that the historical novelist has his plot outlined for him. Not so, says Cecilia Holland in her prefatory note to *The Firedrake.* The author says she stuck to historical details as closely as possible but did rearrange facts about October 1066 to suit plot and characterization. The reader is asked "to approach the events of this tale not as accomplished facts but as the unfolding of the continual unforseeable present. The decisions of the dark and violent eleventh century were no more inevitable and no less agonizing than the decisions of the dark and violent twentieth century."

In "Revising a Historical Novel" (*The Writer,* October, 1969), Cecilia

Holland recalls her problems in plotting *Until the Sun Falls*. The rough draft was rambling and discursive, some 400,000 words, in contrast with her earlier works, *The Firedrake, Rakossy,* and *The Kings in Winter,* none of which in finished form exceeded 250 pages. The author realized that her usual device of throwing in a new character whenever a plot drags would only burden a long novel with too many people. Even her practical methods of handling a mass of notes by tacking them to the wall above her desk or filing them in the pages of the phone book led to no solution. For *Until the Sun Falls* the author's approach to revision was to "chop like a headsman" whatever was not absolutely necessary, whether lengthy scene settings, information on the past lives of characters, material on battle tactics and formations. Her basic rule has become "anything I like too much draws attention not to the story but the way it's written." Although writers of historical fiction must be concerned with matters of style, they should avoid getting carried away with their own narrative and losing the line of the story. The problem of how to end *Until the Sun Falls* was not solved by a battle but by the Mongols' withdrawal because thousands of miles away their Kha Khan has died and the warriors had to return to elect a new leader. Much of the conflict inherent in the plot is conveyed through the differences between characters. The contrast between the Russian woman Ana and her Mongol captors creates a sense of changing attitudes and the end of an era.

In his foreword to *One Million Dead* Jose Maria Gironella discusses the plotting of his novel. For this sequel to *The Cypresses Believe in God*, the Alvear family remains the "psychological nucleus" of the characters. The city Gerona is the geographic center, but the action extends throughout Spain. *Cypresses* had ended with the death of an early victim of the war, young Cesar Alvear: "Then his heart closed." *One Million Dead* begins as an immediate continuation with Ignacio Alvear visiting a Gerona cemetery in search of Cesar's body. The novel closes with the end of the war announced. Gironella's plan was to show a "panoramic view of what our struggle was and what it meant." In terms of plotting, his approach required a balancing of incidents, sometimes the cancellation of one event by another, and the synchronizing of situations on both the "Nationalist" and the "Red" sides. The reconciliation of diversities on both sides took the author five years and three writings of the entire manuscript. The first version was a chronology of facts and catalogue of horrors; the second writing deleted much anecdote and stressed logical situations. This revision, says Gironella modestly, "succumbed to the grandeur and the poetry that can doubtless be found wherever man dwells." Many novelists might have stopped there, but Gironella pushed on to the third and hardest writing, giving his book verisimilitude. The events of the period were so crowded and complex that any onesided statement of what happened "falls a thousand leagues short of the detached story of humanity."

Gironella sees his story as a reply to influential works written by foreigners such as Malraux's *Man's Hope*, Hemingway's *For Whom the Bell Tolls*, Bernanos' *Les Grands Cimitieres sous La Lune*, Barea's trilogy *La Forja, La Ruta*, and *La Llana*, Koestler's *Spanish Testament.* Admitting their literary value, Gironella says these works discomfort the informed reader.

The author sees his work also as a chronicle of participants, each of whom remembers his own saga, not understanding the stories of others. The plot is not confined to its setting in Spain, for in 1937 in both zones of the war many foreigners fought — Germans, Italians, French, English, Belgians, Americans. Moreover, in the wake of the Spanish Civil War, civil wars in which communists intervened broke out in other countries. The struggle in Spain effected a political evolution. By experience and research Gironella became aware of so much information and its implications that the plotting of his work was extremely difficult. Often the sacrifice of fine details was required to preserve the emotional rhythm of the novel.

The elements of plot may be examined in any good historical novel, but for purposes of analysis it is helpful to consider in detail the plot of a shorter work, Hawthorne's "My Kinsman Major Molineux."

Having left his father's farm, young Robin comes to town to seek his fortune with the help of his cousin Molineux. The search for his kinsman takes Robin through crooked streets and a dark and smoky tavern, and his inquiries are met with rebuffs. Since what Robin wants, an improvement in fortune, is dependent in his mind on the help of Molineux, each act of rudeness he meets seems to thwart him in his purpose. An old man whose tones are sepulchral, a barber, an innkeeper, a demoniac inn patron, a scarlet woman, a watchman — all seem to conspire against him. Finally, someone tells him to wait an hour and Molineux will appear; Robin recognizes the speaker as the inn patron whose face is grotesquely divided, half red, half black. Robin waits by the church steps, falls asleep, dreams of home, the door of which is closed. Waking or dreaming, he thinks he sees his kinsman's face in a window. Then, a stranger, who appears friendly but whose "singular curiosity to witness" Robin's meeting with Molineux may be cause for suspicion, appears to wait with the youth. Sounds of a parade are heard. The procession comes, led by the double-faced man, and featuring in a cart, tarred and feathered, none other than Robin's kinsman, Major Molineux. The discovery scene is intensified by Molineux's recognition of Robin: their eyes meet. Robin feels pity and terror, but suddenly he is caught up in the feelings of the mob. Robin joins in the shouting against his kinsman. The expectations of both Robin and the reader have been reversed. The procession ends; the stranger-companion asks Robin if he is dreaming. Robin asks for directions out of town, but the stranger urges him to stay, telling him he may succeed without Molineux's help.

Recognition and reversal signified by the shout of another of Hawthorne's characters occur in his "Young Goodman Brown." Like Robin, Brown is a young man on a journey — in this instance that of the husband's night out. In spite of his wife Faith's misgivings, which increase the reader's expectations that something will go wrong, Brown sets out to meet a strange man in the woods. The story's episodes are carefully balanced: Brown's meeting with Goody Cloyse, his old catechist, against the meeting with the minister and Deacon Gookin. The characters' speeches are also balanced: the woman speaks of the young man to be taken tonight into the communion; the men, of a young woman.Since there are only one young man and woman in the story, the reader can guess to whom the strange travelers through the woods refer.

Brown makes discoveries along the way that things are not what they seem. Horrified by the realization that the man he went into the woods to meet is the devil in the guise of Brown's grandfather and by the blood curdling remarks of Goody Cloyse, Brown can say only "That old woman taught me my catechism." The great recognition scene, in which Brown is overcome by the hypocrisy of those whose authority he had venerated, takes place at a witches' meeting. Seeing now where the path through the woods has led, Brown shouts, "Come, devil, for to thee is this world given." Brown goes home, but the wife he kissed at the beginning of the story he now regards sternly and sadly, ignoring her wish to kiss him, passing her without greeting.

The reader who has finished "Young Goodman Brown" will probably ask what it all means, but questions of interpretation depend on an analysis of Hawthorne's careful manipulation of the plot to allow for ambiguity, and his use of balance and contrast. In thinking of Hawthorne, the contemporary reader is often struck by the way the author's stories transcend their time. The sense of the past is there, but so is the tone of the present. Readers and writers interested in exploring this phenomenon further are directed to *A Casebook on the Hawthorne Question*, edited by Agnes McNeill Donohue (Crowell, 1963).

No discussion of plot would be complete without some comment on historical fiction for the young reader. It may be true that there are no such things as good or bad adult books or good or bad children's books, that there are only good or bad books, but there is such a thing as the juvenile market. For many writers the existence of this market has meant no sudden windfall of royalties but a steady period of royalties coming in. An author who has written historical novels for readers of all ages, Eloise Jarvis McGraw, has pointers about juvenile historical fiction. The writer must simultaneously appeal to the young reader -- and to children's librarians who are among a book's best promoters. The author should concentrate on telling a good story with a fast paced plot, clear background, and economy of style. The length of the work should run 60,000-70,000 and no more than 90,000 words. A central character a year or two older than the intended young reader is desirable, as is that character's struggle with a problem that will stretch his abilities. Research must be accurate, but it should support the story and not get in its way.

With the possible exceptions of the length of the novel and the age of the main character, most of McGraw's criteria are applicable to any historical novel, regardless of intended audience. Equally helpful are the author's comments on why novels fail (also in her *Techniques of Fiction Writing*). Briefly, there are five major faults: weak plot, wooden characters, poor or dull style, dragging pace, lack of a clear story. McGraw also enumerates eight minor flaws: grammatical errors, boring or confused passages, near miss passages, overstatement, understatement, rough passages, faults in dialogue, passages that need clarification.

Anyone who has ever received a rejection slip is probably familiar with one or more of the terms McGraw uses. Nor does publication insure that the author's work is free of flaws, but that he constantly works at rooting them out, trying for perfection. As J. Middleton Murray says, "Style is perfect when the communication of the thought or emotion is exactly accomplished." Another scholar, Thomas M. Raysor, used to arm his students with a list of questions on plot in the novel. Writers who are stuck somewhere in their plotting may extricate themselves and their stories by asking these questions:

1. Is the plot structurally unified so that incidents are connected by cause and effect?

2. If not, are there principles of unity, of impression?

3. Is the plot concentrated on one situation like a play?

4. If not, are there parts of it so concentrated?

5. Are there unrelated episodes?

6. Is the plot probable?

7. Does the plot contain the essential element of struggle?

8. Does the struggle rise out of character?

9. Does the struggle involve great issues or ideas?

10. Are there tragic or comic faults in the principal characters?

11. Is there dramatic discovery? Or reversal of a character's course of action?

12. Can the chief elements of the plot be summarized for analysis?

No two novels are alike. Each writer finds his own answers to the questions.

FOUR

CHARACTER

The reader who closes *Kristin Lavrandatter* at the end and says, "How deep it is," is probably not thinking of Sigrid Undset's extensive knowledge of fourteenth century Norway but of the character Kristin and her story. What keeps a reader reading a historical novel is not the author's erudition but the illusion of life given through lively characters in a sound plot. The reader wants to see what happens to characters and how they feel about it, what they do, why they do it. The historical novelist takes into account that while societies have changed, people in many ways have stayed the same. The question of the individual in relation to society is not the preserve of the historical novelist but is also raised in that remarkable rabbit saga *Watership Down* by Richard Adams.

In Plutarch's view, character is fate. How do modern writers feel about their characters? Cecilia Holland once spoke of having to remove a shrinking violet of a hero to a quiet court in Flanders in order to toughen him for the plot of *The Firedrake.* The novelist Delderfield advises, "Never make a firm plan for your story line." If an author is flexible enough to *let* a character behave and develop, the narrative will be kept fluid. Delderfield describes having tried vainly five times in five pages to kill off a character with a mortar shell in *The Avenue,* only to settle for letting him lose an arm. As to whether his characters are based on actual people, Delderfield says that some of his fictional characters are composites: nineteen real life figures went into the five characters of his play *Worm's Eye View.* Finally, says the saga writer, it helps to love one's characters. Galsworthy, after all, made a hero out of the character he had begun by loathing, Soames Forsyte.

Character in the novel is vital, not only because readers as people are naturally curious about other people, but because in the modern novel it is through character that the reader preceives the action. Gone are the days of the omniscient and ubiquitous author with his essay comments on plot and character. The contemporary novelist is invisible, the true drop-out. Perhaps he works unseen through the exclusive single point of view of one character in the novel, making every effort to get that key witness in the right place at the right time for the right reason, since the reader can perceive nothing except through that character. Or perhaps the novelist solves the problems inherent in so severely limited a point of view by shifting the perception to another character or two.

The history of the novel registers movement away from exposition and into drama, but even the most recent novel is narrated. The writer's challenge is to preserve the illusion that the events in the novel are actually happening *now*. The historical novel set in the distant past is no exception; the illusion of the present must be sustained. This necessity creates difficulties for the historical novelist who lodges the point of view in a character the reader knows will die in the end. How can such a character be telling the story now? Not all readers may be so literal-minded; still, the writer would do well to play down the inevitability of the conclusion. A vivid character keeps the reader's attention where it should be, on the here and now of the novel.

Like the dance the novel is not static but dynamic. In a recent dance by the Joffrey *(As Time Goes By,* choreographed by Twyla Tharp) the illusion is deliberately broken when the dancers slump suddenly. The audience is made aware not only of a strangely ordinary group of rather stoop-shouldered men and women, but of the choreographer's role. How can we know the dancer from the dance? It's easy. Break the illusion. The audience in the darkened theatre will suppress a nervous laugh at the trick. The dancers restore the illusion in an instant. The audience may not have liked the incident, but they have already paid for their tickets and would resist the effort of getting up and going home, anyway. But it takes little effort to close a book when an author breaks its illusion. He is an intruder and if he is not careful, the reader may avoid his company for good.

The author of *Pharaoh,* Eloise McGraw, believes that writers only half create their characters; the characters do the rest. Citing an example from her own cast of characters—three kings, all named Thutmose, and a queen Hatshepsut -- the author says that little information was available on Thutmose II and, what little there was, was negative. His lack of historical importance made him so negative he was positive. The novelists began by making him a foil for his strong father, but he ended up as a principal character. Similarly, a character in another McGraw novel, this one *Moccasin Trail,* a young people's book, exceeded his author's expectations.

A rather dull character was transformed by the sudden appearance of a half-Indian boy who in the writer's imagination came hurtling out of a trading post with a skunk hidden in his shirt. This character evolves into a third character who replaced the original character whose dullness threatened the plot.

In the process of writing the novelist comes to know his characters so well he may forget their existence is imaginary — and even actual historical characters are imaginary in fiction. The writer must work to make these characters vivid to the reader. It is not always necessary to explore a character in depth to make him memorable. In fact, the writer may have to guard against any latent tendency to make universal statements; he may even have to suppress poetic impulses. "What a miracle she was," or "As much beauty as could die," or "Full fathom five" belong to a different realm of literature; such phrases might provide material for the titles of fictional works but not for the development of their characters.

On the other hand, the prose writer who concentrates too closely on external details may fall into caricature. Intentional caricature is another matter, of course, as a study of that art in the novels of Dickens reveals. In *Great Expectations,* the reader does not know the stream or even the trickle of Wemmick's consciousness, yet who can forget him hoping for a nod from his Aged Parent? Caricature did not die with Dickens; the art lives on in moments of high comedy in Thomas Pynchon's *Gravity's Rainbow* and other works which reveal all — well, not quite all — the reader needs or wants to know about a character. The only danger to the historical novelist is unintentional caricature which results in an undesirable comic effect. Who is sadder than the historical novelist who did not mean to be funny?

While good caricature is permissible in the historical novel, it works only for minor characters. No novel can survive unless some character is developed to the depth that will distinguish him or her from other characters. Besides appearance, what differentiates one person from another? Certainly the author who confines himself to the point of view of one character as narrator has one person in depth: consider the intimacy of Geoffrey Turton's *My Lord of Canterbury* or William Styron's *Confessions of Nat Turner.* Should the point of view shift to other characters, they will stand out for the reader and may also shed light on the first character. Characters of obsessive or even mild interest to these witnesses will in turn catch the reader's attention. But the good reader on whom, in Emerson's words, good books depend, however much he may sympathize with a character or identify with him, remains outside the character. This distance enables the reader to see what the author wants him to see but the character cannot see — human faults. Who does the reader remember better.Thackeray's Becky Sharp or Amelia Sedley?

Excesses may be committed through the warts-and-all theory of portraiture. Characters can be buried somewhere under their faults. The classical idea of *hamartia,* by which the ancients probably meant the missing of the mark, has much merit. *Hamartia* has come to mean the single fatal flaw in a character which may be the source of both his good and bad qualities and the seed of conflict in the plot. "Fatal virtue" might more aptly define what it is in a character that may or may not lead to his downfall but is certain to make him credible to the reader. Consider the nuances of *tenacious* in relation to Robert Aske in Prescott's *Man on a Donkey:* the young squire shows the strength of perseverance and the weakness of being stubborn. Or consider Christabel Cowper in the same novel: the prioress is calculating, which means she has a gift for efficient management at best, and a talent for manipulating people at worst. Robert's cluster of words suggests his virtue to the reader, Christabel's, her vicious nature, but both characters have in them the source of their own downfall. In one catastrophe the reader mourns; in the other he rejoices.

John Gardner has succeeded in creating a sympathetic character out of unlikely material in *Grendel.* This revisionist novel, told from Grendel's point of view, wins the reader over to the "true story." Although he calls himself a "pointless, ridiculous monster," Grendel bawls "Blind prejudice!" when a doe stiffens at his sight, and bellows "Mama! Waa! Waaa! ... I'm going to die ... Poor Grendel. Poor old Mama!" These characters are not the Grendel and Grendel's dam the reader knows from previous experience. This Grendel knows the mindless brutishness of things, and even when the harper plays hopeful songs, endless darkness reaches out and snatches Grendel's feet. Grendel wants a world lovingly made by a god, the world of the shaper's song, even if he himself must be an outcast "cursed by the rules of his hideous fable." The reader sympathizes with Grendel, grinding his teeth in his own absurdity, feeling that tedium is the worst pain, or saying, "I am mad with joy — at least I think it's joy." In fact the reader may feel much closer to Grendel than to a host of existential anti-heroes, but that is just part of the fun.

Upon the arrival of the Geats, Grendel observes that the Danes are unhappy with the visitors who have come to save them, and the priests are unhappy after all those years of saying the Ghostly Destroyer would set things right. Danish honor is threatened; religion is unmasked. Grendel is disturbed by one visitor whose sea-pale eyes focus on nothing and whose mouth moves independently of his words. This, of course, is the stranger ordinarily assumed by the reader to be the hero of the epic. The character of the usual villain of the piece is rendered sympathetically, while that of Beowulf is seen as inhumanly withdrawn, almost as if his body were a disguise for some unknown horror. All the strangers move like a machine, their weapons clanking, while poor Grendel's heart aches to know what goes on at the meadhall.

In the great meadhall scene all the familiar characters are present, but they look different. Unferth, son of Ecglaf, who has "a nose like a black, deformed potato, eyes like a couple of fangs," asks the stranger about his meadboast with Breca. Unferth's inquiry is complete with comic gestures; Beowulf's eyes are like empty pits, his weird gaze focusing nowhere as he answers. Grendel believes Beowulf's story and concludes the stranger is insane. When Wealtheow, old Hrothgar's wife, speaks to Beowulf courteously about his strength and trustworthiness, he simply says, "We'll see." Eventually Grendel moves through the hall to kill and eat everyone, but he wears his gore with a difference, even tying a tablecloth around his neck. After polishing off one victim Grendel reaches for another's wrist: "Mistake!" The monster tells himself "Grendel, Grendel, hold fast to what is true!" But Beowulf triumphs, and in the end Grendel whispers to the animals watching his agony: "Poor Grandel's had an accident," adding, "So may you all."

The reader's pleasure springs from Gardner's fidelity to the original plot and from his reversal of the reader's expectations about character. The character "man" emerges as less attractive than the subhuman characters in another novel, William Golding's *The Inheritors*, which might be classified as prehistorical fiction. In the final pages the first representatives of *homo sapiens* arrive, and the reader knows they will subdue the simpler characters, gentle missing links, who can only see pictures and can form no concepts, and who have won sympathy as the book's main characters.

The idea of presenting a monster as the hero or a humanoid as truly human may seem ridiculous, but Gardner and Golding show what skilled novelists can do in characterization. Both *Grendel* and *The Inheritors* illustrate a technique important to the historical novelist, the ability to begin with unsympathetic historical or legendary characters and make them sympathetic.

Another revisionist achievement is Jeremy Potter's *Trail of Blood*, a detective novel which clears the name of Richard III through the sleuthing of

Brother Thomas, "a real historical person about whom little or nothing is known." (See "Anyone for History?" *The Writer,* September 1970.) Potter, whose monk in 1536 investigates the murder of the princes in 1483, urges the potential writer: "You too can answer the call of history and rehabilitate the worthy dead. Don't be put off by the historians."

Another novel based on the investigation of the alleged murder by Richard III of the little princes is Josephine Tey's fascinating *Daughter of Time.* In this book the author uses a contemporary detective, Inspector Grant, to explore the past and solve the case. Both novels have in common a character who may be fixed in the reader's mind as a villain but who is exonerated, changing the reader's mind, or at least making change possible.

The transformation of character is accomplished in part by examining recorded history for traces of propaganda. Hugh Ross Williamson in *Historical Whodunits* clearly and briefly discusses the sources of beliefs about the villainous character Richard III. A chronicle, no longer extant, is said to have been written by Thomas More. Since More was five years old at the time of the murder, he could not be considered a credible witness. What is more likely is that, if there really was such an account in More's writing, it may simply have been dictated to him by an older "witness," Cardinal Morton, in whose house More lived for a time as a young man. According to some historians, Morton was a lawyer who became a priest for financial reasons, a political opportunist who quickly changed to the winning side, a breaker of the seal of confession, and the mastermind of the Woodville faction who promoted the cause of Henry Tudor against Richard. Morton's credentials, then, are not those of the fair-minded historian. Yet the interpretation of evidence in itself is not enough to explain the success of historical detective novels like Potter's *Trail of Blood* and Tey's *Daughter of Time.* Plantagentets and Tudors are important characters, but even more important are Brother Thomas and Inspector Grant.

The historical novelist fortunately does not have to redeem every character he treats. Not all characters are so unlikely as Grendel or Richard III, who are exceptions included in the discussion to show what an imaginative author can achieve. The reader admires the audacity of Gardner's *Grendel* or the novels by Potter and Tey because the authors take on *Beowulf* and Shakespeare's *Richard III* and the concept of character perpetuated by those works.

More often, the writer dealing with a well known historical figure is intent on developing the character along the lines of popular tradition. The reader's understanding of the character may be modified through information the author provides as part of the novel. With less well known historical figures, or with wholly fictitious characters, the novelist is less dependent on recorded facts but not entirely free of their pull, for even an invented character lives in the novel's time and place, and the author must be accurate about whatever he presents as factual.

Characters existing in history or legend come to the novelist half-formed, and that is how they will remain unless they are created anew. The writer may have some evidence to work around, some to play up, some to play down; this only increases the challenge.

Theseus, for example, whose story is told by Mary Renault in *The King Must Die* and *The Bull from the Sea*, is not a totally new character in the reader's experience. Banking on that experience, the novelist builds on the original character. The foundation, then, is the character Theseus, as readers familiar with the mythic sources might expect him to have been, had the original versions developed his character in the modern sense. *The Bull from the Sea* is told from Theseus' point of view, beginning with the return from ruined Knossos. For a moment he regrets having left the triumphs of the Cretan Bull ring, but he says, "Now it was time to be my father's son," and, "What is written in blood cannot be washed away." Theseus calls his father's death his "grief forever"; the grief springs less from a feeling of personal loss from Theseus' sense of responsibility since he had forgotten to change his ship's sail from black to white to signal his safe return, and his distraught father Aigeus plunged from a cliff. Actually, it was the grandfather of Theseus who reared him, not his father. The link between father and son is nevertheless established which makes Theseus sympathetic and real: Aigeus' boarhound which had been keeping vigil near his dead master's body leaves to follow Theseus.

Later in an encounter with the lordly cattle raider, Pirithoos, with whom he trades insults and threats, Theseus suddenly sees in the man not an enemy but a friend: "One's heart must love him, whether one will or no." But the hero's greater love is reserved for Hippolyta, a warrior maiden of Pontos, in the service of Artemis. Through Theseus the reader sees Hippolyta, gray-eyed, strong, free of any tendency "to put other women down to prove herself regarded." Theseus says further, "She would keep one perfect thing with her all day, to feel and understand it. Bards loved to sing for her, for, as one told me [more objectively than a lover can] she never asked a foolish question, and saw straight through to the core." It is Hippolyta who bears Theseus' favorite son Hippolytus. In the usual version of the story, Hippolyta dies beside Theseus in battle, after which he sends for and marries the Cretan princess Phaedra. Mary Renault alters the story to allow greater interaction among characters. The dynastic marriage to Phaedra takes place before Hippolyta's death; in fact, she sacrificially tells Theseus to marry the princess to whom he had been betrothed in order to keep Crete from rising against his rule. When Theseus expresses concern about their son, Hippolyta says she is confident that he is under some god's protection.

Theseus plans to marry Phaedra, but since she can inherit Minos' land only if she remains in it, he decides to leave her in Crete and visit her there. In contrast to Hippolyta, Phaedra wears her dark hair in long serpentine ringlets, her eyes shadowed with kohl and lapis paste, her breasts painted with powdered coral, her toenails with henna. She needs to say nothing. Her hand lies motionless in the hand of Theseus, and she does not look at him. The fire he wakens in her burns ultimately not for him but for his son Hippolytus. In the Renault story, Phaedra lies to Theseus that Hippolytus has ravished her and that he had sworn he would restore the old religion. Although he learns the truth too late to save Hippolytus, Theseus takes vengeance on Phaedra, "a lying slave, the daughter of a thousand years of kings." To insure that her slander will not survive, Theseus strangles her, arranging the death to look suicidal. He also writes a note in Cretan style exonerating Hippolytus. The reader does not dwell on the elements of concealment and forgery, devices necessary to explain the death of Phaedra. Besides, the reader's perception is within the character of Theseus.

On Skyros, near the end of the novel, Theseus is older but wiser: "Hope comes in these waves, like water filling a dried up pool." He feels it is time for his own death, yet he thinks that if he jumps from the balcony people may accuse his host Lykomedes of murder. So Theseus climbs among the crags, looking for a place that will make the death he offers Poseidon appear accidental. Technically, there is a problem with a narrative told by a suicide, but Mary Renault manages the conclusion without jarring the reader's disbelief.

Like *The Bull from the Sea*, James Sherburne's *Way to Fort Pillow* is told through a first person narrator. As in all such novels, the narrator becomes part of the process he observes, which tends to work against the character's reliability as historical witness. To counteract this tendency, the novelist must make the narrator at once shrewd and likable. Sherburne's Hacey Miller, introduced in an earlier novel as a thirteen year old Kentuckian, is now a teacher at Berea in the tense days before the outbreak of the Civil War. Through Hacey, fighting on the Union side, the reader sees the Miller family conflict, epitomized in his brother's position as a Confederate medical officer, the abolitionists Clay and Higginson, and several other characters who, like Hacey himself, may not have existed but well might have.

A character in this novel may be described by a simple observation: "He looked like an unmade bed." Or the description, via Hacey, may go deeper: "There was a broad strain of kindliness in his character, but often it didn't surface for days at a time." In a novel with several characters, some are bound to be more typical than individual, such as Robin Ledyard Miller, Hacey's sister-in-law, a young woman loyal to the old South. At first even Hacey's wife Ellie may appear typical, a lovely mountain girl whose hair is the color of woodsmoke and smells of lilac soap, who worries that she is too bone ignorant for Hacey. As the plot unfolds, Ellie emerges as an individual character. Also memorable is Star, a black man who had influenced Hacey when he was growing up. But it is Hacey himself who holds first place in the reader's attention, a character who emerges as recognizably human as he is heroic. It is Hacey who tells his own story with its external conflicts as well as his inner struggles between following truth at the expense of one's loyalties, or loyalties at the expense of truth.

A novel narrated in the third person with much of the action perceived through the central character is Duggan's *Right Line of Cerdic.* The novelist examined history and legends but went beyond these sources to create his Alfred. To introduce his character sympathetically and get the plot started, Duggan shows Alfred in the first scene as a boy of four, allowed to stay up for a banquet after a papal ceremony but given only porridge since roast pork is not good for small children at bedtime. The conversation of the adults is over young Alfred's head but prepares the way for future developments in the novel.

Back home at Wantage, the older children in the Cerdinga family are introduced. Although Alfred is the parental favorite, his siblings do not hold it against him since he never curries favor or tells tales. With his brothers Alfred learns to ride, to manage hounds and hawks, to read, sing, and play the harp. Duggan's Alfred is clever but not prodigiously so. He also suffers from a tragicomical physical disability — loose bowels which cause him to retreat at inconvenient times. Nor is Alfred's character without flaw, though he does respond to correction. When he once complained about a group of yokels who kept him from this dinner, his conceit was punished with a slap from his cousin, the monk, Neot. The immediate result was Alfred's embarrassed rush to the privy, but the ultimate effect was graciousness to social inferiors.

Character can be revealed through contrast: Alfred's father Ethelwulf is almost but not quite a great king who plans so carefully for the future he neglects the present; Alfred is shrewd and pragmatic. Alfred's qualities may make a good king but not a lovable character; so, Duggan adds wisdom, humor, and courage to his virtues.

When Alfred succeeds his brother King Ethelred, he must defend all Wessex. "My own family will be as well defended as the rest of my people, and no better," he says. The speech is not heartless, for the reader sees the inner thoughts of Alfred and knows his double sorrow over the loss of his brother and the painful responsibility of kingship.

No kingly legends are present to help or hinder Zoe Oldenbourg in the creation of characters from what the author considers to be a neglected group in historical novels: the poor. In her *Heirs to the Kingdom*, the main characters are weavers who embark upon the first crusade to Jerusalem. The narrative is in the third person, but the impressions of the crusade are chiefly those of Jacques and Marie, a young couple who set off on a religious adventure turned arduous trek. Not only does Zoe Oldenbourg create two memorable characters, she offers a fresh perspective on the history of the crusades.

In *The Kings in Winter,* a novel set early in eleventh century Ireland, Cecilia Holland features several actual historical figures among her characters but invents Muirtagh and his family. With his brother, Cearbhall, Muirtagh is summoned to join forces with Brian Boru. At the hall of the high king, Muirtagh reveals his witty and sharp tongue. To an advance rider who had once asked Muirtagh, then stringing an arrow, " 'Can't you read my device?' " Muirtagh had answered, " 'So near Dublin, nobody reads.' " Remembering an old feud, Cearbhall says to his brother, " 'They thought perhaps we'd forgotten.' " Muirtagh replies, " 'They thought they'd forgotten. That's the way with them.' "

When Brian Boru asks Muirtagh to take up his harp (Cearbhall, he says, is the warrior in the family), the song describes the old feud which nearly destroyed Muirtagh's clan. Several listeners stiffen, but Muirtagh says that those dead were long ago, thay twenty years would have been enough to restore Judas to good company, that Christ died for our sins. Although Muirtagh is not given to long speeches, the reader might tire even of one liners. Cecilia Holland shows Muirtagh in homelier moments — being wakened from a sound sleep or trying to catch his ponies. Through dialogue and incident in the first fifty pages, Muirtagh emerges not as some grand, never flinching hero but as the human chieftain of a clan who knows, as Cearbhall does not, the difference between the trouble a man chooses to get into and the trouble that comes against his choice. Muirtagh is willing to forgive old wrongs, particularly that done by the MacMahon clan on whom Cearbhall would take vengeance, but his efforts to keep peace are in vain. Muirtagh is trapped in the old feud when his brother is hacked to death. After avenging himself on some of his brother's killers, Muirtagh renounces his position as leader, passes the title to his son Eoghan, and goes into the wilderness.

Realizing that he will be regarded as an outlaw and that he will have to kill anyone who happens upon him, Muirtagh misses his wife Aud and their children. He manages to survive the winter in a ruined hut, a hiding place which is discovered by the same monk who attended his dying grandfather. To Muirtagh's remark that outlawry is less bitter than it is boring, the monk says there is no school where one can learn to be an outlaw. Muirtagh flashes back, proving his wit has not dulled in exile. " 'The neglect of it's a scandal. Send to Clonmacnois, tell them they must widen the cursus — put outlawry next to Latin.' " When the monk suggests that he seek sanctuary in a monastery, Muirtagh rejects the temptation to the quiet life and shares his plan to join Maelmordha's rebel forces and the Danes against the high king. The monk tries to dissuade him from further vengeance but accepts his decision and prays with words that seem to sink into Muirtagh, giving him peace. Such a scene works because Muirtagh has been shown observing simple religious rituals, puzzling about God, struggling over his course of action.

Although he joins the rebel Irish and Danes against Irish forces in which his own son fights, and although he kills many with his bow, Muirtagh is ever the true Irishman. As a character he is at once individual and typical, complex and simple. Eventually captured by his son and freed by Maelsechlainn (the high king having been killed), Muirtagh returns not to his clan but to the life of a wanderer. Given back his bow and a case of arrows, Muirtagh tells the king and his men they will hear from him but not for some time. The novel ends with Muirtagh going to retrieve his harp which Eoghan had sent him, his mind already shaping the music of his story. Because of the novelist's development of his character, the reader remembers Muirtagh, whose story is the very plot of the novel, as a civilized man among barbarians.

In a long historical novel with a large cast, keeping characters straight can be a problem for the reader. An author can help by listing the characters at the beginning of the book, not only by their full names but according to any name or title by which they are referred, a device particularly useful in long Russian novels where the characters are sometimes known by their patronymics. In a historical novel, a list of names may also serve to distinguish between actual and fictional people. Jose Maria Gironella provides such a list at the end of *One Million Dead.* Not only are separate lists given for fictional and historical characters, identifications are made according to family, occupation, and political alliance. In his *Cypresses Believe in God*, a two volume novel set in the period immediately before the Spanish Civil War, Gironella lists the names of numerous political parties during this confusing period. Such lists keep the text uncluttered and provide a quick source of information to the reader who needs or wants to be sure about a reference.

The background of characters in historical novels can be made more clear by the presence of a diagram or family tree. The family need not be royal to merit such treatment: R.F. Delderfield provides a tree for the Swanns of Tryst. The diagram at the beginning of *Theirs Was the Kingdom* shows nine children and the ward of Adam and Henrietta Swann, their marriages and offspring up to 1889, exactly one hundred years after the birth of Adam's father, Colonel Edward Swann. The novel itself opens with the death of the colonel in 1879 and the thoughts of various family members at his funeral. Although the leisurely pace of Delderfield's novel allows him to develop characters separately in chapters, the funeral offers a chance to assemble several of the cast.

When Adam first told the family of his father's death, the reactions of family members differed. Henrietta had wept; Giles, turned silent and pale, had gone to be alone in the winter woods. Stella could not know until word would be sent her in the next county. Alex would remain unaware until some time after the funeral, since he was soldiering in Africa. At the funeral the younger children follow the cue of sixteen year old George and put on pious expressions that fail to hide their enthusiasm over the prospect of being part of a military funeral.

Such an assembly gives the author an opportunity to sow the seeds of character; however, full growth comes only through attention to the individuals as the plot develops. Delderfield presents his characters in a third person narrative voice which he can make intimate enough to sound as if it comes from within various characters or sufficiently distant when objectivity is needed. Characters are shown in their inner thoughts as well as in their external actions. Situations in the novel are often a blend of pure reflection and straight incident. In Henrietta's thoughts about family in "Change of Landscape," for example, the reader senses that her reflections will lead directly to action. The climactic incident of Denzil Fawcett's midnight arrival and news that Stella has run away from Courtlands leads to the almost immediate formation of a plan by Henrietta. The second section of this chapter backtracks to Stella's reflections as a still unravished bride on her strange life at Courtlands. The third section shows Stella in action on the same blustery February night of section one, which was devoted to Henrietta's thoughts. The next chapter shows Henrietta actively executing her plan, now according to what seems her blueprint, now according to her instinct, as she confronts Stella's father-in-law, the lecherous Sir Gilbert Moncton-Price, and declares the Swanns' intentions of removing Stella's belongings from "this ratty old house" and seeking the annulment of her marriage to Lester, Sir Gilbert's homosexual son. For good measure Henrietta throws in social commentary: insulted by Sir Gilbert, she points out that the Swanns' money comes from the honest work of hauling goods, and that his kind live off generations of the poor "without putting a penny-piece back into the country." After her ultimatum, Moncton-Price admits to Henrietta that she is a remarkable woman and a credit to her husband.

That husband, although he has been notified of a crisis, has not yet returned from a business trip; yet, Henrietta has concealed her nervousness and acted as bailiff's man. The reader is impressed but not surprised by her actions. As early as the carriage ride back from the cemetery and the colonel's grave, this development in character had been anticipated by Adam's thoughts about his wife. Searching for the right word to describe her, Adam rejects *staunch*, *stalwart*, *intransigent*, and *resolute*, finally settling for *indomitable*. Indomitably is how Henrietta, in Adam's view, and that of the reader, meets every new situation.

Later, in the chapter "Time Miracle," a menopausal but serene Henrietta thinks of Adam, who has just surprised her by announcing that after his retirement he plans to leave something permanent — like trees. Henrietta finds Adam's knowledge of trees, new to her, one of the rewarding things about life with Adam: "You never stopped learning about him." She responds that he ought to begin immediately with his plans, but her response comes only after she has taken a moment to absorb the plan and assess the probability of his achievement. The scene reveals as much about Henrietta as about Adam.

In American historical novels, the theme of the westward journey has helped many writers develop character. One thinks of Vardis Fisher's *Children of God*, a novel which follows the movement of the Mormons from New York to Illinois and Missouri and finally to Utah. Religious persecution of the sect forced its migration west. The main events are historical as are characters such as Joseph Smith and Brigham Young. Character dominates plot and setting. In their struggles some of Fisher's people reveal deeply flawed human nature, others show strength and courage that enables them to endure against all odds. Even when Utah has been reached, only relative peace ensues. Characters are further developed through a period of internal strife until the novel's end, when some of them set out on another religious journey, away from the mainstream of the church.

Another westward journey prompted by religious reasons is Willa Cather's *Death Comes for the Archbishop*. In the prologue the reader learns that the candidate designated for the bishop's post must be able to cope with savagery and ignorance, with dissolute priests and political intrigue, with a world whose floor is cracked open by canyons and arroyos. What if the character turns out to fit this description? Will the reader be bored by someone too good to be true? Or will the character be unequal to the conflict promised by the environment described? But the reader for the moment is taken up by the four speakers in the prologue, particularly with the Spanish cardinal and the missionary from America. The contrast between the two men is more than personal; it is the difference between the old and new worlds. The reader's anticipation of the yet unmet character, Latour, is increased by what they reveal about themselves. The missionary knows the rigors of the land but has confidence in his candidate; the cardinal remembers that a valuable painting from his family's collection is now in the southwestern United States, and he hopes the new bishop will reclaim it for him.

The new world turns out to hold all the dangers and hardships foreseen in the prologue, and more. Latour and his friend Vaillant meet one of their challenges when they stop in a storm at what turns out to be a murderer's hideaway. In making their escape and in keeping with their characters, Vaillant relies on the protection of his patron St. Joseph while Latour draws a pistol, an action which works although the weapon is not in firing condition. The priests escape and are followed by the murderer's woman who has been more a captive than an accomplice. At the next town, Latour and Vaillant seek out the civil authorities. The murderous Buck Scales is found, tried, and hanged. Latour provides a place for the outlaw's woman, Magdalena, who had watched him murder not only strangers but the three babies she bore him; she is to work in the house of five sisters of Loreto whom Latour invited to find a school in letterless Santa Fe.

Among his letterless friends, Latour counts Kit Carson, who could read a landscape or a face but not a book, whose brain was the most reliable map of uncharted mountain ranges, and whose discriminating intelligence and compassionate heart put him "ahead of books, gone where the printing presses could not follow." Carson "not only had a story, but seemed to have become his story." Latour sees the man, not the legendary hero, and during the period when Carson carries out orders to move the Navajos out of their territory, the bishop sees him as his "own misguided friend."

A short dialogue between Latour and Carson's wife, contains a portrait of a minor character, Trinidad Lucero, a priest's nephew. Alleged by some to be Padre Lucero's son, but according to Senora Carson more likely the son of Padre Martinez, Trinidad had participated in the previous year's celebration of Holy Week by the Penitential Brotherhood. Tied to a cross, to his humiliation his weight pulled it down on top of him. When the bishop asks whether she thinks he should stop the excesses of the Penitentes, Senora Carson does not answer him directly but says she has advised her husband against suppressive measures which set people against authority. (This is not the sort of advice Carson originally followed on the Navajo question, although he and the government did reverse their stand on boundaries eventually.) Latour, in listening to people native to the area, is an effective administrator; he is also a character who wins the reader's sympathy and through whom the reader receives information and perceives the action of the novel.

The relationship between character and setting is close. On one of his journeys, Latour visits the grim and warlike church of Acoma, in whose gray walls and gray light he feels he is celebrating mass at the bottom of the sea for shelled antediluvian creatures beyond the reach of Calvary. Feeling inadequate and defeated, Latour later examines the church and concludes that the early missionaries must have been powerful men to have drafted Indian labor to build the massive structure. His reflections begin with the understatement that the missionaries were not altogether innocent of worldly ambition. Neither for that matter is Latour, but his dream of a cathedral in Santa Fe is more in keeping with the desire of the people, a plain honest building with good stone cutting.

Of all the tribes in the area Latour most admires the Navajos, although they are more resistant than the others to Christianity. He learns Navajo ways through his friend Eusabio, a chieftain who shows a hospitality that never intrudes, an ability to communicate deeply through a few words and gestures, and a reverent attitude toward nature. In traveling with Eusabio, Latour thinks of the differences between the white man's style of asserting himself against the landscape and the Indian's way of vanishing into it, obliterating all traces of a temporary campsite "as if it were his business to pass unseen and unheard through a country awakening with spring."

As Latour had visited Eusabio after the death of his only son, at the novel's end Eusabio comes to the archbishop. After Eusabio's departure, Latour says he has lived to see two wrongs righted, the end of black slavery and the restoration of the Navajos to their own country. The dying Latour had decided against returning to his native Auvergne, for he knew he would be homesick for the open sky, and the floor of that sky, "the desert where the wind made one a boy again." Willa Cather solves the problem that arises when the character in whom the novel's perception has been centered must die by shifting the perspective in time and place through a reference in a letter the archbishop had written to Vaillant's now dead sister, found among her possessions, "the full period of reflection that is the happiest conclusion to a life of action." Willa Cather, through Latour and his circle of characters, has, like the archbishop "accomplished an historic period." The reader feels he has been given an objective view as well as having been taken into the subjectivity of a character, to the place where "he sat in the middle of his own consciousness."

H.F.M. Prescott in *The Man on a Donkey* presents the reader with six main characters and a chance to change perspectives: the Prioress of Marrick, Christabel Cowper, Thomas, Lord Darcy, Julian Savage, Robert Aske, priest Gilbert Dawe, and the serving woman Malle. What moves these characters? At opposite ends of the scale, Malle loves but cannot hate; Gilbert hates but cannot love. Christabel loves power; Darcy, honor. Julian loves Robert, and Robert loves — but that is not so easy to say. Is it wholeness?

Robert is introduced as an otherwise happy boy with a temper and a brother with whom he does not get along well. In one of their fights Robert loses an eye, but he makes up in moral integrity what he lacks in physical wholeness. Prescott does not set Robin up as the brave though maimed hero. His teacher, Dom Henry, who taught his older brothers Jack and Kit and like all teachers tends to make comparisons, sees the boy is changing and that he will not grow up to be a quiet man, whatever he may be. Through the eyes of his father, Sir Robert, the reader sees his little sisters crying when Robin leaves to serve in the house of Northumberland, although he had teased and tyrannized over them. Three years later his sisters see him as a young man, almost a stranger. Dom Henry sees Robin now as having something that even-tempered Jack, with his wife and three children, and clever Kit, who has his books, do not have — strength.

When Robin, bored in the service of his new master, decides to turn to the study of law, the reader sees him bent over his Bracton, pushing his hair back and stuffing his thumbs in his ears to shut out his servant Will Wall's snoring. The next scene shows Robin studying at the family home in Aughton, where this time he is plagued by the bustle of women clearing out the old rushes from the floors and the presence of a flea-bitten spaniel. As a crowning interruption he is given a wet baby nephew to hold. The reader sympathizes with Aske in his frustrations but notices his perservance. Other characters may find him stubborn; a friend who loses an argument with him over a point of law tells him he is as set in his opinions as a boarhound hanging on by its teeth and that such tenacity will get him in trouble some day. The good-humored prophecy turns out to be true. Robert Aske becomes deeply involved in the uprising called the Pilgrimage of Grace, the event to which the plot leads and in which the various themes of the whole novel merge.

The divisions of Sigrid Undset's *Kristin Lavransdatter* have titles reminiscent of *kinder-kuche-kirche*, or, in Norwegian, *Kransen, Husfrue, Korset*,--*The Bridal Wreath, The Mistress of Husaby, The Cross*, in Charles Archer's translation. Yet, as any reader of the three part novel knows, characters are memorable not because they are typical representatives of Medieval Norway but because they are fully developed by the author as individuals. For this reason, although it is not a cult book in the sense of works by Golding, Salinger or Tolkien, *Kristin Lavransdatter* continues to rouse in its readers an almost personal loyalty to the central characters.

The reader's perception of the novel comes mainly through Kristin, but Undset does shift the point of view. Inside Erlend Nikulaussen, for example, the reader sees his thoughts about his quarrels with Kristin. Always he had blamed his own moodiness and outbursts of temper, but he begins to notice that his wife, for her part, stores up offenses and later hurls them at him as weapons. Another character through whom part of the story is seen is Ragnfrid, Kristin's mother, who has many visible disappointments as well as a hidden grief and who thinks of what she has lost rather than what she now possesses. In one scene she goes to sleep alone in a loft room, diving into a bed as soft and cold as a snow bank, weeping quietly. Later, after their daughter's marriage, Ragnfrid reveals to Lavrans that she was no maid when she married him and that their first child, a boy who did not survive infancy, may have been the other man's child.

To Lavrans, distressed by his knowledge that Kristin was carrying Erlend's child well before their wedding, Ragnfrid's confession about her own past brings much pain, but also a new understanding between the couple. The scene is incredibly moving and revelatory of character, as is a later dialogue between Lavrans and Kristin. Lavrans knows he is dying and Kristin visits him with her sixth son, a baby named after his grandfather, who delights in his daughter's role as a loving mother. Suddenly Kristin begins to cry wildly, thinking how much she does love the children, "But none had rightly loved them with her...'twas not Erland's way." After the death of Lavrans, Ragnfrid and Kristin tell each other their innermost thoughts. The mother embraces and kisses her daughter many times; "She had not done this before in all the years since Ulvhild died," Kristin's sister who had never fully recovered from an injury in childhood. During the time after Ulvhild's accident, Kristin had found a mother figure in the lady Aashild, who some said was a witch woman but who came to nurse Ulvhild. Kristin helps Aashild gather herbs, learning many ancient customs from the kindly old woman, one of the novel's vivid minor characters. Kristin also keeps praying for her sister, particularly on one summer night when the landscape seems to come to life. The scene foreshadows a much later incident in the novel; when her nephew is near death Kristin tells her brother-in-law Simon that she will dare to stay God's hand by a method taught her long ago by Aashild. In the light of the risen moon Kristin takes some turf from a grave in the local churchyard and buries her grandmother's betrothal ring in return. Her courage in performing the rash and blasphemous deed grows out of her desire to repay Simon (to whom she was originally betrothed) for the generosity he always shows to her family. The reader sees the incident from Kristin's point of view, sharing her fears and sense of determination.

Still later, the reader through Kristin reflects on her parents' life and the strong currents of joy and sorrow that must have run between them: "But she had begun to understand how much there was she did not understand." One of the things she does not understand is her life with Erlend. The reader remembers his various thoughtless acts, such as his failure to summon the lady midwives to assist in and legally witness the birth of his heir, but the reader may also remember Kristin in the first stages of labor as almost too thoughtful, wondering whether the servant has remembered to cook the fish in buttermilk which the priest had said would not break the fast since the broth would not be consumed.

Yet when their marriage ends with Erlend slain in her sight, Kristin, feeling that she herself still bleeds from his death-wounds, realizes "the whole of her life had lain within his arms." Character is fate: Kristin thinks of her sons and the uncertainty of their future, "All that had befallen, and all that was yet to befall was their doom — all things fall out as they are doomed to fall." Kristin eventually comes to have a more hopeful attitude, but by then she is near the end of her life.

A novel like *Kristin Lavransdatter* lives on to be discovered by new generations of readers and writers. The work is now over fifty years old, but it is less tarnished than some and brighter than many of last year's historical novels. Today's writer may feel he cannot achieve the level of Sigrid Undset's novel, but he should take heart. He should also take pleasure in the research and in the writing, remembering Delderfield's advice: "Enjoy your work. For if you don't nobody else will."

**The Writer's Manual
Book 5**

How to
Write
Articles
for
Magazines
and
Newspapers

By
Arthur Gould, Sr.

ABOUT THE AUTHOR

Arthur Gould, Sr.

has published widely in the article

and short story forms including the novella.

A former newspaper columnist and theater and music critic,

Dr. Gould has taught thousands of journalism students at

Northwestern University's

Medill School of Journalism.

CONTENTS

CHAPTER I

Specialization

There are somewhere between 15,000 and 20,000 magazines in America, nearly all of them in specialized areas--and many of them, literally thousands, willing to buy articles from free lance writers who send them stories *well directed to their readers.*

Today, specialization--meeting the specific needs of a particular magazine or newspaper--is the surest way of getting into print. For better or worse, the day of the big general magazine is dead. Readers go to magazines for special interests. It's up to the writer to know the special interests of the magazines he or she wants to write for and to slant the article--material as well as the writing itself--to those readers.

The writer who sells knows the markets. He or she has thoroughly researched the requirements of the magazines and newspapers in a specific area before writing and submitting the article. Querying an editor about article ideas will produce a specific response that will pinpoint needs even further. An honest, well written article about something that interests the writer and meets an editor's requirements will be published.

The premise to keep in mind is that every publication either wants to, or does not want to, print certain ideas, concepts or notions. Monographs on comparative philology, or structural linguistics will certainly be rejected by *Playboy,* although such essays may be welcome, and well paid for, by *The New York Review of Books.* A nostalgic look at the "super-cars" of the 1950s has virtually no chance at *Ms. Magazine,* but such an article was readily acceptable to *Esquire.* Erotic material should not be submitted to religious magazines; *Sports Illustrated* has no interest in gay liberation, even in sports. The obvious needs of editors are apparent to anyone with common sense. More subtle are differences among magazines of the same type. The only way a writer will know if an idea is more suitable for *Redbook* or *McCall's* in the women's market is by carefully comparing the magazines. When the writer has a *feel* for the market, he or she has acquired professional understanding. Given some hard work, the author will sell.

The policies of a magazine editor are difficult to second guess. Most editors are free to choose content without publisher interference, unless, of course, the editor offends advertisers (or caters to them), or alienates any great group of readers. The editor is free within the general structure of policy set by precedent and the publisher's direction. As a rule nearly all magazines adhere to the same basic principles: they must have advertising dollars and they must have readers. As a result, articles attacking financial backers are unlikely to run in a magazine. Two famous magazines, *Collier's* and *American Magazine,* were forced out of business in part because advertisers were offended by editorial content. (A young reporter at the time, Vance Packard was so outraged at the treatment of these two magazines by the advertising industry that he wrote *The Hidden Persuaders,* the expose of the ad-business that catapulted him to international fame as an author.)

Because advertising revenue depends on high circulation figures (the same is true of newspapers as well as magazines), editors in the past have been careful not to offend readers. During the late 1960s and into the 1970s, however, the question of what offends readers has gone up for grabs. In the past, anti-racial, anti-religious, anti-American, and anti-sectional articles were banned outright. This is not true today. The fall of Richard M. Nixon is due entirely to newspaper and magazine writers who shook the very foundations of the country with their stories. The same kind of questioning attitude in such magazines as *Esquire* and *Ramparts* was partially responsible for getting the U.S. out of Vietnam.

Even the question of good taste has given way to an attitude that prescribes: if it feels good, do it. In terms of magazine policy this can mean-- if it captures readers, print it. The writer will have to use his or her own judgment based on knowledge of current markets.

What may be offensive to one class of readers will appeal to another. Cynicism and irony--two elements traditionally edited out of article copy-- now are often major attractions. Sincerity and unsophisticated praise of life's simple pleasures and virtues appears less frequently in the pages of the slick national magazines, the ones that make the Big Dollar and pay authors the best fees. They appeal to a young, well educated, highly paid, urban audience. Such magazines as *Playboy, Esquire, Vogue, Penthouse, Redbook, Cosmopolitan, Glamour,* and *Ms.* fit this "now" category.

Generally, there are three kinds of magazines--the excellent, high paying, high circulation magazines and newspapers; the majority of adequately written, generally read publications, and the low-quality, violence-and-sex tainted "rags." Many writers scorn this last category, but what writer can say he or she hasn't sometime written for a low quality newspaper or magazine? As glamorous and rewarding as it is to publish in the great national slicks, practically all beginning authors start writing for lower quality publications. There's a lot of money to be made from these magazines; they are less choosey, but they do demand professionalism from their authors.

There are five generally recognized viewpoints of magazines: conservative, ultra conservative, middle-of-the-road, liberal, and radical.[1] Although editorial policy is a changing and subjective element, consistent examples of the five are: *Saturday Evening Post, The National Review, Redbook, Esquire, and Ramparts.* A good free lance writer reads these magazines, or ones like them, to keep abreast of attitudes, issues, interests, and subjects that are currently appealing to the great classes of readers. A writer should never consider sending an article exposing the weaknesses of the capitalist system in America to the *Saturday Evening Post.* Likewise, a complimentary profile of J. Edgar Hoover is unlikely to find space in *Ramparts.* The writer must understand the basic point-of-view of a publication, and it's important that the free lance feel comfortable writing for a particular slant. Insincerity is the easiest fault to spot and the most damaging for the writing. Since editors will not, or cannot, change the basic policies of their magazines, it's up to the writers to seek publications that agree with their own beliefs.

At the same time, it's foolish for a writer to be dogmatic. Most American readers have catholic tastes--they'll read anything that interests them, to their benefit--and those aspiring to be professional writers should be willing to mirror that eclecticism. For instance William F. Buckley's conservatism is not so closed-minded that he's unwilling to appear in *Esquire* or *The New York Times Sunday Magazine,* two traditionally liberal publications.

Recognizing the reader of a magazine is the best way for a free lance writer to begin specializing. To know who reads a magazine, the potential contributor must study the publication. Read all the ads — to whom is the product appealing — the wealthy, the well educated, the white or blue collar worker, union or management? All of this information can come from the ads. The cost of the magazine and the number of readers lets the writer know something about the audience, too. If the magazine sells for $1.50 on the stand, has a 200,000 circulation, and carries ads for expensive restaurants, travel, and cars, chances are good the reader is a wealthy executive, man on woman, white or black with college education and a relatively bright outlook on life.

The slicker the magazine, physically the greater the appeal to a sophisticated reader. A comparison of *Gentlemen's Quarterly*, published by *Esquire*, and *The National Enquirer* will make this point clear. The latter is a pulp newsmagazine, with a weekly circulation of 3 million copies, that uses human interest, off-beat, occult, and self-help material to attract a wide audience. *GQ's* reader, on the other hand, is attracted by the expensive color photography, featuring exotic travel and expensive clothes for men. The paper is of the highest quality and the type and layout are sophisticated.

Other ways of identifying readers are: the kinds of articles the magazine uses; the vocabulary used in the articles; the technical terms--exact, or general--; the slant for education or entertainment; the size and number of columns per page; the length of sentence and the article itself.

Most magazines will vary the length of sentences and paragraphs to avoid monotony. The writer should be aware of the maximum and minimum length of articles for a specific magazine. It's a waste of time to send a 700 word article to a magazine that sets a 1500-word minimum. Editors have to fill white-space around ads and they can get desperate for adequate amounts of copy. If you are on assignment, don't put the editor on the spot by turning in a story that's too short, or too long. It's easier to cut copy than add it, but no editor wants to waste time rewriting an article he has paid for and expects to be correct. The writer won't have a second chance to treat the editor that way.

Titles and sub-titles should be studied carefully to tell the editor's philosophy of "grabbing" the reader: emotional, sensational, or sophisticated appeal are possibilities. The titles of the articles and stories do a great deal to set the tone of the magazine, and they indicate the kinds of material the publication is looking for.

In studying illustrations, it's a good idea to find out if the writers have supplied the art work themselves or whether the magazine has assigned the pictures. There's extra money for the free lance who can take his or her own pictures. Nearly all magazines purchase photographs, black-and-white (b/w) glossies, usually 8 x 10, as well as color transparencies. All magazines that buy photos pay extra if a picture is used on the cover. It's important to pay attantion to captions and cut-lines that go with a picture. The caption is a title that usually appears above the art work. A cut-line is made up of a few sentences of copy describing the picture. They appear below the photo. Technically, the smaller the size of the magazine page the less room for illustrations; the larger the page the better quality of dramatization through pictures.

In examining magazines for editorial policy a writer should read at least 30 issues of a monthly and two or three issues a month for three years for weeklies. Examine each of the issues for the characteristics that will tell you what kind of people read the publication as well as the needs of the editors. Newspapers publish articles by free lance writers in their Sunday magazines, feature sections, entertainment reviews, and in some instances in spot news columns. Newspapers and magazines are closer today in speed of production, color equipment, use of wire services and typographical excellence and style, as George L. Bird points out. Writers should approach both in the same ways as far as knowing markets and submitting material. Newspapers, like magazines, need interpretive articles, profiles of prominent people, think pieces, interviews, food articles, fashion, and others. The major difference between the two is the money that papers and magazines pay their authors. While magazines will pay outstanding fees, $2000 and up, newspapers pay notoriously low commissions, just as they generally underpay their full time staff reporters.

Since the amount of space filled with copy determines how much the newspaper editor will pay, it's profitable to write as much as you can and hope enough of it survives the editor's blue pencil to cover expenses. To compound the situation, many newspapers will refuse to give the free lance a by-line; or, more agonizing, the material may appear as part of someone else's article, or under another by-line. This isn't stealing by the newspaper; it's the way papers use copy they buy from stringers. Unless a writer can work for *The New York Times Magazine,* or others like it, that give by-lines and pay competitive rates, he or she must be prepared to serve a difficult apprenticeship at newspapers in return for the experience of getting into print. The pay may be as low as $1.50 for a local column and may go up to $15 to $20 per column. Writers should check *Ayer's Newspaper and Periodical Directory* and *Editor and Publisher's International Year Book Number* for rates in their regions.

Reproduction of illustrative material--photographs, charts, tables, line drawings, maps—will not have the quality or impact in a newspaper that we expect in magazines. But the newspaper is the place for the stark, dramatic story picture. Although color process is improving, color may bleed on newsprint. It's impossible to achieve much drama with a blurred color photograph.

The same kind of research used in learning magazine markets should be applied to newspapers. The advantage with papers is obvious: every area has local newspapers. Writers should get to know the editors personally. In larger towns and in cities with medium size and large dailies the writer should get to know the Sunday editor, sports editor, city editor, and managing editor. On many papers, the editor-in-chief does not get involved in the day-to-day work of running the paper. In most instances, the managing editor directs the newsroom and he, or she, is the person to see about free lance assignments. Since it's difficult to second-guess newspaper editors, the only way to get the *feel* for a market is to read the "target paper" every day and to follow all the special departments where features are published, especially the family interest sections and the women's departments. These sections often welcome contributions from readers and will pay something for short human interest and how-to articles. Papers are always looking for articles on murder mysteries, important crime, inside political news, high society divorces, run-a-ways, and new angles on old stories. Historical material is popular, as well as the six generally accepted types of magazine articles.

1.) Profiles, sometimes called personality sketches, emphasize the individual and his or her achievements. As a human interest story, the person only has to attract the reader by entertaining, or inspiring. But the author must make the person come alive for the reader by using characterization, physical appearance, dress, habits, interesting biographical material, mannerisms, and the opinions of others. The reader wants to know what's in the subject's head, how he or she feels, and what are his or her beliefs. Anyone living in a large metropolitan area will have access to entertainers and famous personalities who pass through the city. But wherever the writer lives, he or she must watch newspapers for advance notice of visiting dignitaries and other famous people. In almost every instance, the writer will have to acquire advance permission to interview a public personality for a profile article. As a matter of expediency and courtesy, the writer should contact the prospective subject's managers or agents in advance to set up an interview. This will insure the writer's getting in to see the person. Most people in show business, and most politicians, want and need the publicity of magazine or newspaper articles. They're happy to talk with writers and pose for photographs.

In writing a profile, after the initial interview, use devices such as anecdotes, minor incidents and major experiences to relate the character of the subject. Use direct quotes to add authority, authenticity, and to *liven-up* the copy. The article should be written with a clear, confident, and fast paced style that grips the reader's attention.

2.) First person narrative articles include essays and how-to stories.

Although the personal essay is not a popular genre today, many magazines will occasionally publish such articles by well known writers, experts, or outstanding personalities. Beginning writers have trouble finding outlets for their opinion pieces, because the reader must recognize and trust the authority of the narrative voice. Magazines such as *The Atlantic Monthly, Esquire, Harper's,* and *The New York Times Magazine* run essays.

First person narratives in these magazines are characterized by clarity of thought, freshness of style, authority, original ideas, declarative statements, humor, irony and startling comments, and observations on the human condition. The writer's goal is to entertain, to educate and to change the reader's point of view. The facts must be on the writer's side and they should convince the reader that the essay's premises are correct. The most convincing presentation follows a reasonable and valid line of argument that draws a valid inference in the conclusion.

First person is most often used in how-to articles telling the correct way to build a patio, repair an automobile, grow a herb garden, paddle a canoe. . . anything that appeals to readers of a particular magazine. The trick in this kind of article is to write clearly and logically enough so the reader can successfully follow the process step-by-step, like a good recipe. At the same time, the copy must be presented in an interesting, personal way so the reader isn't bored. Encouragingly, more how-to articles are sold than any other type of story.

The writer should be sure that he or she understands how-to-do-it before writing the article. Then present the process step-by-step including only material that will explain how-to and that will keep the reader's attention. The use of technical terms depends on the audience, but generally they should be explained as soon as they're mentioned.

Structurally, the title and the lead should explain the purpose of the article. Further down should come an explanation of why the reader should be interested in the process. In the body, the writer should give definitive directions in a logical and orderly way. Examples should be included and faults detailed for the sake of honesty. Above all, the article must be genuinely helpful.

3.) Third person narrative articles sell best. They tell about the experiences of someone, or something, using the devices of the short story: description, conversation, and suspense. As Bird points out, they tell how something was done, but not how-to-do it. The events and persons written about must be real, but the style can be impressionistic and interpretive in the vein of so-called *new journalism.* Any subject is open to this kind of handling.

4.) Confession articles are always popular because of readers' interest in the motivations and actions of others. Subjects for a confession range from the baldly lurid to the sophisticated and intellectual. But whatever the story, the article must convey a feeling of intimacy, depth of personality and revelation. The confession implies the author is seeking atonement for *sin.* Told in the first person, the writer should give the impression that he or she is *letting it all hang out* in order to clear the air and be forgiven. Since the subject is asking forgiveness, a repentance is a necessary part of the story. The material should be factual and realistic, as well as exciting and suspenseful. The events must have happened to someone, but the as-told-to format is out in a confession article.

Careful study of the confession magazines is necessary for a writer to break into the market. Although such articles may appear easy to write, because of their usually simple and direct style, confessions are actually difficult to produce. For instance, the writer has to be able to handle emotional description well. Without fictionalizing the material, the author must be able to adopt the first person voice of someone else. If the story is truly personal, the writer will probably want to use a pen-name for the by-line.

5.) Interview articles are a type of third person narrative. The words of the subject are the story, although the writer may use description, characterization, and other comments to bring correspondence between the reader and the subject. This use of extra material may not always be the case, however. The body of a *Playboy* Interview, for example, is straight dialogue between the magazine and the subject. But it's important to inform the reader about the person and that biographical material may appear as a separate insert at the beginning, as *Playboy* handles the background of the subject, or brought out in the article itself as part of the author's narration. At the same time, the article is *not* a profile, and the biographical material should apply directly to what the person says during the interview.

The writer should conduct the interview only after thoroughly researching the subject. There's no point in wasting time discussing personal matters readily available elsewhere. The subject's date and place of birth, educational background, marital status, number of children, heritage, wealth, and so forth, should be part of the author's background for the interview. The writer's questions should reflect that knowledge as he or she probes the subject for more important revelations.

The writer's goal should be the subject's feelings, and to capture them in quotes. A writer may put words in the subject's mouth, if the quote reflects the true impression of his or her thoughts. As a rule, if the free lance is unsure whether the subject would agree with a statement, the quote should not be used.

A celebrity's agent or manager should be contacted to arrange an interview. It's unlikely a writer, no matter what his or her status, will get an interview without setting it up first. Such contacts have to be negotiated, often far in advance, because of scheduling problems. At the same time, these people want publicity and they'll usually make every effort to cooperate with a writer, even a beginner.

6.) The potpourri article is a miscellaneous collection of items generally related to one another written under a unifying title. An article listing 72 ways to save money and fight inflation sold recently to a family magazine is an example. Such articles are usually short, under 1000 words, although they can run longer when they are played as features, such as Christmas-gifts-you-can-make-at-home types that show up in family and women's magazines during the holidays.

Subjects for potpourri articles are all around us: timesaving items, menus, inventions, parties, special events, to list a few. The style should be fast-paced, concrete, and condensed. Such articles are often unillustrated and they are usually assigned after an author quiries an editor.

It's important to stress that these six kinds of articles can be sold to newspapers as well as magazines. But the writer should keep in mind that newspapers most often buy stories with local angles. A newspaper's national news and features are supplied by wire services, or the paper's own bureaus. The home staff covers local spot news and local features. It's up to the free lance to search out items of local interest and expand on them on a way that has not been covered by the paper. There may be spot news that a reporter doesn't have time or inclination to expand on for an article. Stories appearing in out—of—town papers about a local resident, or happening, may miss the eye of the local editor. Government bulletins about local agencies may be ignored by staff writers. Interesting events of local clubs or personalities may get by the city editor. All of these circumstances offer a way for the free lance writer to sell his or her material to a newspaper.

When a writer considers that over 100,000 issues of publications appear annually, and that each issue has from one to 20 feature articles, the chances of getting into print, even for the beginner, are excellent. With that kind of broad support, the writer increases his or her chances of selling articles by knowing the markets, specializing and slanting the story for a particular magazine or newspaper. The formula for each publication is found by studying and analyzing past articles. Although the larger magazines receive over 3000 manuscripts a week for consideration, a writer who has learned market requirements, knows something about the editors and how to impress them will get published.

As a rule most readers are interested in other people's achievements, pursuits, economic success, health and happiness. Successful articles deal with these subjects, using concrete examples, direct quotations and interviews. As Helen Patterson points out, the average American reader wants to be healthier, wealthier, wiser, and happier. Readers want to know about others who have achieved more efficiently, more satisfactorily, or more profitably than they have.

CHAPTER TWO

THE FOUR
MAIN MAGAZINE FIELDS

The thousands of magazines published in America fall into four general categories for the free lance writer to study in his or her pursuit of specialization and publication. There are consumer magazines; business publications; association magazines; and company publications. The majority of the magazines in each group publish non-fiction, articles and features, and most purchase illustrations--black and white glossies, color transparencies, line drawings, maps, tables and charts. The rates vary from 1/2 cent a word to $5000-plus per article. Subjects are virtually unlimited--a competent writer should be able to find a magazine in these four categories for any kind of article, from lurid sexual material to the most sophisticated and intellectual essays and reviews.

1.) Consumer magazines are what most readers think of as magazines-- from *Ladies' Home Journal* and *Esquire* through *Better Homes and Gardens* to *Playboy.* They include the name publications that people subscribe to at home, buy on the newsstands, or browse through at the library. They are also the literary and little magazines, religious publications, sports journals, regional magazines, and others that share a general interest appeal.

The big name magazines are the cream of the crop. They are tough to break into and they pay top rates--$750 to $5000-plus per article. However, there are 12 major categories of consumer magazines that include publications that are easier for writers to break into. The majority of these magazines pay lower rates.

There are more literary and little magazines (206 publications) than any other type of consumer magazine.[2] About ninety percent of them publish non-fiction of all kinds-- humor, interview, general interest, and reviews. The tone of such articles is generally sophisticated and the research and authority must be unimpeachable. The fees these magazines pay range from nothing, or subscription copies, to about $150 per article. Many pay 1c to 5c per word.

Typical magazines and their specifications, in this group, are:

Pyramid (circulation 500) which accepts non-fiction articles on any subject with no special slant or taboos. The editors are interested in reviews of books of poetry. Articles should not exceed 3000 words. The magazine pays $3 to $20 per printed page, plus copies and a free subscription:

The Southern Review (circulation 3000) is a well known university magazine that publishes non-fiction, particularly essays with careful attention to craftsmanship, technique and seriousness of subject. The editors advise authors to avoid extremism and sensationalism. The length of articles should be 4000 to 10,000 words. Writers are paid 3c per word.

The Ohio Review (circulation 900) buys non-fiction, think articles only. Length is open and there are some cash payments: $25-$100.

Fiction International (circulation 5000) publishes non-fiction--interviews with well-known fiction writers, and book reviews. Articles run from 1000 to 10,000 words. Payment is $5 to $25 per article. This magazine also buys photographs, as do many of the magazines in this group. Payment for photos varies. They should be 8 x 10, b/w glossies.

The American Scholar. (circulation 47,000) which pays top rates for articles ($150) in this group, is looking for nontechnical treatments of science, art, religion, politics, national and foreign affairs. Length: 3000 to 3500 words.

Religious magazines are second highest in number of consumer publications, with 134. All the magazines in this group accept non-fiction on religious subjects, or life and religion. Some publications run material with moral and philosophical overtones. Here is a market for educational and inspirational articles, too. There are non-denominational magazines and publications for-and-about particular religious groups, sects, and orders. The pay range is from 1½c per word to $300 per article .

Typical magazines and their specifications in this group are:

Annal Of Good Saint Anne de Beaupre (circulation 75,000) accepts articles on devotions to St. Anne, major current social problems, education, ecumenism, family, interviews, profiles, inspirational and think pieces. Material must have a Roman Catholic slant. Length of articles runs from 800 to 1800 words. Authors are paid 1c-to-2c per word.

The Baptist Herald (circulation 12,000) buys articles of general religious interest. They are looking for articles that are precise, concise, and honest. The editor will accept interviews, inspirational, and personal experience. The length of articles runs 700 to 2000 words. The magazine pays $5 to $10 per article.

Canadian Churchman (circulation 250,000) accepts non-fiction on religion, social action, morality, social conditions, new religious trends, entertainment, and politics. The articles should be 750 to 1200 words and the rate is $35 to $250.

Jewish Social Studies (circulation 1200) is concerned with sociology and contemporary and historical aspects of Jewish life. Article length is open. Pay is $5 per printed page.

Columbia (circulation 1,000,000) uses non-fiction for the Catholic layman and family. Articles should deal with current events, social problems, Catholic apostolic activities, education, rearing a family, literature, science, the arts, sports, and leisure. 8 x 10 b/w glossies are required for illustration. Authors are paid a package price--article and photos--of $100-$300.

There are 120 sports-and-outdoor publications slanted for sportsmen, sports fans, or both. All of these magazines accept non-fiction with heavy emphasis on how-to and where-to perform ... and cover all aspects of sports. The many sub-categories in this group include magazines on archery and bowhunting, basketball, bicycling, boating, bowling, billiards, football, general sports interest, golf, guns, horse racing, hunting, fishing, material arts, mountaineering, skiing and snow sports, swimming and diving, tennis, and wrestling. Fees for writers range from 50c per column inch to $750 minimum and negotiated payment in the thousands of dollars for professional writers who are well known for their sports copy.

Typical magazines and their specifications in this group are-

Bicycling (circulation unavailable) uses articles on unusual bicycle adventures, bike racing, family bicycle trips, vacations, surveys of technical problems, equipment reviews, health articles, bicycle commuting and bike history. The editors advise writers that all articles should encourage the reader to ride a bicycle and must be informative and authentic. Articles should run 1000 to 4000 words. The magazine pays 50c per column inch.

Sail (circulation 100,000) is looking for articles on sailing technique written in technical language. They also want feature stories, how-to, personal experience, profiles, historical, new products and photo articles. The author should emphasize the excitement of sailing and its human aspects. Article length runs 1000 to 2000 words. The magazine pays $50 to $300. Black-and-white glossies purchased with the manuscript are bought for $10 to $125; color $35 to $200; and $200 for a photo used on the cover.

The American Rifleman (circulation 1,068,735) is concerned with hunting, target shooting, shotgunning. conversation, firearms repairs. The editors *do not* want semi-fictional or "me and Joe" yarns. Length is 1-4 magazine pages and they pay $75 to $750 per article.

Gambler's World (circulation 300,000) insists that the writer know the gambling topic he or she is writing about. They are looking for informational, how-to, personal experience, interview, profile, humor, think pieces, exposes. Article length should be 100 to 5000 words. Payment depends on subject matter, quality of writing, and article length. Pays $25 to $500.

Sports Illustrated (circulation 2,150,000) has two general categories for non-fiction: regional and long text. The magazine runs a great deal of regional advertising and pegs regional stories to it. The regional material should be 600 to 2000 words, with timeless quality: humor, reminiscence, personality in some aspects of sports. Authors are paid $250 for regional articles. The long texts run 2000 to 5000 words with emphasis on major personalities, personal reminiscence, authoritative look into aspects of sports with broad appeal. The magazine pays a minimum of $750 for long text. *SI* negotiates fees for articles by well known authors, in the sports area.

The fourth largest group of consumer magazines is the regionals, and metropolitans with 79 publications. They are general interest magazines for residents and visitors to a specific region or city. Pay ranges from 1½c per word to $500 per article. All these magazines accept non-fiction.

Typical magazines and their specifications in this group are:

Coast Magazine (circulation 15,000) accepts material about Western America and California. Emphasis is on pulse of the west--life styles, arts, politics, ecology, business, education, sports, food, and fashion. Article length should run 300 to 10,000 words. Pay rate is 1½c to 5c per word.

New England Galaxy (circulation 130,000) accepts non-fiction on New England history, biography, and social customs. Length should be

2000 to 3000 words. Pays $50 to $150.

New York Magazine (circulation 325,000) looking for new or important aspects of the New York scene. Articles should run 1000 to 3500 words. The magazine pays $100 to $350 per article.

Chicago (circulation 100,000) accepts non-fiction dealing with the quality of life in Chicago, its past, present, and future. The magazine is also looking for personal experience, think pieces, interviews, profiles, humor, spot news, historical articles, and exposes. Length should be 2000 to 6000 words. Writers are paid $100 to $500 per article.

Minnesotan (circulation 70,000) accepts non-fiction concerning facets of the state, its history, and people living within 100 miles of Minneapolis and St. Paul. Articles should run 1000 to 2000 words. Writers are paid $100 to $250 per article. The magazine also buys photos, as do most of the magazines in this group, and pays an average $25 to $50 per b/w glossy.

Teen and young adult publications are plentiful--59 such magazines-- and they are slanted for young people 12 to 26 years old. They are general interest magazines that all accept non-fiction. The pay rate is 1/2c per word to $500 per article.

Typical magazines and their specifications in this group are:

Alive (circulation 19,000), looking for first person articles about outstanding young people and issues that they must deal with. The length of an article should not exceed 1500 words. Writers are paid 2c per word. The magazine pays $5 to $10 per b/w glossy.

Campus News, (circulation 25,000), accepts reviews of records, films, how-to, columns, and articles that tell about campus life. Article length --200 to 1500 words. Writers are paid 25c to 60c per column inch.

Exploring (circulation 2,300,000), looking for non-fiction concerning careers, colleges, exploring, travel, music, contemporary youth, sports, how-to, personal experience, interviews, profiles, humor, think pieces, photo essays. Do not submit sexual material or particularly contro-versial issues. Articles should run 2000 to 2500 words. The magazine pays $250 to $500 per article. Photos are purchased for $100 per b/w glossy; $150 per page for inside color; and, $250 to $350 for a cover shot.

The New Ingenue (circulation 1,000,000) is looking for general interest with a strong emphasis on personal identity, health, drugs, sex, school, family, peer groups, travel, sports, political and social trends, how-to, "now". Writers should send outline and query letter including a summary of the idea for an article. Article length: 700 to 4500 words. Pay: $175 to $500 per article.

Seventeen (circulation 1,994,318) accepts non-fiction with general interest, but the emphasis is on topicality and helpfulness. Writers should sent outline and query. Length: 2000 to 3000 words. Pays: $100 to $500. Photos on assignment.

There are 59 juvenile publications appealing to children 2-12 years old. Many of these magazines are published by religious groups. Pay ranges from 1/4c per word to $200 per article.

Typical magazines and their specifications in this group are:

Adventure (circulation 206,000) accepts non-fiction on children's experiences, adventure, nature, travel, biography, hobbies, how-to, science, history, pets, home, school, nature, love, God, animals, and Bible related activities. Writers should keep in mind for this magazine and all magazines in this group that they are writing for a young reading audience. Articles should not exceed 900 words. The magazine pays 2½c per word.

American Red Cross Youth News (circulation 258,000) non-fiction emphasizing service, positive side of life for and about children, humorous, seasonal, games that teach, science experiments, health, well-being. Articles should run 1000 to 1500 words. Writers are paid $100 to $150 per article.

Highlights For Children (circulation 1,000,000) looking for non-fiction emphasizing factual features, history, science by experts; also looking for articles on children living in other countries; sports and biographies. Articles should not exceed 1000 words. The magazine pays a minimum of $50 per article.

Kidstuff Magazine (circulation 75,000) accepts articles that interest parents and teachers on education, health care, how-to, crafts, and the creative talent of children themselves. Articles should run 300 to 1500 words. Writers are paid $25 to $100 per article.

Ranger Rick's Nature Magazine (circulation unavailable) accepts non-fiction on anything concerning nature, conservation, environmental problems, natural science. Length of articles should not exceed 750 words. The magazine pays $200 per article.

A recently popular group of consumer publications is the alternate, and radical magazines. There are 48 of them currently in print. They all accept non-fiction that expresses generally anti-establishment or minority ideas and views that are unlikely to be accepted by a more commercial press. The pay for articles ranges from nothing at all to $150 per story.

Typical magazines and their specifications in this group are:

The Advocate (circulation 30,000) accepts news and features concerning homosexuals. Articles should run 1000 to 3000 words. The magazine pays $15 to $30 per article.

Both Sides Now (circulation 6000) accepts non-fiction concerning counter-culture, radical/liberal politics in the U.S. and the world. Also looking for well researched articles about health foods, religion, women, how-tos, personal experience, interviews, profiles, inspirational, humor, spot news, new products, photo features, travel, and reviews of film, music, and literature. Article length is open. Pay is in copies of the magazine.

The Boston Phoenix (circulation 200,000) wants non-fiction covering movies, rock music, books, politics; the articles should emphasize the experimental. There is also an interest in humor. Article should not exceed 5000 words. The pay rate is $50 to $100.

New Earth Tribe News (circulation 500) is looking for articles that stress humanistic/positivistic consciousness. Writers should encourage self-responsibility, self-discovery, and solidarity among people. They use articles on recycling, living off the land, community living experiments, ecology, yoga, health, organic-foods, the arts. Articles should not exceed 750 words. The magazine pays from $5 to $10 per article.

San Francisco Bay Guardian (circulation 25,000) is looking for investigative reporting, features, analysis, interpretation, how-to, consumer reviews with a San Francisco angle. Advocacy journalism is the style required by this publication. Needs features on how to survive in the city. Also looking for interviews, profiles, think pieces, historical, expose, nostalgia, photo, travel, and pop culture. The length of reviews should be 800 to 1500 words and the pay is $24; short articles should run 1500 to 2500 words and the pay is $25 to $50; long articles run 2500 words, or more, and pay $50 to $75.

Newspaper Sunday supplements make up another large group of popular consumer magazines. The articles they publish should be about persons, places and events in their specific circulation areas. Payments range from 2c per word to $750 and up per article.

Alabama Sunday Magazine (circulation 80,000) accepts non-fiction concerning people and places in Alabama, or people from the state; how-to, or general features concerning holidays or events. There is a market for humor, historical nostalgia, and photo essays. The articles should run 300 to 1500 words. The magazine pays $10.

The Blade Sunday Magazine (circulation 200,000) is interested in general feature articles on personalities, life style, leisure, unusual happenings, and adventure. The emphasis should be on local-northwestern Ohio and southeastern Michigan. The articles should run 800 to 2500 words. The magazine pays $20 to $65 per article.

Chicago Sun-Times' Midwest Magazine (circulation 714,164) accepts non-fiction of general interest with topical features focusing on Chicago or the Chicago area. Writers should submit brief queries and story outlines. Articles run 750 to 2500 words. Writers are paid $50 to $300 per article.

The New York Times Magazine (circulation 1,412,017) is looking for background articles on national and international news developments, science, education, family life, social trends, the arts, entertainment, personalities, sports, the changing American scene. Also, timely articles based on specific news items, forthcoming events, significant anniver-saries. They use humor with a news peg. Full length articles, about 3500 words, pay $750 and up; shorter articles, 1000 to 2000 words receive $75 per column.

Tahoman (circulation 97,129) is looking for articles of general interest to readers in the Pacific Northwest, particularly the Puget Sound area and photos on the same subject. The interest is in historical, biographical, and recreational material. Article length is open. The magazine pays $25 per printed page.

There are 56 hobby and craft publications for collectors, do-it yourselfers, and craft hobbyists. The magazines in this group pay from 1c per word to $400 per article.

Typical magazines and their specifications in this group are:

Acquire (circulation 50,000) accepts non-fiction news articles on trends and specific events in the area of contemporary collectibles; profiles and interviews. The articles should be tightly written, fact-filled, and informational. They use how-tos, personal experience, humor, expose, nostalgia, personal opinion, travel, and all types of reviews. The magazine is always on the look-out for spot news, successful business operations, new products, merchandising techniques, and technical articles. Stories should run 250 to 5000 words. The magazine pays $45 to $250 per article. B/w glossies are purchased for $10 to $100 per picture.

Boat Builder (circulation 50,000) accepts how-tos on building boat models, in clear semi-technical language. Articles should run 250 to 1500 words. The magazine pays $25 to $300 per article.

Model Airplane News (circulation 100,000) is interested in articles dealing with model airplanes in all phases. The appeal is for general aviation news if it has a tie-in with model airplanes. Writers are encouraged to submit photos and drawing with articles. Length: 1500 to 2000 words pays $50 to $300 per article.

Railroad Modeler (circulation 75,000) wants non-fiction in all areas of model railroading, building, layouts, new ways of producing models. Writers must have first hand knowledge of model railroading. Photo features in color are accepted. The market is informational, how-to, historical, and technical material. The articles should run 1000 to 4000 words. The magazine pays $25 to $100 per article. 5 x 7 b/w glossies are purchased with articles. Writers receive a minimum of $10 for color transparencies.

Postal Bell (circulation 300) wants non-fiction for the stamp collector.. Stories related to stamps and the countries that issue them. Technical articles on stamp issues are used. Articles should run 500 words. The magazine pays $10 per article.

The women's market, with 38 publications, has the highest paying magazines, 8c per word to $5000 per article. This group includes many of the major consumer magazines. They are slick, high quality, expensive, mass circulation publications. They carry the most advertising and publish only the best commercial writing, in most general interest subject areas. They appeal to women and the family, including men, although the audience is predominantly female.

Typical magazines and their specifications in this group are:

Cosmopolitan (circulation 1,500,000) is *not* interested in unsolicited manuscripts or queries. Writers who want to break into this market must work through agents. *Cosmo* will consider unsolicited queries only from top professional writers with wide publishing background. Articles are aimed at young women—18-34—who are intelligent, good citizens and who are interested in a more rewarding life. There is a market for how-to, self-improvement, careers, part-time jobs, diets, food, fashion, men, entertainment, material dealing with emotions, money, medicine, and psychology. Writers are discouraged from submitting material on war, poverty, and civil rights. Short articles, 1200 to 1500 words pay $200 to $500. Long articles, 3000 to 4000 words, pay $750 to $1500. Photos are on assignment only.

Glamour (circulation 1,500,000) does not need articles on fashion, beauty, decorating, entertaining, and travel. Articles in these areas are staff written. There is a market for current interest articles, and helpful, informative material, as well as humorous or series articles on all aspects of a young woman's life. The appeal is for women 18-35 years old. *Glamour* also needs articles on medicine, mental health, travel, society, and economics. Articles should run 2000 to 3000 words. The magazine pays $300 to $500 for short pieces and a minimum of $750 for long articles.

Modern Bride (circulation 300,000) accepts non-fiction of interest to brides-to-be concerning etiquette, marriage, planning a home, and honeymoon travel. Articles should run about 2000 words. The magazine pays $150 and up.

Ms. Magazine (circulation 350,000) needs non-fiction on the arts, women's minds and women's bodies that relate to explaining a new life style for women, and changes in their roles in society. There is special interest in articles that tell how a woman may gain control over her life. In all instances women must be treated as human beings, not sexual objects. There is a market for how-tos, personal experience, interviews, profiles, humor, and historical material. Articles should have a minimum length of 1000 words. Writers are paid $100 to $500, per article.

Vogue (circulation 458,555) does *not* need fashion articles, as they are staff written. But the magazine does use general interest feature articles of high quality. Length: 2000 to 2500 words. The magazine pays $300 and up.

The men's market, with 50 publications, also pays the highest rates, 3c per word to $4000 per article. The magazines in this group include some of the slickest, highest paying consumer publications. The subject range is wider than in the women's market, however. The men's field includes magazines from luridly sexual to first rate, literary publications. Circulations are high and advertising space is enormous. Men's magazines publish a broad spectrum of articles from sexual material to well researched and authoritatively written think pieces.

Typical magazines and their specifications in this group are:

Playboy (circulation 7,000,000) uses carefully researched articles on men, sports, politics, sociology, business, finances, games--anything of interest to the affluent, urban male. The magazine uses little or no adventure or how-to. Review of movies, records, theater, books, food and drink are staff written. Articles should run 4000 to 6000 words. The magazine pays $3000 for a lead article, and $2000 for a regular feature. The regular Playboy Interview, 8000 to 15,000 words pays $2000. The annual Playboy Panel Discussion, with 7 to 10 people on a topical subject, 8000 to 12,000 words, pays $4000. The magazine also pays $50 to $250 for article ideas. Authors are paid a $400 kill-fee for assigned material that is later rejected.

Argosy (circulation 1,400,000) accepts articles on personal adventure, off beat and exotic travel, treasure hunts, unusual outdoor stories. Writers should not submit overly sexual material. Articles run 2500 to 3000 words. The magazine pays $500 to $3000.

Fling (circulation unavailable) editors advise writers to query on all article ideas. The slant is to the adult male. The magazine uses personality profiles from show business (living or dead), male success stories, off beat material, social-scientific-sexual fads. They also use controversial national issues. Length should be 3500 to 5000 words. Writers are paid $125 to $300. A special department, "Fling Report," deals with first-hand investigation of a new sexual phenomenon, but not expose. The editors are looking for straight reporting. "Fling Reports" should run 20 typewritten pages and they pay $150 and up.

Esquire (circulation 1,250,000) accepts articles slanted for the sophisticated, intelligent reader, with a wide interest range. Articles should run 4000 to 5000 words and be of the highest literary quality. magazine pays $350 to $1250 per article.

Adam (circulation 500,000) uses sexual material that is sophisticated and erotic. Adam's reader is a hip young swinger. Articles should run 1500 to 3000 words. Writers are paid $100 to $200 per article.

The general-interest magazines form another group with 32 publications. They are slanted for a wide national audience. The Magazines use articles on any subject that will appeal to a broad spectrum of people. The pay ranges from 2c per word to $1500 per article.

Typical magazines and their specification in this group are:

The Atlantic Monthly (circulation 325,000) does not have any particular specifications for non-fiction. The editors suggest that potential writers for the magazine read back issues. Generally, however, *The Atlantic* publishes articles of intellectual sophistication, of the highest quality writing, appealing to well educated readers on subjects of current interest in the field of literature, politics, social conditions, and the arts. Length is 2000 to 5000 words. The magazine pays $100 per published page.

Country Clubber (circulation 22,000) needs articles on golf, tennis, swimming, boating, good food, gourmet cooking, travel, entertaining, gardening, and business. Articles should run 1000 to 2000 words. The magazine pays 5c to 7c per word.

Holiday (circulation 1,036,016) buys articles on travel, regions, communities, and resorts. International in scope, *Holiday* has recently been emphasizing travel in the U.S., Canada, Mexico, Caribbean, Europe, and the Mediterranean. There is a market for unusual trips, and remote but unusual places. Articles should run 1000 to 2000 words. Writers are paid $50 to $1000 per article.

The New Yorker (circulation 475,840) uses single factual pieces running 3000 to 10,000 words. Everything else in the magazine is staff written. Editors say the magazine pays good rates.

The National Insider (circulation 500,000) accepts non-fiction that is sexually oriented and that which is general, in depth reporting, on people of significance. Article length is open. The magazine pays $75 to $300.

Other magazines in the consumer category include publications on animals, the arts, astrology and psychic, automotive and motorcycle, aviation, black, confession, consumer service, detective and crime. There are consumer magazines concerned with education, food and drink, health, history, home and garden, military, and music. Other magazines in this area publish articles on nature, photography, politics, retirement, science, social science, theatre, the movies, television, entertainment, travel, camping, and trailer life.

2.) The second major magazine category is made up of business publications, trade, technical, and professional journals.

There are two kinds of business magazines: those appealing to a general audience, including business people, interested in trends, theory and practice, and financial management. There are 30 important magazines, regional and national. There are also 34 additional business publications with a highly technical, professional slant, appealing to specific readers who are interested in highly sophisticated business material.

These business publications are a great market for writers, even beginning writers, to sell to. The main thing here is to know the field of information, the magazines' requirements and the readers.

Among the first type of business magazines, the general, mass circulation publications such as *Barron's, Money, New Englander Magazine* and *Voice of Business,* free lance writers are paid from 2c per word to $500 per article for material on such subjects as industrial investment, corporate wealth, and popular investment information.

Typical magazines and their specifications in this group are:

Barrons' National Business and Financial Weekly (circulation 225,000) uses material concerning investment in industry, short articles on individual companies and corporations, including their past performance and future prospects, with an eye to industry trends. Articles should run 2000 words or more. The tabloid type magazine pays $200 to $500 per article.

Black Enterprise (circulation 125,000) is slanted for the black person interested in finding out how to break into business in the U.S. There is a market for articles on economic developments, business trends, and career opportunities; also informational and analytical pieces. Length varies and pay is negotiable.

The Exchange Magazine (circulation 122,000) needs articles of current interest with strong reader identity. There is a market for profiles of industries, trends in business, investment, finance, economics, and government. Articles should run 1800 words. The magazine pays up to $350 per article.

Business West (circulation 10,000) is interested in profiles of West Coast companies only. Length 1500 to 5000 words. Writers are paid $10 to $50 per article.

Florida Trend Magazine (circulation 34,000) wants articles on how people succeeded in business in Florida only. The magazine also considers articles on general Florida financial news. Writers must query editors about stories. Articles should run 500 to 2000 words. The magazine pays $1 per inch of copy for shorts; $50 and up for profiles, and $100 to $300 for major research stories.

Michigan Banking & Business News (circulation 5000) is concerned with business and banking in Michigan. Length 1000 to 1200 words. Writers are paid 5c to 15c per word.

The 34 magazines with a highly technical, or professional slant include publications for business management, industrial management and supervision, and financial management. The readers are owners of businesses and top level business executives, bankers and investment counselors. Some magazines are aimed at the insurance industry and lower level business and industrial managers. Pay for articles ranges from 3c per word to $500 per article.

Typical magazines and their specifications in this group are:

Harvard Business Review (circulation 134,700) is concerned with business trends, techniques, and problems. Articles should run 3000 to 6000 words. The magazine pays $100 per story.

Financial Quarterly (circulation 64,000) wants material on trends in banking and bank product information. They publish how-tos, interviews and merchandising techniques and materials. Length 500 to 750 words. The magazine pays $200 to $500 per article.

Investment Dealer's Digest (circulation 9,252) wants articles on professional investment concerning banks, bankers, investment trusts, and insurance companies. Articles should run 1500 words. Writers are paid 3c per word.

Insurance Journal (circulation 4300) needs news interviews, feature articles about property casualty insurance. They use how-tos, profiles, humor, historical, think pieces, and spot news. Article length is open. Pays $50.

The Foreman's Letter (circulation 9,800) buys interviews with industrial foremen in the U.S. and Canada. The style should be newspaper or magazine feature article. Interested only in how foremen manage people working for them. Maximum length 1000 words. Writers are paid 6c to 7½c per word.

There are three types of trade, technical, and professional journals within the business publications category; those slanted for retailers; those slanted for manufacturers, and those slanted for educated, skilled professionals. They buy articles concerning difficulties in the trades they appeal to. These magazines want straight reporting with a clear, simple style that gives plenty of practical information. There is a market for profiles of manufacturing plants, and people. Writers must know the trade and its magazine thoroughly. There are about 495 such publications appealing to 80 trades and professions. Writers are paid from 2½c per word to $300 per article.

Typical magazines and their specification in this group are:

The Counselor (circulation 3200) is slanted for sales management. The magazine accepts case histories of specialty programs, interviews with industry suppliers and distributors. Articles should have a 2000 word minimum. Writers are paid $35 to $75 per article.

Better Vending and Catering (circulation 3456) wants articles of a technical nature on marketing material related to vending and catering. Length: 200 to 800 words. The magazine pays 2c per word. B/w glossies are purchased for $3 to $5 per photo.

American School and University (circulation 45,000) wants articles on planning, designing, constructing, equipping, maintaining, operating and renovating school and college facilities. There is a market for how-to articles, and interviews. The articles should run 500 to 2000 words. The magazine pays $25 to $200 per article.

Southern Lumberman (circulation 5000) accepts articles concerning logging production, manufacturing and marketing of lumber, new developments in the use of wood and news of the industry. Article length is open. The magazine pays $1 per inch of published copy.

Shopping Center World (circulation 15,000) wants articles on specific shopping centers concerning cutting construction costs, promoting a center, increasing its cash flow, and selecting a site. Articles should run 1000 to 3000 words. Writers are paid $75 to $150.

3.) Association publications make up the third major category of magazines. They are slanted for members of specific associations; the general public interested in those associations and persons interested in certain institutions. The magazines set forth the ideals, objectives, projects, and activities of the sponsoring organization. There are hundreds of these magazines and they pay from 1c per article to $400 per article.

Typical magazines and their specifications in this group are:

The Kiwanis Magazine (circulation 280,000) is looking for articles on social and civic betterment, business, education, religion, domestic affairs. The editors request objective and intelligent analysis of the subject. The writing must be concise. Articles run 2000 to 4000 words. Writers are paid up to $400.

Minnesota AAA Motorist (circulation 230,000) accepts articles concerning foreign and domestic travel, motoring and car care. The copy must be of interest to car owners. They use how-to, personal experience, interviews, humor, historical material and photo essays. Articles should run 800 to 1500 words. The magazine pays a minimum of $150 per article. B/w 8x10 glossies are bought for $10 to $15 per photo.

National 4H News (circulation 100,000) wants articles on education and child psychology from authorities, how-to, and material that tells about children's activities outside school. Articles run 1700 to 3400 words. The magazine pays up to $100.

Wisconsin Alumnus (circulation 30,000) for and about graduates of the University of Wisconsin. It's typical of most alumnus magazines. It accepts articles containing the authoritative views of UW faculty and alumni on any subject of public interest, using an interview format. They publish student-authored articles concerning campus issues or national issues affecting them as UW students. There is a minimum of 500 words per article. Contributors are paid $10 to $50.

Woodmen of the World Magazine (circulation 390,000) accepts articles that appeal to the American family with subjects such as travel, history, art, new products, how-to, sports, hobbies, food, home decorating, and family expenses. Writers should stress group social and recreational activities. They print seasonal material. Length--600 to 2000 words. The magazine pays a minimum of $10 per article.

4.) There are two kinds of company publications, the fourth major category, those for customers and those for employees. Generally these magazines promote the company, its products and services. The aim is to cultivate good public and employee relations and to help dealers, franchisers and agents. Payments range from 5c per word to $600 per article.

Typical magazines and their specifications in this group are:

American Youth (circulation unavailable, published by General Motors Corporation) asks that writers query with ideas before submitting articles. The emphasis is on general interest articles for young people. However, editors say that the chances for new writers are slim. Most material is written on assignment. The articles run 1000 words. The magazine pays $150 to $600 per article.

Ford Times (circulation 1,600,000) accepts articles relating to American life--motor travel, sports, fashion, vacations, nostalgia, and humor. Articles run 1500 words maximum. Writers are paid $250 per article, and sometimes more.

Conoco Today (circulation unavailable) is slanted for Continental Oil Company service station operators and wholesale distributor operations. Wants news and ideas. Length 1000 words. Pays 7c per word.

The Kraftsman (circulation unavailable, published by the Kraft Food Co.) is slanted for the company's 20,000 employees and retirees. They accept anything with company, employee or product tie-in. There must be a human element. They use personal anecdotes. Articles should run 1000 to 4000 words. The magazine pays $20 to $100 per article.

TWA Ambassador (circulation 321,000, published by Trans World Airlines for its flight passengers) The magazine is international in scope. It accepts travel with TWA route city angle, but does not want where to stop, where to eat, what to see articles. Writers are warned to avoid flying type articles. No first person or news stories. The writer should entertain, inform reader on sports, business, personalities, and human interest. Articles should run 1000 to 1500 words. The magazine pays up to $500 per story. They buy color photos for $50 inside the magazine and $250 for cover shots.

CHAPTER THREE

WRITING A
GOOD MAGAZINE ARTICLE

Understanding the need for specialization is important for a writer, but no matter how knowledgeable the author, he or she has little chance for a sale unless the article is well written. So what makes a good magazine article?

First, the writer should choose a subject of compelling interest to the magazine's particular audience. If the writer knows the markets and their readers, selecting a topic of interest will not be difficult.

Second, the author should plan to use colorful or useful or entertaining material--examples, anecdotes, and facts.

Third, there must be a strong element of reader identity, so that he or she gets involved with the article, so that it seems to bear directly on his or her interests or concerns.

Fourth, the writing should be clear, absorbing, and to the point.

Fifth, the article should contain a strong element of appeal. Some subjects have more appeal than others: what's closer to home is of more interest to readers than what's far away; what's bigger is usually more interesting than what's smaller. Other elements of appeal, in addition to proximity and magnitude are: glamour, sex, success, conflict, human interest, competition, and uniqueness.

Sixth, in combination with all these points is timeliness. There must be an interest in the material, or the author must show the reader why there should be such interest. The events in the article should be fresh, or viewed with a fresh eye so that they seem important now. Unless dated material is sufficiently explained, it should not be included in an article. You may have a compelling fact, but it's two years old. If it no longer applies, it should not be included.

Every author has to consider these six main points in creating a good article. But there are more specific points, too. For instance, the writer should carefully plan a goal, or purpose for the article. What point will it make? How will it help, educate, or entertain the reader?

As the author begins to write the article, he or she may be concerned first about the title--will it grab the reader; does it let the reader know what the article is all about? The opening should compel the reader to keep turning pages to find out what "happened next," in the same way a good short story keeps a person reading. The body of the article must be clearly developed to show the points the writer is making. There must be a convincing conclusion that persuades the reader. Finally, the author should think about the kinds of illustrations needed to make the article a convincing one-- photos, line drawings, maps, charts or tables.

All articles have three primary goals: to inform, to offer help, and to entertain. An article may include one, or all three goals.[3]

An article that conveys information emphasizes facts important to readers. The writer wants readers to think about what's being said, because the information is vital to understanding an important facet of life. The subject may be political--an explanation of how one-man-one-vote affects a specific locale. The article may explain the causes of inflation, or how the stock market responds to the foreign policies of an administration. An informative article explains what something is and why it's that way. In a successful information article the material must be worth remembering.

An article that offers help to the reader tells how-to-do something. The material may include definitive directions so the reader will be successful at a specific task; or, an article may advise the reader in less concrete areas, such as psychology or mental health care.

An entertaining article may use humor, suspense, adventure, romance, or pathos to keep the reader's attention. Illustrations are important. Photographs make the subject come alive for the reader. The article is a visual experience, too, and the more specific the writer is the greater the article's impact. Language should be crisp, imaginative, clever, colorful, and fast-paced.

A good article, whether it is one of the three basic types, or a combination of them, must have a clearly defined goal. The writer should have purpose in mind before he or she begins writing. Then keep the goal out front during the whole process. Is the purpose being served? Only relevant material should be included, no matter how interesting or important a particular piece of information may be. If it is a digression having little or nothing to do with the subject, then it should not be used. Copy has two functions: the material must adhere to the purpose of the article and it must appeal to the reader. A reader is grabbed by a startling lead and then interest is maintained paragraph by paragraph.

The writer can count on capturing the reader's attention by relying on the reader's identity with people, places, and things. As Helen M. Patterson points out, the most successful articles contain a simple subject with broad appeal.[4] The writer must judge how wide an interest there is for the subject and how great the appeal will be within a particular publication.

Critics, teachers, and professional writers know that authors can count on certain subjects of perennial interest to readers. Current events that are timely and important enough to outlast spot news columns are popular subjects. Unusual happenings raise reader cusiosity. The unexplainable, the chaotic, the mysterious have wide appeal. Sex is the strongest drive and love the most popular emotion--both are timeless subjects. Most readers enjoy heroic actions of their fellow men and women. High adventure and accomplishments of impossible tasks offer readers a chance to identify and escape with present day heroes.

There is always a market for articles telling how people enjoy themselves. Stories about animals—pets and wildlife—are particularly popular with the current interest in ecology and conservation so high. Children are as popular as pets and many magazines are looking for profiles, interviews and articles for-and-about juveniles and young adults. Success stories are in demand in sports, business, and politics where stakes are high and superhuman effort is needed to reach the top. What's well known to the reader can always be written-up and sold, if it is written well. There are social, business, professional, and home interests that offer subjects.

As long as the material reflects the interest of readers, the writer has a chance for a sale. With that reader interest foremost in the writer's mind, with facts, thoughts, and words that accomplish the purpose of the article, it will not be difficult to interest an editor in a story.

A successful free lance knows the work must appeal to what an editor believes his/her audience wants to read and what an editor is actually willing to buy and run in the pages of the magazine, or newspaper. But to second-guess an editor is a very subjective game. The author must approach it with knowledge of what has been printed in a specific publication. Knowing the kind of material a magazine has published, the writer can submit an idea or an article with reasonable certainty that it will be accepted. The kinds of articles a successful magazine publishes represent empirical evidence of what readers of that publication want. But no matter what the particular slant of a story, most articles share a similar structure.

Reporters are familiar with the inverted-pyramid structure of news stories, in which the most important facts appear at the top, with general information broadening out the story as the writer works down. This allows a copy editor cutting room without fear of losing important details.

But a good magazine article has the opposite structure. An article lead will grab the reader, but not necessarily with all the important facts. The reader of an article will have to go through the whole story to understand the writer's goal. Significant information will appear throughout the article, and not just at the top. In fact, the most important part of an article is the body, or middle section, in which the central ideas are developed. The beginning and the end of an article are relatively less important.

There are a number of effective article leads that grab the reader and bring him or her into the story. The writer may give an overview--what, who, why, how, where, and when--in a summary lead. The grabber may be a startling statement that arouses curiosity. The expression should be unique, unusual, paradoxical, novel, with a strong, crisp style. A fiction-like tone is characteristic of a narrative lead. Dialogue may be used, too, for personal experience and adventure articles, using strong incidents, examples, and interesting events. The question lead is another curiosity-raiser. There may be a single question or a number of them put to the reader in direct address. A descriptive lead uses impressions to interest the reader. The appeal is to the senses and the emotions. Detailed facts may appear in the body of the article but not in this kind of lead. High impact language should be used. Quotes are used as a lead when they apply specifically to the purpose of the article. Generally, however, a writer should begin and end an article with his or her own words. Direct address, or second person leads, are used most often in how-to articles in which the author speaks personally to the reader. Finally, an article may open with two or more of these leads in combination.

The second-lead consisting of a few paragraphs following the opener, draws the reader further into the story, securing his or her interest.

After the opening paragraphs comes the body of the article in which the writer spells out the information concerning the goal of the story. The writer should be confident of market appeal and reader interest by the time he or she begins writing the central section. The research should be completed and the writer should have an idea of how long to make the article. A style should be set, development planned, and transitions worked out from opening to middle and from middle to end. When this groundwork has been accomplished, writing the body should not be difficult. The words should flow easily and confidently with a simplicity of style that reinforces ideas and allows for spontaneity, at the same time.

The conclusion justifies the article as a whole, by creating the impression that the material in the body is worth knowing. There should be a tone of finality, a sense of ending and satisfaction.

As far as title is concerned, many writers wait until the work is finished before scanning the article for a telling phrase or idea that can be used as a head. Others, like to have the title first, as a sign post guiding them through the writing. The process is a subjective one and whatever works best for an author or for a particular article is the way it should be done.

Ms. Patterson has summed up the important points:[5]

Capture the reader's attention with a title that gives the reader a picture of the subject.

Grab the reader with a startling lead in the first sentence and paragraph.

Continue to attract interest in the first few paragraphs leading into the body of the article.

In the central section keep reader sympathy through well developed ideas that show the information is worth reading because it adds to the reader's knowledge, wealth, and health.

The end of the story should convince the reader that the article was worth the time.

The writer should be aware of a publication's length requirements--500 to 6000 words are the minimum and maximum for magazines, with the average about 1500 to 3500 words.

An outline may be helpful in keeping to the subject and avoiding irrelevant digressions. Many writers, however, do not write from an outline, but use their notes in an orderly way.

The writer should make sure that development is effective and that the goal is maintained. The sections of the article should fit together naturally with effective transitions.

All devices should be used to insure that the reader understands the author's viewpoint.

The purpose of an article is to entertain and to inform. Incidents and anecdotes concerning the subject are used to illustrate and to make a point but more important to entertain. Statistical material on the other hand is used to inform, although the details should be presented in as interesting a way as possible. The same is true of scientific material, which should be made simple and clear enough for readers to grasp without losing the authority of the facts. Factual material can be presented effectively through narration and description. Other ways are interviews, dialogues, quotes, charts and tables. Specific examples should be concrete and readily understood. Any hypothetical material must be authentic and plausible according to the circumstantial evidence of the case.

The most universal writing styles are exposition, argumentation, description and narration, and they are usually supplemented with dialogue, interviews and illustrative material -- photographs, maps, charts and tables.

Generally, sentences and paragraphs in an article for magazine or newspaper publication are short and to the point. A sentence should run about 10 to 25 words and each paragraph should contain a transition, a subject, explanation, examples, or facts, and a conclusion that leads to the next thought.

The writer should know that editors are looking for articles that 1) appeal to their particular readers, 2) are written in logical, or chronological order, 3) have current interest to readers, 4) entertain, as well as inform, 5) contain information that is true and easily understood and 6) cause readers to see material from the author's point of view.

CHAPTER FOUR

SOURCES
OF MAGAZINE ARTICLES

A professional writer knows where to look for article material. He or she has a regular plan for digging out subjects from newspaper, radio and television, and personal experience. The writer always watches out for over-used subjects, or ideas that lack substance. They are immediately rejected. The most successful writers have specialized and not only know their markets, but editors count on them to consistently submit material they can use.

The writer has to develop a news-sense. In going through newspapers, for instance, he or she will spot stories that can be turned into good articles with just a small amount of additional work. Other ideas will need a great deal of development, but the work is worthwhile if it means a sale. For the magazine article writer, newspapers offer what's going on in the world in quick surface form providing the leads to stories that can be researched into the fuller story that a publication would want to buy.

Most daily newspapers publish a Sunday edition, with their own magazine section, or one of the national syndicated magazines like *Parade*. Since these magazines cover a wide variety of subjects pegged to a specific item, free lance writers will find material with potential for other markets.

An article about an archaeological dig in a Sunday Magazine was recently the basis for a sale to the publication of a heavy equipment company. The alert writer noticed the brand name on a caterpillar tractor in one of the photos that illustrated the original article. With some further research, he was able to write an article on the same dig, from the tractor company's point of view.

Another author was sparked by a spot news item concerning a hold-up murder to write a human interest feature about the restaurant owner who disarmed the killer.

A profile of a prominent person led to a more specific article on her antique glass collection for a glasswares magazine.

The same approach should be used with radio and television. Newsbroadcasts, specials, and media features can offer countless suggestions for a writer. The media doesn't have time, staff, or money to follow up many of the interesting leads they uncover. Small mention may be made of a subject and that's the most the station can afford to do. The free lance has the advantage of relatively low expenses and all the time he or she is willing to spend on an article. At best a television special will run 90 minutes. Most run less and a feature, or a personality profile on radio, may last only a minute or two. Interest in a subject is demonstrated by the media's willingness to devote time to it. The perceptive writer will pick out the areas that are inadequately covered and find a market for them.

Magazine themselves are sources of articles. Ideas cannot be copyrighted, only the way they are expressed--the specific order of words the author has used are copyrighted. The writer should look through back issues of target-magazines for ways to update, or put a fresh face on an interesting idea. Many subjects are worth more than one article; another author may have exploited only a limited angle. Scanning also tells the writer what has been done and what's unlikely to interest the editor.

A common source for articles in both newspapers and magazines is the letters-to-the-editor column. Readers are concerned about what appears in print. Although they usually write about issues that are close to them, a reader will sometimes raise a point with broad enough appeal to suggest a subject for a wide audience.

Personal observation and conversation offer the greatest number of article ideas. A writer is always on the lookout for material, often senses a story in what he overhears, or sees while walking, riding or flying, at parties, or visiting, or while working on another story. Anything in a writer's experience may be a subject for an article.

Other sources are:

Scientific reports—newspaper reporters have an advantage in the advance-report area, because institutions and companies wanting maximum publicity on new inventions, or scientific break-throughs, send releases to city editors who pass them along to reporters for rewrite. This offers a good chance for a reporter to use the material for his or her own article writing. Writers without this kind of contact can solicit such information from individual scientists or the universities, institutions, and companies where they work.

Government bulletins—these documents are also filtered through the newsrooms of most papers, especially when the information applies specifically to a certain region or city. Free lance writers can get the bulletins by writing the agencies.

Trade journals—many tips are found in the publications aimed at specific, professional audiences. The writer should read the trade journals in areas that interest him, or her, for leads on subjects that can be worked into articles for other markets.

Current books--all writers have access to popular books through stores and libraries.There are markets, for essays, profiles, and interviews concerning a book and its author. The subject of a book may suggest articles in the same area.

Experts —there are experts in every field who are willing to lend their authority to articles about their work. They may suggest ideas or in some cases co-author the material. A great deal depends on the writer's interests and who he or she can contact for advice.

Magazine editors—as a rule, editors should not be solicited for article ideas. They expect authors to query *them*. Editors don't have time to think up ideas for free lance writers. Anything that comes to an editor's mind will usually be given to a staff writer of dependable ability who is paid to handle such assignments. Sometimes, however, writers can get to know an editor well enough so that he or she will give the ideas to them. More often, editors will contact an agent and ask them to line up material from their stable of authors. In any case, it's worth free lance writers' time to get as close to editors as possible, as well as working with agents, who can find work for them.

Conventions—metropolitan areas are often hosts for conventions and an alert free lance will keep track of these happenings. Markets may range from the host city's newspapers to the organization's publication. If the group is of national significance (VFW, American Legion, Shriners) an article might be written for a mass circulation market.

Addresses—newspapers of every city and town are interested in speeches by prominent local personalities, or politicians. A writer should keep track of these addresses and be aware of what may be significant for the community. When a person of national stature is speaking, the free lance should be there even if local and national papers have reporters on the scene. The free lance may pick up a point the others miss that will be the basis for an article.

Museums—exhibits and shows by local artists, or persons of national and international fame are subjects for articles. The writer's community may have a natural history museum, or an industrial or farm museum that is a source for stories. The free lance should establish contacts with persons or the museum staff to be kept informed about significant events and projects. The writers should maintain the same kinds of contacts at zoos and theaters, too.

Holidays and anniversaries—magazines and newspapers are always looking for seasonal material. The writer should keep a file of important dates and try to write an article for each one. Since magazines and newspapers prepare features on such subjects far in advance, the writer should submit the material three to six months before the date. Obvious ones are Christmas, New Year's, Easter, Hanukkah, Fourth of July, centennials, bi-centennials, birthdays of important persons, founders-days, grand openings, the seasonal equinoxes, Memorial Day, Veterans' Day, Fathers' and Mothers' Day, and elections. A free lance should have a good almanac for the source of these holidays and anniversaries. Often an almanac will provide information about dates, explaining their significance and why they are remembered. The library should be used for further research.

Newspaper files—these are open to all reporters, but some papers will allow free lance writers to search their morgues for ideas and information. However, the writer may find it difficult to get access to these files unless he or she is a well known author or has contacts at the paper who will have authority to admit them--the managing editor, city editor, or head librarian.

Article sources must be reliable and the author should be prepared to check the credibility of a tip, lead, or idea. Whether the source is another article, or an anonymous phone call, the writer should spend time on further research to insure the truth of the material at hand, and to avoid plagiarism. There is a great deal of difference between using an interesting idea and developing it into an article of your own and simply rewriting someone else's work. In doing the latter, a writer not only runs the risk of lawsuits, but also kills his or her reputation as an author. The trust of an editor may take years to build up, but it can be destroyed instantly if a writer uses false information, or steals someone else's writing.

A free lance should carefully check sources, give credit and attribution where it is due, and tell the truth. If an author follows these rules of common sense and courtesy he or she will not run into problems.

Once a writer understands where to find sources and how to use them, it isn't hard lining up information for stories.

There are three main sources: printed (books, newspapers, magazines, public records), tapes, and live. Of the three, more often than not, a writer's most vital sources are live ones--people themselves. By talking to people, interviewing them--live research--the writer will get the latest information directly and will be able to question the persons about anything that is unclear or contradictory.

Although live research may be the most interesting and the most productive, printed sources are most commonly used. For one thing, it may be difficult, if not impossible, to reach the live source. Or, the person may be uncooperative, or misleading. In any case, research from printed material is necessary to collaborate a person's story and to find more facts. Most articles can be written from printed sources alone. There are volumes of published material on almost every subject and the most recent publications will keep the writer up to date. Whether a writer has access to live research, he or she should count on printed sources, too, in combination.

Tapes are often used as secondary sources related to live research. Obviously, the writer can't ask a tape questions and such material has to be used in the same way as printed material. Ideally, an author will use all three sources. Most likely, he or she will have to depend on tapes or printed material. When a live source is available, however, it should be exploited.

Information-gathering should begin at the fountainheads, as the writer gets as close as possible to primary sources. This may not always be live-research. For instance, the primary source of an article on an archeological excavation would be the dig itself and the artifacts discovered there--pots, arrow-heads, bones, whatever. If the writer is familiar with the field, the material will tell him or her more about the sight than an interview with one of the people working there. When the subject is a complicated one, involving more than one source, the writer has to chart the most likely primary and secondary sources and work from the best to the worst. If an author is writing an article on some aspect of highway safety engineering, he or she shouldn't start with a local traffic cop. Go to him last. Start out with the people at the National Safety Council. Then to the state agencies, including safety and highway engineers, and on down to the municipal director of public safety, then to the police traffic inspectors and local street engineers.

If a writer is doing an article on farm production in America, he or she shouldn't go to a farmer first; go to him last. Go first to the Department of Agriculture, the state farm agencies or farm cooperatives, etc. The writer has to recognize where the right information will be found. To do this he or she must know the subject by specializing in it. A writer may have more than one area, but those subjects must be so familiar to the author that he or she knows instinctively where to get the information.

The writer must be familiar with the tools and techniques of information gathering, as well as the sources.

In the case of live research, the author should find out, or sense, whether the person objects to tape recorders or a lot of note taking. If such is the case, keep these to a minimum and count on memory, then make detailed notes as soon as the interview is over. If the subject doesn't object, use the tape recorder--then all the material is on record. But the writer should be sure that he or she knows how to handle the equipment easily.

Often the person being interviewed will demand that the writer take extensive notes, or use a tape recorder so that the information is correct and the subject is not misquoted. Sometimes the person will ask to look at the writer's notes, or listen to the tape, to make sure no mistakes have been made. This kind of cooperation is not rare and, if the author established a friendly rapport with the subject, there should be no problems. But the author may encounter someone who is suspicious, reticent, or has something to hide. In such a case the author must be as shrewd as possible, without being openly offensive. Watch for signs in the subject's expressions that tip when he or she is lying, with-holding information or changing the subject to lead the writer astray. Make a note of these points and go back later to check the story, or dig out material that the person was reluctant to talk about. Most good newspaper reporters know these techniques of getting a story when the principle live--source is tight-lipped.

In doing an interview, the writer will want to appear as professional as possible. Some note paper folded lengthwise that the writer can casually take out and scribble notes on is far less intimidating than a large pad, or clip board with a fat stack of paper. The notes a writer takes during an interview should be short and used to recall important points. It's impossible for the writer to get the whole interview down verbatum, so don't try.

Beforehand, the writer should jot down some questions that will lead to the heart of the information. Nothing will distract, bore, confuse, or irritate a busy person, who's taken time to grant an interview, more than an unprepared writer. Of course, questions may come to mind on the spot, as the subject talks--an unexpected revelation may be made, or the person may use the writer as a "news-leak." Be prepared for the unexpected, but always have a set of basic questions to keep the interview running smoothly.

Aside from these few technical rules, common sense should be used in conducting an interview--be polite, friendly, and unpretentious. Don't try to impress the subject with the fact that you are an important writer. At the same time, don't fawn over the person. He or she will respect you as a professional writer on assignment. The writer should be firm and knowledgeable without being aggressive or pedantic. Be relaxed without being sloppy. If the subject thinks the writer knows his or her work, that confidence will be reflected in the way the author is treated. Most persons with important information want to cooperate with a writer. Politicians and performers not only want to get along with writers, they depend on good press relations to enhance their images. The writer always has the upper hand, but don't rub it in or embarrass the subject needlessly. When all goes well, a feeling of comradery will develop between the person and the writer and he or she can count on help in the future from that subject.

Free lance writers should know how to use a library--the card catalogues, the documents and periodical rooms, and the kinds of research material available, such as *The Reader's Guide To Periodical Literature, Ayer Directory*, and *Books In Print*. Librarians are always willing to cooperate with a writer, but the author should show his or her respect for the librarian's profession by knowing the basic ways in which a library functions.

At the same time, the writer should keep a record of all sources, live and written, so he or she can backtrack, if necessary. A writer who sells consistently knows how to pick a market, find the right subject, and write a good article based on sound research from the best sources.

CHAPTER SIX

ILLUSTRATIONS

Many magazines pay extra for illustrations supplied by the author. A good photograph, map, chart, or table--one that clearly explains an aspect of the article--may be worth a great deal to an editor. Sometimes the quality of the illustration is so high that it is used for the cover and the article as the lead piece in the magazine. If this is the case, the cover illustration may be worth more than the article itself. In any case, if the author can supply illustrative material, he or she should do so by all means.

But the pictures must be of good quality and glossy prints, usually 8" x 10", black and white (b/w), or color transparencies (slides) suitable for reproduction. If the writer cannot take the pictures, he or she should line up a free lance photographer to do the work, sharing the fee, or suggest to the editor the kinds of pictures or illustrations that are available for the magazine to get.

Each illustration should be accompanied by a cutline (an explanatory note that will appear below the picture), or a heading (a title that will run above). The cutlines should be well-written, lively, and refer to the picture in the present tense; for example "A million dollars in old money is burned by employees of the treasury department."

Generally, a free lance writer should not depend on someone else to take pictures for an article. The writer should know the basics of photography and illustrate the story. This know-how will pay off, and add dimension to the author's range. A free lance who knows photography can pick up extra work with photo essays, or by doing other writers' illustrations.

Whether the writer takes the pictures or not, the illustrations should be an important part of the article. Some magazines do not run art, as it's called, with stories, but they are the exceptions. Most publications want photographs or other illustrative material, and pay from a few dollars per item to a few hundred. Professional photographers for the top slicks are paid thousands for their work, but that is another field. What we're talking about are the "news" pictures that show the subject of an article.

There are sources for photographs, if the author cannot take the pictures and does not have access to a good photographer. They are syndicates that specialize in supplying illustrations to newspapers and magazines. They sell to individuals, too. *Literary Market Place* lists 90 such agencies, including Black Star Publishing Company, College Newsphoto Alliance, Globe Photos, Inc. Photography For Industry, Pictorial Parade, Inc., and Wide World Photos, Inc.

The rates set by these agencies vary, but, generally, the pictures are expensive and the free lance should make sure that the purchase of illustrative material will be worthwhile. Certainly, a writer shouldn't buy photographs, or other material, until he or she is absolutely sure that the article is sold. Then if there is no alternative, the writer can hopefully afford the high price per picture, from a syndicated source.

CHAPTER SEVEN

THE SUBJECT SHOULD BE

RIGHT FOR THE WRITER

A free lance writer working on assignment for a popular men's magazine was asked by the editor to do a profile story on an entertainer. Although the fee was good, the author turned down the assignment.

"I spent fifteen years as a newspaper reporter getting those kinds of assignments. I didn't do them well then, and I'm not going to suffer it now that I'm on my own. The superficiality of many of the celebrities depressed me and I couldn't write that kind of story," he said.

The author understood something very important to all writers: a subject must be right for the author, as well as the publishing source.

Most newspaper reporters have had to write stories that didn't particularly interest them, but there were copy editors to improve the writing, or kick it back at them for rewrite. The reporter's pay check would be there no matter how disinterested he or she happened to be. Writing dull, or distasteful copy is part of every reporter's job. He or she can consent to do it, or quit. But a free lance writer has no copy editor to put punch in a poorly written story, and no accounting office to send up a check each week, whether the writer has written one good story or ten bad ones. When a poorly written, or half-hearted effort is rejected by a magazine editor, there's no second chance for the writer, and no pay check, either.

Being a free lance writer is a lonely occupation, especially for a beginner. Chances for success often seem slim and it may take years before the writer has a reputation and expertise to command the highest prices. That level of work and pay isn't going to be achieved by writing a lot of articles that don't really interest you. If the writer isn't enthusiastic about a subject, it will be difficult to make editors and readers interested. Inevitably, the writing will reflect the degree of the author's commitment to the subject. A badly written article may mean the author has no talent, or that he or she doesn't care enough about the subject to do a good job.

As a rule, the free lance should work only on subjects that he or she cares about. The free lance doesn't have a boss, and doesn't have to accept every assignment. The markets for articles are wide enough so the writer will be able to make a living writing about people, places, and things that interest him, or her.

With this in mind, before committing yourself to all the time and energy and, sometimes, expense, of researching and writing an article, you should ask several questions and be able to answer yes to all of them.

Is the subject of interest to me? If not, it's better to go on to something than write an article that will almost certainly be rejected. If the subject interests the writer, then he or she must find out if it will interest a particular magazine. We've discussed this aspect of market research earlier in this section and seen how important it is to know the target-publication.

Is there plenty of interesting, fresh, informative, colorful, or useful material on the subject available? Some subjects are worthwhile, but they don't have lively material. Many worthy education, or governmental subjects, for example, have this handicap. By definition, a *well written article* on a dull or complicated issue means that the author has made the material interesting. But sometimes, the raw data has no entertaining or lively aspects the writer can draw on to keep the reader awake. If that's the case, the free lance should find some other subject, or resign himself, or herself to the documents section of a library.

If there is such a body of good material available, is it available to me? Some stories are available only to certain writers, or even to a single writer and not to others. The chief of the Washington Bureau of the *New York Times*, for example, might be able to get information that is not available to other writers. A reporter assigned to the Moscow bureau certainly has the edge on a story concerning strife within the Politburo. During the closing months of the Nixon administration, it would have been very difficult for a free lance writer to scoop Woodword and Bernstein of the *Washington Post* on a Watergate story. So be realistic. Know what kinds of stories are at hand. There are all sorts of stories available to any writer who is willing to dig for them. As a writer becomes more experienced, he or she will develop special areas that will provide inside tracks to information. A magazine writer must always try to build up such contacts.

If the material is available, is it economically sound to get it? If a writer lives in the Midwest, why think of going to California to get a story that he or she might sell to a magazine for $350. Some high paying magazines will pick up the author's expenses on a story, but even well known writers aren't sure of collecting that extra money.

A name writer on assignment for a national magazine recently had to face the grim reality of seeing his article edited beyond recognition. He would not allow his name to go on the piece. As a result, he was paid half the original fee and the magazine refused to pay his expenses that they promised at the start. In the end, the assignment *cost* the author over $500.

Is there a market for the article, or has the subject been overdone? The best way to find out if an editor might be interested is to ask him, or her.

Which brings us to the matter of the *query letter* and selling an article.

CHAPTER EIGHT

SELLING ARTICLES

Query Letter

The query letter is the single most important element in the writer's quest for sales. Many magazines will not read unsolicited manuscripts. It's a waste of time and money to research and write an article no one will consider. To prevent this writers query editors with ideas that are likely to appeal to the magazines' readers.

An editor's response to a query may be a definite commitment for the article, or it may express interest in the work on speculation. In the first instance, the query has interested the editor enough so that he or she is willing to offer a commission for the work. In such cases, a kill-fee, a future-rejection-fee, is decided upon, so the author will be paid part, or all of the original commission, whether the magazine uses the article or not. Obviously this is the best protection for a writer. Usually, however, only the pros can command such agreements.

More likely for the beginner the editor will agree to pay for the finished article, if it lives up to expectations. Under these circumstances, the risk remains on the author.

A query letter must be polite, friendly, confident, attractive, and persuasive. The letter is the writer's contact with the market. It may be a highly personal, hand-written suggestion for an idea, if the editor is a childhood friend, or a former college roommate. But for most free lance writers, the editor is a name and a reputation who much be convinced of an idea without being bullied or offended. It's not wise to tell an editor what *should* appear in the pages of his or her magazine or newspaper. In the first place, an editor may have nothing to do with the general editorial policy of the publication: and in the second, an editor has had a difficult struggle to reach this position and, like anyone else who has achieved prominence, should be treated with respect. On the whole, editors know more about magazine article writing than many writers. An editor can't be fooled, cajoled, or tricked into something he or she doesn't want. An editor may have to run items out of necessity, but that's different from running something of low quality, or that serves no purpose for the magazine. So the query letter must be honest, forthright, and to the point. It should be as short as possible and still state the idea fully. A query letter may be long, but never superfluous.

As George L. Bird points out, the query is used especially for limited markets, to save extensive research, to save expense and time, and to get ahead of others on a popular subject.[6]

A query letter proposing an interview/profile for *Sepia Magazine* read:

Dear Editor (use name of editor):

Madame X, internationally famous opera singer will be performing in concert in Chicago, Aug. 3. I'll be in the city at that time and would like to interview her for Sepia. The article will stress Ms. X as a black woman, as well as a performer. Recent Sepia articles indicate your appeal to readers with stories about outstanding blacks in the arts, business, and in politics. I would show the reader a black woman who succeeded in opera, a field that is characteristically Caucasian. Ms. X is married to a German white composer and that would interest Sepia readers, I think. I can supply black and white, glossy prints to illustrate the article. I look forward to hearing from you. My most recent publications include:. . . .

Sincerely,

Keep Research Records
on Articles and Magazines

Keeping clear, orderly records is a task any free lance writer undertakes in order to sell articles. Keeping such records is tedious and it's not very glamorous, but every professional writer has files on magazine markets and story ideas.

Anyone who has been a newspaper reporter knows how important it is to keep records of stories, sources, and leads. Every paper has a morgue, a library, for clippings on every subject the staff covers. This facilitates research for the reporters. For instance, if a reporter is assigned to cover a politician, local or national, who is making important news, a reporter first goes to the newspaper's morgue to get all the clippings about that person. The reporter will find important information--biography, career, criminal records, anything that has ever come to the attention of other reporters, or the newspaper's librarians. The data will come in handy when the reporter sits down to write a specific story on the person. The background material may be used to fill out the story, and to keep a reporter informed about the subject. Without this kind of systematic compilation of material, each story would have to be written from scratch and the results would be time consuming, and probably chaotic.

Most writers keep three kinds of files: cards on stories, cards on publications, and newspaper and magazine clippings. Story-cards are records of ideas, leads, sources, interesting persons, places, and points or issues that may be used for articles. It's easy to jot down an idea for a story and file it away. Or perhaps a subject will interest the writer so that he or she will open a file on it and whenever information comes to light make a note of it until there is enough raw material to develop an article. A subject index for this kind of file is best and the writer may keep a master list showing where ideas and subjects have been filed. The more orderly the better.

Magazines should be listed alphabetically. The name of the magazine should appear on a card, as well as the editor the writer deals with, the general editor policy of the publication, the rates it pays, the circulation and, of course, the address. The writer should also list the number of articles he or she has sold to the magazine and how much it paid for each work.

A writer should keep a file of all his or her published work, not only for future reference but for credentials to show editors, in applying for assignments. Anything that catches a writer's eye, however, should be clipped and filed away under an appropriate heading, and especially any material that applies to the author's special fields of interest. Such work is time consuming, but can pay off, if the writer is on deadline and needs a filler, or a particular fact. The writer should be able to turn to his or her files for any information on the subject at hand. Over the years, a good free lance writer will build up an impressive collection of facts, biographical material, historical data, statistics, tables, charts, maps, and photographs. Hopefully, when the writer gets an assignment he or she will have to look only to the cards and clippings on file.

Know What Rights You Are Selling

Magazines and newspapers may buy first magazine rights, or first serial rights, world rights, all rights, and second serial rights. A publication usually is not interested in dramatic, photoplay, book, foreign or translation rights. The writer must be aware of what rights he or she is selling.

Normally, a publication buys an article for first-time North American use. This means the magazine has bought the material for one-time use in a serially issued number of the publication. The magazine pays a fee to the author for the privilege of running the article, and after a period of time, usually three to six months, will reassign rights to the author. The writer can then use the article again, in a collection for instance, as long as the magazine in which it was originally published is given credit, such as "First appeared in X Magazine, July 10, 1968." The same is true of a magazine with international distribution that buys world rights for an article for one-time, first-time use.

When an author has sold a book manuscript, and before the book is published, a magazine may buy a chapter, a condensation, or a "creative rewrite" of a chapter or chapters. The publication has one-time, first-time rights on the material. A magazine may buy an excerpt from a book already in print for second serial or syndicate rights.

Sometimes a magazine will buy an article that has already appeared in print--they are purchasing the reprint rights. The best example of this is *The Reader's Digest.* Most writers and readers are familiar with this magazine and the way it operates. They reprint what they consider the best articles and stories that have recently appeared in other magazines and newspapers. They buy reprint rights, pay the author well for them, and credit the original publication. Sometimes, the magazine that first published an article will insist on splitting the reprint fee with the author. This is rare, however, and most magazines are happy to see their author's work picked up by another publication, as long as proper credit is given.

A literary agent keeps track of this kind of information for authors and negotiates the rights and fees, which brings us to the question of whether a free lance writer needs an agent.

Agents

Many of the large, general interest, national magazines and newspapers with mass circulation--the ones that pay the highest rates for the most professional work--will not read material unless it is submitted by an authors' agent. More and more, the smaller publications--even the ones in specialized markets, company magazines and business publications--will consider only those articles that are sent to them by an agent. The reasons for this are spelled out in the section dealing with agents in *The Writer's Manual*, but, in short, editors, today, count on agents to screen manuscripts so that only the best material arrives on their desks. Magazine and newspaper editors do not have the staffs, nor the time, to read and consider every piece of writing sent in over the transom. Most free lance writers have received form rejections-- "Dear Author: We're sorry but your manuscript does not meet our editorial needs at the present time...." In other words, the writing is so bad the editor won't take time to scrawl a personal note; or, no matter how good it is, the editor will not look at an unsolicited submission.

An agent acts as a foot-in-the-door for the writer. He or she receives a percentage of the writer's income because the agent has the contacts to sell the articles and to solicit assignments. Often, editors go directly to agents with article assignments and ask them to "sub-let" the work to writers in their stables. The agent then considers a file of writers until he or she finds the right author for the right story. The agent is an influential and lucrative contact for an author.

No writer is too famous, or too "big" for an agent. Like thousands of authors, Norman Mailer has an agent and Vance Packard has a literary-lawyer to negotiate his contracts. Every beginning writer should do whatever he or she can to get agency representation.

Aside from finding assignments and selling articles, agents negotiate the best possible contracts, from positions of strength--editors respect agents because they are dealing with professionals within their trade, men and women who themselves have spent their lives in publishing and who are editors and writers too.

Agents also function as book-keepers for writers, processing income checks, preparing tax information, and other financial responsibilities, and detail work that takes an author away from the typewriter, where he or she belongs.

The writer-agent relationship may be a subjective one, too, with the agent offering editorial assistance, and advice on the direction of an article or book. A writer must be able to trust an agent's judgment on market and on quality of the writing itself. When an agent offers direction, the author should be willing to consider the potential market. Like editors, agents know the literary market and what material sells.

It's not easy to get acceptance for representation by an agent. Many agencies will not consider representing an author who has not established a set annual income. Other agents are willing to work with new authors, but on a fee-basis and only when they can afford the time away from publishing authors who are earning income for the agency. The best advice for a beginning writer is to keep trying for an agent, while building up a good number of publishing credits. Eventually, if the writer is selling well, an agent will want to represent him, or her.

Article Writing

Article writing is one form of the writing field. Like all forms of writing, it requires constant attention and practice if you are to succeed in acceptance and publication. A poet does not arrive full-blown; neither does the novelist or the biographer. Any form of writing demands an inquiring mind, a concern for style and technique, not only in your own writing, but in the writing of others as well. Perhaps the greatest mistake most writers make is to leave a particular writing form too soon or to work in another before mastering a form in which you begin to achieve some success. The step from article writing to a book of nonfiction can be a wide leap. Success in the writing of articles does not mean you can string a series of articles together for book purposes simply because they are loosely related. The writing of a book requires different techniques. Many writers who work effectively in the newspaper and magazine fields flounder when they tackle a book length subject. It is far more than a shift of gears. It is a giant step into another form.

The sooner you learn to be objective about your writing, the quicker you will evolve and succeed in any form in which you work. In "How to Write Articles for Magazines and Newspapers" we've examined the basic elements in selling an article -- the four main magazine fields, sources, the choice of the right subject, gathering material, the writing itself, illustration, rights, the query letter, research records, and agents. The desire to write is widespread. The ability to write is another matter. Anyone can improve their mechanical ability to write. In the writing of "Article Writing," we assume some preparation to write exists. If you require other foundation, that is covered in *The Writer's Manual* in sufficient detail to satisfy your needs.

Good luck to you and may you have a promising article writing career.

BIBLIOGRAPHY

Bird, George L. *Article Writing and Marketing.* rev. ed. New York: Rinehart & Company, Inc., 1956.

Brennecke, Ernest, Jr. and Clark, Donald Lemen. M*agazine Article Writing.* New York: The MacMillan Company, 1947.

Gehman, Richard. *How To Write and Sell Magazine Articles.* New York: Harper & Brothers, 1959.

Gunther, Max. *Writing The Modern Magazine Article.* Boston: The Writer, 1968.

Henry, Omer. *Writing and Selling Magazine Articles.* Boston: The Writer, 1962

Patterson, Helen M. *Writing and Selling Feature Articles.* 3rd Ed. Englewood Cliffs, N.J.: Prentice-Hall Inc., 1956

Root, Robert. *Modern Magazine Editing.* Dubuque, Iowa: William C. Brown Company, 1966.

FOOTNOTES

1. George L. Bird, *Article Writing and Marketing* (New York: Rinehart & Company, Inc., 1956) p. 56.

2. *Writer's Market 1974,* edited by Jane Koester and Rose Adkins (Cincinnati: Writer's Digest), is the source of factual material for the listing of sample magazines in this section.

3. Helen M. Patterson, *Writing and Selling Feature Articles* 3rd ed. (Englewood Cliffs, N.J.' Prentice-Hall Inc., 1956), 99. 211-229.

4. Ibid. pp. 211-229.

5. Ibid. pp. 211-229.

6. Bird, *Article Writing and Marketing*, p. 91.

**The Writer's Manual
Book 6**

How to
Write
for Children

By
Roy E. Porter

ABOUT THE AUTHOR

Roy E. Porter
writes out of a wide publishing background,
twenty years of it with Rand McNally & Co. and
teh as a partner in Chicago's largest author's agency,
Porter, Gould & Dierks.
After study at the University of Chicago,
he had a variety of administrative experiences
with Rand McNally.
He organized the company's
first institutional trade book department,
representing all company products purchased by the library field
including maps, globes, and atlases.
Eventually he became senior editor and
head of the adult trade book department,
a position he held until becoming a partner in the authors' agency,
Max Siegel & Associates.
At the death of the founder in 1972,
he reorganized the agency, became its president,
and added two additional partners.
The firm operates under the name of
Porter, Gould & Dierks,
maintaining offices in Evanston, Illinois.

CONTENTS

ACKNOWLEDGMENT

Grateful acknowledgment is made to
Mary Cornelia Aldis Porter
for permission to quote extensively from
Ride the Wild Waves throughout the chapter,
"An Analysis of a Juvenile Book",
and the poem, "Hiding",
both by Dorothy Aldis.

Lord Curzon's golden rule of foreign policy
might well apply to all communications,
but most particularly to writing.

*"Know your own mind and make sure
the other party knows it as well."*

CHAPTER ONE

A LOOK BEHIND THE SCENES

Book selection, at the editorial level, is a subjective process. It also is dependent on many variables not the least of which is the capability of the editor; the attitude of publishing management; the availability of creative capital; and, finally, the dimensions or limitations of the publisher's sales, advertising, and promotion staffs. In addition to these internal considerations, there are many variable external circumstances that also have great influence on the acceptance and success of a book: the critical acceptance in some review sources may hang on who is chosen to review the book; a similar book or a book in the same subject area that comes out in the same publishing season diminishing the effect of both (this competition can have a positive effect if they compete with each other well); the availability of funds to buy (during economic imbalance of any sort, book budgets get trimmed before administration is cut back, for instance); how effectively the author can be used for promotion and exposure; and many other factors.

If we can assume an ideal situation, where the editor is impeccable; the management willing to grant the editor the authority to exercise selection; the balance between design, illustration and all other creative handling is well worked out; the necessary creative capital is available; the manufacture is more than adequate; the book is sold and distributed well; there are still other problems to be solved before a good book is printed. The editor has to find, or attract, the writing calibre to make a worthy book possible. If all other factors converge, at the right time, in the right degree, and the writing talent is absent, mediocrity is all that can be expected in the final result.

In the purely subjective area of manuscript selection, the criteria may be based on need (has the subject been covered in the literature?) or market appeal (will a wide segment of children, and, more importantly children's specialists, respond to the treatment and subject matter?) or is the handling deft enough that an emotional impact will carry the book? All of these elements are operative where book quality is the over-riding consideration, either when it is by conscious choice or through luck of choice, but any one of these elements may also dominate, and prevail, as the basis of manuscript selection.

Just as it is true that a writer's output will tend to ebb and flow, so too will the editor's ability to select good manuscripts be uneven over a period of time. Editors are human, as subject to needs and satisfaction as any other segment of people. If the eggs are over-cooked for breakfast, they respond to the upset as much as anyone else, and that fact can start the day off poorly. It may be the very day when a crucial decision has to be decided: 'Shall I publish or reject John Doe's manuscript, when every other book of his has been successful and made money for the firm, when all my instincts tell me this one will not?' How that question is decided has little to do with quality, if the editor is right and the book does not measure up to expectations. It is a tough, hard decision to make, and may cost an editor a valuable author if the decision is against acceptance.

Successful publication often has little to do with the quality of writing. The ability of the writer to handle relationships, to handle character development, to depict emotion within a strong story line often is more important than the writing style. Perhaps no juvenile author has ever written more successfully for children than Marguerite Henry. Yet, despite her considerable and successful output, none of her books can measure up to any one of the three written by E.B. White, not even his *Stuart Little*, which children's specialists and critics found disturbing because Stuart was the product of a human family. White is much more brilliant in style; Marguerite Henry is a craftsman, a good one, who dogs a manuscript all the way to the presses, making changes in an effort to polish and improve.

By and large, White's books appeal to adults as much as to the special child. It is this writing ability which hurtled him over the objections of the children's specialist and critics and that make his books classics. Marguerite Henry aims at broad appeal. When she uses "embarrassing" concepts, such as the account of the rape of Roxana by the Godolphin Arabian in *King of the Wind,* she handles it so gingerly as to make it meaningless to any child. Mrs. Henry's eye is on the book selection committee and too little on the force of her narrative line. White makes no such compromises.

Illustration can be an enormous decision to successful publication. Again, the Marguerite Henry books are interesting to illustrate the point. The majority of her books were illustrated by Wesley Dennis, and four color art is generously spread throughout the text and jackets. The marriage of writer and illustrator became so strongly identified in the minds of book buyers and book selection specialists, it was really a matter of keeping author and artist working together, on the publisher's side. When Lynn Ward was used to illustrate *Gaudenzia,* acceptance reflected the change. Yet, Mr. Ward is an infinitely more gifted illustrator than Wesley Dennis by any artist's judgement of technical skills. To the credit of the Caldecott Award Committee, Lynn Ward won the award for his *The Biggest Bear.* Wesley Dennis never made the grade.

Why do such problems exist? Because authors, illustrators, publishers, and editors are human, trying to make the best out of what can be no more than a potpourri of human limitation — a good seasoning of human limitation and a lot of deft handling and negotiation on the part of people who are thrown together in the pursuit of producing a book that sells well. When the market place and critical acclaim takes over, it can often perpetuate the process, obscuring the case for quality and accepting second best. Public acceptance can sometimes over-ride children's book specialists, such as in the case of E.B. White, *Stuart Little,* but when a publisher exercises a strong merchandising sense, such as in the case of the Marguerite Henry books, the broad appeal to emotions can often support a lesser degree of quality which is ultimately reflected in larger author's royalty statements.

Compromise may well be necessary to successful legislative deliberations, but in the creation of children's books it is unfortunate. Ideally, a good children's book should be a collaboration of people who work together toward a common end: to make the book the best human ingenuity can devise. When this happens, the writer, the editor, the illustrator, the publisher all recognize the need for the other; each functions in a specific area of expertise; each respects the others' special ability and no one intrudes in the others' domain. Needless to say, such a blissful state rarely happens.

Perhaps there is no area of publishing where more effort has been aimed and utilized to assure the success of producing meaningful books than in juvenile publishing. Locating an editor who has the ability to select manuscripts that possess literary merit is not the simplest task to solve. Locating an editor who can satisfy this requirement and also select books that sell well is another matter. Many editors can locate and consistently select books that will sell out a first edition of five thousand copies, perhaps even seventy-five hundred copies. However, that kind of list will neither attract much notice, make much income, or create much impression. The books will settle into the market place and struggle through annual sales of two or three hundred copies a year once the initial sale is over. That is hardly sufficient volume to justify the warehouse space necessary to carry the book stock in today's cost structure. It is the book that sells upwards of ten thousand copies and settles into an annual sale of 1000 to 1500 copies a year that begins to have impact on the profit side of the publishing operation. In some publishing houses, when a book falls below a thousand copy sale a year, the accountants will begin urging the sales departments to write off the stock, and close out the stock balance. That usually means remaindering -- selling out the stock for as little as ten cents on the dollar in investment at cost.

People who work in other areas of the business world rarely understand how any area of business that functions in such an irrational manner as publishing does can persist for long. Tens of thousands of dollars may be risked on publishing a book because an editor recommends it. Contracts are one-sided, almost always favoring the publisher. The publishing of a book assumes an act of faith on the part of several people, but most particularly this must exist between the editor and the writer or nothing much of a positive nature can happen. Publishers attempt to develop market analysis, but how can you assess market in any scientific sense when its acceptance is dependent on what motivates the deep-seated ideas of the mind and emotions of the book-buyer! You can stand quietly in bookstores and watch how a buyer selects a book. You may deftly probe into the book-buyer's reasons for purchasing a book, but all this has been tried many times over, with little positive results. Judging the public's taste for a given book is still a matter of good editorial instinct. If we knew how that was developed, we could produce nothing but successes and remainder outlets would disappear from the face of the earth.

Within these imperfect boundaries, vague and amorphous though they may seem, juvenile publishing exists and, not infrequently, produces a fair number of useful books.

Publishers often are very concerned about standards. They set up requirements ranging from house style on the one hand, to whether a book should be produced with head bands -- that decorative cloth edge that appears next to the binding on the top and bottom edge of the spine of a book -- it is not functional, but adds a finished touch to a book that is well designed and manufactured.

In most large publishing houses, the juvenile department is an area apart. It can be significant to the over-all income the publisher enjoys, but, if that is the case, management has found a solution in the choice of the editor who heads it up and may not be quite certain why, but is content to admit it is successful. In the inner circle of the publishing house, it is not unusual to have the juvenile department discussed as "kids books," or almost idly as "the juvenile side," or worse, as "juvies." That may sound harsh to the uninitiated, but the very nature of juvenile publishing encourages such terms, no matter how distinguished the list may be. Among general publishers, it is the successful adult book that brings in large income publishing season after publishing season. It is the adult book that is sold for large advances to paperbacks, the adult book that brings in huge income in the sale of movie rights, that is sold into foreign editions. Few juvenile books reach such heady levels. A sale to the largest children's book club will mean the author and publisher will share in a four to five thousand dollar total income; sale to a paperback house is routinely negotiated for less, on the whole, rarely more.

Then, there is that area in which the juvenile department functions, where the editor makes a decision to publish only after obtaining reports from outside consultants - librarians and teachers who advise editors by reading manuscripts for them, on a fee basis. By and large, adult manuscripts are read and appraised in the adult editorial department and only when some specialized knowledge is involved will an editor seek outside opinion. Adult editors tend to expect such capability from juvenile departments and find it odd that a juvenile editor must consult outside sources, consistently, before recommending a book for publication. Such terms of derision - "juvies," and "kids' books," - creep into publishing vernacular, defensive - to be sure - as a means of separating the two areas. It also spills over into the specialized areas of book wholesalers, rebinders, and bookstore buyers.

The juvenile editor, often feeling less than understood or accepted by publishing colleagues, tends to seek understanding from educators, librarians, or other specialists who work with children and books. Many juvenile editors become closely identified with the professional organizations of such specialists, participating in meetings as panelists and speakers, and becoming familiar with the officers and officials of such organizations. Publisher's booth income at professional conventions often provides the basic cost for convention housekeeping costs, may, in fact, provide the professional organization with a profit. In addition, editors entertain hundreds of librarians at, for instance, the annual meeting of The American Library Association, and conduct open-houses or cocktail parties for hundreds more. Other professional organizations receive the same attention.

In the best sense, it is no less than old fashioned public relations activity at a very soft-sell level. At times it can get rather commercial, where a publisher will offer an expensive fur coat in a drawing among booth registrants. By and large, this is considered too crass for professional taste, whereas a luxurious dinner at an expensive restaurant is acceptable, particularly if other guests represent the upper echelons of the organization and the editor can host it all with finesse and keep the conversation sparkling.

Although it is the professional organizations, and their review services, which can make or break a book, it is fair to say no amount of publisher/editor public relations activity can alter the nature of a review in such organizations as The American Library Association's *Booklist* or *The School Library Journal,* as two such examples. Here the professional line is drawn, no matter how friendly the association might be. The publisher's book gets handled, as it is received, in the way it deserves to be reviewed. (Books not recommended for purchase are not reviewed by *Booklist; Library Journal,* and *School Library Journal* attempt to review all significant books published, but will publish reviews where the book is not recommended for purchase.)

Outside the professional organizations, privately owned book review services have appeared, but they just as often languish and disappear. One that did not is The Virginia Kirkus service. It will review books from publisher's galleys and makes every effort to cover all trade books published, offering reviews sooner than most other services, including professional organizations. It is a useful service, but should be considered in tentative terms and until other reviews appear. *Kirkus* reviews can often misjudge a book's contribution, perhaps because of the need to get a review into print before anyone else. Anyone in publishing has smarted when the *Kirkus* review appears on a book that has taken all the editor's best effort, only to have it autocratically consigned to oblivion by *Kirkus* standards. However, *Kirkus* reviews have been disproved, time and time again and a seasoned editor, wise in the ways of reviewers, will sigh, scrawl a note to the Agent or author -- 'obviously this reviewer did not read the book we published' -- send it off in the mails and wonder what *Publisher's Weekly* or *School Library Journal* will report. Not infrequently, the same book will pass those professional judgements with flying colors.

The Bulletin from the Center for the Study of Children's Books is published by the University of Chicago. Its standards are very high, but it tends to be rigid in its handling and often out of touch with the real world. Not all children are University of Chicago Lab-school material, but no effort to make this point has ever succeeded with the staff that turns out the Center's Bulletin.

Many large city school systems and metropolitan libraries review books independently of all review services, making their judements of what to buy and what not to buy on the basis of local needs and curriculum considerations that are established by the system they represent. They utilize personnel who understand the needs of the system and consider a book wholly in those terms. Increasingly libraries cooperate on a country or regional basis and share the costs of book selection, reviewing, and even buying books for the member libraries.

Smaller city systems make accommodations, too, sometimes cooperating with the local public library in book selection and buying. They sometimes place a standing order with their book supplier to send them one copy of every book reviewed by, for instance, *Booklist,* making their decision to buy by considering only those books.

We may lament the cumbersome aspects of book buying and grouse about how poorly books are distributed, but, on the whole, the system works reasonably well, if slowly. No book worth merit is wholly ignored and libraries and schools have available to them a variety of services and methods in deciding how their book buying purchases can best be handled.

CHAPTER TWO

SO YOU'RE THINKING
ABOUT WRITING A JUVENILE BOOK?

It is a common misconception for many writers to think of writing a juvenile book — or short story — because they are short and, therefore not too demanding. Nothing could be further from the fact.

Parents, and particularly mothers, sharing in the experience of child rearing become convinced their insights, their observations, have to be recorded for posterity. Rarely do they consider writing ability or question if they possess any writing skill. They roll the paper into the typewriter, or scrawl out page after page of long hand, intent on piling up pages of verbiage. The larger the stack of pages grow, the more convinced they become that what they are doing is destined for publication.

Such people appear to be amazed when you point out that any good library will have fifteen to twenty good books on juvenile writing and that it would be wise to begin there. It's much like the incessant stream of people who apply for a position as editor at a publishing house and when you suggest a reasonable beginning is a job selling books in a good bookstore, they look at you in disbelief convinced you are using that as a dodge to get them out of the office so you can get back to reading manuscripts.

It is equally odd to discover that such people aren't readers, that they know very little about any books, and particularly about juvenile books. Yet, any public library will have a juvenile section today or it doesn't deserve to be in existence. Where else would logic suggest a better beginning than by selecting books that have already made the grade of publication, and read them. It seems so obvious as not being worthy of mention. Busy editors soon find ways of protecting themselves from such interruptions.

Reading to your own children can prove instructive, if you can disassociate yourself from the experience enough to stand back and consider what is happening. You can learn what makes them respond, what triggers their imagination, what holds their interest. It is difficult for a parent to do, but if you do nothing more than provide a warm period of experience between yourself and the child, surely that, in itself, is worth the time.

Writing for children does not mean you write in simple terms. We all know what adverse affect the Dick and Jane series had on reading habits when they were almost used exclusively in school reading programs. Children are very complex beings. They are constantly acquiring knowledge from the time the eyes begin to focus and they are glorious creatures to watch until the time we begin to socialize them by introducing them to schooling.

Perhaps the best juvenile book is one that will also interest an adult, where the handling is clear enough that each level of reader can take a dimension of experience from the book. Many adults never quite give up Lewis Carroll's *Alice in Wonderland*. They never tire of reading *Alice* every year or two throughout life. The Beatrix Potter books fall into the same category. Grandparents can hardly wait to share them with grandchildren, or parents, re-discovering them with their children.

Such genius as Carroll and Potter possessed is rare and to place yourself into that league may be asking too much. We are lucky to have it come along once or twice within any century. Yet, if you intend to write fantasy, you should certainly read *Alice* and all the Potter books, and learn as much as you can from them.

We often think of childhood as the age of innocence, and it surely is that in many ways. Who, for instance, cannot marvel at the two and a half year old little girl, rich with blonde curls, with eyes that twinkle, a nose that wrinkles up, who positively dominates a Fourth of July block picnic? She deserts her parents and moves among the guests, securely and confidently. She finds the refrigerator, points to it and her paper cup. You open it and she points to the milk, expecting you to fill her glass. And, when you do, her face erupts in triumph and pleasure. Surely this is innocence. Her pleasure is a glass of milk. Yet, even at two and a half, such a child presents unusual problems to everyone with whom she comes in contact. She is not usual. She is untouched and so marvelous to watch, you immediately wonder how it all can be preserved and kept from being blunted and negated.

On the other hand, consider the child of a large urban ghetto. Watch him adjust and accommodate to the environment to which he was born. Watch him dart across a busy street as you feel the pull in your stomach, realizing he isn't more than five years old and your first impulse is to look up and down the busy street to see if he will make it across before cars converge. In his joy and impatience, he must be on the other side of the street, to be with a friend who is playing with a plastic beach ball on the hot, cement sidewalk, almost too hot for their bare feet. They aren't yet burdened by such adult considerations. Catching the bright colored beach ball is all that matters and a look at their faces will convince you as you see the expressions reflect their satisfaction and watch the lithe bodies dart and twist to avoid all the pedestrians that are in their path.

Consider, also, the upper class child reared by a sadistic governess. The parents believe they are providing the best of care, a full-time companion for the child. The governess will cautiously keep her sadistic treatment hidden from the parents. She will know how bestial she can risk being to the child, without the child letting the parents know what a wretched life she has to live. True, the child may be able to play in the large city park, under the watchful eye of the governess, but only with those children who are approved. That child, if she is to survive, soon trains all her attention to ways in which she can survive, learning what the boundaries are and staying well within them in order to avoid punishment.

These three extremes, the untouched two and a half year old; the ghetto child; the upper class, mistreated child; all these, and more, are your audience, if you are going to write a juvenile. You may appeal to one aspect of this range, but you will likely overlook the rest, if you do. If you are going to write to them all, you must choose material that will prove as universal as *Peter Rabbit* or *Squirrel Nutkin* - stories that will jump regional, national and international barriers and speak to all children.

Children are incredibly resilient creatures, but just as you would not want to see a child subjected to unduly harsh treatment, so too, you must cast your subject matter in terms that will treat life honestly, but within the age experience of the level to whom you expect to address yourself.

Every child probes for knowledge and to advance his experience. He seeks to relate to the world about him, to define his boundaries in some respects, and expand them in others. When he has explored the block, he must find out what is beyond. He seeks love and security, but that can be expressed in thousands of different ways and be totally different than in the way his sister or brother expects it, no matter how evenly rearing techniques may have been applied.

To many children, books become the ideal means of the search for growth and learning. For the pre-school child, the solution may be in one of Dorothy Aldis' poems once the Mother Goose rhymes begin to pall. "Hiding" is one such poem, about a mother and father that participate in the world of the child. It is written without any condescension, reflecting the need of any child in wanting a happy parent-child relationship.

HIDING

I'm hiding, I'm hiding,
And no one knows where;
For all they can see is my
Toes and my hair.

And I just heard my father
Say to my mother--
"But, darling, he must be
Somewhere or other;

Have you looked in the inkwell?"
And Mother said, "Where?"
"In the ink well," said Father. But
I was not there.

Then "Wait!" cried my mother--
I think that I see
Him under the carpet." But
It was not me.

"Inside the mirror's
A pretty good place,"
Said Father and looked, but saw
Only his face.

"We've hunted," sighed Mother,
"As hard as we could
And I am so afraid that we've
Lost him for good."

Then I laughed out loud
And I wiggled my toes
And Father said--"Look, dear,
I wonder if those

Toes could be Benny's.
There are ten of them. See?"
And they were so surprised to find
Out it was me!

If you choose to write a picture book, there are many excellent examples already in print that satisfy this age need. Any juvenile librarian will gladly make these available or advise you know to obtain them.

Whatever you do, don't assume you have arrived full-blown and that you are capable of writing any juvenile book. Study children's books that are already published and try to determine if you can work in that area of interest. The field is wide you'll soon discover, just as wide as in adult books. Yet, it is very specialized. Try to find an area where your interests and abilities fit before you begin to write. You will surely find challenge in such an approach, if you honestly do your home work, and it may save you considerable time and output. It may keep you from clogging the channels of juvenile submissions, with an unpublishable manuscript, hardly an unworthy pursuit in itself.

By and large, we remember the pleasant memories of our youth, but lock out those that were distasteful or disquieting. That is the reason so many of us romanticize our past. We actually begin to believe growing up was a blissful period of blue-blue skies, one long stretch of bright sunny days when everything was sereve. We forget those terrors of the dark nights, the bully down the block that kept us in constant terror, the autocratic teacher that made us quiver every time she looked our way. It's natural enough for this to evolve, but it is no accurate reflection of growing up.

Children live with many terrors, some of them real and many of them imagined. Even the outwardly happy child experiences inner fears at times, fears that often aren't articulated and sometimes never understood. It is during these periods of stress in growing up that books can supply outlets of escape, relate the real world to life, help children realize their emotional growth has been shared by others and that solutions are possible.

It does not follow that the books we read as children will serve the same purpose for our children. We have all heard the adult who talks about discovering Dickens as a child. A curious child, inclined toward reading, and growing up forty years ago would find Dickens absorbing reading. The literature available to him was very limited. If he was fortunate enough to have books in his home, it was likely a handsomely bound set of Dickens would be among them, perhaps with those of Browning, Thackeray, Shakespeare, and any others that publishers might print, bind and be able to sell. It was the age of richly bound sets of books, often sold on a subscription basis. People regarded books as part of good living room furnishings. Today, when you come across such sets in rare or second hand bookstores, not infrequently you'll find uncut pages in many of the volumes, convincing proof that no one ever read the book at all.

CHAPTER THREE

SOME BACKGROUND
ABOUT CHILDREN'S BOOKS

It does not follow that because you one day found a handsomely bound set of the complete works of Dickens in your grandmother's library and read all of them as a child that children of today will be equally satisfied. In fact, it is more than romanticizing, perhaps, that you did.

A Christmas Carol, A Tale of Two Cities, maybe even *Oliver Twist,* would hold the attention of any avaricious young reader, but more than likely, Dickens' work was seriously read only because it was assigned reading in high school or college.

There has been an enormous amount of children's literature published since the turn of this century, much of it building on the legacy of children's books that began with *Aesop's Fables* when William Caxton translated them in 1484. If you examine children's literature closely, one point stands out above all else: it has assimilated the best of the old and added a good deal that is new. Like all life, change is inevitable and sure. If change bothers you, the best solution to that problem is to help create it.

Children need change or they will not grow. When a writer faces up to creating something original in children's books, he suddenly begins to realize how difficult that is. The world is never abounding with genius that can and will create new ideas. Most of us examine the world to which we were born and spend our time re-shuffling old forms and ideas about in a fresh structure. Don't, therefore, be content to replow old fields. Look for an area to write about that is as new and fresh as you can possibly make it. In anything as limitless as fiction, the solutions are endless. However, it is not every writer who can handle juvenile fiction well. Be sure you can demonstrate an ability to write in juvenile fiction before you go too far.

Perhaps the greatest mistake in beginning to write is to start before you know what you are going to do. Once the seed of an idea is clearly established in your mind, nurture it with care. Support it with research; read other books that have attempted to handle the subject area, both adult and juvenile. As it grows, you may find it taking on a form of its own. You will find yourself asking questions about how the character would act and react: she wouldn't express a point in flowery verbiage, because her thought processes are too precise; he wouldn't react so hesitantly because he is a sure man, certain of his reactions. As this all takes place, you will find yourself sorting out choices of handling, keeping this and discarding that. You begin to know what situations will bend to the need; what others are too elaborate to serve your purposes well. Throughout this process, it is wise to commit all of this to notes, even if you possess the most retentive mind. At a point, when you begin to assemble your notes to hammer out a structure, you will be grateful to bring back all the feel and thinking a good note will evoke as you begin to write.

The tone or tenor of any manuscript must be kept in careful control. You can use shading of tone to emphasize a point, but it must be just that, subservient to the major theme with which you are working. You can create tone with a blend of exposition and dialogue, but each has to be complementary to the other. Good dialogue develops action and keeps it moving. Yet, when dialogue becomes too drawn out, a reader begins to think of himself as viewing a fast ping gong game, the head flits back and forth across the net, trying to keep track of the ball as an observer, not a participant. You will have to learn how long you can sustain such passages and when you must allow the reader a break, so he can assimilate your point and be prepared for further action. Ordinarily, exposition serves this purpose, to allow the reader to breathe, to reflect and understand where you are taking him.

Juvenile readers are harsh in their judgements of what they read, and what they will suffer. They will not allow the writer long passages of philosophic discourse, where all the strands of the thread are laid out for the reader to examine such as adult writers often do in their writing. A juvenile reader has no such conditioning. He has no reluctance in laying the book down and looking for a better substitute.

Juvenile readers sense pretense quicker than any other reader, and they are not tolerant about accepting such writing flaws. Choices can be presented, but they want the ultimate solution to be real, justified, and clearly the logical choice to be made.

Perhaps no question is asked juvenile writers more than, "Is the story true?" The reason is simple enough: children want to identify themselves with real situations. Even when a writer works in fantasy, it has to be contained and predictable. Once we are prepared to accept the fact that Alice has fallen down a rabbit hole, almost any creation of the imagination can follow, if we can find it reasonable and supported by the narrative line.

Just as adult tastes shift and adjust, so do children's. We may criticize the influence of mass media on juvenile minds, but it is impossible to keep them protected from it. When television was new, many parents felt their children should be shielded from its influence. You would hear them proudly say, "We do not have television in our home." Quite quickly, they discovered their child not turning up after school, only to find him plunked on the living room floor of a friend's home with the television set blasting away.

We may find the local scene deplorable when we have to deal with a young girl who is wildly running down the middle of the street with the police in pursuit, even when we learn that the girl is half-crazed with drugs. It is all a nasty business, a by-product of an obscene war that exposed millions of young men to drug use. Among those that eventually came home, many returned with well developed drug habits. Logically enough, we want to protect our children from even witnessing such distasteful scenes, only to find that he or she can talk about it rather objectively -- "the police were trying to protect her from herself;" "the police were reasonable in the way they handled the circumstance" or "unreasonable," as the case may be. And, suddenly, you realize their experience level for such scenes is far greater than your own, that they have seen such scenes at school, about the playground, or in parks. They can be objective about them, perhaps far more so than we can, because we have lived a protected life and continue to keep the same walls securely about us.

Children can be harsh when they are among their peers. In the raw give and take of the playground, they can, and do, gang up on anyone that challenges their preconceived notions. They can be utterly brutal about a weak member of the group, punishing him and ostracizing him with a venom that makes a sensitive adult wonder about the future of the world if it depends on such potential. At the same time, they can, and are, extraordinarily kind and generous. Like any other human on the face of the earth, they possess emotions, emotions that must be sorted out and developed and employed. Ultimately, for good or bad, they become socialized and they begin to relate to life and the world, even when they choose to "drop out" and establish a new culture of their own, no matter how much it apes old norms that have long since been tried and discarded.

The writer of juveniles must take all this into account. Good juvenile books are instructive, always will be. But, they are not sentimental or moralistic. Children learn about morality today, just as they always have. They are not willing to have it rammed at them, pronounced from on high. They come into the world too soon aware of the frightful possibilities life presents to them. To venture around the block is not the same experience it was for their parents. The mailman still comes, but chances are, it isn't the same one each day. The milkman is fast becoming a remnant of the past; it is too expensive to have milk delivered to the steps outside the kitchen door. The electric light meter is placed outside the house, where it can quickly be read and the child may never see the "meter-man." The grocery deliveryman is still available, at a delivery charge, but it won't be kindly "Henry," who ran his own grocery store just ten years ago and who would, if asked, put the meat in the "frig" because mother had to attend a P.T.A. meeting or work for a school bond issue. For who would comfortably leave the back door open, today, and go off to a meeting? Is that why Thornton Wilder's *Our Town* is so popular for high school performances, because the young are nostalgic about life as it used to be? That surely is true to some extent, but it probably is also a question of knowing that Wilder anticipated women's liberation themes, pointing up how mothers of that long since dead day were subservient to family and their husbands, first and foremost, and always considered their needs last. There are, of course, many other rich themes in that remarkable play, but even small children know "You've come a long way, baby. . ." as the advertisers point out.

If a writer's intent is to recycle his or her narrow social experience, it's best to inflict it on the adult market. It will find fertile enough acceptance there, if it is worthy enough, but it will not filter down to the children's market -- not today.

Good children's books are almost as interesting to adults as they are to children. They are honest, without prejudice, and deal with the world of today. They are books that communicate to children, deal with ideas and themes that children understand and need to learn more about. They are books that touch the imagination, that relate the child to life and the world about him, the world in which he must learn to live and exist.

Children are born to their parents. They do not choose them. We understand that, more widely, perhaps, than any other generation. Nonetheless, when we watch what goes on about us, we sometimes become aghast, and fearful for the future. For example, take a late-fortyish couple, out from under their children and who are beginning to enjoy, perhaps, a segment of twenty years for themselves. They find themselves in a summer resort and the table they are assigned to is between two family groups, both with three children ranging from five to nine years in age. One family is very appealing. When the five year old became upset at dessert because the dessert she chose was not what she expected once she saw her seven year old brother's, she began to pout, and eventually cry. The father leaned over toward her and quietly said, "Beth, if you are going to cry, you'll have to cry all by yourself. None of us are going to join you." That so confounded her, she perked up, looked to see if anyone was ready to cry and when they weren't, she jabbed her spoon into her ice cream sundae. The other family had wrangled their way through the dinner and there were threats and pronouncements from both parents all through the meal. When the parents doddled over their dessert and many cups of coffee, the children became restive and wanted to wait for their parents outside, on the lawn. The mother pointed out, "We have drug you kids all over the place all day. We want to enjoy our dinner and you can just sit there and wait." Of course, that didn't work for long. Finally, the father, in a loud, exasperated voice yelled, "You are here for our convenience — not yours. Now, shut up!"

Consider these two approaches for a moment and you begin to understand why children often are unmanageable on playgrounds, in school, and in almost any social experience outside the home. All counties and municipalities in the United States pass laws about how meat producing animals are raised and handled. But, at the same time, because two parents are able to conceive and produce a child, they do. It is left to society to correct the abuses of child rearing and in this area, books serve an enormous purpose.

A child who does not get proper instruction at home can learn what is expected of him through books. A child who has been born to limited home experience can expand his horizons through reading books. A bright, introspective child who is the product of an overbearing father can find solace in a book which deals with a real, but sympathetic family relationship. Books save children from harsh family and social experiences, making life bearable until such time as they can take matters into their own hands and, hopefully, avoid repeating such mistakes with their own children.

If you have traveled, you can't help but wonder why the Italian family can, even today, maintain such cohesive family unity. Sunday is a day when the family spends the day together, on a picnic, in the parks, visiting museums and public works. Yet, the Italian cannot govern himself. Governments fall constantly; mail is sold for scrap when innumerable postal strikes make it impossible to deliver it. They are almost incapable of establishing institutions that function and are respected such as we find in the United States, yet, they sprung from the Romans, a people who once ruled the world and were more than successful in doing it.

To watch a French child in a family situation can be a stark experience. The average Frenchman must believe a periodic blow to the head of a child is the only way to handle child rearing. They inflict this punishment for any and all reasons, and constantly.

The English still believe the only salvation for a male child is to send him away to school, the earlier the better. No matter that he is disciplined, often severely, by both headmaster and upperclassmen. In time the child will also be an upperclassman and have his turn at the satisfactions.

Child rearing is far from perfect in the United States, but compared to many other countries, we have moved a long step ahead. It is only since the turn of this century that any mandatory public school was enacted into law. We are the only nation in the world that makes any effort to educate any child that is educable. To do this, we largely depend on books.

We are just beginning to examine our attitudes and laws as they relate to children. Children are the most disposed group in the country. They have been, and still continue to be, regarded as property. We must begin to learn that they are people, with rights and privileges. Our law has been derived from English common law. We still face the task of enacting new legislation and correcting old laws that discriminate against children. We need a whole new genre of children's books to handle this adjustment in children, for parents are so imbued with old molds, they can't be expected to adequately interpret this massive change.

The child usually begins his introduction to books through the picture book. It is a deceptively simple book to the adult mind. Yet, it is one of the most difficult books to write and create. It cannot be elaborate in approach. It deals with a single theme and the text has to suggest, and depend, on illustration. In fact, the best picture books are a blend of text and illustration each necessary to the other. It can involve poetry, or prose; it can be fiction or non-fiction. Because of the wide use of illustration, almost always in some color - and sometimes four color art - it is a costly investment for the publisher. Largely for cost reasons, picture book format is rigidly prescribed. Economical use of the press requires that the book be printed in series of eight-page sections. Therefore, you will find most picture books run 32 pages, or 64 pages. A text that doesn't fit these mechanical requirements, that interests an editor, will have to be revised. It is best to study the format of picture books already in print before beginning writing one, and to remember that prelims (the front matter, such as title page, copyright page, acknowledgment, etc.) and the pages that appear at the end of the book are included in the count of pages that make up a picture book.

Picture books assume a unique writing ability and may be best considered after you acquire some publishing experience. It is as difficult as working in poetry, where every word counts, each sentence carefully drafted.

The picture book is used for the pre-school child and will be part of the book experience of children up to the third grade. From that time, they may be considered "baby books" by most children and many will reject them on format alone.

The average third grade child begins to look at books of conventional format for his needs. Text length will vary according to publisher, but will range from ten to twelve thousand words on the low side and up to twenty to twenty five thousand.

If a writer can handle concepts that interest the fourth and fifth grade child, this area, or one of the higher age ranges among juveniles, is often the best area to begin writing for children. Not because the demands are less, but because the range of material is wider as the child grows. You may find a more comfortable niche in this area than in books for younger readers.

Well over 80 percent of all children's books are bought by schools and libraries. Some publishers expressly build their juvenile list for this market, by-passing the bookstore markets entirely. Therefore, it is wise to keep a close eye on what is going on in education at the elementary level and be mindful how your book would fit curriculum needs. Do not become confused with publisher's readers, a genre of books that are often edited by well established names in the field of reading. *Their* names will appear on the title page as editors or consultants and suggest authority to other reading teachers. This "pre-sells" the books with book selection committees.

Textbook publishers' readers are often "in-house books," written by people who must use certain words that are expected to be introduced into a particular grade level. The old Dick and Jane books are examples of this genre. Authors names rarely appear on such material. The publisher will buy the piece outright rather than pay royalty.

Within the last ten years, textbook publishers' readers have altered considerably. They are less rigid in the mechanical requirements such professionals demand, less romanticized in the art they use. The change came about when publishers began losing adoptions to schools who insisted on more realistic handling, material that dealt with the world of the child today and, not unreasonably, employ some ethnic contributions in illustrations and text. Trade book publishers were more responsive to such needs, less concerned about word level requirements, published books about racial and ethnic problems, used more interesting art and, according to many authorities, selected manuscripts, edited them better, and turned out more attractively manufactured books.

The battle between textbook publishers and trade publishers has by no means subsided. Text readers were often printed in huge printing quantities - 100,000 and 150,000 copy editions were not uncommon. They were fantastically profitable for the publisher, even after paying a percentage point or two of the income to the editorial consultant who loaned their names and reputation to the publisher's title page.

Many school systems now depend wholly on trade books for teaching reading and as supplementary material in teaching the social studies. Nonetheless, education specialists still wage the battle. They cry for more "professionally trained people" at the editorial level in publishing, regard William S. Gray as "the father of reading programs" in the United States. (William S. Gray was the force behind the Dick and Jane series).

The use of trade books in teaching, often referred to as an enrichment supplement, is perhaps, acknowledgement of the problem itself. Books, other than texts, make the subject matter more palatable for the student. As new teachers are trained, they tend to use supplementary material as teaching sources, departing from the old, standard textbook with the teacher's edition which made the teacher's course preparation minimal. Competent teachers have always been willing to invest time in course preparation and tended to use lectures or discussion to supplement textbook instruction. At the same time, school boards that authorized payment for an expensive textbook purchase tended to resist a substitute or replacement text until it was painfully necessary, content to buy additional books of the same edition for books that were worn out, lost, stolen, or strayed.

The appearance of the paperback also facilitated the shift from textbooks. Textbook publishers reacted by publishing books in stiff covers (hard book binding is one fifth of the cost of manufacturing a book.) As trade publishers began to establish their own paperback lists, and paperback publishers moved into the juvenile markets, a rich diversity of material became available for teaching.

There are many writers content to work in the textbook publishing area, contributing articles and short stories to in-house publishing projects, realizing that even after hundreds of such contributions, they will earn no more and have no greater reputation as a writer than they did the day they received their first acceptance.

Writing ability ought to be acknowledged and recognized and it is in the trade books area where this is almost uniformly the case. True, there are some trade publishers who publish for the institutional markets and buy manuscripts outright, even though some of them do acknowledge authorship, but these do not tend to be prestigious publishers and good writers soon move away from them.

Curriculum Libraries are often used as a research area by many writers with good profit, but a knowledgeable writer will distinguish between textbook readers and trade books, quickly. A Curriculum Library can point up educational usage if you do not have access to a professional source with whom you can discuss this area. Colleges and universities that offer a degree in education will have such a collection.

It is well to remember that a professionally trained educator is not necessarily a good editor, any more than an editor with a Ph. D. in literary criticism would make an excellent teacher. You quickly come to the realization in publishing that even an outstanding teacher who is adoringly regarded by his students and voted the most popular teacher of the year is not necessarily able to select or work with raw manuscript. Teachers read and use books that someone has already anguished over, suggesting where areas of revision will make the manuscript clearer, more useful, more meaningful. Manuscript selection is a profession all its own. It involves instincts that successful editors develop and employ, almost intuitively. It is a quality much like the singer or musician possesses: an ability to function because you sense what is right and go about working to bring it out in the writing, or recognize it in writing that comes into the office almost full-blown. It is anticipating trends, sensing market changes and shifts, a sensitivity that is almost impossible to define, and is rare in existence.

Perhaps it is this ephemeral quality that makes trade publishing more responsive to changes. There is no question that trade publishing has been accountable for innovation to a far greater degree than educators themselves. It is axiomatic that textbook publishing has been less responsive to change, largely because it depends on education for direction and guidance. It is significant that textbook publishers continued to publish many books in two editions in the fifties and sixties: one acceptable to the South and the other for the sale to the North. In some instances, they printed a third edition, appealing to the black market of Puerto Rico. Trade books had long been pointing up this disparity. Finally teachers and librarians themselves joined the battle, putting publishers on notice that they would print supplements to correct the texts on hand and refuse to buy additional books if the problem was not corrected, despite the fact that educators, usually at the administrative level, were guiding publisher concepts.

As a writer of juveniles, you will find other areas in which to concentrate your time and energies, as long as you wish to stay the course. It is a very diverse field, ranging from an enlightened direction to the ultra conservative position. You may wish to take the activist route, and if your writing is worthy of publication, you can find a publisher who will consider your point of view valid enough to have its hearing. At the same time, if you can find something new to record about McKinley and his period, you will find an editor who will see a worthy book in that area into print. The market place is another matter. Critics who support your point of view will applaud you; those who see it otherwise will cull through your material with an alert eye and pounce on any seam or defect that you have allowed to see print. In the final analysis, it is the author who must stand behind a book. The publisher has been persuaded that there is a market for what you have written and will attempt to find it. The publisher may be roasted for poor editorial work, bad design, poor manufacture, but it is the thrust of the text for which the author is accountable, and critics will treat your book accordingly.

If you choose to write a juvenile, and succeed, your book will join millions of books that set on library shelves, and are in The Library of Congress. If it is a good book, it will touch the lives of tens of thousands of children in each generation. If you are fortunate enough to write a *Winnie-the-Pooh*, hundreds of thousands will read you, each taking their special demands from your text, passing it along to other children as long as the book is available. It is a sobering undertaking to write a juvenile, an awesome task worthy of the very best any writer can give it.

CHAPTER FOUR

A FRUITFUL AREA OF INQUIRY

As our world becomes more complex, so does children's literature. Yet, there are fundamental themes that have always been part of children's literature as long as it has existed as a genre. Peter Pan did not want to grow up and go to school, but when the adventures of Never Never Land are over and Peter, Wendy, and Tinker Bell return to face growing up, a hint of unreality is left with us as Peter tries to save Tink, whose life is in danger, by turning to the audience and asking all children, "Do you believe in fairies?" And, the children in the audience, having enjoyed the fantasy, all cry out, "I Do!" confirming that strong element of faith children possess.

Peter Rabbit is very disobedient and, because of it, he ends up in Mr. MacGregor's cabbage patch, happy in his disobedience, at first, then roundly frightened when he is chased by Mr. MacGregor. But, Peter triumphs. He keeps his wits about him, hiding in the watering can. Eventually he gets home and in the last scene, is snug in his own bed, loved and secure.

Beatrix Potter did not write *Peter Rabbit* as a book she expected to publish. It was written and illustrated for a small, invalid child, to cheer him up, and sent to him as a letter. Once it found its way into print it has delighted children ever since. No child that knows Peter Rabbit ever sees one of those furry creatures, in the wild or as a back-yard pet, that he doesn't think of Peter Rabbit's escapades.

Peter Rabbit is a good stepping stone to that second English masterpiece for children Kenneth Grahame's, *The Wind in the Willows*. It, too, was not originally intended as a book. Kenneth Grahame had a small son who was nicknamed "Mouse." The father, gifted in storytelling, began telling the son related tales as bedtime stories. Mouse once refused to go away for a seaside holiday because he would miss his father's stories and the father agreed he would send Mouse a chapter through the mail each day. Mouse's governess realized the value of the letters and carefully mailed them back to Mrs. Grahame. Ultimately they became *The Wind in the Willows.*

Each chapter covers an adventure of four friends: Mole; a genial old Water Rat; the timid Badger; and Toad, a rich, bothersome, creature who is very conceited. Their adventures range from picnics to getting lost in Wild Wood, but they also rescue Toad from his indolent life style. It is a special book for many children, but not all children respond to it. Those that do never quite forget it, even as adults.

Mother Goose persists despite constant criticism from children's specialists over the years to bring children into the present world with "now" subject matter. The battle began as far back as 1833, yet children hang on and find these folk rhymes necessary and relevant. Perhaps they are the best of what was handed down from the minstrels, passed on by generations who responded to ballads and ditties, remembering them and sharing them with others. We know that many of them originated in England, and some came from France. Although the history of Mother Goose is fairly well documented and available to readers in a variety of sources, May Hill Arbuthnot provides a good summary of it in her *Children and Books.* It is sufficient that children still respond to Mother Goose verses as mothers play with their toes, or make "Pat-a-cake" games out of their attention as they chant the rhymes. Children like the musical quality of them, their humor, their action and they especially like the illustrations of the Blanche Fisher Wright edition with its simple, bright colors as well as those of Kate Greenaway with its quaintness and detail.

Perhaps of all children's books ever published, a popularity poll would find Mother Goose and *Peter Rabbit* to top the list.

There is no question that many of these old classics would not find much sympathy among juvenile editors if they were offered today for the first time. They would be rejected as old fashioned, not relevant, unlikely to meet present day need. We may lament that fact, but it is a reality of our time.

If we are beginning to examine the legal rights of children, we might well begin to think of what we impose on them in the literature we publish for them. There is no doubt that adolescents grow up with imagined or existing fears. It is very easy for adults to forget what growing up is all about, to forget the uncertainties and groping of children as they reach out to find their place in the world about them. The world they see facing them is frightening beyond comprehension. They quickly see the adult's duplicity and begin to question its purposes. If the parent still believes children should be seen and not heard, they will get few good answers, but they will find their own, because they must have answers to these perplexing questions. We have exposed them to remarkable experiences through schools, media, travel and with incredible ease and opportunity. But we leave relating themselves to an adult world as part of finding the hole in the pattern to which they can respond and into which they can fit. No one wonders much about how they can possibly feel part of the mammoth institutions to which we subject them - the high school with five thousand students, a monstrosity in which you have to carry a floor plan to find where you are going. We press them to make career choices early, because specialization requires they make the correct choices in the courses they take. If they show broad interests, we discourage it and make them fearful that such apptitudes are not marketable. We do all we can to discourage the very point we hope we are working toward, to get young people to feel they belong to a meaningful, rewarding life.

True, youth has always had to find itself. We may countenance divorce, for instance, where children are involved, because children are enormously resilient and can make adjustments quickly. However, once career counselors began complaining about the price children paid when divorce was forced into their lives, books began to appear to help young people to handle such adjustments. The books became a reaction to an imposed problem. Surely that is some help, but it did not alter the ever escalating number of broken families whose children often have to fend for themselves in whatever way they can.

The social chaos of the 1960's leaves us with a legacy that will have to be corrected for several generations. Somehow we must make it clear that the technician is important to our well-being, but not as important as the human being. We must find ways to still the anxieties of the young, release them from the pressures schools impose in their desire to "place" their students in prestigious colleges. We must find ways to keep the young from becoming cynical toward the society to which they have been born, alienated from it and embittered by it. We must find ways to allow them time, to test and ponder, to make mistakes without making them feel guilty. We must find the time to communicate, with wholesome, genuine concern, with love and understanding. We must help them away from the terrible feeling that they must "make it" or "drop out." We must not judge them by preconceived standards that applied to another generation. If we have grown accustomed to the frenzied existence in which we live, we must not expect our children to passively accept it as well.

When Cornelia, the mother of The Gracchi, was asked about her jewels she pointed to her children and said, "These are my jewels." We have an odd penchant, as parents, for bestowing on mankind the greatest gift of all, life, without the other responsibility, to provide that life with a chance to grow up humanely.

Books can right some of this mal-alignment, good books that speak to the inner uncertainties of childhood. At a time when non-fiction pours out in juvenile lists, we must find ways of publishing more fiction, excellent fiction, to which children can relate and, in the absence of any sure direction, find their social and moral solutions in literature.

CHAPTER FIVE

HOW TO WRITE A

SUCCESSFUL CHILDREN'S BOOK

A wise resort owner once commented about his patrons, "On the whole, I enjoy people who come here as guests. They are at their best because they expect to have a good time, and they are willing to pay money to have that happen." Children approach the reading of a book in much the same way, knowingly or unknowingly. They are prepared to enjoy what they want to read. It depends on the author as to whether they are fulfilled.

There always has been, there always will be, children who are avid readers. Although most parents do not have to worry about an over-preoccupation with reading, we all know that comment, usually attributed to the female child, "She always has her head buried in a book." Such children grow up "hooked" with the reading habit. As adults, they can't go to sleep at night without reading a chapter or two of a book, no matter how late they retire. They haunt libraries, checking out a half dozen novels, or mysteries, or gothics, week after week. They are what constitutes the core of readership for books and their number grows year by year.

Interest Areas

For the most part children are like adults in that they read in interest areas. Stories about horses have always been popular. They adore stories about animals, even about animals that we don't usually think of as pets, such as Elsa in *Born Free*. When they empathize with such an animal, they will read and re-read the same book, quietly sobbing their way through it, sometimes audibly, as they turn the pages. They have so successfully lost themselves in the narrative line, they are transported from all their uncertainties and frustrations into a world of imagination where the author leads them through thickets of ideas to a resolution, almost always, a happy one.

What we will examine in this section is that quality in writing, not the mechanical aspects of writing itself. That can be best served by studying manuscript preparation, the book on style or others that pertain to particular needs.

Children's Books Come Of Age

Early children's books were unusually heavy in instruction and the theme was simple: follow the Puritan ethic and all will be sweetness and light in the end. Yet, for most of those earlier children, life was very stark. Children were an adjunct to the family work force, property in which parents invested and out of which they should expect a return. Of course, there were the rebels who for one reason or another slipped out from under the yoke, and sometimes simply ran away from home. Children's literature is well peppered with such examples, sometimes suitably sugar coated to make it less disturbing. Even Dickens, who did much to bring the abuse of children to society's conscience, cast Pip as an orphan in *Great Expectations.*

Child labor laws were a long time coming in the United States, but once they were enacted, another link in the chain of children's emancipation was added and with the reality of compulsory education, children who would never have been exposed to ideas that books promulgate took a great step up the ladder to a better life.

Think, for a moment, of the children, tens of thousands of them, who grew up in the mining areas of the United States, who worked long hours, picking slate out of the coal that was mined to run the factories and heat homes; who worked in oppressive factories, poorly lighted, unventilated, harbingers of maiming machinery, all for a pittance. All of this was still acceptable even during the early part of this century.

However, with the arrival of the twentieth century, enormous social change came. Children's books began to be printed in greater number, but it was not until 1919 that the first children's book department was founded in this country by the MacMillan Company. For many years the number of new children's books hovered around a thousand a year. Today it is in excess of 2,500.

Non-Fiction

In the writing of non-fiction for children, your research will bring you quickly into contact with the published literature. A more practical way to approach any non-fiction writing is by checking the Subject Guide available in any creditable library and, more recently, *Children's Books In Print.* If you find the subject has not been treated, you have discovered a "hole" in the published literature, clearly a green light to press further. If you find the subject well represented with published books, you may be persistent and want to check out how thoroughly and competently the literature covers the area, but be objective in this. Don't assume that you can do better - and that is exactly what you will have to do - if you are to locate a publisher who will seriously consider your manuscript. It is always possible to build a better mousetrap, to be sure, but it is also an uphill battle, unless you have some important and convincing research where you can expand or correct the information already published.

Non-fiction sells better than fiction, both in children's books and in adult books. As a result, some publishers do not publish any juvenile fiction. Fiction demands an editorial capability quite different than what is used in publishing non-fiction. And, if fiction does sell in smaller quantities, that is not to say that non-fiction is easier to write. It simply means that fiction requires a different writing capacity, one that keeps the battle raging between those who consider fiction more creative. Suffice it to say, they require different talents and it does not follow that the writer of fiction is equally comfortable in writing non-fiction. More frequently, it does not follow that the writer of non-fiction can write fiction.

You will have to experiment with your talents and discover in which writing form you can work best.

Professional Assistance

Many writers lean heavily on a librarian in choosing a book subject. Librarians are an enormously helpful professional group, and they will go through endless inconvenience to help any serious patron answer a question. Like any other professional who serves the public, it is not the case that every librarian is the right solution in your search. Nor should you impose unreasonably on a librarian's time, even if you pay your taxes promptly and are the biggest owner of real estate in town. Like any other relationship, it is a question of give and take. If you demonstrate that you are capable, serious, and do not impose, few librarians will refuse you help. You can also find this sort of direction from an equally capable teacher at times. But, be careful of either when responses are very general -- "I can't get enough books in that area;" or "Children read every book on horses we can buy." If you ask a question, you should expect an answer. Whether the answer is informed you will have to check out and decide for yourself. But, when you find those informed professionals, respect them and don't make them want to duck behind the shelves every time they see you come through the door.

Writing Out of Total Life-Experience

Perhaps the worst aspect of many writers is the limitations out of which they write. A good writer has the experience level, the facility to use research and expression in an artful way. Good writers are great note-takers. Watch them reach for a bit of paper and scrawl down a statement as they move about, responding to some felicitous expression or point that is made in conversation. Watch their faces react to an elegantly turned phrase, a succinct observation. If they are social beings — and many writers sometimes are not — they are working at their craft, even when away from the desk. They store away experience and, not infrequently — if you have the ability to see ideas freshly, transform the commonplace into concise, original expression — you may find yourself turn up in a writer's published book. It is the lot of most mortals to live and savor; it is up to the writer to use and record.

Most writers write out of a total experience. Bits and pieces swirl around in the storehouse of the mind, find themselves in notebooks and files. All of it surfaces when the writer's creativity is flowing, to be fitted in and used.

The Demands of Juvenile Writing

The writing of a juvenile is just as demanding as any other form of writing, and many authorities would agree it is far more so. The juvenile writer carries an additional responsibility in his work, for he is dealing with a young mind, one that is emerging and shaping. The pebble of impression the writer leaves with the children that read him can expand and have its usefulness for years to come, perhaps for all of life. Children react to experience in their own special way, just as keenly as an adult, but in quite different ways. They are less inhibited, not yet socialized into predictable molds. They feel emotion intensely, even when it is for short periods of time. Their time span is the immediate, the moment of the present. Within that moment, they can live the tortures of the damned or the ecstasy of all life. It may all be transient, but it can lurk in the convolutions of the brain as a moment never to be quite forgotten.

Point of View

Any good writing has to make a point. It is what point of view is all about. Children prefer answers, specifics that contribute to an effect. Factual material cannot be laid on a manuscript. It has to be integrated in the narrative line so that it is logical and part of the whole. Learn to know when your material is carefully woven into the prose you write, and when it won't bend to your creative needs. If you cannot write it so that it is a seamless flow, discard it. Good writing draws on research that moves a storyline, an expression that moves and advances the writing pattern and design. Keep the reader sufficiently in mind so that you learn how to read your output with fresh eyes, able to disassociate yourself from what you hoped to do, and to determine if you have done it. It is a difficult stance to develop, and some writers never develop the talent. You will be better off if you can master it.

The Writer as a Storyteller

A good writer is basically a storyteller. If your writing makes a moral point well, it is because you have confronted the same point, either imaginatively or through experience. If you must preach, find a pulpit. Your task is to illuminate in so telling, in so convincing a fashion, the moral point is self-evident. If you have to lard your writing with moralistic pronouncements, editors will respond with form rejections.

It requires strong dedication to write well. It also requires will power and a willingness to work quietly and alone. It does not follow, however, that any of these qualities are sufficient to see you into print.

We all know the story about the young farmer who visited his minister and announced that he was going to become a minister. "What leads you to that decision?" the minister asked. "Pastor," the young farmer began, "It's cause I had a dream. In my dream, I saw a field of corn. But though the corn was high enough to be in tassle, most of the stalks warn't. How-some-ever, some of them was in tassle and they just marched across the field, spelling out two great letters: a great P and a great C, right in the middle of the field. I take that as a sign that I been called and that them letters mean preach Christ." The minister knew the young man, knew his limitations well, and he pondered the statement. Then, he suggested, "Did it ever occur to you those letters might mean plow corn?"

Realism in Children's Books

If children insist that the stories they read have to have a start, a middle, and an end, that something has to happen, right up front, and it has to be built upon, moved between a number of possible solutions and eventually come to a reasonable and understandable end, that does not mean they are timid little people who have to be protected with soft-soaping prose.

Today's books deal with all the ramifications of life, from the influence of divorce to certain death through leukemia and every other shade of existence in between. Television and movies have exposed children to both real and unreal life, perhaps unduly so. They are amazingly well informed, handling concepts and ideas that most adults did not learn about at all, or learned about poorly. They are more humanistic, without being sentimental. They care about their environment in greater numbers than their parents ever did. We deal with many by-products of this knowledge explosion and social awareness, but other generations have had to cope with such intrusions, too. Young men walked for hundreds of miles to hear Martin Luther lecture in the sixteenth century, living in hovels so they could listen to his teachings, wearing long hair and despised by almost everyone but the academic community. In our own country, New Harmony was a communal experiment that flourished from 1815 until 1928. Social change can be ignored or we can try to understand why it has occurred. With the first position, little happens; in the other, real change, good change, can come about.

Books that contain a strong point of view, that test the existing social mores still are suspect, perhaps always will be to some extent. There are authors whose prisms of sight see issues in that vein. They ride the crest of debate for a time and eventually find their niche or are forgotten. If they are effective in their reasoning and persuasion, they deserve their place, no matter how controversial their import. But, at any one time, they are a thin layer of the output. The vast majority of juveniles are reasonable in content and many others are simpering nonsense.

Good books are written out of the background and experience of the author. In a country as large and diverse as the United States, with authors representing the regionalism that has shaped and nurtured them, it is reasonable to expect the arc of viewpoint to be wide and rich. No idea deserves to be suspect simply because it ruffles complacency, disjoints the social process, or disturbs the grain of public thought. No nation ever was too rich in originality of ideas. New ideas in the market place are always tested for their value and contribution. When they prove wanting, they are discarded. When they are accepted and assimilated in the population, good changes usually result.

Age Level

Most publisher's books contain symbols that indicate age appeal. They vary from publisher to publisher, but all suggest the age level to which the book is aimed. These can appear on the back of the book or on the inside flap of the jacket. If you see, 4-10 printed on the jacket, it means the book is expected to appeal to the four to ten year olds; 12 up means a twelve year old should find the book interesting and any child above that age bracket. This device was used when bookstores handled more of the juvenile sale of books and was intended for the harried book clerk who could quickly determine the book's age appeal. It is helpful to a librarian or teacher today, even though professional reviews may ignore the reference and state the use in terms of curriculum needs or grade levels.

The juvenile author quickly realizes that such age level references are rough indications of appeal. An ardent horse fan who happens to be a fourth grader will sometimes select a picture book format, even though that format is considered by his peers as a "baby book." In the same sense, a child will often reach beyond its age level for reading material. The answer lies in the wide diversity of interest, development, and ability that exists in any segment of the juvenile market.

Bookstores Versus the Institutional Markets

Although many publisher's juvenile books are not sold through book-stores, others continue to work this area. Publisher's lists that appeal to the bookstore market are known as merchandise lists. Such books often contain greater use of color, and are manufactured in over-sized formats that are referred to in the trade as flats. Frequently they do not contain jackets and the book covers are laminated with plastic or sprayed varnish. Many of these are non-royalty books, put together in the publisher's editorial departments from writing that has long been in the public domain or they may be adaptations of old classics written by a staff member. Others contain writing the publisher has purchased outright from the author. Often such books are not exposed to school and library markets for a variety of reasons: the binding does not meet library standards; they are not written well enough or are so slight in content that they simply would not pass professional muster. Such books are merchandised and their success is dependent on sales programs the publisher devises where discount offered dealers is more important than the quality of the book in question.

Now and again, an author and publisher can cut across both areas, selling equally well to bookstore trade and the institutional markets. Such authors are few and far between and when a publisher finds one, concessions are made, all along the line, to keep the author safely in his stable.

Today, bookstores depend on their income from walk-in trade or what they can generate through mailings, advertising, and charge customers. Increasingly they move into other lines of merchandise to keep profits up. If you have ever stood in a large bookstore, where a reasonable juvenile section is possible, you may have thought of publishing juveniles as a very satisfactory and rewarding way to live your life. The two divisions in juvenile books, the merchandise book and the institutional book, either hardly compatible with the other, argue against such a conclusion. Most bookstores write fifty or sixty percent of their income in the last three months of the year when most books are bought, and this is as true about adult books as it is about juveniles. Publishers that depend on bookstore trade stick rigidly to two book lists a year, spring and fall. Salesmen quickly form opinions at the publisher's sales conference and they know when a book is basically aimed at the institutional market, even though the juvenile editor is doing his or her level best to wring a bookstore sale out of the book. It may have a seasonable appeal, such as an Easter Story, tied to the coming of spring, or travel. But whatever the reason for publishing the book in the spring, the salesman subjectively knows the book will not sell as well as a book that has merchandise appeal and appears on the fall list. The salesman thinks in terms of piling up books in the store. A large stack of books, no matter what the book may be, suggests importance to the public and will get more attention in that frantic book buying period of October through December.

Consequently, the new author will do well to think carefully about this built-in distribution and consider the more stable juvenile market, the book that is aimed at the institutional market.

Publishers may well support newspaper's book sections that issue summer reading lists, attempting to stimulate a larger book sale, but they also know the summer is the slowest sales period of the year and little that they have ever done has changed the circumstances.

Although sources that sell lists of bookstores for advertising and promotion purposes often exceed 2,500 such outlets, it is generally agreed there are no more than that number which are legitimate book sales sources. Of that number, perhaps a thousand do a reasonably good job of selling books. If each good bookstore bought two copies of a juvenile, and sold them, that would increase the sale by two thousand copies. Assuming a 10% royalty on a $5.00 list price, that would add $1,000 of income to the author's royalty, perhaps enough to repay the advance the publisher pays the author (a $750 advance, for a first book author, in juveniles, is not unheard of, even today, among some publishers, when the manuscript is submitted without an Agent.)

If all this unvarnished discussion begins to pall and you begin to wonder why anyone would want to invest time in writing a juvenile book, take heart. There are many compensations, sometimes even fair income. This chapter began with a quote by a resort owner. He too has his limitations in how far he can guarantee his guests will have a good time, no matter how well appointed his facilities happen to be, no matter how his guests try to enjoy themselves. The resort owner can't control the weather. He can, however, provide a good game room for those inevitable periods when the skies cloud over and, day after day, rain descends. If his cook suddenly quits because the Land's End Inn happens to woo him away for more money, his dining room will suffer and nothing he can do will right that until he hires another cook, as good, or better than the old one. In short, then, the resort owner has to anticipate his problems and be ready to find substitute solutions at any moment, unless he is content to see his accommodations stand idle.

A Check List for Writing a Successful Children's Book

So it is with books. There are many practical considerations to bear in mind. A checklist of those considered in the writing of a successful children's book is worthy of repeating.

1. Write a book that will appeal to children.
2. Know your audience and write for a broad interest area.
3. Consider your own capability and be convinced that you have the ability to write a good children's book.
4. Be sure you know how to structure a children's book.
5. You can write in any subject area, but know what is workable for the age level to which you are aiming.
6. You have to have a point of view.
7. Be a good storyteller, but don't preach or moralize.
8. Know your strengths and limitations and learn to improve the former and diminish the latter.
9. Non-fiction sells better than fiction.
10. Use the library tools available to you.
11. Aim at curriculum usage.
12. Differentiate between markets by knowing what fits a bookstore or institutional market.
13. Don't anguish over the book that is in production. Use your time positively and begin working on another manuscript.
14. Write the best book that's in you.

CHAPTER SIX

SOME INITIAL CONSIDERATIONS AND

AN ANALYSIS OF A JUVENILE BOOK

Perhaps the greatest mistake most writers make - and it is as true for juvenile writing as it is for any other category - is they simply begin. They sit down and begin writing. It is possible the result will be published, but not probable.

A better start would be to spend a period of time finding out what you are best fitted to write.

There are two broad fields of juvenile literature, fiction and non-fiction. Both demand creativity from the writer, but fiction also requires a creative imagination. There are writers that can move from fiction to non-fiction, but they are rare creatures. It will be more practical to make your choice after a careful analysis of your capabilities. If you have a fertile imagination, fiction would be a better choice for a beginning; if you tend to factual material in your interests and reading, non-fiction will be a better solution.

In deciding on subject matter, it is wise to take careful stock of what has interested you. What are your interests, your hobbies? What kinds of material do you read and what kinds of courses interested you most during your education? Somewhere in that morass you should find an area that surfaces as a special interest and that is usually the best starting point. It may be sensible to consider a skills analysis evaluation such as is offered at many educational institutions today if you have any doubts about your particular talents.

Once your choice is made, begin modestly. Work in a smaller form before launching into a book project. Study juvenile publications to learn what interests particular magazines and pay close attention to how other writers work out their articles and short stories. If you possess the ability to write in the juvenile field, you'll quickly discover other writers who are able to present their material in a manner that is acceptable to the age level for which it is intended, interestingly, without being patronizing and, most important, entertainingly.

All writing requires patience and endurance. If you write an acceptable article or short story that makes it into print, the income should be secondary to the satisfaction you will realize in knowing you can write for publication.

If you have children about you, listen and observe them while they are playing. Watch how they conduct their relationships with each other. Spend some time reading their school books. If they are children of average intelligence, you will begin to understand how they respond and what interests them in a way that should recall some of your own childhood. It is absolutely essential to have this ability to deal with children, on their interest level, to know their levels of joy and their periods of disquiet and uncertainty if you are to succeed in writing for them. Most adults are so busy maintaining themselves in the adult world they forget what it was like to be a child, and many of them can never recapture the feel of childhood again. If you are one of these, you will have difficulty writing juveniles and it may be well to concentrate in some aspect of adult publication rather than attempt to work it out.

Children's books can be used as a substitute, in the absence of children of your own, but it also puts the whole experience a step removed from the primary source of knowledge. Direct contact with children is, of course, the best solution.

Once you have settled on a subject, the next step is research. Read everything you can find in the subject area, both juvenile and adult. Fiction writing means you will rely more on imagination, but it will help you to read how other authors have handled their material. Background must be convincing and that means solid research at the library.

If you are working in fiction, the short story will force you to write economically. If you can create interest, develop a start and a middle and an ending, handle characterization well and tell a story, all in 2,500 words or less, you are on your way to a writing career. The test is in submission, but if you have done your work successfully, acceptance will follow.

Although children learn to read at varying rates and increasingly know a good bit about the process before they begin formal schooling, for our purpose we are concerned with the average child. Kindergarten introduces the child to a variety of concepts in preparing him for education and a good deal of stress is placed on reading readiness, or preparing the student for reading, the first stage of learning to read. The second stage begins in earnest in first grade, and by the time the year ends, the child will be reading, with a vocabulary of about 300 words. Reading studies tell us that children in the primary grades are most interested in animals, the familiar turf, and about other children of the same age. It is also interesting that *they* prefer this instruction as stories rather than non-fiction or other types of material.

Although books are often coded as appropriate for the six-through-eight-year-old, you'll quickly realize some of the problem when you decide where to aim your writing: at the minimal vocabulary of the first grader with an animal story or the more advanced reading level of the third grader where you can begin to introduce more challenging concepts. Fortunately, the interest level and the reading ability range widely in these early years. Some students at the end of first grade are reading at a third grade level and, because of emotional or social factors, not to ignore physical problems, others will require supportive work in reading for another year or two, possibly longer. Your answer, of course, is to aim for the middle of this group and how well you achieve that will determine how widely your book is accepted.

The third stage of reading is concerned with building on this base already established, plus working toward progress in an enlarged vocabulary (1,500 to 2,000 words that are recognized by sight) and to develop the ability to sound out words independently. A first grade student reads about equally fast in either oral or silent performance. By third grade, silent reading becomes accelerated and the student will read faster in silent reading than in oral reading.

It is the fourth stage of reading where a wider concern with interests and tastes begins and during this period all other concerns of the first three stages are reinforced and refined. As the student's reading background improves, ability to interpret increases, vocabulary is enlarged, and he seeks out broader concepts and more challenging ideas. Books of the 1,000 to 10,000 word range fit the six through eight age level, but the eight through twelve wants a fully developed plot and is ready for books that run as high as 40,000 words in length. The material has to have good pace and lots of action. Adventure is popular, hero worship and factual books on hobbies and science also are in demand for boys while girls enjoy fantasy, romance, and some adventure. Both groups enjoy mysteries and books about horses.

The teen-age or young adult book, ages eight and up, developed in the late forties and early fifties. It is a step beyond the average juvenile, eight through twelve range, but not yet the full adult book. The subject matter is broad, including anything that covers teen-age problems and interests, but handled more as an adult book is written.

In addition to aiming your manuscript at the proper age slot, you will also have to decide whether you are going to write for boys or girls. A nine year old girl may well read a boy's book, but a nine year old boy will have nothing to do with one intended for girls. You can introduce plot elements that recognize this problem once you have gained some success in publishing, but it is more sensible, as a beginner, to make a choice and stay with it, the boy's or girl's market. A quick look at the published literature makes the point: men write for boys; women for girls. There are exceptions, but they usually can be explained once you get to know something about the author. For instance, a woman teaching in a boys' boarding school, has her own special solution.

Editors, agents, and teachers who work with writing groups often speculate why the new writer so often turns to fantasy. Perhaps it can only be explained as misdirected effort. Any writer who takes the time to study the juvenile field will quickly realize there is no place for another book on Santa's Elves or the little Christmas tree that makes some child happy even though it was gnarled and overlooked by the tree cutters. No established writer would touch the subject, and only a novice might. Resist tackling any fantasy until you develop some writing experience. Chances are, you never will attempt to write in that area if you do.

The possibilities for subject matter are endless, if you approach your writing realistically. Most published writers rarely want for subject matter. It is a question of time to write all the books they want to write.

Although you may begin writing shorts and articles, eventually you will begin thinking in terms of book subjects. Don't hurry the process. Writing a book is far more demanding, more substantial in contribution, and, if it is a good book, will be read and reread by generations yet unborn. We owe Thomas Carlyle for pointing out: "No book is worth anything that is not worth much; nor is it serviceable until it has been read, and reread, and loved, and loved again."

Reading is the chief means we have for gaining knowledge and books preserve all that has been recorded from the past and up-dates the present for future readers. Books are the means of understanding and preserving our culture. Writing any books should never be approached lightly.

Lord Houghton (1809-1885) lived a very active and colorful life as an English poet and man of letters. He is chiefly known today for his contribution in molding public thought on literary matters of his day and for his assistance to young writers, including Alfred Lord Tennyson, Ralph Waldo Emerson, and Algernon Charles Swinburne. It was Lord Houghton who wrote: "Think what a book is. It is a portion of the eternal mind caught in its process through the world, stamped in an instant, and preserved for eternity. Think what it is; that enormous amount of human sympathy and intelligence that is contained in these volumes; and think what it is that this sympathy should be communicated to the masses of people." Additionally, we are considering books for children. They deserve nothing but the very best.

At all times, remember that you are a storyteller and if you are inform-ing your reader, you must also entertain. Perhaps this is doubly true today when we are confronted with a knowledge explosion. Reading is used to obtain information, but it is also used for stimulation and inspiration.

Don't write off the top of your head. Know what you want to convey and don't begin to write until you have defined your purpose. If necessary, commit it to paper and keep it close at hand to keep your thinking concentrated on your purpose. Any piece of writing must have a central theme or purpose and offer a point of view.

In fiction, narration dominates the writing; facts are secondary and should not intrude on the narrative development. Good background material is just that. It must not take over, acting only as a backdrop against which action is presented.

In juvenile books, we never have too many that deal with human values at their best. The child that comes from limited background, social or familial imbalance, has a second chance to learn what his adjustments should be through books. The writing has to be realistic, part of the real world in which he will eventually live, and should not be so sugar-coated or romanticized as to be meaningless.

Once you have established your purpose, begin to define your plot. What characters best represent your purpose? What kind of situation will permit you to make your purpose clearly? It is time for note making, time for writing character sketches so that you can begin to develop a plot.

The question of how you develop your plot is a matter of personality. Yet, whether you commit it to paper in elaborate notebooks or block it out in your mind, you must pit your actions and characters against each other in the final analysis. For the new writer, it is undoubtedly easier to get it all down on paper before you begin writing. You must know your characters, know their limits and dimensions. They must be believable and each of their actions, must be convincing to the reader or you have not kept characterization in control.

In juvenile writing, a slow beginning often loses the reader. Start the story off with a crisis or some tension. Your characters have to have problems through which your purpose is presented. There must be conflicts, pitfalls to overcome, tensions to be eased and used to build good emotion, a climax and solution. One character must be central to the story and it is best to relate the story through his or her point of view. In time you may wish to introduce an objective point of view, but this is best left to the seasoned writer as it is a harder technique to employ.

Work in third person. Children are not very responsive to first person stories. Keep the age of your children a year or two ahead of the age level for which you are writing. Children are interested in what lies ahead of them and less interested in reading about children their own age.

Any manuscript you write must have a beginning, a middle, and an end. Make the opening strong. The middle is the development section, where possibilities are offered and explored, each contributing to a probable solution that should conclude in a strong ending. There is much tinkering that must be done as you work. There may be frustrations, times when nothing seems to be working out, that the characters won't bend to your needs. None of these problems are unique to any writer. If you have strong characterizations in your writing, you must expect some fight and resistance from them when you want to maneuver them to your needs, into positions in which they do not fit. Stay the course. Learn to consider other alternatives. Test them out in other situations. Don't lose sight of your purpose and it will, eventually, work itself out, hopefully, well.

The Outline

A good outline brings a writer to grips with intention. Well done, it is the essence of what will follow in the writing stage. Once a writer becomes established, it also can be a selling tool and result in a contract when offered to an editor. But, editors who offer a contract on the basis of an outline must be convinced of potential and that means your initial work has been done so well that you have actually blocked out the book before writing it.

In writing either fiction or non-fiction your options and alternatives as to how you proceed are so rich with possibility you can easily get bogged down before you begin. An outline will help you focus your intention, give you a frame within which you can work. It can't be written before you have completed your research in the case of non-fiction or before you have worked out your plot in fiction. It should not be considered restrictive, but it should clearly explain your purpose and how you expect to develop it. Even if that work is done well, changes often assert themselves at the writing stage, but deal with that later. A good outline is a starting point, the keel laid, about which all else fits and depends.

Some writers work from notes and research notebooks. They may construct an outline after the first draft is completed, to test the text and decide how well organized it is. They keep the details of organization in mind and can sense what is necessary to add, what needs to be supported, as they write. A tidy mind, a well organized mind can work this way. For most of us, working from an outline is a safer bet. If you have trouble establishing direction, if your ideas come in spurts and bursts, if you tend to flounder in research details, aren't sure how long the manuscript will run, aren't certain how many chapters you will use, can't decide how to maneuver your characters, which one should be dominant, and all the other problems that plague a writer, an outline will help solve the problem.

An outline should present the significant features of your purpose. You may choose to use headings and subheadings under which you amplify a point. You may prefer to use topical sentences and, under them, list other points that must be covered. You may choose to write chapter descriptions, each working to advance your intent. As long as order and general relationship are kept in mind, how you work out the mechanics is a matter of personal choice and what works best.

The Beginning:

To get the first paragraph written is often difficult for many writers. The only sound advice to follow is to get it down. It is yours to change and alter in whatever way you please, later and, chances are, you will rewrite it, many times, until the right solution is found. True, it can be crucial in establishing setting, time, place, and characters. But it doesn't have to be perfection to do this in first draft.

Keep economy of expression in mind. It can suggest pace and action better than any other writing device, two requisites in juvenile writing.

In Dorothy Aldis' *Ride The Wild Winds,* an adventure story about English Puritans that immigrate to Salem, Massachusetts, she begins her first chapter in this way:

"A boy of twelve stood staring out an upstairs window. His name was Samuel Dudley. Over three hundred years ago he lived in Northampton,

a fair-sized town in England, and although St. Peter's church loomed
directly across the street from his home and one would think he couldn't
help but see it, all he saw were his own troubles."
In sixty words, less than eight full lines of print, we know a boy of twelve,
Samuel Dudley, lived over three hundred years ago, in Northampton, England,
and that he was, like most twelve year olds, wrapped in the flannel of his own
troubles.

Dorothy Aldis quickly introduces her second character, Patience,
Samuel's ten year old sister. She is working on a sampler, sympathetic to
Samuel's wish to be outside playing football, an activity that Puritans
regarded as wicked. Although Samuel is the main character throughout the
book, Patience plays a sufficiently strong part to keep a girl reader interested.
Patience learns to make candles, soap, butter and collect herbs for medicinal
value, all occupations that occupied a young girl of that period.

Themes and Devices:

One of the underlying themes of *Ride the Wild Winds* is witchcraft. In
the period of this story, many women who possessed what we today know as
extraordinary perceptions became suspect. If they had a knowledge of herbs
and their use, that only compounded the suspicion. To treat illness with
potions meant the practitioner was in league with the devil. The "witch
hunting bell" is introduced by the second page and we learn that townsmen
are stalking the streets looking for Elinor Shaw.

Elinor Shaw, in real life, was hunted down in Northampton, tried and
executed for practicing witchcraft. Dorothy Aldis, in her author's notes,
admits Elinor Shaw never went to Salem, Massachusetts, but uses her as a
fictional creation as the primary tension between Samuel and Patience.

What to Tell the Reader, and When

We do not know the reasons for Samuel's belief in witches at this point
in the narration. We only know he accepts the fact that witches exist. However, the author knew she had to offer a strong justification for Samuel's
belief and she does this, but not until the end of the second chapter when we
learn that Samuel witnessed a disturbing experience, the delirium of a small
boy, William Adams, and hears him cry out:

"Elinor Shaw!" . . . "Yes, I promise not to tell my mother I talked to
you, only don't bewitch me, please."

Patience, on the other hand, considers Elinor Shaw an old woman misused.

She persuades Samuel, against his better judgement, to help rescue her and together they hide her in the Widow Law's house, a neighbor who is not in sympathy with the witch hunting craze. Widow Law is a minor, but necessary character. She is introduced as Samuel and Patience go fishing early one morning. The section also serves to fill in setting and provide period flavor.

> "It was a perfect morning; the sun not yet up, but the wide sky cloudless. Square and solid against it loomed St. Peter's tower. In the small, triangular churchyard, larks were dipping and singing. Quickly Samuel and Patience skirted the town pond where six swans were conceitedly swimming. They walked through Market Square bordered with its many selling booths for shoemakers, butchers, bakers and fishmongers."

Samuel speculates about catching an eel because

> "...they bring in much the most money."

then

> "They turned up Laundry Street, hurried past Samuel's free school and the old Hynde Inn, turned left on Checker Street where Mercy Doolittle (a friend of Patience's who is mentioned earlier in the text) and the Widow Law lived. Mercy's house was still so thoroughly locked and shuttered it looked asleep, but the Widow Law was already up and sweeping her front doorstep."

This makes it possible to use the Widow Law, later, to perform an adult function beyond the action level of the children. Patience wants to stop and visit with Widow Law hoping they will get something to eat since they left their house so early, not wanting to rouse anyone with getting themselves fed. At the same time, we get to understand the Widow Law's attitude toward the witch hunt.

> "Soon they were seated in front of the Widow Law's huge fireplace, each munching away on a venison pasty. The fireplace had a border of stone apples curving around it. The apples were painted bright red and the surrounding leaves bright green. The Widow Law was as cheerful as her fireplace -- a round bustling little body whose rosy face was forever creasing into a network of smiling wrinkles.
>
> "You know," she said happily, "I said to myself as soon as I saw you two that you wouldn't have had breakfast this early in the morning." She hurried off across the rush-strewn floor to get still another pasty apiece for her hungry guests."

Next, the author fortifies the witch bell suggestion in yet another way with Samuel.

The Widow Law explains it is just her goat.

> "Only my poor old Nana who keeps wandering off all the time. I've had to tie a bell around her neck so as to have some idea where she's got to. But I know what you thought it was," the Widow Law added, all her cheerful wrinkles smoothed away. "Thanks be they haven't caught her (Elinor Shaw) yet. When they do we'll certainly hear soon enough."

When the witch hunting bell is first introduced in the chapter, we also learn Samual believes the stories that have been circulating in the town — that Elinor Shaw has bewitched eighteen horses to death, and all of Mr. Mathews' sheep. A more grisly bit of lore, true of the period, was that poor Elinor also greased her broomstick with freshly stewed babies when she went riding at night. Dorothy Aldis used it. However, to temper the effect, as Samuel tells stories to Patience, his fifteen year old sister comes into the room. Anne scolds him, reminding him that

> ". . . father would punish you severely if he caught you trying to frighten Patience with any such stories."

The older sister provides a means of weighing the witch hunt scare, allowing Patience's and Samuel's attitudes to be developed. Here we learn that the Widow Law doesn't believe in Witches; that Thomas Dudley, the children's father and Mopsa, the housekeeper, agree with the widow. But, Anne's point of view is ambiguous when Samuel asks her:

> "Don't you believe there are witches?"

and Anne replies:

> "Well, Samuel, yes. A few, I guess. At least I suppose so."

The children discuss the possibility of their father hiding Elinor Shaw in their house since he doesn't believe in witches. We also learn that if he was caught the King had ruled the punishment would be life imprisonment.

At this point, Anne, older and, therefore, privileged to more of the family's plans, hints at a change that will influence the whole family. Patience wonders if it has anything to do with the visit by the Earl of Lincoln and Minister Dod who had recently called on their father. Patience overheard them talking about Northampton getting too much like London, a subject which distressed "all good Puritans." They discuss that people smoke and swear, and

> ". . . the king encourages them to play games and bait bears and have maypole dances even on Sunday . . . At the same time food is so scarce it's almost impossible to raise a family."

Mr. Dudley comes into the room and attempts to distract the children. He reminds Samuel he was supposed to fix a shelf in the buttery and Samuel agrees with, "I'll do it now." Patience, knowing something is afoot, attempts to learn about it from her father with:

> "I do wish something would happen to us that's never happened before."

Mr. Dudley, indulging his youngest child asks her:

> "Then how would you like to go live in a castle?"

After the father leaves, Anne tells Patience their father is going to give up his law practice and help the Earl of Lincoln with his estates. The next week the family will move to Tattershall Castle, but Anne suggests not telling Samuel as she doubts he will like the idea of a move, nor living in a castle so far away from their home.

It is the next morning that Patience persuades Samuel to take her with him as he goes fishing and the Widow Law feeds them venison pasties. All of the background information has been supplied. We know the times are troubled; that Puritans were displeased with the social mores and the king's support of them. We know that witch scares are commonplace and each of these strands of idea suggest troublesome ferment. The Widow Law's goat ringing its bell serves a double meaning: to further explore the difference of opinion in Samuel and Patience, and to indicate that not all adults believed in the king's edicts, even when it was against witches. While Samuel and Patience are eating venison pasties in the Widow Law's cottage, Samuel takes the subject back to Mr. Mathews' betwitched stock with,

> "Well, I hope it will be Mr. Mathews who finds her because think how you'd feel if all of your sheep had been bewitched to death."

The widow responds with:

> "Now Samuel Dudley, there's no proof that she can bewitch one sheep to death, not even my poor old Nana who's about to drop dead with no help at all. Mr. Mathews' sheep could perfectly well have died of cholera."

And Patience adds:

> "In any case, think how she'd love one of these, she must be so hungry." And licking her thumb so pastry crumbs would stick to it, she started picking up the few scattered over her dress."

Samuel wants to go fishing as "early morning is the best time" to fish and the widow sees them off with:

"Good luck," the Widow Law called after them.

"Catch something big."

And the children reply with:

"Oh, we will.

The author shifts the scene to fishing at this point.

"In a few minutes they reached the river's banks. This morning the Nene seemed to have more to talk about than ever as it rushed and babled along. It was the clearest, cleanest river. Watercress grew at many of its quieter turns. Samuel and Patience were well acquainted with these places since their mother was forever sending one or the other of them out to gather cress for salads.

"About half a mile north of St. Andrew's Mill, the Nene entered a peacefully flowing stretch bordered on either side by tall rushes... The sun, well up now, was turning a heavy dew into millions of diamonds. Millions of very wet diamonds the Dudleys discovered as they pushed through the rushes."

After they bait the hook and Samuel has his line in the river, Patience hears a noise. Samuel suggests it is an animal in the tall rushes, so tall they hide the children "in a small, secret world." But, Patience hears a second sound just as Samuel gets a bite. As he pulls in his line, Patience finds the sight of the eel distasteful and turns her head away.

"What she did see was worse -- two eyes staring at her through the rushes out of a wild white face."

The narrative elements are set in this first chapter. We know that the main character, Samuel Dudley, 12 years old, has a sister, Patience, 10 years old, and a second sister, Anne, who is fifteen. Since the subject is history adventure, it will fit the fourth through sixth grade reader, both boy or girl audience, and could find interest at the seventh grade level as well. Therefore, the readership is established. We know the children come from an English Puritan family in the early part of the sixteenth century, that the father, Thomas is a lawyer, is about to give up his practice and work for the Earl of Lincoln, that the family will move to Tattershall Castle. We know the town is searching for Elinor Shaw who is suspected of being a witch, that Samuel accepts the fact that she is, that Patience does not, that Anne is uncertain. We also know Thomas Dudley does not accept the witch craze, that Mopsa, the housekeeper agrees with him as does a neighbor, the Widow Law.

The chapter ends with Samuel and Patience fishing and, we suspect, they stumble across Elinor Shaw hiding in the rushes along the river bank.

We do not know why Samuel disagrees with his family about witchery. Their mother has not been introduced. We do have an explanation as to why the father is giving up his law practice and moving the family to live in Tattershall castle, but that seems like a great gyration and we wonder what is really behind it, especially since the Earl and Minister Dod have called at the Dudley home and discussed the unrest in Northampton. The chapter opens on a note of tension and ends on an element of suspense.

We do not know that Dorothy Aldis visited Northampton when she researched the book, that she walked along Market Square of the town, along the River Nene, saw St. Andrews Mill, the town pond with the six "conceited" swans, saw St. Peter's towers "looming" against the sky. But, she did.

We don't know, after reading this first chapter, that she also would have to visit Salem, Massachusetts, for where the story begins in Northampton, England, it will end in Salem. We do not know that she visited the Boston Athenaeum to see the portrait of Simon Bradstreet -- who later will marry Anne in the book -- and to see his grave in Salem. We don't know that it was reading Anne Dudley Bradstreet's poetry that suggested the idea of doing a book on the Dudley family. As Anne Bradstreet, she became the mother of eight children and wrote poems to all her children — "I had eight birds hatcht in one nest — as well as many long poems. She was the first American poet and Dorothy Aldis, who is best known for her poetry, found that of more than passing interest. She also found the last house Anne Bradstreet lived in, still standing, in North Andover.

There was so much to research, so many books to be read, if she was to get the feel for life during that period, what they ate, how they lived, what it was like to cross the Atlantic on a sailing ship, what Salem would look like when they arrived.

The Aldis library was extensive, over 14,000 volumes. Book shelves lined the living room walls, all the walls of the wide hallway on the second floor and at least one wall of every bedroom - sometimes more. It was a family library and since the Aldis family had immigrated to America in 1639, much of the collection dealt with New England.

When Dorothy Aldis' oldest grandchild was five he once lost himself in exploring the Aldis house, going up the back stairs to the second floor and roaming the bedrooms, eventually coming down the front staircase. As he walked into the living room, he burst out with, "Grammie, this house is like a liberry!" She agreed, thought it was a perceptive observation, and, was pleased that her grandson saw it that way.

A great deal of her research came from the Aldis library, but not all of it. There were books to check out from other library collections, and books to buy because she had to use them for long periods. When the research period was completed, she often donated books she didn't wish to keep to other collections, and, not infrequently to the University of Chicago's Harper Library.

Her daughter, Mary Cornelia, later a student at the University of Chicago, wrote her Master's thesis on pacifism in the United States. During her research, she took out some books that Dorothy Aldis had also used in her research, in exploring the origins of pacifism, each with a gift acknowledgement pasted in the inside of the front cover, ponderously proclaiming, "Harper Library gratefully acknowledges the gift of Dorothy and Graham Aldis in making this book available to the library." Mary Cornelia once impishly complained about having to pay library fines on books her parents had donated to Harper Library. Her father agreed it was unfair but questioned whether he, even as a trustee, could "buck library bureaucracy by asking that Aldis family be exempt from paying library fines on books they had donated." The matter ended there.

In one of the books Mary Cornelia used, she found a pencil margin notation in her mother's handwriting, "Puritans," with a light line down the page to mark the area with which she was concerned. A few pages later, another margin notation was "More Puritans." A few pages later, another: "And still they come!"

So, it was from all of this that *Ride the Wild Wind*s came, much of the research coming out of family diaries and family histories that had been in Aldis book shelves for generations, including a copy of the collected works of Anne Bradstreet's poetry. Book ideas are often sitting righr under our noses, waiting to be recognized.

* * *   * * *   * * *   * * *

In chapter two, the first paragraph is both transitional and explains Patience's fright.

"Patience tried to call out to her brother but found she had no voice. Worse still, her feet refused to move. Momentarily frozen by fear, there seemed no way for her to turn Samuel from the business of removing his eel from the hook. Then with a rush of courage, she grabbed Samuel's rod and shook it, sending the eel into fresh convulsions of coilings and uncoilings. Looking up from his task, Samuel saw the terror in his sister's face. His gaze followed hers."

The motif of chapter one is picked up here and expanded — Patience's openness; Samuel's caution.

> ". . .Almost in spite of herself she stepped forward and spoke.
> "Good morning!"

> "Oh miss, good morning to you." The deep voice was warm with surprised relief. "And God bless you and yes I am Elinor Shaw but you mustn't believe the terrible wickedness they say I do."

> "How long have you been hiding in these rushes?" Samuel's stern question brought back the hunted look to the red-rimmed old eyes.

> "Three days. Three nights."

> "Could you hear the searching bell in town?"

> "Indeed, young master, off and on."

> "How near did they come to you?"

Elinor Shaw shuddered. "Quite near enough." Next there is some description of Elinor Shaw:

> "She started toward them through the bushes, a ragged shawl clutched around her shoulders, her brown calico dress torn and filthy, her feet all but bare, so shredded were her sad old shoes."

Patience begins to persuade Samuel they must take her to the Widow Law's where she can be fed and where she can hide out when Elinor Shaw interrupts their plotting with:

> "Dear young master, dear young miss, I won't have you getting into trouble over me. Tell me the way to go and I'll get there."

Here is the opportunity for Samuel to give somewhat. He begins to enter into the plan.

> "You couldn't" burst out Samuel. "You'd be sure to stumble into the wrong house and get caught." And be hanged, he almost added before swallowing the words."

At that point, something to provide a keener edge to the tension is added when John and Wolf Adams appear along the river's edge on a fishing trip of their own. These boys are the sons of the Mr. Adams who is one of the band the children see in the street while the searching bell is rung in the streets in the first chapter. It is their younger brother, William, who was supposed to be betwitched by Elinor Shaw. Patience comments:

> "And they're every bit as excited about witches as their father. Even poor little William who's so sick," added Patience."

Samuel tells Patience and Elinor Shaw to hide in the rushes and he goes off to distract the Adams boys from coming any closer. There is an interesting example of device used in covering this action: a summarizing of action in exposition:

> "Elinor Shaw needed no persuading; before Samuel had disappeared through the rushes, she was running as quickly and furtively as an animal toward the spot he'd suggested. Patience followed. Curling up beside the old woman, she heard her brother speak with a cheerful heartiness she could only hope sounded natural. He told the boys he'd had no luck, not even one bite, he was about to move on. Where to? they wanted to know. Oh, just around a couple of bends, said Samuel. Then they'd come with him, said John."

As the boys discuss all this, a new paragraph shifts the action back to Patience and Elinor Shaw, with a local flavor touch that denoted the passage of time.

> "As the boys' voices grew fainter, St. Andrew's Mill began to turn upstream. To Patience, laying concealed, this familiar sound was somehow comforting."

While Samuel is leading the Adams boys out of the area, Elinor Shaw uses his knife to cut some rushes. The idea is that she will carry them on her back as they walk to the Widow Law's cottage, as though she was out cutting them for the thatching of a roof. Samuel returns on the premise that he left his knife. It is also the time for him to decide how he will line up in handling this development.

> "I told the boys I had to come back for my knife. I think it's safe for us to go now."

> "You mean for the *three* of us?"

> "Yes."

> Patience felt like throwing her arms around her brother but Samuel didn't look as though he wanted to be thanked."

They proceed to the Widow Law's where Elinor is fed "Half a cold partridge and some newly baked bread." The Widow Law cautions: "But people as hungry as you are should eat slowly," and while Elinor is eating, the widow explains to Samuel how he should remove bricks from one end of the fireplace. When the opening is large enough, he looks in and discovers there is a "hiding hole!" It is lined with straw and,

> "No one knows about it except you two--and a very special visitor who stayed with me once."

The Widow adds about Elinor Shaw:

> ". . .she'll be comfortable. She'll be safe too, that I can promise you. But I can't keep her long."

So, the solution of one problem is a step toward another. The threat of the king's edict about protecting witches is mentioned by the Widow Law. And, Patience chooses to take the opportunity to tell Samuel that the family is moving to Tattershall Castle where their father will manage the Earl of Lincoln's estates. They could take Elinor Shaw with them, she proposes, if the Widow Law can keep her for a week.

In handling this revelation, from all points of view, the author brings in further fact about the period, through the eyes of the adult, Widow Law.

> "What tidings!" exclaimed the Widow Law. Observing how stricken Samuel looked, she walked over and put both plump hands on his sagging shoulders. "Look at me, Samuel. No more are English people allowed to live as they please or worship as they please. Our own good Minister Dod was kept stretched out in the stocks for two whole days when he refused to light candles in his church and wear a scarlet robe. Now he lights candles, *now* he wears that robe. Because he's afraid to endure the stocks again? No, not that. But rather because he knows his next punishment might be death and death would keep him from serving his people. You must see how wicked and wrong it is not to be free!"

At this point, Elinor Shaw cries out, *"Merciful heavens!"* and the emphasis shifts as the Widow Law runs over to assure her

> "Please don't be alarmed, that's only the bell my old Nana wears around her neck."

The children leave, get back home with no more than a scolding from Mopsa, who, we learn had been their mother's nurse when she was a child, and we are introduced to Mrs. Dudley, busy at preparing inventory of the house as it has been rented after they leave for the castle. She enlists the children in this project.

The next three days, the children are kept busy getting ready for the move and have no chance to discuss Elinor Shaw. On the pretext that he is going to see the Adams boys, Samuel escapes the household. Of course, he goes to the Widow Law's. When he returns, Patience sees him coming up the street and rushes out to learn what has happened. Samuel reports

> "You'll be pleased with the news. The Widow met our father in Market Square and reported everything--don't interrupt! What's more, she persuaded him to tell mother we should bring two servants with us to Tattershall instead of only Mopsa--don't interrupt! Well, so father promised to say to mother, and perhaps he's already done so, that most fortunately an excellent old servant of the Widow Law's would like to come along with us."

Patience tries to get Samuel to admit that he should be pleased about all this. She begins to question if it is fair to have Elinor Shaw as a servant when the ladies of the house won't know that she is Elinor Shaw.

> "I never thought about how mother and Anne and Mopsa wouldn't know our new servant is supposed to be a witch. I don't know that I like that part of it, Samuel."
>
> "Why, when you yourself are so certain she isn't a witch?"
>
> "I'd feel better if they were certain, too. The way you're beginning to be. Aren't you, Samuel?"
>
> "No."
>
> "But how can you not be, after having been with her and seen she's only a poor old woman?"
>
> "Perhaps I know something you don't know." Samuel said darkly."

It is at this point we learn why Samuel is still unpersuaded about Elinor Shaw. The reader learns about it as Samuel thinks back on the scene, but Samuel doesn't explain it to Patience or anyone else, carrying it as his unsolved problem to the very end of the book. He is disturbed by what he knows and attempts to resolve it with his father on a number of occasions, but always unsuccessfully. However, he never uses the knowledge in any unfair way against Elinor Shaw.

The chapter ends as they say goodbye to friends and before sun-up on August 23, 1628 when the Dudleys are all settled in their coach with their two grey horses, Rookbie and Okeley in the harness and the carter,

> ". . .a small fat man well pleased with his own importance, hustled and

bustled about. Finally satisfied that all was in order, he climbed into the driver's seat and raised his whip."

The Carter stops at a house at Mr. Dudley's direction and Elinor Shaw comes out, ready to join them. Mr. Dudley introduces her as Sara Goney. Mrs. Dudley comments:

"Oh!" said Mrs. Dudley, "that must be she coming out of the door. How willing and pleasant she looks!"

The moment that Patience and Samuel dreaded passed calmly enough. Their new servant looking rested, and dressed in neat and suitable clothes, greeted the Dudley family respectfully. Moving toward the space which Mopsa and Anne squeezed out between them, she gave no sign of ever having seen Samuel or Patience before."

These first two chapters of *Ride the Wild Winds* are interesting to analyze for their effect. Chapter one introduces the principal characters and established setting. Quickly tension is interjected and the chapter ends with a heightening of that tension.

Chapter two sustains the tension and ends on a note of temporary resolution, a pause to take stock and establish where we have been and yet, open the door for further plot development. We are waiting to discover what Tattershall Castle has in store for the Dudleys.

In both of these chapters themes are presented that are reinforced and supported, sometimes expanded more fully where they serve a stronger purpose. Meantime, we get a clearer picture of the day amd what life was like in that early sixteenth century, but pace is quick, the setting drawn with quick word strokes -- "all he saw were his own troubles;" "larks were dipping and singing;" "six swans were conceitedly swimming;" "so thoroughly locked and shuttered it looked asleep;" "a round, bustling little body whose rose face was forever creasing into a network of smiling wrinkles:" "the rush strewn floor;" "not even my poor old Nana who's about to drop dead with no help at all;" "the Nene seemed to have more to talk about than ever as it rushed and babbled along;" "turning the heavy dew into millions of diamonds. Millions of very wet diamonds the Dudleys discovered as they pushed through the rushes;" "two eyes staring at her through the rushes out of a wild white face;" "sending the eel into fresh convulsions of coiling and uncoiling;" "a cheerful hardiness she could only hope sounded natural;" "this familiar sound was somehow comforting."

Chapter three works as a transition from Norhampton to Tattershall Castle. Samuel and Patience look at the scenes of home as the coach carries them from all that has been familiar. It is handled quickly and the focus shifts to the effect of the swaying coach on the passengers.

Incident fortifies the period, but also serves the purpose to establish relationships. Mopsa resents the intrusion of Sara Goney, but when Sara takes "a dried bouquet from her apron pocket" and suggests Patience "Smell this," we know Sara is better prepared than anyone else in the swaying coach. Patience smells the bouquet and finds it to be "a strong wild aromatic odor" and "her sick feeling" vanishes. It is tansy, an herb that was used for its tonic value in medicines and this is made clear between the conversation that the tansy makes possible, between Sara and Mopsa. Through it, the stiffness betweem them is broken. But, Samuel, still suspicious about Sara, and as much in need of the tansy as any of the group, refuses it. The tansy is introduced to emphasize the period, is the means of drawing Sara and Mopsa together, and also serves to show Patience's openess to Sara, while Samuel remains unpersuaded. Mrs. Dudley is not coach sick, but Mr. Dudley and Anne sniff "gratefully."

In discussing the hamlets the coach passes through, the term "bede house" is used:

> "Grimden was even smaller with only three cottages, a bede house and a church."

It was a term in common usage in sixteenth century England and not unknown in New England, even today. More commonly, the term would be manse. Dorothy Aldis uses it in connection with the mention of church and leaves it at that, a word to look up, if it bothers you, perhaps even hopeful it will and so expand the vocabulary of the reader. Touches of this sort should be used sparingly and only when they fit well and add to the color of the writing.

The perils of traveling in seventeen century England are handled next after the tansy incident:

> "However, in spite of his suspicions and his stomach, Samuel enjoyed the first few hours of driving. The day was fine, the horses moved along so briskly. Once their carter pulled over to the side of the road to give way to an oncoming coach rattling toward Northampton. Out through its windows came a flurry of waving handkerchiefs. Another time, four dashing horseback riders overtook them with backward halloos and an enveloping cloud of warm dust."

They pass several villages
> "Then no more hamlets."

A bridge paragraph knits the handling together, moving from the general to the particular.

"The day which at the beginning of their journey had been a musty gray, then pink with dawn, then yellow, was now a bright, windy blue. .

They approach a bridge and Samuel asks

"What river is this?"

The carter explains

"The Nene."

Samuel is surprised at how broad it has grown and that it is the same river Nene in which he had fished among the rushes such a short time ago, then asks:

". . .Why are we stopping, is something wrong?"

The carter replies:

"Twice before this bridge has gone down when the water was high. So all out, all out unless you prefer to drown." And clambering from his seat the little man loaded his passengers' backs with boxes, hung buckets and baskets from their hands, waved them imperiously ahead. . . . . .

Nothing disasterous happens, but Samuel speculates about the prospects:

"On the way across, Samuel stepped into one of the scallops fashioned for the safety of foot passengers when a drove of cattle was being driven over the bridge. Only two feet below the water roared and swirled. Samuel wished he couldn't hear the sounds of a disintegrating bridge so clearly nor see the sight of Rookbie and Okeley struggling in the water as the weight of their harness and coach slowly, slowly pulled them out of sight. . . .

"A crack of the carter's whip brought the coach, back to real life. He ran after the coach, reaching the opposite side of the Nene only a few seconds later than Rookbie and Okeley who stood heaving and panting, their sides white-flecked with foam."

The next problem is to allow the feeling of time passing, and a typical reaction for a boy of twelve years, cooped up in a traveling coach is also added.

"By the time they were all on their way again it was noon. Only noon. Samuel felt as though he'd been driving forever.

"However, he'd become used to the swaying and jolting of the coach. Instead of making him feel sick, he felt sleepy. He dozed, woke up, dozed again, and so it went until hours later they pulled up in front of the White Lion Inn in Higham Ferrers where dinner was served immediately: boiled crane, a green and gold salad of nasturtium leaves and flowers, cherry tarts, sugar sops and fruit-shaped marchpane candies. Breakfast in the morning was another candle-lit meal--a hurried one, as their carter was anxious to be off."

The use of marchpane is interesting. An adult, perhaps a child who has eaten marzipan which German pastry shops in this country offer for sale during the Christmas holidays, might think it was a printer's error. However, march-pane was a popular sweet in England during the seventeenth century, as well as in other European countries. It is made from almonds, sugar, and whites of eggs, molded into the shape of vegetables and fruits, dyed with vegetable dyes, is ladened with calories and is, delightful to the taste.

The first day of travel is over. The second day would take them out of the hilly country and into flatter land, easier on the horses and travelers. The carter tells Samuel,

". . . If the road should be muddy, I have ropes for pulling us out of trouble and an ax for chopping up any large trees fallen across our path."

Samuel asks about the woods and the carter tells him they will pass through "very deep woods." They have to stop for herds of sheep, twice and once for "the looming forms of oxen." The market square--"Even at this dim hour of the morning there was bustle and stir in Higham Ferrers."--gets mention, with carts being unloaded and there is the "frenzy of miserable quacks" that "made it certain a good duck dinner was about to be eaten."

Then, the new day starts with,

"After that brief spell of feeling part of the human family again, the Dudleys and their two servants had the road completely to themselves. No riders appeared. No cart, no coach, not even a herd of sheep or oxen.

They are in open country. By noon they reach the "very deep woods" but the most they see are "furiously busy squirrels" and Patience is "relieved" when they emerge "into broad daylight again."

By dusk, they reach the Rose and Crown in Thrapston and Samuel is, of course, fascinated with "a huge cage placed in the middle of the square" and begins to tell Patience all about it.

> ". . . inside it would be instruments of torture for punishing people who went against the king's laws."

Patience asks,

> "Like those stocks Minister Dod was stretched out in?"

And Samuel responds with,

> "More cruel than stocks. Thrumbscrews. Racks. The Scavenger's Daughter: that's the king's favorite--manacles press a person's head down to his toes and keep it there for days. . ."

Mr. Dudley intervenes with,

> "Samuel!" His father spoke so meaningfully that Samuel looked to see whether Sara Goney was listening, but no--she and Mopsa were companionably engaged in gathering up their belongings."

Here is an example of using Samuel's natural interest, as a boy, in the instruments of torture as a means to bring in the father, and to touch on the rescue of Sara Goney, and, at the same time, to show that she and Mopsa have begun to establish a relationship.

The night spent in the Rose and Crown is covered in three lines with:

> "Another fine dinner was produced by the Rose and Crown. Another night in strange but comfortable beds. A brief breakfast before-dawn, and once more the sights and sounds of a waking town."

The detail of the first night spent in the White Lion Inn in Higham Ferrers is, in effect, depended on to cover the second night of the trip. The problem is to cover the five days it would take to travel by coach from Northampton to Tattershall castle and Dorothy Aldis used it to fortify the threads of her narrative, provide period flavor, cover the geography, create some apprehension in the problems of travel of the day, and introduce us to the castle. The terrain becomes very flat so that you can see for miles. "A. . . hamlet was visible for a long, long while before they reached it." They pass through Titmarsh and, later, Winwick,

> ". . . where they paused long enough to water their horses. Here two riders, halting for the same purpose, told of traveling friends who'd only recently been cruelly beaten by robbers: conealed in the underbrush, they'd sprung upon their prey armed with knives and hatchets. A silence followed this tale. Thomas Dudley broke it by asking the riders if they themselves had had any midadventures. The younger of the two said no. But the howl of panthers gave us a mighty scare last night."

All of this fills the needs of the writer, to fill a time period that must be covered, provide authentic background, yet keep the reader interested. The mention of panthers furthers the solution.

To modern day readers, it is likely the use of the name panther would connote leopard, particularly the black leopard of Southern Asia, and in the United States, the puma. However, during the seventeenth century, panther referred to any large feline carnivore. Again, it is historically accurate and if any reader cares to dispute the point, it means turning to an encyclopedia or or reference work to clarify the issue. Not an unworthy suggestion for any young mind that is inquisitive.

Thomas Dudley explains the road they are traveling along was built by the Romans.

> "Samuel found this bit of information as tiresome as the road which, like a ribbon on a table, lay flat with no sign of trees or underbrush on either side--no possible place for robbers to lie in wait."

After lunch the next day, Samuel falls into "a post-lunch drowsiness" when Patience wakes him up with,

> "There it is. There's Tattershall!"

They see the castle from a distance,

> ". . .A great tower culminated in four turrets each, at this distance, distinct and visible. Two wings stretched out on either side of the tower reaching halfway up. Close around the castle clustered a flock of small buildings like children hanging onto their mother's skirts."

Anne says,

> "It's the finest castle in all England" as everyone takes turns craning out of the coach windows. Eventually they pass through the deer park, "a small, beautifully groomed forest," and Mr. Dudley points out where the tiltyard used to be, explaining, with disapproval, the sport in which mounted knights charged each other using lances to unseat an opponent. They pass through the gardens where vegetables and fruits were grown as well as "beds of bright flowers."

> "Patience exclaimed over marble statues in a rose garden, Anne over a fountain guarded by cupids."

Thomas Dudley tells them Ralph Cromwell built the church:

> ". . . Squared towered like their own St. Peter's at home, this church

had a row of small brick houses angling off from it.

The servant's quarters, Thomas Dudley told his family."

They pass the castle stables just as the sky has turned cloudy.

> "Rain on the way," shouted down the carter."But that's all right, it may rain any time it wants to now."And having given his permission to the heavens, he cracked his whip to get a last spurt of speed out of Rookbie and Okeley."

Chapter three moves the setting from Northampton to Tattershall castle. We have a better grasp of what it was to live in the early part of the seventeenth century, something of the food that was eaten, the time it took to travel, some of the problems and threats in travel and all the characters are more solidly etched. We still wonder why the family is making the move, what Tattershall and the Earl of Lincoln have in store for us. For a student who has taken his fifth or sixth grade history seriously, the suspicion might occur that the Earl may be involved in organizing groups of Puritans that will eventually secure land grants from the Crown and leave for the New World, but we have no solid evidence of that in the way the narration is handled up to this point.

It is exactly what will happen at Tattershall, and Samuel is invited to sit in on the meeting where it all unfolds the first day he spends in the castle. The meeting is held in the state room and he recognizes faces that he had seen the night before in the Great Dining Hall where they all take their meals. Sara Goney

> ". . . waxed enthusiastically over the Master's table in the dining hall . . ."With branched candlesticks parading down its whole long length, and what silver, what china, and how glad I was to see that even in so splendid a place as Tattershall they have the good sense to spread wormwood on the floor!"

Samuel has an hour to himself and he explores the castle. He first finds out where the state room is then winds his way up a circular stairway, pausing to look in rooms on various floors he reaches, until finally he gets to the roof and "those towers." One is a library, but the others contain cannons "their big, black snouts thrust through the turret windows."

Samuel begins to wonder if that is what the meeting in the state room will be about, "making plans for their defense?"

> ". . . Wasn't it possible, perhaps likely, that a number of influential Puritans had taken refuge here in this wonderfully fortified castle to withstand a monarch who wanted to destroy them?"

This is the first concrete hint of what is to come at Tattershall castle and Samuel "buoyed by this wishful thinking. . ." concludes as he looks out over the surrounding landscape and thinks how easy it would be to see a foe for as much as twenty miles away

> "And who would give the warning the day the king's soldiers came marching over that far horizon?
> Samuel knew. Samuel!"

In the state room he learns of a new "outrageous tax" the king has levied, a tax against swearing. Mr. Winthrop points out the inequity of it with

> "There's nothing wrong with a nobleman's swearing, of course, but let a poor over-worked servant indulge and from now on he'll be fined a penny an oath!"

Mr. Winthrop also reads a letter from Captain Smith who wrote about the difficulty with Indians, but concludes with,

> "Nevertheless, in this new country a man may live contented and free. Free in person, free in religion. And most wonderfully well fed. For there are plains, valleys, rivers and brooks all running most pleasantly into a fair bay surrounded by fruitful and delightsome land."

Sir Isaac Johnson points out that Captain Smith is writing about Plymouth and not Salem, but Mr. Winthrop also had a letter from John Endecott, who had been sent as a representative from the group to make a personal assessment of Salem where they hoped to settle.

Mr. Winthrop reads John Endecott's letter and it, too, speaks to the abundance of the land, that the bay is full of lobster, that fresh cod "seems but course meat to us." He reports a rumor that "our company" has "now paid in full for the wide strip of land between the Charles and Merrimac Rivers." and asks to have it confirmed "whether this rumor is true."

Mr. Winthrop mentions the letter took four months to cross the Atlantic ocean, but everyone is very pleased with its news. Mr. Dudley, however, raises the question of how they will raise the money to buy a fleet, when they already have raised

> "so much. I believe it likely we now have enough supplies, equipment and possible provisions for a fleet. But remember, gentlemen, we still have a fleet to buy."

Mr. Winthrop also reads a letter from a carpenter who accompanied Mr. Endecott. The carpenter wrote a letter to his wife in Souhampton. The carpenter wrote,

> "The winds and seas were as mad as fury and rage could make them. There was not one moment in which the sudden splitting or instant oversetting of our ship was not expected. Our sails, wound up. Lay without use. Fury added to fury and one storm, urging a second even more outrageous, struck at our ship amongst women and children not used to such terrible hurly-burly."

Samuel, getting some idea of what is in store is full of questions.

> "Indians, what were they? This new country, where was it? What of Plymouth? What of Salem? What of this strip of land between the Charles and Merrimac Rivers? And, most important, what does all this have to do with us."

After the meeting, Samuel races from the castle, to the stables, where he was forbidden to go because the Earl had his mastiffs there and Thomas Dudley didn't think a boy of twelve should be around dogs that were well known for their meanness. In this confusion, he decides to go to the stables, non-the-less. "Surely, with such extraordinary events brewing, his father would pay little attention to one small act of disobedience."

In chapter five, Samuel talks to his mother and learns the decision to leave for the New World has not been made, that he will accompany his father the next day to a nearby town, in Boston, where the company expected to meet and decide on what shall be done.

Samuel gets to know Simon Bradstreet on the trip to Boston and it is clear Simon is more than casually interested in Anne Dudley. He asks if Samuel knows she writes very fine poetry, but Samuel admits he wasn't aware.

At the meeting, some opposition develops to leaving England, but when the Earl of Lincoln rises to his feet and says,

> "Your attention, gentlemen. We have heard enough. As many of you as believe the government of our company should be transferred to New England, hold up your hands."

After the count is made, the Earl announces,

> "Thirty-nine to two. It appears by general consent that our government shall now be settled in New England, where we shall be free."

Samuel rides back to Tattershall with Simon Bradstreet and when he asks if Samuel's sisters know they are leaving England, Samuel tells him his mother asked him not to tell them until it was certain. Simon suggests "Let me tell Anne."

Chapters six through nine deal with the preparation for the trip and the crossing of the Atlantic. Disease breaks out, violent storms occur, food is short, but seventy seven days later, their ship, the Arbella reaches mainland and Salem. The company is The Massachusetts Bay Colony and they do get their charter, financing, and the fleet - the Talbot, the Ambrose, the Jewel, the Eagle, the Whale become known as The Winthrop Fleet. The Eagle is renamed the Arbella and is the ship on which the Dudleys sail. Anne marries Simon Bradstreet before they sail and Samuel is constantly trying to find some solution for that doubt he holds about Sara Goney.

Getting to Salem is more than bleak. There was only one house, John Endecott's, and a half dozen thatched roofed cottages. There were some "English wigwams" constructed, dug-outs, with three sides being earth walls and a front wall of timber holding up a roof.

Everything is in short supply. Breakfast was coarse bread and acorns. There are no fresh vegetables and many of the people have died from scurvy. The people are too busy clearing land and building shelters to grow anything and they depend on wild fruit and fish from the bay to eat. Joining the new settlers a few days later, the Talnot, Jewel, and Ambrose arrive, all on the same day.

In Chapter eleven, John Endecott and his family move out of their house and it becomes Hospital House. Mopsa and Sara Goney live there, as nurses to the sick. Samuel and all other boys are pressed into the work of establishing the colony. The Dudleys share an "English Wigwam" with another family, the Gridleys. Patience gets sick. The new immigrants aren't really wanted in Salem as it simply means what food there is has to be spread among them. Mr. Winthrop, who has been appointed governor, takes a party up the Charles River and locates land that is healthier than the low land of Salem. And, since food is more plentiful, a number of families plan to leave for Charlestown within a week. Before Samuel left Tattershall castle, he made friends with the Earl's mastiffs. They are on the Trial, a smaller ship on which animals traveled. When Samuel learns from his father about the move to Charlestown, he also learns that Patience is too sick to travel with them and that she will have to remain in Hospital House until she is better. His father also tells him the *Trial* is in port and that the mastiffs are aboard her, a concession his father knows will please Samuel as a distraction and a remembrance of home.

In Chapter ten, Samuel's doubt about Sara Goney comes to a head. He does not want to leave Patience behind, in her care, and he finally forces the issue with his father. He tells him about his experience when William Adam, in his delirium cries out, "I won't tell my mother I talked to you, only don't bewitch me, Elinor Shaw!" He believes Elinor Shaw had good reason in "planning to do away with everyone who knows she was hunted as a witch back in Northampton, Patience. You. Me."

> "It was out. It was out.
> Samuel stood trembling, but relieved."

His father misjudges the significance of a boy's mind and the terror it can create, sometimes with less foundation. He is sympathetic, but neither able to believe "his eyes nor his ears" he puts a hand on Thomas' forehead and finding it "beaded with sweat but cool," counsels,

> "Work will make you feel better, Samuel. The best specific for worry is to keep busy with one's hands. . ." Automatically Samuel said those two words: Yes Father. But he was frantic. Here he'd forced himself to speak out. And been ignored. Brushed off like a fly. How monstrously unfair. For had he not been treated as one of the men back at Tattershall? Had he not worked like a man here at Salem? And now: *go away little boy, I'll talk to you later.*"

Samuel turns to the task at hand, as his father urged him and begins to work, peeling bark from pine logs, for covering roofs. In his frenzy, he cuts himself, badly. His friend, Henry with whom he is working, yells for Sara Goney, for help. And, with Samuel protesting, Sarah comes to help.

Sara applies a tourniquet to stop the bleeding then sends Henry for bandages and "plaintain leaves. Mopsa will give them to you. Don't tell her what's happened--she has enough to worry about with a new patient just gone out of his head."

When the blood stops running, Samuel begins to feel better. He asks about Patience and Sara says she is so much better she thinks she can go to Charlestown with the family. But, she says, "I'm not, because I prefer to stay here in Salem where so many are in need of nursing. But I truly cannot imagine why you think Patience--"

Samuel listens, still unpersuaded and decides he must level with Sara Goney.

> "A deep and terrible concern froze the small staring-back face. For a moment Samuel was reminded how Elinor Shaw had looked in those tall rushes by the River Nene.
>
> "Samuel!"

Sara Goney explains that it would surely mean death to her to be the cause of three deaths.

". . .A small matter since I have few years left. But a long life stretches ahead of you and somehow you must purge this poison from your veins".

"What poison?"

"Suspicion, darkest of· all poisons tormenting the human soul. Unless you rid yourself of it, it will spread, stunt your growth, render you useless."

Sara Goney reached Samuel.

"Right then and there something took place in Samuel's heart. As he looked into those dark imploring eyes, scales fell from his own. Instead of an evil witch he saw a brave old woman.

"He spoke his understanding. Forgive me, Sara Goney! He knew the horror of Elinor Shaw was gone for good."

Samuel finally breaks through, to reality, and the book ends on this note of discovery.

This skeletal outline of *Ride the Wild Waves* lays bear many of the writing elements out of which a successful book is developed. Tone is closely involved in writing style and the author's use of it is quickly established and plays an important part of all the writing. The research out of which the book evolved is carefully integrated and the author uses official documents to maintain pace and move the narrative line along so professionally the reader loses recall of the fact that he is reading from a colonist's letter or a charter paper. In good writing, such seams must never show.

Pace is always strong and when the author faced the need to transport The Massachusetts Bay Colony across the Atlantic, a long, tedious voyage of some months, she keeps her characters sharp and engaged with life at sea, relating incidents and developing sub-plots that provides color, develops character further, while maintaining interest. Consequently, suspense is high as we follow the family during their perilous trip from England to the New World.

The book is written from Samuel's point of view against a back-drop of authentic history, with the same keen sense of understanding of children's thoughts that is so strong in Dorothy Aldis' poetry.

The majority of writers of adult books are agented. That is not the case with juvenile writers. There is good reason for this difference to exist.

Any writing, even when it is unsuccessful or unpublishable writing, inevitably becomes a very personal preoccupation by the time a manuscript is ready to offer. It is something like sending a child off to his first session of summer camp, or his first day at school. Emotions well up and the writer has a feeling of being bereft, as though a part of him has been severed from his life and a great void persists. Doubts suddenly develop. In reflection, the writer begins to wonder and have second thoughts. Should I have handled the ending differently; should I have created more tension; did I make my point clear in that first chapter. Such second thoughts can be endless.

Editorial Guidance

No matter how you evolve your relationship with an editor, nor no matter how solid it may be, the editor is an extension of the publisher, a part of "them." Hopefully, it you publish a second manuscript with the same publisher, you will have respect for the editor. Yet, you may have some doubts that the editorial suggestions are correct. After all, you are writing about a family setting, yet she wants you to develop a main character more. He/she wants you to cut some of the community flavor and concentrate more on the inter-actions of the family members. He/she wants fewer characters while you see a rich fabric, with all the threads showing up in the pattern.

Perhaps you have relied on Aunt Fanny who taught social studies all her work life, who spent years developing curriculum programs, who was on the book selection committee, and helped decide what books went into each classroom library collection. Aunt Fanny generously read your manuscript — and made very good suggestions, all along. Doesn't she know as much about what makes a good book as the editor! Can you go against her advice and risk a fracture in what has been a wonderful, life-long relationship?

If you, as a writer, don't confront these questions, you will have a set of your own. You may feel cut off, unable to talk intelligently to anyone, and you don't want to pester the editor too much or he/she may decide against another reading, even if you do wade in and do all the revision suggested.

Suppose you sent the manuscript off and you eventually get that letter in the mail and it says, almost too simply:

Dear Mr. Harrison,

Several of us have now read your manuscript, with pleasure. You write well and handle your material interestingly. Yet, the subject area in which you have written is so well covered, we can't see risking our limited budget money to offer a book contract for your manuscript, Young Abe Lincoln.

If you had written about another subject, we might have felt differently.

With regrets, therefore, I am returning your manuscript under separate cover by manuscript rate and wish you the best in finding another publisher who may not agree with our assessment.

Sincerely yours,

Jane Fletcher
Director, Children's Books

You read it; you ponder. After all, haven't you personally walked the very streets Lincoln walked in your research? Didn't you read all the existing literature and haven't you written your book in a far more convincing way than most everything you read?

Finally, you let some objectivity surface. What you need is some professional advice, but who can offer that?

Such anguishing goes on all the time with writers. It has never admitted to ready solution; with an Agent, the odds can be improved.

The Agent As the Author's Confidant

Agents represent authors. As such, they are the writer's confidant. Chances are an agented author would never have risked so much investment of time in writing a manuscript about Abe Lincoln at all, but he surely wouldn't have considered it without talking it out with his agent.

Agented authors do work closely with their editors, but in almost all instances, they conduct such contacts on a purely editorial level, and their agent has long since talked over the book idea with the author. In many instances, the agent has made the first approach to the editor. If the editor is receptive, the agent gets the author into direct contact with the editor, but remains active in the proceedings, at least until the contract is signed. The agent may read drafts of the manuscript as it is under preparation, offering guidance or direction, watching for possible rights sales that have been retained for handling by the agency.

It is the author's responsibility to write. It is the agent's work to represent that writing in the best possible way and to secure for the author the maximum benefit, in placement, sales, and income.

A Limited Number of Agents Represent Juvenile Writing

If you study directories where agents are listed, you will discover many do not represent juvenile books. Children's books are a world unto themselves and many agencies have not developed the knowledge necessary to handle such work. For any number of reasons, they prefer to work in the adult book field. Consequently, the number of agents available to authors who work in the juvenile field is limited. Among those that do work with juveniles, agency time may not be available to take on an emerging author. Even if you have a list of juvenile acceptances that runs into several pages in length, the total income can be less than attractive to a busy agent who has to, inevitably, consider 10% of a thousand dollars is, after all, $100. He well knows how many hours of his time will go into a new writer, all risk investment, that may or may not pay out, long term.

In addition to these limitations, juvenile editors have tended to encourage the editor-author relationship, even when they are inordinately slow in response or reaction. They can, on the one hand, put together form rejection letters, pre-printed form letters or those which a secretary — or the typing pool — will dash off for signature. On the other hand, they not infrequently will talk about author relationship, in public, explaining it is utterly necessary in the publishing of a good juvenile book.

The truth of what works best is somewhere in between.

The Shift of Juvenile Editors to Use Agented Authors

Juvenile editors increasingly realize manuscript screening is costly. The adult side of publishing recognized that fact many years ago. Today, juvenile editors are more receptive to agented authors if for no other reason than that submissions are screened before arriving at the editor's office. They also realize that the difficult area of negotiating contract terms can be handled outside the author contact idea, often with better and more realistic understanding. They are willing to pay a price for that, alone, ready to settle for U.S. and Canadian publishing rights, foregoing the possible lucrative movie rights areas, and acknowledging that the terms written for one contract do not necessarily preclude changes in a subsequent contract that may be negotiated.

This is not to say that any editor is out to take advantage of an author. It does mean they are interested in increasing the profits the juvenile department generates and if they can do that at more profitable terms, they will.

Advances

Publishers become known for advances they offer for any type of book. Among the large, well established houses, advances are set in terms of what the history of the department has established. If the average advance is $1,500 or $2,000, it simply means the average book that publisher published managed to return sufficient income to justify such an advance.

Should the editor offer a larger advance than the average usually written in contracts, it will be done for reasons that can justify the exception -- to attract an established author or because the manuscript in question is so obviously superior.

Large advances reported in the press inevitably are concerned with adult books. An aggressive rights department will have copies made of a manuscript under consideration and offer or discuss a sale, to paperback publishers and to the movie industry, sometimes while an editorial department is making a decision on whether to offer a contract for the manuscript. There is little to risk if the editorial department considers the work promising, especially if the book is backed with a half million dollar subsidiary rights sales. The publisher knows he has his sales program well developed, in advance, if he can present the book at sales conference with that kind of promise to the salesmen as they go out to sell their wares. It does not function in the same way in the juvenile area.

Right Sales

In the juvenile field, few books are pre-sold either as paperbacks or to the movie industry. That activity comes after the book has been published and becomes a success. True, editors are very interested in securing awards and accolades for the books they publish, but, for the most part, it is the rights department that does the real work, although the editor will support it in maintaining contacts with juvenile book club personnel and other contacts that are important to special awards and rights sales of juveniles.

Agents who represent rights areas in juveniles tend to work such sales as far as possible. With modern copying facilities, it is cheaper to work with copies of a manuscript, in selling foreign editions and movie sales, once a publisher's contract is secured than to wait for publisher galleys. Working with copies of a manuscript shortens the time for rights sales to be completed, getting income in quicker, and has the added effect of clustering activity where foreign editions come out sooner and tend to create more attention and excitement for a book.

Sales of editions abroad, compared to the adult book field, are cautious in advances and terms, but, depending on the book, the aggregate influence of this activity can be remunerative and it certainly builds the name and reputation of the author if he is published widely in other countries.

Agents, depending on 10% of what a piece of writing brings in, are anxious to work such rights areas vigorously and as soon as possible. Publishers who work such areas themselves, on unagented books, usually work them from galleys or after the finished book is available. Moreover, if they do not contract with an overseas agent to represent the book, it is a slow and cumbersome process. Agents, almost universally, work their overseas sales through resident agents in the country in which they expect sales to result. The agent to agent contact is a more responsive structure and works quickly and efficiently.

Book Income

The crucial test for any book is to sell it in sufficient quantity to pay back its advance and make income beyond that amount. Some books do and many do not.

Before a book is published, for the author to speculate on what a book might earn is a dubious use of time. An agent or editor will have some general idea of what a book can produce in income, and some authors get pretty accurate about this second-guessing, but no one can supply real figures until the book appears and you get some market feed-back. It is an improvident author who spends such income before a royalty check is in hand. Once you develop some pattern of how your books sell, you can begin to judge royalty income, but it can fluctuate up and down from royalty period to royalty period.

Paperback sale terms vary widely, but if a book does well in such a market, it can have a continuing influence on future income. However, 4% or 6% of a paperback list price means 4¢ or 6¢ on the sales dollar, it must be remembered, and paperback list prices are aimed at the widest possible sale, and therefore, at the lowest possible list price. For the most part, such income is split evenly between author and publisher. Juvenile editors resist changing this formula wherever and whenever possible.

Movie sales for juveniles do not bring the prices for which adult's books are sold. A producer will often take an option on a particular property for a nominal amount - a thousand or two dollars, and, depending on how the option is drawn-up, can successfully tie up the rights for a year or more. Film companies often buy film rights for something under five figures, despite the fact that profits more than justify larger outlays. However, the appearance of a movie always creates interest in book sales and it has always been considered more positive in that area than in direct income.

A publisher that is well organized for sales to the institutional markets will notify pre-binders about the publishing list in sufficient time to allow the pre-binder to purchase unbound sheets. Such orders are shipped, ordinarily, before the edition is bound, and while unbound sheets are on hand at the bindery. If the book meets the elementary library/school need, several thousand sets of sheets can be sold in this area. If the book is the author's first book, or, perhaps, even the second or third book, with none of the others making much of an impression on reviewers, it may be ignored completely or represented in token orders.

Pre-binders came into existence at a time when publisher's binding standards did not meet library binding specifications. Pre-binders moved into this market providing more durable bindings of publisher's books by binding publisher's stock in a good grade of cloth, better sewing and binders board. They sell their books under their own imprint and deal wholly with libraries and school markets, issuing their own catalogs, maintaining their own promotion and sales programs.

Sheet sales usually are reported in publishers' royalty records as an exception to ordinary sales and the rate of payment is often based on net income or sales that fall below maximum discount usually allowed. (See *A Typical Book Contract* in *The Mechanics of Writing and How to Get Published.*)

State and municipal approved lists, as well as reading circles, are an additional sales area that capable publishers solicit for book purchases. It is a complicated area of contact that usually is handled under the publishers school and library sales department or in the promotion department.

The capability of the publisher is closely studied by the agent and he will channel manuscripts to publishers that can best serve the book he is offering for contract. Changes in personnel or where key specialists work in such sales or promotion can affect a publishers success materially. The agent will watch such shifts and be governed by them in what publishers he solicits for sales.

The Second Book

A serious writer soon realizes the best use of his time is in writing. A portion of the writer's time can be well spent in promotion work, assuming the inclination and capability of the writer to that end, but if these areas intrude too greatly, they will, of course, affect the amount of writing time left to the writer. Productive writers organize their time and fit in any activity that supports their success to the extent that it doesn't dominate or eat into writing time. There are many good reasons for this.

Launching any book well is an expensive and time consuming process. If a publisher's personnel work well to that end, it is a frustration of the writer's contribution if too much time passes before another book appears in print.

A good publisher will prepare promotion releases, announcements, and catalogs and each book published will receive its share of attention. Advertising will be placed in media aimed at calling the attention of buyers to the publisher's books. For the most part, such ads appear in library and school media — *School Library Journal, Booklist, Grade Teacher*, etc. Books are shipped to exhibits at professional conferences that publishers attend where booth space is rented and the publisher displays his wares. Exhibit copies will be sent to special displays and exhibits that are constantly organized for a variety of reasons, as well as to such organizations as the Combined Book Exhibit which makes an effort to cover most professional conferences.

Each new book published is widely sampled to libraries and schools, to evaluation and selection committees. A good promotion sample list will run from 350 to 400 sources in the library/school area alone and each will be sent a review copy. If the book has bookstore interest, as many as 150 to 200 additional review copies will be sent to newspaper, magazine, column and other promotion sources.

From all this support, it soon becomes clear that successful promotion can best be built on and advanced only if a writer continues to be productive. Once these promotion channels are exposed to a book, selection and review personnel build up a familiarity with the author's writing capability. A second book is less of an unknown quantity. It may well be weighed in terms of the earlier book — is it as good; is it a better story; is the writer improving, evolving and showing promise; all those subjective questions that selection personnel must bring to bear in evaluating the second book. If the writer has, indeed, succeeded in writing a better second book, both books may be mentioned in the written comment that is eventually prepared and distributed.

In any aspect of publishing, a good book, well received, is only helped by the appearance of a second book, if it is likely to be equally well received. One supports the other, calling attention to readers the earlier publication in the event they haven't read it, and, subliminally, creating an interest in other writing of the author.

There is something suggestive when you page through a publisher's catalog and come across the name of a writer who is working in an area of reader interest, especially if he has published a number of books and they are now known to you. As the list of titles published increases, the more this factor compounds.

From a publisher's point of view, the backlist represents capital investment that is unproductive until it is sold. A new book by an author already in the list is an opportunity to "push" the backlist. The books will begin to suggest promotion ideas to bring the books to the attention of special interest areas -- how they fit into social studies, for instance, or enrich fifth history studies. Any new book announcements inevitably refer to backlist titles by the same author and frequently will draw on reviews obtained for earlier books. When advertising and promotion budgets are established, all these factors are considered and money is allocated in such a way as to derive the most income from the money spent, from new titles as well as backlist.

Clearly, therefore, a manuscript accepted for publication ought to be a signal for the writer to get back to the desk and typewriter. That does not mean that an editor will quickly contract for a second book. Juvenile editors think in terms of list make-up. If they publish fiction at all, the list surely will be heavily weighted with non-fiction. If the list runs to twenty books - a large list can run that high - a percentage will be devoted to picture books, while the largest number will be aimed at grades three through six, as one area, and the seventh grade through the teen-age market as another. Editors tend to shy away from publishing an author in two successive lists. They argue, and rightly so, the books tend to get confused and neither gets fair exposure.

If you are a very productive writer, it is well to think of several areas in which you can work. You might choose to write books in the sports area, block out some biographies, some books in history, pacing them so that each can be published at intervals of approximately two years. Such scheduling generally works well, and it almost always means each area will be published by a different publisher. There was a time, when juvenile publishing was smaller, that editors considered such publisher "hopping" with some distaste. Editors were very possessive about the authors they published, expecting to handle all the output of an author. This attitude has tended to give way, today, but editors do continue to think of their authors in terms of subject areas in which they publish a given author. "We publish his sports stories. . ." or "We handle his biography."

When Editors Move

Nothing can be more disturbing than to be in the midst of manuscript revision work with an editor and suddenly discover the editor is leaving for a position with another publisher. Such work is very personal and it does not follow a new editor will see the work shaping up in the same light. An author may know something about the new editor, if unagented, but it is more likely an agent will know a good deal more. If the book in question is under contract, it is not impossible to "move" with the editor, but that generally means repaying advance money and canceling out the contract. Many editors who move under such circumstances aren't likely to encourage such a step. It is considered pirating and questionable ethics. A contract with a publisher is negotiated with the publisher, not with a specific person that works for the publisher. Therefore, a publisher can insist the agreement is valid and expect to proceed with publication. Practically speaking, few publishers exercise that right. If an author is unhappy in being published under the publisher's imprint, most publishers will agree to cancel the contract.

The question really begs some very careful consideration. If the author has already published with the publisher in question, he will, no doubt, have been satisfied with the publisher's performance and handling of his book. If the relationship with the editor was thoroughly satisfactory, the time for change might be when the next book is ready for submission. Any editor of merit does tend to "take" authors with them when they move to a new publisher. It doesn't follow that includes work in progress. Furthermore, editors influence a publishing list, but it usually takes a year or two before that effect will show up.

Other Functions of the Agent

Juvenile publishing is a complicated process, where an error or delay in scheduling may cause a book to miss major children's book review sections, so necessary to acceptance of the book. For this, and many other reasons, editors work in advance, by list. Books being selected may not appear for a year or more, after acceptance. An editor's spring list is so organized that it can be presented, in many instances, as finished books to the publisher's sales conference. Other books will be presented in jacket proofs, perhaps, bound galleys and a completed catalog which will contain copy on each new book to be issued.

The agent knows all this background and works with publishers whose capability has been demonstrated to work well in all these areas.

In addition to this specialized knowledge, the agent guides the writer in whatever special needs may be required. The agent may put the writer in touch with sources and contacts that are useful in researching and writing of a book, evaluate drafts of a manuscript, discuss handling, and offer editorial direction.

Not infrequently, writers travel a good deal. The agent can speak for the author in matters that have to be decided in the author's absence. A writer that has to spend several months in Siena, Italy in researching a book on the famous annual horse race held there can be pretty inaccessible. Mail in Italy is slow and uncertain as a means of contact and trans-oceanic phone calls are expensive as well as difficult in Siena. If the research work happens to be in Puerto Rico, contact is almost impossible.

The agent can - and often does - arbitrate points of dispute when a writer is writing about a famous personality and differences about handling arise. The agent can be the dispassionate voice, guiding each through the literary thickets of getting a manuscript written.

The agent can protect the writer from intrusions on his time, screening and handling disturbing contacts the writer wishes to avoid. A phone call in the midst of writing a difficult passage can often mean the loss of half an hour in writing time in losing the thread of thinking and getting back into the material again, not to mention the time spent talking on the phone.

In placing rights, the agency's objective is to secure the best possible income. Selling first serial rights can boast interest in a book when it is published, but the appearance of that material must be timed so that the interest it creates isn't dissipated by too early an exposure. Sometimes it may be advantageous to place an excerpt of a book in a publication primarily for promotion purposes and where income is a secondary consideration. The agent, therefore, often acts as an adjunct to the publisher's support of a book, obtaining promotional exposure in the placement of rights.

Writers, intent on working with research materials and writing a manuscript, not infrequently operate on verbal agreements, assuming their own good will is shared by everyone else. The agent will watch for such developments and see that agreements are drawn up so that everyone's interest is protected and made a matter of record. In this respect, the agent often acts as a legal counselor to the writer, avoiding future misunderstanding and making certain all parties proceed according to terms that are clearly defined and agreed to in writing.

Writers are often criticized for making poor business decisions about how their writing income is derived. The charge is probably unfair for writers are like any other segment of people; some possess excellent judgement about money matters and some do not; some have inflated notions about what their writing should produce and some underrate their writing. To make certain this unevenness is kept in proper balance is the agent's job.

Writing is a solitary preoccupation for the most part. The agent knows the by-products of it all, the uncertainty and anguish of the writer when work is not proceeding satisfactorily, as well as those periods when the material takes over and what comes out of the typewriter is as near perfect as any writing can be. The agent is helpful during both extremes, offering encouragement when it is needed and direction or suggestion when required.

CHAPTER EIGHT

An Overview of the Field

Too often the public thinks of books much in the same terms as they do breakfast cereal or soap powder. Editors, publishers and agents are constantly asked, "What is selling today?" the indirect question being, "What kind of book should I write?" Bennett Cerf, had a standard answer to that question. He suggested humor, because people always enjoy laughing.

Good children's books are published each year that run the range of the literature, and humor is a part of that span. Humor isn't a large part for the simple reason that it is very hard to write, either adult or juvenile. Certainly we need more of it today than ever before, to distract and entertain, to transport us from the harshness of jangling headlines, screaming sirens, traffic jams, bomb threats, and all the other disturbing aspects of modern life. The problem for agents and editors is to find the talent.

Trendish issues often influence what books editors select, but other books fill a niche and they appear year after year on juvenile publishers lists. People of other lands, in non-fiction, pour out, endlessly as enrichment for social studies programs. Good fiction in the same subject area is viewed cautiously for no other reason than it doesn't sell as well. No one knows what would happen if children's specialists suddenly became more receptive to such books, on the sales side, but many of us suspect children would be receptive to them if they were urged on them as much as non-fiction. Such fiction as does find its way into print is likely to reflect societies' tone for the moment simply because editors, conditioned by the specialist and reviewers, accept that fact. It is appalling to have one of the brightest editors in the field write: ". . .Children are bound to today, but looking for tomorrow, and books must give back to them the spirit of what they know." If this is true, heaven help us, for they will also repeat all the mistakes of the past, simply because they haven't been exposed to them.

Historical fiction, well layed out in terms of curriculum use, is a useful area for any author to work in. It is not a large market, but some distinguished publishers work in it and if you are accepted in it, it is a steady market once the books settle into approved lists. The only criterion to keep in mind is that it requires thorough and objective research so that the period is presented as accurately as possible. Concepts are handled in relation to the age level in which you are working.

Adventure stories, like mysteries, are escapist reading, just as they are in adult books. Emphasis must be placed on strong plotting and characterization with an element of continuous tension and incident that builds logically to a believable end. Background is important and can sometimes, when well done and accurately handled, be instructive as well as entertaining. All of this must be carefully fused into the writing so that it adds and advances the narrative line.

Fantasy in children's books can arouse spirited discussion among children's specialists, and some editors. As a category, it has always been a part of children's literature and will continue to be in the future. Once the author is able to convince his reader to suspend disbelief, almost anything is possible, within the structured setting. A wise children's editor once remarked at an educational conference, "Fantasy must be contained." A novice writer asked for elaboration and the editor replied, "If you ask for elaboration, you may never understand what the statement implies."

There are children who prefer reality in their reading and no amount of prodding or any inducement will change that. There is no reason to encourage them to read fantasy. On the other hand, the child who enjoys fantasy is not unusual or trying to escape the real world. The child may possess a vivid imagination and not only understand what Peter Pan and Wendy are up to, but may well identify with Tinker Bell and feel quite comfortable with Tink, in every way. There is always a great need for fantasy, good fantasy, in children's books, although it is not a writing form that a novice should undertake.

The areas of non-fiction are not unlike those of the adult world, but for the most part they are curriculum oriented, largely in the sciences, and social studies. There are biographies, craft and how-to books, books on geography, and others on history. There are career books, books on psychology and books on sociology. There are books on all aspects of the arts, and, there are books of poetry.

Children's tastes are just as wide as those of adults. There are children whose interest is factual and they gravitate to non-fiction. There are children who enjoy fiction and books are available to satisfy them, too. There are children who read and there are those who do not. Books must satisfy all this need and the better they are, the better the need is fulfilled. For the non-reader, perhaps the best solution is to see that his needs are satisfied in other ways, in whatever is required to spark interest, be it picture books, film strips, photography, or audiovisual material.

Not infrequently, when parents complain about how little children read, it is not uncommon to discover they come from a house devoid of books. Busy fathers may read professional or trade publications, often in an evening after the children are in bed. Any curious child that looks into such magazines or journals is likely to consider that reading as an extension of what "daddy does at the office." It is associated as part of a job, or earning a living for the family, but hardly the kind of reading that sets an example.

A child should be comfortable with books. They should be part of growing up, preferably part of his own room — his book shelves; his books; ideally, books he has selected to own. It does not necessarily guarantee developing a reading habit, but, it could.

Today, with children's sections one of the most inviting areas of the library, it is pitiable how few parents make a trip to the library a routine part of rearing children. No parent should deny a child this privilege, not even the working mother when libraries stagger hours and remain open on week ends for that very purpose.

If children are the hope of the future, their education is more important to the national welfare than any other item in our public expenditure. Yet, we annually approve military budgets that allow for expenditures in covert activities alone that would more than cover all costs of education, including those of our colleges and universities.

We are a young nation, accustomed to squandering our resources, both human and natural. Perhaps, entering our third century, we will re-examine our values, to direct our energies more pointedly. Sheer numbers in the population explosion demand this, if any reasonable degree of civility and individual satisfaction is to be assured in the future. Time is not in our favor.

This short overview touches on a wide range of subjects. The public attitude toward books; a quick survey of the juvenile book field; types of books published; children's tastes; children's specialist's needs and influences; and, finally, some parental attitudes that influence books and children's use of them. They are not as disparate as they first seem, all part of the world of juvenile literature, a segment of the commercial world we live in, but one that exerts enormous influence, far beyond the dollars spent to create it.

Bibliography and Notes

From Childhood to Childhood, by Jean Karl (The John Day Company). A distillation of more than twenty years in publishing by an editor whose books have won great prestige and honors. It is an insider's view and rich with information and direction, for the writer, the specialist and those interested in children's literature.

Your Child's Reading Today, by Josette Frank (Doubleday & Co.). One of those remarkable people that devoted themselves to working for excellence in children's books at all levels, and for which there will always be great need. A practical, thorough examination of books and reading for children, helpful to the parent and anyone else interested in the writing or use of juvenile books.

Children and Books, by May Hill Arbuthnot (Scott, Foresman and Company). A definitive guide and source book for those concerned with children's literature. It is written in a warm, inviting style, reminiscent of her lectures for which she was widely known and appreciated.

Writing Books for Children, by Jane Yolen (*The Writer, Inc.*) An excellent book for the perceptive novice. Perhaps not the first book to tackle, but one that deserves attention, ultimately. The author has editing and teaching experience and is the author of some twenty books in the children's field.

Writing Juvenile Fiction, by Phyllis McGinley *(The Writer, Inc.)* A basic book for the beginning writer. Doesn't assume you have arrived full-blown. Informative, instructive, and down-to-earth. A successful writer of both juveniles and adult books.

Books, Children and Men, by Paul Hazard, translated by Marguerite Mitchell (The Horn Book, Inc.) A slim volume of 176 pages, and hard to locate, it is worth any juvenile writer's time as a general survey of children's literature from the beginning of its history to the time of the book's publication, in 1944. Starting with Charles Perrault's *Tales of Mother Goose*, published in 1697 in France, he covers John Newberry's first children's bookshop in England in 1750, Germany's contribution, in 1765, when Christian Felix Weisse published his songs for his children, and others who have contributed to children's literature. He also examines European and England's juvenile contributions, as well as those of the United States, with keen perception and persuasive understanding. In his last chapter Hazard discusses "The World Republic of Childhood," admitting that children's books keep alive nationality, "but they also keep alive a sense of Humanity."

The Writer's Manual
Book 7

How to
Write
Poetry

By
Arthur F. Gould

ABOUT THE AUTHOR

Arthur F. Gould was a founding editor of
Tri Quarterly magazine
responsible for the publication's poetry selection.
He served in that capacity for three years
during his undergraduate period.
He also was chairman of Northwestern University's Poetry Club
at a time when Stephen Spender was in residence
at the university and an active member of the club.
He has published poetry in a number of student publications.

As a partner in the authors' agency,
Porter, Gould & Dierks,
he handles the agency's poetry submissions.
He did graduate work at the masters and doctoral levels in literary criticism.
He has taught classes in writing, Adult Education Program,
Evanston Township High School, and is a lecturer,
English Department, Barat College, Lake Forest, Illinois.

CONTENTS

INTRODUCTION

A sense of beauty, insight, a moment of inspiration and a good deal of hard work are required in creating a poem. There are rules to follow, break and ignore. Poetic forms offer such a variety of structures that no poet can master them all. A beginning poet, however, should be familiar with the various forms, and all their technical aspects. A serious poet should be able to recognize and work with more than one form. He or she should experiment and, perhaps, create a new form as Spenser did in the 16th Century. The English poet added an Alexanderine line to Chaucer's familiar eight-line Monk's Tale Stanza to create the Spenserian Stanza of the "Faerie Queene". The famous stanza was adopted by Keats, Byron, and Shelley, the second generation Romantic poets, who used it in their poems "Eve Of St. Agnes", "Childe Harold's Pilgrimage", and "Adonais."

Our purpose, then, is to provide the fundamentals of writing poetry. A poem is more than self-expression. There must be structure to allow ideas and emotions to develop in an orderly way for the reader. Even free verse is bound by the pattern of the strophes as they work to develop meaning. An Italian sonnet must have 14 lines of iambic pentameter arranged into an octave rhymed abba abba and a sextet rhymed cde cde, cdc cdc, or cde dce. There are rules for writing odes, as well as the strictly formal French forms like the villanelle, or the rondeau. In many instances, the poet must pay close attention to metre and rhythm to achieve a desired effect. There must be considerations of language, as well, even though today we tend to shy away from the idea that there is a specific poetic diction. In the hands of a master most words can be made to work in the context of the poem. However, everyone recognizes that some words are so clearly cliches that no poet can use them.

No one can promise that knowing fundamentals will allow a person to become a poet. However, without a knowledge of the basics the task is considerably more difficult.

It must be kept in mind that poets are concerned with the implications of words more often than with their literal meanings. For instance, when the word moon appears in a poem, the author's intentions are likely to rest in references to love, life cycles, classical mythology, rather than a lifeless satellite circling the earth:

> O more than moon,
> Draw not up seas to drown me in thy sphere;
> Weep me not dead, in thine arms, but forbear
> To teach the sea what it may do too soon.
>
> from "A Valediction: Of Weeping"
> John Donne

Donne uses the reference to the moon's control over the tides to create a complex metaphor in which the moon is passion drawing the poet's tears in a way that the moon, itself, draws the tides. The success of the lines depends entirely on the image of love that's impressed upon the reader by the word moon. The meanings of the word, therefore, shimmer through, providing the desired depth of feeling. The effect is a tangible sign of Donne's great appreciation of the language.

As a rule, subtle language creates better poetry. If the other elements of poetry work well in a poem, the author's efforts will be sound.

> Surprised by joy--impatient as the Wind
> I turned to share the transport--Oh! with whom
> But thee, deep buried in the silent tomb,
> That spot which no vicissitude can find?
> Love, faithful, love, recalled thee to my mind--
> But how could I forget thee? Through what power,
> Even for the least division of an hour,
> Have I been so beguiled as to be blind
> To my most grievous loss!--That thought's return
> Was the worst pang that sorrow ever bore,
> Save one, one only, when I stood forlorn,
> That neither present time, nor years unborn
> Could to my sight that heavenly face restore.

Wordsworth's sonnet is about death, but he talks about it in a special way: the process (almost unconscious) of getting used to death and yet to honor the dead. That subtlety of thought expressed through the discipline of the Italian sonnet structure gives the poem its power. We move from the specific--the poem was actually the result of Wordsworth's remembrance of his daughter some years after her death--to the universal statement of salvation and hope contained in the words at the end. The movement from the particular to the general is another sign of well executed poetry.

That is not to say a poem should self-consciously open with a particular subject and move to a grand cosmic statement. But our mood should become reflective as we understand the correspondence with a common idea. The subject of a poem may be what T.S. Eliot refers to as an "objective correlative," energizing the universal vision of truth. Certainly, the subject is in the idea behind the images, metaphors, personae, and other poetic furniture.

No one has ever made love to an abstract concept. That's one way of remembering to be concrete in writing poetry. Relate through the real world to the ideas that are important. If you want to write a poem that will give the emotion love, the poem must involve people. We must taste their love and we must consume it to understand it. We see this in the following poems:

UPON JULIA'S CLOTHES
Whenas in silks my Julia Goes,
Then, then, methinks, how sweetly flows
That liquefation of her clothes.

Next, when I cast mine eyes, and see
That brave vibrations, each way free,
O, how that glittering taketh me!
                              Robert Herrick

TO HELEN
Helen, thy beauty is to me
        Like those Nicean barks of yore
That gently, o'er a perfumed sea,
        The weary, way worn wanderer bore
        To his own native shore.
On desperate seas long wont to roam,
        Thy hyacinth hair, thy classic face,
Thy Naiad airs have brought me home
        To the glory that was Greece
And the grandeur that was Rome.

Lo! in yon brilliant window-niche
        How statue-like I see thee stand!
The agate Lamp within thy hand,
        Ah! Psyche, from the regions which
Are Holy Land!
                              Edgar Allan Poe

J. 1078

The bustle in a house
The morning after death
Is solemnest of industries
Enacted upon earth--

The sweeping up the heart,
And putting love away
We shall not want to use again
Until eternity.

                    Emily Dickinson.

There is something specific in each of the poems to make each one home to a special scene. At the same time, we experience the general vanity, grandeur and loss of love.

If we assume, as Colerage did, that an author creates illusions of reality that call upon the reader to willingly suspend his or her disbelief, the poet's task is to dramatize emotional energy in a convincing way. An idea is understood through the images the poet employs. The more concrete and clear the images are, the better chance the poet has of communicating. A poem is often less complete, structurally, than a short story or a novel, but its form and technique will say as much about reality and truth.

Therefore, as poets our eyes should be on ourselves and not on our gods. The cosmic approach in poetry is often meaningless vis-a-vis our daily hum-drum lives. The best poets draw material from the worldly milieu for situations: images, symbols, language, and the rhythms of life. This was as true of Shakespeare, Milton, and Donne, as it is of Hopkins, Eliot, and Plath. Poetry is written for people to understand and a poem relates through familiar objects and characters:

TO A COMMON PROSTITUTE
Be composed--be at ease with me--I am Walt Whitman, liberal
        and lusty as Nature.
Not till the sun excludes you do I exclude you,
Not till the waters refuse to glisten for you and the leaves rustle
        for you, do my words refuse to glisten and rustle for you.
My girl I appoint with you an appointment, and I charge you that
        you make preparation to be worthy to meet me,
And I charge you that you be patient and perfect till I come.
Till then I salute you with a significant look that you do not forget
        me.   Walt Whitman

SNAPSHOTS

I

it is a bicycle
rit-clicketing
on the street.
    it could have been
    crickets
    shivering in the snow

II

on the back steps beside milk bottles
the squirrels waited
for bread and stale cookies.
they will never guess that
the clock is on the mantle watching
a couch, some pictures and an oriental rug.

III

water from a drain pipe
keeps time
by well-shaped drops
into a muddy puddle.

a puddle does not keep time
but dries in the sun.
                        D. Keeley Porter

    We respond to a poem because it shows us something valid and accurate about life. As in any kind of writing, the less the author tells and the more he or she shows the reader, the more effective the work will be. It's not enough to write words such as love, truth, and beauty, by themselves, and expect to raise emotional and intellectual responses. The subject must be so clear that we feel the meaning of the verses. Emily Dickinson's poem J. 1463 is an example of how an author creates a feeling for a subject without ever mentioning it directly. She captures all the effects of a hummingbird in sunlight like this:

        A route of evanescence
        With a revolving wheel;
        A resonance of emerald,
        A rush of cochineal
        And every blossom on the bush
        Adjusts its tumbled head,--
        The mail from Tunis, probably,
        An easy morning's ride,

The last two lines may seem obscure, but it's not difficult to see a reference to the sun: only the sun could serve as such a mailman, ". . . from Tunis, probably/An easy morning's ride." Thus the bird is set in the sunlight completing the image. But how masterfully she handled this. Not content to say, "The morning sunlight playing with the colors of a humingbird," she makes a tangential reference that brings up the right image of the sun in order to have the right emotional tone of adventure in a flower garden.

In his excellent book *First Principles of Verse,* Robert Hillyer points out that poetic diction must be simple, definite, and fresh in order to make language create the author's conception of reality clearly to the reader. How well the poet uses language will affect the clarity of the poetry. The primary and secondary meanings of a word are important to an author. We have seen how the word moon functioned in Donne's poem. Sometimes, however, the secondary meaning of a word may no longer convey freshly enough to be used persuasively. If the symbolic meaning has become cliched, the poet may use the word for its literal effect. (It's interesting that the literal meaning of a word never becomes jaded: tree, sun, ocean, stars, and so on.) Words such as rose, swan, sun, thorn, cross have appeared so often as symbols of love, religion, mythology, and life-cycles that their referential use today may endanger the integrity of a poem. However, if a poet can use such words with little symbolic intention, they may function as strong words.

Some reference is inescapable, of course, but the poet can direct the meaning of a poem according to the value placed on the secondary and primary meanings of words. The quest for literal interpretations is common fare in contemporary poetry and the reader will find abundant examples of this in most modern poets. Basically, it's a question whether the poet's intention is to interpret a rose as a symbol of the Virgin Mary, or spiritual love, or to use the word only to mean a flower of great beauty. How literally we take a word depends on the poet and his or her specific intentions. Interpretation is a very subjective task.

But the way we understand the meaning of words depends on the overall sense of the poem. The total effect of the poem gives back a meaning to each word and image. For instance, Edmund Spenser's concern for a sacred and spiritual quality in profane love gives deeper meaning to the language of "Sonnet 68" than simply a praise of the Lord. It is a poem of seduction, as well. Spenser is saying that we can understand the power of spiritual love through passion. He is trying to get his lover into bed. There is sexual connotation in the words death, blood, joy, and in the image of the Lord descending into hell; and the last two lines of the sonnet make it clear that the author is speaking to someone in a pleading voice: "So let us love," is an active declaration.

> Most glorious Lord of lyfe, that on this day
> Didst make thy triumph over death and sin:
> And having harrowed hell, didst bring away
> Captivity thence captive us to win:
> This joyous day, deare Lord, with joy begin,
> And grant that we for whom thou diddest dye
> Being with thy deare blood clene washt from sin,
> May live for ever in felicity.
> And that thy love we weighing worthily,
> May likewise love thee for the same againe:
> And for thy sake that all lyke deare didst buy,
> With love may one another entertayne.
> So let us love, deare love, lyke as we ought,
> Love is the lesson which the Lord us taught.

The subtlety of poetry depends so much on the author's sense of language. The poet's aim is to entertain, to enlighten, to create beauty, to tell the truth. But all successful poetry will have a degree of sophistication in the way the author uses words, whether it is a heroic couplet by Alexander Pope:

> All seems infected that the infected spy,
> As all looks yellow to the jaundiced eye.

Or a simple strophe by Dickinson:

> Apparently with no surprise
> To any happy flower,
> The frost beheads it at its play
> In accidental power.

Pope's writing is clever and expresses truth through a turn of a phrase that delights the reader. Dickinson's vision is more direct, but none the less pleasing. The impersonal power of nature and nature's happy resignation shown in her lines helps define the human role as much as the Augustan wit. Pope would certainly scorn Dickinson for her "ludicrous" departure from form and gross lack of style. We, however, have the advantage of time and a freer attitude toward composition in order to appreciate both their intentions. The heroic couplet sounds dated to us, but Pope's words are as meaningful today as when he wrote the lines.

We are really talking about two kinds of language: the diction in which the author expresses the thoughts--that which reflects common usage of the day--and the ideas behind the words that can be translated, at any time, into current thoughts and feelings. The second is a language of emotion in which the words are symbols for feelings.

Good poetry cannot be defined solely on the choice of words. To use an extreme example, in a post-beat, post-1960s world, in which language has been "liberated," even the most stogy critic has accepted the fact that *motherfucker* can be just as effective a phrase as *lovers' infiniteness.* Context--situation, mood, image, tone, rhythm, and rhyme--must be used to judge whether a word is appropriate. Words must work in relationship to one another and then to the poem as a whole. This gives the poet a great deal of freedom and that is the way it should be. There should be no restraints except those the poet imposes through his or her own structures, or the imposed, but flexible, structures of poetic forms such as sonnet, villanelle, and so on.

Poetic structure is how the author visualizes what has to be said. An idea may develop best as a sonnet, or as a five line image. Final form depends on how the poet feels about the poem while the idea is taking shape in his mind, before anything is put down on paper. The decision may be instantaneous: I'll write a sonnet about this incident, or mood. Or, it may take weeks before the poet realizes that the best way to express the idea is with a tanka. Structural discipline may give meaning to the words. On the other hand, free verse may best show the thought, as in this poem on mortality by Mary Aldis:

BARBERRIES
You say I touch the barberries
As a lover his mistress?
What a curious fancy!
One must be delicate, you know,
They have bitter thorns.
You say my hand is hurt?
Oh no, it was my breast,
It was crushed and pressed--
I mean--why yes, of course, or course--
There is a bright drop, isn't there?
Right on my finger,
Just the color of a barberry,
But it comes from my heart.
Do you love barberries?
In the autumn
When the sun's desire
Touches them to a glory of crimson and gold?
I love them best then.
There is something splendid about them;
They are not afraid
of being warm and glad and bold

They flush joyously
Like a cheek under a lover's kiss,
They bleed cruelly
Like a dagger wound in the breast,
They flame up madly for their little hour,
Knowing they must die--
Do you love barberries?

Some poets work best with great discipline; others are stifled by it. But a claim for freedom should not be used as an excuse to ignore poetic techniques. You have to know the rules in order to break them with revolutionary effectiveness.

A subtle quality of expression in poetry also demands clarity, like the first keen scent of salt-air breathed in as you approach the shore. Our senses tell us that the ocean is not far away, although it remains hidden behind trees and bluffs. Yet the smell of the sea stimulates images of sand, white-caps and strands of colors--black, blue, green, gray--swelling to the horizon. The language of a poem functions in much the same way. Words are important as long as they stimulate an impatience in the reader to find the sense of what the author is saying, as the smell of the ocean makes the traveler anxious to get to the beach.

Christina Rossetti, sister of Dante Gabriel Rossetti, devout High Church Anglican, Pre-Raphaelite poet and one of England's outstanding female poets, expresses something of this in her work "Uphill". It is a poem of death-or is it? We ask, who are the speakers? How allegorical and how literal is it? What is the Inn? The road? Is the day's rest really death, or the satisfaction of passions? We have a "scent" of all of these questions that bring up images of life and death, of vast, frightening and wild proportions. The questioner is a traveler. The one who answers is a narrative voice--the poet-- a man or woman by the roadside, or Death itself, or God, or the dead, or all of these. The Inn is heaven, or hell, or it just may be an inn. The road is life and day's end is death. A psychoanalytic interpretation would lay great emphasis on the pathway to the inn, the beds, the sensuality of it all. The sexual energy is there:

Does the road wind uphill all the way?
     Yes, to the very end.
Will the day's journey take the whole long day?
     From morn to night, my friend.

But is there for the night a resting place?
     A roof for when the slow dark hours begin.
May not the darkness hide it from my face?
     You cannot miss that inn.

Shall I meet other wayfarers at night?
    Those who have gone before.
Then must I knock, or call when just in sight?
    They will not keep you standing at that door.

Shall I find comfort, travel-sore and weak?
    Of labor you shall find the sum.
Will there be beds for me and all who seek?
    Yea, beds for all who come.

The poem is good because the language excites the imagination. We are in the presence of truth and we want to explore the poetry until we understand the author's vision. We may never fully appreciate it, but that is an element of great poetry, too. It is not necessary to find answers to all questions. Some questions are better left unanswered, appreciated as questions. This is a truth that poetry teaches, if not science. Keats appreciated the point:

Thou still unravished bride of quietness,
    Thou foster child of silence and slow time,
Sylvan historian who canst thus express
    A flowery tale more sweetly than our ryhme:
What leaf-fringed legend haunts about thy shape
    Of dieties or mortals, or of both,
            In Tempe or the dales of Arcady?
What men or gods these?   What maidens loath?
What mad pursuit? What struggle to escape?
    What pipes and timbrels? What wild ecstasy?

Heard melodies are sweet, but those unheard
    Are sweeter; therefore, ye soft pipes, play on:
Not to the sensual ear, but more endeared,
    Pipe to the spirit ditties of no tone:

A person's vision of the world is a result of outside stimuli. Just as the salt-smell of the ocean leads to something greater than itself--the sea itself--so language lets us see the abstract world of thought. The images created by words show the poet's ideas. The ocean creates a scent that guides one back to the sea. The author's vision stimulates a poem in words that brings the reader back to the poet's original ideas and feelings.

At the end of the "Ode On A Grecian Urn," Keats says of the urn:

'Beauty is truth, truth beauty,' that is all
    Ye know on earth, and all ye need to know.

It is all the urn needs to know about the nature of truth and beauty, Keats is saying, but not all that men need know. Because beauty fades, in reality, mortality--the loss of beauty--is Truth for mortals. It is a complicated and perceptive idea. Although books of philosophy could be written on the idea, Keats used a few lines of poetry to express the vision. The language is the bridge between Keats and the reader, and unless the words convey effectively, as they do here, the whole idea is lost.

In Keats' poem the idea is definite, strong, and original enough to be worth the effort of discovery. The thought that stimulated the poetry is significant. We are indeed in the presence of Truth and Beauty.

If asking an author for clear expression, mastery of language, subtle use of words, and significant ideas with a strong sense of mood, tone, and emotional involvement seems like a great demand to make on a poet, *it is*. Poetry is the most demanding of the written art-forms. We believe it is in the same relationship to prose as music is to the plastic arts. One is not potentially greater than the other, but one more technically difficult to achieve than the other.

> Contemplate all this work of Time
>   The giant laboring in his youth;
>   Nor dream of human love and truth,
> As dying Nature's earth and lime;
>
> But truth that those we call the dead
>   Are breathers of an ampler day
>   For ever nobler ends.
>   from "In Memoriam"
>   Alfred, Lord Tennyson

Poets do more than relate experience, or comment on various activities. They offer subjective relationships between persons and apparent truths. The subjectivity--spirituality--is beautiful. Part of the beauty comes from the assumption that the relationship is a natural bond. What the poet sees and then shows the reader is something that is true and in which we all share. The specific is an example of the universal. As part of a shared sensibility, men and women are generally affected by the same kind of emotional reality: we recognize love, hate, fear, and so on. We know pain so that any kind of pain is imaginable, and the poet takes advantage of that assumption. In the following lines from "Sonnet 71," Shakespeare shows something about the selflessness of love. If you have never feared a lover's rejection, such terror is in these lines:

Nay, if you read this line, remember not
The hand that writ it; for I love you so,
That I in your sweet thoughts would be forgot,
If this thinking on me than should make you woe.
Oh, if, I say, you look upon this verse
When I perhaps compounded am with clay,
Do not so much as my poor name rehearse,
But let your love even with my life decay;
Lest the wise world should look into your moan,
And mock you with me after I am gone.

The basic elements of verse can be visualized in terms of a vague dialectic: there is the poet's imagination, intuition, and inspiration on the one hand and on the other is the content, rhythm, form, and diction with all the other other rules of versification. The synthesis is the finished poem. Anne Hamilton, in her book *The Seven Principles of Poetry*, stacks the elements in a display of evolutionary aspects. To think of the poetic process in dialectical terms seems more current and closer to the truth of the creative act. But however one wishes to talk about the writing, a poem is created from what goes on inside the poet's head combined with the mechanics of writing poetry.

The narrative voice in Shapeskeare's sonnet is able to grasp his own demise: the poem illustrates that. However, it is doubtful that Shakespeare summed it up that way before he began writing. Perhaps one of the lines came into his head and he built the poem around it. Maybe the whole poem came to him as he wrote it down, the unconscious doing the real work of creating. Shakespeare was probably suffering the anguish and fear that he recorded. The emotions sparked the imagination, intuition, and inspiration. We can assume that, but specifically what went on inside his head in creating the poem is lost.

What we have is the poem on the page and we can talk about the mechanical elements of the sonnet form. Since our concern is with the technical aspects of writing poetry, we'll have to ignore, without denying, the validity of such probers of literature as the psycholanalytic critics. For the interested reader the works of Normand Holland, Simon O. Lesser, and Ernest Jones are definitive in this area. Hundreds and hundreds of books have been written on the interpretation of poetry. These are all available at a good library. Anyone interested in speculations on how the mind creates should begin by studying Arthur Koestler's *The Act Of Creation.* In this section, we will study only the basic elements of poetry.

The basic metrical unit in poetry is called a foot. There are four common feet: iamb, trochee, anapest, and dactyl. Each one is characterized its own pattern of stresses or emphasized syllables.

An iamb is made up of two syllables: soft then hard (U—). A line of iambic verse consists of a number of such stressed feet.

This line from the preceding sonnet is an example:
U – U – U – U – U –
When I I perhaps I compoun I ded am I with clay.

Notice how the emphasis rises within each foot so that we end with the hard stress on *clay*, which is the moment of greatest despair at the end of the line.

A trochee also has two syllables, but the emphasis is hard then soft (—U) the opposite of an iamb. A trochee has a falling action that affects the tone of a line. In the following line from Shakespeare's "The Phoenix and The Turtle" notice how the poet caused the line to end on an up beat by omitting the final unaccented syllable of the trochee. Often a poet will cut a syllable of a foot, or use an extra one, for full effect.

```
  -   U     -   U     -   U     -
```
Let the I bird of I loudest I lay,

Here we see that such words as *the* and *of* usually don't receive great emphasis. Certainly, a line of poetry should never end with a weak word.

An anapest is a rising foot made up of three syllables: soft, soft, hard (UU−). In the line from Shelley's poem "Cloud" notice the distinct rhythm of anapestic verse. There is great potential for monotony caused by the sing-song effect of the stresses.
```
   U  U  -      U  U   -       U U   -        U   U   -
```
Like a child I from the womb, I like a ghost I from the tomb,

The dactyl is the opposite of an anapest. Both have three syllables, but the dactyl is a falling foot, hard, soft, soft (−UU). A common example is the word mannequin.

English poets make use of some other feet to break up the patterns of emphasis of the four basic feet. These are the pyrrhus, soft, soft (UU)‐ spondee, hard, hard (−−); amphibrach, soft, hard, soft (U−U); amphimacer, hard, soft, hard (−U−); the paeons: first, hard, soft, soft, soft (−UUU); second, soft, hard, soft, soft (U−UU); third, soft, soft, hard, soft (UU−U), and fourth, soft, soft, soft, hard (UUU−). The different paeons get their names according to where the so-called floating accented syllable appears in the foot. Two other feet are the choriamb, hard, soft, soft, hard (−UU−), and the monosyllable, hard (−).

A poem is a "rhythmic expression in words" as Ms. Hamilton says, and the 11 feet give the stress patterns for the metrical beat which moves through the lines of a poem. Metre is also determined by how long a line is. Length is measured by the number of feet. For instance, the monometer--a one foot line --opens Robert Herrick's iambic ode to Ben Jonson:
```
  U   -
```
Ah, Ben!
Say how or when

The following line from George Herbert's "Aaron" is a dimeter--a two foot line--of two amphimacers:
```
  -   U  -     -  U   -
```
Holiness I on the head

Henry Vaughan's last line of "Peace," made up of three iambs, is an illustration of trimeter:
```
  U    -     U   -     U    -
```
Thy God I thy life I thy cure.

One of the most famous examples of tetrameter--a four foot line-- is found in the couplets of Milton's companion poems "L'Allegro" and "Il Penseroso." Note the tendency toward a singsong effect in the following lines. Tetrameter is very difficult to write well:

Of for / ests and I enchant I ments drear,
Where more I is meant I than meets I the ear.

Pentameter is a five foot line and the most famous use is the iambic pentameter of Shakespeare's sonnets:

Shall I I compare I thee to I a sum I mer's day?

The Alexandrine is a good example of a six foot line. Spenser's innovative use of iambic hexameter was mentioned earlier. The following example is the last line of the first stanza of his great romantic epic "The Faerie Queene:"

Fierce warres I and faith I ful loves I shall mor I alize I my song.

Heptameter is based on the classical Latin septenary. The heptameter is sometimes called a fourteener because it is often made up of fourteen syllables. The following line from Thomas Hardy's poem "The Convergence of the Twain" is interesting: it's seven feet long, with four kinds of feet (anapest, iamb, trochee and monolyllable), and 14 syllables.

And the Pride I of life I that plan I ned her, I stilly
couches I she.

Feet and line length determine metre, which is the felt rhythm of the ideas. When the reader feels the movement of language, he or she is experiencing the rhythm of thought. In the past, metre was more structured and therefore more predictable. The expression was expected to conform to exact externalizations. The metre of a Shakespearean sonnet, for instance, grew from a combination of iambic feet and pentameter verse. The poet's thoughts were expected to find expression within those structures.

Iambs and trochees create two part metre, while anapests and dactyls allow for three parts. The other kinds of feet we have discussed create their own metres with the hard and soft beats showing the emphasis--the stress composition--of the metre.

The foot, the line, and finally the stanza are the units of recurrence that determine metre. The stanzas within a poem should be similar enough in their patterns so that each one is characteristic, while each is unique enough to avoid monotony of idea, image, metre, and rhymes.

The opening stanza should act as a touchstone for those that follow. The first stanza may establish metre, rhyme scheme, if any, mood, rhythms, intellectual and emotional levels, and the basic poetic techniques employed. The ideas and images will be developed through the middle of the poem, and at the end there should be a feeling of completion. This development may be quite apparent from stanza to stanza.

The features of a stanza--also called a strophe, or a stave--include a set number of lines, feet per line, and a rhyme pattern. There are specific ways of talking about a stanza. For instance, rhyming lines are assigned an identifying letter with an accompanying numeral to indicate the number of stresses per line:

So runs I my dream I but what I am I?	a^4
An in I fant cry I ing in I the night;	b^4
An in I fant cry I ing for I the light,	b^4
And with I no lang I uage but I a cry.	a^4

The quatrain--a four line stanza--in iambic tetrameter is from Tennyson's "In Memoriam." Quatrains have many variations in line length and rhyme scheme, which may be *aabb, abab, aaxa, axax, xaxa, or axxa (x* is a common way of showing a non-rhyming line). The *abba* pattern of the preceding stanza is known as the In Memoriam Stanza, as it was popularized by Tennyson in that poem. Not all stanzas are named after the poet or poem that popularized them, but there are a few that we will consider: The Monk's Tale Stanza, The Spenserian Stanza, and Rhyme Royal, which is also called the Chaucer, or The Troilus Stanza.

The Heroic Couplet is a two line stanza with matching end words which may be four or five feet in length. Alexander Pope is known for his use of the stanza:

'Tis hard I to say, I if great I er want I of skill	a^5
Appear I in writ I ing or I in judg I ing ill;	a^5
But of I the two I less danger I ous is I the offense	b^5
To tire I our pat I ience than I mislead I our sense.	b^5

A tercet is a three line stanza with varying line lengths and a triplet rhyme scheme. The Herrick poem, "Upon Julia's Clothes" is composed of two tercets, also called triplets. (In the following stanzas through-out the chapter the reader may find it good practice to scan the lines for the number of feet and the pattern of the syllables, as well as the rhyme patterns.)

Whenas in silks my Julia goes,
Then, then, methinks, how sweetly flows
That liquefaction of her clothes.

Another three line stanza, Terza Rima, is Italian in origin and was adopted by English poets during the 17th Century. The best known use of

Terza Rima is in Dante's "Divina Comedia." The metre is usually iambic pentameter and the rhyme scheme is aba, bcb, cdc, ded and so on, with the end-word of the second line of each stanza determining the rhyming sound of the next stanza. Terza Rima has been popular with English poets from Milton to Eliot. In "Ode To The West Wind," Shelley used four triplets in Terza Rima and a couplet to create the distinct pattern of the poem; the following is the first stanza of the poem:

> O wild West Wind, thou breath of Autumn's being,
> Thou, from whose unseen presence the leaves dead
> Are driven, like ghosts from an enchanter fleeing,

The five line stanza has always varied in length and rhyme scheme-- ababb, abbaa, abbxa, for instance. The stanza does not characterize a particular poet, or poem. The example is from "Song'" by John Suckling:

> Why so pale and wan, fond lover?
>   Prithee, why so pale?
> Will, when looking well can't move her,
>   Looking ill prevail?
>   Prithee, why so pale?

Another with a different rhyme scheme and line length is the fifth stanza of Dryden's irregular ode "A Song For St. Cecilia's Day:"

>   Sharp violins proclaim
> Their jealous pangs, and desperation,
> Fury, frantic indignation,
> Depth of pains, and height of passion,
>   For the fair, disdainful dame.

The six line stanza is common, too, appearing with either an ababab, aaxbbx, or other variations. The stanza that appears below is from Henry Vaughn's "Cock-Crowing:"

> Father of lights! what sunny seed,
> What glance of day hast Thou confined
> Into this bird? To all the breed
> This busy ray Thou hast assigned;
>   Their magnetism works all night,
>   And dreams of paradise and light.

George Gascoigne, the 16th Century poet, dramatist, soldier and diplomat called the seven line stanza, "a royall kind of verse, serving best for grave discourses." This was Rhyme Royal, and it was first used notably in

Chaucer's "Troilus and Criseyde." The stanza is also known by his name and the title of the poem. The rhyme scheme of the stanza is ababbcc and the lines have five stresses. Spenser used Rhyme Royal for "An Hyme In Honour of Beautie:"

> Ah whither, Love, wilt thou now carrie mee?
> What wontlesse fury doest thou now inspire
> Into my feeble breast, too full of thee?
> Whylest seeking to aslake thy raging fyre,
> Thou in me kindlest much more great desyre,
> And up aloft above my strenth doest rayse
> The wondrous matter of my fyre to prayse.

Ottava Rima, an eight line stanza in iambic pentameter, was probably created by Boccaccio, in Italy, in the 14th Century. Other Italian poets that used the stanza were Tasso and Ariosto. Although the normal rhyme scheme is *abababcc*, Chaucer, who used the stanza in the "Monk's Tale", rhymed the lines ababbcbc, in iambic pentameter.

> And lik an egles fetheres was his heres;
> His nayles lyk a briddes clawes weere;
> Til God relessed hym a certeyn yeres,
> And yaf hym wit, and thanne with many a teere
> He thanked God, and evere his lyf in feere
> Was he to doon amys or moore trespace;
> And til that tyme he leyd was on his beere
> He knew that God was ful of myght and grace.

Other English poets to use Ottava Rima included Spenser, Milton, Keats, and Byron. The following stanza is from Byron's "Don Juan":

> And Juan throttled him to get away,
> And blood ('twas from the nose) began to flow:
>   At last, as they more faintly wrestling lay,
> Juan contrived to give an awkward blow,
>   And then his only garment quite gave way;
> He fled, like Joseph, leaving it; but there ,
> I doubt, all likeness ends between the pair.

The nine line stanza is the famous Spenserian Stanza discussed earlier. Taking Chaucer's eight line Monk's Tale Stanza, Spenser added a ninth line, one foot longer, which was the Alexandrine. The first eight lines are in iambic pentameter. The rhyme scheme is ababbcbcc. The last line is then in iambic hexameter. Burns, as well as the three Romantic poets, made good use of the

Spenserian Stanza. The interlocking rhymes and the sweep of the Alexandrine make this stanza imposing and worthy of grand subjects.

The example is from "The Faerie Queene", Book I
Then groning deepe, "Nor damned Ghost," quote he,
"Nor guilefull sprite to these wordes doth speake,
But once a man Fradubio, now a tree,
Wretched man, wretched tree; whose nature weake,
A cruell witch her cursed will to wreake,
Hath thus transformed, and plast in open plaines,
Where Boreas doth blow full bitter bleake,
And scorching Sunne does dry my secret vaines,
For though a tree I seeme yet cold and heat me paines:

A variation of the Spenserian Stanza has ten lines and is rhymed ababbcdcdd. But this may vary, too, as in the following excerpt from Donne's "The Sun Rising"--abbacdcdee:

Busy old fool, unruly sun,
Why doest thou thus,
Through windows and through curtains call on us?
Must to thy motions lovers' seasons run?
Saucy pedantic wretch, go chide
Late school boys and sour prentices,
Go tell court huntsmen that the King will ride,
Call country ants to harvest offices;
Love, all alike no season knows nor clime,
Nor hours, days, months, which are the rags of time.

The eleven line stanza also appears with different rhyme schemes. Obviously, poets used the patterns to best advantage and changed them when it suited their purposes. In the past, there was more criticism of variations than today, when any kind of expression is tolerated as long as it's meaningful to enough people. Both Browning and Keats used eleven line stanzas. The following example is from "To Autumn," by Keats. There is a line in this stanza in which he captures the effect of wind in a woman's hair that is very beautiful:

Who hath not seen thee oft amid thy store?
Sometimes whoever seeks abroad may find
Thee sitting careless on a granary floor,
Thy hair soft-lifted by the winnowing wind;
Or on a half-reaped furrow sound asleep,
Drowsed with the fume of poppies, while thy hook
Spares the next swath and all its twined flowers:
And sometimes like a gleaner thou dost keep
Steady thy laden head across a brook; Or by a cider-press, with patient   k
Thou watchest the last oozings hours by hours.

The 14th Century poem "The Pearl" uses a twelve line stanza which Tennyson adopted for "Mariana", a poem based on the Shakespearean character who, in *Measure for Measure*, awaits her lover in a moated grange-- but who never shows up. There are seven stanzas in the poem. Six have a rhyme scheme *ababcddcefef*, and one *ababaccadede:*

> About a stonecast from the wall
>> A sluice with blackened waters slept,
> And o'er it many, round and small,
>> The clustered marish mosses crept.
> Hard by a poplar shook alway,
>> All silver-green with gnarled bark:
>> For leagues no other tree did mark
> The level waste, the rounding gray.
>> She only said, "My life is dreary,
>>> He cometh not," she said:
>> She said, "I am aweary, aweary,
>>> I would that I were dead!"

Edgar Allen Poe's "Ulalume" offers an example of the rare thirteen line stanza:

> Then my heart it grew ashen and sober
>> As the leaves that were crisped and sere--
>> As the leaves that were withering and sere;
> And I cried: "It was surely October
>> On this very night of last year
>> That I journeyed--I journeyed down here!--
>> That I brought a dread burden down here–
>> On this night of all nights in the year,
>> Ah, what demon has tempted me here?
> Well I know, now, this dim late of Auber--
>> This misty mid region of Weir--
> Well I know, now, this dank tarn of Auber,
>> This ghoul-haunted woodland of Weir."

Or this simply rhymed stanza from "A Fable For Critics" by James Russell Lowell:

> "There is Bryant, as quiet, as cool, and as dignified,
> As a smooth, silent iceberg, that never is ignified,
> Save when by reflection 'tis kindled o'nights
> With a semblance of flame by the chill Northern Lights.
> He may rank (Griswold says so) first bard of your nation

(There's no doubt that he stands in supreme iceolation),
Your topmost Parnassus he may set his heel on,
But no warm applauses come, peal following peal on,--
He's too smooth and too polished to hang any zeal on:
Unqualified merits, I'll grant, if you choose, he has 'em,
But he lacks the one merit of kindling enthusiasm;
If he stir you at all, it is just on my soul.
Like being stirred up with the very North Pole.

The Sonnet Stanza, fourteen lines in iambic pentameter, is covered in depth in the chapter on poetic structures. There are various rhyme schemes and patterns within the stanza, but Shakespeare's sonnets are probably the best known use of the fourteen line stanza. The rhyme scheme is *ababcdcdefefgg* in iambic pentameter:

My mistress' eyes are nothing like the sun:
Coral is far more red than her lips' red;
If snow be white, why then her breasts are dun;
If hairs be wires, black wires grow on her head.
I have seen roses damasked, red and white,
But no such roses see I in her cheeks;
And in some perfumes is there more delight
Than in the breath that from my mistress reeks.
I love to hear her speak, yet well I know
That music hath a far more pleasing sound;
I grant I never saw a goddess go;
My mistress, when she walks, treads on the ground.
And yet, by heaven, I think my love as rare
As any she elied with false compare.

If you want to be a poet, you must know these elements of poetry--the kinds of feet, the line lengths and metres, and the stanzas. You must be able to recognize them, to talk about them in someone else's writing, and to work with them in our own poetry. Writing is a craft, with rules and mechanical means of achieving an effect. Important poetry is written by geniuses with great sensitivity, but such poets share a common technical knowledge of writing with good poets and with mediocre ones. There are more basic elements of poetry which we will discuss in the next chapter.

CHAPTER THREE

Elements of Verse II

A problem for beginning poets is establishing a sense of coherent movement--rhythm--in their work. Prose statements set down in short lines and broken into stanzas do not make a poem. Self-expression that is understood only by the author is not a poem. Unassociated images strung together with comments is not a poem.

One of the elements that helps to identify a poem is rhythm. Without it language is flat, monotonous, and static. Rhythm is motion. It causes thoughts and words to move together in a pleasing pattern creating impressions similar to the disciplined movements of music. Poetry and music are similar in the ways they achieve their effects: tones, beats, rhythms, stresses, themes, cords, and so on. Rhythm is important to both.

Rhythm in poetry is the flow, the beat of the words. As was explained in the last chapter, rhythm is externalized in metre, the stressed feet and the line lengths, and rhymes. Most readers are caught up by the rhythm of Poe's "The Raven," for instance. The effect depends on the distinct beat, which is achieved by the predominately imabic feet, the rhymes within the lines, and the strong rhyming of end-words:

Once upon a midnight dreary, while I pondered weak and weary,
Over many a quaint and curious volume of forgotten lore,
While I nodded, nearly napping, suddenly there came a tapping, As of
someone gently rapping, rapping at my chamber door,
"'Tis some visitor," I muttered, "Tapping at my chamber door
    --only this and nothing more."

There is a rising quality, a marching quality to the words. The pattern is established and the rest of the stanzas meet our expectations. Patterns and expectations are the elements of rhythm. Whatever is established at the beginning, the best poetic effect is achieved by repeating the patterns. The reader expects repetition. There may be variations, but the reader should be able to recognize the basic combination of stresses and the number of syllables per foot, line, and stanza. The rhyme scheme may change, the feet may be shorter or longer, but the sense of flow and motion should be consistent.

Along with technical rhythms, there are rhythms of thought, too.

J. 1052
I never saw a moor,
I never saw the sea;
Yet know I how the heather
    looks,
And what a billow be.

I never spoke with God
Nor visited in heaven;
Yet certain am I of the spot
As if the checks were given.

In Dickinson's poem on faith, the secular thought of the first stanza is reflected in the religious belief in the second. The idea is based on a logical assumption; without seeing moor or sea, the poet can see a heather and a billow, because she has reason to believe in their existence. With the same faith, without having a *sign* of God's existence, she finds Him real. Technically, the rhyme schemes of the two stanzes are the same, abcb. The repitition "I never saw" in the first stanza is echoed by "I never spoke" in the second. This is poetic continuity. The *assonance* (a similarity of vowel sounds followed by different consonants) in heather-heaven, know-spoke, how-God, and billows-given create a bond of sound between the stanzas thus enlarging the rhythm.

Basically, the rhythm--sometimes called cadence in free verse--of the poem is created by sound similarities and repetition of words and phrases, as well as thoughts. In this instance, the beat would become monotonous if the poem continued, but Dickinson stopped at the right point, when the thought was complete. Any more would belabor thought and rhythm.

Usually, when a poet knows what he or she wants to say, the rhythm of the poem accompanies the thought. There will be a unique sound to the verses. The poet's task is to decide on the language that will best enhance the patterns and convey the meaning to the reader. As Ms. Hamilton points out, poetic rhythm is the balancing of metrical emphasis with speech emphasis, emotion, and thought.

Of course, not all poems--perhaps not many contemporary poems--are based on classical or traditional metrical structures. Free verse hasn't set

rhythms based on predictable structures. A poet writing in this genre
depends on cadences--sound without metric regularity--to achieve strong
impressions on readers:

At My Grandmother's Funeral

I

The coffin is an ancient flowerbed
Where a tired face is growing small
I stand in the doorway, waiting for rain.
What the room needs is a flashflood.
The silver-handled box is not so indispensable.
It is beginning to turn to stone.

II

The open air is still. The flowers are breathing.
They are manufacturing reveries,
Morning in a farmhouse in North Dakota

When a young girl is just waking.
Her body is a field of wild daisies.
We lower a boxful of dark petals.

Thomas James

The cadence of James' poem depends on the association of ideas and
images. We are carried along by the flowers, rain, and flood--the physical
reality of the scene. The flowers take us back in time, when the grandmother
was a child. They bring us to the present, again, as "We lower a boxful
of dark petals." There is hardly any attempt to rhyme--breathing/waking,
reveries/daisies is all and rather weak. The lines are irregular, while the words
are exact. But there is a symmetry to the lines, a cyclical movement from the
present to the past and back to the present. It is charged with delicate
emotional energy that takes the place of metrical rhythm.

James' use and association of metaphors in the last two lines is very
good, as it causes the move from past to present. A metaphor, which says
that a person or object *is* something else, creates an image as a result of the
reference. (A simile, which also creates an association between two
subjects, does so by saying that one thing is *like* another.) The image created
by a metaphor, in turn, conveys the author's meaning through the words. In
the second to the last line, her youthful beauty passionate nature are made
real for us through a direct association with a field of wild daisies. Symbol-

ically, a daisy is a first-rate, or exemplary person. The cadence from past to present is made possible through the second metaphor in the last line: the body in the coffin is *dark petals.* We have death of flowers, death of a grand-mother, and death of us all. The wild daisies--the beautiful child--have become dark petals, an aged corpse. James' comment on mortality of beauty is not unlike Keats' in "Ode On A Grecian Urn." A study of the two poems would be a worthwhile comparison of free verse and a more structured form: one working with cadences and the other more technical rhythms.

A unique rhythm achieved by technical use of metre is Sprung Rhythm. Dating as far back as "Piers Plowman" in the late 14th Century, Milton used it in the chorus of "Samson Agonistes," and it appears in old nursery rhymes, too. But Gerard Manley Hopkins identified and named it at the end of the last century. His use of Sprung Rhythm has popularized it in the 20th Century. Although Hopkins wrote during the 1870s and '80s and died in 1889, the first volume of his work did not appear until 1918.

Hopkins was dissatisfied with the idea that rhythm must be governed by set metrical patterns--so many feet per line, with each foot having a regular number of stressed and unstressed syllables and little choice of variation. Hopkins stressed flexibility of rhythm. To do this, the poet should base rhythm on the stressed syllables and ignore the number of those that are unstressed, he said. The first syllable in a foot was accented and, therefore, the feet might be monosyllabic, trochaic, dactylic or the first paeon. Unavoidably, there is a falling effect to the lines of such poetry, although a poet might split a foot at the end of a line to finish on a stressed syllable. Most critics, including W.B. Yeats, agree that Sprung Rhythm is very difficult to scan, because it is sometimes most difficult to say where the accent should fall.

Generally, Spring Rhythm is characterized by a swinging pace of the lines which is achieved by trochees and first paeons. Hopkins strove to choose exactly the right word so his meaning would explode. This was an idea that the Imagists picked up early in the 20th Century and used effectively.

For example, the following lines are from "Piers Plowman" and were written some 500 years before Hopkins:

In a summer season when soft was the sun
I shaped me into shrouds as if I a shepherd were,
In habit like a hermit, unholy of works,
Went wide in this world, wonders to hear.

Only the stresses have been marked to show the sprung quality of the rhythm that also appears in Hopkins' work which was achieved with the monosyllables, trochees, first paeon, and the uncounted unstressed syllables such as *In a* that open the first line.

Sometimes, in poetry, the emphasis of the ideas will coincide with the metrical emphasis in scanning the lines, but this is not always the case. The technical rhythm and the rhythm of the thoughts may parallel each other in a poem, or the emphasis of thought may run through the lines without regard to stressed and unstressed syllables. For instance in the following lines from Shakespeare's "Sonnet 97", the emphasis of the idea is on absence and the rest of the words and images illustrate, or modify, his feelings about it. But we don't read the word and accentuate it: "How like a winter has my ABSENCE been." Although the word absence contains the essence of the thought, the word is treated like the other iambs:

How like I a wint I er hath I my ab I sence been
From thee, I the pleas I ure of I the fleet I ing year!

The poet should be acutely aware of speech rhythms and try to apply the most effective ones to his or her writing. There are the natural patterns of speech and the images of free verse, the more frigid metrical rhythms of traditional poetry, and the sophisticated swing of Sprung Rhythm.

One of the most easily recognized contributors to rhythm is rhyme. Rhyme has been defined in many ways, but most critics agree that the repetition of identical or closely related sounds at definite intervals creates a regular pattern the reader experiences as a rhythmic entity. For instance, notice the rhythm of seduction created by the end-rhymes in these selected lines from Andrew Marvell's poem "To His Coy Mistress:"

> Had we but world enough, and time,
> This coyness, lady, were no crime.
> We would sit down, and think which way
> To walk, and pass our long love's day.
>
> . . . .
>
> But at my back I always hear
> Time's winged chariot hurrying near;
> And yonder all before us lie
> Deserts of vast eternity.
>
> . . . .
>
> The grave's a fine and private place,
> But none, I think, do there embrace.
>
> . . . .

. . . .
Now let us sport us while we may,
And now, like amorous birds of prey,
Rather at once our time devour
Than languish in his slow-chapped power

The clarity of thought and tone is due in large part to the perfect rhymes of the couplets. In perfect rhyme, such as hear/near, the last accented vowel sounds of the two sounds are the same, as are the following consonant sounds. The consonant sounds preceding the last stressed vowels in the two words must be different. In the lines from "To His Coy Mistress," time/crime, and place/embrace, are perfect rhymes. Notice the correspondence is between stressed syllables. Rhymes on unstressed syllables are very weak: hunting/haying.

Different kinds of rhymes have individual names. A masculine rhyme, for instance, ends on the stressed syllable. In the poem above, lie/eternity is masculine, or *strong*. Marvell would have pronounced the "y" as "i". A feminine, or *weak,* rhyme has two syllables, stressed and unstressed: lying/ dying. Multiple rhymes consist of a stressed syllable followed by two or more unstressed: opportunity/impunity.

In a mixture of masculine and feminine rhymes--hermaphrodite or wrenched rhyme--the masculine rhyme is matched to the last syllable of the feminine.

Analyzed rhyme is a complicated scheme used in quatrains. Given four lines of poetry, the end-rhymes of the first and third lines share a common vowel sound, as do the second and fourth lines. The final consonant sound of the first and fourth lines are the same, as are the sounds of two and three:

I ran through the night,
Looking in vein for stars,
Hearing shots and singing cries
Of guns and my broken heart.

AFG

Imperfect rhyme involves changing the basic vowel sound to create a slant rhyme, as the classic example of love/prove. This is also known as near rhyme, or approximate, embryonic, half, off-rhymes, and paraphones. Assonance is another form of imperfect rhyme. Also called vocalic assonance, the stressed vowels of the words have similar sounds, but the consonants do not. This is different from dissonance in which the consonants before and after the vowel sounds are rhymed, but the vowels are not: better/bitter, vine/vane. In another kind of imperfect rhyme, consonance, the final consonants of stressed syllables of end-words match, but the preceding vowels do not: begun/afternoon.

Rhyme is an important element of poetry, because it helps create the rhythm and it contributes to the poetic effect. But it does not follow that rhyme is the key characteristic of poetry. Nor is it the single most important element of rhythm. Rhyme can add a pleasing effect, but it should never intrude so as to change or limit ideas, mix-up word order, or alter the sense of expression. It is one of many elements that may, or may not be used in writing a poem. Whether it is employed depends on the poet's conception of a poem and poetry in general.

The elements discussed in this chapter, and in the preceding one, are foundations for verse. You cannot write a poem without a knowledge of how these elements function, so that you can decide wisely when to depend on them. Not every element appears in every poem, but some of the elements are used in all poems. You have to discover them, yourself, by reading as much poetry as you can and then practicing over and over. Just as someone cannot compose music without first playing scales, you cannot write worthwhile poetry without learning metres, rhythms and all the elements of verse.

Many kinds of poems have been written in the past, and in this chapter some of the ones that are helpful for a beginning poet to study so as to learn how to write poetry will be discussed. Only small sections of poems are quoted here. It's expected the reader will complement the suggestions by reading the complete works.

Probably the oldest form of poetry is the narrative poem which tells a story about heroic events. The narration is non-dramatic, but epic in scope with an elevated style and central characters who are important to the history of a nation or race. Unpopular today, narrative poetry has a long history in both folk and literary epic and ballad forms. A folk epic is distinct because it lacks certain authorship. Some of the best known folk epics are *The Iliad* and *The Odyssey*, by Homer, an arch-type of a poet who may really have been more than one person; *Beowulf, Mahabharata, El Cid,* and *Song Of Roland.* Literary epics include Dante's *Divina Comedia,* Tasso's *Jerusalem Delivered,* Milton's *Paradise Lost,* Longfellow's *Hiawatha,* Whitman's *Leaves Of Grass.*

The setting in which the legendary, or culturally important characters act is vast and exotic, covering great distances. The scene of Milton's *Paradise Lost* is the universe--Heaven and Hell. Action is superhuman, often drawing on the influence of gods, as in *The Odyssey.* Supernatural forces are always included as inhabitants of the landscape, although they may not always work for the benefit of the heros and heroines. The author's style should be grand, but objective, simple, and straight forward. The opening of *Paradise Lost* represents high epic style which includes the traditional invocation of the Muse to guide the poet's pen in telling the story:

> Of man's first disobedience, and the fruit
> Of that forbidden tree whose mortal taste
> Brought death into the world, and all our woe,

With loss of Eden, till one greater Man
Restore us, and regain the blissful seat,
Sing, Heavenly Muse, that on the secret top
Of oreb, or of Sinai, didst inspire
That shepherd who first taught the chosen seed
In the beginning how the Heavens and Earth
Rose out of Chaos:

Milton's is a Christian epic, with references to Biblical mythology, the story of man's fall and redemption and an invocation of a "Heavenly," not a pagen, Muse. As we discover a few lines later, Milton began *in medias res*, in the middle of things which is traditional epic form. Background material will be worked in later, as well as catalogues of warriors, ships, armies which is good epic style in order to convey to the reader the scope, grandeur, and impressiveness of the story the poem tells.

Here is the opening of The *Odyssey*:
Sing in me, Muse, and through me tell the story
Of that man skilled in all ways of contending,
the wanderer, harried for years on end,
after he plundered the stronghold
on the proud height of Troy.

Another form of narrative poem is the ballad which is a prose legend adapted for singing. The following "Bonny George Campbell" is characteristic of the form. There are mysterious disappearances, suggestions of the supernatural, common people as central characters, a single episode, a domestic setting, lack of characterization, use of dialogue, and repetition of the sense of the second stanza which provides a chilling refrain:

High upon Highlands
    And low upon Tay,
Bonny George Campbell
    Rade out on a day.

Saddled and bridled
    And gallant rade he:
Hame cam his guid horse
    But never cam he.

Out cam his auld mither,
    Greeting fusair,
And out cam his bonny bride,
    Riving her hair.

Saddled and bridled
    And booted rade he:
Toom hame cam the saddle,
    But never cam he.

"My meadow lies gree,
    And my corn is unshorn,
My bar is to build,
    And my babe is unborn."

Saddled and bridled
    And booted rade he:
Toom hame cam the saddle,
    But never cam he.

Dramatic poetry, another verse genre, includes plays, dramatic monologues, and dramatic lyrics. The form may make use of most dramatic elements to achieve poetic effect. Shakespeare's plays in blank verse are examples of dramatic poetry as are such famous closet dramas as Shelley's "Prometheus Unbound" and "The Cenci." Robert Browning's "Pippa Passes" is characteristic of the form. More popular among modern poets is dramatic monologue. T.S. Eliot's *Love Song of J. Alfred Prufrock* is well known. Browning used dramatic monologue in *My Last Duchess.* From the conversation, the reader is able to tell the circumstances--past and present--and to understand the central characters; the duke speaks:

That's my last Duchess painted on the wall,
Looking as if she were alive. I call
That piece a wonder, now: Fra Pandolf's hands
Worked busily a day, and there she stands.
Will't please you sit and look at her? I said,
"Fra Pandolf" by design, for never read
Strangers like you that pictured countenance,
The depth and passion of its earnest glance,
But to myself they turned (since non puts by
The curtain I have drawn for you, but I)
And seemed as they would ask me, if they durst,
How such a glance came there; so, not the first
Are you to turn and ask thus. Sir, twas not
Her husband's presence only, call that spot
Of joy into the Duchess' cheek: perhaps
Fra Pandolf chanced to say, "Her mantle laps
Over my lady's wrist too much," or "Paint

Must never hope to reproduce the faint
Half-flush that dies along her throat.": such stuff
Was courtesy, she thought, and cause enough
For calling up that spot of joy. She had
A heart--how shall I say--too soon made glad,
Too easily impressed. . . .

Lyric poetry is the most inclusive. Hymns, sonnets, songs, odes, elegies are among the many forms. This broad category includes such French forms as ballade, rondel, and rondeau. As Thrall, Hibbard, and Holman point out in their *Handbook To Literature*, lyric poetry is not so much a form as a way of writing in which subjectivity, imagination, melody, and emotion are the primary elements. Free verse can be lyric as well as the most structured of forms. In general, the basis for lyric poetry is the personal expression of the poet's emotional state:

Shall I compare thee to a summer's day?
Thou art more lovely and more temperate:
Rough winds do shake the darling buds of May,
And summer's lease hath all too short a date:
Sometime too hot the eye of heaven shines,
And often is his gold complexion dimmed;
And every fair from fair sometimes declines,
By chance or nature's changing course untrimmed:
But thy eternal summer shall not fade,
Nor lose possession of that fair thou ow'st ;
Nor shall death brag thou wander'st in his shade,
When in eternal lines to time thou grow'st:
So long as men can breathe, or eyes can see,
So long lives this, and this gives life to thee.

Shakespeare's Sonnet 18 certainly shows the poet's emotional state. Structurally, the sonnet is made up of three quatrains with their own rhyme patterns, and the poem ends with a rhymed couplet. The verses are iambic pentameter. The musical quality comes from the pattern of the rhymes contained within the fourteen lines. As a result, emotional energy is compressed and heightened by the limitations of line length and the total number of lines.

Anyone learning about poetry should understand two other sonnet forms: Petrarchan or Italian, and Spenserian. The first poems of a sonnet form were written in Italy in the 13th Century. The form was later developed and made popular by the 14th Century Italian poet, Petrarch. The Petrarchan sonnet consists of two parts--an octave and sestet. The rhyme scheme of the octave is *abba, abba;* while the sestet may be *cde, cde; cdc, cdc;* or *cde, dce.* The octave must contain some problem and the sestet offer an answer. As in any other poetry form, the structure is not always adhered to and individual poets may make changes to suite their own purposes. Good poets play successfully with form, while bad poets always read as having made mistakes.

The beginning poet should stick with accepted form until it is mastered, just as in painting one must know how to draw, apply paint to the canvas, break up space into a good composition, master perspective and dimension before experimenting. All the arts have this characteristic: their structural elements must be mastered before the rules can be broken and revolutionary uses made of those elements. Creativity and innovation in art follows a period of learning in which the most outdated and time worn procedures must be learned in order to modify and discard. Paint thrown on a canvas, or words typed randomly on a page by a novice may be interesting, but is not art. Art is calculated illusion and nothing in art should be accidental. Certainly a formal structure such as a Spenserean sonnet makes this apparent. The sonnet is of three quatrains and a couplet. There are linking rhymes between the quatrains: *abab, bcbc, cdcd, ee.* It might best be thought of as a combination of the English and Italian sonnets.

There is another form of poetry, blank verse, which is a line of unrhymed iambic pentameter, strictly speaking. But as a general category it includes any line length and any metre as long as the lines are unrhymed. The form is usually found in long poems that are of great significance with fine, noble subjects and sublime expression. Effect is achieved by the placement of stresses which may vary from the iambic penatmeter pattern and by the use of pauses (caesura).

Although free verse has been in vogue in Western literature in the 20th Century, it is not a new form of poetry. Many of the great poems of the Bible were written in free verse, as the Psalms and Song of Solomon. Primarily, free verse has served to liberate poets from the cumbersom structures of the past that seem outdated. Again, the basic units in traditional poetic structures are the foot, line, and stanza. In free verse, the unit is a strophe. Like a paragraph in prose writing, the strophe is a unit of thought rather than a metrical unit of verse. But free verse is not prose because of distinct cadences that are poetic in their rhythms and unique to individual poems. Whereas prose has an extended sense of style that is unpoetical because of length, and a more liesurely attitude toward description, metaphor, and image. Poetry, whether a sonnet or a dramatic monologue, says a great deal in a few words, depending on a compression of thought and language, while prose in short story or novel form conveys ideas in terms of lengthy development of character and situation.

The cadence of free verse is subtle and is larger as a concept of communication than metre. but it is not so free in its execution as prose because it involves an emphasis of rhythm that is easily recognizable as being poetic. The works of Carl Sandberg or Amy Lowell are good examples of this genre.

Conclusion

The emphasis in the preceding chapters, and in the glossary that follows, is on the elements of poetry that a beginning poet should know in order to pursue the task of writing good verse. Writing successful poetry is an art. Anyone can put words on a page in order to say how they feel, what they think, where their emotions are in relationship to the rest of the world. Nearly everyone has felt the urge to write a poem. But those who wish their work to be taken seriously by editors must study the elements of good poetry. This section shows what goes into writing a poem. It does not tell *how* to write a poem. No poet can teach someone else how to write a great poem any more than Picasso could have taught a young artist to paint with genius.

Advice and criticism can be given. Whether the individual response will meet expectations is an unanswerable question. Shakespeare never took a college course in creative writing, but he was aware of what was being written by others. If you really want to be a good poet, read all the good poetry you can get your hands on. Study the history of poetry. Read the poets and critics of poetry who make up the poetic tradition in our literature. Imitate the works of our great poets, as you begin, until you understand how they achieved success. Then write your own poems building on what they learned.

BIBLIOGRAPHY

Abrams, M.H., et al. *The Norton Anthology Of English Literature, Vols.1 & 2.* New York: W.W. Norton & Co., Inc. 1962.

Altenbernd, Lynn, Lewis, Leslie L. A *Handbook For The Study of Poetry.* New York: MacMillan Co. 1966.

Barnard, Ellsworth, ed. *Shelley Selected Poems Essays and Letters.* New York: Odyssey Press. 1944.

Beatty, Richard Croom, et al. *The American Tradition In Literature, Revised.* New York: W.W. Norton & Co. Inc. 1962.

Beaty, Jerome, Matchett, William H. *Poetry,* New York: Oxford University Press. 1965.

Bennett, J.A. W., et al. *Early Middle English Verse and Prose.* Oxford: Oxford University Press. 1968.

Boynton, Robert W., Mack, Maynard. *Introduction To The Poem.* New York: Hayden Book Co. 1965.

Breduold, Louis I., ed. *Lord Byron Don Juan and Other Satirical Poems.* New York: The Odssey Press. 1935.

Cawley, A.C., ed. *Geoffry Chaucer Canterbury Tales.* London: J.M. Dent & Sons LTD. 1958.

Chew, Samuel C., ed. *Lord Byron Childe Harold's Pilgrimage And Other Romantic Poems.* New York: The Odyssey Press. 1936.

Deutsch, Babette. *Poetry Handbook, 4th Edition.* New York: Funk & Wagnalls. 1974.

Eliot, T.S. *On Poetry & Poets.* New York: Farrar, Straus, & Co. 1957.

Hamilton, Anne. *The Seven Principles of Poetry.* Boston: The Writer, Inc. 1940.

Hibbard, Addison, et al. *A Handbook To Literature.* New York: The Odyssey Press. 1960.

Hillyer, Robert. *First Principles Of Verse.* Boston: The Writer Inc. 1967.

Holmes, John. *Writing Poetry.* Boston: The Writer Inc. 1966.

Korg, Jacob. *The Force Of New Words.* New York: Holt, Rinehart & Winston, Inc. 1966.

Kreuzer, James R. *Elements of Poetry.* New York: MacMillan. 1955.

Lewis, C. Day. *Poetry For You.* New York: Oxford University Press. 1947.

Spender, Stephen. *The Making of a Poem.* New York: W.W. Norton Inc. 1962

Thorpe, Clarence DeWitt, ed. *John Keats Complete Poems and Selected Letters.* New York: Odyssey Press Inc. 1935.

Abstract poem: one in which words are used for their auditory value with little concern for their ordinary connotations. Similar to abstract painting in which colors and shapes are arranged which do not represent physical objects, an abstract poem achieves its effect through patterns of sounds, rhymes, and rhythms. Obvious meaning, or sense, is not a concern of the poet as much as overall impressions. Dame Edith Sitwell who named this kind of verse is probably best known for her collection of abstract poems, *Facade.*

Acatalectic: the term is applied to a line of poetry that is metrically complete, representing the basic metrical pattern of the poem. For instance, a line of iambic pentameter from a Shakespearean sonnet would reflect the basic meter of the poem.

Accent: emphasis in language in reference to a single syllable, word, thought, or metrical unit. Accent may be called stress, although some critics reserve accent for refering to syllables and stress for whole words. The three basic kinds of accent are *word accent,* which is the proper stress on the syllables: *thought accent,* which is the natural stress on the important rhetorical points, and *metrical accent,* which emphasizes the stresses according to a metrical beat. In poetry, the natural accents of speech are made to coincide with the metrical patterns of stressed and unstressed units. Rhetorical accent, or the emphasis of the thoughts, may not always correspond with the metrical and the word accents. This is acceptable, but when the metrical accent destroys or alters the natural accent the result is called *wrenched accent.*

Alcaics: named after the Greek poet Alcaeus, this manner of writing verse is characterized by poems of four stanzas in length, with each stanza four lines long, and each line containing four stresses. The best example of alcaics in English poetry is Alfred Lord Tennyson's "Milton."

Alexandrine: a twelve syllable line (six iambic feet), it is the *heroic verse* in Old French Romances of the 12th and 13th Centuries, concerning Alexander The Great. Thrall, Hibbard, and Holman in their *A Handbook to Literature* suggest that the line receives its name from a French poet, Alexander Paris, who often used the line. The classical French alexandrine is characterized by two principal stresses on the sixth and last syllable and a floating light stress that may fall anywhere in the line. The metre of classical tragedy in French, the alexandrine was later used with great flexibility. The number of syllables may range from eight to fourteen and the number and place of the stresses may vary.

Two English poets writing in the 16th Century, Sir Thomas Wyatt, The Elder, and Henry Howard, Earl of Surrey, are usually credited with introducing the alexandrine into English poetry. The greatest example in English, however, is Spenser's use of the line in creating the Spenserian Stanza by adding the verse of iambic hexameter after a stanza of eight lines of pentameter from Chaucer's "Monk's Tale."

Alexander Pope's couplet, which ends with an alexandrine, sums up the use and abuse of the line:

A needless Alexandrine ends the song,
That, like a wounded snake, drags its slow length along.

Allegory: a form of *extended metaphor,* allegory is a narrative in which persons, events, and objects have meaning outside the context of the story. The material in an allegory must attract the reader's attention both for the story and for the ideas that the events, characters, and situations convey. The allegorical meaning of a narrative may be political, moral, religious, personal, or satiric. For instance, Bunyan's *Pilgrim's Progress* allegorically is a moral and religious treatise disguised as a story about a pilgrimage. The key to allegory is that the ideas have a formative influence on the story.

Symbolism is different from allegory because it doesn't have that kind of influence while it attempts to suggest more than one level of meaning.

Famous allegories include *The Faerie Queene* and *Gulliver's Travels.* Some examples of allegory are parables, fables, apologues, and beast epics.

Alliteration: consonantal alliteration occurs with the repetition, or echo, of initial consonant sounds which are the same. For instance, this line from Poe's *The City In The Sea:*

(Time-eaten towers that tremble not!)

Vowel alliteration follow the same pattern, as in this line from "Piers Plowman":

In a somer seson. Whan soft was the sonne,

Sometimes called *head rhyme* and *initial rhyme,* alliteration was first used in Anglo-Saxon poetry in which the consonants marked the stresses and the vowels alliterated with each other.

Amphibrach: a metrical foot in a verse of poetry made up of three syllables which are unaccented-accented-unaccented.

Amphimacer: a foot of verse with three syllables which are accented-unaccented-accented.

Anacrusis: one or more unstressed syllables at the beginning of a line of poetry that appears before the metrical pattern of the line begins. In the following stanza by Shelley, the word "From" begins the third line, while the lines before and after start with accented syllables:

What thou are we know not:
What is most like thee?
From rainbow clouds there flow not
Drops so bright to see
As from thy presence showers a rain of melody.

Anapest: a metrical foot of verse of two unaccented syllables followed by one accented syllable.

Anthology: a collection of an author's or authors' writings, usually poems. Literally, the word means a gathering of flowers. *The Anthology* refers to the collection of some 4500 short Greek poems composed about 490 B.C. to 1000 A.D. Among the great anthologies of the world are the Bible and the Koran.

Anistrophe: see *Ode*

Assonance: a similarity of two vowel sounds followed by dissimilar consonants in two or more stressed syllables, as in afterwards and absently.

Ballad: part of a culture's oral or spoken history, it is an anonymous narrative song. A ballad is characterized by alteration from one generation to the next without ever being written down. A ballad may have been founded on legend and old romance. There is usually a romantic theme which is impersonally handled in simple language. Strict rhymes are not necessary. The *ballad stanza* is characteristically *abcb* with four syllables in the first line, three in the second, four in the third, and three again in the fourth. Common to our culture are the ballads of the English-Scottish border region from the late Middle Ages; ballads of the American frontier of the last two centuries; ballads of the Southern Appalachian mountains in the United States; the bush ballads of Australia, and the calypso music of the West Indies. Some common

English ballads are "Lord Randall," "Edward," "Barbara Allan," "The Wife of Usher's," "The Three Ravens," "Bonny George Campbell," and "Robin Hood and the Three Squires."

The *literary ballad* is one written by a known author in imitation of the folk versions. Keats, Coleridge, Kipling, and Dylan Thomas wrote ballads.

Ballade: a French verse form of great popularity, the ballade is complicated and of unique structure. The ballade is most often composed of three stanzas with an envoy following as a summary statement of the thought which is addressed to an important person or personification.

The number of lines to a stanza and the number of syllables per line may vary from poet to poet. Most critics recognize three common characteristics, however: a refrain containing the basic that appears at the end of the stanzas and the envoy: the envoy, itself; and three or four rhymes in the poem which appear in the same place in each stanza, all dissimilar, except in the refrain.

The most common ballade form is the eight line stanza, *ababbcbc*, with *bcbc* as the envoy. Another is the 10-liner in pentameter, *ababccdcd*, with the envoy as *ccdcd*. The envoy is usually half the length of the stanza.

Chaucer's "Balade de bon Conseyl" is an example of the form, as well as Swinburne's version of Francois Villon's "Ballade of the Hanged," or Rossetti's rendering of Villon's "Ballade of Dead Ladies."

A double ballade is made up of six octaves, or 10-line stanzas. There may be three, sometimes four rhymes and a refrain, but hardly ever an envoy in this variation.

There have been *triple ballades* of nine octaves and an envoy written. *Chant royal* is still another version of the ballade using five stanzas of 11-lines, with a five-line envoy and refrain. The rhyme scheme here is *ababccddede*, with *ddede* as the envoy.

Beginning rhyme: rhyme in the initial syllable or syllables of a verse.

Blank verse: unrhymed lines of poetry. Milton defined blank verse as "English Heroic verse, without rime. . . ."

Broken rhyme: the questionable practice of dividing a word at the end of a line in order to create a rhyme.

Cacaphony: denotes a harsh, unpleasant mixture of sounds and tones.

Cadence: as an element of movement in verse, such as rhythm, cadence has to do with the recurrence of stress and with rising and falling patterns of thought and speech in poetry. While rhythm is created by metrical patterns, cadence is less structured, less regular, less objective in its elements. Cadence gives a feeling of patterned movement where strict metrical structure is lacking.

Caesura: a stop in a line of poetry. A caesura is used to divide a foot between two words. It often appears in the middle of a verse although diversity may be achieved by placing it anywhere in the line.

Canto: a unit, section, or division of a long poem. Such poems as Byron's *Childe Harold's Pilgrimage,* Dante's D*ivina Comedia,* and Pound's *The Cantos* are divided into cantos.

Carmen Figuratum: also called *concrete poetry,* or *picture poems,* carmen figuratum is a poem written to look like, or represent the form suggested by the subject.

Catalexis: dropping the last syllable (unaccented) of the last foot in a line of verse. This is also called *truncation.* Catalexis is used to achieve metric variation. When it occurs at the start of a line, dropping the unaccented syllable makes the verse *headless.* Lines in which catalexis does not occur are called *acatalectic.*

Choriambus: a metric foot of two accented syllables enclosing two unaccented, such as "year upon year."

Cinquain: a five-line poem with lines of two, four, six, eight, and two syllables. Invented by the poet Adelaide Crapsey, it is an Americanized version of Japanese *haiku.*

Closed couplet: one line of poetry following another with a rhyme of *aa* in which a single thought is completely contained.

Common measure: also known as *common metre* and the *hymnal stanza,* common measure consists of a quatrain, *abcb,* or *abab,* with the first and third verses in iambic tetrameter and the second and fourth in iambic trimeter. Common measure (CM) is one of a number of variations such as *Short measure* (SM), another quatrain with an *abab* or *abcb* rhyme scheme. In SM, the third verse is in tetramter and the first, second, and fourth are trimeter. *Long measure* (LM) uses either rhyme scheme, but all four verses are in iambic tetrameter. *Common particular measure* is a stanza of six lines with tetrameter in the first, second, fourth, and fifth verses and trimeter in the third and sixth. *Short particular measure* has trimeter in the first, second, fourth, and fifth verses, with tetrameter in the third and sixth.

Compensation: the substituting of pauses or rests for omitted stresses which are usually unaccented as in these lines by Tennyson:

Break, break, break,
   On thy cold grey stones, O Sea!

The compensation comes in the first line in which rests should follow each "break" which are the three accented syllables in the line.

Consonance: also called *half-rhyme,* and *slant rhyme,* consonance occurs when the consonants in the last stressed syllables of two lines of poetry rhyme but the vowels that precede them do not, as in deed/dead, jump/cramp.

Couplet: two verses together with similar end-rhymes and often in the same meter. The *closed couplet* is always grammatically complete. An *open couplet* is one in which the sense is run-on from line to line in a series of couplets. Variations on the *heroic couplet* include Dryden's addition of an alexandrine creating three lines on the same rhyme. The *short couplet* is iambic, or trochaic tetrameter and is characteristically octosyllabic.

Crown of Sonnets: a series of seven sonnets which are interconnected by having the last line of the first sonnet as the first line of the second and so on, until the last line of the seventh sonnet is the first line of the first. John Donne's "La Corona" is an example of the difficult piece of versification.

Dactyl: a metrical foot of poetry of three syllables: accented followed by two unaccented.

Decasyllabic verse: a 10 syllable line which was best used by Milton in Paradise Lost:

As he I our dark I ness can I not we I his light
Imitate when we please?

Denotation: the literal definition of a word free from emotional influence.

Didactic poetry: verses that are meant to teach. They emphasize ideas, theory, dogma, rather than emotional feelings, or sensuous understanding. Usually, didactic poetry is tedious, pedantic, boring. At its best it's seen in the works of Alexander Pope in a poem such as *Essay On Criticism:*

   'Tis hard to say, if greater want of skill
Appear in writing or in judging ill;
But of the two less dangerous is the offense
To tire our patience than mislead our sense.

Dimeter: a line of poetry consisting of two feet.

Dissonance: an abrupt interruption in the music of the poetry. Characterized by harsh words, phrases, and inharmonious sounds. Sometimes dissonance is used intentionally for effect. But if it occurs unintentionally, it is a major flaw. Dissonance may apply to rhymes that have slight variations in vowel sounds, enough to prevent them from being perfect rhymes.

Distich: a couplet in classical elegiacs.

Distributed stress: also called *hovering accent,* or *resolved stress,* it is a term used to describe a situation in which the reader is uncertain on which of two consecutive syllables to place the stress.

Doggerel: less than perfect poetry (often quite bad) which is sometimes unintentionally humorous, or absurdly truthful. Mark Twain summoned up an example of doggerel by the morbid young character Emmeline Grangerford, in *Huckleberry Finn:*

> And did young Stephen sicken
> > And did young Stephen die?
> And did the sad hearts thicken
> > And did the mourners Cry?
> No; such was not the fate of
> > Young Stephen Dowling Bots;
> Though sad hearts round him thickened,
> > Twas not from sickness' shots.
> . . . .

Double rhyme: also called *feminine rhyme,* identical stressed syllables are followed by the same unstressed. For instance, say/hay is a rhyme; saying/haying is a double rhyme.

Elegiac: a classical form currently used to describe poetry expressing lamentation. Originally, elegiac was used in the *distich* in classical poetry; the metre is made up of a verse of dactylic hexameter and then one of pentameter. Most popular in Germany, Longfellow's translation of Schiller's couplet offers an example:

> So the Hexameter, rising and singing, with cadence sonorous,
> > Fall, and in refluent rhythm back the Pentamater flows.

Elegy : a poem of meditation on death, loss, or other grave subjects. Characteristically, elegy has come to mean any poem in which the author dwells on his or her sentiments. Well known eligies in English are the Old English poem "The Wanderer", Chaucer's "The Book Of The Duchess," Donne's

"Elegies," Grey's "Elegy Written in a Country Churchyard," Shelley's "Adonais," Yeats' "In Memory of Major Robert Gregory," Tennyson's "In Memoriam," and Whitman's "When Lilacs Last in the Dooryard Bloomed."

Elision: o're for over, th' for the, ne'er for never are examples of one kind of elision--the leaving out of letters, or syllables to enhance the reading of a verse. In another kind of elision, syllables are slurred in order to strengthen the stress value of the line, to quicken the pace, to add tension.

End-rhyme: rhymes occurring at the ends of verses.

End-stopped lines: ones in which the sense and the grammatical structure coincide at the end of a line without running on to the next.

Epic: a long poem in narrative form that tells the adventures of a single hero of great stature. This central character is usually of importance to the history or tradition of a locale. The style of such a poem is elevated. There are folk epics such as *The Iliad* and *The Odyssey* which are of questionable authorship and literary epics written by known authors in imitation of folk epics such as Milton's *Paradise Lost.*

Equivalence: a form of *compensation* in metrics in which a foot other than the one expected appears in a line of poetry. The substitute should be the same length as the expected foot, as an iamb when a trochee is expected.

Eye-rhyme: rhyme that appears perfect by spelling but is *slant* or *half-rhyme* according to pronunciation, such as hatch/watch.

Feminine-ending: also called *light-ending,* the term applies to an unstressed syllable at the end of a line in iambic or anapestic metre. Most often used in blank verse, feminine-endings give a lightness to the poetry.

Feminine-rhyme: see *double-rhyme.*

Foot: the basic metrical unit in poetry. A foot consists of syllables accented and unaccented, according to the stress, and functions as a unit of metrical rhythm.

Fourteener: a verse fourteen syllables long, usually in seven iambs.

Free Verse: a descriptive term coined in France in the 1880's, *vers libre,* referring to the poetry of the day that rebelled against strict formal requirements. In English poetry the outstanding characteristics of free verse are lack of adherence to metrical structures, the use of cadence rather than metrical rhythm, and the substitute of strophe (a thought unit in stanza form) for foot or verse as the basic unit in a poem.

Free verse is a self-defining term in that it may be as free of form as the author wishes and is not limited to a set style or period in literary history. The great songs of the Bible are written in free verse, such as the Psalms and the Song of Solomon. Whitman's poetry is written in free verse, as are many of the works of Milton, Dryden, Blake, Arnold, Pound, and Wallace Stevens.

Haiku: a form of poetry which is very structural with three lines. There are five syllables in the first verse, seven in the second and five in the third. The poetry is intended to create an exact picture of an emotional mood. A Japanese form, haiku had great influence on the Imagist poets earlier in the 20th Century and has been popular with Post-World War II poets, as well. A related form is the *tanka* composed of five lines with the first and third lines having five syllables and the second, fourth and fifth seven syllables, 31 in all.

Half-rhyme: see *consonance.*

Heptameter: a line of poetry containing seven metrical feet.

Heroic couplet: two rhymed lines of iambic pentameter. Heroic couplets were used by Chaucer in "The Legend Of A Good Woman." In the 17th Century heroic couplets were used in poetic drama. The heroic couplet is most often associated with the works of Alexander Pope.

Hexameter: a line of poetry containing six metrical feet.

Iamb: a metrical foot of two syllables with the first one unaccented followed by a second accented.

Ictus: the stress, itself, on an accented syllable.

Image: a verbal communication of a sense perception. An image not only represents the subject, as in a metaphor, or compares it as in a simile, it includes the sensuality, as well. An image is a concrete appeal to the imagination which is asked to appreciate an aspect of existence within an object or person.

A sculpture of a person, for instance, is a concrete image through which the beholder sees the essence of the subject recreated in stone. The same kind of comparison in poetry creates the image which evokes a desired response in the reader, a twisted hand as an image of anguish, for instance. Or, as in Donne's simile:

And like a bunch of ragged carrets stand
The short swolen fingers of thy gouty hand.

The image of goutiness is felt in the simile by the mention of the commonplace *carrets* as the hand. The *carrets* represent the hand, the hand like the *carrets* as a blending of identities which creates the successful image.

Images may evoke a uniformly expected response, or they may mean different things to different readers, just as images may have literal or figurative meanings.

There is thought, idea and calculation in an image. It might be argued that all poetry is image making, if you consider a broad definition of the term as a means of representing thought in word pictures. The essence of poetry is found in the images a poet creates to make clear his or her vision. Images are weak when they fail to truly represent the poet's intentions. They are strong when they capture exactly what the author wants to say. In a sense, then, judging an image is a subjective process appealing strongly to the imagination. An objective image is a contradiction in terms.

We feel the truth of an image, instinctively, in a subjective, irrational way. We experience the image while we read the words and the effect is in the image itself. It is firm, clear, and concrete in its outline. It stimulates greater understanding.

Poets who used the image to develop a genre known as Imagism in the first quarter of the 20th Century include Ezra Pound, William Carlos Williams, John Gould Fletcher, Amy Lowell, and Carl Sandburg.

Inversion: defined as the conscious reversing of the normal word order for poetic effect in order to give extraordinary emphasis and to keep a particular metre or rhyme scheme. There is really little excuse for inversion. Poetic effect is achieved by writing good poetry, not by inverting words to make them look, or sound poetic. Today, certainly, inversion is treated with suspicion as a cheap way to write poetry.

Ionic: a classical metrical foot consisting of four syllables, the first two accented followed by two unaccented. This is called *a greater ionic,* strictly speaking. When the syllables are arranged with the two unstressed ones first, it is a *lesser ionic.*

Lay: a short poem in four stress couplets meant to be sung. Scott's "Lay of the Last Minstrel" is an example of a literary version of this form of narrative verse. Folk lays, which were actually sung, are rooted deep in Anglo-Saxon and French cultural history.

Light stress: words that are not emphatically stressed or accented in normal speech receive a light emphasis in a line of poetry, words such as *a, and, an, the,* and so on.

Light verse: poetry in a humorous, or nonsensical vein which includes *limerick, parody, epigrams, clerihews, occasional verse,* and *vers de societe.*

Entertainment is its primary purpose. Anything didactic, heavily intellectual, or serious is not allowed. Light verse may be satiric, but it must be kept at a bantering level. It is often lyric in style.

Limerick: humorous poetry of three long and two short lines, *aabba*. Written in anapests, the first, second, and fifth lines have three feet and the third and fourth lines have two feet. Chiefly concerned with manners and morals, the limerick was popularized by Edward Lear's *Book on Nonsense* publishes in 1846. Lear is said to have discovered the form in this anonymous limerick:

There was an old man of Tobago
Who lived on rice, gruel and sago:
Till, much to his bliss,
His physician said this:
To a leg, sir, of mutton you may go

The limerick has gained its widest popularity for the chances it offers one to be cleverly obscene.

Long Measure: four lines of iambic tetrameter.

Lyric: a kind of poetry characterized by a strong expression of the poet's personal feelings. Lyric poetry is probably the most inclusive of all poetic genres—sonnet, songs, odes, hymns, elegies, ballade, rondel, rondeau, ballads, and free verse. There is a heightened use of subjectivity, imagination, melody, and emotion. There is no single lyric structure, but the various forms mentioned provide their own structures.

Macron: the symbol —, or / to show a long, *stressed, or accented* syllable.

Masculine rhyme: when the rhyme falls on the stressed and final syllable of the rhyme-words, the rhyme is said to be masculine, as in strike/bike.

Measure: a term meaning a metrical foot in poetry.

Metaphor: using language to imply a relationship between objects to enhance our appreciation of one or the other, or both. The similarity of elements of the first object to elements of the second creates an emotional and intellectual bond between the two. In the following metaphor from *J 76*, Emily Dickinson compares an event with a feeling and finds enough similarity to define exultation as the exhalaration of an *inland soul* going off to sea:

Exultation is the going
Of an inland soul to sea.—
Past the houses, past the head-
   lands,
Into deep eternity!

In the critic I.A. Richards' terms, the tenor of the metaphor is the idea, here exultation. The vehicle conveys the idea—the image of the land-lubber experiencing a sea voyage

A *complex* or *telescoped metaphor* is one in which the vehicle becomes the tenor of another closely related metaphor. A *subdued metaphor* is one that exists only by implication.

A good metaphor is more than a decorative comparison in which an idea or person is represented by other things. The metaphor must be *organic* in the sense that it is *alive* in a functional way. The vehicle must present a specific tenor in which the vehicle may be read symbolically. The tenor may be the power of faith and the vehicle may be roses, crosses, the seasons, the sun, the moon and stars which are conveyers of the tenor that can be seen as religious symbols of faith. It is a far more complex, or living metaphor than one that represents faith as a shield against despair, as a knight's armor.

A *mixed metaphor* is one which makes such an absurd comparison that the reader is unable to suspend his or her disbelief and accept the image. An example would be: the thunder storm was a furious one and brought a rain of ballbearings on our heads. To unmix the metaphor, an author might say, the thunder storm was a furious one and brought a rain of irrational spite on our heads. It's easy to see the thunder storm as a vehicle for the tenor of spiteful nature.

Metre: in poetry the pattern of movement established by the recurrence of similar units of rhythm. A *quantitative* rhythmic pattern is classical metre established through the use of long syllables and short syllables in regular succession. *Accentual* patterns are determined by the occurrence of stressed, or accented, syllables without regard to the unstressed, or unaccented, syllables. Both *sprung rhythm* and Old English Versification use accentual patterns. Another rhythmic pattern is *syllabic.* Although the accent varies, the number of syllables per line is predetermined. A fourth pattern is one in which the number of syllables and the number of accents are set.

The *foot* is the basic unit of rhythm. The basic feet are iambic, trochaic, anapestic, dactylic, spondaic, and pyrrhic. The number of feet per line is another element of metre. The standard lines in English poetry are monometer, dimeter, trimeter, tetrameter, pentameter, hexameter, heptameter.

Metonymy: using a word related to the subject for the subject itself: the administration advised Congress to accept its economic package. Here, the administration means the President.

Monometer: a line of poetry of one metrical foot in length.

Narrative poem: a poem of any length that tells a story in a narrative, non-dramatic way.

Objective Correlative: the use of objects, persons, circumstances, situations, and events to evoke the correct emotional response in a reader that the author has in mind without directly refering to the emotion. A term first used by T.S. Eliot, he said that an objective correlative was the formula of a particular emotion that will always evoke that emotion under the correct circumstances, "when the external facts, which must terminate in sensory experience, are given . . . ."

Occasional verse: poetry written specifically to mark an event such as a birthday, national holiday, or a death.

Octameter: a line of poetry eight feet long.

Octave: usually the term is used in reference to the first eight lines of an Italian sonnet; a division of such a poem is called an octave. The last six lines are the *sestet.*   In an Italian sonnet the octave rhymes *abba abba.* An octave may also be a complete poem of eight lines.

Octosyllabic verse: a line of poetry made up of eight syllables.

Ode: an elaborately designed lyric poem which is enthusiastic and exalted in tone and which has a fixed purpose dealing with a dignified theme.

The *regular,* or *Pindaric Ode,* which is of classical origin, was a part of Greek dramatic poetry. It consists of three parts: *strophe, anti-strophe,* and *epode.* The strophe in the ode originally refered to the first turning across the stage of the dramatic chorus, which sang as it moved to one side. The *counterturn,* or anti-strophe represented the reversal of the chorus' direction, and the epode was sung while the chorus was standing still at the end of the play.

The strophe and anti-strophe in a regular ode should be similar in form, while the epode is always unique. Metrics and line-lengths may vary within a strophe, but when the strophe is repeated within the ode (strophe, anti-strophe and epode are repeated four times) the metrics and line-lengths should be similar, only with different rhymes. Sometimes, strophe, anti-strophe and epode will not alternate regularly within the ode. The epode may appear only at the end, or inconsistently through-out.

The *homostrophic,* or *Horatian Ode,* is a form containing one stanza-type which is repeated. But both the Horatian and the *Irregular Ode,* a third type, are characterized by great freedom within the strophe. However, in the irregular ode, all pretense to order may be given up and no recognizable stanza pattern emerge. Line lengths may vary, as well as the number of lines per stanza. The poet's mood will determine the pace of the metrical movement.

Examples of the three kinds of odes in English poetry include the earliest of the Pindaric form, Jonson's ode to the memory of "Sir Lucius Carey and Sir Henry Morison;" Collins "Ode To Evening" and Keats' "Ode On A Grecian Urn" are Horatian Odes, while a well known example of the irregular ode by a modern poet is Allen Tate's "Ode On The Confederate Dead."

Onomatopoeia: words used so that their sound, or pronunciation, imitates the sound, or meaning, of the subject. The example most often cited is from Tennyson's "The Princess:"

The moan of doves in immemorial elms,
And murmuring of innumerable bees.

Ottava Rima: a stanza of eight iambic pentameter verses rhyming abababcc. Originated by the Italian poet Boccaccio, English poets adopted the form and examples of it can be found in the works of Milton, Spenser, Keats, and Byron.

Paeon: a metrical foot made up of one stressed and three unstressed syllables. The stressed syllable floats from first to last position. Paeons are called first, second, third, or fourth depending on the position of the stressed syllable.

Pantoum: a poem containing an indefinite series of quatrains in which the second and fourth lines of the quatrains appear as the first and third lines in the following. In the final quatrain of such a poem, the second and fourth lines must repeat the first and third lines of the opening quatrain. The form was originally taken by the French from the Malaysian literary tradition and somewhat resembles the *vilanelle.*

Pastoral: a poem treating rustic life, particularly shepherds and other herdsmen in exaltion of their life-style. A form of pastoral is the *idyl,* which is a short poem praising country life. Another is the *ecologue,* or *bucolic* also dealing approvingly with country themes, but usually in the form of a dialogue between two herdsmen. There are pastoral lyrics, eligies, dramas and epics, such as Milton's "Lycidas," Shelley's "Adonais," and Spenser's "The Shepherdes Calender."

Pathetic fallacy: a critical term to denote a writer's overly impassioned attribution of human emotions to nature. In general, the pathetic fallacy refers to any false emotionalism that leads to an overly sympathetic or elaborate description of nature.

Pentameter: a line of poetry five feet long.

Pathos: the tenor, or quality, in writing that evokes pity, tenderness, or sorrow.

Personification: attributing human characteristics to inanimate objects, to animals, to abstractions, or to ideas, in a figure of speech.

Poem: a structural reference to a composition which is characterized by the presence of imagination, truth, emotion, sense perception, and specific language. Movement is achieved through rhythms that may involve formal elements such as rhyme, metre, and stanzaic structure. The use of metaphors and similes to create images is characteristic of poetry. The language is heightened by compressing as much meaning into as few words as possible, to create effects of great emotional and aesthetic impact. Any poem represents the *idea of poetry,* although the definition of poetry is highly subjective, mutable, and depends on the attitudes of the specific period of history in which a poem is being written and evaluated.

Poet: generally someone actively involved in the craft of writing poems. A person may be a poet, and have poetic sensitivity, and never write a verse. As the 16th Century English poet Sir Philip Sidney said, "One may be a Poet without versing, and a versifyer without Poetry."

Poetic diction: language used specifically because it separates poetry from prose. Poetic diction developed to its extreme creates a special vocabulary for use only in poetry. The first generation English Romantic poets, especially Wordsworth, rebelled against the decorum of poetic diction of the Augustan Age which flourished at the end of the 18th Century. Wordsworth argued that there was no essential difference between the language of poetry and prose and everyday speech. In the 20th Century, poets have sought objective correlatives to exactly express their thoughts and feelings using the language of the streets. It is a characteristic of contemporary poetry. The idea that a specific poetic diction exists, or ought to exist, is out of fashion.

Poetic drama: plays written in verse that are intended to be acted. *Dramatic poetry, or closet drama,* is not intended for stage production and therefore distinct from poetic drama.

Poetic license: a freedom to vary pronunciation, diction, or facts for the sake of a poem as a whole, or for considerations of rhyme and metre.

Poetry: three qualities are generally recognized as common to all poetry: a specific content; some sort of form, and an effect. Much has been written on the subject of poetry, more than we can go into here. Poetry is a highly complex and subjective concept. The reader wishing to get an understanding for the meaning of poetry should read what some of the following poets have written in prose and verse on their art: Samuel Taylor Coleridge, William Wordsworth, Edgar Allan Poe, William Blake, Walter Pater, Matthew Arnold, Gerard Manley Hopkins, William Butler Yeats, T.S. Eliot, Ezra Pound, Amy Lowell, e.e. cummings, Babette Deutsch, W.H. Auden, Stephen Spender, Sylvia Plath, Emily Dickinson, Robert Frost, Carl Sandberg, Edna St. Vincent Millay, Wallace Stevens, Allen Tate, Marianne Moore, and others.

Polyphonic prose: poetry written as prose which has elements such as metre, assonance, alliteration, rhyme, and symmetry. Amy Lowell is the best known advocate of polyphonic prose.

Psalm: a lyric poem in praise of someone or something. The term is commonly applied to the *Book of Psalms,* in the Bible.

Pyrrhic: a foot in which both syllables are unstressed.

Quatrain: a stanza of four lines with a variable rhyme scheme, from unrhymed to any variation of one-rhyme, two-rhyme, or three-rhyme lines. Popular rhyme schemes are: abab, aabb, abba, aaba, abcb.

Rest: a pause, but one that counts, in a verse.

Rhyme: a characteristic of poetry, rhyme is a matching of sounds— vowels, consonants, or a combination of these—in one or more syllables within one, two, or more lines. The rhyme is created by the similarity of sound between the vowels and following consonants of the accented syllables.

End rhyme, internal rhyme, and *beginning rhyme* are so called because of the placement of the rhyming syllables in the verse.

Masculine rhyme: feminine rhyme, and *triple rhyme* indicate the number of syllables in which the matching of sounds takes place.

Poor rhymes, to avoid, include: same sound, but different spelling, as in *night* and *knight;* matching of unaccented syllables, as in *loving* and *beating;*

lack of rhyme in syllables following the accented syllable, as in *heating* and *beater:* although the same vowel sounds appear in different rhymes they should not appear near each other; at the same time, rhyme sounds should be spaced close enough to maintain the continuity of the rhyme scheme.

Rhyme Royal: iambic pentameter stanza seven lines long, rhymes *ababbcc.*

Rhyme-scheme: the sequence of rhymes in a poem or stanza, as in a Shakespearean sonnet, *abab cdcd efef gg.*

Rhythm: recurrence of similar time intervals between specific events. Rhythm, in poetry, is determined by three basic elements: *quantity, accent,* or *stress,* and number of syllables. The pattern of accented and unaccented syllables gives pleasure to the reader by building up a system of expectations and rewards. There are rhythms of iambs and trochees, quick two-beats, and longer three-beats of dactyls and anapests. All four with rising or falling action. These are the classical rhythm patterns, but there are others such as *sprung rhythm* and *free verse.*

Rondeau: a French form popular for light, fanciful expression. A rondeau is 15 lines, with the 9th and 15th coming as short refrains. The rhyme scheme is *aabba aabc aabbac* with the refrain lines rhyming. The lines are usually octosyllabic. Another kind of rondeau consists of 12 lines, *abba, abc, abbac.* Still another, known as *rondeau redouble,* is made up of six quatrains rhymes *abab.*   The first four lines—the first quatrain—are the last lines of the second, third, fourth, and fifth stanzas.

Run-on lines: verses in which the sense and grammatical construction are carried on from one line to the next.

Scansion: a study of the metrical pattern and other poetic elements in a line of poetry.

Similie: a comparison of two objects in which one is *like* or *as* the other. In a m*etaphor* one object is the other, creating a blended image of comparison. When one element is shared in common by two objects, there is basis for a simile. For instance, in the following lines from Shakespeare's Sonnet 60, *change* is the element common to both time and waves:

Like as the waves make towards the pebbled shore,
So do our minutes hasten to their end;
Each changing place with that which goes before
In sequent toil all forwards do contend.

Slant rhyme: an *imperfect, near,* or *approximate rhyme.*

Sonnet: a fourteen line lyric poem in iambic pentameter. It may be divided into an octave and a sestet, three quatrains and a rhymed couplet, or any combination, or variation of the two.

The *Italian,* or *Petrarchan,* sonnet has two distinct parts: first, eight lines rhymed *abba, abba,* called the octave, followed by six lines that may be rhymed *cde cde, cdc cdc,* or *cde dce.* The octave contains a problem or question. The last six lines (the sestet) offers the solution.

In practice, the Italian sonnet has suffered many variations and mutations in English poetry. The octave and sestet divisions may not be kept, the rhyme scheme may vary, and the metre may be anything but the usual iambic pentameter.

The *English,* or *Shakespearean,* sonnet has three quatrains, each with individual rhyme schemes, and a final couplet. The rhymes are *abab cdcd efef gg.* The couplet at the end is an epigrammatic statement on the sense of the quatrains.

The *Spenserian Sonnet* is a third kind. It combines the Italian and English to form three quatrains and a couplet, but with interlocking rhymes, thus: *abab bcbc cdcd ee.*

Spondee: a foot of two stressed syllables.

Sprung rhythm: popularized at the turn of the 20th Century by the English poet Gerard Manley Hopkins, it is a form of rhythm set according to the number of stressed syllables in the line, with no attention paid to the unstressed. In all instances, the first syllable of a foot is stressed. Thus, the kind of metrical feet that can be used is limited to monosyllabic, trochaic, dactylic, and first paeon. Variation is achieved by breaking up the feet at the beginning or end of a line, or dropping an unaccented syllable.

Stanza: two or more lines of poetry set off to form a unit within a poem. A stanza may be a division of a poem according to length, metrical pattern, rhyme scheme, or thought. Other terms for stanza are *strophe* and *stave.* Stanzaic forms include *couplet, tercet, quatrain, rhyme royal, ottava rima* and *Spenserian Stanza, Monk's Tale Stanza, In Memoriam Stanza.*

Stress: accent or emphasis a syllable, or word, receives in a verse, as a light or hard stress.

Symbol: in poetry, the use of a word, such as cross, to convey more than a literal meaning. A cross is both two pieces of wood, or metal, joined at right angles to each other and is the symbol of Christianity, Christ, sacrifice, redemption, and salvation. Usually, a symbol will refer to some arch-type in a culture's history, mythology, and emotional composition. A rose is a flower that also symbolizes love, Divine Love, and other religious and secular ideas.

Tanka: see *Haiku.*

Tercet: a triplet, or three line stanza, with each line having the same rhyme.

Terza rima: a poem made up of three line stanzas rhyming aba, bcb, cdc and so on. Dante used the form in Divina Commedia and English poets who used terza rima include Robert Browning, Milton, Shelley, and Byron.

Tetrameter: a verse of four metrical feet.

Tribrach: a foot of three unaccented syllables.

Trimeter: a line of three metrical feet.

Triple Rhyme: rhyme in which the sounds of three consecutive syllables are matched.

Trochee: a metrical foot of two syllables, the first accented, the second unaccented.

Variable syllable: a syllable whose stress, or accent, is determined by the context.

Verse: a line of poetry. Verse may also be used to refer to metrical composition and is sometimes used interchangeably with *poetry.*

Villanelle: a French form of 19 lines—five tercets and a concluding quatrain, with a rhyme scheme aba, aba, aba, aba, aba, abaa. The first line is used to form lines 6, 12, 18, and line 3 is also used as lines 9, 15 and 19. Eight of the 19 lines are refrains.

Virgule: the symbol I dividing feet in a verse.

Weak ending: a word ending a line that has metrical stress, but is commonly unaccented in normal usage.

Wrenched Accent: changing the normal pronunciation of a word to fit the needs of metrical accent in a line of poetry.

**The Writer's Manual
Book 8**

How to
Write Scripts
for Theatre,
Television and Film

By
Dale Miller
and
Michael Springer

ABOUT THE AUTHORS

Dale Miller

Dale Miller's background covers two fields:
education and the professional theatre.
His PhD is in Theatre from Northwestern University.
He had additional training in acting, directing, and theatre history
at the University of Minnesota, Denver University and the
Foundation for the Extension and Development
of the American Theatre in New York.

Dr. Miller has been an instructor of theatre arts at Northwestern University,
Stephens College, and Huron College and has served as guest director
Of other universities. Chairman of the Theatre and Dance Department,
Barat College, Lake Forest, Illinois, 1967-1976,
he is presently Director of Theatre, Purdue University.
He has directed productions of
*Medea, Romeo and Juliet, Showboat, Man and Superman, Man of La Mancha,
Butterflies are Free, Best of Friends,
The Owl and the Pussycat* and *Madam Butterfly,* and nearly 100 others.
As an actor, he has appeared in
*The Sound of Music, Who Killed Santa Claus?,
Best of Friends,* and *How the Other Half Loves.*
He has also acted in television commercials.
He is a member of Actor's Equity and Screen Actor's Guild.

In addition to a successful career as a director and actor,
Dr. Miller's knowledge of the theatre is both academic and professional.
He is an authority on the theory and practice of theatrical plays.
As a theatrical pro, he understands the problems and demands
of creating and presenting drama.
As an educator, he is able to explain
the creative process in clear, constructive terms.

Michael Springer

Michael Springer is a professional scriptwriter,
one of the new generation of young writers
who grew up with the television medium,
and who tailor their work specifically to television and film presentation.
He wrote his first screenplay while an undergraduate
at Northwestern University where he studied radio, television, and film.
After receiving his degree,
he worked in various forms of television writing
including commercials, documentaries, and news.
He now devotes full time to dramatic writing,
primarily in made-for-television films and dramatic specials.

In addition to his work as a screenwriter,
he has had experience in production of television and motion pictures
and has served as a director, actor, and producer
in addition to working in radio and the theatre.

As a working member of the scriptwriting craft,
he has a thorough knowledge of the latest techniques
in the writing and production of television programs and feature films.
He writes out of his personal experience on such matters
as current production techniques, contacting agents and producers,
making the first sale, etc.
Familiar with the ins and outs of the television and motion picture industries,
he understands the questions new scriptwriters in the '70's need to know.

ACKNOWLEDGEMENTS

The authors are grateful for permission to quote from

The Effect of Gamma Rays on Man-In-The-Moon Marigolds.

Copyright © 1971 by Paul Zindel.

Reprinted by permission of

Harper & Row, Publishers, Inc.

Illustrations and charts
by Dale Miller

CONTENTS

FADE IN

Introduction

The craft of scriptwriting, like all forms of creative endeavor, presupposes two elements on the part of its practitioners: talent, and training. Of these two, talent is by far the more important. Talent is a natural endowment; it cannot be imparted. From this truth springs the conviction that writers are born, not made, and that writing cannot be taught at all. It is true that the would-be writer must be blessed with certain qualities before he even sets pen to paper: vivid imagination, a strong creative drive, a flair for the dramatic, a fluency with words. These intangibles cannot be absorbed from the pages of a book or a series of lectures. Therefore, genuine writing talent is rare and most people are disqualified from becoming first-rate scenarists, regardless of how much training they may receive.

However, if the innate talent for writing is available in an individual, professional training will be invaluable. Though instruction can't bring certain necessary abilities into being, it can nurture and develop those abilities if they already exist. It is upon this premise that our discussion of scriptwriting is based.

This examination of the craft of scriptwriting is intended primarily for the beginning writer. It should, nonetheless, be of use to writers who have proven themselves in other areas of writing and want to try their hand at a new and exciting literary form. It can be used by playwrights who would like to write a script for television or film, and for screenwriters who would like to try a theatrical play. Finally, this discussion may also be enlightening for individuals who are simply interested in scriptwriting and who would like to acquire some general sophistication about the field.

The text covers all the basics of scriptwriting, with attention to both the theoretical and practical principles. It first deals with those elements which are essential to the creation of a sound dramatic script, and demonstrates the manner in which these elements apply to contemporary scriptwriting. There is also a heavy emphasis on technique; examples and illustrations from some of today's most popular productions are used. There is a section on production elements for those interested in the technically demanding fields of television and film. And finally, we have included a discussion on an often neglected area of scriptwriting, the business aspect of the writing profession. In short, we hope to trace the development of a script (for theatre, television, or motion pictures) from its original conception, through the writing process, to its eventual sale and production.

In addition, we hope to leave the writer with some conclusions as to what it takes to become a professional writer and, more importantly, what it takes to *be* a professional writer. The late Rod Serling once observed that he did not embrace the scriptwriting profession; he succumbed to it. The statement could have come from any full-time writer. A really good writer must have a script he wants to write, as opposed to simply wanting to write a script. Scriptwriting fulfills a personal need. It is more than a job or a way to earn money — it is a way of life. Scriptwriting demands an individual's energy, his time, his full concentration and, perhaps, a piece of his soul. Only those who go into writing who are willing to give everything and expecting little in return can hope to one day become bona fide professional scriptwriters.

At the very least, scriptwriting demands these qualities from an individual: a rare combination of intuitiveness and intellect; the ability to condense and select; strict discipline in terms of work habits; a knowledge of his particular medium; and the ability to follow classic principles of good drama. If there is one prerequisite to the craft of scriptwriting, it is the power of observation. The willingness to observe and interpret life must be at the core of every writer's disposition.

An attribute of good living is the ability to see life steadily and see it whole. It is also a good formula for living for the average person — but it is absolutely essential for the professional scriptwriter.

CHAPTER ONE

THE THEORY OF SCRIPTWRITING

Any discussion of scriptwriting will logically begin with an analysis of the elements of which drama consists: theme, plot, characterization, dialogue, music, and spectacle. Any script, for any medium, will require a great deal of attention to each of these components of drama. These principles date back to Aristotle; they are as timeless as the theatre itself. Even though they were first defined many centuries ago, their essence has not changed over the years. The manner in which these components are used changes from time to time, and we will discuss the contemporary use of each, but for the most part, Aristotle's poetics contained material that is every bit as important and valid to theatre today as it was in his time. The components we discuss here are classic concepts, not out-dated dramatic rules.

THEME

The importance of theme in scriptwriting has been widely disputed for many years. Some feel theme is an essential element of a play; others dispute the necessity of a theme and regard it as a mere dramatic afterthought. Perhaps the importance of theme is a relative matter. But, the fact remains, the most significant and lasting dramas in theatre, film, and television have all been constructed around strong themes. It might be assumed therefore, that the presence or absence of theme differentiates a truly important film or play from a piece of light entertainment. It is the writer, himself, who must decide which type of play he wishes to present to the audience.

When theme is an important element of a script, it must be used judiciously. As Walter Kerr once said, "A good way to destroy a play is to force it to prove something". Theme must be subtly integrated with the other elements of the drama: plot, characterization, dialogue and other mechanical elements. If the script has a statement to make, it must be done in a matter compatible with the story's dramatic requirements. The play must hold the senses while it educates the mind; otherwise, both the play and the message fail to move the audience. The ideal script strikes a balance between entertainment and enlightenment; it draws the audience into the drama, then leaves it with something to think about.

Since the beginning of drama, or perhaps all literature, there have been three basic themes. They are:

> Man against Man
> Man against Himself
> Man against God (or Nature)

Oedipus Rex combined all three of these themes into one of the greatest dramas ever written. It is also a masterpiece of construction and condensation, and worthy of periodic review. Most of Shakespeare's plays can be boiled down to one of these basic themes. Of course, Shakespeare usually had several themes and subthemes running through his plays, just as he had plots and subplots. He was a master of such techniques: It is one of the reasons he is still considered the world's greatest playwright.

But how do today's playwrights apply and develop theme? How do these universal themes apply to modern society? The answer lies in the fact that the nature of man has not changed significantly. People are still engaged in the same struggles they were in Shakespeare's time. They struggle to survive, to live with one another, to avoid pain, seek pleasure, and ward off death, as long as possible. Only the trappings have changed; the fundamental elements of life have not. The nature of conflict remains timeless. The playwright has the prerogative of asking Why? Though he is not always required to answer his own question, he must at least raise it. This is the core of theme.

In order to develop a viable theme, one which will be clear in your mind as you compose your dialogue and plot, you should at some point state your theme in a complete sentence. The writer must be able to grasp his own message before he can transmit it to an audience. As an example, let's take a look at a reasonably commercial play, *The Owl and the Pussycat* by Bill Manhoff. This play will probably never find its way into an anthology of the 20th century's great plays, but it is a successful script, nonetheless, and widely known. It's also a good illustration of how a theme can be defined, even in a play aimed at the mass audience.

The plot of *The Owl and the Pussycat* concerns a young, self-proclaimed intellectual who makes a practice of denying his sexual desires in favor of his intellectual urges. He meets a part-time prostitute who has shied away from all intellectual pursuits and tries to find the meaning of her life in physical love. They battle each other through a series of episodes which are funny, pathetic, and tender. By the end of the play he recognizes his anomaly, and so does she. The play, if not totally resolved, is at least concluded.

What is the theme of the play? First of all it is Man against Himself, and Woman against Herself. But that theme covers a lot of ground; the themes must be more specific. We could borrow a line from *Hamlet* and say that the theme is "To thine own self be true." Taken one step further, the theme could be stated: Normal human behavior occurs when people have recognized both their animal and intellectual needs.

Very few people who see *The Owl and the Pussycat* will have their lives changed by the play's message. Most will regard it as a comedy piece and react accordingly. They will be entertained. But they will also be able to leave the theatre with something more to discuss than just the funny gags. The point is, although the play is lightweight and serves primarily as entertainment, it also possesses a viable theme, one which may give the audience some "food for thought."

There is a difference between a theme and a topic. Theme and topic can often parallel and complement one another in a single plot. But, just as often, they can be separate entities within the same story. For example, the outstanding, made-for-television movie, *That Certain Summer,* dealt with the topic of homosexuality; homosexuality was not the theme. Though the plot centered on a man trying to cope with his own sexual tendencies, the larger theme concerned an individual's right to freedom. Topic and theme were not the same; rather, they coalesce to give the plot both timeliness and significance.

Whether you choose to use theme to its minimum or maximum effect, two points must be kept in mind: first, that theme should make some statement about life; and second, that the theme must always be implicit in the action of the story. If these two requirements are met, theme fulfills its purpose.

PLOTTING

Plot is the common denominator with which an audience identifies. Contemporary scriptwriters have a tendency to forget this important axiom. In the late '60's and early '70's, filmmakers began cranking out motion pictures which heavily emphasized theme and characterization, with little or no attention paid to the story line. The result was disastrous. At first the public was bewildered; they couldn't follow the story in most pictures. They became apathetic to films without plot and stayed away from the theatres in droves. The film industry began to crumble from the lack of box-office response. Lack of plotting is largely responsible for the failure of many recent motion pictures.

If you doubt this as an exaggeration of plotting's importance, check the list of the most popular and successful films of the 1970's: *The Godfather, The Poseidon Adventure, The French Connection, The Exorcist, The Sting, Jaws, The Towering Inferno*. Besides huge box office grosses, what did all these films have in common? Each had a very strong, tightly - structured, exciting plot. Alfred Hitchcock once said: "The question is how to apply glue to the seat of the audience's pants". Each of these films did, through plot. Though some viewers may discount these particular films because they lack "significance," there can be no denying the importance of good plot in terms of dramatic impact and audience appeal. Hollywood has learned this lesson the hard way, and good plotting is once again in fashion.

Television, which by its very nature is geared to a mass audience, has always placed a heavy emphasis on plotting. Too often, a television program's obsession with plot has resulted in a sacrifice of characterization and theme. The effect is every bit as detrimental to drama as the opposite extreme, ignoring the plot.

To be successful, plotting must be integrated; it must work in harmony with all the other dramatic requirements, particularly characterization. Plot is a very important part of the whole effect. But its purpose is not served unless all the other dramatic principles are served as well.

Simply defined, a plot is the sequence of events which constitutes the action of the story, or plot is the presentation of a conflict and its resolution.

John Van Druten makes the distinction between a story and a plot. He says that it is possible to have a story without having a plot. By this he means that a story can go on without end, but a good plot will tie everything together: shape the story, condense it, and present it clearly to the audience. Because plotting must be so concise, it may well be the most difficult part of the scriptwriting process.

Originality is *not* the most important factor of plotting. In fact, there's really no such thing as a "new" plot. As far as the fundamental elements are concerned, theatre historians believe there are as few as seven different plots, all dating back to the theatre of ancient Greece. Strictly speaking, no new plots have been developed since. William Shakespeare's plays can be traced back to other sources, even though no one ever thinks of Shakespeare as unoriginal.

The "originality" aspect of plotting comes from the manner in which the plot is used in the script. The writer provides a new slant to a classic situation dealing with new subject matter, contemporary problems which add freshness to age-old conflicts. The basic elements of the plot will not be new, but the writer's approach and his handling of the conflict may be original with him.

The fact that most plots are not really "new" does not mean that designing a fresh, exciting plot is impossible. In fact, a satisfactory plot is essential. When beginning writers have a problem with a script, the cause can invariably be traced to some deficiency in plotting. Perhaps the plot lacks credibility; or there may be some structural weakness, with an important piece of information left out or scenes poorly arranged; it may be that the script simply lacks action. Individual scripts require individual remedies and it is up to the writer's ingenuity to devise a solution to the problem. But the most promising way to isolate the problem in the first place is to examine the plot closely.

One consideration to bear in mind is that successful plotting depends on sound dramatic structure more than any other single factor. All the material must be unified and integrated in a clear, concise manner. There is a specific dramatic structure that is used to arrange the series of events so that they have a maximum impact. The structuring principles can be considered in the following order:

1. *Status Quo.* Status Quo is an exposition of the way circumstances are at the beginning of the story. Think of it as the curtain-raiser or opening situation. Sometimes the central conflict of the story has not yet begun. Or, the opening scene may find the characters enmeshed in the conflict. Whichever method you choose (the latter is more popular these days), the Status Quo must introduce the characters, hint at the impending conflict, and set the scene for what is to follow.

2. *Conflict.* The conflict that threatens to upset the Status Quo is introduced. The writer must demonstrate precisely what the conflict is, what its implications are, and who it involves.

3. *Rising Action.* The conflict increases. The two opposing forces struggle with each other in increasingly threatening situations. The action builds until a final, decisive confrontation becomes inevitable.

4. *Climax.* The highest and most absorbing part of the story, the climax, is the point at which decisions must be reached and action is taken which makes a return to the original status quo impossible.

5. *Falling Action.* All the loose ends of the plot are brought together. The audience learns the outcome and consequences of the climax.

6. *Denouement* (or *Resolution*). The story is finished and a new status quo has been reached. Sometimes, as in real life, the story doesn't really end; but this particular series of events is concluded. In either case, the status quo will never be quite the same again.

For a standard three-act theatrical presentation, this structure can be diagrammed to illustrate where and when the various crises occur. The diagram usually looks something like this:

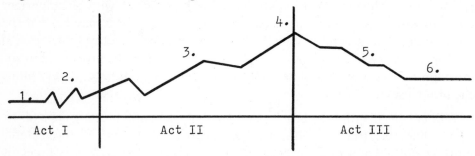

The "peaks" in the diagram denote crisis; the highest "peak" is the climax of the play. As this diagram indicates, crises of varying degrees are distributed throughout the play. In theatre, the end of the first act finds the characters in the midst of a crisis; the end of the second act is where the climax generally takes place. Knowing where in the play these crises will occur enables the writer to build the action of the scene toward each particular crisis.

The structure of a television program simplifies the plotting process even more, since the structure is more rigid in television. A major crisis usually occurs every fifteen minutes or so in a television program, just prior to a commercial break. When the program resumes, the crisis is either resolved immediately or saved for the program's climax. In either case, television presents a ready-made framework within which the writer must build his program. In diagram form, most television programs look like this:

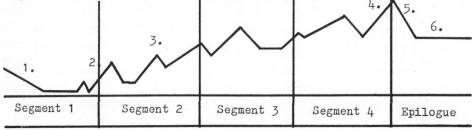

All too often writers have tried to parlay these general structuring principles into a "sure-fire formula" for plotting. To them, constructing a sound plot simply means plugging new information into the same tired old formula. This way of thinking results in stale, hackneyed writing; it is a distortion of the purpose these principles serve. The craft of structure does not represent a formula for plotting; rather, it presents the writer with a framework for his own creative innovations. The components of structure mentioned earlier simply provide a suggested method of general organization that has proven to be the most effective in terms of dramatic impact. The scriptwriter has a free hand in deciding precisely how these structural components may be used to his own advantage. The content of the individual scenes, the nature of the conflict, and its consequences all rely solely on the writer's individual creativity.

The concept of conflict is sufficiently clear to most people. Opposing forces (man against man, man against nature, or conflicting values within the individual) are placed in a situation where they must confront each other. The concept of climax is equally clear: eventually, the conflict must reach full force; one of the opposing forces must triumph over the other. The script-writer's main problem comes between the two. How does the writer intensify the conflict? What constitutes rising action?

Rising action should be thought of as a continual shifting of balance between the two opposing forces. The writer must introduce new complications to the story line that moves the equilibrium back and forth. This constant shifting of equilibrium gives the script its forward motion (i.e. rising action).

There are essentially three types of complications that cause the balance shift: 1) new information can be introduced; 2) another character can be brought into the conflict; or 3) one of the opposing characters or forces can take some action. Any or all of these complications can give the plot a new twist, change the conflict, or otherwise cause complications that move the plot closer to its climax.

Another plotting element that constantly plagues writers is exposition. Exposition is defined as information the audience needs to understand the situation as the play proceeds. For example, perhaps the central character acts the way he does because of something hidden in his past, something that happened before the current conflict began. The audience must be aware of this information if it is to fully comprehend the action. This is the purpose of exposition.

Blatant opening scenes loaded with exposition used to be common in the theatre. The curtain would rise, and the maid and butler would give the whole background of the story while they dusted. This anachronistic device was finally satirized out of existence by Thornton Wilder's *The Skin of Our Teeth*.

In contemporary scripts, exposition must be inserted into the action of the story so skilfully that it seems to be part of the action. One example of how plot and exposition can be joined is Paul Zindel's *The Effect of Gamma Rays on Man-in-the-Moon Marigolds*.

Marigolds is a two-act play with exposition spread throughout. In spite of this slightly unorthodox approach, Zindel is able to let the audience know where they are very quickly, without having to spell it out. He is also able to delineate his main character, Beatrice, so skillfully that the audience knows who she is almost immediately. The audience does not discover the "why" in her characterization until immediately before the denouement.

The main plot is effectively woven around events at a local high school. From Beatrice's point of view, the high school represents a malevolent, omnipresent character. From the author's point of view it serves as a backdrop and sounding board for the entire play.

Zindel's script, reduced to its most basic plot components, illustrates how he has used the basic structural principles outlined earlier:

1. *Status Quo* is partially established by means of a prologue; statement of theme occurs; a tape recorder functions as narrator.

2. *Conflict* begins as soon as the phone rings; conflict continues during Beatrice's phone monologue with the high school teacher. (The status quo is completely established by the end of the first scene.)

3. *Rising Action*
   a. Beatrice discovers that Tillie was laughed at during a recent high school assembly.
   b. Nanny, the old invalid, is introduced.
   c. Thunderstorm occurs which parallels Ruth's epileptic seizure.
   d. Beatrice reminisces about her childhood.
   e. Tillie's project is chosen for the science fair; Beatrice is petrified when she discovers that she is expected to appear on stage with the other mothers.
   f. Ruth informs Tillie that when Beatrice was in the same high school she was called "Betty the Loon."
   g. Beatrice appears and tells Ruth to stay with Nanny while they are at the assembly.

4. *Climax*   Ruth is furious and tells Beatrice "They're all waiting for you
   . . . Betty the Loon."

5. *Falling Action*
   a.   Beatrice orders the girls out of the house and begins to sob softly.
   b.   the science fair is held and Tillie wins.
   c.   Beatrice destroys whatever she can and is left with nothing.

6. *Denouement* and epilogue
   a.   Beatrice is destroyed - an unsuccessful mutation.
   b.   Tillie has triumphed over her environment and will continue to
        grow - a successful mutation.

In graph form Zindel's play looks like this: (parallel lines indicate
exposition; peaks indicate conflict):

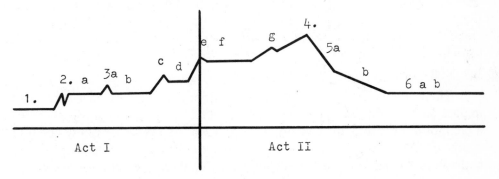

This rather detailed look at Paul Zindel's plot is not held up as a perfect
example of modern plotting, nor is it intended to serve as a model for any
other script. It is simply one example of how an author arranged his material
to suit his needs, blending exposition and plot successfully and dramatically.
This type of structural analysis can be performed on any play, film, or
television program.

The best way to become acquainted with different ways of plotting is
to study the methods other writers have used. Watch different plays or
movies; analyze an episode of *Police Story*, or any other interesting television
show. Study the story's construction. Do all the elements build to the climax?
At what point do different crises occur? What about the show's pacing? How
is exposition included? When your analysis is done, you will be left with one
important question: could the plot have been better, and if so, how?

By studying the plots of various programs, you will be able to draw some
inferences as to how a good plot is constructed. The idea, of course, is not to

learn to imitate what others have already done, but to learn from their successes (or failures) the principles of plotting that work most effectively. Watching enough plays and programs, both good and bad, you'll undoubtedly be left with one very important conclusion: that good plotting combines both creativity and good technique. Technique can be studied, as we've examined it here. The writer must supply the creativity himself.

CHARACTERIZATION

Characterization is one of the most important elements in the script-writing process. The development of interesting, believable characters is absolutely crucial, and represents one of the writer's most pressing challenges. Depending on the treatment and the demands of the script, all of the other elements of drama — theme, spectacle, even plot — may be subservient to characterization. The examination of one intriguing character has served as the key to many powerful plays and motion pictures. The vivid impressions created by some of theatre's immortal personages — Don Quixote de la Mancha, Stanley Kowalski in *A Streetcar Named Desire* — remain long after the details of the plot are forgotten.

There are a number of reasons why fictional characters have such great impact on an audience. First, fictional characters are larger than life; they are a composite of several different real-life personalities. A writer rarely creates a character from a single impression; he usually collects the traits, mannerisms, and values he has observed in various people, then compiles and rearranges these characteristics until a totally new and arresting personality emerges. A fictional character is far more complex and compelling than anyone found in real life. Second, the author has taken this already interesting character and placed him in a dramatic situation, a set of circumstances fraught with excitement, humor, terror, or whatever devices the author chooses. Third, actors and directors have added their observations and interpretations, hopefully reinforcing the character's personality. Finally, the audience's collective attention is focused on the story and the characters exclusively. For a period of two hours, these people and their circumstances become real.

Even if the script is not dominated by such powerfully impressive characters as Don Quixote or Stanley Kowalski, each writer still bears a responsibility to create viable and lifelike characters, characters who will serve and be served by the plot and theme.

The difficult process of characterization consists of two steps: creation and revelation. The writer must first determine who the people are he's writing about and what they are like; he must come to know them and understand them. When this is done, he faces the task of revealing his creations to an audience by means of the dialogue, setting and plot. Let's address the problem of creation first.

Character Sources

Someone once asked the accomplished filmmaker Federico Fellini where he found the unusual and sometimes grotesque characters that appear in his movies. His answer was: "I go down to the street corner." Every author must also "go down to the street corner," if not literally at least figuratively. The author's power of observation is the key to characterization. The encounters the writer has with people in real life represents an invaluable character source. The world is rife with characters waiting to be discovered. By observing human beings wherever he goes — in a department store, at a party, anywhere people are engaged in activity — the writer will enjoy an unending supply of character types.

But before the writer pounds the pavement of the world looking for interesting characters, he should first reflect on the people he already knows, his own family and friends. Each of us is already acquainted with enough characters to cast several plays. By drawing on personal relationships, the author also has the advantage of several years of exposure of his "characters"; he already knows them well and understands their values and their quirks. Many fine writers have drawn on their family and friends as a source of characters, among them Tennessee Williams and Eugene O'Neill.

An even more valuable character source is the author himself. Most scripts are, in a sense, autobiographical, since the author almost always projects something of himself into his characters. He infuses his own values, his own personality, and problems into the characters he creates; the things that concern him most are often reflected in his characters. Some writers even go far as to create characters who literally represent themselves (Eugene O'Neill is such an example.)

Many writers try to keep their own personalities separate from those of their characters. They are either afraid of revealing too much of themselves, afraid of what they may find, or they regard this device as "cheating." But no matter how hard the writer tries, leaving his personal imprint on his characters is unavoidable. There's no such thing as a completely "fictious" character; central characters often represent, unconsciously or otherwise, what the author is, what he would like to be, or what he's afraid he might become were he confronted with the character's circumstances.

Whichever source of characters the author chooses to use (and he will use them all eventually), he must remember that these potential characters cannot be translated to the stage or screen without some modification. They must become *dramatic* characters, since they will be confronted with a dramatic situation. The writer must add new dimensions to the character, accentuate others, building and shaping until the character fits the requirements of the script. To do this, the writer will want to concentrate on the general human qualities of which characterization is comprised: values, traits, and mannerisms.

Character Qualities

Characters, like human beings, are composites of various traits, mannerisms, and values. The writer will want to spend some time thinking about these general qualities as they pertain to each individual character featured in his script.

The first matter to consider is the character's values. What are the driving forces that dominate his life and thus motivate his actions? Is his behavior determined by love, or greed, or selfishness, or a lust for power? The writer must reflect on the wide gamut of human emotions and decide which ones apply to his character. Every character must have a reason for what he does; the reason is found in his own sense of values. The writer must completely understand the character's motives, so that he can predict how he will act in a given situation.

The character may not be aware of his own motivations, of course; this can be used very effectively in drama. The character's own self-discovery may be used as an integral part of the script. His struggle to learn something about his own values may capture the imagination of the audience; they will struggle along with him. At the story's climax, the character may be confronted with his true feelings or he may not; but the audience will have reached some conclusions of their own if the treatment has been handled effectively. The result can be very satisfying statistically. But whether or not the character understands himself, the author himself must know, even if he never shares this knowledge completely with either the character or the audience.

Characters cannot be one-dimensional. Real people are seldom driven by a single force; rather, they possess a number of different values. This reality also applies to characters. When a character's opposing drives clash, the result is drama's most important element: conflict. The character must wrestle with his conflicting values until one conquers the others at the story's climax. This sense of inner conflict is a very important dimension in contemporary characterization.

A trait is defined as a distinguishing quality or characteristic. The character's traits will be determined by his system of values. For example, Dr. Benjamin Franklin (Hawkeye) Pierce, the central character in the television series *M*A*S*H*, has a clearly defined system of values; his overwhelming concern is the value of human life. This sense of priority is reflected in one of his most outstanding traits: his dedication to medicine. From his values comes another trait as well: his rebellion against war and the army, an instrument of war. Hawkeye rebels because these two institutions, which he confronts every day, are directly opposed to his own values. The purpose of war is to take lives; his is to save them. Consequently, two of Hawkeye's distinguishing traits are the direct result of a clearly defined set of values.

Mannerisms come next in this progression of human qualities. A mannerism is any pecularity in speech, dress, or behavior. Mannerisms are the external clues to a character's values and traits. Let's take the character of Hawkeye again. His sense of values involves a deep respect for human life. The resulting trait is a rebellion against the military establishment. Hawkeye's mannerisms resulting from this trait are disrespect, irreverent wit, and often chaotic behavior. Hawkeye totally disregards the army's rules and regulations. He is always out of uniform and wouldn't know how to salute if he had to. He shows no respect for superior officers unless they've earned it; their rank doesn't automatically command his respect. He is insolent, especially toward his major protagonists, the "major," in this case, are Frank Burns and Margaret ("Hotlips") Hoolihan. He has no use for discipline and order; he drinks, parties, and breaks rules with abandon. Finally, his barbed wit is directed consistently against the army and the war.

Obviously Alan Alda, who plays Hawkeye so expertly, and Larry Gelbart, *M*A*S*H's* creator, have taken extreme care with characterization. *M*A*S*H's* writers have carefully nurtured each layer of characterization—values, traits, and mannerisms — not just in Hawkeye's case, but with every character in the show. In so doing, they have provided some of the best examples of richly textured characterization in contemporary television.

It should be pointed out that each of these human qualities must be present in order to achieve richness in characterization. Mannerisms alone will not characterize; they only work if they are the result of the character's more meaningful subtext. The character's values and traits must also be revealed. If a character is created from mannerisms alone, he will be a caricature rather than a character.

*M*A*S*H* has enjoyed tremendous success in characterization; but the program also had several years in which to develop its characters. Most writers don't enjoy such luxury; they are constantly confronted with the limitations of time. They are only permitted an hour or so in which to develop their characters.

Obviously, it's impossible to display every facet of a character's personality in such a short period of time. How can a writer solve this problem? The best solution is to select and condense. Choose one or two pertinent characteristics and concentrate on them in your story. Create different situations in which the characteristics can be displayed. Choose those qualities which have the greatest bearing on the plot. Highlight the character's values and traits that will be brought to the surface by the situation the story presents, then develop them as vividly as you can. Other character values not directly related to the plot may either be simply hinted at or set aside entirely.

Even if all the qualities of a character might not be needed to move the story forward, these qualities must still exist. The writer must know every facet of his characters before he starts to write about them, whether he intends to make use of all of them or not. The creation must be total before anything about the character can be revealed. Ibsen summed it up well when he said of Nora, the central character in his play *A Doll's House:* "The things I know about that young woman that aren't in the play would surprise you."

Revelation

Once the creation of a character is complete, the writer faces the real test of characterization: translating that character to an audience successfully. There are several ways by which this revelation is accomplished, all of which will probably be incorporated into the script. They are: physical appearance of the character; what the character says; what the character does; other people's reactions to the character.

The audience usually views a character before he has a chance to do or say anything. Therefore, the first impression is created by the character's physical appearance. The writer must determine what his character will look like. Is he handsome (a positive impression) or unattractive (a negative first impression)? Is he neatly dressed and groomed (appealing) or sloppy and careless in his appearance (repugnant)?

Today, even the character's age may be a factor in the type of impression he creates. The contemporary (i.e. youthful) audience automatically associates certain age groups with certain traits and values.

There is an immediate (if short-lived) identification with a younger character; the audience assumes he must be the "hero," rightly or wrongly. Older characters are instantly associated with rigidness, power, and oppression; therefore, they are initially regarded as the "heavy," rightly or wrongly. (The exception to this rule are very old characters, who are thought to be harmless and thus represent no threat to the hero; it's okay to like old people in the audience's mind.)

The vastly successful motion picture *Shampoo* is an ideal example of the importance of physical identification in characterization. In that film, physical appearance, age, costume, and setting were all used to immediately characterize. The audience is introduced to George (played by Warren Beatty) first. George is young, handsome (perhaps too handsome), dressed in casual California costume, and riding a motorcycle. All these are positive associations with the 18-to-35 year-old movie-going crowd. George is contrasted with Lester (Jack Warden) physically. Lester is middle-aged and coarse-looking. He wears $400 suits and, worst of all, drives a Rolls Royce, the overworked symbol of affluence. He is first discovered in his oppulent office overlooking the city (another symbol of his position and power.) The audience automatically assumes that he must be the villain, a typical "establishment fat cat." While both these characters represent hopelessly outdated ideas of characterization (the "new cliches," if you will), they also represent the immediate effect physical appearance, costume, and setting have on today's audience.

The first impression, though revealing something about the character, need not necessarily be accurate. It's possible to create an illusion of the character, then go on to reveal that he is not what he seemed at first. Work against type occasionally; make the handsome guy a bum, the ugly one the hero. Contrast the character's external elements with his inner self. Characters don't have to be what they seem to be on the surface. This device adds depth and complexity to the characterization, and makes the character infinitely more interesting. In *Shampoo* George, for all his appealing physical traits, is revealed as a weak and shallow individual as the story progresses. (He was weak and shallow by design, of course; not accidentally.)

A character's personality is also partially reflected in his dialogue. In *Shampoo* again, George's dialogue reveals his lack of substance. His usual reply to anything is an inarticulate "Great." His lack of conversational ability contributes to his characterization. Dialogue reflects both the character's individuality and his nature. What the character says reveals what he thinks; this in turn tells us something about his values.

In terms of characterization, an unoriginal but accurate adage applies: "Actions speak louder than words." Action is essential, both to drama in general and characterization specifically. The actions of a character not only affect the story line, but also reveal his nature. The decisions a character makes, the path he chooses as the alternatives are presented to him in the story, represents the key to character revelation. His outward appearance and everything he says may be overturned by a single action. Weak men become heroes, successful men failures. In drama, what a character *does* ultimately determines what he *is*.

Reactions are an important part of characterization, too. What other people say about a character and how they react to him can add insights into that character's personality. Other characters' reactions also say something about those doing the reacting, and thus adds to *their* characterizations as well.

All these general principles of characterization are guidelines for the creation and revelation of characters. The implementation of these principles, like all the principles of scriptwriting, depends on the individual writer's creativity and skill. Hopefully, the writer will use these principles, combined with his own observation and imagination, to create original, provocative characters, as well as novel and dramatic ways of presenting them. But one point is clear: whoever the characters are, whatever the manner in which they are presented, the writer's ultimate purpose is to show the audience real human beings in crisis. If the audience cannot get interested in the characters or their situation, if the audience simply doesn't care what happens to the characters, then the story is doomed to failure.

DIALOGUE

Most of the action in contemporary dramatic scripts depends on the interaction of characters. This interaction almost always takes the form of dialogue. Without good, dramatic dialogue the impact of this interaction is diminished; it becomes dull and disinteresting. Without strong dialogue there is no movement, no conflict — in effect, no story. For this reason, the ability to write good dialogue is essential to the scriptwriter.

Dialogue is purposeful language; it serves a wide variety of functions critical to the scriptwriting process. Through dialogue, the theme of the story is revealed. Most of the script's action takes the form of dialogue. The characters are drawn and revealed by the words they speak. Dialogue is the primary vehicle of exposition. It provides humor and emotion. With all the functions dialogue must serve, it becomes apparent that most of the components of the script — plot, characterization, theme — rely heavily on the success or failure of the dialogue.

Each line of dialogue performs double and sometimes triple duty. Each sentence must serve a specific purpose. Ideally, each line of dialogue moves the story closer to its climax; it must add to the suspense, establish a mood, provoke a laugh, reveal something about a character, or provide an essential piece of information. Every line should be in the script for a reason. And every line must work. The dialogue must be packed, not padded. Writing lines so characters have something to say to each other is not enough. If specific lines or even whole passages of dialogue can be omitted without significantly altering the story, then the dialogue is badly defective. The writer is allowed a very short period of time in which to make his point; he cannot afford to waste words.

This doesn't mean that dialogue must be reduced to bare bones, of course. Some pleasantries, even small talk, may be included to make the dialogue sound realistic. But again, even chit chat can serve a purpose. Innocuous conversation can be used to disguise something else. So long as the exchange has more meaning than appears on the surface, a more important subtext, it can be termed effective dialogue.

Some writers and directors feel that scripted dialogue must duplicate real-life conversation exactly in order to be authentic. They are only partially correct. Dialogue must indeed sound authentic; but it must also have greater content than everyday speech. Normal language often consists of trivial exchanges, awkward phrases, long pauses, improper grammar and endless social amenities. Most everyday conversation may mirror reality, but it is meaningless from a dramatic standpoint. Even worse, most everyday conversation is deadly dull. Real speech must not be confused with realistic speech, just as real life should not be confused with good drama. The writer cannot present conversation exactly as it would occur in real life; rather, he shapes the conversation to meet the dramatic requirements of his script. Duplication is not art; art is selectivity. It is for this reason that naturalism in dialogue is unsuccessful; directors like John Cassavetes (*Husbands, A Woman Under the Influence)* have met with only sporadic success using "natural" (i.e. ad libbed) dialogue. Dialogue requires the condensation and selection a scriptwriter can give it. Capturing the literal quality of speech is not necessarily a criterion for writing good dialogue.

Rather than trying to make his dialogue sound exactly like everyday conversation, the writer must try to reflect only the *quality* of everyday speech. There are many aspects of everyday language the scriptwriter can adapt to make his dialogue sound natural without going overboard. For example, most dialogue will contain a heavy use of contractions, since this demonstrates a familiarity with the language and establishes an informal conversational tone. Sentences should be kept short and simple, as they are spoken in real life. Characters can interrupt each other from time to time; they can also grope for a word occasionally. The writer can also infuse his dialogue with the verbal "shorthand" we all use; grunts, groans, and simple "mmhms" qualify as language. And, of course, no character will ever speak in paragraphs. By absorbing these characteristics of real speech, developing a good ear for language, the writer can capture the essence of conversation while tailoring its content to fit his script.

Scriptwriters must keep in mind that, unlike a novelist or short story writer, they are creating dialogue that is meant to be spoken rather than read. As Thornton Wilder observed, a script is always in the present tense, meaning of course that it is meant to be heard as it happens, not second hand. Therefore, dialogue must sound right when spoken aloud. If it does, then it has faced one of the most crucial tests and succeeded.

Dialogue must also possess a poetry of its own. Lines must flow naturally from one to the next. Take for example a brief dialogue passage.

Woman

How can you love her and still play around?

Man

Who says I play around?

Woman

Don't all men?

Notice how naturally one line leads to the next, how one character's thought inspires another's. There is a continuity in this brief exchange, which enforces the impression that the two people involved are really talking to each other, not just reciting lines.

Here is a less successful exchange:

Woman

How many times have you threatened to
elope with me to Bermuda?

Man

Any time you're ready.

These lines are incongruous. The two characters obviously aren't really talking to each other, or even listening to each other. The lines do not possess the necessary fluency of thought. Unless the conversation is meant to be incongruous, continuity is essential.

Besides bringing a poetic quality to conversation, dialogue is also one of the best ways to delineate characters. In terms of their dialogue, Bob must be different from Ted, Carol from Alice. Each line of dialogue must be consistent with the personality who speaks it; lines may be out-of-character only if the writer means for them to be. If lines can be switched from one character to the next without sounding out-of-place, then the dialogue or the characterization is deficient.

Dialogue is also an effective way to characterize. If a character is poor and uneducated, this will be reflected in his speech — limited vocabulary, poor grammar, double negatives and so on. The reverse is also true. Each character's background, education, and personality should be revealed by the manner in which he talks.

In the television series *M*A*S*H*, each of the central protagonists, Hawkeye Pierce and Frank Burns, has a separate and distinctive way of saying things. Hawkeye's dialogue reflects a quick, sarcastic wit; it is colored with puns, putdowns, and double entendres. In contrast, the fatuous Frank Burns shows neither humor nor originality in his speech. The writers have wisely imbued his language with an almost archaic quality; he expresses himself in innocuous cliches. (He calls Hawkeye a "wisenheimer" and cautions him to "mind his own beeswax.") Dialogue for each of these characters is consistent in every episode, and the friction between the two is one of the highlights of the show.

*M*A*S*H* also makes use of a popular tool of dialogue: slang expressions. The slang characters use can help convey the feeling of a past time period — in *M*A*S*H*'s case, the early 1950's. On programs like *Police Story*, contemporary slang is used to keep the dialogue topical and current. (A robbery is "going down," an informer is a "snitch.") The excellent, fast-paced dialogue on *Police Story*, checkered with slang, makes each episode authentic and up-to-date.

A word of caution about using slang in dialogue: slang can date your material — intentionally or otherwise. When writing a script set in contemporary times, the author must be able to distinguish slang expressions that become part of the language from the transient, "fad" expressions which disappear almost instantly. (Watch a rerun of *Mod Squad*, produced just a few short years ago; see if you don't flinch every time someone says "groovy.' The material is permanently dated.)

The scriptwriter encounters a special set of problems when he tries to write dialogue for characters who speak a different dialect or who speak with an accent. Obviously, the writer must have a working knowledge of the dialect in question; he must be familiar with the pronunciation of words, the cadence, rhythm, and syntax of the dialect if his dialogue is to be effective. This familiarity is most easily acquired through the writer's personal experience, if he lives in the area where the dialect is used or knows someone who speaks it. If this type of exposure is unavailable, however, the writer is obliged to do some research. There are many books available to writers and actors on the subject of dialect and accent. Also, the writer can study other films where the dialect or accent has been used.

Once you've mastered the accent well enough to work with it, you are faced with the problem of putting it down on paper. This presents the writer with a dilemma: should he try to mimic the pronunciation by using sound spelling, or should he write the lines out as he would normally and let the actors worry about pronunciation? George Bernard Shaw used to go to great lengths to convey the exact pronunciation of every word; he wrote out lines which called for a Cockney accent using sound spelling. The method was meticulous, but of minimal use. As in Shaw's case, there is such a thing as being too exact; his sound spelling often confused the actors stuck with the part.

Most writers will not face an accent as challenging as the Cockney; but they will be called upon to use regional American speech from time to time. Instead of writing every word out in sound spelling, the writer should concentrate on rhythm and syntax. For instance, a character with a Yiddish accent might have a line like this: "You're telling me something I don't know already?" The rhythm of the line, the sentence structure, and inverted word order will convey the feeling of the dialect and serve as a key to pronunciation.

It is also permissible to alter the spelling of certain words slightly. If a character drops his g's at the end of words, you can indicate this. Just don't overdo it. All the writer has to do is give the performer indications as to how the character talks. He pays close attention to syntax and rhythm, and lets the actor worry about the exact pronunciation of various words, Sometimes a simple sentence in a stage direction is all that is required. ("Character speaks with a light Viennese accent.") So long as the performer is given some indication of the dialect, and the syntax is correct, the writer need not worry too much about accent and dialect; this is the province of the performer.

When writing dialogue, the author should also keep one point in mind: silence can be eloquent, too. Sometimes a look or a visual reaction can have more power than a whole page of dialogue. Besides knowing how to use his dialogue effectively, the scriptwriter must also learn that, sometimes, no words are necessary at all.

MUSIC

Music is the Aristotelian principle which will probably concern the scriptwriter the least. Historically, music has played an important role in drama; the early tragedies were, in many aspects, musical performances with much choral singing, rhythm, and dancing. Some mention of the role of music and sound may also be pertinent to contemporary presentations. For the sake of clarity, the use of music has been divided here into musicals, plays with music, incidental music, and sound effects.

In the case of a musical, the scriptwriter (the person who writes the "book" for the show) will probably work in tandem with a collaborator who will compose the music. There have been few cases, (e.g. Stephen Sondheim) where one person has possessed enough talent and skill to write both music and lyrics. Whether the script or the music first appears is decided by the individual creators involved in the production. In the case of Rodgers and Hammerstein, Hammerstein's words usually appeared first. Whatever arrangement the writer and the composer reach, the writer must bear a double responsibility: he must have the ability to write lyrics and must also be more concise in writing the dialogue sections.

The American musical was once the staple of Broadway and Hollywood. Today, the successful formulas of teams like Rodgers and Hammerstein have become stale and outdated. This very difficult medium is currently in a state of decline, perhaps facing extinction. Of course, there's always a chance that a new, creative approach might be discovered which could bring this once-popular art form back to life, stronger and better than ever. Until that time, devotees of musicals will have to content themselves with revivals like *No No Nanette!*

Plays with music are a common form. Most of Shakespeare's plays called for some music, songs, dances, and even underscoring. A more recent example is *Dark of the Moon,* a play set in the Smoky Mountains. It makes extensive use of the folk songs sung in that area and in so doing adds verisimilitude to the play. If the writer feels his script needs a specific song or piece of music, he should include it, or at least consider doing so. But again, the script must be packed rather than padded; including music just to fill time in a play is a poor idea.

Even in a straight, non-musical play, incidental music can play an important role. One of the best contemporary examples of an author's use of music can be found in Tennessee Williams' *A Streetcar Named Desire.* The atmosphere of New Orleans is quickly established by featuring the strains of a blues piano in the distance. In addition to this background of jazz music, music is used as "exposition" and even "characterization." Every time Blanche's mind drifts back to the night of her young husband's suicide, the dance music of that evening is reproduced. The effect is poignant and haunting. Mr. Williams was not the first author to use specific music as an aid to flashback, but he certainly used it effectively in that great dramatic play.

Incidental music can be used by an author to suggest a locale. For example, a script might include the notation: "The sound of a carousel is heard in the distance." Or sound can be used to motivate a specific action, such as "suddenly a burst of acid rock emerges from the adjoining room." Not all requests for incidental music will come from the scriptwriter. Often the director will add music during the rehearsal period, to help set the mood of the play.

Incidental music is used much the same way in television and film as it is in the theatre as far as the author is concerned. The scriptwriter will only suggest music or sound effects when he wishes to create a specific mood, or when the music or sound serves a special function. The film or program will be "scored" (that is, the background music will be added) when the entire script has already been filmed and edited. Most background music is not the scriptwriter's concern.

Beyond the use of music, the scriptwriter has a whole spectrum of options open to him which all fit under the heading of sound effects. Basically there are two categories of sound effects: action sounds and sounds that determine the setting. Action sounds are generally created by some sort of movement; an example of an action sound might be a car door slamming outside, or the sound of a gate being opened. Examples of setting sounds are traffic noises to denote the big city, or crickets chirping quietly to give the scene a country setting.

The selection and use of sound effects depends on the author's sense of observation. Chekhov was masterful at calling for the exact sounds needed to recreate a specific location and period — the sound of wagon wheels on gravel, the rustle of wind across the field, dogs barking, a thunder storm.

Every setting the author selects for his script will have its own set of sounds. While he is not expected to describe sounds for every scene, the occasional use of sounds (and silences) can add a great deal of reality and atmosphere to the script. The writer may wish to consider such options when composing or polishing his work.

SPECTACLE

Theatre

Aristotle called it *spectacle;* the French refer to it as *mise-en-scene;* and Americans often call it the setting. Whatever the writer prefers to call it, he must give some thought and attention to the physical production of his play. Unlike film productions, a theatrical play is confined to a relatively small area where the conventions of the theatre prevail. In the theatre, the components of spectacle are sets, set pieces, furniture, props, lighting, and costumes — in other words, the total visual concept of the play. These components must complement each other and, together, make a statement which re-enforces the plot, character and theme of the script.

If the potentialities of scene, costume and lighting design are unknown to the writer, if the writer is unaware of the different types of theatrical presentations, this brief summary will be of value.

Most modern plays are written with a proscenium stage in mind. A proscenium theatre is one where a wall separates the auditorium from the stage house and where the actors play in a "picture frame." In a standard, legitimate theatre you can expect to find:

    a. a center performing area
       (which can be framed in flats or curtains)
    b. wing space
    c. fly galleries
    d. pin rail
    e. curtains and battans
    f. an orchestra pit
    g. lighting ports

(Consult Illustration #1).

On such a stage the illusion of a realistic set can best be accomplished. It is also possible to abandon realism and use set pieces and curtains. Scenery can be moved on and off with wagons, up and down with battans, and around with the use of a turntable. Lights can be hung on all four sides of the center acting area without shining into the patrons' eyes. For most plays the proscenium stage is satisfactory.

Stage House

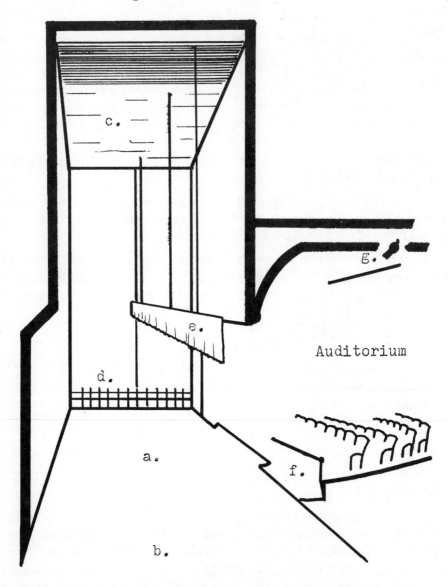

Auditorium

Illustration 1
The Proscenium Stage

During the mid-1950's there was a swing away from the proscenium stage, toward thrust and arena stages. Part of this change was artistically motivated by such people as Tyrone Guthrie. Mr. Guthrie felt the proscenium theatre separated the actor from the audience; he wanted to "break out of the picture frame" and get closer to the spectators. The use of thrust and arena stages was also motivated by economic reasons: thrust and arena stages are cheaper to build and operate.

The thrust stage (See Illustration #2) is really 3/4 round. The audience sits on three sides and furniture and other pieces are placed on the thrust. The actors perform on the thrust with only one back wall of scenery. In a thrust theatre wings and fly galleries are of minimal use, and are therefore rarely included in the structure. Realism is confined to set pieces rather than total sets; consequently, the cost of mounting a production is significantly reduced. The play can be lit from four sides, but three sides run the risk of shining light into the audience's eyes.

The arena stage is the most intimate and economical stage to operate. The audience sits on all four sides so there are no walls, no stairways, rarely any doors, and only occasionally a platform or level variation. Intimacy is an advantage, but with the exception of costume, the spectacle impact is nil.

Once the writer understands some of these basic approaches he will be able to say something about what he wants for his setting. It is not up to the author to design his set, lights, or costumes, but to simply outline the atmosphere and basic needs of the set. He tells the producers what contribution the spectacle, sets, lights, and costumes should make to the play. Describing the set as "bright and cheerful" or "old and dank" will be helpful. The designer will design the sets and arrange the lights; the director will also make some technical contributions. A general description with some specific requirements from the author will make their job much easier and more successful.

With production costs soaring, it is advisable to keep the play to one set. Multi-set shows simply cost too much to produce, especially in a proscenium theatre. Twenty years ago it was not uncommon for a three-act play to be presented in three sets. Neil Simon demonstrated how far the pendulum has swung in the opposite direction when *Plaza Suite,* three one-act plays, used only one set throughout.

There was also a time when a set could have several rooms, as in *The Desperate Hours.* However, writing a script that requires extra rooms, or an upstairs, or several exterior scenes limits the chances of an initial proscenium production. It will also be practically impossible to adapt such a production to an arena or thrust stage.

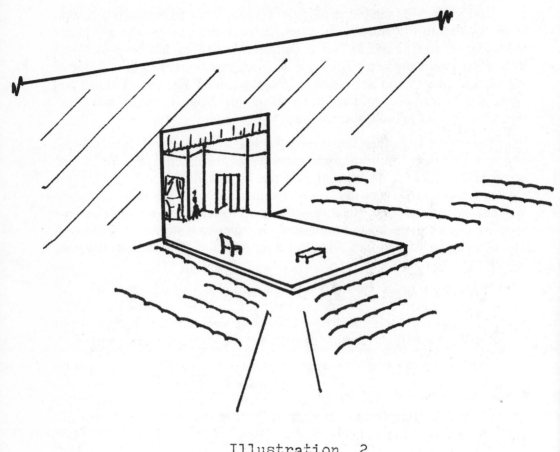

Illustration 2
The Thrust Stage

If the play absolutely demands a set change, then this major change must occur during the break between acts. There are exceptions to this rule, e.g. in musical productions where sets are flown in with great rapidity. (However, even this practice is coming to an end. A recent musical *The Chorus Line* is done with minimal scenery.)

Costume is also a part of spectacle and makes a considerable contribution to the color, atmosphere, and mood of the play. One of the fastest and most efficient ways of announcing the period of the play is to have the characters wear the correct period clothes. In revivals, the period of the play is sometimes changed simply by moving the costumes into a different period.

Whether on stage, film, or television, costumes make their own statement about each character. The author's stage directions may therefore include some mention of the character's costume. The author need not dwell on costume too much, trying to decide the exact color, texture, and style of the apparel. Costume designers will create the costume with great care if the characters are well drawn. They will also see that the costumes blend and contrast with each other properly, and with the set as well. The writer's responsibility is to give the designers a few significant details and, if characters change costume during the show, give the actors enough time to make the changes.

If a writer comes up with a terrific idea that will require an elaborate spectacle, he should first check it out with a competent theatrical designer. Amazing things can sometimes be done at minimal cost. In general, it's a good idea to: 1) limit the action to one set; 2) make sure the set complements the other elements of the play; 3) remember the contribution lights can make to the mood of the play; and 4) don't try to compete with film or TV in terms of spectacle. It's impossible.

Television and Film

Though some marvelous effects have been created in the theatre in terms of spectacle, the stage is by nature limited. Spectacle in the theatre relies heavily on the imagination of the audience. Even the most spectacular theatrical set is always just that — a set. Theatrical conventions can only create the *illusion* of reality.

The filmmaker, on the other hand, need not settle for an illusion; he can show the audience the real thing.

Film provides an unlimited stage. The motion picture form moved drama from the confines of the theatre's walls into the world, thereby removing all limitations from the phenomenon known as spectacle. With the mobility of the camera, the entire world is available as a set. Film not only uses spectacle to make a statement; the spectacle has greater impact because it is accurate, exact, and real.

This quality of reality has not always existed in motion pictures — far from it. In the days of the great Hollywood studios, spectacle simply moved from the theatrical stage to the sound stage. Filmmakers failed to take advantage of the camera's portable quality. If a motion picture was set in Paris, for example, the studio would construct a *duplicate* of the city on the back lot; location shooting was simply too easy. The question of which is the more expensive undertaking —shooting on location or building an entire city from scratch — is debatable. But this monumental waste played no small part in the decline and eventual extinction of the major studios. It was also detrimental to the concept of spectacle, since all credibility had to be suspended. Nothing was real in motion pictures.

In the '70's, there can be no artificiality in terms of spectacle. Audiences today are far too sophisticated to be impressed or fooled by dummy buildings and painted backdrops. Today, everything in films must at least look real. And the easiest way to make the setting look real is to make sure it *is* real — by filming on location.

After World War II, documentary films and feature films began to borrow from each other in terms of technique. Feature films inherited the documentary legacy of genuine settings. The camera was taken into the streets, into the home, in order to absorb the atmosphere and tempo of real-life settings. Because of this, spectacle is a prominent, integral part of contemporary film-making. Film today not only says something about the characters, but about the world they live in, the world we all live in. Spectacle today constitutes a reflection of contemporary life. At its best, film fulfills the real promise and purpose of spectacle, and remains popular in terms of audience appeal.

Film's greatest advantage in terms of spectacle is its ability to use exteriors. More and more exterior shooting is being done every day — not just in feature films, but in television as well, where the concept was practically unheard-of twenty years ago. Westerns were the first to make use of natural settings through exterior shooting. Some of the best examples of exterior shooting are found in the films of John Ford, whose breathtaking outdoor photography remains unmatched. In his work, the settings were not only visually beautiful, but said something about the characters who inhabited that world.

Today, exterior scenes are used regularly. Outdoor shooting provides a visually appealing setting, helps space the film and enhances the dramatic action.

Location shooting, both here and abroad, is common practice today, even in television. *I Spy* in the mid-1960's was the first series to film regularly in foreign locations; episodes were shot in Italy, Greece, Spain, Japan, all over the world. Programs like *It Takes a Thief* and *Name of the Game* followed suit. In today's economy, locations are not quite so exotic, but many series' still film away from the studio.

The biggest detriment to location shooting used to be the cost. Moving thousands of dollars worth of equipment made filming on location economically prohibitive. A few years ago, a gentleman named Fouad Said introduced an idea that has proven a boon to location shooting and the entire film industry in general.

Said, the former director of photography on *I Spy*, is the creator of a phenomenon known as Cinemobile. Cinemobile, a copyrighted idea, is essentially a studio on wheels, a truck containing all the cameras and portable equipment necessary for location shooting. As a result, professional production facilities are available, anywhere, at a fraction of the cost. Cinemobile has revolutionized location shooting and made it a viable alternative for every television series and feature film. The credit "production facilities by Cinemobile" has become a commonplace and permanent fixture in contemporary film productions.

All these innovations spawned by film — location shooting, exteriors, Cinemobile — have radically developed the concept of spectacle. With such means available to him today, the scriptwriter is virtually free to use any setting to fit the purposes of his script.

GENRE

In scriptwriting, genre is the key to treatment. It is what makes Feydeau's treatment of infidelity different from Tennessee Williams' treatment of the same subject. Whether to treat the subject in question humorously or tragically is a question of genre.

Some theorists maintain that there are only two different genres, comedy and tragedy; others maintain there are as many genres as there are scripts. As Elton Elder explained it, it all depends on whether you're a "lumper" or a "splitter." We are not concerned with developing a deep philosophical discussion of the comic and tragic muse; nor is there much point in trying to come to grips with the myriad of different "isms" (expressionism, naturalism, and so on ad infinitum). However, contemporary scriptwriters should at least be aware of the basic genres in order to 1) consider the various approaches to his story available to him and 2) know which genre he is using so as to write with consistency.

There are three basic categories of genre: realism, fantasy, and farce. These categories can be defined by applying the maxim "Is it possible or probable?" If the story is both possible and probable, the writer is working within the category of realism. Both comedy and drama can be treated realistically and both can be used within the same script. When this occurs the script is referred to as a tragi-comedy. If the material in the script is possible but not probable, it is considered farce. John Guare is a modern playwright whose approach to plot and character would be stifled if he were forced to stay within the bounds of realism. His characters say things and perform actions which may be possible but are often highly improbable. (The Marx Brothers are another example of farcical performers.) Finally, if the action in the script is neither possible nor probable, the writer is working in the area of fantasy. The script for the motion picture *The Exorcist* might be considered a fantasy; another, less controversial example, is *Peter Pan*, Almost everyone agrees that people cannot fly by means of fairy dust.

Realism, farce, and fantasy are the basic genres with which the writer will be concerned. It is possible to write comedy, tragedy, drama, mystery, or any combination under any of the three categories. Combining these sub-categories (for instance, writing a comedy-drama) was at one time frowned upon, but in the 1970's this is a completely acceptable practice. It is unacceptable, however, to interweave the primary categories of realism, fantasy, and farce.

There are many examples of modern scenarists who successfully combine comedy and drama within one basic genre. Sean O'Casey, although hardly a writer of the '70's, brought tragi-comedy to a state of near-perfection in his play *Juno and the Paycock*. The two male leads, Captain Boyle and Joxer, could most aptly be described as an Irish version of Laurel and Hardy. Against the backdrop of war, death, unwanted pregnancy, and poverty Joxer spouts a multitude of "darlin' proverbs" while Boyle complains of pain in his legs whenever there's work to be done. They are united in their fear of Mrs. Boyle. These characteristics, combined with their laziness and charm, provide a great deal of comedy in a very serious setting.

A more recent example is *The Effect of Gamma Rays on Man-in-the-Moon Marigolds*, where Paul Zindel introduced Beatrice, a tragic figure who occasionally displays flashes of deliberate wit (albeit menacing). An example of Beatrice's humor is provided when Beatrice becomes upset with her studious daughter, Matilda, for keeping a white rabbit in the house. Beatrice crosses to the medicine cabinet and returns with a bottle saying "Here it is. Here's a new word for you, Tri. . .trichloro. . . .methane. Do you know what that is, Matilda? Well, it's chloroform. I'm saving it for that Angora manure machine of yours." Later in the play Beatrice refers to the rabbit as a "cotton-tail compost heap." Zindel's sense of humor may not be on the same level as Neil Simon's (who also blends comedy and drama consistently), but this excerpt illustrates that comedy and drama can be (and often are) used within the same script, be it a comedy with tragic elements (a la Simon) or a tragedy with comic elements (a la Zindel).

But while comedy, drama, and the other sub-categories can be blended successfully, the three basic genres cannot. Scriptwriters are wise to select one genre at the outset and stick with it throughout the script. One test of a good script is its consistency.

Of special consideration is the writing of melodrama. Since the 19th century this sub-genre has been one of the most popular forms of entertainment. Audiences have long enjoyed booing the villain and cheering the hero. Motion pictures used to fulfill the audience's appetite for melodrama; that responsibility has since been relegated to television.

In pure melodrama, the following conditions exist:
1) The characters are two-dimensional.
2) The forces of good and evil are only discussed on an elementary level.
3) There is an emphasis on physical action.
4) There is usually an exciting climax just prior to the conclusion.
5) There is a dual ending; good wins out and evil is vanquished.

The term "two-dimensional characters" means that the characters are usually easily identifiable and are quickly established at the beginning of the program. Once they are established, they never change; they are either good or bad, or stupid or humorous. They remain that way until the show is over. Most actors become bored with a long-running series for this very reason; the characters they play are not allowed to expand. There is no progression, growth, or exploration into the character's mind and emotions. In well written scripts, characters must grow, change, and learn something about themselves and the world around them.

Television has matured rapidly in recent years. More and more attention is being paid to intelligent characterization and plot. Scripts that would have been handled as melodrama ten years ago now arrive as full-fledged, legitimate drama. But the staple of television is still melodrama, and perhaps always will be.

CHAPTER TWO

TECHNICAL ELEMENTS

One of the most desirable tools of the scriptwriting trade is a basic knowledge of the medium in which the author wishes to write. For the theatrical playwright, a simple understanding of stage directions is sufficient. But the television and film writer deals with a far more complicated medium; he must have some understanding of camera movements, placement, angles, and effects. While scriptwriters don't have to be technological geniuses, they must know enough about their medium to be acquainted with both its scope and its limitations. Under such conditions, they can take full advantage of the technical miracles available to them. Scriptwriters must also be able to translate their ideas into the functional jargon used by those who translate those ideas into action — the directors, cameramen, and engineers.

Here, we are only concerned with those technical elements of film and television production that are pertinent to the writer. Script writers are only concerned with the fundamentals of production, since it is the director who determines the actual shots and decides all technical matters.

Much to the writer's relief, there will actually be two different scripts used during the production. The first is the author's script, which, technically, describes the basic action without too much mention of specific shots and camera angles. The second is the shooting script in which the director has listed each specific shot, angle, movement, and effect to be used in the production. The shooting script bears almost no resemblance to the author's script, since it is highly detailed and very technical. The writer need only concern himself with a concise description of the action, and let the director worry about the rest.

If the writer would like additional information about the technical elements of film production, if only to satisfy curiosity and broaden his horizons, there are several fine books available that deal exclusively with this subject. For television production, one of the best is Herbert Zettl's

Television Production Handbook (Wadsworth Publishing, Belmont, California) the bible of television students everywhere. Zettl's book will tell the writer more than he'd ever need to know about television production.

For our purposes, the basic terms and definitions the writer will use from time to time follows:

Camera Shots

The distance from which the audience sees the action is determined by 1) the placement of the camera and 2) the position of the zoom lens. Specific shots most commonly called for are the Long Shot, Medium Shot, and the Close-up.

Long Shot (abbreviated LS) A long shot is a full view of the scene, including the background. A long shot of an actor will frame his entire figure, like a full-length portrait. The camera is placed a considerable distance away from the subject; the zoom lens is generally fully extended as wide as it will go.

Close-up (CU) The object or individual is only a short distance from the camera, tightly framed. A close-up of a person photographs him above the shoulders, framing his face. Close-ups are used when the character's facial expression or visual reaction is important, especially in scenes of high emotional intensity.

A close-up that focuses on one feature of the performer's face (for instance, his eyes), or which tightly focuses on a single object is called a *Big Close-up or Tight Close-up.*

Medium Shot (MS) A medium shot is the midpoint between a long shot and a close-up. A medium shot of an individual photographs him from the waist up.

There are variations of the above shots as well. Terms like *Medium Long Shot* (MLS), *Medium Close-up* (MCU) and *Extreme Close-up* (ECU) define the distance between audience and subject more exactly. But such exactness is not the writer's responsibility. These are directors' terms.

Number of Characters The number of characters photographed in a given shot is designated by the terms *one-shot, two-shot, three-shot,* and *four-shot.* A shot grouping more than four people is termed a *group shot.*

For example, a scene consists of two characters talking; it is important that they be photographed together, for dramatic reasons. You would include this direction in the script:

TWO-SHOT, BILL AND JANE.

It is not necessary to list the number of characters in every given shot, as that is the director's job. The writer doesn't have to call for a two-shot or a three-shot every time the scene changes. He will only use these terms when he has to, when there is specific reason why a certain kind of shot should be used.

CAMERA MOVEMENT

Dolly. To dolly in means that the entire camera is moved closer to the subject; dolly out is the reverse. A dolly shot increases or decreases the field of vision.

Zoom. Through the movement of the zoom lens, the camera can vary the distance between the audience and the action. For instance, if the camera is on a medium shot of a performer and a close-up is required, the camera can simply *zoom in;* the reverse is a *zoom out.*

The resulting effect (changing the distance) is similar to the one produced by a dolly shot. But with a zoom, it is not necessary to move the camera; the lens does all the work.

Pan. Turning the camera to the left or to the right is called *panning.* By panning, the camera can sweep a scene, follow a moving character or object, or turn its attention to something else in the scene. A pan is indicated by the terms 'pan left' or 'pan right.'

Tilt. The camera is moved up or down.

Truck. Instead of turning the camera to the left or right on its axis (panning), the entire camera moves to the left or right. The truck shot is used to follow the action. For example, two characters are walking down the street; a pan cannot follow them. Call for a trucking shot, as follows:

BILL AND TOM START WALKING DOWN THE STREET.
TRUCK WITH THEM.

CAMERA ANGLES

High angle shot. The camera shoots down on the scene from above (from a high angle.)

Low angle shot. The camera shoots up at the action from below.

Overhead shot. A camera is placed directly above the action and shoots down. Overhead shots were used to photograph the June Taylor dancers on the *Jackie Gleason Show:* they were also used frequently in the film *The Cincinnati Kid.*

Over-the-shoulder shot. The camera sees the action over the character's shoulder. The over-the-shoulder shot is often used when two characters are engaged in dialogue.

Reverse-angle shot. Let's say the script calls for an over-the-shoulder shot as described above; the camera shoots the face of one character, over the shoulder of a second; next, the camera will shoot the second character over the shoulder of the first. This is called a reverse-angle shot. Reverse angle shots are used frequently on *Columbo*, to name one example. (They are much easier to point out than they are to define.)

Point-of-View. The shot is described by referring to the way in which a character sees it, in terms of his perspective. Point-of-View is one of the most common directions, and is abbreviated POV.

Example:

JOHN WALKS CAUTIOUSLY DOWN A DESERTED CITY STREET LATE AT NIGHT.

SUDDENLY A MAN STEPS OUT OF THE ALLEY AND BLOCKS JOHN'S PATH.

JOHN'S POV, THE MAN
JOHN FIRST SEES THE MAN'S HARD, MENACING FACE. HE LOOKS DOWN UNTIL HIS EYES COME TO REST ON THE GUN IN THE MAN'S HAND.

TRANSITIONS

A transition is the device used to move from one scene to the next (that is, replacing one shot on the screen with another.) Transitions are always noted at the end of a scene in television or film. At the end of a television act (i.e., before a commercial break), the term FADE OUT is used. This will be discussed in greater detail in the section on script format in the next chapter.

At the end of a scene, whenever the location or the period of time changes, one of these two directions will be given:

Cut. A cut is an instantaneous switch from one scene to the next, or one shot to the next. Cuts are the most common transitions in both film and television today since many productions try to maintain a fast pace. Unless otherwise noted, the director will always assume that a cut is to be used whenever a new shot is introduced.

Cuts are not only used at the end of most scenes, but are also used *within* the scene, whenever a different view of the action is required.

Dissolve. To dissolve means to slowly overlap the end of one shot with the beginning of the next. A dissolve is most commonly used to denote the passing of time. Dissolves are used infrequently these days, since most television and film directors favor the quick transition the cut provides.

Dissolves were used frequently in the early days of television, and also in films until recently. A dissolve is a rather old-fashioned transition device, and can be used most effectively in old-fashioned period productions.

Some television programs develop their own special transition devices, a trademark of the series. For example, *Man from U.N.C.L.E* used a whip pan between scenes, a sort of on-screen blur; *Batman* used to spin the camera rapidly, a variation of the whip pan. Some programs will defocus the camera, then refocus on another scene. The writer will substitute the special transition device for the cut or dissolve when writing for a show that has its own visual trademark. Every few years, a new transition "fad" will be introduced to television. The writer will simply have to watch for them and use them at his own discretion. As a rule, the direct cut and the dissolve serve the writer's needs well; let the director worry about the visual gimmicks.

CHAPTER THREE

THE TECHNIQUE OF SCRIPTWRITING

The actual writing of a script for theatre, television, or film is divided into five stages: the idea stage, the treatment, the step outline (or scenario), the first draft, and the final polish. These five steps trace the progression of a story from the embryonic idea form to its completion as a polished, marketable script. All five stages are interrelated; each depends on the quality of its predecessor in order to work. When the writer pays proper attention to the early, preparatory stages, putting the final script together is relatively simple. But if the early stages are neglected, the script will not develop as it should.

Too often, new writers (or lazy ones) try to find shortcuts in the scriptwriting process; they omit the treatment stage or the step-out stage (or both) and try to jump directly from the idea to the first draft. The standard rationale for this shortcutting is, "I've got the whole story in my head. All I have to do is put it down on paper." This is mindless thinking for any writer, especially one whose experience is limited. A contractor doesn't start putting up a building until he has a detailed blueprint in front of him; a well-constructed script requires a blueprint, too. The writer is doing himself a great disservice if he tries to cut corners in order to "save time." His work will undoubtedly show the effects of sloppy preparation; and ironically, shortcutting only makes the entire writing process harder, not easier. A Noel Coward can take liberties with the scriptwriting form, but there are few Noel Cowards among us. New writers are cautioned against departure from the standard scripting procedure until their genius is fully established; even then they should think twice about such deviations.

Each of the five stages has its own form and its own specific function. If each step receives proper attention, that combined with the author's creativity and dramatic instinct, should result in a solid, well-crafted script. Laboring over each step will demand a great deal of time, concentration, and energy, true; but who ever said scriptwriting was easy?

The Idea Stage

One of the professional writer's primary concerns is to develop new story ideas. Writers are constantly searching for fresh ideas that will spark their imaginations and set the creative juices flowing. They must always be aware of people, places and events around them. A good writer must also be an avid reader; his work requires solid research and a knowledge of his own culture. Newspapers, magazines, and books are professional necessities. The writer must absorb as much as he can from life, and he must do so consciously. Observation is part of his trade, for from his observations come ideas for future scripts.

Professional writers know that a good story idea can come from anywhere — from a character one has met or heard of, from a conversation overheard in a restaurant, from an item in the newspaper, from an everyday occurrence. The quality that separates the writer from the layman is the unique ability to see a dramatic potential is an unlikely source. Writers must also be blessed with the talent to develop the idea through their own imaginations, to shape it, and to find a logical and dramatic conclusion to bring the idea full-circle.

Sometimes a story can find its origins in a philosophical observation or perception on the part of the author. The author begins with a theme he would like to explore (greed, love, hate, revenge, whatever) and tries to build a story to fit the theme. However, when a story is written to fit a theme, (as opposed to finding the theme of the story), it usually results in a lumbering, self-conscious, pretentious piece that is more mess than message. Thematic considerations generally come later in the scriptwriting process. If the story is good, if the conflicts are solid and dramatic, if the characters are well-defined, the theme will practically develop itself and will become an intrinsic part of the story. Although there are inevitably exceptions to every rule, theme is usually an unlikely source for a story idea. Drama does not live by theme alone.

Character is a more likely source of story ideas. Developing a story around the personality of an interesting or unusual character is a current trend. This approach has mushroomed in the past few years; many motion pictures are television series have been based on an idea for a character. For example, real life undercover policeman, David Toma, was the inspiration for a moderately successful 1973 series, *Toma,* which in turn led to a top-quality 1975 series, *Baretta.* Both of these programs are built around the exploits and idiosyncracies of the central character. *Baretta* particularly depends on its vibrant, irreverent hero for its excitement in what would otherwise be a mere potboiler. Thanks to the careful attention the writers give to characterization (not to mention the considerable talents of Emmy-Award-winning Robert Blake) Tony Baretta has become as life-like a character as one is likely to find on prime-time television.

Another example of an interesting character providing the story idea comes from the series that probably started the trend in the first place. In the late 1960's, writers Richard Levinson and William Link created a TV detective totally different from the quick-witted, physically flawless heroes of *77 Sunset Strip* and *Mannix*. Their hero was a rumpled police lieutenant who cloaked his sharp detective skills beneath an illusion of ineptness and a coffee-stained raincoat. His name, of course, was Columbo. (To this day, no one knows his first name.) Columbo, played so expertly by Peter Falk, made his debut in a made-for-TV movie; later the *Columbo* series became one of the most popular detective shows of all time. At the beginning of each episode, the audience learns who the murderer is; the fun is in watching Columbo wear down his suspect with his bumbling, annoying persistence. It is Columbo's relentless pursuit and his personal style that make the series unique (and highly rated).*

In the wake of *Columbo's* success there came a flood of imperfect TV detectives: Ironside was confined to a wheelchair; Longstreet was blind; Cannon was fat; Kojak was bald. Each of these series' had as its base a novel idea for a central character. Quite often, the style of that character took precedence over the plot. The series was used as a showcase for the central character, with varying degrees of success.

Sometimes an idea for a character can be the basis for an individual episode in a series as well. An original character, played by a talented guest star, can be worked quite comfortably into the established format of the program. This is especially true of anthology series like *Police Story*. This high-quality series has no regular cast and features a different lead character every week. There is a heavy emphasis on characterization as well as plot. *Police Story* has dealt in the past with ambitious cops, psychopathic cops, cops on the take, women cops, self-styled supermen, and on down the line. In each case, a strong character is blended with an action-packed story line; the result is one of the most consistently fine programs on television today.

Most television series do not enjoy the freedom of *Police Story*. Usually the series format is firmly established, and the regular characters have been

---

*(A little-known footnote in television history: the character Columbo was originally created for was Bing Crosby!)

developed as far as the producers intend to go. Writers must therefore devote their energies to finding ideas for possible plots.

Many writers find viable plot ideas in contemporary events. A real-life crime, an unusual robbery or scandal can provide the idea for a script. As society becomes more and more bizarre, all the writer has to do is pick up the paper; his scenario will already be drawn out for him. Some recent examples: a series of murders in Boston was the inspiration for two films — *The Boston Strangler* and *No Way to Treat a Lady; Dirty Harry* borrowed its plot from a series of homicides in the San Francisco area; *All the President's Men* is the story of the *Washington Post* reporters who uncovered the Watergate scandal; *The French Connection* is a true story; the *Pueblo* incident was recreated in a TV movie starring Hal Holbrook. In a lighter vein, a newspaper report of a 200-pound man who claimed he was raped by a 110-pound woman was the inspiration for a TV movie with the droll title *It Couldn't Happen to a Nicer Guy.*

Television is especially good at taking controversial topics and building a story around them before the controversy dies down. Once again, newspapers and magazines can supply the source material. Some examples from the '70's: *Maude* combined character and plot in a two-part episode on abortion; the current concern over the increase of rapes and the treatment of rape victims resulted in two TV films — *A Case of Rape* and *Cry Rape;* homosexuality was dealt with in *That Certain Summer;* runaway wives were the subject in *The Last Good-by.* In each case, the story idea came from a topic that concerned the public. The writers obviously paid close attention to newspapers and magazines to find the subjects people were talking about. Television, by virtue of its immediacy, is able to dramatize these controversial topics and events before they become passe.

There is one rather grim twist in contemporary society of which the writer must be aware. When Oscar Wilde observed that "life mirrors art," one wonders if he was anticipating television and films. Life in the '70's does have an alarming tendency to mimic what it has seen on film. Sometimes this phenomenon is amusing, as in the case of a convict who escaped from prison by helicopter after seeing the stunt in a Charles Bronson movie, *Breakout.* But in other cases it can prove tragic. In 1974, a gang of teenagers murdered a young woman by dousing her with gasoline and setting her on fire; they had seen the same act on *Kojak,* the night before.

Contemporary scriptwriters must realize that, sometimes, they will have to disregard a sensational idea because it is too graphic or too real. If a scenarist comes up with a fresh idea for a murder, a robbery or a kidnapping, he should be warned that in the 1970's the odds are very good that some kook will run out and try to live the scenario. While this fact should not cramp the writer's creative powers entirely, he should be aware of the moral responsibility he assumes when writing for a mass audience. In some cases, discretion is the better part of writing. Television and film receive enough criticism as it is without being accused of serving as an audio-visual aid for potential criminals.

Just as the study of current events can serve as a source of story ideas, so can past history. Many great scripts have had their beginnings in the discovery of a little-known historical incident or a new twist on one that is well-known. Robert Parker and Harry Longbaugh were little known until William Goldman and George Roy Hill unearthed their story and turned it into a film — *Butch Cassidy and the Sundance Kid.*

A popular trend or fad in motion pictures can also serve as a source for story ideas (albeit a dubious one). This phenomenon is known in Hollywood circles as "jumping on the bandwagon." Filmmakers have a habit of trying to capitalize on a trend by mimicking an already successful picture. For instance, films set in the 1930's have enjoyed great popularity the past few years; next year, writers won't be able to give away scripts set in the '30's when the market is glutted. The same is true of disaster pictures. After the enormously successful *Poseidon Adventure,* every major studio rushed into production with its own sensational calamity — crashing airplanes, earthquakes, towering infernos. The point is, some writers (and most studios) find their "inspiration" in what the other guy is doing. Time and time again, this has proven disastrous. It takes a year to put together a major motion picture and release it; by that time the public has turned to something else for diversion and the trend is dead. Unless a writer can work quickly (or a studio commissions him), he should never try to cash in on a current fad. Don't follow a trend—start a new one.

These examples of possible sources for story ideas — themes, characters, current topics and events, historical characters and incidents — is not a definitive list. It is intended to give the writer some idea of where to go and what to watch for in his search for new ideas.

If there is one invaluable source of story ideas, it is the writer's own personal experience. The writer's background, his youth, his family and friends, jobs he held, hobbies, and interests — all of these represent a wealth of potential material. A script drawn from a writer's personal knowledge can be authentic, rich in detail and, above all, true to life. Joseph Wambaugh, novelist and creator of *Police Story,* parlayed his experience as a Los Angeles policeman into a highly successful writing career. Author Eric Monte drew upon his youth in the Chicago ghetto as a source of material; the result was TV's popular *Good Times* and the 1975 film *Cooley High.*

Two crucial points about personal experience: It's a good idea for the writer to stick to what he knows about, at least in the beginning of his career. If the author knows something about medicine or law, he should try to write about those topics; if he has a special interest in the Old West, he should use it. Writers who tackle a subject they know nothing about usually find themselves in over their heads. If you happened to grow up in the ghetto, write about that; don't try to do a comedy about high society — at least not right away.

The second point is: Always remember that a scriptwriter must be selective. The most exciting experience of an author's life may not necessarily make a good script; perhaps no one cares but the author. Keep in mind that drama is bigger than life, and that any story has to have good dramatic potential. If the author's objectivity and editorial judgement are diminished because he's too close to his story, the result can be a one-sided or, even worse, a tedious script.

For the most part, developing story ideas from one's own experience can be very pleasurable work. The demand for new ideas dictates that the scriptwriter must expose himself to new surroundings, people, and experiences all the time. It's all part of the profession and, as a rule, an enjoyable part at that.

No discussion on story ideas would be complete without some mention of the biggest problem writers face: what happens when you get stuck for an idea? The answer is: don't panic. Writers can go for weeks or even months without finding a story idea that has potential. It happens to everyone, and there's no way to prevent it. All you can do is keep looking and keep thinking. Worrying about a dry spell only makes it worse. A story idea can come from anywhere; just when the writer is convinced he can never think of another subject, a brilliant idea will come to him. Don't be alarmed by an occasional fallow period. Sometimes, instead of the writer finding a great idea, the idea has to find the writer.

Once a promising idea has been found, the writing process begins. The idea should be written down in a single, concise paragraph. It should indicate who the central characters are, which program type the idea is intended for (if applicable), what the major action or conflict is and how it will be resolved.

A story idea in its initial paragraph form may look something like this:
"Wide World of Mystery"

"A series of Jack-the-Ripper-style murders plagues a quiet resort town. All the police know is that a scalpel was used as the murder weapon, and that the wounds on the victims, all young girls, indicate that the killer may have had some training as a surgeon. The sole suspect is the town's physician, Dr. Arthur Dawson; Dawson, a quiet, rather mysterious man and a newcomer to the town, has no alibi for any of the murders. When the police try to arrest him he runs, which seems to prove his guilt. In reality, the doctor wants to catch the real murderer before the police catch him.

The mystery is resolved when the doctor catches the real killer, a waiter at one of the hotels who, during the academic year, is a medical student."

Any promising idea the writer comes upon should be written down in this form. It is often possible to tell just from working with these few sentences whether the idea has any real potential or not. Writing the idea in paragraph form capsulizes the idea, reduces it to its most basic ingredients — character, conflict, and resolution. If these concepts work together well once they're on paper, the idea may be worth pursuing.

Any story idea, however good or bad, should be written down and saved for future reference. Sometimes the writer will find an idea that he knows he won't be able to treat, an idea ahead of its time; but perhaps he will be able to use it at some future date. Sometimes an idea just won't click; but six months later, the writer may stumble across the missing ingredient that makes the idea terrific. Frequently an idea simply isn't strong enough for a full-length script; but the idea may make an excellent subplot in another story. For all these reasons, the writer should record all his ideas for that time when they might come in handy.

Coming up with a fresh story idea is one of the most difficult tasks of being a scriptwriter. Rehashing an old idea is fairly simple; coming up with something really special is quite another matter. It is for this reason that the idea stage is so important. Fresh ideas are the reason most young writers are given a chance. Television, with its voracious appetite for material, consumes approximately two thousand story ideas each year in prime time alone; since the demand for fresh ideas is so great, there is usually room for new talent with new ideas.

The idea stage can be very important to the writer, in both an artistic and commercial sense. The first essential part of the writer's craft is the ability to find and cultivate promising story ideas.

The second part is knowing what to do with an idea once you've found it.

The Treatment

Once you have decided on the general elements of the script — character, conflict, and resolution — you must start fleshing the story out; you will add more detail and start shaping the story. In short, you start concentrating on the details that will make the story more than a good idea — this is the purpose of the treatment stage.

The treatment, quite simply, is an expansion of the idea. It is the basic framework around which the script will be built. The treatment deals exclusively with the plot and develops the general story line. When you have finished the treatment, you will have clearly outlined the story's major crises, its turning points, its climax, and resolution.

In the theatre, this process is sometimes referred to as "developing the spine of the play." "Spine of the play" is a particularly apt term, since a sound script relies heavily on the strength or the weakness of the treatment. Drama is, after all, the story of characters in conflict; a good script must have a clearly-defined major conflict which can be brought to an exciting conclusion. The treatment defines the conflict and conclusion; the rest of the action in the story may then be built around this central action.

Using the idea given in the last section, the subsequent treatment would look something like this:

"Wide World of Mystery"
"The Doctor's House"

1)   Late one night, a girl walking alone on the beach is suddenly attacked. A man strangles her; she falls to the ground. The man reaches into his pocket and takes out a gleaming scalpel.

2)   The girl's mutilated body is discovered the next morning. The police have no leads and no witnesses to the crime.

3)   Two nights later, a waitress at a restaurant in the local hotel is attacked by the same man while going home from work.

4)   An autopsy reveals that the murders were not the work of a mad "butcher"; all the wounds were made with the neatness and precision of a surgeon. A scalpel is the probable murder weapon. Both women were strangled, then systematically dissected.

5)   All evidence points to one man: Dr. Arthur Dawson, the town's only physician. Dawson is new in town, a mysterious character and a natural suspect. The police bring him to headquarters for questioning.

At the station, the police are questioning the employees from the hotel to see if they saw or heard anything the night before. One of the employees, a young waiter working to send himself back to graduate school in the fall, says he thought he saw a tall man running toward the woods soon after the crime was committed. Dr. Dawson is a tall man; the police become more suspicious of him. When questioned, the doctor has no alibi for either night — he was at home, alone. Although the police are suspicious, they don't have enough evidence to hold the doctor.

6) The next evening, Dr. Dawson's nurse is working late. As she is leaving, she is attacked. The doctor, who lives nearby, thinks he hears something, goes to investigate. He doesn't see anything and goes inside again.

7) Next morning, the police arrest Dawson. His nurse's body has been found, with a bloodied scalpel, belonging to the doctor, next to her. The doctor escapes.

8) The doctor spends the day trying to elude the police. Late that night, he waits in the woods next to the hotel. He sees a young woman leave the hotel. She is walking. He follows, quietly.

9) The girl walks about two blocks when a man steps out from the shadows and attacks her. She screams and struggles. Suddenly the doctor appears and grapples with the man; he wrestles a scalpel out of the man's hand, finally subdues him.

10) The police arrive. The doctor hands over the killer. It is the young waiter who claimed he'd seen a man running away when the police questioned him. The doctor had not been waiting at the hotel for another victim. He hoped the young man might attack again. When the police ask how he knew the young man was the killer, he tells them he heard the young man mention that he was in graduate school at State University. It wasn't until later that the doctor realized the only graduate school the university had is a medical school. Therefore, the young med student would be knowledgeable in the handling of a scalpel.

11) The police apologize to the doctor and take him home.

Although not one of the great mysteries of modern time, the treatment does set down the major conflict of the story, all the major crises, the climax and the resolution. Once the foundation for the plot is set down, the writer can build his action toward the crises. He is also free to add subplots and incidental action to make the story more interesting and enjoyable. But first he must have an overall structure for the script, as the treatment demonstrates.

Sometimes it is also helpful to diagram the action, as illustrated in the section on plotting. The diagram of this particular story looks like this:

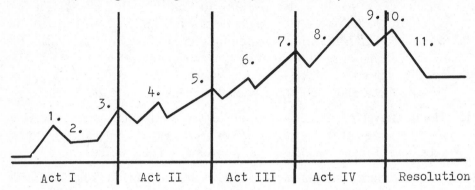

Since the treatment only establishes the basic structure of the plot and is therefore not too detailed, it can usually be set down in a well-written page or two. As this treatment indicates, it is intended for the writer's use, and may not mean too much to anyone else. But the treatment stage is important to the writer himself; it serves as his general outline, and helps him decide what is supposed to happen and when it is supposed to happen in his script. If the treatment works, if it includes exciting or significant crises, if the action builds to the story's climax, if the plot holds together, then the writer probably has the makings of an acceptable script. The purpose of the treatment is to show the writer whether the idea is really dramatic or not; if the treatment is solid, the script will usually be solid, at least in terms of plot.

Once you have the basic plot laid out, you move to the next step: the step-out stage.

The Step—Out

The next, and perhaps, the most critical stage in the scriptwriting process is referred to as the step—out stage. The name is an abbreviation for "step-by-step outline." There are other names for this stage — it may be called an "outline," a "scenario" or even a treatment. All these terms are acceptable and interchangeable. For our purpose, the term "step-out" will be used, since it is probably the most common term, and is also the most descriptive.

A step-out is a complete description of the entire story, broken down, scene by scene, and written in prose form. It is the most comprehensive outline the writer will use. It describes all the action in the script, all the characters, the locales, and might even include some dialogue. Just as the treatment stage expands the idea, the step out fills in all the details and expands the treatment.

The step out is of inestimable value to the writer. By putting a good deal of time and energy into writing a comprehensive step-out, the writer makes the actual writing of the script much easier. As the writer starts to work on the first draft, he will have a complete description of the story in front of him. If the step-out is through enough, the script itself is practically written. In fact, most writers could put together an entire script following someone else's step-out, if it was done properly. From a writing standpoint, the step-out is a crucial step. In many cases, a script could be described as an elaboration of a well-written stepout.

The step-out also serves an important commercial purpose. In almost all cases of scriptwriting, especially when the work has been commissioned, the step-out is the first piece of material the producer (i.e. potential buyer) will see. On the merit of the step-out, he will decide whether or not he wishes to invest money in the project. If the step-out is good, the producer may offer to buy the subsequent script; if the step-out is poor, he will likely turn it down.

The step-out is also worth money in itself. If the producer decides the step-out has potential, he has one of two options: he can pay the writer a "deposit," perhaps a thousand dollars or so, and commission the writer to complete the script. Or, he can buy the step-out from the author outright and commission another writer to do the script. In either case, the producer will pay the writer for the work he's done. In terms of dollars and cents, the stepout is worth one-quarter of the sum paid for the completed script. For instance, if the going rate for a completed script is six thousand dollars, the step-out is worth fifteen hundred. The step-out, therefore, has both artistic and commercial value.

What should be included in a step-out? In a word, everything. A step-out should contain all the information pertinent to the telling of the story. It is a prose version of the script, minus the embellishments. Write the step-out as though you were describing the story, in detail, to a friend. Step by step, and in proper sequence, describe the action of the story— plot, subplots, characters and locations.

A step-out written for the story we treated earlier follows:

After receiving the results of the autopsy report, Chief Larraby decides to pay a call on Dr. Dawson. He drives to the doctor's office on the outskirts of town. As he drives, he sees the beach on his left and the spot where the body of the killer's first victim had been found. Further down the road he sees the woods, the scene of the second murder. Ahead, obscured by some tall pines, is Dr. Dawson's clinic.

Larraby parks his car and goes inside. He talks to the doctor's nurse, Mrs. Davis, a handsome woman in her late thirties. Mrs. Davis, like the rest of the townspeople, is very upset about the murders. She asks the chief if he has any suspects. Larraby is non-committal. He changes the subject and asks the nurse about the doctor's nightly routine as casually as he can. The nurse says there's nothing too unusual about it; the doctor sees patients until six most nights, then goes home. Sometimes she works late to set up for the next day or catch up on paperwork. Larraby asks her what kind of man her employer is. Mrs. Davis says she doesn't really know. In the office, he's quiet, polite, very professional. He keeps to himself. She doesn't really know what he's like outside the office. Larraby asks if he can have a word with the doctor.

This brief example illustrates the type of description used in a typical step-out scene. There's really no need for flowery, expansive prose — just tell what happens in the scene as concisely and lucidly as possible. The step-out should be conversational in tone, so that the material is understandable and easy to follow. Lengthy exposition, poetic descriptions and rich metaphors aren't necessary in the step-out. Don't be self-conscious about style — just tell the story.

Some purists maintain that a step-out should be straight descriptive prose, with no dialogue included. This attitude is a bit too pure, since what characters say is often as important as what they do. Entire passages of dialogue should not be included; in fact, dialogue will ordinarily be kept to a minimum. But an occasional line of dialogue, used judiciously, can add impact to a key scene and make it a little more interesting to the producer who reads it.

Brief snatches of dialogue can be included if dialogue is one of the writer's strengths. Perhaps the characters phrase things in a fresh, crackling style that makes the story even more interesting. It might not be a bad idea to give the producer a small sample of the merchandise; let him know, subtly, that you have a flair for dialogue. While the step-out's immediate function is to describe the story, it's secondary function is to advertise the talent of the scriptwriter.

The step-out generally runs about 12 to 15 pages, double spaced, for an hour-length story, and may run as long as 20 pages for a longer work. The length, however, is rather arbitrary. The important consideration is to remember that a step-out is a comprehensive work-up, long enough to cover the topic completely. Also, the step-out must be clear and meaningful to a number of people, to the writer himself and any potential buyers who read the material.

Besides being an important organizational tool, the stepout provides essential information for the producer. Before the producer even sees the completed script, he will know how large a cast the film will require, where the production will be filmed, how many sets will be used, and other pertinent production details. Not only does the step-out tell the producer how good a story is, it also tells him how involved the production will be and how much it might cost.

Many producers will not read a completed script unless they've seen a step-out first and have approved it — simply because they don't have the time. Why read one-hundred pages of script when the story can be fully explained in twelve or fifteen pages? The abbreviated story description is a time saver for producers and agents; it can also save the writer time. An agent or producer can look at the step-out and recommend changes at the outset of the project; this avoids the problem of having to rewrite whole sections of the script. It is much easier to spot a problem early and solve it immediately, before the actual script is written.

The step-out "saves time" for the writer in other ways. Just as a story can be approved on the basis of a good stepout, a story can also be rejected on the basis of a step-out. No matter how high the quality of the work might be, stories can be rejected for any number of reasons (Too expensive to produce, too outlandish, the studio bought a property just like it last week). Circulating the step-out will often tell a writer whether he has a market for the script or not. While having a step-out rejected won't make the author jump for joy, it will at least spare him the trouble of writing a script that can't be sold. "Testing the waters" is also part of the step-out's purpose.

Many writers work up an outline for their use; then, after they have a high-quality script already finished, they write a new step-out to show producers. This can work well for the amateur writer, since many producers are reluctant to read a full-length script from an unknown writer; the step-out may sell the script. Once the writer's career is rolling, this trick won't be necessary. But, at the beginning, it's a good idea to have a topnotch script prepared before showing anything to a producer. If the producer wants to see more, the writer will have to be able to come up with something fast. The step-out is only a promise — the script is a fulfillment of that promise.

The First Draft

Most beginning writers have a preoccupation with learning proper script format. This format is really quite easy to master, much easier than it may appear. The standard script format is to an experienced writer what basic mathematics is to an engineer — a fundamental knowledge. And, like multiplication tables, once script format has been absorbed and practiced for awhile, it becomes second nature to the writer. Professional writers are far more concerned with the content of their scripts than with its form. However, it is a good idea for the beginner to become acquainted with script format so that he may become comfortable with it. After you have written a full-length script or two, the form will come naturally and easily.

The main reason the beginner should want to master script format is that he will want to make his scripts as professional-looking as possible. Letter-perfect form will not disguise a poor script, of course; but proper form will encourage a producer or story editor to look further. Proper script form can help dispel the "amateur" stigma, as it creates a favorable first impression.

There may be some initial confusion as to what the correct script format looks like, since there have been (and still are) three or four different formats in common use. There is a play script form, a radio script form, and two television script forms. (Twenty years ago, the last two were divided into "TV script format" and "movie script format," a distinction no longer valid). In the early days of television, when most programs were presented live, everyone used the "TV script form." The audio portion of the program was listed on one side of the page, the visual portion on the other.

VISUAL	AUDIO
TWOSHOT, BILL AND JANE AS THEY TURN AND FACE EACH OTHER.	1. JANE: I thought you were 2. leaving.
CU BILL	3. BILL: I started to. But I 4. got to thinking. . .about us, 5. about all the good times 6. we've had together.

Though this format is still used from time to time, particularly in commercial copywriting and documentaries, it is hardly ever used for television dramatic programs. The older TV script form was specifically tailored to programs either presented live or recorded continuously in a studio.

Since primetime programming is now either filmed or videotaped, borrowing its technique from the motion picture form, the movie script form has been adapted. This is the form now being used almost exclusively, and is the one with which this section will deal. While there are some variations used by script-writers, the format provided here is both the most common and correct in use today.

Every television and film script begins the same way, with the notation FADE IN. The FADE IN is the electronic equivalent to the theatre's "At rise." FADE IN means to go from a blank screen and gradually introduce the picture and the sound. FADE IN always opens the story, and also introduces a new act after a commercial interruption. Example:

ACT I

FADE IN:

INTERIOR, COUNTY JAIL — DAY

FADE OUT is simply the reverse of FADE IN. With a FADE OUT, the picture and sound gradually disappear until the screen becomes completely black. FADE OUT is used at the conclusion of every script, or at the end of an act, just before a break to a commercial. Example:

THE OLD MAN TURNS AND WALKS SLOWLY BACK INTO THE HOUSE.

FADE OUT.

Whenever a scene changes, that is, whenever the location of the action or the time sequence changes, the writer immediately establishes three conditions: 1) where the new scene takes place; 2) whether the setting is an INTERIOR or an EXTERIOR; and 3) whether the scene occurs during the day or at night.

This information is not only used dramatically, to define the setting, but provides a guideline for the set designers, the lighting director, and especially the director. Glancing through the script, it will be possible to tell what sets will be required, how many there will be, and how they should be lit, either for day or night.

In a continuing series, where many of the sets are already well-established and familiar, a simple direction is sufficient.

INTERIOR, DR. WELBY'S OFFICE — DAY

When a script requires a new set, or when the set is particularly important (perhaps it reveals something about one of the characters), the writer may want to add some description.

INTERIOR, HAMILTON'S OFFICE — DAY

ONE LOOK AT THIS ROOM AND WE REALIZE THE MAN WHO USES IT HAS BOTH EXQUISITE TASTE AND THE MONEY TO INDULGE IT. THE OFFICE IS PANELLED IN DEEP MAHOGANY; ORIGINAL PAINTINGS ADORN THE WALLS, AND A DEEP, RICH CARPET COVERS THE FLOOR. THE ROOM IS DOMINATED BY A MASSIVE MAHOGANY DESK.

The designation DAY or NIGHT is supposed to provide general information. Phrases like EARLY EVENING, LATE AFTERNOON, are unnecessarily specific. If the time of day is crucial to the story, indicate that fact in an additional description.

EXTERIOR, FORT DODGE — DAY

DAWN IS BEGINNING TO BREAK. AS THE SUN COMES UP, THE SOLDIERS STEEL THEMSELVES AGAINST THE IMPENDING INDIAN ATTACK.

All the directions are typed in capital letters. *Everything* in a script appears in upper-case letters, except dialogue.

JOHN CROSSES THE ROOM AND SITS DOWN NEXT TO LOUISE, AS CLOSE AS HE CAN.

JOHN

> You know I love you. I've told you so
> often enough.

SPACING

A script written in the proper form leaves a lot of white space on each page. Spacing between lines, knowing when to indent may seem arbitrary; but such details work toward making the script "look right."

For all directions, descriptions, and technical instructions — everything that's capitalized — start at the lefthand side of the page, allowing a one-inch margin on either side of the page. Unlike prose writing, new paragraphs are not indented.

The only time indentation is used is in the case of dialogue. The name of the character speaking the line appears in the middle of the line. The dialogue is also set in, with about two inches left on either side of the page.

MILLER ENTERS THE WAITING ROOM AND CROSSES TO THE RECEPTION DESK. THE RECEPTIONIST DOESN'T LOOK UP FROM HER TYPING.

                              MILLER
          Excuse me. I'd like to see Mr. Hamilton, My name's
          John Miller.

THE RECEPTIONIST STOPS HER TYPING AND LOOKS UP AT HIM, ANNOYED.

It's also a matter of form to skip three spaces between the directions and the character's name above the dialogue. Skip two spaces between one character's line and another's. Everything else will be single-spaced. A typical page of script spacing follows:

INTERIOR, WAITING ROOM OF HAMILTON'S OFFICE — DAY

MILLER ENTERS THE WAITING ROOM AND CROSSES TO THE RECEP-TION DESK. THE RECEPTIONIST DOESN'T LOOK UP FROM HER TYPING.

                              MILLER
          Excuse me, I'd like to see Mr. Hamilton. My name's
          John Miller.

THE RECEPTIONIST STOPS HER TYPING AND LOOKS UP AT HIM, ANNOYED.

                          RECEPTIONIST
          Mr. Hamilton's in conference. He won't be available
          until day after tomorrow.

MILLER
But I have to see him today. It's important.

RECEPTIONIST
I'm sorry, but you'll have to come back another
time. He can't be disturbed.

MILLER
But he told me. . . .

RECEPTIONIST
If you'd like to leave your name and number,
I can give him the message. He'll get back to you.

MILLER TURNS TO GO, SHRUGS. SUDDENLY HE TURNS AROUND
AND BOLTS FOR THE DOOR TO HAMILTON'S OFFICE. HE OPENS IT
AND GOES INSIDE.

TRANSITIONS

Scriptwriters are expected to indicate the method of transition that will
be used to proceed to the next scene. As described in the section on Production Elements, the two most common transitions are the CUT and the
DISSOLVE. The cut will be used almost excusively; dissolves in contemporary
scripts are rare. Also, whenever a specific transition method is not indicated, it
is presumed that a direct cut will be used.

Transitions are indicated as follows:

MILLER TURNS TO GO, SHRUGS. SUDDENLY HE TURNS AROUND
AND BOLTS FOR THE DOOR TO HAMILTON'S OFFICE. HE OPENS IT
AND GOES INSIDE.

CUT TO:
INTERIOR, HAMILTON'S OFFICE — DAY

ESTABLISHING SHOTS

An establishing shot is used to define the locale in which the scene, or the entire story, is about to take place. An establishing shot may be used to identify the city in which the story takes place, as was the case in the openings of each episode of *I Spy* and *The Saint* ; these programs always opened with a panoramic view of a foreign city (the "setting of the week"), sometimes with the city's name superimposed ("Rome", "Paris", whatever applies.)

On a more modest scale, establishing shots are used as a transitional device. Series' like *Marcus Welby, M.D.* and *Mary Tyler Moore* often preceed a change in setting with an establishing shot.

CUT TO:
ESTABLISHING SHOT:
EXTERIOR, DR. WELBY'S HOUSE — NIGHT

CUT TO:
INTERIOR, THE LIVING ROOM — NIGHT

On some programs an establishing shot seems redundant (the writers seem to think the audience couldn't recognize Mary Richards' apartment unless they saw the front of the building first), yet it is probably as good a transitional device as any. An establishing shot gives the audience a moment to make the change mentally and to anticipate the upcoming scene.

An establishing shot is also a way to introduce the audience to an unfamiliar location. Rather than run the risk of momentarily losing the audience while they try to figure out where the characters are, filmmakers tell them, right away.

For instance, private investigator Frank Cannon goes to see the district attorney. Location and identity can be established this way:

ESTABLISHING SHOT:
INTERIOR, CLOSE-UP ON DOOR MARKED 'DISTRICT ATTORNEY'S OFFICE — DAY

This brief, visual image tells the audience two things: 1) that the scene is set in the DA's office and 2) the man Cannon will be talking to will be the DA. Establishing shots can save the audience a lot of guesswork.

For examples of how establishing shots can be used, the following programs feature them in nearly every episode: *Mary Tyler Moore, The Bob Newhart Show, Marcus Welby, M.D., Medical Center, Little House on the Prairie.*

INSERTS

Sometimes the writer (or director) may want the audience to have a closer look at an object — a book of matches with a phone number written inside, a monogrammed handkerchief left at the scene of the crime, some object that has bearing on the plot. This is accomplished through the use of an INSERT.

An insert is a close shot of an object that is filmed separately, then inserted (i.e. edited) into the film later. In Alfred Hitchcock's *North by Northwest* it was important that the audience get a close look at Cary Grant's monogrammed matchbook; this matchbook would be used later to send a clandestine message to Eva Marie Saint. Hitchcock used an insert of the matchbook so that it made a greater impression on the audience's mind; they would remember it later.

Inserts are very useful visual tools. An insert saves the actor the trouble of having to say, "Oh, look, a book of matches with a message inside". Film is a visual medium — an insert lets the audience see for themselves.

The use of an insert in the script is an follows:

INTERIOR, HOTEL LOBBY — DAY
BRENNAN CROSSES THE LOBBY TO THE FRONT DESK.

CLERK

Yes, sir?

BRENNAN
Any messages for 312?

THE CLERK CHECKS, HANDS BRENNAN A SLIP OF PAPER. BRENNAN LOOKS AT THE MESSAGE.

INSERT: PAPER READING 'CALL MR. DELANEY — URGENT'.

BRENNAN GOES TO THE PAY PHONE NEARBY.

STOCK SHOTS

Suppose the writer is working on a script for an episode of *Rhoda*. He wants to do a scene showing Rhoda's husband, Joe Girard, on the job. The problem is, Joe Girard owns a wrecking company. To really see him "on the job," the scene would call for a shot of a building being demolished.

Obviously MTM Enterprises is not about to pay to have a ten-story building knocked down so they can photograph it for the scene. In a case like this (and this is not too outlandish an example), the script would call for a STOCK SHOT.

Every major studio has a library (or stock) of hard-to-get shots which might be called for in a script. These are stock shots. A stock shot can be located in the studio library and edited into a film. Any studio's supply of stock shots will include shots such as an atomic bomb exploding, a building collapsing, a battleship sinking, a jet taking off. Stock shots are collected from various sources — newsreel footage, photography, army combat films, even other productions — and saved for future use. The 1960's series *Twelve O'Clock High* was famous for its use of aerial combat footage — bombs dropping, fighters attacking, flak bursting, planes crashing — all were stock shots from 20th Century Fox's library, originally collected from World War II films.

Many films and TV series call for stock shots at one time or another. If the shot required is not too outrageous, the odds are good the studio library will have it on file.

A stock shot is called for as follows:

THE B—12 IS NOW DIRECTLY OVER ITS TARGET.

                    MURPHY
          Bombs away.

STOCK SHOT: BOMBS BEING DROPPED, EXPLODING ON CONTACT. A DIRECT HIT.

THE USE OF VOICE

Voice-Overs

A VOICE-OVER is a term used to describe narration over a silent picture. Voice-overs (abbreviated VO) are used frequently on news programs, commercials, documentaries, and sometimes, dramatic presentations. In the 1940's, especially, voice-over narration was used in feature films.

In the '70's, voice-overs are used infrequently in dramatic scripts. The trend is to let the story explain itself rather than have a narrator explain it. One of the best-known television series to use the voice-over regularly was *Dragnet*. This program, originally a radio series, used Joe Friday's distinctive drone as the program's signature. Though the voice-over is not used as extensively today as it once was, it does enjoy an occasional revival. *The Waltons* and *Little House on the Prairie* both use voice-overs occasionally, and the detective series *Harry—O* features the technique in every episode. Harry's (David Janssen's) world-weary commentary on each case is a throwback to the hard-boiled private eye genre of the 40's in the great tradition of Humphrey Bogart.

Voice-over narration is indicated as follows:

FADE IN:
ESTABLISHING SHOT:
EXTERIOR, A PANORAMIC VIEW OF LOS ANGELES — DAY

FRIDAY (VO)
This is the city — Los Angeles, California.
My partner and I were working the day watch
out of homicide.

Off-Camera Voices

Sometimes a character's voice will be heard even though he is not seen. The character is referred to as being OFF CAMERA. The term OFF CAMERA (abbreviated OC) should not be confused with VOICE-OVER. Voice-over deals specifically with narration. A voice off-camera means that the character speaking is in the scene; the camera simply doesn't photograph him. A voice-over is a disembodied voice, a voice belonging to someone in the scene but not photographed.

The abbreviation OS may also be used to designate an off-camera voice. In film, OS stands for "Off-screen"; in the theatre, OS means "Off-stage." For film or television, either OC or OS is acceptable, OC being more commonly used.

When a character is heard, but not seen, his line is written as follows:

BOB WALKS INTO THE LIVINGROOM LOOKING FOR JANET.

BOB (CALLS)

Janet!

JANET (OC)

I'm in the kitchen, Bob.

Telephone Conversations

Telephone conversations represent another use of voice, both on-camera and off, the writer will use frequently. Young writers sometimes make scripted telephone conversations more complicated than necessary. Dialogue over the telephone is really quite simple to script.

There are four methods of writing a telephone conversation. All are equally appropriate; the writer's own discretion determines which method he will select. It also depends on the demands of the scene and the importance of the conversation to the script. Different methods can also be used within the same script; having selected one, the writer is not necessarily obligated to stick with it throughout.

The first method involves the use of a split screen. The audience sees both parties simultaneously as they speak to each other. The split screen technique reached its zenith in the 1960's. It now seems a little too gimmicky for a dramatic script, as it detracts from the illusion of reality the writer is trying to create. The audience becomes too conscious of the film-making technique when a split screen is used. Of the four methods, the split screen is probably the least used and least desirable.

A more practical and satisfying technique is the use of intercutting. To intercut means to cut back and forth between one image and another. Intercutting is probably the best way to create the effect of two people talking to each other on the phone. It's especially effective when the characters' facial expressions and reactions are as important to the scene as their dialogue. Intercutting has all the advantages of the split screen technique without the drawbacks. It also breaks the visual monotony of a single static image, particularly if the conversation is a long one.

When writing a telephone scene in which intercutting will be used, it is not necessary to write "CUT TO: JOHN'S OFFICE" every other line. Simply state who the two parties are, where they are, and add "INTERCUT WHERE INDICATED". The script will look as follows:

MORGAN, IN SHIRTSLEEVES, SITS AT HIS DESK, READING.

THE PHONE RINGS, HE ANSWERS.

>   MORGAN (TO PHONE)
>   Yes?

CUT TO:
INTERIOR, MAGGIE'S LIVINGROOM — NIGHT
(INTERCUT WHERE INDICATED)

>   MAGGIE (TO PHONE)
>   How's the private eye tonight?

CUT TO: MORGAN. HE SMILES.

>   MORGAN (TO PHONE)
>   Better now. You couldn't have picked a
>   better time to call. I've just been going
>   over the coroner's report on Larry Connors.

CUT TO: MAGGIE

>   MAGGIE (TO PHONE)
>   Anything suspicious?

Another method that's used often is the filter technique. The camera stays on one character exclusively; the party on the other end is heard talking over the phone. That dialogue is recorded using a microphone with a filter that distorts the voice, makes it sound as it would over a telephone or an intercom. Using the filter technique, the camera can stay on character and yet pick up both conversations.

The filter technique is especially useful when a telephone conversation is brief or of little consequence. If the character at the other phone only has one line, it makes more sense to use the filter than to intercut. The filter is also a handy device when you wish to keep the caller's identity a secret, as in a kidnapping story or a mystery.

A phone conversation using a filter is written as follows:

> PERRY (TO PHONE)
> This is Dr. Perry calling. Let me
> speak to Dr. Baker, please.

> NURSE (OVER FILTER)
> I'm sorry, Doctor. Dr. Baker isn't
> here at the moment. He went out
> a few minutes ago.

> PERRY (TO PHONE)
> Are you sure?

> NURSE (OVER FILTER)
> Yes, Doctor, quite sure.

The filter technique is also used for voices over an intercom, a car radio or short wave set, or any other type of electronic speaker. The lines are written in the same manner with the designation (OVER FILTER).

Very often these last two techniques, intercutting and the filter method, are used together in the same scene. This combination is very effective since it allows for some variation in the visual image and maintains the realistic feeling the filter creates. Combining the two methods is especially appropriate when the conversation is a long one. The writer's (or the director's) own sense of pacing will dictate which method or combination will work best for the scene. (An example of combining techniques appears at the end of this section.)

For an excellent example of how the telephone can be used as a dramatic device, watch for the made-for-television movie entitled *A Cry for Help,* starring Robert Culp and written by Peter S. Fischer. The film made extraordinary use of intercutting, filters, and pacing. It is a model of telephone technique since the protagonist, a radio talk-show host, is seated in a sound booth for the entire 90 minutes. The telephone was his only means of contact with all the other characters.

The fourth, final, and simplest method of writing a telephone conversation is to write half the conversation. This is the method used exclusively in theatre, since the stage lacks film's electronic advantages of intercutting, filters and such. The scene is written as though the audience were overhearing a conversation, but can't hear the party on the other end of the line.

In both television and film, this "eavesdropping" method is sometimes used when the writer wishes to build suspense. The audience sees the character on the phone, hears his remarks, and sees his reaction to the conversation. They naturally wonder what the other person is saying to cause such a reaction. Then comes the "snapper" — the hero hangs up and reveals the dramatic news he's just heard. Usually what he says will surprise the audience. The suspense created by the eavesdropping technique has piqued their curiosity making the message more important and dramatic when it's finally revealed.

Such an example follows:

TOM SITS CLOSE TO THE PHONE, ANXIOUSLY WAITING FOR WORD FROM THE HOSPITAL. DAVID SITS NEARBY WORKING ON A CROSS-WORD PUZZLE, TRYING TO DISTRACT HIMSELF.

THE PHONE RINGS, THEY BOTH JUMP, AND TOM ANSWERS.

> TOM (TO PHONE)
> Yes?. . . .Yes, Doctor. How did. . . .

A DISTRESSED LOOK SWEEPS ACROSS HIS FACE. DAVID LOOKS AT HIM ANXIOUSLY, MOTIONS FOR TOM TO TELL HIM WHAT THE DOCTOR IS SAYING. TOM WAVES HIM AWAY.

> TOM (TO PHONE)
> No no, that's all right. I'm sure you did every-
> thing you could....Thank you for calling,
> Doctor... Good-by.

HE HANGS UP. HE TURNS TO DAVID AND GIVES HIM A SOLEMN, SILENT LOOK BEFORE DELIVERING THE NEWS.

TOM
She died on the operating table a few minutes ago.

By building the suspense, making the audience wait for the news, the information has greater impact when it finally arrives. If the audience had heard the information at the same time Tom did, the rest of the conversation would have been anticlimactic. The audience begins to fear the worst from the look on Tom's face. Whether the news is bad or a pleasant susprise, the audience is satisfied, dramatically.

In the theatre, and in some television series (*Bob Newhart, Rhoda*, other programs filmed before a live audience), the eavesdropping method is always used. Sometimes it can be a disadvantage. The biggest problem is that actors are always obliged to either repeat or paraphrase what the person on the other end of the line has just said. ("What do you mean, 'did I go to the store'? Of course I did...How was it? Oh fine.") Such redundancy is unnatural and sometimes annoying; the audience (and the writer) must really stretch to make the conversation believable. Try to avoid this pitfall.

Ultimately the writer's selection of which technique he will use depends on the methods available to him. He will also want to consider which technique is best suited to the needs of the script. Does the conversation give the character a piece of information, or is it a significant part of the plot? Choose the method that is most appropriate and best serves the script dramatically. All four methods may be used in a single conversation if the writer so desires, or any combination, but, keep two points in mind: 1) telephone conversations in a script should be brief — the audience did not tune in just to watch someone talk on the phone; and 2) phone conversations are dialogue; like dialogue, they must be dramatic, concise and well-written.

Actors' Directions

There is one fool-proof way to spot a script written by an amateur: the script will have a brief direction before almost every line of dialogue: JOHN (ANGRILY), FRANK (COOLLY), HARRY (SURPRISED), MARY (QUIETLY).

Nothing is more annoying to producers, directors and actors than a script with profuse, unnecessary dialogue directions. Directors and actors are intelligent people — they understand what a line means and how it should be said just by *reading* it. There's no need to precede every line with an explanation. As in the case of elaborate camera directions, the writer must resist the temptation to direct the script from his typewriter. Give the other specialists involved some credit for interpretive ability.

If a line of dialogue is well-written, it will usually be self-explanatory. If the writer finds he must use dialogue directions extensively, perhaps his dialogue simply doesn't make sense. The precise reading of a line is the jurisdiction of the actor and the director; usually their interpretation will jibe with the writer's. If it doesn't, it is usually a case of either a poor actor or a poor script.

The sense of any given line of dialogue is determined in two ways: 1) by what the line says, or the content of the line; and 2) by the context of the scene. If, for instance, the scene involves a confrontation between a father and son, the dialogue may be written as follows:

MARK OPENS THE FRONT DOOR TENTATIVELY AND LOOKS AROUND THE LIVINGROOM. SEEING THE COAST IS CLEAR, HE ENTERS QUIETLY AND CROSSES TO THE COFFEETABLE WHERE HIS SCHOOLBOOKS ARE SITTING.

                    FATHER (OC)
          I thought I told you not to come back here
          again.

MARK FREEZES AT THE SOUND OF HIS FATHER'S VOICE. HE LOOKS UP AND SEES THE OLD MAN STANDING IN THE DOORWAY TO THE KITCHEN.

                    MARK
          I just came back to get my. . .

                    FATHER
          I don't want to hear any more of your
          excuses. I've heard enough. Now, get
          out of here! Before I have you arrested
          for trespassing.

MARK DOESN'T MOVE.

FATHER (CONT.)
Go on!

From the sense of the lines, and from the context of the scene, the friction between Mark and his father is keen. The father is obviously angry; to write FATHER (ANGRILY) is unnecessary. Your lines should speak for themselves. If a line doesn't achieve its purpose or have the proper impact, don't try to explain it away — rewrite it.

The only time dialogue directions can justifiably be used is when the sense of the line intentionally differs with the common meaning, for example, when a line is sarcastic or ironic.

MOTHER
Did you have a nice talk with your father?

MARK (IRONICALLY)
Terrific! Just terrific.

Used properly (and sparingly) dialogue directions can be a great help to actors and directors. When a direction is really is necessary, when a line *must* be said a certain way to get the point across, by all means say so. Don't, however, overdo it; actors, directors, and producers are the last people a writer wants to alienate unintentionally.

DESCRIBING THE ACTION

One question that always arises is: how explicit, how complete, does a script have to be? Unfortunately, there is no really definitive answer to such a question. Simply put, a script is a thorough description of the action, written as clearly and concisely as possible. It's up to the writer to find that precarious balance between underwriting and overwriting. Beginning writers frequently make the mistake of offering too much description, too much information. Afraid they might leave something important out, they overcompensate.

Writing a script is like any other form of writing: offering too much can make the work verbose and confusing. A basic rule of thumb in scriptwriting is "never write a paragraph when a sentence will do." Directions and descriptions must, of course, be clear to whoever reads the script; but clarity is achieved by the *choice* of words, not the number of them.

One vivid example of how *not* to describe the action is found in the film scenarios written by F. Scott Fitzgerald during the last days of his life. Fitzgerald, one of the great prose writers of his generation, would include breathtaking descriptions of actions, characters and locations in his scripts; so well written are these passages that they could easily have been excerpts from one of his novels. Fitzgerald's scripts are a delight to read; they were also unproduceable. Going through his scripts, producers would find little material that could actually be translated to the screen. His error was in writing reading scripts rather than scripts that could be translated into stage action.

The scriptwriter must always keep in mind that he is writing a work that is meant to be performed. The action must be vivid, the directions clear. A gift with prose can be an asset as well as a hindrance to the scriptwriter, whichever he chooses to make it. Simple, straightforward sentences will describe the action well. The writer may add some literary flair if he wishes, so long as the action is clear, concise, and described in visual rather than abstract terms.

Scriptwriters are not obliged to describe absolutely every movement, every gesture, every activity a character performs. Concentrate on the action that is necessary to the story's development. "JOHN CROSSES TO THE DESK, PICKS UP THE DOCUMENT AND TEARS IT UP" is a necessary description; "JOHN SCRATCHES HIS HEAD AS HE THINKS" is not — unless that action is pertinent to the story. In the theatre especially, the specific movements and gestures the actors make in any given scene (when they stand up, sit down, cross left and cross right will be blocked out by the play's director, with help from the performers. Such activities are not the author's problem. The writer should confine his descriptions to action that is either revealing, moves the story along, or is otherwise important to the development of the action. And he must keep his descriptions as uncomplicated as possible.

Physical action is almost always the director's responsibility; this is particularly true in such film phenomena as fight scenes, gunfights, and car chases. The writer is not required to give a blow-by-blow account of such action sequences; a general description is sufficient. The director, his stuntmen, and his technical advisors will provide the specific sequence of the action. Many directors build their reputations on their ability to stage physical action sequences; sometimes a separate director is engaged for such scenes. (For example, Robert Culp of *I Spy* also happened to be a talented director; he directed and often staged all the fight scenes on the series.) Unless the action sequence the writer envisions is involved, unusual, or otherwise demands a complete description, he need only provide general information, the highlights of the sequence.

There is one type of "action" that is the writer's responsibility: scenes in the operating room on medical programs. It's surprising how many beginners ask, "Who does all the research on those shows? Who stages the operations? Who writes in all the medical terminology?" The answer is, the writer does. Considering the number of medical shows for which the writer might want to prepare a script (1975-76: *Marcus Welby, Medical Center, Medical Story, Doctor's Hospital*) this is a pertinent piece of information. Writers must have a working knowledge of the "disease of the week"; they must know how to treat it, what drugs are prescribed. They must also describe, step by step, the scenes in the operating room. Every show has a medical advisor who will correct any mistakes the writer makes; but the burden of research for a medical "action" series is on the writer.

When describing the action, keep in mind that all scripts should describe what is to be seen; the director will decide *how* it should be seen. Always bear in mind, don't try to direct from the typewriter. As Freddie Prinze of *Chico and the Man* might say, "Ees not your job, man."

LENGTH OF THE SCRIPT

The inevitable question is how long should a script be? When writing a television script, one fact must be taken into consideration: a one-hour television show doesn't contain an hour's worth of material. By the time you've subtracted minutes here and there for commercials, credits and (sometimes) teasers, the length of the program itself is closer to 52 minutes. For the same reasons, a half-hour show runs about 23 minutes in actual playing time. The writer has to gauge his script to fit the time limitations of the commercial series format. A general rule of thumb is: subtract about 8 minutes per program hour to find the actual length. This will give you a rough estimate for any type of television presentation — a one-hour dramatic series, a half-hour sitcom, or a 90-minute movie of the week.

Time restrictions on feature films and theatrical plays are not as stringent. The running time of a feature film varies from 90 minutes up to four hours; the average is between two hours and two hours and twenty minutes. Most two-act plays last an average of two-and-a-half hours.

What the writer must know is how long the script should be, and the formula is for converting the number of script pages to the running time of the presentation. Some people suggest reading the script aloud and timing it to see how long it will run. This demands time and is not particularly accurate anyway. There is an easier method; if the script is written in proper script format, one minute of film time is roughly equivalent to one page of script. This is an estimate, but one which is pretty accurate. In scenes without dialogue, allow more time or less, depending on the action in the scene and the length of the writer's description. As a general guide, a 51-minute show will have a script about 52 pages long; a 24-minute show will have a 24-page script. A feature film script will run about 140 pages.

When in doubt about the running time of a particular script (especially one for time-conscious television), it's better to have the script a little long than too short. It's much easier to delete a scene or two than it is to beef up a script.

LENGTH OF SCENES

Anyone who watches television critically will notice that most scenes are very brief, about two minutes long or less. Obviously scenes are kept short so that the action keeps moving (for fear the audience will tune out). Most scenes are also exchanges of dialogue, with individual lines running no more than a sentence or two. Therefore, most scenes for a television program will be fairly brief, perhaps two or two-and-a-half pages on the average. A TV scene that runs three pages or more is considered lengthy, unless it is an unusually important scene.

Feature films and plays are not subjected to such limitations. A movie scene can run anywhere from one minute to ten minutes. A scene in a play is, of course, quite long, perhaps fifteen or twenty scripted pages.

TITLES

A good title represents an attractive wrapping for the package the writer presents to his audience. Titles should serve two purposes: 1) they are an attention-getting device. Before an audience knows anything about a presentation, before they know who directed it, who wrote it, who stars in it or what it's about, they hear the title. A title must entice the audience by being intriguing, powerful, revealing or just plain "catchy." As the old joke points up, "First you have to get their attention." 2) The title should match the script; it should give the audience some idea of what they're about to watch, tell them what to expect. While a title can be unusual or even cryptic, it can never be misleading.

The importance of titles is illustrated every year by the shenanigans of the three major networks' programming executives, The fuss that is made over program titles is amusing. In the 1975-76 television season, several new series' underwent title changes before they premiered in the fall. A program originally entitled *Sunday Dinner* was scheduled to appear on Thursdays; since that didn't make much sense, the title was changed to *The Montefuscos.* A new police series, *Metro Man,* had its title changed to *Joe Forrester,* after the central character — presumably the executives were afraid no one would know what a "metro man" was — because the audience might confuse the show with *The Six Million Dollar Man.* A series starring Glenn Ford, entitled *Holvak,* featured Ford as a Depression-era country preacher; however, the title sounded more appropriate for a police show (a la *Kojak);* the title was subsequently changed to *The Family Holvak,* a remarkable improvement.

The point is worthy of consideration if only to illustrate how important titles can be. The executives of the three major networks, as well as creators, producers and writers, realize that titles can have either a positive or negative effect on an audience. Titles are an integral part of any presentation. They deserve careful attention, even if the networks carry that attention to ridiculous heights. Johnny Carson tells the story of the network executives trying to select a title for a sitcom starring Jimmy Stewart. Meetings were called, "think sessions" were held; the matter was debated for days. Finally, the executives arrived at a title — they called it *The Jimmy Stewart Show.*

In television, many dramatic programs have a title for each individual episode. *Medical Center, Marcus Welby, Police Story, Little House on the Prairie* each feature titles for every program. Writers are required to come up with appropriate titles for their individual scripts.

Selecting a good title is initially the responsibility of the writer for any type of presentation. Titles may be suggested or changed by a producer later. If creating imaginative titles is not one of the writer's strongpoints, he can use what is known as a "working title." A working title is simple a functional name given a production until the actual title is selected. For example, the Barbra Streisand remake of *A Star is Born* was completely finished shooting before a title for the film had been selected. A good script by an established writer does not go unproduced for lack of a title. In a pinch, a working title will do.

The most important point to remember about titles is that the title represents your script. If for no other reason, the title should be appealing and appropriate. The title will always be associated with the script and with the writer himself.

THE TITLE PAGE

Writers will frequently be required to provide a title page for their scripts. The title page should include the name of the series, the title of the specific episode, a list of the characters, and a list of the sets to be used.

A title page is always required for a play script, and contains all this information.

A typical title page follows:

PREPPIES

written by Michael Simon

Cast of Characters

Ridgely Potter

Marc Silverstein

Wendy Kaplan

Caroline Morency

Walter Hoesel

A Nurse

2 Policemen

Sets

1)   A dormitory room at a boarding school

2)   A restaurant in downtown Chicago

3)   The livingroom of the Silverstein home.

NAMING THE CHARACTERS

It's standard practice to name most of the characters features in the script, excluding those characters whose part is really insignificant (BELLBOY #,1, POLICEMAN #3 etc.). This practice is more for the self-esteem of the actors than for any artistic reason. As the standard cliche goes, There are no small parts; only small actors. But by giving any character a name who has a line or two of dialogue, the part seems more significant than it actually is. Most actors prefer to play "Harry Adams" than "The Storekeeper." It's well to make everyone in the production feel a little special, within reason, of course.

The days when all characters had to have Anglo-Saxon names are long gone. Characters should have names that represent a variety of backgrounds and ethnic cultures, as in the case of Theo Kojak, Mike Stivic, and other popular contemporary characters. For the sake of reality, scripts with contemporary settings should feature a variety of ethnic types.

It's difficult sometimes to come up with names that sound like they belong to real people, not fictional characters. When such is the case, there are two great sources of character names. One is the telephone book. The other, a personal favorite, is the paging system at the airport. No one knows why, but the names being paged at an airport all seem to have a ring to them.

TEASERS

Teasers are strictly a television phenomenon and, as such, do not apply to feature films and/or plays, as do the other elements discussed. Commercial television demands that all programs be built around intermittent commercial breaks; because of these interruptions in the program's continuity, television has had to develop a form of its own. The form encourages the introduction of crises just prior to a station break, in order to sustain viewer interest. It also presents different requirements for opening a program. It is necessary to capture the audience's attention in the first few moments of a program, before they switch to some other channel. For this reason, most television programs use what is known as a "teaser".

A teaser is a brief scene that precedes the main body of the program; it appears before the first commercial break and before the title and credits are shown. The derivation of the name is apparent — the brief scene is used to "tease" the audience, to whet its appetite.

There are two types of teasers. The first uses a string of short excerpts from the drama itself, a sort of preview of coming attractions. This method was borrowed from motion picture advertising. It is the method favored by programs like *Marcus Welby* and *Little House on the Prairie.* The director chooses the scenes to be used for this type of teaser; it's not the writer's concern which scenes will be used.

The second type of teaser is not an excerpt; teaser in this case means the actual opening scene of the story. Since this type of teaser is part of the action, it *is* the writer's concern. This opening scene sets the stage for what follows; it introduces the central characters and the setting, and gives the audience some hint as to what the story will be about. The scriptwriter has a great responsibility in this type of scene, since he has only a minute or two to get the audience hooked. Teasers that are part of the action are used weekly on programs like *Hawaii Five-O* and *Medical Center.*

Some programs don't use a teaser at all. The writer will simply have to check the program for which he wishes to write and see which type of teaser, if any, the show uses.

PUTTING IT ALL TOGETHER

This discussion of script format has covered a lot of ground — from camera directions to punctuation and spacing. Though there is a great deal the scriptwriter must remember, knowing how and when to employ all these concepts gets easier with each script. To illustrate the simplicity with which these rules can be used (and in order to provide an additional example of TV and film script format) there follows a brief scene in which many of the principles described in this section are applied. It should also give the writer some idea how sample script pages should look.

ACT III

FADE IN:
ESTABLISHING SHOT:
EXTERIOR, THE MOTEL — NIGHT

CUT TO:
INTERIOR, MOTEL LOBBY — NIGHT
CARLSON CROSSES THE LOBBY TO THE FRONT DESK AND ADDRESSES THE CLERK ON DUTY.

CARLSON
Any messages for room 312?

CLERK
Just a moment, sir, I'll check.

CLERK REACHES BEHIND HIM, LOOKS, TURNS AND HANDS CARLSON A SLIP OF PAPER.

CARLSON
Thank you.

HE LOOKS AT THE MESSAGE; AN EXPRESSION OF CONCERN CROSSES HIS FACE.

INSERT: PAPER READING 'CALL MR. RACLIN — URGENT'

CARLSON LOOKS AROUND, CROSSES THE LOBBY TO A ROW OF PAY PHONES. TRUCK WITH HIM.

CUT TO:
INTERIOR, RACLIN'S OFFICE — NIGHT

(INTERCUT WHERE INDICATED)

RACLIN SITS AT HIS DESK, PUFFING NERVOUSLY ON A CIGARETTE.

PHONE RINGS. RACLIN POUNCES ON IT.

RACLIN (TO PHONE)
Hello.

CUT TO:
INTERIOR, MOTEL LOBBY — NIGHT
CARLSON AT PAY PHONE

CARLSON (TO PHONE)
I got your message.

CUT TO: RACLIN. HE LOOKS AROUND TO SEE IF ANYONE'S LISTENING.

> RACLIN (TO PHONE)
> I. . .I have the information you wanted. I
> think we can do business now.

CUT TO: CARLSON

> CARLSON (TO PHONE)
> What made you change your mind?

CUT TO: RACLIN

> RACLIN (TO PHONE)
> Let's just say I've done a lot of
> soul-searching since this morning.

CUT TO: CARLSON. HE LOOKS AT HIS WATCH.

> CARLSON (TO PHONE)
> Okay, I can be at your office in half an
> hour. Make sure you're alone.

CUT TO: RACLIN

> RACLIN (TO PHONE)
> Count on it. . . .Good-bye

RACLIN HANGS UP. HE SITS FOR A MOMENT, STARING AT THE
PHONE, WONDERING IF HE'S MADE THE RIGHT DECISION.

A NOISE FROM THE OUTER OFFICE. RACLIN LOOKS UP, ALARMED.
HE SWITCHES OUT THE LIGHT ON HIS DESK, RISES, AND CROSSES
SILENTLY TO THE OFFICE DOOR. TRUCK WITH HIM.

HE OPENS THE DOOR.

RACLIN'S POV, A MAN WITH A GUN STANDS ON THE OTHER SIDE,
POINTING THE GUN DIRECTLY AT RACLIN.

THE INTRUDER FIRES THE GUN.

ON RACLIN. HE FALLS TO THE FLOOR.

WE HEAR THE SOUND OF FOOTSTEPS IN THE OUTER OFFICE. A DOOR OPENS, THEN CLOSES. THE INTRUDER IS GONE.

CUT TO:
EXTERIOR, THE OFFICE BUILDING — NIGHT

CARLSON'S CAR PULLS UP IN FRONT OF THE BUILDING. HE GETS OUT OF THE CAR AND ENTERS THE BUILDING.

CUT TO:
INTERIOR, RACLIN'S OUTER OFFICE — NIGHT

ON THE DOOR. CARLSON ENTERS, LOOKS AROUND THE DARK ROOM.

              CARLSON (CALLING QUIETLY)
      Raclin?

HE STEPS INTO THE ROOM CAUTIOUSLY, AND MOVES TO RACLIN'S PRIVATE OFFICE.

AS HE STEPS INTO THE DOORWAY, HE SEES RACLIN'S BODY ON THE FLOOR IN FRONT OF HIM. HE KNEELS NEXT TO THE MAN AND HE CHECKS FOR SIGNS OF LIFE; THERE ARE NONE.

CARLSON STANDS UP AND CROSSES TO RACLIN'S DESK. HE STARTS TO PICK UP THE PHONE. THEN SEES THAT ONE OF THE DRAWERS IS OPEN.

HE RUMMAGES AROUND INSIDE AND REMOVES A SMALL BLACK BOOK. HE TUCKS IT IN HIS POCKET, THEN TURNS AGAIN TO THE PHONE.

HE DIALS '0.'

              CARLSON (TO PHONE)
      Get me the police.

FADE OUT.

For more complete examples of television and film script format, there are a number of film scripts readily available to the general public, most in paperback. William Goldman's screenplay of *Butch Cassidy and the Sundance Kid* is available from Bantam Books; MGM puts out a series of classic screenplays, including *North by Northwest.* For a minimal cost, the writer will have full-length, professional examples of proper script format to which he can refer whenever he's not sure exactly what to do. These scripts will provide the proper guidelines.

Theatre Script Format

It is not necessary to dwell too long on the subject of theatre script format for one reason: play format is not nearly as intricate as film script format. The playwright does not have to worry about technical directions, camera shots, and such; the only technical concerns which may merit his attention are lighting cues and an occasional sound effect. For the most part, the playwright is free to concentrate on the more basic elements of drama. As in a television or film script, the playwright's major task is to describe the action.

A theatrical script is written in both upper-and lower case letters, like prose; only the names of characters above each line of dialogue need be capitalized. It is also a good idea to capitalize character's names when they appear in a stage direction, so that the actors can spot their actions easily. The spacing for a theatrical script is essentially the same as it would be for a TV or film script — dialogue is indented, the character's name directly above the line, in the middle. The playwright must describe the essential action of the story as he goes along; however, elaborate stage directions are not necessary ("Jim crosses to the stove, stirs the stew.") Specific movements and bits of business will be added by the director in the play's first production.

Most modern plays are divided into two acts; each act will be divided into scenes of varying length.

An example of play script format follows:

ACT TWO

SCENE 3

JIM TYLER, dressed in a tuxedo, emerges from the bedroom, diligently struggling with his bow tie. He hears the door buzzer.

JIM (calling)
Come in, it's open!

The door opens and Karen enters. Jim turns and is obviously surprised to see her. He stops fumbling with his tie.

JIM
Oh, hello. . . .I was expecting someone else.

KAREN
So I see. I hope I'm not intruding.

JIM
Oh no, no. . . .I was just going out.

Uncomfortable, he turns to the mirror and tries to fix his tie again. Karen crosses to him.

KAREN
Can I give you a hand with that?

JIM
I need all the help I can get. (Karen starts to tie his tie for him. Jim smiles slightly) You were always good at this. I don't know what I'd do withou.....(He realizes what he's saying.) I'm sorry.

KAREN
I understand. Force of habit, I guess.
It takes a long time to adjust.

JIM
Too long, if you ask me.

He tries to look into her eyes for a reaction. Feeling awkward, she finishes the tie and steps back from him.

The theatre script format is quite undemanding. There are really no hard-and-fast rules for the theatrical script — the writer should simply concern himself with the quality of the script; in the theatre, script format almost takes care of itself.

For reference, there are any number of fine play scripts available to the public. They may be found in any library, most book stores, or through the Dramatists Play Service in New York.

THE FINAL POLISH

All the steps in the scriptwriting process — the idea, the treatment, the step-out, and the first draft — have followed one another in fairly rapid succession. Writing the script has a momentum of its own. With the first draft (a complete script) finished, the momentum comes to an end. It is time for the writer to tuck his script safely away and take a breather.

There's a practical aspect to this "rest stop." No one deliberately writes something that isn't good. But the writer can get so caught up in the material that he fails to spot errors and imperfections in the scripts while he's writing it. After a brief rest, some time away from the script, he can be more objective about his work and make whatever corrections or improvements are necessary.

Several points should be in the back of the author's mind as he rereads his script: does the script make sense — does the material hold together? Do scenes flow naturally from one to the next? Could the dialogue be improved? Are descriptions and directions clear? Has anything been left out? The ultimate question the writer asks himself is: How can I make the script better? Unless he's an extraordinary genius (and who is?), there's always a way. That's the purpose of the final polish.

The final polish is an exceptionally satisfying part of the scriptwriting process. It is a stage of refinement, not a major task. The story has already been carefully planned; all the details have been brought together effectively in the first draft. The writer's purpose, at this point, is to make a good script better.

When polishing a script, the writer's biggest enemy is his own ego, being faced with the difficult proposition of criticizing his own work. If he lacks the necessary objectivity, he should seek the opinion of a neutral party, someone whose opinion he respects — an objective and talented friend, a teacher, or another writer. Good, constructive comments or criticisms will be helpful, since criticism is the first step toward revision. The writer should first step toward revision. The writer should avoid being defensive; justifying weaknesses in the script will not improve its quality.

Just as he must learn to accept constructive criticism, the writer must also learn when to leave well enough alone. There is an old saying in the script-writing trade, "The first script is never finished." This means that, because a beginning writer may not know what a good script looks like, he's never satisfied with his own first effort. He keeps trying to improve it, since he may not realize how good his script really is. Some very fine scripts have been "tinkered" to death because of this problem. The young writer has to realize there is a limit to the expertise he can bring to his first work. If he's not exactly sure what to change, or where, he should leave well enough alone; let the producer or story editor suggest changes.

Also, remember that the term "final polish" is a misnomer. This is not the ultimate rewrite of a script — rewriting will take place up until the moment the film is "in the can". Once a script is purchased, a whole new rewriting session begins, with producers, directors and even actors adding their own suggestions; rewriting becomes a collaborative effort. Writers must adjust to the fact that their work may be changed once it becomes someone else's property.

But during the final polish stage, the script is truly the writer's own; for the moment, he has the ultimate editorial power. He should strive to make the script as good as his own personal concept allows. When the writer is satisfied that he has done his best, when he feels he's taken his material as far as it can go, the script is finished.

The process that separates writing as a hobby from writing as a career begins at this point — the process of selling the script.

CHAPTER FOUR

THE BUSINESS OF SCRIPTWRITING

The writing of scripts is only a part of the writing profession. Once the writing is finished, the writer faces an equally formidable task — marketing his material. The first script is always the hardest to sell; at times, it seems almost impossible. Scriptwriting is a business — an intricate and demanding business, rife with rewards and accolades for those who succeed; and, like any other business, it's hard for the beginner to get his foot in the door.

There is no easy way to sell the first script. But there's no reason to make the process more difficult than it already is, either. There is a procedure for making the initial venture into the marketplace. The writer's ultimate success will depend on equal measures of persistence, personal talent, and luck.

With this in mind, let's address the question, "How do I get started?"

Into the Marketplace

Truman Capote claims he never received a rejection notice; if so, he's probably the only writer around who can make that statement with a straight face. Rejections are an inevitable part of the writing profession, particularly in the beginning. It is a lucky writer who can sell a script on the first try. The beginning writer must realize that acquiring his first credit will be a long, arduous process; it can take years. Young writers should not be terribly discouraged if their first attempts at selling a script are unsuccessful. They will have something in common with the most successful writers working today.

The first question a writer must consider, before he even starts writing the script, is "Who should I write for?" Should he attempt a feature film script, or a movie-of-the-week? Should he write an episode for a series? If so, which series?

The market for scripts fluctuates all the time. At times, for example, producers desperately need TV movie scripts; other times, writers can't give them away. In part, this is the result of the fact that most producers and studios work on a kind of quota system; a producer of a television show will only buy up to thirteen scripts at a time (enough for half a season) since the show may not be around after that; or, a studio decides they will only film five TV movies in a particular season. The writer has to consider such limitations, and, in effect, try to second-guess the producers in trying to determine what the producers will be looking for, and when they will need it. Trying to decide who to write for can be a gamble for the beginner.

Of the three major options (feature films, TV movies, and television series), feature films are the most difficult to break into. The motion picture industry suffered a major slump a few years ago; though it had a record recovery in 1975, producers and studio executives are still very cautious about what properties they buy — and from whom. A motion picture represents an investment of (conservatively) at least two million dollars. Producers are reluctant to risk that much money on a script from an unknown writer. It is wise, then, for the would-be scenarist to work in television, first.

The made-for-television film format, begun by NBC with *Fame is the Name of the Game* and extended by ABC with *Tuesday Movie of the Week,* used to be an ideal place for the new writer to start. *Movie of the Week* was the contemporary equivalent to the anthology series' of the '50's: *Playhouse 90, Climax* and *General Electric Theatre.* These last programs were a showcase for young writers of their time, giving writers like Rod Serling and Paddy Chayefsky their first big break. But anthology series lost favor in the early '60's. Movies made for television revived the concept in the '70's; TV movies reached their peak in 1974-75, when three new TV films were shown in prime time every week (two on ABC, one on NBC).

Movie of the Week and *World Premiere Movie* allowed writers a great deal of creative leeway, just as the "playhouse" programs of the '50's had. Writers were not restricted by a set weekly format; they were free to develop comedies, contemporary dramas, fantasies, or science fiction. Any genre could be fit into the movie-of-the-week concept. A wide variety of material was needed, and this worked to the advantage of writers. Also, because so many TV movies were being done, the medium was accessible to younger writers.

Unfortunately, in the spring of 1975, the networks surprised everyone, when all three regular movie nights were cancelled, victims of the same plague that had killed the "playhouse" programs: anemic ratings. TV movies are by no means dead; the networks will continue to substitute the less-expensive TV films on some of their feature film nights. However, the demand for TV movies has decidedly decreased. Most of the TV films to be shown during the season are high-quality specials, written by established writers. There's always the chance that TV movies will be revived sometime in the future, for to some extent, they are a permanent television staple. In the meantime, the beginner might best try something else.

The best bet in the television industry is the faithful standby, the regular dramatic series. But, the question is "Which series?" Here again, it's a matter of second-guessing.

In California, "the word" will sometimes go out to agents and freelance writers that *"Marcus Welby* is looking for scripts," *"Medical Center* is buying". But the outsider doesn't have access to such information ordinarily; all he can do is anticipate.

Many people think it would be easier to sell a script to a new series, since a new series has the greatest need of good scripts. That reasoning is wrong. By the time the general public hears that a new series will premiere in the fall, the script quota has already been filled — by established, commissioned writers. When a network purchases a new television series, it commissions thirteen episodes, enough for half a season. Of these, the show's creator, producers, or story consultant may write about six; the rest are parcelled out to writers with a proven track record. If the show is picked up for another thirteen weeks, the same writers get the assignments.

It's virtually impossible for a beginner to sell a script to a series in its first season. The show is usually struggling to find the right "chemistry," a successful format, tone, and approach. The producers entrust this challenge to writers whose work they know and respect, or to the creative people permanently established with the program.

The best series to write for are those which have been on the air three or more years. These programs have already run through a lot of material; they need new blood, fresh ideas. Producers of older, more established shows are frequently willing to consider scripts by young writers. *Gunsmoke* was a classic case-in-point; that historic series was on the air for twenty years and used hundreds of scripts, many written by non-professionals. Currently, the beginning writer might consider a script for a series such as: *Marcus Welby, M.D.; Medical Center; Cannon; Barnaby Jones; The Rookies; The Waltons; Emergency; Streets of San Francisco; Hawaii-Five-O.*

If a series has been on the air for a long time, it's pretty safe to assume they need scripts. The question is when to make contact? There's always a chance an older series might be cancelled, leaving the writer stranded with an unsalable script. Producers usually wait until the show's renewal is certain before they start collecting scripts. Do the same thing the producers do: check the ratings occasionally; see if the series is slipping. If a show has dropped to the bottom 30 in the Nielsens, the cancellation is almost guaranteed; shows in the middle 30 are shaky, but still a possibility; a program in the top 30 still has a lot of life in it. The networks announce cancellations in February and March, and present the complete fall line-up in May. If the series is not axed in March, the producers heave a sigh of relief and start buying scripts for the new season. April is the best time for the young writer to make his move.

Like everything else in scriptwriting, there are very few hard and fast rules. If the fledgling writer wants to write a script for a relatively new series, he should feel free to take his chances. But these are the patterns that have emerged over the years; exceptions are infrequent. There's no point in writing for a series that will probably be cancelled or will simply not buy from beginners; it's a waste of time and energy, if the script can't be sold.

Once the writer has selected a promising program, and has written a competent script, the process of trying to sell it begins.

Finding an Agent

Some writers in other fields, particularly those who write articles on a freelance basis, manage their business dealings without the benefit of an agent. In the business of scriptwriting, finding an agent is a prerequisite.

Producers rarely, if ever, give serious consideration to a script that has not been submitted through a reputable agent. Even if the writer should be able to break through the barriers on his own, representation will be to his advantage when he becomes established. Therefore, before one can hope to enter the market as a full-time professional writer, he must find an agency willing to represent him.

"Represent" is the key word here, since that is precisely what an agent does. An agent is an extension of the writer, his link to the marketplace; he is the middle man between a creative talent and his potential "employers." Agents manage the selling part of the writing profession — they negotiate contracts, handle salary matters, offer career advice, and sometimes find commissions for their clients. In short, an agent is responsible for merchandising the "product" his client has to sell: his writing talent.

We've all been conditioned to think of agents as fast talking hucksters who reap the fruit of their poor client's labor, This image of agents is fiction, and a tired cliche at that. A capable agent can be a writer's most valuable asset. At the risk of making a sweeping generalization, most writers, historically, have been vulnerable people; writers are defensive of their talent, sensitive to criticism, and naive in contract and money matters. Many writers prefer not to see rejection letters — they let their agent handle that; many have no idea how much their script may be worth — the agent handles that, too. Most writers prefer to work on their creative projects and let someone else worry about knocking on doors, finding a buyer, haggling over price and drawing up contracts. A good agent does all these things for his client, and more — all for the reasonable, tax-deductible fee of ten per cent.

Some scriptwriters do manage without an agent, but they are the exceptions. A beginning writer needs an agent to get him started — to make the contacts, show him the ropes, and to make the first few sales. A well-established writer, one who's in demand (a "hot property") needs an agent even more — to handle his business as it becomes more complicated, to sort out all the offers that come pouring in.

Most talent agencies aren't standing there with open arms waiting for new writers to walk in off the street, however. Because agencies work on a commission basis, the amount of money they take in is directly related to the writer's earning power. Writers are an investment for agencies; a writer without promise or earning potential is a bad investment. For this reason, agencies must be selective. Many are reluctant to take on a writer who doesn't already have some credits.

This fact results in one of the most maddening aspects of starting a writing career, the "Catch 22" of show business: a writer can't sell a script unless he has an agent; he can't get an agent unless he's already sold a script. After running around this treadmill a few times, the writer may wish he'd opted for the aluminum siding business instead.

But to the fearless, agents' societies like the Society of Authors' Representatives in New York are willing to furnish a list of reputable agencies upon written request. Another list can be found in a book entitled *Writer's Market*, published by the *Writer's Digest*. The book not only features a list of agencies, but tells what kind of material they handle and what their policy concerning new writers is. *Literary Market Place* is another similar source.

Many agencies set down requirements before they will consider a new client: 1) The writer must have sold material previously; it's helpful if he is making at least five thousand dollars a year from his writing; or 2) the writer must be referred by someone who is presently a client of the agency.

Neither of these conditions is particularly helpful to the beginner. The best solution for a novice is to get in touch with agencies which say they are willing to read unsolicited manuscripts. Agencies usually charge a nominal fee for this service, to pay for the time spent reading and evaluating the script. Many will give the writer a critical evaluation. Even if the script is rejected, it can be worth the writer's investment to get a professional opinion. All of this can get a little costly; but, after all, there is an element of gambling in professional writing. It may pay off.

Finding an agency willing to handle him can be a trying experience for the writer. But once he has found one, he has taken a monumental step forward professionally. Therefore, before a writer tries to sell his script, he should first try to sell himself to an agency. The initial contact should be made through a letter of inquiry.

The Letter of Inquiry

The letter of inquiry to an agent (or producer) may be the single most important piece of "creative writing" the scriptwriter ever does. The purpose of the letter is to capture the agent's interest in the writer himself and the script he's offering. If it creates a favorable impression, the author may be invited to submit his material for appraisal.

The opening paragraph of the letter should be used to introduce the writer himself. If he has a degree or has otherwise had some experience in writing or broadcasting that should be mentioned first. If he has had no related experience of any kind, it is permissible to refer to himself as a "freelance writer"; though that may be stretching a point, the term is partially deserved if you have written a script. The object of the first paragraph is to give the agent or producer the impression that the writer knows what he's doing, and that it will be worth the agent's while to read the letter.

After he has introduced himself, the writer introduces his material. He must explain to the agent, briefly, what his script is about. Obviously the writer will want to furnish enough information to make the script sound of interest, but not so much that he gives the whole story away. It is wise to experiment with this description to find the proper balance.

In the next paragraph, the author will ask whether or not the agent might be interested in reading the script, on a speculative basis with no obligation. In a final sentence or two, thank him for his time and consideration.

The writer should also enclose a stamped, self-addressed envelope with his inquiry. This increases his chances of getting a speedy reply. The agent will respond positively or negatively, and will include any information about reading fees if applicable.

The writer may send out as many letters of inquiry as he wishes. However, it's generally best to send them out in groups of three or four at a time. The chances of receiving a favorable reply are good, so there's really no reason to blanket the country. If an agent (or a producer) does show an interest, it is good form to show the script one at a time; simultaneous submissions (sending copies to everyone) is frowned upon.

Be sure the letter of inquiry is business-like, i.e. properly typed on good quality paper, with no typographical errors. The letter should be precise and, above all, brief. Long letters wind up in the agent's "circular file."

An example of a letter of inquiry follows:

831 Forest Avenue
Evanston, Illinois 60466
August 4, 1976

Mr. Mark Bauer
Mark Bauer and Associates, Inc.
2343 Sunset Boulevard
Los Angeles, California 90069

Dear Mr. Bauer:

I am currently working toward a degree in television from Northwestern University. I have recently completed a 90-minute television motion picture script which I feel may merit your consideration.

I have a strong background in both writing and production. Several professional writers have praised this script for its content, characterization, and dramatic sense.

Briefly, the story is this: Through a series of events brought about by a case of mistaken identity, a doctor in a small Midwestern town is accused of a murder he didn't commit. The story deals with the doctor's fight to exonerate himself, as well as with the actions and reactions of the people around him.

If you are interested, I would be happy to send you the film treatment and/or the completed script. I will also be happy to pay whatever reading fee might be required.

Thank you for your time and consideration.

Sincerely yours,
Grier Raclin

Contacting Producers Directly

If the writer's attempt to engage the services of an agent is unsuccessful, or if he prefers to represent himself, he can try to contact producers directly. This tactic is not always successful, but it may be worth a try.

The writer starts by assembling a list of names of producers he might want to contact. If the script is for a television series, watch the credits at the end of the show and find the names of the program's executive producer, producer, or story consultant, as well as the name of the company that produces the show and the studio where it is filmed.

If the script is for a movie-of-the-week or a special, watch the credits of various TV films and find out who produces them and where. You'll discover that only a handful of production companies are responsible for most of the television movies; Universal, Spelling-Goldberg Productions, and Lorimar Productions are leaders in the field. Watch for the producer's credit when these studios are involved. Also, the program's final credit will usually list an "executive in charge of production"; he is probably the best person to contact initially, since he is in charge of developing TV movies for the company. Devotees of television credits quickly learn that the same names keep popping up; this will give you some idea of who is currently in power and additionally, which producers have the muscle to purchase a script and develop it.

Try to match the script to the studio that deals in your type of material. If the script is an action-adventure story, Universal and Spelling-Goldberg would be the logical companies to send it to, since these studios specialize in action stories. If the script is a topical, contemporary drama, it may appeal to Lorimar Productions or Wolper Productions. Try to determine the type of material each studio and producer handles; in effect, try to second-guess what they may be looking for in a script.

Once the writer has his list of producers, executives, and studios, go to the library and find the Los Angeles telephone directory; there you will find the addresses of the studios and production companies.

Beginners who have written to producers directly are always surprised at the courteous replies they receive; at times they're amazed they received any reply at all. The film industry is not the hard-nosed, heartless business everyone thinks it is. Some of the biggest names in the industry are willing to give the beginning writer advice, encouragement and, occasionally, an opportunity to prove himself. The majority of production outfits have a policy of only accepting material submitted through an agent. But most companies are at least polite enough to write back to the author and tell him so, with regrets. Some producers (usually the ones who started as scriptwriters themselves) take the time to write a personal note; if they're not at liberty to read the script, they will at least offer some suggestions as to how the author may get started. Any correspondence with the studios and producers is valuable to the beginner. It is not unreasonable to anticipate a reply from everyone he writes to. Even the rejections are polite and sincere.

Depending on which companies the scriptwriter contacts, (the large studios are best), the odds are that for every reply that says "no thank you" he may receive one that says "We're willing to read it." Sometimes, one is all it takes.

Release Forms

When a producer for a major studio receives a letter of inquiry from a writer, he will often turn it over to someone in the studio's story department. Any correspondence will be between the story editor and the scriptwriter.

If the studio is willing to look at the script, the story editor will write to the author with this information, and will send along release forms. A release form is an official-looking document; it is an agreement between the studio and the author which sets down the terms under which the studio consents to read the script. By signing the release form, the writer certifies that his material is original, and that he holds all the rights to the material and the proposed title to the material.

The standard release form sets down these conditions between author and studio: 1) The author agrees to keep at least one copy of the script on file; the studio will not be obligated to return their copy. 2) The studio acknowledges that they cannot use the script unless they pay the writer for the privilege. 3) If another writer or an employee of the studio submits material that is similar in some ways to the author's own, since there may be some elements of the script that are not novel or original, the studio is not obligated to pay the writer.

The last clause is reasonable on the studio's part; it is not a potential "rip-off." Let's assume the studio receives an unsolicited manuscript which contains a scene involving a car chase; for whatever reason, the studio rejects the script. Later, if the studio produces a film with a car chase in it, someone might accuse them of "stealing the idea." Logically, the studio didn't "steal" anything; the writer making the accusation was not the first, nor the last, to write a car chase — the material did not originate with the author signing the release. Rather than risk a tiring legal entanglement with writers, the studio asks the writer to acknowledge the fact that the studio is not responsible in such cases.

Don't be intimidated by the legalistic jargon contained in the release form. It protects the author as much as it does the studio. If the studio likes the script, rest assured, they will pay you for it; if they don't like it, or if something similar is already in the works, they are under no obligation. It isn't the studio that tries to rob the writer; often its the other way around. The release form is essential and protects the rights of both parties.

The release form also asks the author to describe his manuscript — number of pages, title, date submitted, physical characteristics. All this is to help identify the material and assist in the handling.

Release forms will be in duplicate (at least). Fill out all the copies, keep one for your personal records, and send the remaining copies back with the script. Address the package to the story editor who requested it, and be sure the return name and address is clearly printed on the envelope. If the editor can't tell who the manuscript is from, they may not open the envelope.

How Long Should I Wait?

The story department of a major studio is a very busy place. Story editors have dozens of scripts on their desks at any given time, all crying out to be read. Though it isn't easy, learn to practice patience and wait for a reply.

First of all, consider mail delivery. If the writer lives in the Midwest or the East, it will take the script several days to reach California, even if sent first class. It will take the editor several weeks to get around to reading the script. All in all, it will be at least a month or two before the writer hears anything.

If at the end of two or three months the writer still hasn't heard anything, he may write a polite letter asking if the script has been received or whether or not any decision has been reached. Keep the contacts restrained. It's a poor policy to create a negative impression on the person who may hold your literary future in his hands.

If four or five months elapse and still nothing happens, the writer may wish to write and request the script be withdrawn so that you may submit it elsewhere.

As a rule, the length of time a writer will have to wait when submitting a script through a studio story department is measured in months rather than weeks. A script may be read and reread by the story editor. If it shows potential, it may be circulated among various producers for their consideration. A script can make the rounds for several months before any action is taken, one way or another. Unless the writer has someone else dying to look at the script, all he can do is wait.

Remember, the writer's the one who's in a hurry; not the studio.

How Much Will I be Paid?

The minimum fee for a half-hour television script is about $3,000. A script for a full hour television script is worth at least $5,000. A 90-minute script will bring about seventy-five hundred dollars. These are the fees that would be paid to a beginning writer with no previous credits; the price increases dramatically once you are established. A single television script can earn tens of thousands of dollars for a top professional.

Payment for feature film scripts starts higher than television's base fees. For a beginner, without the benefit of an agent, a full-length motion picture script may bring about $10,000.

Everyone has heard stories about writers who were paid 10—$15,000 for a film script; however, after the picture became a hit, the next script was sold for a quarter of a million dollars. Those stories are true. There is no ceiling to the amount of money a motion picture script can bring. The film industry is becoming increasingly aware of the importance of a good script; top writers are being given a larger share of Hollywood's profit pie than ever before. It is not unusual for an established, "name" scriptwriter to earn upwards of $200,000 per script. One huge hit behind him, and the author can name his own price for, at least, the next three years.

In exchange for the fee, the writer of a television script gives the studio or network the rights to the original television presentation, plus the right to. one free rerun. For each telecast of the program thereafter, the author receives a smaller, additional payment, a residual, according to the rules set down by the Writer's Guild.

Rewrites

When the writer sells his script, he is really selling a whole package. The author, in exchange for his fee, sells the stepout, a first draft, and a rewrite (final polish); he also promises one free rewrite thereafter.

As mentioned in the discussion on the final polish, later rewrites are a collaborative effort; additional input is received from producers, directors, and story consultants. Changes, additions, and cuts will undoubtedly be suggested by one or all of the persons involved in the production. Writers, particularly those who hold their text inviolate, must remind themselves that material becomes the property of others, once it's sold. Compromise is often the name of the rewrite game. The original author may explain and defend his concept; but ultimately all parties must reach accord. The executive producer always has the final say in rewrite matters. The script is, after all, his property and his responsibility.

Television and film writers who do not learn to bend, who consider their text sacred, are in for trouble. There have been innumerable cases of uncooperative writers being barred from the set; and it is not unthinkable that the producer may dismiss the writer from the project entirely and hire someone else to make changes in the script — the way the producer sees them. If the writer wants to have any say in the rewrite procedure, it is wise to cultivate a reputation as a "team player" early in the game. If he does not, "unreasonable" may become a synonym for "unemployable."

In theatre and, to a lesser extent, motion pictures, the rules of rewriting are not as stringent. Writers are often welcome to contribute ideas well into the production stage. In film, in recent years, writers have acquired new status — their creative input does not stop when the original script is finished. (For instance, scriptwriter Robert Towne reportedly contributed as much during the filming of *Shampoo* as he had when he originally wrote the script.) And the theatre has a traditionally high regard for a well-written play; little or no "tinkering" is allowed.

Whatever his medium, the writer's importance in the rewrite and production stages is in direct proportion to the writer's professional status. Beginning writers have little or no authority — first-timers are often urged to "leave it to the pros." This may make you chafe a bit; but the more credits the writer accumulates, the more willing producers are to listen. Like everyone else in the film industry, and the theatre — directors, producers, actors — the scriptwriter is required to "pay his dues." This applies to rewriting as well as every other aspect of the writing business.

What to Do If You Think You've Been Had

There are those unfortunate instances when a writer may see material being performed that is too similar to something he has written to be explained as "coincidence." The film industry, thanks to the protections initiated by the Writer's Guild, has a standard procedure for dealing with possible plagarism cases.

In an effort to prevent a possible court fight, the matter is first submitted to arbitration. The arbitrator will be mutually selected by the studio/producer and the writer, and will be someone experienced in the industry. If the two parties cannot agree on the selection of an arbitrator, one will be chosen by the American Arbitration Association.

If the arbitrator decides that the author's claim is valid and the studio/producer did use his material without permission, the studio/producer will be obliged to pay the writer an amount equivalent to what they would have paid had they bought the material originally. (For example, if the writer is a beginner, the standard fee for a TV script is about $5,000; that is the amount he will be paid for his claim.)

If the studio/producer is not willing to submit the dispute to arbitration, the author has no recourse but to take legal action. Whatever the decision, whether the matter will be settled in arbitration or in the courts, the writer should consult an attorney before starting any proceedings.

Cases, such as this, are infrequent, but they can occur. They are time consuming, and debilitating. Hopefully, in your script writing career, you can avoid the experience, first-hand.

Contests

Every year some studios hold a contest to select two or three promising scripts by non-professionals. Recently, Walt Disney Productions and Twentieth-Century Fox have held such contests. First prize is usually a cash award in the area of $5,000. These contests are conducted through the instructors of universities with broadcasting departments; information about current contests may be attained from the department chairmen; also, submissions usually are faculty sponsored.

Though the immediate financial reward is not huge, scriptwriting contests do represent a tailor-made opportunity for the beginner to get his foot in the door.

There are some additional points about the writing business which may be of interest to the scriptwriter later in his career. Most won't concern the beginner too much, but they are important to anyone who plans to earn a living writing scripts.

Credits

To a professional writer, the screen credit is almost as important as his fee. For providing the script and doing some rewriting, the author is entitled to a solo screen credit.

The business of credits can get clouded when other writers are brought in to work on the script. For example, we've all seen film credits that read, "Written by Joe Writer and Jane Doe"; we naturally assume that the two writers whose names are listed in the credits collaborated on the script. In reality, it's highly probable those two writers have never even met each other, much less collaborated. One writer may have written the original script while the other was brought in for some rewriting. All the writers have in common in a case like this is the credit.

The assigning of credits is further complicated by a Writers Guild rule which states that only two authors may be given credit as the program's authors. What happens when three or four writers work on the script altogether — one writes it, another rewrites it, someone else rewrites the rewrites? In that case, the credits read something like this: "Written by Writer A and Writer B — Story by Writer C and Writer D".

There are times when an author's script is rewritten so extensively by others that the end product bears no resemblance whatsoever to the script he originally wrote. Even in a case like this, the original writer is entitled to screen credit. If the author feels his work has been written out of existence, or if the final script has become such a mess that the author's association with the production might damage his career, he can have his name omitted from the credits.

Many scenarists choose to write under a pen name for a variety of personal reasons. In the wake of the McCarthy era writers on the blacklist were forced to use assumed names, if they could find a writing job at all. It's acceptable to do a script under a pen name, so long as there is no fraudulent intent.

Matters pertaining to credits are usually dealt with during negotiations between the writer and the producer. The author's right to credit will be protected both by his contract and by the Writers Guild.

Collaborating

Writers, like everyone else, may have strong points and weak points among the different elements of scriptwriting. Some writers are terrific at writing dialogue but have trouble plotting; others are plotting geniuses but weak on dialogue. It is sometimes beneficial for two writers to combine their talents, compensating for their individual weaknesses and concentrating on their specialties. The process of team writing, or collaborating, is a time-honored Hollywood tradition.

Since writing is such a personal and lonely endeavor, finding a partner whose style, ideas, approach, and philosophy blend with your own is not simple. A successful writing team must function as a unit; the two writers must reenforce each other. This doesn't mean that the two writers have to be identical twins, but there has to be a chemistry between them. The work they produce jointly must be superior to anything either could have done separately, or else there is no point in a team effort.

The merits of collaboration can currently be considered by the success of such writing teams as Bill Persky and Sam Denoff *(The Dick Van Dyke Show)*, James Brooks and Allan Burns *(The Mary Tyler Moore Show)*, and Richard Levinson and William Link (*Columbo, That Certain Summer, The Execution of Private Slovik).* Collaboration is not for everyone, but it can be a tremendous advantage to those who are suited for it.

Spec vs Commission

Writing on speculation means that the author writes the script, without the benefit of a contract or a guaranteed buyer. He submits it to producers, who are free to purchase or reject it. Speculation is just what the name implies: writing the script and taking your chances on being able to sell it to someone later. All beginning, unproven writers do their work on speculation.

Professional writers with proven ability have neither the time nor the inclination to play such games. Professional writers are guaranteed a buyer, before they will spend up to three months writing a script. Once a writer has made his mark, once his position is secure enough, he will submit a story idea or an outline to a producer for approval. If the producer finds the idea promising and knows the writer's previous track record is good, he will commission the writer to do the entire script and pay him an advance. (The payment will range anywhere from a thousand dollars to a maximum of 25 per cent of the purchase price for the whole script.) When the script is completed, the producer has first refusal rights. If the script is good, he'll buy it, as arranged in the contract; if the script does not meet his expectations, the producer does not have to buy it. The author is then free to sell the script to someone else; the writer also keeps the advance. All the terms and technicalities are agreed to before the writer begins to write the first draft. This is a much more secure and business-like arrangement.

Having his work sold before he has even written it is one of a writer's great luxuries. When a writer can get assignments on a commission basis, he knows he has arrived. And like everything else, working on commission depends entirely on the writer's previous credits and experience. The beginning writer has to pay his dues, first.

Copyrights

Copyrighting unsold material can be a complicated matter. It is impossible to copyright an idea for a story. It is also impossible to copyright characters' names and story titles.

However, there are ways to protect a claim on completed written material (the first draft of a script) prior to its sale:

1) The Writers Guild will issue a temporary copyright on unsold material to its members.

2) Correspondence with an agent or a studio, someone who has read the finished script, will establish a prior claim. For instance, if a writer sends a script to a studio story editor on speculation, the editor will make record of the material as received: *"The Great Script, written by Joe Writer. Received 6-24-75 by Mark Editor, Warner Bros. Story Dept."* If there is ever a question of prior claim, the writer will be able to prove, through letters from the studio and with the studio's corroboration, that his material existed on a given date. Such proof will be sufficient for his claim.

3) This is perhaps the simplest method of protecting unsold material — and it does work. When the writer finished a script, he should always keep, or make, a copy. A registered copy mailed to himself is another such protection. When he receives the parcel, he should leave it *unopened* and put it away for safe keeping. The postmark is sufficient proof of when the material was written, so long as the envelope is left sealed and intact.

For further information about copyrights, refer to *The Writer's Manual.*

Postage Rates:

It costs about two dollars to send a full-length script by first-class mail. Unless the writer is in a hurry for some reason, it is much cheaper to use special fourth class manuscript rate. The same package can be mailed for a quarter of the cost of first class postage.

If a letter is enclosed in the fourth class manuscript package, an extra charge for the letter, at first class mail rates, must be added to the mailing costs. If the writer sends the parcel first class, the letter rides free.

Postage prices are subject to change practically without notice; but the special manuscript rate will always represent a substantial savings to the poverty-stricken young writer.

Business Managers

The financial rewards for a first-rate scriptwriter are great. Many writers struggle along for years and then, one day, after a few successful scripts, they find they have become corporations, capable of generating hundreds of thousands of dollars in income. The problem in a sudden income jump such as that can be staggering. Also, "hot properties" can cool off just as quickly. True, a good feature film writer can earn millions in his career. But consider this: a writer is unemployed every time he finished a script. The trick to remaining financially solvent in this crazy business is to make as much as possible, then hang on to it.

Many writers engage the services of a good business manager for this very purpose. An agent is not a business manager; the agent is concerned with selling the property; the business manager takes care of the resulting income. The business manager handles tax matters, makes investments, budgets the money, and tucks some away for the future. The standard fee for these services is five per cent of the writer's gross income, not unreasonable considering that writers as a group are notoriously bad businessmen; the business manager's fee can be money well spent.

With ten per cent going to his agent, five per cent to his business manager and thousands of dollars more for attorneys' retainers and upper bracket income taxes, the writer will undoubtedly start to wonder if success is all it's cracked up to be. It's ironic that many writers may, in fact, — in terms of anxiety quotient — have been better off before they made it than after. But again, it's all a part of the business the writer has chosen. You have to learn to live with the irony if you want to be a successful professional writer.

Where to Live?

Many beginning writers ask: "Is it necessary for a scriptwriter to live in California?" It all depends. If most of the writer's assignments are scripts for television series, then living in the Los Angeles area is almost a prerequisite. The writer must be near the studios so that he can get assignments quickly and work in tandem with the producers and story consultants during the writing process. To be part of the thriving television industry, the writer has to be where the action is.

If, on the other hand, the writer makes his living writing feature films, then he probably only works on one or two projects a year, and independently at that. So long as the writer is available for further work on the script after it is sold, where he lives and works is pretty much his own decision.

Many writers, directors, and actors, shunning the glitter and hustle of Los Angeles, make their homes farther north, in Carmel or the San Francisco area. Some entertainers don't live full-time in California at all — Bill Cosby lives on a farm in Massachusetts, Alan Alda makes his home in New Jersey; and these performers don't work in soltitude the way writers usually do. With jet travel, Chicago and New York are almost as convenient to Los Angeles as San Francisco. If the writer really wants to, he can live anywhere.

However, wherever he chooses to reside, periodic trips to Los Angeles are inevitable; sometimes these "visits" last for months. It's up to the writer to decide where he lives and how he will resolve this problem. Whatever his decision, commuting problems can be worked out.

Unions

Anyone who intends to become a professional scripwriter will have to join the Writers Guild of America (Writers Guild West for screenwriters, Writers Guild East for playwrights). The Writers Guild protects authors' rights and sets down guidelines on such matters as wages, credits, working conditions, residuals, and other matters pertinent to the business of writing.

Not everyone can join the Writers Guild; only those writers who earn income from their scripts are able to join. The first script a writer has produced is considered a "freebee" by the Guild — it may have been a fluke, or perhaps the writer is a non-professional who just wrote one for fun and doesn't intend to write any more. It is not necessary to join the Writers Guild to sell one script. Should the writer sell a *second* script, however, he takes on professional status — it's obvious that the writer is not just doing it for fun, that he plans to keep writing and selling. For the writer's protection, and to protect the other writers with whom he competes, the author will be asked to join the Guild after he has sold his second script. If he does not, he represents unfair competition to all the writers who do belong to the union.

There is a nominal membership fee initially; annual dues are one per cent of the writer's annual income from his scripts every year thereafter. The Guild realizes that beginning writers can least afford a membership fee, and they are reasonable about spreading out the initiation fee, if the writer so desires.

The Writers Guild also offers a copyrighting service for unsold material to its members.

For more information about the Guild, write:

> Writers Guild of America (West)
> 8955 Beverly Boulevard
> Los Angeles, California 90048

or: Writers Guild of America (East)
>   1212 Avenue of the Americas
>   New York, New York 10036

Writing as a Steppingstone

A well-written, original script is proof positive of creative talent. For this reason, scriptwriting may be the best way to enter the theatrical, film, or television world today. Many scriptwriters use their writing ability as a steppingstone to other endeavors within the creative field. Scriptwriting can open many doors, often leading to assignments as a director or a producer.

Many writers opt for the director route. They try to combine their writing ability with the ability to see their script treated faithfully by taking on the dual role of writer-director. One recent example of this trend is John Milius, who wrote and directed *The Wind and the Lion,* a successful picture both critically and financially. However, many writers have not made the transition as successfully as Milius. Writing talent is no guarantee of directorial ability — but some producers are willing to take a chance. The writer should at least be aware that directing is one option that may be open to him; whether or not to take the plunge is a matter of personal decision.

Most writers who move on to another position in the industry choose to become producers. This is especially true in the television field, where the credit "produced and written by" is not uncommon. The producer's role, again, requires a special ability which not all writers possess. But for those who have it, becoming a producer is a good way to guarantee control over the way your script is handled.

In television, writers are often asked to serve as story consultants or script supervisors for a series. The story consultant is responsible for collecting and assigning scripts for the series, has a hand in rewriting scripts for the series, and sometimes writes scripts of his own for the show. The position of story consultant represents steady, lucrative employment, it is also an important job, since the writer/consultant will be largely responsible for the quality of the scripts.

For some, dual roles like writer-director and writer-producer are too schizophrenic. There is nothing shameful about sticking to what one knows best — writing. It all depends on the writer's personal goals. To some, writing is only a step toward becoming a producer; to others, scriptwriting is a desirable end in itself. Whatever the writer decides is right for him, he should at least be aware that the opportunities open to him are not strictly confined to scripting.

FADE OUT

Conclusion

One fact bodes well for those with a desire to become professional scriptwriters: writers are currently enjoying a status they've never known before. During Hollywood's "Golden Age," the screenwriter was a forlorn and underrated creature forced to churn out scripts by rote, confined to the dungeon known euphemistically as the Writers' Building. Many a promising talent was stifled and eventually snuffed out by that demanding monster known as the Studio System. Some writers survived; a few flourished — Ben Hecht, Preston Sturges, Howard Koch, Joseph Mankiewicz. But for the most part, the Hollywood scriptwriter was an underappreciated commodity. Many writers were driven back to the city they had deserted—New York; others vanished into obscurity.

Times have changed. Today, many intelligent people in the film industry are coming to the realization that the cherished "auteur theory" of filmmaking is bunk. The emphasis on the director's role has been inflated for so long that it was bound to burst eventually. There are few directors — perhaps a Bergman or a Fellini — who can really live up to the artistic expectations of the auteur philosophy. Most people have awakened to the fact that filmmaking is, almost exclusively, a collaborative effort. A film represents the sum total of the collective talents of the director, the writer, the producers, and actors. Only a handful of directors can fashion a good film from a poor script, but it is distressingly simple for a director to make a poor film from a promising script. Every element must hang together if the film is to ultimately be successful — the writing, acting, direction and production values. Just as writers are now free to share some of the credit for a good film, they must also be prepared to share the blame for a bad one.

This new realization of the author's significant role has elevated the scriptwriter's stature to dizzying heights. Writers are the film kingdom's new celebrities, perhaps because they were neglected as a group for so long. The creative energy of a top screenwriter is at a premium, making scriptwriting one of the most rewarding occupations in the film-making industry, financially and otherwise.

Perhaps the film medium is finally taking a cue from its elder cousin, the theatre. Theatre has long recognized the playwright as the only truly creative artist involved in a production, from its inception to its performance. The rest of the collaborators recreate the ideas the author originally brought into being. They may embellish the author's ideas, they may shape them and perhaps take them a step further — but they are all beholden to the script-writer for the material he gives them to work with. As the saying goes, "The play's the thing" — and there is no play until someone writes one. Theatre has known this for ages; film and television are learning the lesson.

Scriptwriting is a noble craft, an art unto itself. For those with the talent, skill, and good fortune to become a part of it, the scriptwriting profession can be fulfilling; it brings personal satisfaction, financial reward, and a tremendous sense of artistic achievement. In fact, the ability to create good scripts may be the most sought-after attribute in theatre and film today. There are far more directors, actors, designers, and technicians than there are positions. But a talented scriptwriter will always be in demand — once he has proven his talent.

Finally, there is one more fact worthy of mention. Of the thousands of writers today, a select group of two hundred writers prepares the scripts for every television program and film we see. This group by no means represents the greatest wealth of talent necessarily. Though the odds against the individual becoming one of those two hundred writers may seem insurmount-able, it is by no means an impossible goal. With talent, training, diligence, and a lot of luck, it is still possible to become a successful professional writer. And even if he doesn't penetrate the "in" two hundred, the bona fide writer will still find the craft of scripting exciting, challenging, and rewarding. To a true professional, the act of creation provides all the satisfaction he needs.

The Writer's Manual
Book 9

How Books
are
Promoted

By
Fred Hahn

ABOUT THE AUTHOR

Fred Hahn

is the founder and president of Hahn-Crane & Associates,
Chicago, the first Midwest advertising agency
to specialize in serving publishing and education.
He has received several national awards for work in direct mail.
After taking a BA, Roosevelt University (Philosophy),
he earned an MA at Columbia University (Comp. Lit/Philosophy).
During 1953-63 he was an advertising executive
for Kroch's & Brentano's (world's largest bookstore.)
He served as director of educational information
for Roosevelt University for 1963 — 1964
and also as an instructor at the university (1963-67).
He was an advertising executive for Rand McNally & Company (1964-67)
and vice president of Holtzman-Kain Advertising, Chicago, (1967-70).

PROMOTING THE BOOK

This section of the *Writer's Manual* traces the promotion process from the time a book is accepted for publication until it goes out of print. It is a "how-to" approach to the subject in a limited sense only. It tells when and where the author effectively can help in the promotion of his* own book and the ways to make that assistance most efficacious. The major emphasis is, necessarily, on the publisher rather than the author. As a result, there are explanations of *what* is done by the publishers in book promotion, *who* does it, and *why*. How to do it in the sense of how to write an effective book ad is the subject of an altogether different matter and one I am in the process of living long enough to learn enough to write.

A few words and terms used throughout "Promoting the Book" have special meanings when used in advertising or publishing. They include the following:

Trade and Book Trade

Anyone and anything involved in the publishing and selling of books is in "the trade." Sometimes, but not always, the usage also includes authors, librarians, and reviewers.

Trade Book

All fiction, general interest non-fiction, and books for children are Trade Books. Trade books are those found in a general bookstore.

Juvenile

In the book world, "juvenile" is a book aimed at children's interest level. Juvenile author and juvenile editor are common terms in the trade.

Library or Institutional Books

Almost any book may be found in a good library. However many books

---

*Throughout this text. "he" and "his" are used as neuter pronouns. "When sex is indeterminate, the masculine embraces the feminine." —

Mrs. Wolf, 6th-grade teacher.

are published specifically for the library market with no expectation of, nor much attempt, at sale to the general public through trade bookstores. Such library books include the following:

1.   JUVENILES. Children's books, like paperbacks are divided into "mass market" and "quality" with the former referring to methods of distribution and sale rather than intrinsic worth. Mass market juveniles are those sold in discount outlets, toy departments, supermarkets, and anywhere else children's books can be sold on a self-service basis, including book and department stores. The quality juvenile, on the contrary, is handled by comparatively few bookstores and by no non-book outlets. Its major sale depends upon a specialized evaluation of its suitability for library use. Once gained, such approval practically guarantees a book's immediate as well as long-term success. Since quality juveniles are purchased by school as well as public libraries, this market can be quite large and profitable to authors and artists who meet its standards.

2.   SCHOLARLY BOOKS. Many scholarly books are published with the expectation that they will be ordered by the larger public and most college and university libraries — and no one else. Few such books are actually purchased by scholars for their personal use. Printings are therefore comparatively small, generally 5,000 copies or less, and in some instances, as few as 500 copies.

3.   REFERENCE WORKS. Some reference works, such as the unabridged *Oxford English Dictionary*, are found in just about every library and in practically no private home.

Text Books

Not every book used in the classroom is a textbook, but for our purpose, "textbook" is used in its narrow sense and does not include supplemental reading nor "non-text" materials that may incidentally be suitable for instruction.

Promotion

Promotion encompasses everything that is done to help sell a book. Promotion includes, but is not limited to, jacket design, jacket blurb, catalog listing, advertising, public relations, and special offers.

Sell-In

The "sell-in" is the number of copies of a book ordered by retailers and wholesalers before publication, also referred to as "the advance sale" or simply as "the advance" — the number of books sold before publication date.

Promoting the Trade Book

The promotion process begins long before the trade book is published and often before a manuscript is completed by the author. In chronological order, these are the initial steps in book promotion:

1. The author or his agent discuss the book idea with an editor. The process will be the same whether the idea originates with the publisher or author and whether the book is completed or yet to be written.

2. The editor prepares a summary of the book and an estimate of its potential sales.

3. Summary and sales forecast are submitted to the publisher's editorial board.

4. Summary and sales forecast* of approved books, with expected publication date and tentative promotion budget, go to the publisher's promotion department.

The book summary is the information upon which the initial — and often total — promotion is based. To make certain that the promotion department understands how the author views his own book, he can and should submit his own summary to the editor. In many publishing houses, he will, in fact, he asked to do this. In submitting this summary, follow these Three Commandments.

---

*In recent years, almost all first novels have lost money for their publishers. Many other first books have barely broken even. It is only with subsequent works that most authors become "established" and profitable — for their publishers as well as for themselves. Forecasting accurately the number of copies that *will* sell and the promotion program needed to achieve this goal is a critical function of the editorial-promotion partnership.

I. *Thou Shalt Be Intelligible*
Technical jargon, especially in non-fiction, becomes a habit. Assume that the promotion manager has a limited knowledge of your field and if you must use specialized terminology, translate it in to standard English.

II. *Thou Shalt Be Complete*
This is your one chance to tell the publisher how you think the book should be described . . . and have him listen. Do it right. And do it in no more than two pages.

III. *Thou Shalt Not Embellish*
Let a becoming modesty and total honesty be your guide.

In addition to the summary of book content, include the following:

Biography. Very briefly and in outline form, the basic dates, places lived, education, employment, spouses and children.

Bibliography. Your published writing, if any; include magazines as well as books, with publishers and dates.
Competition. For non-fiction, include your evaluation of the competition, if any. If your book is best, say so; if not, tell why you wrote it ("his is definitive, mine is readable").

Armed with the summary, the estimate of sales and a tentative publication date, the advertising department begins, the actual promotion of the book.

Pre-Publication Advertising

Trade publishing is tied to a three-season schedule of Fall (September through December and including the all-important Christmas season), Spring (January through May) and Summer (June through August). *Publishers Weekly*, the most important journal of the book trade, publishes seasonal announcement numbers in which practically every publisher advertises the books he expects to produce during the season. These advertisements serve as an invaluable overview of a particular season and the industry-wide reference for booksellers, librarians, reviewers, and all others who need information about new books. Almost all trade books published in the United States appear in such "announcement number" advertisements. For many titles, it is the only *advertising* they will ever receive, though by no means the only promotion.

Dust Jacket Design

The dust jacket is the one promotional device for the book that is seen by *everyone* — publisher, bookseller, reviewer, librarian, casual bowser, and ultimate buyer. It is essentially a miniature billboard and like all billboards must make an instantaneous impact to impel further investigation. For many titles, the dust jacket is the most important consumer promotion. It either motivates a sale or fails in its intended purpose.

Jacket Blurb

Most book-browsers look first at the jacket, then leaf through the book - especially if it is illustrated — then read the jacket blurb before deciding to buy — or not to buy. The blurb has the immediate task of selling the book. With the possible exception of a display sign, the blurb is the only advertisement *addressed to an individual holding the physical book in his hands* and should be written with that fact in mind.

Trade Catalogs: Forthcoming Books

What jacket design and blurb are to consumer promotion, the catalog is to the trade. The catalog of forthcoming books describes the titles to be published during a specified period, generally four to six months. This catalog is used as a basic sales tool by the publisher's salesmen in meetings with booksellers, wholesalers, and librarians and mailed to those not called on in person. Since catalog descriptions are written months before the books are actually published and often before the finished manuscript has been delivered, they are almost always prepared from the editor's summary rather than a reading of a finished book.

Catalog copy, like the jacket blurb, describes the book. Trade catalogs, however, have the additional function of telling the reader, and especially the bookseller, why the book will sell. Consequently, catalogs often include information on size of printings, advertising budgets and schedules, and other details of promotion plans that will help the bookseller judge likely customer demand.

Library Catalogs

In addition to the general catalog of forthcoming titles, many publishers also issue catalogs to various specialized audiences. For trade books the most important of these catalogs is the one addressed to librarians.

Librarians take their responsibility seriously in spending public funds. In the selection of titles for their shelves, they are guided by professional evaluations of books that appear in a variety of review journals. Since it is common for such "library" reviews to appear months after a book is published, libraries tend towards "second season" and even "second year" purchases. The library catalog, and much other library promotion, are designed to take advantage of this buying pattern.

Unlike the seasonal trade catalog that emphasizes new books, the library catalog provides equal, if not major, emphasis to books already published. When favorable reviews have been earned, they are quoted or abstracted. If no such review is available, the description of the book highlights the features particularly important to the library patron — validity and ease of use for non-fiction; literary merit for fiction; and for juveniles, the merit of both text and art — and for all books, aesthetic appeal and likely reader demand, not just today, but for years to come. *For the librarian, book evaluation is less concerned with keeping the worthless out than with giving the valuable a home.*

Promoting For Impulse Buying

How a publisher views his book and the sales he expects from it are controlling factors in how it will be promoted. Comparatively few books are expected to be best sellers, and of those which are, fewer still are marketed as true impulse items — books purchased on the spur of the moment by the browser or casual passer-by. In impulse sales, two factors are critical to the publisher's success:

1. The title must be ordered by the retailer in large quantity, forcing them out of the stockroom and onto the sales floor.
2. The title must be displayed so as to attract a large number of potential buyers.

The vast majority of books will not generate impulse sales no matter how prominently displayed. For those which are potential impulse items, the publisher often makes a "Special Offer" to induce the needed initial sell-in. The most common such offer is:

1 copy FREE with each 10 ordered before publication

Such offers are viewed as a promotion expense exactly as if the cost of the "free" books had been used for advertising. For the impulse title, the offer is often the most effective promotion since it works to the advantage of both publisher and retailed in four ways:

1. The retailer increases his book order since the free books give him, in effect, additional discount and profit.

2. The publisher's total sales to all sources make practical a large first printing, lowering the production cost of the individual books.

3. The retailer, because of the quantity of books ordered will intensify his selling efforts to his customers.

4. Because of the large inventory of *returnable* books held by the retailer, the publisher promotes aggressively, often by way of "co-operative advertising."

Co-operative Advertising

Co-operative advertising, or "co-op," is the key to advertising by retail booksellers for impulse, and all other books. Practically 100 percent of all secular bookstore advertising and perhaps 80 percent of religious bookstore advertising is co-op; So important is co-op, and so critical to retail book promotion, that is is worth examining in detail.

Over the past hundred years, a two-track system of costs or rates for newspaper advertising has become the rule throughout the United States. To encourage advertising by local merchants, most newspapers have established a "retail" rate which is appreciably less than the "national" rate charged to manufacturers, including publishers. As a result, a full-page advertisement placed by a book publisher will cost approximately a third more than exactly the same ad placed by a local bookseller. And this holds true for the book publisher located in Los Angeles as well as one headquartered in New York. It is the type of business rather than location which controls the rate.

Under a plan of cooperative advertising, the bookseller shares with the publisher his local "retail" rate. Co-op does *not* mean that the retailer placed the publisher's advertisements in the local newspaper. Rather, the retailer advertises the publisher's book as he would advertise any other item. The publisher "co-ops" by paying *to the retailer* an agreed upon portion of the advertising cost. This system has several advantages to publisher and retailer alike:

1. Cooperative advertising stretches promotion dollars by using the lower retail rate and by sharing this lower cost between publisher and retailer.

2. Like the impulse book, co-op books are usually stocked in large quantity, prominently displayed, and vigorously sold by the bookseller — his way of protecting his investment in the coop promotion.

3. Many publishers make available at no charge to the bookseller professionally prepared retail co-op ads.

Co-operative advertising promotes traffic-building books, does so in a professional manner, and does this on a shared-cost basis. And most important, co-op multiplies by 200 percent to 400 percent the amount of book advertising retailers would place without it.

Nevertheless, the majority of book advertising is not co-op. Retailers cannot, even on the shared-cost basis, absorb all the advertising publishers wish to place in local newspapers, and few retailers have any interest in advertising in national magazines. Perhaps even more important, retailers and publishers have different, though not conflicting, goals for cooperative advertising.

For the publisher, co-op is one phrase of a total promotion. Since few retail customers have "brand" loyalty *to a publisher,* it pays him to advertise through a retailer who does have an established following. Furthermore, most customers know that they can purchase any advertised book through *any* bookstore. For the publisher, co-op with a single retailer is an advertisement for his at *all* retailers, exactly as if it ran under his own name.

Retailers are, of course, aware of this also. But unlike the publisher, they are less concerned with selling a particular book than with promoting books as such, *and with promoting their establishment* as the place to buy them. If any book advertisement attracts a potential customer to the store, he may buy something — perhaps even the advertised book! The same ad that serves as product advertising for the publisher served as product *and* institutional promotion for the retailer. Each gets his value from their joint co-op dollar.

Beyond the Co-op

Like the retailer who uses book advertising to promote his store, the publisher, too, has promotion goals beyond the immediate sale os a book. Through his own advertisements, the publisher sells himself to that audience to whom publisher identity *is* important — to authors, agents, reviewers, booksellers, librarians, and others inside and outside the trade. But ultimately, the publisher must generate the income that makes everything else possible. Therefore *he advertises in order to sell his books* in newspapers which offer retail discounts and in magazines which don't, with co-op and on his own; wherever he believes he will find a responsive audience that can be reached within the limits of his promotion budget.

Getting Reviews*

Only a fraction of the fiction, non-fiction, and juveniles published each year is reviewed in any consumer media. Some titles, because of the fame of their authors, the importance of the subject, or the undeniable brilliance of the writing, gain practically universal notice. Less than half of all books published fail in these happy categories. Other books will be reviewed because of the specialized interests of a reviewer, and sometimes through sheer luck; but most often because its publisher mounts a campaign on that book's behalf.

The long-held belief by publishers and booksellers that *paid* advertising on radio or television is economically unsound is gradually disappearing. In fact, for books of very broad appeal such as paperbacks, the electronic media may be the only practical way to reach potential buyers.

A promotion that is planned to influence reviewers may use extensive and elaborate advertising designed to convince them that a title is worthy of their notice. Or it may be limited to a quiet lunch during which the publisher discusses his book. Either will work . . . sometimes. The actual influence reviews have on the sale of books is much debated, but no publisher will gladly do without them — and many will rather have unfavorable reviews than none at all.

Unreviewed books have been successful and many seeming failures have brought benefits — even profit — to their authors and publishers.

Some of the ways of profiting from a flop are:
1. Become an expert (after all, you *have written* a book on the subject).
2. Become a public speaker by registering with Lecture Bureau (after all, you *are* an expert).
3. Become a teacher (after all, you have been lecturing on the subject).
4. Get a better contract on your next book (after all, you *are* an established author).
5. Write a book on "How to Make a Flop Work for You!"
   (after all, you are far from alone).

Publication Parties

A publication party is an occasion during which an author meets those persons who, hopefully, will be instrumental in getting his book talked about, asked for, and sold. Guests include reviewers and other members of the press, radio and TV, booksellers, and other opinion molders. A publication party is

---

*See "Public Relations," page 675

not an autographing party, although autographed copies of the author's book often are given to those attending. For new author's publication parties work best when the book or author are newsworthy beyond the pure aesthetic merit of the work so that its publication will become a news story as well as a literary event.

Autographing Parties

The autographing party, as distinct from the autographed book, has become a comparatively minor factor in book promotion. Historically, few autographing parties have paid for themselves through books sold while the author was actually in the store. And such a party causes undeniable interruptions in normal business routine. Most attract more voyeurs than buyers. But they generate excitement and a feeling of being present at an event that more than makes up for their real or imagined failings.

Though the autographing party may disappear, the autographed book is very much with us. There is little question that an autographed book will outsell its non-autographed twin; so much so that more authors should make greater effort to sign their books, whether under the auspices of their publisher of on their own.

The Author on His Own

Few authors are satisfied with the quantity — if not the quality — of the promotion effort generated by their publishers on their behalf. First books especially are often left to "prove their worth" in the marketplace. And even after showing the prerequisite "signs of life," all too often the advertising budget is depleted, the sales staff is concentrating on a new list and the cost wouldn't be worth the likely return — or so the author is told.

Unless he has very good reasons to believe the contrary, he will be wise to listen.

Authorship brings with it numerous "natural" opportunities to sell ones own books. Some of the more practical of these are outlined in the pages which follow. Beyond this, few authors should try to go. If you are absolutely convinced that your book has not gone to the proper individuals for review, by all means purchase some copies from your publisher and send them. If you have an attention-getting idea that your publisher refuses to execute for you, by all means do it yourself. If you know better than your publisher how to sell your book' become your own best salesman. But remember that your publisher is also interested in selling — perhaps just as much as you. Balance your expenditure in time, effort, and dollars against the probable gain;

especially the gain spent in writing your next book. And there *are* all those opportunities that *do* come to you for promotion, almost without trying.

Authorship often brings with it a prominence that generates invitations to participate in panel discussions, to speak before civic or social organizations and generally to become a public figure.

Such public occasions give the author unparalleled opportunities to sell himself, his authorship, and his book — if only he will grasp them. The following are some practical steps to follow in achieving these goals:

1. Prepare, if you have the expertise, or ask your publisher to prepare for you, a simple press kit containing a press release about your book, a press release about yourself, and photographs of the book and the author.

2. Send the press kit to the head of the group before which you will speak,* and ask him to use it as part of his own announcement to the local newspaper. In smaller communities, send several kits and ask that they be sent to local radio and television stations, also.

3. If a photographer covers the event, try to be photographed holding your book so that the cover will show.

4. Ask if the group will permit a local bookseller to sell your book before and after the meeting. If such agreement is reached, *let your publisher handle the arrangements.* Do not try to do this yourself and do not expect this service from the group which has asked you to speak.

5. Prepare a fact sheet about yourself and your book and give it to the person who will introduce you.

6. Take along a copy of your book and ask the person who introduces you to show it as part of the introduction.

In all such appearances, work closely with your publisher's Public Relations Director. He will give guidance, good cheer, and much help.

Public Relations

Public Relations, or "PR," has the responsibility for calling favorable attention to books and authors by methods other than paid advertising. On a practical level, PR tries to get books reviewed, calls attention to aspects of books and authors which are newsworthy, and attempts to place some authors

---

*If you have been dealing with the Entertainment Chairman or some other officer, continue to do so.

on radio and television talk shows. The key to successful PR is in not trying to place *all!*

The public relations function is a very personal one. It depends on trust by the person who controls, for instance, a TV talk show in what a PR Director tells him about a writer. It is essential to an ongoing relationship between them, that PR does not use this trust to "sell" a TV dullard. The ability to write brilliantly has little relationship to television showmanship, and it is the showman who is most successful as a speaker, at publication parties, in newspaper interviews, and on radio and television. Siegried Mark, the philosopher and great friend of Nobel Laureate Thomas Mann, once said of him, "To find the true Mann, one must flee from his conversation to the world of his books." Most authors are best left to readers for discovery.

Nevertheless, it is a rare author who is not convinced that he, too, can sell a million copies of his book if only his publisher will get him on "The Tonight Show." There are several things you can do to help your publisher get you there:

1. Tell your publisher that you *want* to appear on talk shows and are prepared to make yourself available around publication day. Most books are *news* only at publication and that is the easiest time to get placed.
2. "Try out" on a local show before attempting a national program. Such local exposure gives invaluable practice in radio or television technique and, even more important, makes possible a sample tape of your appearance for other producers to see and hear.
3. Most national talk shows are filmed in New York or Hollywood. If you want your publisher to send you there, decide in advance who will be responsible for expenses.
4. Successful talk shows are built on having something to talk about, and few interviewers are prepared to discuss *fiction*. If you are a novelist, and even if you write non-fiction, be sure your publisher knows *all* the subjects in which you can display expertise. This is often critical in placing the right "mix" for a group discussion in which a book may be seen and mentioned, but not the actual subject of the discussion.

The Advertising Agency

An advertising agency is expert in media selection, creativity, and production. Few publishers find it economical to employ a staff that is as knowledgeable as an agency in these areas — and fewer still could bring to their advertising the breadth of experience gained by agency personnel in their daily contacts with a variety of clients.

Media Selection

Book advertising appears in well over 1,000 different magazines and newspapers, as well as on radio and television. The decision of where and when to advertise to best advantage is the contribution of the media expert.

Creative

Book advertising is written to the following formula:

Imagine the particular group of readers who will want to know about the specific book in question: then tell them about it in such a way as to make them buy it.

What the promotion says and how it looks is the contribution of the Creative Staff.

Production

Production makes certain that the message that actually appears in print, on radio or on television looks and sounds the way Creative has designed it. Production is to Creative as the builder is to the architect — the unsung hero who makes reality out of vision.

Promoting the Textbook

A basic or "basal" textbook is marketed with the same care, planning, effort, excitement — and only slightly less cost — as the introduction of a new car. A publisher may spend several years and up to a million dollars in the production, testing, revision, and ultimate publication of a text. With so much at stake, promotion tends to be comprehensive, elaborate, and widespread. But even the most successful textbook promotion will only get it into the hands of the educator who makes the final purchasing decision. Ultimately, the text stands, or falls, on its own merit — a merit not unmindful of, but also not awed by, the author's expertise, authority, and prestige.

The *Adoption System*

Practically every textbook used in an American elementary, junior high school, or high school requires an initial approval or "adoption" by an individual or committee assigned to evaluate and approve texts for a particular course. From that group of approved books (and it is almost always a group rather than one only) a teacher or department then selects the particular textbook to be used in each classroom. The problem textbook promotion must solve is therefore twofold:

1) Who gives initial approval and how can the publisher reach and influence them?

2) After adoption, who makes the actual buying decision and how can the publisher reach and influence them?

Numerous surveys indicate that *everyone* in the school system, with the possible exception of the crossing guard, has an important voice in textbook approval and adoption: teachers, department chairmen, principals, curriculum supervisors; the list is endless. It is also accurate, at least in part. Therefore, to successfully sell within this market requires a highly professional and coordinated effort among advertising, public relations, and the publisher's sales staff. Within this orchestrated endeavor, the author plays at best but second fiddle.

The College Textbook

In promoting a textbook to the college and university market, the author plays a more important role. His expertise is sometimes sought in the selection of professional journals in which to advertise to best advantage, professional meetings at which the book can most profitably be displayed; professional colleagues to solicit for advance comments and post-publication reviews.

Some schools, even large universities, use a single basal text for required courses, but this is the exception rather than the rule. In the majority of classes, the college teacher has complete autonomy in the selection of a text. He is selection committee and adoption committee all in one, therefore, promotion tends to concentrate on ways to make the text seem so enticing that he will request a copy for personal evaluation. Since even the most dedicated professor seldom reads textbooks for pleasure alone, every such request is a battle the publisher can consider half won.

The Author and Textbook Promotion

Authors of textbooks tend to be articulate, forceful, and professionally competent in speaking before a lay audience as well as before their peers. It is in just such appearances that they can best promote their texts. Every publisher welcomes his textbook authors' help in the areas where the authors do have expertise. It is to be hoped that they will not confuse this with universal competence in everything, including promotion. In the words of an advertisement from Chicago's Harris Bank:

THE UNSHAKEABLE BELIEF THAT YOU CAN DO ABSOLUTELY ANYTHING
IS A SOLID CORNERSTONE ON WHICH TO BUILD DISASTERS

The Writer's Manual
Book 10

How to
Write
Term Papers,
Theses,
and
Dissertations

By
Lynda Hungerford

ABOUT THE AUTHOR

Lynda Hungerford
has taught composition and literature
since 1966
with a two-year break in between
to complete her own dissertation on the Middle English lyric.
She is now teaching at Illinois State University.
In addition to her academic career,
she has served as a consultant
to the authors' agency, Porter, Gould & Dierks,
in manuscript evaluation, for over five years.
She and her husband, also an academic, have two small boys.

ACKNOWLEDGEMENTS

I gratefully acknowledge the courtesy of the following publishers
for permission to reprint from their works:

Doubleday & Company, Inc.:
From *A Child's Mind: How Children Learn During the Critical Years
from Birth to Age Five* by Muriel Beadle.
Copyright © 1970 by Muriel Beadle.

Cambridge University Press:
From *Literature and Pulpit in Medieval England: A Neglected Chapter
in the History of English Letters and of the English People* by G.R. Owst.
Copyright © 1933 by Cambridge University Press.

Harcourt Brace Jovanovich, Inc.:
From *On Aggression* by Konrad Lorenz, translated by Marjorie Kerr Wilson.
English translation copyright © 1966 by Konrad Lorenz.

Random House, Inc.:
From *Crisis in the Classroom:
The Remaking of American Education* by Charles E. Silberman.
Copyright © 1971 by Charles E. Silberman.

Routledge & Kegan Paul Ltd.:
From *The Language and Thought of the Child* by Jean Piaget,
translated by Marjorie Gabain and Ruth Gabain. 3rd ed.
Copyright © 1959 by Jean Piaget.
Published in the United States by Humanities Press.

The Pennsylvania State University Press:
From *Academic Women* by Jessie Bernard
Copyright © 1964 by The Pennsylvania State University Press.
Reprinted by permission of The Pennsylvania State University Press.

The University of Michigan Press:
From *The Assault on Privacy: Computers, Data Banks, and Dossiers*
by Arthur R. Miller.
Copyright © 1971 by The University of Michigan Press.

ONE — RESEARCH AND WRITING

Introduction

Some people undertake an ambitious research project with unmixed enthusiasm. Experience has taught them that they have the knowledge of libraries and bibliographies, the intellectual strength, and the writing ability to see a project through to a happy end. Others undertake such a project with unmixed dread; they don't like doing library research, and they either do not like to write or feel they cannot do so well. The first fortunate group have no need for a guide, and it is hoped that the second will not put themselves in a position which requires one. Most, however, begin such projects hoping that once finished, they will be pleased with their work, but knowing that there will be false starts and frustrations. They may even fear their enthusiasm will so wane that they may end with a half-hearted effort or even quit. This guide is intended to help them reduce false starts and frustrations and to provide knowledge of research and writing techniques needed to produce a report which represents their best work.

A research project for an advanced course or degree needs to satisfy someone other than the writer himself. It must meet the standards of an instructor or director. Although such standards may include an idiosyncrasy or two, there are many common standards by which reports are evaluated. First, the report should present complete and valid data. Second, it should bear evidence of the writer's having weighed and measured the work of others on the subject. Third, its arguments and interpretations should be at least tenable and at best demonstrably valid. Finally, the report should have a strong informing principle, that is, a principle of organization provided by the author.

This guide can provide some direct help in meeting these standards. First, you will acquire and verify much if not all of your data in the library, and the guide describes what kind of data you might find in what kind of library and the easiest way of getting it. Some of the arguments and interpretations you present will be your own, some will be those of other scholars, and the guide can help you find the work of other scholars and show you the ways you can legitimately use their work. On the other hand, your evaluation of the work of others and the construction of arguments and interpretations of your own depend on your understanding of the discipline within which your project falls. Thus, if your project involves evaluating a social scientist's argument based on a statistical survey, you will need a knowledge of the valid use of surveys and statistics, knowledge beyond the scope of this guide. After all, research projects are routinely assigned to give the student a chance to show how he can apply the principles he has learned to an independent project. Many of those principles are specific to the subject and thus are not to be found in a general guide to research.

As for the organizing principle, the guide discusses some of the ways authors arrive at one for their work, but that principle must come from the writer, that is, from the powers of your mind and imagination. Those powers will have been heightened by what you have learned about the discipline and what you have discovered in your research, but in the end they are your own.

So far, however, we have talked only about the substance of the report. The form remains. While a discussion can leave the form and substance tidily separate, such an abstraction is misleading. Bad writing is confusing and unconvincing. Since the reader has only the written report, he cannot be expected to discriminate between an argument which is bad because it is poorly thought out and one which is merely sloppily presented. Indeed, the two often go together. An argument is likely to be badly written because it has been poorly thought out, and a poorly thought out argument is bound to appear so in writing. A few scholars have distinctive styles which actually add to their work, but for the apprentice in research writing, the best prose style is probably a self-effacing style, which instead of drawing attention to itself presents arguments in a clear, convincing way, and this guide describes the processes of revision which create such a style. Adding the characteristics of an especially incisive mind or quick wit is beyond our scope.

Prose style is not the only element of form in a research report. Documentation, that is, the use of footnotes and bibliographic information to support assertions and arguments, is a second element. The reader experts to know at a glance where he must go to check the accuracy of a fact or of an opinion attributed to another scholar. The reader can know this only if he and the author share an understanding of what goes into a footnote and where. So the guide includes information about the standard forms of footnoting and presenting bibliographic information in the text and bibliography.

The form given in this guide for the arrangement of information in the footnote and bibliography is the fullest form in use today and the one that has the widest acceptance, for it is used throughout the humanities. Mastering this form will put the student in sufficient command of the details of bibliography that he will easily adapt to any of the several forms used in the social and natural sciences. He will know, for example, what constitutes a full author entry, what to do with a corporate author, and the difference between a new edition and a reprint. Such knowledge makes the superficial rearrangement of the information a minor problem. Thus, once the student knows how to determine the correct date of publication, it is a simple matter for him to put it after the place of publication or the name of the publisher, according to the demands of his particular field.

We cannot and will not try to provide a formula by which someone can effortlessly or thoughtlessly produce a good report. There is no such formula. Neither good research nor good writing comes easily, and a report of any sort is almost certainly doomed if the writer is unwilling to devote sufficient time and energy to the project. But the addition of know-how to diligence does save time, energy, and frustration. For example, if you make a complete bibliography card the first time, you will not find yourself frustrated by having to go back to the library to verify a page number or an edition number only to discover that the book is out on loan or lost. The techniques presented here will not guarantee that you will not find your best lead in a totally unexpected place, that you will not suffer a sudden attack of writer's block, or that your typist's toddler won't cast your footnotes into the fireplace. We hope that the techniques will, however, divert you from paths that lead inevitably to frustration.

Some kinds of frustration can be avoided, but not all, simply because writing is more than a stimulus response pattern, and, therefore, writing a research report is creative. Two people following the same approach will not always perceive the same facts, and having found the facts they will not interpret them the same way. Looking at a field of daffodils does not elicit a poem from all of us, and "I Wandered Lonely as A Cloud" is a unique poetic response to a field of daffodils. Likewise, assuming legend trustworthy, many observed apples falling before Newton described gravity. Although logic as well as the standards of an academic discipline prescribe limits for a research report, within those limits the mind is free to discover, or to fail to discover, patterns and relationships.

The techniques of research given here are designed to suggest routines to minimize the thought given to the uncreative aspects of research. None of us can afford the time it takes to track down the quotation we forgot to document in our notes. Such a task can take several days of unproductive time going over books and articles already surveyed. Mental notes are easily forgotten, and making a point of remembering something rather than writing it down invites confusion and frantic re-researching. Most of us have time for only one round of research. Thus, by establishing a routine in which we always document a note in the same unambiguous way, we leave ourselves free to devote most of our conscious thinking to the interesting problems encountered in our reading. Tedium cannot be eliminated, but it can be reduced. Intellectual creativity, on the other hand, cannot be forced, but it can be encouraged.

WHAT MUST BE DONE

The assumption that the research paper involves creativity will not alter dramatically the four steps usually prescribed for research reports: (1) choice of a subject, (2) research, reading, and note-taking, (3) writing, and (4) revising. But here the steps are given with the warning that the four activities do not go on in pristine isolation, but are, instead, intimately related. Often your research will show good and sound reason for altering an early conception of your topic. Often too the act of writing will reveal a gap in the research which must be filled by more research and reading. Finally, ideas exist only as they are expressed, and in a written work that means they exist in the language in which they are stated. Thus, you define the limits of your topic even as you revise the final draft.

The interrelationship of the four steps of research can be seen in a hypothetical example. A student choosing a subject might decide that he wanted to study the Middle English lyric. After reading several anthologies of Middle English lyrics, he might decide to limit his reading to the religious lyric and after reading many such lyrics and perhaps several books about them, he might then conclude that the penitential lyric of the fourteenth century provided a subject with manageable boundaries, with possibilities for original analysis, and for which he had access to the relevant library resources. He could feel confident that he had a sound topic, but the confidence would be possible only because he had done some of his reading and bibliographical work.

Our hypothetical researcher had to avoid two dangers in selecting a topic: (1) selecting a topic so broad that he exhausted his research time before he mastered it, and (2) limiting himself early in his work to a topic on which he would exhaust his time trying to ferret out non-existent material. By far the greater of the two dangers is postponing narrowing the topic. At the doctoral level, a prospectus, or description of proposed research, usually must be approved before a student's topic is accepted. Even at this advanced level, and even with graduate instructors in general agreement that the prospectus is closer to a hunting license than a description of exactly what prize will be brought home, the most common reason for rejecting a prospectus is that the topic is too broad. One can stake out an acre or so in hopes of finding gold; one cannot stake out the whole of California. Sooner or later the prospector has to give up his airborne scanning of the landscape and begin to dig. He may not find gold when he does dig, but he most certainly won't find it from the airplane. Fortunately for the researcher, a rigorous examination of some aspect of his subject is much more likely to yield new insights than mining the average rock is likely to yield gold. The principle is the same for any research project, whether or not the researcher must have his topic formally approved or not; the sooner he narrows the topic, the less time he spends on peripheral reading and research.

The ideal subject is narrow enough to be examined completely within the scope of your time and ambition. You will also have to appraise realistically the resources of the libraries available to you, for to put together a short report of twenty-five pages or so you will need two or three books basic to your subject and some additional material — chapters from other books, articles in periodicals, or the results of original field work and experiments. Research does not, of course, end with this material; it begins with it. The basic core will probably contain bibliographical material that you will want to follow out, and when discrepancies show up, you will need to consult other works to resolve them. In addition you will have to search bibliographies in the library to discover less obvious sources that might directly bear on your topic. But without the basic core of four or five sources at hand you have no beginning.

As you narrow your topic and read your basic books and articles, you develop your bibliography and take notes. To develop the bibliography you record, either by listing or on separate cards, references, books and articles which you will want to examine in the course of your research. Typically, notes contain the factual information, interpretations, and arguments which you will examine in the report, and they can be taken in a variety of ways. Some people prefer larger note cards with one note to a card. Some people prefer notebooks, or large sheets of paper. Note cards are flexible because they can be shuffled and rearranged easily. But notes in notebooks are easier to carry and harder to lose than separate cards. Also, a notebook sheet allows for a more complex or extensive note, though for the inexperienced or undisciplined researcher, that can, as we shall see later, be a temptation to postpone the intellectual work that should go into note-taking. The sooner you establish a routine for yourself in regard to how you take notes, the more distractions you will eliminate from your work.

When you have taken notes on a significant portion of your research you can and should begin writing, even though the research writer is sometimes advised to complete his note—taking before writing. That is a fine idea if you are secure in your ability to pace yourself and have done your research so thoroughly that discrepancies in fact or gaps in argument do not appear when you begin to write. For many people, however, writing is an internal dialogue which reveals the exact subject and the arguments related to it. In addition, experience is needed to gage accurately the number of words needed to express an idea or couch an argument. The sentence that you thought would easily expand to fill several pages, sits before you still a sentence, an important one, but a sentence nevertheless. The point that you thought might take a paragraph to develop may take several pages of expansion and development to be clear. Most important, the ideas that are foggily in the back of your mind for inclusion may, when you get down to expressing them clearly, not look nearly as interesting to you, or they may need more rigorous examination and working out before they can be included. The sooner you express your ideas on paper the sooner you can examine and evaluate them. So, if it is possible to work up the research on separate aspect of your subject, do so. Then you can begin writing on one aspect while you pursue the research on another.

When your research is complete and you have followed out all the pertinent leads on your subject, then you will want to finish a preliminary draft as soon as possible. If you have written a few sections or done other forms of preliminary writing while you were doing your research, this task will seem less formidable. It will be easier too, if in writing the subsections you have developed something of a routine for writing. For your first draft you may have prepared an outline in advance or you may simply have jotted down the subtopics of your subject and the order in which you plan to treat them. Ready and easy guides to writing usually prescribe outlines, but the more creatively you are working with organizing your material the less likely you are to produce a tidy outline, since the organizing principles have to be clearly in mind to make the outline. Moreover, struggling with the outline may just be a way of postponing writing. Revising and refining an outline is not a substitute for beginning to write.

Once you begin your first draft, press through to the end. You can afford to be sloppy with grammar and diction. You can afford even to leave blanks when you can't think of any word that would do or when you discover you don't know an important date or name. Once you have begun the first draft, the highest priority is to finish it, and you can afford to be sloppy because when you finish the first draft you begin to revise.

Rewriting is absolutely essential, and it is the step that inexperienced writers and harried students are most likely to try to eliminate or to scrimp on. Good, responsible writers just don't let first drafts go unrevised into the world. The revising of a research paper involves weighing the arguments anew, examining the order of presentation of subtopics and ideas to see if some other arrangement would be more effective, verifying names, dates, quotations and facts, and, finally, seeing that the words into which all is put are the clearest and most direct possible,

All of these steps take time. Surely everyone knows that he is supposed to budget his time. For research and writing most of us need to budget liberally. One graduate instructor has commented, "The secret vice of every graduate student is optimism." At the time he was examining the projected dates of completion of dissertations. That the vice prevails far beyond the final stages of graduate work is attested to by the innumerable papers sloppily finished in the early morning hours of the due date. To have to begin writing when you know you have not gotten to some relevant sources is debilitating. How can you confidently pursue your argument when you know you have examined only some of the evidence? Failure to rewrite will simply muddle your work and may result in your best ideas going unrecognized and unrewarded. To avoid such traps, realistically assume that every phase of your work will take longer than you expect and plan accordingly.

There are, then, four steps in the research project: choosing the subject, research and note-taking, writing, and revising. The first two steps will bring you to the library, and the kind of library you have available will help to determine the procedures you follow in your research.

LIBRARIES

The large research library of a major university attempts to buy every scholarly book by a reputable publisher and to acquire all scholarly journals. Your problem in such a library is to find in a mass of two to ten million books those few that are relevant to your particular topic.

A special library is one that is devoted to one or several particular fields. The John Crerar Library now at Illinois Institute of Technology has over a million volumes on scientific and technical subjects. Thus, although it has fewer volumes than the more academically oriented libraries of Northwestern University and the University of Chicago, it might well have more thorough coverage of some technical subjects, such as architecture. A special library may have specific limitations. The library of the American Medical Association, for example, tries to maintain complete world coverage of journals in clinical medicine, but it has not retained most journals before 1962; hence its collection would be most useful for recent material. Another example is the Huntington Library and Art Gallery, which is devoted to rare books and modern English and American first editions. Special libraries often have reference sections which are broader in scope than their general collection of books and periodicals, and which can be used for verification of facts outside the field of special interest and, perhaps, for bibliographic purposes.

In addition, some libraries maintain special collections. For example, Northwestern University maintains a separate, large collection of materials relating to African history, literature, and linguistics. The Directory *of Special Libraries and Information Centers,* edited by Anthony T. Kruzas (Detroit: Gale, 1968) has an index in which you may be able to locate a special library or special collection covering your subject. In the directory, for example, you could learn that the Illinois State Historical Library in Springfield is one of several libraries with a special collection devoted to Mormon history.

If you are lucky enough to know the author or title of a good general book on your subject, you are almost certain to find it in the stacks of a major research library or a special library in your field, and you can begin your reading and bibliographic search with that book. If your topic is narrow enough and if the subject catalog of the library is detailed enough, you may be able to find two or three relevant books through the subject catalog, and those books can provide your beginning leads. However, if your topic is at all general, you will soon discover that the library has an unmanageable number of books on the subject, and you will need to begin work in the reference room.

An undergraduate college library may be a carefully selected collection of the hundred thousand or so books deemed most useful for the research projects of undergraduates. Such libraries usually belong to major universities which also have graduate research libraries or to a very select few of the best and oldest undergraduate colleges. In such a library you can proceed as in a university research library with the additional advantage that you are unlikely to be overwhelmed by the sheer volume of material. Unfortunately most undergraduate colleges have libraries which, like Topsy, just grew. Hence their collections are likely to be lopsided and patchy. The number and kind of books in a particular field may well be determined by the interests of particular faculty members. Moreover, a thousand of its 33,000 volumes may have been donated by the local minister in 1929 and reflect his passionate interest in marble effigies or African ceremonial masks. In such a library you are probably best off beginning your research in the reference room, especially if the solid general book you had hoped to find in the library is not there.

Public libraries, with rare exceptions like the New York Public Library, are not intended to serve in-depth research. If you must work in an ordinary public library, you will be more limited than in an even modest college library, and you will have to expect to depend on interlibrary loan and other tedious procedures. Even the reference collection is likely to be disappointing. Before accepting such limitations, at least explore the possibility of using a nearby college or university library.

THE REFERENCE ROOM

The reference collection of any library is used for several purposes. You can find direction there to the general works you need to read before narrowing your subject and to the best basic works in your field. When your subject is further defined you can return to the reference room for a thorough bibliographic search for relevant materials, and, in the case of a dissertation, to guarantee that your project has not been done, or not been done adequately, before. The reference room also provides specific facts and information you need for your project, for example the date when the rosary took its present form, the population of London after the great fire, or the source of a literary quotation or allusion.

A number of guides to reference books are available, some of them in inexpensive paperbacks. Constance Winchell's *Guide to Reference Books,* 8th ed. (Chicago: American Library Association, 1967) with its three supplements compiled by Eugene P. Sheehy (1968, 1970, 1972) is an extensive guide to reference material published before 1970 and should be available in any library. Winchell's *Guide* is organized by subject and then by class of reference work (bibliography, guide, bandbook, etc.), and it includes descriptive comments from a few sentences to several paragraphs in length. For example, of Richard D. Altick and Andrew Wright's *Selective Bibliography for the Study of English and American Literature,* 2nd ed. (New York: Macmillan,

1963) she says, "A highly selective guide to research materials; classified arrangement with author, title, and subject index."

In addition to directing students to bibliographical material and handbooks, reference guides such as Winchell, Frances Neel Cheney's *Fundamental Reference Sources* (Chicago: American Library Association, 1971) or Mona McCormick's *The New York Times Guide to Reference Materials* (New York: Popular Library, 1971) can direct you to the most appropriate encyclopedias, almanacs, statistical abstracts, or dictionaries for verifying or discovering specific facts. When, in your search for a particular fact, your ingenuity combined with the information in such guides fails, the reference librarian may be able to help you find the right source.

THE GROWTH OF A BIBLIOGRAPHY

At the beginning of a project you want quick direction to the best basic books. Such books can be found directly in Winchell, or in the guides and handbooks to various subjects that she cites, such as Frederick Bateson's *A Guide to English Literature,* 2nd ed. (Chicago: Aldine, 1967), or a history of the subject, such as *The Oxford History of South Africa*, edited by Monica Hunter Wilson and Leonard Thompson, 2 vols. (New York: Oxford University Press, 1969-71). If the broader subject is limited to a particular individual, a biography or biographical dictionary might provide leads to basic material. Occasionally encyclopedias can be used for preliminary research, but it should be remembered that encyclopedias have distinct limitations and are not entitled to awed respect. Articles for encyclopedias are necessarily finished long before the encyclopedia is published, so that the information is not usually current even with the date of publication. Moreover, the articles are brief and seldom prepared with the care that goes into a book or journal article which will prominently display the author's name. Sometimes, too, encyclopedia articles are left unrevised or are only partially revised for new editions.

You go to a guide or handbook, a history of your subject, or an annotated bibliography to find the titles of the best books and articles related to the aspect which interests you. You go to such guides rather than to a comprehensive bibliography in your field so that you will learn early in your research the books and articles which are judged by scholars in the field to be significant and accurate. The fear of reading a masterly work on the subject because it might leave you with nothing to say or prejudice your judgments should pale into insignificance beside the possibility of being seduced into a deadend investigation by the meanderings of an ill informed writer or crank.

In addition to providing references to what becomes the basis of the research, the guide, history, or handbook may provide additional leads to useful books and articles. These references, of course, will be noted down as they are found on bibliography cards. A bibliography card is usually a three by five inch card containing the information needed to find the book and all of the information needed for a bibliographic entry in the final paper.

A complete card for a book might look like this:

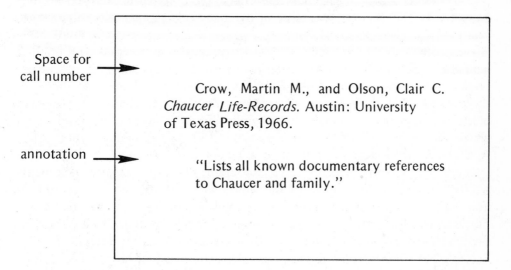

Space for
call number

Crow, Martin M., and Olson, Clair C.
Chaucer Life-Records. Austin: University
of Texas Press, 1966.

annotation

"Lists all known documentary references
to Chaucer and family."

Of course you may choose any size card or slip of paper you like, but you must be consistent about how you arrange information on the card so that you can automatically retrieve it. If you are inconsistent, you may find yourself wondering if Henry Regnery is the editor or publisher. An omission on the bibliography card will usually entail an extra trip to the library to recover the missing information. It may seem like a short cut to note merely the author and title for a book, but if the book must be ordered from a bookseller or requested on interlibrary loan, complete bibliographical information is essential. If all the information you need is not given in your source, leave ample room to add it in the appropriate place on the card. The blank spaces will remind you to write down the information when you do find it, and preparing your bibliography will be easier if all the cards follow the same pattern. A list on a sheet of paper is less convenient than a pack of individual cards because the entries on the list cannot be reorganized and references cannot be easily discarded.

Once the subject of the report has been narrowed down sufficiently, you are ready to do a thorough bibliographical search to find references to all the material which bears on your subject, or at least to as much of it as you can cover before the project is due. In the case of a doctoral dissertation the search must ensure that you are not duplicating the work of another scholar. Indeed, any researcher wants to find the place where he can begin to build on the firm work of others and thus, in his more or less ambitious way, expand the frontiers of knowledge.

To expand and supplement the collection of references found in your basic books you may explore some of the many other kinds of bibliographies. For example, *The Readers' Guide to Periodical Literature* (New York: H.W. Wilson, 1900—date) provides an index for a selected number of popular manazines. Scholarly journals sometimes provide annual indexes of current books and articles in the field. *PMLA*, for example, attempts to index all the current scholarly work on all modern languages and literature. A selected bibliography is one in which the compilers have included only those works which they believe significant and important. "English Literature, 1660-1800: A Current Bibliography," published annually in *Philological Quarterly,* is a selected bibliography which is also annotated; that is, descriptive comments are included for at least some of the works listed. If you are very fortunate, you may find a comprehensive annotated bibliography covering your topic. For someone interested in the application of linguistic theory to the study of literature, for example, Richard W. Bailey and Dolores M. Burton's *English Stylistics: A Bibliography* (Cambridge: Massachusetts Institute of Technology Press, 1968) provides such a tool.

It is a rare research project, indeed, for which a search of just one or two bibliographies will guarantee thorough coverage. A good handbook or guide should help you assemble a list of sources of bibliographical information in your field. To make sure that you are getting the coverage you need, check for each bibliography you use the material surveyed for the bibliography and the cutoff dates for inclusion. For example, some bibliographies include dissertations and some do not. The *PMLA* bibliography looks deceptively comprehensive, but before 1956 it is limited to works by American scholars, so that the earlier bibliographies must be supplemented by other bibliographies which cover work by non-American scholars.

Rather than consult annual bibliographies of current publications over a long period of years, try to find a bibliography which covers a long period of time in your field, such as the Bailey and Burton bibliography of style. As a general rule, it is wise to begin with the bibliography that is most closely confined to your subject and, if possible, to begin with an annotated bibliography. Thus, for a project on Wordsworth, a student who consulted either Winchell or Bateson's *Guide to English Literature* would learn of Elton F. Henley and David Stom's *Wordsworthian Criticism, 1945-1964: An Annotated Bibliography*, rev. ed. (New York: New York Public Library, 1965). It is obviously preferable to consult this single 107-page volume than to plod through twenty to thirty-two separate annual bibliographies of English literature. Of course Henley and Stom would have to be supplemented to cover the period after 1964. This could be done through "The Romantic Movement: A Selective and Critical Bibliography" published annually in *English Language Notes*, 1964-date, or in the *PMLA* bibliography.

There is no point in searching for bibliographical references you will not have time to read or even acquire. For most researchers this means that a standard selected annotated bibliography is more useful than culling many comprehensive bibliographies which include material that is of doubtful value and available only in the largest libraries. It takes at least four to six weeks, for example, to acquire a dissertation on microfilm or in photocopy form, and the time for interlibrary loan can be even longer. Even the dissertation author who must prove that his work is original is better off using a limited bibliography, doing his preliminary reading, and narrowing his subject as much as possible before doing the comprehensive search. To copy down all of the bibliographical entries pertinent to Wordsworth is a futile exercise of the worst sort. There is no way you can read everything before the seminar paper is due, the dissertation deadline has passed and left you in permanent academic peonage, or your publisher has found someone else to do the book.

Your goal should be to have a small, carefully selected pack of bibliography cards all of which are pertinent to your narrow, defined subject. This scant, unpretentious list of books will grow as you pursue your work and ask questions of your own that entail going to sources not previously applied to your subject; the answers to those questions may well be the heart of your paper. Keep in mind that the research paper is not an exercise in making a long bibliographical list, nor is it designed to show that you have read a lot of books. At whatever level you are working, the goal is to assemble and present true, verifiable information in a way in which it has not been assembled and presented before. It is more important that the information you collect be true and complete and that your presentation of it put it in a new perspective than that you have made a futile effort of doggedly going over vast amounts of information only tangentially related to your subject. One test of the researcher is how well he exercises his judgment in determining what is important for his work and what is not.

Unlike Wordsworth, some topics offer little or no choice of bibliographical tools. Before 1968 there was no bibliography for English stylistics. In the case of no bibliography at all, the researcher can only follow the leads he finds in his core material and use his wit and intuition to discover other relevant material. On obscure subjects which have been little studied, it may be feasible to collect a comprehensive bibliography and read all the material in it. The *PMLA* bibliographies, supplemented before 1956 by other annual bibliographies, would yield most of what had been written in scholarly journals about a very minor literary figure. The topic with an ideally limited bibliography, however, may have other flaws, such as dullness. Not only each field, but each topic, has its own bibliographic problems, and the solution of those problems is part of the researcher's task.

You need to remind yourself, too, that current bibliographies lag behind what is already printed and available. To catch up on the most current publications you must depend on your imagination and the familiarity with your field you have acquired. All books appearing in the catalogs of most publishers are included in the *Publishers' Trade List Annual*, which is indexed by author and title in *Books in Print: An Author-Title-Series Index to "The Publishers' Trade List Annual,"* 2 v. (New York, R.R. Bowker, 1874-date), and by subject in *Subject Guide to Books in Print: An Index to "The Publishers' Trade List Annual,"* 2 v. (New York: R.R. Bowker. 1957-date.) You can also check the tables of contents of periodicals which you know publish work on your subject.

In addition to the authors and titles of published works, the person undertaking a long-term, probably book-length project may find a list of works in progress. No research project should be abandoned, however, because something similar appears on such a list. Projects are sometimes abandoned, and often two researchers approach the same subject from perspectives so different that both make genuine contributions. Should you discover that someone else is working on the subject of your thesis, you can write to him inquiring about his approach and progress. It is entirely possible that an exchange of information would be beneficial to both projects.

THE CARD CATALOG

Once you have a clear idea of what material you are looking for in the library, the next job is extracting it from the stacks and other sources. The usual place to begin is the card catalog, which will normally contain for every book an author card, a title card, and at least one subject card. These cards may be interfiled into a single catalog, or one catalog may contain cards for authors and titles and a second subject cards. A separate catalog or list is sometimes maintained for periodicals. The cards themselves will probably be Library of Congress cards or cards that closely follow the Library of Congress format. Here is an example of a Library of Congress card:

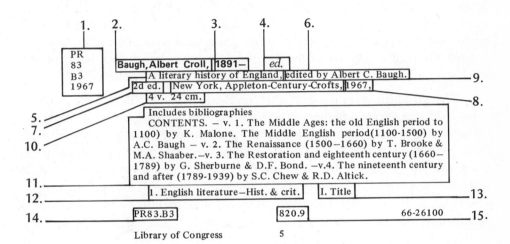

1. The call number for the book in this library.
2. The name of the person or institution responsible for the book — the author or compiler.
3. His birth date and, if he has died, his death date.
4. His role if he is not the author.
5. Title of the work.
6. The author, editor, or compiler's role as given on the title page of the book.
7. Edition number if other than first.
8. Place of publication and publisher.
9. Date of publication. Brackets indicate that the information was not on the title page. Here 1967 is the copyright date taken from the reverse side of the title page.
10. The number of pages or volumes in the work and the height of the book.
11. Information about the contents of the book.
12. Arabic numerals indicate Library of Congress subject classifications. In this case there is only one.
13. Roman numerals indicate additional cards printed for the author and title catalog. In addition to the card to be filed for the title, cards might be printed for a second author or a series title.
14. Library of Congress call number.
15. Dewey Decimal Classification number. In a large library using the Dewey Decimal system an additional number, the Cutter number, would be added.

Of course, the call number in the upper left hand corner, in this case a Library of Congress number, tells you where the book is located and enables you to go to the stacks to get it yourself or to call it from the shelves if the stacks are closed to the public. The card gives other information which may be useful. For example, it gives the complete name of the author and his dates, information that is useful in cases where two authors have similar names. For example, several authors have the name Paul Goodman; the middle name separates the books of one from the books of another, and even though the reader may not know the middle name of the author he is seeking, the dates and subjects of the books together provide telling clues.

The card also gives the publisher and date of publication, which provide some evidence about whether or not a book will be useful. For example, if a scholarly book is privately printed, the author may have paid to have the book published because no commercial or scholarly publisher thought the book worthy of publication. Moreover, in some subjects information rapidly becomes obsolete. If a researcher is interested in the most recent information, the date of publication tells him how old the material had to be to be included in the book.

The card also gives the number of pages or volumes and their size. From the sample card we can see that this particular literary history contains four volumes, and we can, therefore, expect substantial coverage. The title of the fourth volume indicates that the history stops at 1939. Thus, although we can hope the discussion of the periods covered will be updated to approximately the date of publication of the second edition, 1967, we can eliminate this history if we are interested in English literary history after World War II. The card also indicates that bibliographies are included (actually the bibliographical information is contained in footnotes), so that while we might not expect to find extensive coverage of any one literary figure, the bibliographical information could provide useful leads.

Finally, the card indicates what other cards there are for the book, in particular the subject heading that the Library of Congress chose for the book. Thus, if you know of one book on your subject, the catalog card for that book would indicate the subject heading for other books on the same subject. Notice that the sample book has only one subject heading which is quite broad. Despite the lengthy treatment of Middle English literature, no subject card would lead you to it, an example of the trend to fewer subject cards for books. The trend assumes the library user will explore the printed bibliographical sources of the reference room.

Using a card catalog effectively requires knowledge of the finer points of the library's system of alphabetizing. The larger the library, the more important this is, and in a large library with an interfiled subject and author catalog, it is imperative. Common problems include:

Does the library alphabetize letter by letter or word by word? In a letter by letter system word boundaries are ignored, so that "classical antiquities" would come before "classic *sculpture*." In a word by word system, all entries with the same word are filed together, and, therefore, "classic sculpture" would come before "classical antiquities."

How does the library file German Ö? Often this is filed under oe. In general, when a diacritical mark appears in a foreign name or word, you need to know what the diacritical mark means and how it is alphabetized by the library.

Where does the library file M', Mc, and Mac? Often these are interfiled together at the beginning of M. How are the subtopics of a subject ordered? And how are subject cards ordered in relation to authors who may also be subjects?

After you find an appropriate card in the catalog, you need to be able to interpret any code marks the library uses. Your library may have a system of marking a card when a book is temporarily removed from the general collection and placed somewhere like the reserve room. The key which deciphers red lines, blue dots, and other code marks is usually posted near the catalog. If when you find an appropriate card you record the call number directly on your bibliography card, you should never have to consult the catalog again for that particular book.

LIBRARY STACKS

Libraries with closed stacks have the reader fill out a call slip with the catalog number and, usually, the author and title of the book. Although closed stacks mean that you will not be able to browse through the books, you have at least the consolation that fewer books are misplaced, lost, or stolen from closed stacks than from open stacks. If you keep a record of the books you called from the stacks, you will know which books are not brought to you, and if neither the book nor the call clip is returned, you can assume that the first call slip was lost and submit another.

If the stacks are open, you can browse among the books near the ones you have found to see if there are others which might be useful. The price you pay for this privilege is having to find the books yourself. The better you know your library, the more of your books you will find. Some libraries, for example, store books that are too large for the regular shelves on a separate set of shelves for oversize books. That the book is oversize may not be indicated on the catalog card or in the number, so the reader must remember to check the oversize shelf. Also, books that have been returned by previous readers are usually sorted in some preliminary fashion and stored in a place convenient to the stack area where they are to be replaced. Knowing where these areas are provides another place to check if the book is not on the shelf.

Some libraries which have outgrown their present facilities store little-used books in another building known as the annex. If your book, or more likely periodical, is not on the shelf and is either old or esoteric, a check of the shelf list should indicate if it has been moved from the stacks. The shelf list is a catalog in which a card for each book is filed according to catalog number. Often the shelf list card is the most carefully maintained for changes in location, and the shelf list card may contain the most accurate record of holdings for periodicals.

If you fail to find a book, usually the clerk at the circulation desk can tell you if it has been checked out, and, if it has, you may request the book be held for you when it is returned or even have it called back to the library for your use. If the book is not checked out, and if your own detective work fails, then you can ask to have the book traced. It is, however, usually faster to do as much of the tracing as possible yourself.

INTERLIBRARY LOAN

To use a book or periodical which your library does not own you can buy it if it is still in print, have your library borrow it from another on interlibrary loan, or go to another library and use the book there. Since the General Interlibrary Loan Code of 1952 specifies certain materials which should not be requested by interlibrary loan, including current issues of periodicals and items which are in print and can be bought inexpensively, a check of *Books in Print* may make the choice for you. In addition, libraries may not request a large number of books for a single borrower, for the borrower's library or the borrower himself is expected to buy the bulk of material needed for a major research project. Moreover, libraries are naturally reluctant to send out rare and valuable material.

The request form for interlibrary loan asks for two bibliographical sources for the book. The first would be the book or bibliography in which you found the reference. The second, which verifies the existence of the book or article and the accuracy of the citation, can be found in another bibliography. For a book, one obvious source for the second reference is the appropriate catalog of cards printed by the Library of Congress.

Rather than lending a periodical, libraries prefer to photocopy the relevant article, and if you know what part of a book you want, and if copying that section is not construed to be a violation of copyright by the lending library, portions of books will be photocopied in preference to loaning the book. Thus, complete accurate bibliographical information is essential. Convenience as well as the restrictions of the Interlibrary Loan Code discourages heavy dependence on the procedure, for it can take several weeks for the book to arrive. Finally, you may be asked to pay a fee for interlibrary loan, the amount of which may be unknown in advance and which can be quite high.

An alternative to interlibrary loan is to organize your research so that you can go to a larger library if there is one close enough to make such a trip feasible. To do this you would want to have references for enough sources to make the pilgrimage worthwhile, enough so that if one book or periodical were missing you could look at other sources instead. Also, it is wise before you make such a trip to inquire into the library's policy concerning "visiting scholars," for you may need a letter of introduction from another librarian, a dean, or a similar authority to use the library.

EVALUATING SOURCES

As you acquire relevant books and articles you begin extensive reading and note-taking, although you may have taken some notes during your preliminary reading. During your research you will probably examine both primary and secondary sources. A primary source can be an eyewitness account in a newspaper, diary, or letter; a poem or novel if the paper involves literary study; an historical document; census data; the raw data from a sociological survey; or the uninterpreted results of a scientific experiment. A secondary source is an interpretation, paraphrase or analysis by a student, scholar, or researcher using primary sources. Some secondary sources are secondary in name only and are really much farther removed from the primary material. You must appraise how close the author of a secondary source is to primary sources because you must evaluate all your sources. Primary sources, of course, can be as misleading as secondary sources. The letters of a known braggart or the explanation of someone deeply implicated in an incident which he would want interpreted in a certain way must be regarded with at least as much scepticism as a scholar's analysis of an event or circumstance. The conscientious researcher must weigh the analysis or interpretation of a secondary source against primary source material even when everyone seems to agree.

An example is the long-held notion that the bawdy stories which belong to the medieval genre of the fabliau were bourgeois or lower-class in their orientation and origin. The incongruous picture of the decorous audience of noblemen and noblewomen who listened to tales of courtesy and chivalry also listening to stories and poems much more scatological and sexually explicit than anything in Chaucer led generations of scholars to accept the nineteenth-century thesis that two classes of literature appealed to two social classes. In such a system the fabliau definitely belongs to the bourgeois class. But a Danish scholar, Per Nykrog, went back to the fabliaux and did a systematic study of the literary themes and conventions as well as of the manuscripts in which the fabliaux were recorded, and he found compelling evidence of the appeal of some fabliaux to an aristocratic audience familiar with chivalric and courtly literature. The citation of conventions found in fabliaux and the description of physical evidence in the manuscripts are examples of dependence on primary sources. To cite Nykrog or a different scholar who argues for a bourgeois audience would be using a secondary source in a discussion of fabliaux, but a primary source in a discussion of current arguments about the fabliau.

No adequate research paper relies on secondary sources alone, but a solid research paper is likely to rely very little on secondary sources. Of course the use of previous analysis and interpretation is not a bad thing in itself, for knowledge will not advance if we are not willing to build on the work of others, but secondary sources must be evaluated by the scope and use they make of their primary sources and the findings of one secondary source must be weighed against the findings of others concerned with the same facts or data.

TAKING NOTES

In your reading and note-taking, then, you are at least as concerned with the arguments and evidence a scholar uses to support his statements and the assumptions which underlie his interpretations as you are with the statements and interpretations themselves, and the notes you take should enable you to recall the arguments and assumptions readily. Of course you cannot prove every statement you make, and knowledge advances because scholars and researchers agree to accept certain facts, yet you should be prepared to defend the assumptions you do accept. The quality of your examination of the previous scholarship will weigh heavily in the evaluation of your work by your instructor, director, or peers. Hence note-taking must be an analytical procedure in which you record your ideas and your perceptions of primary and secondary sources.

Because note-taking is analytical rather than mechanical, a photocopy is not a note. Although photocopies cannot serve as notes, they are useful. If you are going to be conscientious about verifying every quotation and citation in the final draft, there are enormous advantages to buying the most pertinent books and photocopying the most significant passages from books and articles that you don't own, especially if your project is long. In all probability, some of your material will have to stay in the library, and if your research goes on over several months, or even years, the librarians may demand you return circulating books before the end of the project. Having photocopies at hand means that you won't have to go back to the stacks or recall volumes you have already checked out once before. But however useful, a collection of photocopies is no substitute for a collection of notes.

A note, then, is a record, most often of ideas, but it may on rare occasions simply record a bare fact, such as "In Utah in 1968 a condemned man selected either hanging or shooting as the method of execution." A note may record a summary of an article which interprets a small number of facts in a relatively simple way. For example:

> John E. Williams and John R. Stables in "If White Means Good Then Black . . ." (*Psychology Today*, 7 (July, 1973), 51-54) cite numerous experiments that show that pre-schoolers have already acquired negative associations with the color black and positive associations with the color white. These associations are found in many cultures, and studies have shown some connection between the strength of such association and racial bias. Therefore, the authors suggest that terms such as Euro-American be used instead of the names of colors to distinguish among races.

Such a summary does not include everything in the article. For example, the authors also describe an educational program which seems to reduce racial prejudice in young children, and they cite some experiments which tested the affective value of color names in adolescents and adults. But the summary does capture the elements emphasized in the article — the response of small children and the authors' concern about the use of color terms for racial distinctions.

A note may paraphrase or summarize a paragraph from a book or article instead of attempting to summarize the whole work, especially if the work is complex or if only a portion of it is relevant to the writer's project. For example, here is a paragraph from Arthur R. Miller's *The Assault on Privacy: Computers, Data Banks, and Dossiers* (Ann Arbor: The University of Michigan Press, 1971):

> Some blacks have argued that many census questions have racial overtones and are designed to identify the black community for possible separation from the larger population should a crisis arise. They see the census as working hand in glove with such legislative proposals as those involving stop and frisk, preventive detention, the establishment of incarceration camps for use during civil disturbances, as well as with what many believe is the white establishment's conspiracy to exterminate black militants. Despite reasoned defenses against these attacks, the government's credibility gap seems too wide for many blacks to bridge. (p. 148)

The paragraph might be paraphrased in this way:

> Blacks who have been sensitized by legislation apparently aimed at them, e.g. stop and frisk, preventive detention, and proposed detention facilities for demonstrators and rioters, resent census questions which they believe could be used to identify and locate them in times of critical racial tension.

The paragraph might be summarized thus:

> Some blacks are hostile to the census because they believe some questions have racial overtones and because they fear the government could use the information to harass or incarcerate them.

Finally, a note may be the simple transcription of a direct quotation. Such notes should be kept to a minimum. If note-taking is to be efficient, you must have a clear enough conception of your subject to separate the relevant fact or opinion from its context when you are doing extensive reading. In the example above, unless the specific legislative proposals which have aroused black distrust are relevant to the topic of the paper, they can be left out. By carefully focusing the note, you save time not only in writing the note out but also in reading and weeding your notes when you are composing your report. Simply transcribing a direct quotation is a mechanical, time-consuming procedure which does none of the intellectual sorting out required to write the report. It is a step to be eliminated whenever possible.

Direct quotations are called for when an author's statement is so striking and concise that it deserves to be reproduced verbatim, or when it could be rephrased only at much greater length. A direct quotation may be necessary if you are going to discuss, analyze, or take issue with it. And a direct quotation might be used to prove that what has been held to be the opinion of its author is inaccurate or even contrary to what he is saying in the passage being quoted. Ideally, in your note-taking, however, you will routinely try to summarize first, then paraphrase, and then, after a conscious decision about the purpose of the quotation, quote verbatim.

The form of a note must include certain features. It must be legible and permanent; hence the frequent recommendation of pen over pencil. It is wise to limit yourself to one vehicle, always using a 4 x 6 inch card or 11 x 8½ inch sheet of paper or whatever suits you. It is bad policy to keep a note on the back of a menu, not because the menu will not fit tidily into a pack of note cards, but because a week later you may well forget the note and discard the menu. Likewise any odd group of notes is too easily set aside and forgotten. The nature of the material you are working with in your research and your own inclinations will determine whether you use notecards, notebooks, or some sort of loose leaf arrangement.

Whatever arrangement you choose, however, if you always use only one side of a card or sheet, you will not lose a note on the reverse side. Whether you use cards or paper, leave some blank space for your comments at a later date. When you take the note you can indicate somewhere the special aspect of your topic with which your note deals, but the extra space allows for changes in that concept as well as other comments such as, "but see Smith on the use of census figures for social planning," or "see also Jones's comment," or "number inconsistent with estimate of Arbuthnot."

Finally, whatever form your note takes, it must include a record of the source such that if you found the note two months later under your desk and isolated from all your other notes, you could go directly to the page of the book or article from which it came. This can be done in the same form a footnote would take in the final draft, or in a shortened footnote form including the author's name, a shortened title, and the page, or even more briefly by some code keyed to your bibliography cards plus the page number. The first pattern is the most tedious and least risky, the last is the fastest and most fraught with danger. If you omit this information, you virtually guarantee having to go back through at least some of your sources to find the origin of a quotation, fact, or opinion that was left partially or wholly unidentified.

In addition to noting facts, interpretations, and opinions, you may also want to note discrepancies you discover and questions that occur to you as you read. If you keep a separate sheet or notebook for such discoveries and thoughts, you can make a quick note and continue your reading. Later you will have a collection of questions and facts that need further research, and you can organize them for efficient use of the library.

PRELIMINARY WRITING

In the hierarchy between the note and first draft may come a written preliminary analysis of a literary work, an argument, or an experiment. If you are working with a project which permits early acquisition of the source material which you are going to interpret in some way, you can write a preliminary interpretation. This exercise can point out those areas which need the most attention before the work can be finished and also those relatively elementary questions which can be solved quickly, sometimes adding a significant insight. For example, if your project includes interpreting a number of poems, the effort you put into an early analysis may point to simple trouble spots — a word, for example, that is used ambiguously, or an inverted grammatical structure which emphasizes a statement, or alerts you to a previously unperceived aspect of an image. Such preliminary writing can clarify your own perceptions and ideas, point to new directions for your research, and give you practice in writing about the subject. Such practice may, in turn, speed the first draft by providing usable passages and increasing self assurance with writing about the topic. Thus the effort put into preliminary writing can save time by focusing research and by cutting the effort needed to produce the first draft.

WRITING HABITS

Writing is difficult at best, and to write well consistently requires discipline. A look into the studies of professional writers shows that most have a routine they follow for writing. Hemingway, for example, wrote every morning. A routine time may be supported by rituals, as in the case of Nabokov, who composes in longhand standing at a lectern. Such routines and rituals have value because they establish writing as a habit in certain circumstances. Thus, anyone who has to write an extensive report or many short reports needs to set aside a time and a place for writing and to accustom himself to writing there and then.

The skill involved in writing is not unlike other skills: it atrophies with lack of use. If when you sit down to write your first draft you have not written for some time, you can expect to have a slow, jerky beginning. Likewise, unless you have become accustomed to writing for long stretches at a time, you probably should not plan on working for more than about three hours at a sitting. For virtually everyone, three hours a day for five consecutive days will prove more productive than fifteen hours crammed into one or two days, especially for someone who has done no writing at all for a while. Although the writing itself will never become routine, you can establish a writing time and a writing ritual. Do you work best composing at a typewriter? Are you more comfortable writing in longhand? Know what you need at hand to write comfortably, have it available, and then sit down and write.

If you have not developed writing habits yet, and if you can type, learning to compose at the typewriter has two advantages. First, your manuscript will always be legible, even to a typist who doesn't know you. Second, once you are used to the typewriter, you will type faster than you can write in longhand and thus be able to record ideas faster.

THE FIRST DRAFT

The poet's advice was to look in your heart and write, but the researcher generally begins by looking at his notes. If your notes are in fact notes and not a collection of quotations, you will avoid the first trap in the way of the writer — the temptation to string together a series of quotations on a slender wisp of tedious, predictable prose. The next temptation, one that has been too often encouraged, is to think that to give your material shape you need merely order your notes and string them together with a similar wisp of transitional remarks. Writing is harder work than that.

You will, of course, before you begin writing the first draft, review your notes and sort them according to the topics which emerge as important and related. If you can possibly put your notes aside and then write, letting your mind select the emphasis and give the material the shape that you are creating for it, your first draft should emerge the honest work of your mind. If you keep your notes at your side instead of simply referring to them to confirm points and check facts, you may unwittingly let them dampen or control your own intellectual processes.

Before you write you will also have made some decisions about the structure of your paper and the elements you want emphasized. The point that you are making should help to determine how it is presented, even though some topics lend themselves to a particular format. Biography, for example, is often presented chronologically, but a biography of Noam Chomsky might reasonably begin with a description of his antiwar activism, and then show how his background led to his study of linguistics as an attack on the structure of the social sciences, thus showing that his work in linguistics is actually based on the same concerns as his political writing and action. That many dissertations and scholarly articles begin with a review of the research does not mean they all have to, or even that some wouldn't have been improved by a less conventional beginning.

If you can construct an outline before you write, and if you find such an outline useful, then make an outline. But despite frequent pedagogical imperatives on the subject, many successful writers do not begin with outlines. If you find an outline constraining or if you find one tedious to construct, don't bother. If you need an outline to go with the paper, you can outline it after it is written. No one consciously parses a sentence before he speaks it, and just as you must have the sentence to parse it, you must have worked out the structure of the paper to outline it. Some people, of course, do work out the structure sufficiently in advance to construct detailed outlines — a room in Faulkner's house is papered with the working outlines of the chapters of one of his novels. Other people prefer working from a simple list of major topics or ideas.

Reports usually follow one of two patterns. In the first, a conclusion is presented and argued for. In the second, a question or problem is presented followed by pertinent data and one or several hypotheses which explain it. If several hypotheses are presented, they are tested or evaluated to demonstrate which are most satisfactory. Although the second pattern appears to represent the actual course of the researcher's work, it is a much simplified representation, for no one wants to read about every mistake made and tangent taken by the writer in the course of his work.

In addition to deciding on a general scheme for the paper, you need to decide exactly what audience you are writing for. A college or university student can assume that he is writing for his classmates. The term paper submitted at the end of American History I is usually addressed to an audience with the preparation for the course even though the only reader may be an instructor who knows much more about American History. Similarly, papers for an advanced seminar, which are often formally exchanged during the term, are addressed to students ready for the advanced work. In the case of a thesis or dissertation, the writer can reasonably assume an audience of scholars in his general field, but not specialists on his particular topic. Anyone on the faculty in the student's department should be comfortable reading the paper. The dissertation writer has become a specialist in his field, and he is writing for intelligent, informed non-specialists.

Having reviewed your notes, selected the general method of presentation and points for emphasis, and reminded yourself of the needs of the audience, begin to write, but not necessarily at the beginning. A systematic person who normally begins at the beginning will probably do so. But if you are less systematic, and you are particularly confident or excited about one particular topic, begin with that, especially since first paragraphs and first chapters are among the most difficult to write. Wherever you begin, you may find your early paragraphs unsatisfactory, but instead of going back to rewrite them, forge ahead. With any luck at all, as you get into writing your ideas will begin to flow and the words will begin to flow with them. Since you will not want to do anything to discourage this, do not stop to look up words in the dictionary, to check a fact, or to go into the next room for a book. Instead of worrying about the antecedents of pronouns, lack of parallelism, or even prepositions at the ends of sentences, work to maintain the momentum of your writing, a momentum highly vulnerable to interruption. You will, of course, want to be coherent and convincing, so you cannot simply proceed on the basis of free association of ideas, but in the first draft two crudely stated ideas are more valuable than one elegantly stated.

If the momentum of your writing stops, simply rereading what you have written may help you regain it. Sometimes you will find that you are trying to trace several different but related arguments or lines of development at the same time. Often a writer begins with one line of development, some aspect of which is linked to the second, and he is sidetracked to the second before finishing the first. If this has interrupted your progress, try to set aside the sections on the peripheral argument, go back to developing the first, and then plan to follow up on second and even third strands at other points.

As you work on an extended project, or as you complete several small projects, you will develop a sense of about how much you can expect of yourself at a sitting. Although some sessions will go better than others, and although if you expect to do much research writing you will try to extend your limits, it is dangerous to try to push too far beyond them. For most people it is better to stop with a few good ideas left, jot them down, and then pick them up at the next session. Then the writer has a running start when he sits down to continue his work.

Even after you have finished your major reading and note-taking, you may find your conception of your subject changing. Such a change can happen even while you are writing. In *Crisis in the Classroom: The Remaking of American Education* (1970; reprinted New York: Vintage, 1971) Charles E. Silberman describes some of the changes that this particular research report, researched and written by a professional, went through. He says of his book:

> . . . the question of purpose kept intruding itself throughout the course of the research, and even more, through the course of writing. Writing is always painful, for it is a continuous process of dialogue with oneself, of confrontation with one's thoughts, ideas, and feelings.
>
> . . . .
>
> It was not until I was well into the writing, therefore — not until I had, over a summer, completed and abandoned a first crude draft — that I began to realize what a metamorphosis had taken place in me and in my thinking about education. In struggling to find my theme, I discovered that my views had changed profoundly. I had not thought hard enough about educational purpose until the agony of writing forced me to; I thought I *knew* what the purpose of education should be: namely, intellectual development.
>
> . . . .
>
> I was wrong. (pp 6-7)

Silberman was a senior editor *of Fortune,* a researcher and writer of experience and proven talent, when he undertook the Carnegie Study of Education and Educators which led to the book. His description of the act of composition ill accords with the portrait of the unruffled student writing sedately at a desk with his detailed outline, in perfect parallel form, at one side, his notes at the other, casually knocking out his term paper. Unfortunately that portrait has often been seriously offered to students as a model for their own work. In contrast, Silberman testifies that writing is not easy, but agony. He found he needed not to revise his first draft, but to abandon it and start over. For that to happen to a student is not evidence of his incompetence and inefficiency. Instead it may witness to his intellectual honesty.

Earlier in the introduction Silberman talks about the mysterious process of change by which books become something other than what they start out to be (p. 3). The internal dialogue which ultimately defines the topic and shapes the paper is the product of the individual researcher's mind coming to grips with the material his research has provided. There is no guide through those dark woods. One can only suggest you keep at the dialogue, that is, keep on writing, until the conversation with yourself reaches a natural, satisfactory end. Then you will have a draft which represents a statement of your work, a draft which you can begin to revise and refine. Such revision is basic to the intellectual quality of the paper, for since — as Northrop Frye has said — "the words used are the form of which ideas are the content," a crudely stated idea is, in fact, a crude idea.

REVISION

Like crudities in our children, crudities in our writing are often difficult to perceive, and the critical objectivity necessary to see them accumulates with time. Ideally the first draft is set aside for several days before revision begins. If several days are out of the question, at least allow several hours of rest and diversion before tackling the revision. Because large important changes should be made first, revision begins with the questions of how convincing is the argument and how well proportioned are the treatments of various subtopics. You may discover you could improve your argument by rearranging the subsections of the paper or that you could significantly cut a section which you found particularly interesting but does not deserve the prominence of your extended treatment. You may find, too, that you have assumed too much knowledge of certain aspects and therefore need to add explanatory sentences or paragraphs. Such large revisions are common to all reports, but since their specific character is determined by the individual report and author, there are no general rules for guidance. Such changes can be made conveniently, however, only if you have allowed plenty of space on the pages of the first draft, double or triple space on a typewriter with wide margins, and if you have written on one side of the sheet only. Cutting and pasting will not solve all your problems, but it can help solve some, and it is impossible if both sides of the sheet have been used.

TRANSITIONS

Although such evaluation of argument, evidence, and proportion is unique to each project, other problems of research writing are widely shared, and can be described more specifically. Transitions, for example, are essential for clarity; indeed, they are at the very heart of your research, for they show how you perceived some new idea, concept, or likeness which put your disparate data into an organized framework. Perception of the whole is only part of the job; you have to make that perception obvious to your reader, and you can do that only through the transitional devices you use among sentences, paragraphs, and topics.

The transitional problems of the paragraphs are similar to those of the larger report. Just as there is no set formula for a research report, there is no set formula for a paragraph. Indeed, it is hard to imagine anything more tedious than a series of paragraphs all constructed on the model of topic sentence — amplification — restatement. Nevertheless, the reader is entitled to an orderly progression of thought which is simple, clear, and direct. That is where transitions guide him from point to point. Thus you must provide early in the paragraph a link to what has gone before, and you must provide links among the rest of the sentences of the paragraph. It is not sufficient that the facts or ideas are related in your intellectual apprehension of the subject, for that apprehension must be made immediate to the reader. Here are five stylistic devices which accomplish this:

1. Maintaining the same grammatical subject in a series of sentences.
2. Using complex sentences which, by virtue of the fact of grammatical subordination, make relationships among the parts clear.
3. Repetition of key words, as opposed to elegant variation.
4. Parallelism
5. Using adverbs which express relationships, such as *moreover, therefore, nevertheless,* and *for example.*

Here is a paragraph from Muriel Beadle's *A Child's Mind: How Children Learn During the Critical Years from Birth to Age Five* (1970, rpt. Garden City, New York: Anchor Books, 1971):

As the varying cultural patterns of the world's peoples attest, young humans are enormously adaptable, and older humans are exceptionally faithful to the ways of their forebears. A baby can learn to sleep upright and tightly swaddled, or prone and without a cover. If his mother elects not to carry him in a sling on her back during the day and keep him in her bed at night, he adjusts very well to spending long solitary periods in his crib or playpen. As a newborn, he feeds whenever he is hungry or according to some externally imposed schedule, and grows into a pattern of eating once a day or five times a day — not because such behavior is best in any absolute sense but because it is customary in his culture. (pp. 218-19)

This typical paragraph from a sound, readable book provides several examples of transitional devices. The words "cultural patterns" in the first sentence refer back to the subject of the previous paragraph, thus linking the two paragraphs. The first sentence is complex, the dependent clause containing the link to what has gone before, and the first independent clause, "young humans are enormously adaptable," is the general statement which is amplified by the rest of the paragraph. All of the examples given in the paragraph show the adaptation as a response to the demands of "older humans," the grammatical subject of the second independent clause of the first sentence. "Young humans" is made more specific in "a baby" in the second sentence, and "a baby," through the pronoun *he*, remains the grammatical subject of the rest of the sentences in the paragraph. The last clause, "not because such behavior is best in any absolute sense but because it is customary in his culture" anticipates the following paragraph which discusses the effect of culture on values and habits which may be seen as absolute by the reader, a view which the author challenges.

While we do not know what changes the paragraph went through in the actual writing, we can imagine how it would look with less care for such verbal clarity:

> People are highly adaptable to the patterns of their forebears, and they perpetuate those patterns. Some babies learn to sleep tightly swaddled in an upright position. In some societies infants are left without a blanket lying down. There are mothers who carry their babies with them in slings and even sleep with them in their bed. Young children elsewhere are content to play by themselves in cribs or playpens. There are cultures in which mothers feed their babies according to a fixed schedule. Other children are allowed to nurse when they are hungry. Such patterns are not adapted to by the child because they are good or bad intrinsically, but because they are imposed by the culture.

This version is inferior because it is a succession of loose and unrelated sentences. Instead of setting cultural contrasts in opposition in the same sentence, the contrasts are stated in separate sentences with emphasis shifting with grammatical subject from mother to child to culture. This constant, unnecessary shifting of grammatical subjects makes the paragraph harder to follow and the pronoun references confusing even though they are grammatically correct. Moreover, the hierarchy in importance for this paragraph of culture, parent, and child is less clearly defined. Thus, in the original, the careful provision of transitional devices creates greater clarity by indicating what is more and less important and by focusing on the subject.

Just as relationships among the sentences of a paragraph need to be presented to the reader unambiguously, so too do the relationships of topic to topic. Depending on the work and the author, such relationships may be indicated simply or may demand extensive statement.

For example, chapter six, "Earth's Green Mantle," of Rachel Carson's *Silent Spring* (Boston: Houghton Mifflin, 1962) begins, "Water, soil, and the earth's green mantle of plants make up the world that supports the animal life of the earth." (p. 63). The first two words, "water" and "soil," refer to the subjects of chapters four and five.

Similarly, Konrad Lorenz restates the subject of the previous chapter at the beginning of chapter five of *On Aggression*, trans. Marjorie Kerr Wilson (New York: Harcourt Brace & World, 1966), but Lorenz explicitly states the relationship of the previous topic to the new one:

> Redirection of the attack is evolution's most ingenious expedient for guiding aggression into harmless channels, and it is not the only one, for rarely do the great constructors, selection and mutation, rely on a *single* method. It is the nature of their blind trial and error, or to be more exact, trial and success, that they often hit upon *several* possible ways of dealing with the same problem, and use them all to make its solution doubly and triply sure. (p. 57)

In this case, "redirection of the attack" has been the subject of the previous chapter, and this chapter will go on to discuss three more mechanisms for channeling aggression in animals which are paralleled in man.

Even more explicit is Jean Piaget's beginning paragraph of chapter three of *The Language and Thought of the Child*, trans. Marjorie and Ruth Gabain, 3rd ed., International Library of Psychology, Philosophy and Scientific Method (London: Routledge & Kegan Paul Ltd., 1959):

> In the preceding chapters we have tried to determine to what extent children speak to each other and think socially. An essential problem has been left on one side: when children talk together, do they understand one another? This is the problem which we are now to discuss. (p. 76)

Another example, this time making use of summary and enumeration, comes from chapter four of G.R. Owst's *Literature and Pulpit in Medieval England: A Neglected Chapter in the History of English Letters & of the History of the English People* (Cambridge: Cambridge University Press, 1933):

> Three distinctive types of medieval sermon-illustrations have already been noticed and discussed, more especially from the point of view of their literary influence, in the chapters preceding. We have seen brief

illustrations drawn from men and things in the current everyday scene. We have had examples of the allegorical *figure* of speech, often Scriptural in origin but non-scriptural in its development; and in addition we have had occasion to observe the part played by Biblical hero and saint in the pulpit legend. There remains yet the commonest type of *exemplum* to be considered, the moralized anecdote, whether historically true or fictitious, drawn from sources both ancient and contemporary, secular as well as religious (p. 149).

Owst goes on in the paragraph to indicate the literary importance of the sermon *exemplum* and to explain why his discussion will emphasize how *exampla* were disseminated in England.

Summaries such as this which are used in transitions to move the reader from one topic to another are not superfluous. Rather than clogging the report with boring repetition they ease the reader from one section to another smoothly and thus support the structure of the paper.

DOCUMENTATION AND CITATION

The need for transitions is matched only by the need for evidence. Indeed, although it is possible to provide too much, it is most difficult, especially if the evidence is not presented in a clearly organized and rational way. The facts and interpretations you have uncovered in your research are equivalent to the individualizing detail of the novel. Without them there is no life in the work. While you do not want to simply string together a series of quotations or paraphrases, you will need to document facts, and you may want to cite the opinions of others. Both can be done gracefully and must be done accurately.

The Muriel Beadle paragraph quoted assumed that some of the wide cultural differences in child rearing were common knowledge. Since most readers will be aware that in some societies children are carried in slings while their mothers work in the fields and in other societies children are left in their cribs while their mothers vacuum the house, a footnote to an anthropological study independently verifying such observations is unnecessary. But one must document more esoteric facts, or ones which the reader might challenge. For example, in *Fire in the Lake: The Vietnamese and the Americans in Vietnam* (Boston: Little, Brown, 1972) Frances Fitzgerald footnotes the statement, "By 1959 South Vietnam was importing twenty million dollars worth of food per year under the Food for Peace Plan though food was still its greatest national resource" (p. 102), The note in this case directs the reader to Bernard B. Fall's *The Two Vietnams: A Political and Military Analysis* (New York: Praeger, 1963), pp. 294-295. Such a note serves two purposes. First, it acknowledges the source where the author found her information, and second, it enables the reader to go to that source to evaluate it for himself and check whether the author has quoted accurately and with due respect for the context.

Just as you provide the source for facts, so you provide the source for interpretations and opinions. Even when you have reexamined the evidence and independently reached a conclusion, if that conclusion has already been stated by someone else, the other author must be clearly acknowledged in the paper. Whether you agree or not, the text of your paper must show just where the interpretation begins and ends with a minimum of fuss and footnotes.

In a paraphrase, the simplest way is to begin with the name of the author as Jessie Bernard does here in a paragraph from *Academic Women* (University Park: The Pennsylvania State University Press, 1964):

> Caplow and McGee report that the evaluation of professors as men-of-knowledge is more difficult in some areas than in others, most difficult in the "feminine" subjects like English and least so in the "masculine" subjects like physics. They found the difficulty of evaluation in the social sciences to lie between the complexity of the humanities and the relative simplicity of the physical sciences. Whether any specific categorization or classification of academic men in terms of content of their contribution, method, or political stance was considered good or bad, they found, depended, of course, on the evaluator. In any event, they concluded, it was based on "performance and is as equitable as conflicts of viewpoint permit." (p. 139)

Because the paragraph opens with the names of the authors of the original work, and since it is clear that only one work is under discussion, the footnote can be reserved for the end of the paragraph, which because it ends with a direct quotation must be documented precisely. Jessie Bernard is here showing her scepticism of the objectivity possible in evaluating professors as men-of-knowledge by pointing to inconsistencies in Caplow and McGee, and, in turn, her scepticism gives greater force to her subsequent quotation of the authors to the effect that women professors are not evaluated as men-of-knowledge at all. Thus, she is quoting for a purpose.

The facts and opinions you document in your paper should be there either to be refuted, or to buttress your own argument or interpretation.

Simple agreement with a previous analysis is seldom worthy of inclusion. To say, "I agree with John Doe who argues that a free press is valuable," with or without either a summary of John Doe's opinion or a quotation from his work, is certain to convince the reader that you are simple-minded, unless you go on to show why you agree and what place agreed upon fact or opinion has in the fabric of your argument.

Usually it is graceless to simply pick up a sentence from another author, quote it, and provide only a footnote. Somewhere in the text you need to acknowledge the full measure of your debt to the ideas you found in the work from which the quotation was taken, for normally you would not be quoting from a work which was irrelevant to your argument or which did not help to shape your thought. It is not only graceless but also dishonest to place a mere suspended numeral at the end of a paragraph which summarizes someone else's ideas. You must indicate in the text where the use of someone else's work begins. Hiding his name amidst a sea of closely typed references at the bottom of the page or at the end of the paper is not sufficient acknowledgment. Moreover, your own ideas and work will be more prominent if you are scrupulous about giving due credit to others in the text of your paper. The solution is not more footnotes, but rather a balanced and thorough assessment of your debt to others.

Ideally, then, the text of the research report should be written so that a reader has to consult a footnote which documents a fact or opinion or acknowledges a source only if he (1) wants to learn more about a subject from a source you have cited, (2) wants to check the accuracy of your report, or (3) wants to use the bibliographical information, such as the date of publication, to evaluate the source. The reader should not have to consult the notes, with or without the aid of a ouija board, to determine what is original to the report and what is second hand.

EXPLANATORY FOOTNOTES

A second kind of footnote, the explanatory footnote, is provided when the author wants to include information peripheral to his argument for most of his readers. For example, the Report of the Traffic and Distribution Panel to the Commission on Obscenity and Pornography titles Section D of Part I, "The 'Under-the-Counter' or 'Hard-Core' Pornography Market." The authors note "Hard-Core" and provide the following comments in the note:

> Some judges have employed the term "hard-core pornography" as a synonym for "material which can be legally suppressed." In this Report,

the term is used as a synonym for "under-the-counter" or covertly sold materials. This is, in effect, the definition of hard-core applied in the marketplace. It can be argued that because of the confusion about the meaning of the term, which stems primarily from an undefined legal concept, it would be well to avoid the use of the term altogether. *(The Report of the Commission on Obscenity and Pornography* (Washington, D.C.: U.S. Government Printing Office, 1970), p. 113).

The note actually restates the definition provided earlier in the text (p. 18) and goes on to defend the report's use of the word to those few in the audience with enough legal experience to know that the word has been used differently in some courts. Clearly, most of the audience of the report would not have that legal experience, and they are free to read the report without attending to the peripheral argument of the footnote. Remember, however, that most academic research reports are addressed to a much narrower audience than that of a report so controversial and publicized that it was commercially reprinted in paperback for newsstand distribution. A careful author can adjust his text to the specific needs of a small audience, and so an academic report normally requires few explanatory footnotes. For those readers who will feel obliged to read all of a report, it is much more convenient to have all of the relevant information incorporated in the text.

STYLE

Although your first concerns in revising the report are for proportion, smooth transitions, and accurate and graceful inclusion of evidence, you will probably make less dramatic changes in syntax and diction while you are attending to the major problems. Often the minor changes will involve little thought or effort, since they consist of eliminating the awkwardness characteristic of early drafts. The changes, however, are important to your presentation, for they affect the way the work is received. Naturally, if your contribution is important enough, it will be acknowledged even if the style is off-putting, but it may be acknowledged only grudgingly. Moreover, to be as clear and concise as possible, that is, to write as well as you can, is a courtesy to your reader.

As you refine your presentation, you can apply three tests to the individual sentence and paragraph:
1. Does it say exactly what you mean, no more, no less?
2. Does it say that as concisely as possible?
3. Does it sound good when read aloud?

In addition, you can watch for a number of stylistic mannerisms which are commonly found in academic writing. None of these mannerisms produces ungrammatical sentences, but they clog the prose and diminish the effectiveness of the report. Once you are used to watching for them, eliminating them can be an easy way to improve your writing.

Because the mind can process an active declarative sentence more quickly than a passive sentence, the passive voice is justified only when the agent of the action is unknown or so unimportant that it is better left out. For example, if in the context of the paper it is important that the streets were clear, then

The streets were cleared of snow.

is preferable to

The Department of Streets and Sanitation cleared the streets of snow.

However, when the agent is worthy of inclusion, the active voice is usually preferable, not only because it is more easily absorbed by the reader, but also because the elements of importance receive the natural emphasis given to the first and last places in the sentence.

Thus,

The neighborhood improvement association found property values declining.

avoids the anticlimax of the prepositional phrase at the end of

Property values were found to be declining by the neighborhood improvement association.

Besides changing passives to actives, the emphasis of the final position in a sentence can be used in active sentences by removing modifying phrases from the end:

Experiments have not demonstrated the worth of computers, television, and other educational hardware.

rather than:

Computers, television, and other educational hardware have not proved their worth in the experiments in which they have been tested.

Another device that contributes to clarity and emphasis is parallelism, that is putting similar thoughts in the same grammatical structure, as Lincoln did in the Gettysburg Address:

. . . we cannot dedicate, we cannot consecrate, we cannot hallow this ground.

Surely oblivion would have swallowed up the same thought differently stated:

Mere civilians cannot dedicate this ground. Nor can we consecrate it. It cannot be hallowed either.

Although the simple active declarative sentence can often be emphatic, too many such sentences create boredom. Thus grammatical subordination, which we have seen was valuable in providing transitions by describing relationships of place, time, and cause, also combats monotony. Thus, the following paragraph is both dull and less than fully explanatory:

Jane Austen portrays society in *Emma* as extremely dull. It is a particularly cruel environment for an unmarried woman. The author portrays the society ironically, so we see that Emma is better off married to Mr. Knightley than with any other possible fate.

Grammatical subordination makes the thought clearer and the prose more interesting:

Because the ironically-portrayed society of *Emma* is shown to be particularly cruel to single women, the reader recognizes that Emma is best off married to Mr. Knightley.

Occasionally, however, a complex sentence takes off in several directions at once and becomes confusing:

Because the reader is sympathetic to Emma, who lives in a society which is particularly boring and restricted for the unmarried woman, the reader is happy to see her betrothed to Mr. Knightley, who has proved true to his name and considerate of her father.

Although all of the elements included in the sentence could be important to the interpretation, and although the sentence is grammatically correct, breaking it down into three sentences makes the relationships clearer:

By the end of the novel the reader hopes Emma will not be reduced to the pathetic existence decreed for unmarried women in her society. He also desires a man worthy of her hand, and because of her devotion to her father, her husband must be able to accommodate to Mr. Woodhouse. Thus, Mr. Knightley is the perfect match.

Just as a series of simple declarative sentences becomes monotonous, so many long, involved sentences, one after another, can be tiring. Variety of sentence structure breaks the monotony and lets the writer use the short declarative sentence for emphasis, as in the last example.

Repetition is another device ordinarily useful for transitions and emphasis but subject to abuse. Used carelessly, repetition impresses the reader as the product of a dull plodding mind:

> The reader of *Emma* wants Emma to marry someone so she will not be trapped into the dull role of a single woman in her society. The reader wants Emma to marry a man who is worthy of her, and the reader wants that man to be considerate of her father. Mr. Knightley is eligible because he is worthy, because he has been considerate of her father, and because he has already demonstrated his concern for her.

We can recognize the problem in this paragraph as soon as we realize how much it could be shortened without diminishing the content or creating confusion.

Needless repetition is not the only reason for pruning. Crutch words and phrases which come easily to many writers under the pressure of composition can also be pruned to strengthen the prose. Frequently used crutch words and phrases include:

There is

> The house on the corner needs painting.
> rather than
> There is a house on the corner that needs painting.

Due to the fact that

> The siding will be damaged by moisture penetrating where the paint has peeled.
> rather than
> The siding will be damaged due to the fact that moisture can penetrate where the paint is peeling.

Who is

> The frank man can be trusted.
> rather than
> The man who is frank can be trusted.
> John, the boy across the street, climbs fences.
> rather than
> John, who is the boy across the street, climbs fences.

The fact that

> My trip to Brazil . . . .
> rather than
> The fact that I had gone to Brazil . . . .

Which is

> This mystery story is set in Galena.
> rather than
> This novel is a mystery story which is set in Galena

Another form of wordiness in research papers comes from unnecessary or careless qualifying. Because the researcher must be scrupulous to separate facts from opinions and to refrain from overstating his case, he may be tempted to qualify unnecessarily his argument or interpretation. The grotesque example of this is the paper beginning "In my opinion, I think . . . ." A writer's interpretation of his data will pervade his report , both in his presentation and selection of facts. He is obligated to represent the facts accurately. But a careful, honest representation of facts does not require unnecessary and debilitating qualification of interpretation. Thus, "It appears" and "It seems" are quite as tentative as "It appears to me" or "It seems to me" and the shorter forms avoid the intrusion of an insecure author. If the facts support a forthright, positive statement, then the statement should be left forthright and positive, without a "perhaps" which leaves the author on the fence.

The need to eliminate wordiness is not a need to eliminate specific, concrete language. An abstract statement is seldom more concise than a similar statement in concrete terms. Look again at the paragraph from Muriel Beadle's *A Child's Mind:*

> As the varying cultural patterns of the world's peoples attest, young humans are enormously adaptable, and older humans are exceptionally faithful to the ways of their forebears. A baby can learn to sleep upright and tightly swaddled, or prone and without a cover. If his mother elects not to carry him in a sling on her back during the day and keep him in her bed at night, he adjusts very well to spending long solitary periods in his crib or playpen. As a newborn, he feeds whenever he is hungry or according to some externally imposed schedule, and grows into a pattern of eating once a day or five times a day — not because such behavior is best in any absolute sense but because it is customary in his culture.

Notice how stilted the paragraph becomes when the concepts are stated in general abstract terms:

People perpetuate the patterns their forebears have passed onto them. Sleeping patterns in babies persist through generations and are culturally determined. Feeding patterns of the young tend to be uniform throughout a society because of the power of cultural patterns which are not absolute values in themselves.

The specific language of the original paragraph is more convincing and interesting than the generalizations of the second paragraph, which resembles more an outline than a fully developed idea.

Nouns which refer directly to concrete objects and active verbs can have emotional power as well as convincing specificity. Thus, when Lear, who has been beggared by the daughters he made queens, meets the ragged Edgar, his compassionate response is:

"Didst thou give all to thy daughters, and art thou come to this?"

Not:

Is your pitiable state the result of filial ingratitude?

The same principle can be found in *The Letters of Ezra Pound 1907-1941*, edited by D.D. Paige (New York: Harcourt Brace and Company, 1950). Affirming that the virtues of good poetry are those of good prose, Pound wrote Harriet Monroe: "Language is made out of concrete things. General expressions in non-concrete terms are a laziness; . . . ." (p. 49)

Earlier in the same letter Pound says that the precision characteristic of good writing is the ". . . result of concentrated attention to what is writing. The test of the writer is his ability for such concentration AND for his power to stay concentrated till he gets to the end . . . ." Unfortunately, the writer of a term paper or thesis is not to the end when he has seen his internal dialogue, Pound's "what is writing," complete and refined, for the writer must still prepare the manuscript in an accepted conventional form. To that form we turn now.

The Final Draft

Once you have finished all of your revising and editing, you are ready to prepare a final copy of the paper or to submit a legible draft of the thesis or dissertation to your advisor. Many students turn in portions of the thesis as they are completed for their advisors to read and comment on. If you have not done this, you will have to prepare a legible draft for approval, because it is foolhardy to prepare the final copy before you and your advisor have agreed on the revisions to be made.

The draft from which you or someone else prepares the final typescript should be as legible as possible, for the more difficult the text is to read and the more often you or your typist must go to a separate page for an insertion, the more mistakes are likely to appear in the final copy. Also, if you are typing the final copy yourself, and if it is psychologically possible, you should refrain from revising or tinkering as you type. Perhaps the greatest advantage to having someone else type the final copy is that he cannot tinker and can, therefore, devote full attention to the typing itself.

The forms prescribed for term papers, theses, and dissertations are designed to make them easy to read. In general, the forms for academic papers follow the form desired by book publishers and editors of scholarly journals, particularly in such things as style, spacing, margins, and paper. The most significant conflict between academic and professional models is the rule for single spacing footnotes and long quotations — publishers want everything double spaced. As for the minutiae of notes and bibliography, there are many forms for different publishers, for different disciplines, and for different schools. For economic reasons, however, many publishers are discouraging the use of notes and bibliography altogether. Just as the notes and bibliography are the most difficult part of the manuscript to type, so they are the most expensive for the publisher to produce.

Although there is disparity on the minutiae of form, particularly in the case of documentation, many of the rules for form are universal, and once you have mastered the basic form for footnote and bibliography, it is easy enough to make small adjustments for one or another style. Here we will try to provide the standards of form usually set for academic papers and a single consistent pattern for footnotes and bibliography. For the notes and bibliography we will provide the fullest form in general use and then indicate ways in which that form is sometimes abbreviated as well as a means for keeping the number of notes to a minimum without compromising the integrity of the scholarship.

All of the rules here assume that the final copy is typewritten. Of course, there is no question of this in the case of theses and dissertations. There should be no question of it for the extended term paper or seminar report for which this manual is also designed. It is an imposition to ask someone to read a long handwritten manuscript, and if a student has decided that he does not need to know how to type, college is as good a place as any for him to accept the financial responsibility and inconvenience of having someone else do his typing for him.

Academic papers are typed on 8½x11 inch paper with margins of at least 1½ inches at the left and 1 inch at the top, bottom, and right. The extra space at the left allows for binding in the cases of theses and dissertations and for comments by the instructor in the case of less august documents. Completing the manuscript can be done in four stages: (1) the text; (2) the notes; (3) the bibliography; (4) the preliminary matter. In practice the notes should be prepared before the final text is typed, for if the notes are typed at the bottom of the page, they will be typed at the same time the text is typed, and if they are typed at the end of the paper or of individual chapters, preparing them in advance will show which can be eliminated by including bibliographical information in the text. Each stage is discussed in the order in which it appears in the final manuscript, even though the preliminary material is usually prepared last.

THE PRELIMINARY MATTER

The preliminary material includes in this order: the title page; the preface; the table of contents; any list of tables, charts, illustrations, or maps that may be necessary.

The title page should be appropriate to the scope of the paper and the institution. It seems pedantic and stuffy to garnish the title page of a ten-page term paper with the words, "A term paper submitted in partial fulfillment of the course requirements of Phenomenology, Philosophy 351." A similar statement is, however, regularly included in the title page of theses and dissertations, and might be appropriate for an honors project or a report on independent study. Many universities have very specific requirements for the format and spacing of the title page of theses and dissertations. Examples of accepted theses and dissertations can be examined in the library of the institution for which a student desires a model. An example of one form is in the appendix. For a term paper, the title of the paper typed in capitals and centered near the top of the page, the author's name in suitably humble capitals and lower case letters centered in the middle of the page, plus the course title, the instructor's name, and the date, all centered at the bottom, should suffice. An example of such a title page is also included in the appendix.

The preface, if there is one, includes whatever the author wants to say about the work which is not included in the text itself, along with any expressions of gratitude he wants to make. Ordinarily, a preface would not be necessary in the case of a term paper, and, if a student had nothing to say about the background and preparation of either the research or the report that was not included in the text, and if he had received no special or extraordinary help from instructors, librarians, or institutions, a preface might be unnecessary in a dissertation. When there is a preface it follows the title page, and its first page has the capitalized, centered heading "PREFACE." Since the preliminary material is numbered in small roman numerals, with the title page unnumbered but taking the place of i, the preface begins on page ii and is so numbered at the bottom center of the page.

The table of contents is also titled at the center top of the page in capitals. It cannot, of course, be prepared until the final manuscript is typed with all the pages numbered. A student usually has considerable leeway in how extensive he makes the table of contents. He may choose simply to give the chapter titles and their beginning page numbers, plus the page numbers of any appendixes and the bibliography. Many people, however, choose to indicate more extensively what is included in the chapters, either through a summary of the contents, indented below the chapter title, or through the use of subtopics, with pages indicated if the subtopics are clearly marked in the text. Examples of each of these are found in the appendix. Some instructors desire an outline. If you are substituting an outline for a table of contents, remember:

1.   The whole outline should be consistently either a topic outline or a sentence outline.

2. Headings are subdivided and enumerated first with large roman numerals, then with capital letters, then with arabic numbers, then with lower case letters, and last with small roman numerals.

3. One heading at any level is bad form. This rule is based on the argument that on each level the headings represent subdivisions of the larger topic under which they are listed, and anything that is divided must be divided into at least two parts.

If you have numerous tables, charts, illustrations, or maps, you may want to number them and include a list of their locations after the table of contents. Each such list should be separately typed, separately numbered, and appropriately headed — again in the center of the top of the page in capital letters.

THE TEXT

After the preliminaries, the pages are numbered continuously with arabic numbers. Pages that have a major heading at the top of the page, such as the beginning of chapters and the titled appendixes, are numbered at the center of the bottom page, two spaces below the bottom margin. Other pages in the text are numbered in the upper right hand corner, two spaces above the top line, with the number within the right hand margin. The heading for the chapter number is centered in the first line below the margin and typed in capitals. Double space is left between it and the heading giving the chapter title, and double or triple space is left between the title and the first line of text:

CHAPTER II

THE NEW DEAL

Here would begin the first line of the chapter.
The text is double spaced except for footnotes, long quotations, and tables.

In the text, footnotes are indicated by arabic numerals raised one half space above the line, immediately following the last word to be noted. The number comes at the end of a summary or paraphrase and directly follows the closing quotation mark in the case of a direct quotation. Thus, it may well come in the middle of a sentence rather than at the end, but if the last word is followed by a punctuation mark, the footnote numeral follows all punctuation marks except dashes. Here are some examples of the placement of footnote numerals with a description of what the reader would expect to find in the note:

> The League of Women Voters of Illinois affirm the need for positive action on the state level to encourage every community to provide its share of low and moderate income housing.[1]
>
> [1] The note should indicate where the reader can find an official League statement of its position on low and moderate income housing.

> The League of Women Voters of Illinois believe that "carefully screened volunteers could be used for probation and parole."[2]
>
> [2] The note should provide the exact source of the quoted words in an official League statement.

> "The ability of the Viet Cong continuously to rebuild their units and to make good their losses . . ."[3] was a mystery to U.S. military officials.
>
> [3] The note should identify the exact source of the words of the military official who is being used as an example of U.S. military attitudes. The context should be consistent with the author's use of the quotation — the official should be baffled by the Viet Cong capabilities.

In term papers footnotes are numbered consecutively from beginning to end. In works with chapters, footnotes are numbered consecutively for each chapter, each chapter beginning with footnote one.

If footnotes are typed at the bottom of the page, the notes should be typed above the bottom margin, so space must be left for them. Usually, two spaces (triple space) are left between the last line of text and the first note, with the break emphasized by a typed line twenty spaces long:

> Here would be the last line of text.
>
> [4] John Doe, The Development of American Trade (New York: Finley Press, 1957), p. 87.
>
> [5] Brown, Trade Barriers, p. 73.

As you can see from the example, a space is left between footnotes.

Special rules of typographical form apply to quotations as well as to footnote numerals and placement. Any quotation three typed lines or shorter can be typed run-on in the text. Then the quotation is set off by quotation marks:

Shakespeare's Brutus said, "The good is oft interred with their bones,"

but in the case of this statesman . . . .

(Notice that a reference note is unnecessary for a famous quotation when its use is incidental to the purpose of the paper. The exact location of the quotation would be necessary, however, in a discussion of the play.) In the case of poetry, line breaks are indicated by a virgule.(/):

The depth of Frost's pessimism is revealed in the final couplet of his

sonnet "Design," "What but design of darkness to appall? —   / If

design govern in a thing so small."[6]

If more than three lines of poetry are quotes, however, even if they could be compacted into fewer than three lines of text by use of virgules, the quotation will look neater if single spaced and indented. Any quotation longer than three types lines should be introduced by a colon, indented to paragraph indention, and single spaced beginning two lines below the last line of text. Since the indented block of single spaced typing sets off the quotation, quotation marks are not used.

If you want to quote less than a complete sentence or paragraph in your paper, you may do so, but since all quotations must be accurate, omissions, should be indicated clearly in the text. At the beginning of a sentence or within a sentence an omission is indicated by an ellipsis mark, that is three spaced periods (. . .). If the omission is at the end of a sentence ending with a period, four spaced periods (. . . .) indicate the ellipsis mark plus the final period. Therefore, if the sentence ends with a question mark or exclamation point, that punctuation follows the ellipsis, which is still marked by three spaced periods (. . . ?) . If a paragraph is omitted in a long quotation which is single spaced and indented, the omission is indicated by a line of spaced dots-

Those religious poems which are structured either as statements or as

arguments I call discursive, those which recreate a specific religious

experience I call representational.

. . . .

The discursive poems in the Harley manuscript include five poems about

repentence and death, two poems which endeavor to persuade the

audience to love Christ, and four vernacular verse prayers.

The same line of spaced periods is used to indicate the omission of a line or more of verse. In short quotations included in the text, such long omissions are indicated by separate sets of quotation marks:

> The critic classifies religious poems as discursive and representational.
> The former ". . . are structured either as statements or arguments." "The
> discursive poems in the Harley manuscript include five poems about
> repentance and death . . . ."[8]

Insertions or corrections are indicated by square brackets, and since few
typewriters have keys for these, they must be added by hand in black ink. For
example:

> "He [John Doe] argues for a stimulus-response pattern for language
> learning."

> "Scientists' and philosophers' descriptions of the scientific method
> differ astonishingly. The scientist is usually arguing from *experience*,
> the philosopher from *logic*." [emphasis mine]

Also, should you want to disclaim a minor error in the quotation, the
disclaimer or correct information is indicated in square brackets:

> "Ben Johnson's [sic] plays remain a staple of repertory groups," or
> "Ben Johnson's plays remain a staple of repertory groups." [the original
> mispells Jonson] or
> "Ben Johnson's [thus in the original] plays remain a staple of reportory
> groups.

If you are quoting material printed before English spelling was standardized, you will want to decide if you are going to represent the original exactly
and follow the old spelling, or if you are going to standardize according to
modern principles. Should you choose to do the latter, you should indicate so
in the text, in an explanatory note, or in the preface.

Accuracy demands that the punctuation of a quotation be reproduced
exactly. However, punctuation marks within ellipses are omitted, and modern
American practice is to include all commas and periods within the quotation
marks, whether in the quotation or simply required by the context. Indeed,
some scholars omit ellipses at the beginning and ends of quotations that make
grammatical sentences without the quoted parts when such omissions do not
significantly change the sense of the passage.

While this manual does not attempt to include a complete description of
the appropriate style of punctuation for academic papers, we can review a few
more problems which are common to, but not confined to, research reports

and which even advanced students may find useful.

The first such problem is a rule with many exceptions. In the text, single numbers of less than three digits are spelled out (sixty) and numbers of three or more digits are typed with numerals or figures (1,250). Now for the exceptions: dates, addresses, and time of day followed by a.m. or p.m. are not spelled out. Nor are numbers used for decimals, measurements (4 by 6 inch cards), dollars and cents ($4.25), and percentages (7% or seven per cent). In addition, in paragraphs where many numbers appear, especially for statistical purposes, all the numbers are typed as numerals:

> As of June 1, 1976, 325 families in Blooming Grove were on welfare. Of these families, only 33 had been on welfare for more than 2 years, and permanent physical disability of a family member was a factor in 30 of those families. A survey of the families which had received welfare for less than 2 years indicated that 75 of them could provide for themselves if adequate, economical daycare were available to them.

But in less statistical writing, numbers are spelled out according to the rules:

> In two years the three brothers accumulated seventy-five impressionist paintings. Thirty of these were stored in a rural summer home which was destroyed by fire at 7:00 a.m. on January 5, 1976.

A second stylistic problem arises with the use of foreign words. The rule says that foreign words are underlined. However, many words have been assimilated into the English language. Some, like "fabliau" and "minutia," have been assimilated recently enough to maintain the plurals of the original language ("fabliaux" and "minutiae"), but they are included in *Webster's Seventh Collegiate Dictionary* and may, therefore, be used without underlining. Any good English dictionary can provide a standard for usage, but since not all such dictionaries agree, to be fully consistent, you should use only one.

For ease of reading as much as for stylistic purposes, abbreviations should be avoided. If, however, you are going to refer to something that is often abbreviated and has a long title, then spell out the title the first time it appears and give the abbreviation you will use: ". . . the United Nations Children's Fund (hereafter UNICEF)."

Underlining is used to indicate the title of anything that is ordinarily published separately, including books, pamphlets, periodicals, newspapers, plays, motion pictures, anthologies, and any poetic work long enough to be published separately, such as <u>Paradise Lost.</u> Quotation marks are used around titles of works that are usually published in something else, such as magazine or journal articles, short poems, short lectures, newspaper articles, short stories, chapter titles, and the titles of radio or television programs. The titles of unpublished works such as dissertations, theses, minutes, or multilithed or dittoes reports are also marked by quotation marks. The names of the books of the Bible are not marked with either quotation marks or underlining. A normally underlined title within an underlined title is marked by quotation marks, as in <u>Interpretations of "Piers Plowman."</u>

Finally, a note on breakover words at the ends of lines. Words of more than one syllable may be divided between syllables at the end of a line if all three conditions apply:

1.   at least three letters carry over to the next line
2.   more than one letter is left on the first line
3.   a hyphenated word is not divided at a point other than the hyphen.

Since the word must be divided between syllables, you may find you have to check a dictionary for the appropriate point to breakover. However, the time taken to look up the word is seldom worth the space saved or the improved appearance of a more perfectly aligned margin at the right, and two or three empty spaces at the end of a line are far less distracting than an awkwardly divided word. So, when in doubt, don't divide the word.

REFERENCE NOTES

In preparation of the final typescript, the reference material, that is the footnotes and bibliography, presents the most problems. A concern for the form of notes and bibliography can become a time-consuming preoccupation. Suppress pedantry by remembering that the purpose of the reference notes and bibliography is to give the reader all the information he needs to check the facts and sources used in the preparation of the paper. Completeness and consistency are essential, and making the information as accessible and undistracting as possible is a courtesy to the reader.

Reference notes are placed at the bottom of the page, at the ends of chapters, or, in the case of short papers, at the end of the paper. Most instructors will accept endnotes in place of footnotes, and it is certainly easier for the student to type the notes at the end of the chapter or paper than at the foot of the page. When the student takes this convenient road, however, he should remember that every footnote numeral on the page may mean an interruption in the reading of the text while the reader goes back to the end to check the note. Except for theses and dissertations, which are ultimately bound, the student can make up for the inconvenience of endnotes by turning the paper in held together by a paperclip. If he does this the instructor can place the notes next to the text while reading the paper. Endnotes are particularly inconvenient for theses and dissertations, which are bound and reproduced on microfilm. Indeed, some universities insist on notes at the bottom of the page. The student whose university does permit endnotes, and who chooses to use them, should at least make every effort to minimize the number of notes and to incorporate reference information in the text.

Endnotes and footnotes have the same typographical form. The first line of the note begins at paragraph indentation with the number of the note raised one half space above the line. Each individual note is single spaced, but double space is left between the last line of one note and the first line of the next.

Any discussion of the form of footnotes and bibliography is detailed and technical. Here we will begin with the form for the simplest sort of book — a first edition, unedited, in the original language, published commercially in a single volume without being part of a series. We will then show how any or all of these complications are added to the basic form. After the discussion of books, we will describe the form used for citing articles in journals, magazines, and newspapers, the form used for public documents; and, finally, the form used for unpublished works. Having shown the complete form for footnotes, we will then comment on how that form is routinely abbreviated in some fields, and how the number and length of footnotes can be reduced in any paper by including bibliographical information in the text. The discussion of notes will end with the standard methods of citing sources after the first full reference note. Our discussion of the form for entries in bibliographies will simply describe the differences between bibliography entries and reference notes. The sample bibliography in the appendix will be a bibliography of all the examples used in the discussion of footnotes.

Although this guide attempts to be comprehensive enough to provide the information needed for a large number of students using a wide range of resources, there will be many examples of bibliographic problems which are not explicitly covered, and there will be cases where individual judgments must be made. Then common sense must dictate the accommodation of form to be made or the emphasis chosen. For example, books sometimes list on their title page both corporate sponsors and individual authors, as in the case of *The Limits of Growth,* subtitled *A Report for the Club of Rome's*

Project on the Predicament of Mankind (New York: Universe Books, 1972), which lists a group of authors beginning with Donella H. Meadows. The Library of Congress provides two author cards for this book — "Club of Rome," and "Donella H. Meadows [and others]." For a reference note, however, you must select only one for the first position, which will get the primary emphasis, and which will serve as the identifying phrase for all subsequent notes. Since publicity and reviews have given more prominence to the Club of Rome than to the actual authors, it is likely that your reader will more easily recognize the "Club of Rome" designation, and it should probably be selected for the author spot.

This is only one example of the choices the research writer must make in preparing the documentation for his report. The most complete guide cannot make these choices for you, and one that is too complete and too rigid may dictate a form that is ludicrously inappropriate in your particular situation. The forms here are offered as a guide, but you must be prepared to accommodate the forms to the idiosyncrasies of your sources and research and to the needs of your audience.

FIRST REFERENCE TO A BOOK

The basic form for the footnote for a book with an uncomplicated origin or publication history is:

footnote number
The author's complete name. <u>Title of the Book or Pamphlet</u> (Publication Information), exact location of the citation.

An example is:

[9]Margaret Mead, <u>Blackberry Winter: My Earlier Years</u> (New York: William Morrow & Company, Inc., 1972), p. 142.

The author's name should be as complete as possible. If the title page does not give the full name of the author, then the catalog card in the library often does. Information which is added to that found on the title page is enclosed in square brackets. Thus, if you discover that J.T. Jones on the title page was Jeremiah Thaddeus Jones, the author entry in the note would be J[eremiah] T[haddeus] Jones. The full name makes a book easier to find for the reader who wants to check a reference or to learn more from a source you have cited. Trying to find "J. R. R. Smith" in a large card catalog can be frustrating and time consuming. But, since the full name of the author is primarily for identification, the initialed form on the title page can be retained for prominent individuals about whom there would be no question, such as T.S. Eliot, J.R.R. Tolkien, and B.F. Skinner. Thus, too, it is ordinarily unnecessary to search for the full names when the name would not be the first choice for tracing the material, as in the case of journal articles.

If a book has two authors, both authors are listed as they appear on the title page:

[10]Albert H. Marckwardt and James L. Rosier, Old English Literature (New York: W.W. Norton & Company, 1972), p. 75.

If more than three authors are listed on the title page, then only the first is given in the note, plus an indication that there are others — either "et al.," an abbreviation for *et alii* meaning " and others," or the English "and others":

[11]Charles R. Frank, Jr., and others, Assisting Developing Countries: Problem of Debts, Burden-sharing, Jobs and Trade, Overseas Development Council Studies 1 (New York: Praeger Publishers, 1972), p. 179.

A committee, corporation, or government office may be responsible for a book for which no author is given on the title page. Since the corporate entity is responsible for the book, the name of the entity is used for the author:

[12]Drug Abuse Survey Project, Dealing with Drug Abuse: A Report to the Ford Foundation (New York: Praeger, 1972), p. 302.

As described earlier, a book may have both a corporate author and an individually named author, in which case you must decide which is more important and list accordingly:

[13]Club of Rome, The Limits of Growth: A Report for the Club of Rome's Project on the Predicament of Mankind, by Donella H. Meadows and others (New York: Universe Books, 1972), p. 35.

Or

[14]Donella H. Meadows and others, The Limits of Growth: A Report for the Club of Rome's Project on the Predicament of Mankind (New York: Universe Books, 1972), p. 35.

If the author of the work you are citing is unknown, then there is no author entry and the note begins with the title:

[15]Sir Gawain and the Green Knight, trans. Theodore Howard Banks, Jr. (New York: Appleton-Century-Crofts, Inc., 1929), 11. 2052-59.

If the name listed on the title page is a pseudonym and you wish to identify the author, the real name can be supplied in square brackets:

[16]Michael Innes [J.I.M. Stewart], <u>One-Man Show</u> (New York: Dodd, Mead & Company, 1952), p. 51.

The second major element of the note is the title of the book or pamphlet. Usually all of the title and subtitle is given, but when the title is exceptionally long, perhaps longer than two typed lines, an innocuous segment can be omitted as long as the omission is marked by ellipsis points. Within certain limits, the note reproduces the punctuation of the title on the title page. One such limit concerns capitalization. In some books the title is printed entirely in capital letters, but the title in the notes is typed in a combination of capitals and lower case letters. The most common pattern is that used in the examples in this manual, that is, the first and last words and all words except conjunctions, prepositions, and articles are capitalized. It is also acceptable to follow the pattern used on library catalog cards. In that pattern the first word is capitalized, and beyond the first word, only those words which would be capitalized in the text, such as proper names, are capitalized. Another modification of the punctuation of the title occurs when there is no punctuation between the main title and the subtitle. Fill such a hiatus with a colon unless some other mark is clearly more appropriate. Titles in foreign languages are capitalized and punctuated according to the conventions of the language.

The basic publication information, the third major element of the note, is given in parentheses in the note and includes the place of publication, the publisher, and the date of the work. In some fields the publisher is not included, and the place of publication and the date are separated by a comma, instead of a colon, in the parentheses. Like the author and title, the publication data is taken from the title page. If the information is missing and you can supply it, it is enclosed in square brackets. If the information is unavailable, this is indicated by abbreviations — "n.p." for "no place" and "n.d." for "no date." When several cities are listed on the title page, only the first is given in the note. Unless you are willing to check in *Books in Print* or the *Reference Catalogue of Current Literature* for the correct abbreviations for all the publishers you cite, give the full name of the publisher as it appears on the title page. Sometimes professional associations, institutions, and businesses publish books, and their names then appear as the publisher.

The date of the work is ordinarily the last date of copyright, which is usually given on the overleaf of the title page. If the date on the title page itself is different from the date of copyright, then either the book was copyrighted the year before it was actually issued (and the date on the title page is the date for the notes and bibliography), or, more commonly, the book is a reprint. A reprint may or may not use the same plates as the original edition, which means that page references to a reprint may or may not correspond with the original edition. If the reprint is by the original publisher, the last copyright date is given. But if a different publisher is responsible for the reprint, then the copyright date is indicated in the parentheses before the place of publication: (1955; rpt. New York: Many Books Inc., 1966). Some reprint publishers do not give the original date of publication for books which are out of copyright, and in such cases it is a good idea to check the Library of Congress *National Union Catalog* or similar source to determine the original publication date, because information in a book published fifty years ago needs to be evaluated differently from information in a book published only a year or two ago; the older book may have been superseded. Also, giving the first date of publication plus the date for the edition you are using tells the reader that the same quotation or information can be found in either 1955 edition or the 1966 reprint.

In a single volume work, the location of the citation is simply the page or pages where the information or quotation can be found. If all the information is on one page, then the abbreviation "p." precedes the appropriate number. If two or more consecutive pages are given, the abbreviation "pp." for "pages" is used. A list of the exact pertinent pages is far more useful to the reader than these abbreviations, which are sometimes used:

"pp. 65 et seq." for "page 65 and following."
"pp. 65 f." for "page 65 and the following page."
"pp. 65 ff." for "page 65 and the following pages."
"pp. 65 et passim for page 65 and here and there throughout the work."

Note that the second form is no improvement over "pp. 65-66," and the other three examples are less informative than an exact reference such as "pp. 65-69" or "pp. 65-67, 69, 73-75, and 80."

In poetry the line numbers are given when the lines are numbered in the text cited. The abbreviations "1." for "line" and "11." for "lines" precede the number(s). When a long poem has been subdivided into books or cantos, the book or canto number, in large roman numerals, precedes the line number. Only the numbers, separated by a period, are used — III. 25-26. If the larger units are subdivided into smaller units within which the lines are numbered, the pattern is to use large roman numerals for the largest unit, small roman numerals for the next largest, and arabic numerals for the line numbers — "IV. ii. 25-30." Quotations to plays follow the same format to indicate the act. scene, and lines — "III. iv. 25" for "Act III, scene iv, line 25."

Multivolume works, works with editors and translators, works which have been revised or have appeared in more than one edition, and works published in series all require citations which include this information, all of which helps a curious reader readily identify the work and find the passage to which you are referring.

Leaving aside for a moment the question of the multivolume work, the other three situations can be handled in this pattern:

footnote number
        Author's name, *Title*, editor or translator, edition number, series title and number (Publication data), exact location of citation.

Consider the following examples:

[17]Ernst Robert Curtius, European Literature and the Latin Middle Ages, trans. Willard R. Trask, The Bollingen Library (1953; rpt. New York: Harper & Row, Publishers, 1963), pp. 39-42.

Note that 1953 is the date that Pantheon Books published the first edition of the translation for the Bollingen Foundation. If the writer citing the book believed the date of publication of the German edition would be of interest to his readers, he could add to the note, "Originally published as *Europaische Literatur und lateinisches Mittelalter* (Bern, 1948)."

[18]"Beowulf"; Reproduced in Facsimile from the Unique Manuscript, British Museum MS. Cotton Vitellius A.xv, transliteration and notes by Julius Zupitza, 2nd ed., Early English Text Society No. 245 (London: Oxford University Press, 1959), p. 21.

The abbreviations "ed." and "trans." mean "edited by" and "translated by," and since, in this example, Zupitza transliterated rather than translated, his special function is spelled out unambiguously. Also note that the number of a volume in a series is given when the series is numbered.

If you are citing the work of the editor or translator rather than the author, then the editor's name appears in the author's place in the note, and, if the author's name does not appear in the title, it is given in the place of the editor with "by" indicating the author's role.

[19]Peter Allt and Russell K. Alspach, eds., The Variorum Edition of the Poems of W.B. Yeats (New York: The Macmillan Company, 1957) p. 354.

The edition number is usually indicated clearly on the title page. If not, the information is given in the copyright statement on the reverse side.

Normally you are expected to use the last revised edition of a work for your research, unless special reasons of scholarship dictate using an earlier edition. Such reasons should be clear from the text or made clear in the note. Classic works of literature, philosophy, and history are exceptions to this rule. If such a work is out of copyright any publisher can produce an edition. Often there are many cheap editions of such works, editions designed to be sold at newsstands. Rarely are these editions satisfactory for academic work, and the researcher is expected to use a standard scholarly edition. Not only are the texts of such editions likely to be more accurate, but libraries which will not attempt to acquire every popular edition of a book such as Huckleberry Finn will be certain to have the standard scholarly edition of the work. Thus, your reader will be able to check you more readily in the library if you have used the standard edition.

Naturally, if the book is the text for a seminar or advanced course for which the paper is being prepared, you will cite the edition assigned for the course, unless your point involves a difference among editions. Finally, in the case of books produced before the introduction of stereotype in the early nineteenth century, if no modern standard edition exists, you may need to learn about early book making practices and technical bibliography.

How you handle a multivolume work of prose in a note depends upon your emphasis. You may omit indicating the number of volumes, and merely indicate the inclusive dates of publication, and then indicate the number of the volume which you are citing:

[20] John Smith, The History and Tradition of Centralia County (Springfield, Illinois: Marigold Press, 1857 − 1865), III, 35-37.

This is the least precise way to cite the sources, for it does not tell the reader how many volumes are in the work or when, exactly, volume three was published.

A second method for the same reference, places the number of volumes before the publication information:

[21] John Smith, The History and Tradition of Centralia County, 4 vols. (Springfield, Illinois: Marigold Press, 1857-1865), III, 35-37

Should you think that your reader would find the exact date of the volume more useful than the total number of volumes, you can put the volume number before the publication information, and then give only the date of publication for that particular volume:

[22] John Smith, The History and Tradition of Centralia County, vol. III (Springfield, Illinois: Marigold Press, 1862), pp. 35-37.

Notice that when the volume number and page number are together, no abbreviations of "volume" or "page" are necessary. Which of the three forms you choose should depend on the needs of your audience.

If the volume is separately titled, or if a multivolume work contains volumes by different authors, the title of the collection is given:

[23]W[illiam] L[indsay] Renwick. English Literature 1789-1815 in The Oxford History of English Literature, ed. F[rank] P[ercy] Wilson and Bonamy Dobree, vol. IX (Oxford: The Clarendon Press, 1963), pp. 78-79.

Similarly, if you are citing an article, poem, or story in a collection of some sort, the author and title of the separate part are given first in the note:

[24]N.K. Coghill, "Love and 'Foul Delight': Some Contrasted Attitudes," in Patterns of Love and Courtesy: Essays in Memory of C.S. Lewis, ed. John Lawlor (London: Edward Arnold (Publishers) Ltd., 1966), p. 151.

If the collection you are using is an anthology of previously published journal articles, citing the bibliographical data for the original publication gives the reader the date of the article as well as a second source for it:

[25]J.R.R. Tolkien, "The Monsters and The Critics," Proceedings of the British Academy, 22 (2936), 245-295; rpt. in An Anthology of Beowulf Criticism, ed. Lewis E. Nicholson (Notre Dame, Indiana: University of Notre Dame Press, 1963), p. 91.

Standard reference books arranged alphabetically are handled somewhat differently. In the case of a signed article in an encyclopedia, the author's name, usually discovered by tracing the initials at the end of the article to the list of contributors, is given first, followed by the title of the article, the name of the reference work, and the year of publication. Since the same article may appear in an edition published in a different year, and since volume numbering and pagination may not be consistent in printings or editions containing the same article or item, the title or topic is the most convenient reference for the reader:

[26]M.M. Hueller et al, "Hymns and Hymnals," The New Catholic Encyclopedia, 1967.

[27]Oxford English Dictionary, 1933, s.v. scatterbrain.

[28]Lionel Cust, "Gentileschi, Orazio," Dictionary of National Biography, 1908.

If you are doing a close analysis of an ancient or modern classic, then your first reference note for the work will give the complete bibliographical information of the edition you are using. For the location of passages you may have to cite page numbers, but you should prefer a method which would allow your reader to locate the passage in another edition. Thus, when citing a Shakespeare play, cite the act, scene, and line, rather than the page of a particular edition. Similarly, when citing the long eighteenth-century novel *Tom Jones*, you could cite book and chapter as well as the page in the standard edition. If, however, you are citing a classic work for a purpose such that your reader need not know the exact edition, then you may simply cite the work and the place, not the page, in the work, without giving a specific edition:

[29]Shakespeare, Hamlet, II.iii.35-37.

[30]Virgil, Aeneid. VI.417-421.

[31]Aristotle, Metaphysics, XIII.4.

Similarly, one need not encumber the reader with page numbers or editions for the Bible. Indeed, all that is needed is the title of the book, not underlined, the chapter and verse. In some cases you might want to indicate the version.

[32]Psalms 22:1 or [32]Ps 22:1

[33]I Timothy 6:2 or [33]I Tim 6:2

[34]Isaiah   12:5 or [34]Is 12:5 (Revised Standard Version

It is better to place short citations like these parenthetically in the text than to interrupt the reader's attention with a note, but the form for the parenthetical citation is the same as for the note.

FIRST REFERENCE TO A PERIODICAL

Fortunately, citations to periodicals have fewer variations and complications than those for books. The basic pattern is:

footnote number
Author's name, "Full title of the article,"
Name of the periodical, Volume number, issue number (Date), Page number (s) of the citation.

Good sense determines how much to include for volume number, issue number, and date. You should include the information necessary to locate the passage easily. For the many journals that page the issues of a volume continuously, the issue number is unnecessary. Indeed, for journals which page the volume continuously and whose volume year coincides with the calendar year, it would be logical to give only the volume number, but it is customary to give the year and the volume as a precaution against error. On the other hand, popular magazines and newspapers begin each issue with page one, so for them the exact date is crucial. Consider the following examples:

[35]Matthew W. Finkin, "Collective Bargaining and University Government," AAUP Bulletin, 57 (1971), 151.

[36]Roger Sale, "England's Parnassus: C.S. Lewis, Charles Williams, and J.R.R. Tolkien," The Hudson Review (Summer, 1964), 204.

The Hudson Review's volume year does not coincide with the calendar year, hence the year alone is not sufficient.

[37]Annie Dillard, "The Force that Drives the Flower," The Atlantic, 232 (November, 1973), 74.

[38]Horace Freeland Judson, "A Reporter at Large (Heroin in Great Britain — 1), *The New Yorker,* September 24, 1973, p. 78.

One could give the volume number in this reference, but that is not usually done when an exact date is given. Note that when there is no volume number given, the abbreviations "p." or "pp." precede the page number.

[39]Marilyn Bender, "The Very Private Pritzkers: Chicago Deal Makers in Publishing Spotlight," The New York Times, Oct. 14, 1973, sec. 3, p. 1.

Since the sections of this newspaper are paged separately the section number must be given. When the place of publication of a newspaper is not included in the title, it is given in parenthesis after the title. In some cases, the town named in the title may not be sufficient identification (almost every state in the union has a town named Springfield, for example), so the name of the state is added parenthetically.

When the author's name is not given, begin with the title of the article. In some cases, such as reviews, it is usual to include an explanatory statement:

[40]"Global Annual," anonymous review of The Statesman's Year Book 1973-74: Statistical and HIstorical Annual of the States of the World, ed, John Paxton, The Times Literary Supplement, Oct. 12, 1973, p. 1235.

Abbreviations are desirable in footnotes. In particular, abbreviate the titles of scholarly journals in your field with abbreviations you can expect your reader to know. For a paper on the literature in a modern language the abbreviations used in the bibliography compiled annually by the Modern Language Association would be acceptable. In medicine, the abbreviations used by *Index Medicus* could be used. By following the practice of a prestigious journal or bibliography, you ensure that the reader who does not recognize the abbreviation will know where to find what it stands for. Be more circumspect, however, where you are citing journals outside the special competence of your readers. For example, *"JAMA"* is an acceptable abbreviation for *The Journal of the American Medical Association* in a paper whose audience would be familiar with medical publications, but a student citing an article from it on Jonathan Swift's dementia for an audience of eighteenth century literay scholars would be well advised to spell out the journal title.

FIRST REFERENCE TO A GOVERNMENT DOCUMENT

The legal world has its own abbreviated form for citing government documents, statutes, and court cases. If you are writing a primarily legal paper for an audience familiar with legal citation, then you need to consult the most recent edition of *A Uniform System of Citation,* published and distributed by The Harvard Law Review Association. If, however, you are citing government documents in a less specialized context, let the following guide and common sense dictate the form of your notes:

> Footnote number
>> Place of jurisdiction, Name of the branch
> of government or department, any subdivision thereof, <u>Title of Document</u>, other information needed to locate the document, place of citation.

Here are some examples:

[42]U.S., Congress, House, Committee on Un-American Activities, <u>Investigation of Communist Activities in the State of California</u>. Hearing before the Committee, 83rd Congress, 2nd sess., 1954 pt 3, p. 54

[43]U.S. Presidential Advisory Committee on Water Resources Policy, <u>Water Resources Policy</u>; a Report (Washington: Government Printing Office, 1955), p. 27.

[44]U.S., Commission on Organization of the Executive Branch of

Government (1953-1955), Paperwork Management; A Report to the Congress (Washington: Government Printing Office, 1955), 1, 35.

[45]Illinois, General Assembly, Legislative Investigating Commission, The Drug Crisis: Report on Drug Abuse in Illinois to the Illinois General Assembly, 1971, p. 325.

[46]U.S. Commission on Population Growth and the American Future, Governance and Population: The Government Amplifications of Population Change, ed. A.E. Keir Nash, The Commission . . . Research Reports IV (Washington: Government Printing Office, 1972), p. 45.

Since libraries seldom list government documents under author or editor, it would be folly to list the name of the editor first in the note. Even official addresses of the chief executive may be catalogued under "U.S., President," rather than the individual name.

[47]U.S., Department of State, Amendment of Article of Agreement of the International Finance Corporation between the U.S. of America and other Governments, Treaties and International Acts Series 7683.

[48]Senator William Proxmire on the appointment of Dr. William John Fellner to the Council of Economic Advisors, Congressional Record, 119 (Oct. 18, 1973), p. S19424.

[49]Illinois General Assembly, House of Representatives High Density Housing Committee, Report, 1970.

[50]Illinois Revised Statutes, 1972 Supplement, ch. 24, paragraph 7-1-1.

[51]U.S., Constitution, article I, sec. 3.

[52]Illinois, Constitution, article II, sec. 10.

FIRST REFERENCE TO UNPUBLISHED MATERIAL

Although no manual can hope to exhaust the kinds of sources a researcher may find, we can conclude the description of citation form with examples of the notation used for the more commonly cited kinds of unpublished material, such as dissertations, letters, lectures, and unpublished papers. No matter how long the work, if it has not been published, the title is put in quotation marks, not underlined. Beyond that, provide whatever information will guide the reader to the source if it is in a library, or at least let him know where it is even if it is not publicly available. Here are the examples:

[53]Michael Gardner Crowell, "The Lexicography of Americanisms to 1880" (unpub. diss., Northwestern University, 1966), p. 36.

[54]From a MS "Autobiography" by John Russell Bartlett in the John Carter Brown Library, Brown University, Providence, Rhode Island, p. 15.

[55]From a MS letter in the Bartlett collection of the John Carter Brown Library, Brown University, Providence Rhode Island. The letter is dated at "Albany, 22d November, 1848" and signed "H. Bleecher."

[56]Paul C. Bucy, "Sitting on a Basketball," Paper presented at The Chicago Literary Club, April 16, 1973, p. 6.

[57]Letter from Edward Madigan, Representative in Congress of the 21st District of Illinois, dated September 25, 1973.

SHORTENING AND ELIMINATING NOTES

The style which we have spelled out here for footnotes to a first reference is a rather elaborate one, but one which has been generally accepted by university presses and, therefore, university graduate departments and instructors. It is used most often in its full form in the humanities, and even there it is acceptable to some schools to omit the name of the publisher. Students often object that the same information is repeated in the bibliography, and, therefore, to give a full footnote and add a bibliography is redundant. The students are right. The journals which use the full footnote rarely include a bibliography at the end of an article, and scholarly books are sometimes published without a bibliography too. In defense of redundancy we can only point out that a complete footnote is a convenience for the reader who wants to check the author or for the reader whose interest has been aroused by a particular point in the report. On the other hand, any researcher soon discovers how useful a complete bibliography is at the end of a book, and how much easier it is to use than the notes. Surely he can imagine that an instructor might want quickly to review his student's sources while evaluating the report, and for that purpose a bibliography at the end is convenient, even though complete information has been given in the notes.

The redundancy of using a full footnote form and providing a bibliography has been eliminated in many scientific fields. In the physical sciences and in some social sciences, a full list of works cited is given at the end of the paper with complete bibliographical information for each work.

References in the paper, either in the text or in footnotes, merely give the information needed to find the work in the list of references at the end and the exact place of the citation in the reference. Sometimes the date of the work is also given in the note. Unfortunately, there is no one pattern for this abbreviated method of citation. Should your field be one in which abbreviated form is acceptable, you will need to find a source which spells out which of the many variations applies to you.

Anyone, in any field, can shorten his footnotes and reduce the number of them by judiciously including bibliographical material in the text of the report. If, for example, you give the full name of the author in the text, you need not give his name in the note; you may begin with the title. If you give the full name and the complete title in the text, you need include only the publication information in the note, and if that information can be stated briefly, it can be included in the text).

The more information you include in the text the less often your reader will have to look at the notes and the fewer interruptions he will have in following your argument. Remember that a footnote numeral does not indicate whether or not substantive comments or explanations are included in the note. Since many typists charge extra for typing footnotes, the fewer footnotes the less expense for a professionally typed paper or thesis. If your work is to be published, and some graduate papers and dissertations are, the publisher will probably urge you to eliminate as many footnotes as possible. Finally, on a practical level, if you regularly include reference material in your text as you write you will have a far easier time preparing the final draft, because (1) no quotation or citation will have become separated from a note indicating its source and (2) you will have greatly cut down the chore of preparing footnotes, since you will have fewer, perhaps none, to prepare. No research paper, not even that onerous and endangered species found in Freshman English, is written for the sake of the footnotes. Neither the best researched nor the best documented paper is distinguished by the number of its notes.

SUBSEQUENT REFERENCES

Once you have given full information for a source, you need not repeat all that information every time you cite that particular source. It used to be customary to use the Latin abbreviations "ibid.," "op. cit.," and "loc, cit." to refer to sources for which full bibliographic information had already been supplied. "Ibid." is an abbreviation for "ibidem," which means "in the same place," and it could be used when the source cited was exactly the same as the one in the note before. When the page as well as the source were the same, "ibid." was sufficient by itself, and if the page changed, the new page number could be added, as in "ibid., p. 45." Notice that if the preceding reference was several pages back, the reader, unless he remembered the source previously cited, would have to turn back to find the reference. In many cases where "ibid." appears on the same page, a judicious restatement of the text could eliminate the need for two notes.

"Op. cit." stands for "opere citato," meaning "in the work cited." "Op. cit." was used to refer to works already cited, but cited two or more footnotes back. To identify which of the preceding references was appropriate the last name of the author was given first, as in "Smith, op. cit., III, 25." If the reader does not remember the previous reference to Smith, he will probably turn to the bibliography to identify the work; if there is more than one Smith in the bibliography, or more than one work by Smith, the reader must go back through the text to find the reference. On occasion you will find an author who uses "loc. cit." for "loco citato," meaning "in the place cited." "Loc. Cit." is used in place of "op.cit." when the citation is to the same page as the citation in the previous footnote in which the work was cited. "Loc. cit." guarantees the conscientious reader a search through the earlier notes.

It is now customary to use a short version of the title of a book or article instead of "op. cit." and "loc. cit." Very little space is saved by the Latin abbreviations, and the short title is not only unambiguous, but much more likely to obviate the need for a search for the full reference. Thus, instead of "Smith, op. cit., III, 25," give "Smith, *Centralia County*, III, 25." While "ibid." is still used by some authors who have abandoned "op. cit." and "loc. cit.," it too can be eliminated easily. If the second reference is several pages away from the first, surely the reader who looks down at the note will find the author's last name and a short title more informative than only "ibid." For a second reference close to the first, a minor rearrangement of the text may eliminate the need for two notes, and there is no excuse whatever for a long parade of one "ibid." after another. If you cite extensively from a single work, give the full biographical information in the first note along with a statement that subsequent references to that source will be included in the text. Thereafter, the text states the source, usually the author's name or the title of the work is enough for this, and the volume and page are placed in parentheses after the quotation or reference. The note might look like this:

[58]All references to the novel are to "The Red Badge of Courage" and Selected Prose and Poetry, ed. William M. Gibson,

Rinehart Editions 47 (New York: Rinehart & Co., 1956; page references will be included in the text.

In this example, the author of *The Red Badge of Courage*, Stephen Crane, had been named in the text. Though the article contains many references to and quotations from *The Red Badge of Courage*, this is the only reference note to the edition, since in every case the text makes clear that the quote or reference is to the novel.

CHECKING YOUR QUOTATIONS

When a scholar completes a report, he goes back to check each note. He ensures accuracy by proofreading every quotation against the original and by checking that every source says what he attributes to it at the place he cites. For a true scholar, accuracy is an end in itself. Moreover, for a publishing scholar, few things can be more devastating than a reviewer who can cite inaccuracies and factual errors. The writer of the thesis or dissertation is held to the same standards of accuracy, and his failures, if undetected by his adviser, are left in the library or on microfilm for generations of sleuths to uncover and describe in their own tomes. Although it is unlikely that reports for classes, seminars, or independent study will receive such close scrutiny, glaring inaccuracies will be detected by an alert instructor, and whatever reward the writer expected for the project will be adjusted accordingly.

Because, despite the greatest of care, mistakes creep into every scholarly work, and because the context of a quotation may change its applicability to your work, you should always check a quotation in the original work. But that is not always possible. You may find someone quoted in a source you are reading, want to use the source, but be unable to find the original work, either because it is rare and difficult to acquire or because the citation to it is incomplete. When that happens, you may use the quotation if you indicate the true source:

[41]H.G. Richardson and G. O. Sayles, <u>The Governance of Medieval England</u> (Edinburgh, 1963), pp. 277-78; quoted by <u>Albert C. Baugh</u>, "The Middle English Romance: Some Questions of Creation, Presentation, and Preservation," *Speculum*, 24 1967), 9.

BIBLIOGRAPHIES

The last pages of the report usually contain a bibliography of some kind. The kind used should, once again, be adapted to the needs of the paper. From the writer's perspective, the easiest kind of bibliography is a list of works cited

— easiest because it requires the least thought. To compile such a bibliography you need only provide a list of all the works cited in your reference notes, all but books of the Bible and dictionaries cited in passing. However, you may choose to use a selected bibliography, for which you would evaluate your sources, whether cited in the notes or not, and select those which were most important or which might be most useful to someone who wanted to pursue the topic of the paper. If you provide comments about some of the works you include in your bibliography, then it becomes "annotated." If you want to list many items which are not in print, or if you want to include all the works you read, some of which were not cited in the notes, you might call your bibliography "List of Sources Consulted" or "List of Works Consulted," for the title of your bibliography should tell the reader what kind it is.

Whatever kind it is, it may be arranged in many ways. The simplest and most common way is to alphabetize everything in one list. Some authors, however, subdivide the list according to the kind of source. For example, frequently one finds separate, alphabetized lists for books and for articles in periodicals. Sometimes one finds separate lists for primary and secondary sources — the subdivisions might be titled "Works by Mark Twain" and "Works about Mark Twain." Such subdivisions are unnecessary for relatively short papers, where the number of sources can be easily managed in a single list. The dissertation writer who decides on subdividing his list should consult his director before committing himself to a scheme that is not in common use. Usually lists for the bibliography are alphabetically arranged. If they are not, the arrangement should be clear to the reader, and the form of entry may need to be changed to fit the scheme.

A bibliography entry includes all the information given in a full reference note except the exact pages of citations. Inclusive page numbers are given for articles in anthologies, journals, and magazines. The form of the entry in the bibliography is somewhat different from the note. First, the author's name is given last name first, since the bibliography is alphabetized according to the last name. The last name is typed next to the margin, and subsequent lines of the entry are indented, which makes it easy to find an entry in its alphabetical place. Usually, individual entries are single spaced, and double space is left between entries. If the "author" is not a person, the entry is alphabetized according to the name of the entity responsible for the work, and if the work is anonymous, it is alphabetized by the title. When the same author or entity is responsible for more than one work in the same list, a line typed ten spaces long is used in place of his name for works by him after the first one listed. The major elements of the entry are separated by periods. Thus, the basic form for a book is:

Author's last name, his first name, *Name of Book*. Translator or editor. Edition. Series. Volume used, or if several volumes were used, the number in the set. Place of publication: publisher, date of publication.

For a journal article, the basic form is:

Author's last name, his first name. "Title of Article." *Name of Journal*, volume number (date), inclusive pages of the whole article.

The Bibliography in the appendix lists, with comments in the usual place for annotations, all of the examples used for the discussion of reference notes; these examples provide models for the material usually cited in research papers.

Appendix One

SAMPLE BIBLIOGRAPHY

Allt, Peter and Russell K. Alspach, eds. The Variorum Edition of the Poems of W.B. Yeats, New York: The Macmillan Company, 1957.

Aristotle, Metaphysics.

   This form is used when a reference to the work was made in the text but a specific edition was not cited.

Bartlett, John Russell. "Autobiography." MS in the Bartlett papers in The John Carter Brown Library, Brown University, Providence, Rhode Island.

_____ Folder marked "Dictionary" containing MS letters, notes, etc. in the Bartlett papers in The John Carter Brown Library, Brown University, Rhode Island.

   The line in place of the author's name means that the first named author in this entry is the same as the first named author in the preceding entry.

Baugh, Albert C. "The Middle English Romance: Some Questions of Creation, Presentation, and Preservation." Speculum, 42 (1967), 1-31.

Bender, Marylin. "The Very Private Pritzkers: Chicago Deal Makers in Publishing Spotlight." The New York Times, October 14, 1973, Sec. 3, pp. 1 and 4.

   For newspapers whose titles do not include the place of publication, that information should be added parenthetically after the title. When no volume number is given, the date is set off by commas instead of parenthesis marks.

"Beowulf"; Reproduced in Facsimile from the Unique Manuscript, British Museum MS. Cotton Vitellius A.xv. Transliteration and notes by Julius Zupitza. 2nd ed. Early English Text Society No. 245. London: Oxford University Press, 1959.

Bucy, Paul C. "Sitting on a Basketball." Paper presented at The Chicago Literary Club, April 16, 1973.

Club of Rome. The Limits of Growth: A Report for the Club of Rome's Project on the Predicament of Mankind. By Donella H. Meadows and others. New York: Universe Books, 1972.

    Had Donella H. Meadows been listed as the author in the notes, then the bibliography entry would appear under that name.

Coghill, N.K. "Love and 'Foul Delight': Some Contrasted Attitudes." Patterns of Love and Courtesy: Essays in Memory of C.S. Lewis. Ed. John Lawlor. London: Edward Arnold (Publishers) Ltd., 1966, pp. 141-156.

    If several of the articles in this anthology had been cited in the paper, then a single entry of the book under the editor's name would be given in the bibliography.

Crowell, Michael Gardner. "The Lexicography of Americanisms." Unpub. diss., Northwestern University, 1966.

Curtius, Ernst Robert. European Literature and the Latin Middle Ages. Trans. Willard R. Trask. The Bollingen Library. 1953; rpt. New York: Harper & Row, Publishers, 1963.

Cust, Lionel. "Gentileschi, Orazio." Dictionary of National Biography. 1908.

Dillard, Annie. "The Force that Drives the Flower." The Atlantic, 232 (November, 1973), 69-77.

Drug Abuse Survey Project. Dealing with Drug Abuse: A Report to the Ford Foundation. New York: Praeger, 1972.

Finkin, Matthew W. "Collective Bargaining and University Government." AAUP Bulletin, 57 (1971), 149-160.

Frank, Charles R., Jr., and others. Assisting Developing Countries: Problems of Debts, Burden-Sharing, Jobs and Trade. Overseas Development Council Studies 1, New York: Praeger Publishers, 1972.

"Global Annual." Anonymous rev. of The Statesman's Year-Book 1973-1974: Statistical and HIstorical Annual of the States of the World, ed. John

Paxton. The Times Literary Supplement, October 12, 1973, p. 1235

Hueller, M. M. and others. "Hymns and Hymnals." The New Catholic Encyclopedia. 1967.

Illinois. Constitution. Article II, sec. 10.

Illinois. General Assembly. House of Representatives. High-Density Housing Committee. Report. 1970.

Illinois. General Assembly. Legislative Investigating Committee. The Drug Crisis: Report on Drug Abuse in Illinois to the Illinois General Assembly. 1971.

Illinois Revised Statutes. 1972 Supplement.

Innes, Michael [J.I.M. Stewart] One-Man Show. New York: Dodd, Mead & Company, 1952.

Judson, Horace Freeland. "A Reporter at Large (Heroin in Great Britain — 1)." The New Yorker, September 24, 1973, pp. 76, 78-80, 85-86, 88, 93-113.

Madigan, Edward. Letter to author. September 25, 1973

Marcwardt, Albert H. and James L. Rosier. Old English Language and Literature. New York: W.W. Norton & Company, 1972.

Meadows, Donella H. and others. The Limits of Growth: A Report for the Club of Rome's Project on the Predicament of Mankind. New York: Universe Books. 1972.

> If the reference note had given "Club of Rome" as the author, then the bibliography entry would also.

Proxmire, Senator William. Speech on the appointment of Dr. William John Follner to the Council of Economic Advisors. Congressional Record, 119 (October 18, 1973), S19424-5.

> An alternative form is under "U.S. Congressional Record." This citation is to the record published daily.

Renwick, W[illiam] L[indsay]. English Literature 1789-1815. Vol. IX of The Oxford History of English Literature. Ed. F[rank] P[ercy] Wilson and Bonamy Dobree. Oxford: The Clarendon Press, 1963.

> If several volumes in The Oxford History were cited, a single bibliographic entry to the history would be used. See the example under "Wilson."

Richardson.
>   The book by Richardson was not actually used. Rather, a quotation from it was quoted from another source. That source is listed in the bibliography, instead of Richardson. See Entry under "Baugh."

Sale, Roger. "England's Parnassus: C.S. Lewis, Charles Williams, and J.R.R. Tolkien." The Hudson Review, 17 (Summer, 1964), 203-225.

Sir Gawain and the Green Knight.   Trans. Theodore Howard Banks, Jr. New York: Appleton-Century-Crofts, Inc., 1929
Shakespeare, William, Hamlet.
>   See comment under "Aristotle." Metaphysics
Smith, John. The History and Tradition of Centralia County. 4 vols. Springfield, Illinois: Marigold Press, 1857-65.
>   Use this form if you have used or cited more than one volume in the set.

Smith, John. The History and Tradition of Centralia County. III. Springfield, Illinois: Marigold Press, 1862. If you have used only one volume in a multi-volume work, cite only that volume.

Tolkien, J.R.R. "The Monsters and the Critics." Proceedings of the British Academy, 22 (1936), 245-295. Rpt. in An Anthology of Beowulf Criticism, Ed. Lewis E. Nicholson. Notre Dame, Indiana: University of Notre Dame Press, 1963.

U.S. Commission on Organization of the Executive Branch of Government (1953-1955). Paperwork Management: A report to the Congress. Washington, D.C.: Government Printing Office, 1955.

U.S. Commission on Population Growth and the American Future. Governance and Population: The Governmental Amplifications of Population Change. Ed. A.E. Keir Nash. The Commission . . . Reports IV. Washington, D.C.: U.S. Government Printing Office, 1972.

U.S. Congress. House. Committee on Un-American Activities. Investigation of Communist Activities in the State of California. 11 Parts. Hearing before the Committee on Un-American Activities, 83rd Congress, 2nd session, 1954.

U.S. Congressional Record, 119 (October 18, 1973).

U.S. Constitution. Article I, sec. 3.

U.S. Department of State. Amendment of Article of Agreement of the International Finance Corporation between the U.S. of America and other Governments. Treaties and International Acts Series 7683.

U.S. Presidential Advisory Committee on Water Resources Policy. <u>Water Resources Policy: A Report.</u> Washington, D.C. Government Printing Office, 1955.

Virgil, <u>Aeneid.</u>

See comment under Aristotle.

Wilson, F[rank] P[ercy] and Bonamy Dobree, eds. <u>The Oxford History of English Literature.</u> 12 vols. Oxford: The Clarendon Press, 1945.

All of the volumes in this set have not yet been published, a fact indicated by the blank space for the closing date of publication.

APPENDIX II

SAMPLE TITLE PAGE: TERM PAPER

TWO MIDDLE ENGLISH ELEGIES

Walter Austen

English 301

Joseph Mayer

December 5, 1976

SAMPLE TITLE PAGE: DISSERTATION

BARTHOLOMEW UNIVERSITY

THE GROWTH OF LOCAL HISTORY IN THE MIDWEST

A DISSERTATION

SUBMITTED TO THE GRADUATE SCHOOL

IN PARTIAL FULFILLMENT OF THE REQUIREMENTS

for the degree

DOCTOR OF PHILOSOPHY

Field of History

By

PEREGRINE CATHERINE SPENSER

BLOOMINGTON, WISCONSIN

June 1976

APPENDIX III

SAMPLE TABLE OF CONTENTS (1)

CONTENTS

SAMPLE TABLE OF CONTENTS (2)

CONTENTS

SAMPLE TABLE OF CONTENTS (3)

CONTENTS

The Writer's Manual
Book 11

How to
Write for
Academic
Publication

By
Carole Fitzgerald Hayes

ABOUT THE AUTHOR

Carole Fitzgerald Hayes

has taught creative writing, freshman composition,
nineteenth century poetry and prose,
a two year program in world literature,
and conducted a seminar in detective fiction
during her teaching career.
She has also published book reviews and written advertising copy.
In addition to serving as a consultant to the authors' agency,
Porter, Gould and Dierks.
for the past six years,
she has also worked as a publisher's proofreader of scholarly books.
Ms. Hayes is married and the mother of two young daughters
in addition to her professional life.

CONTENTS

SCHOLARLY WRITING

Shut not your doors to me proud libraries . . .

Walt Whitman

Scholarly writers need all the open doors they can find, including those which lead into the houses of publishers. Although university presses and learned journals handle works of special interest, some general rules of publishing apply. A writer is often advised to say something new — or to leave the reader with that impression. In some fields that impression is tenuous, since new thinkers may turn out to be careless researchers who have failed to discover the old thoughts of previous scholars. Where nothing new can be said, or where novelty would be a gimmick, the alternative is to say something better or more clearly than it has been said before.

Publishers and literary agents sometimes see academic manuscripts submitted in the hope that they might, with slight revision, their authors admit, become popular. So much depends on an author's concept of "slight revision." Quite often these manuscripts do contain ideas which would appeal to a general audience. The problem is that the works were written for a special audience in the first place. To change the audience without correspondingly changing a manuscript is like altering one side of an equation without touching the other.

If a scholar-author finds a double helix growing in his academic plot, he is naturally tempted to transplant it to a larger field. In such a move the whole environment is changed. The technical discourse native to the academic manuscript does not become popular or even intelligible if the author simply gives it a few common touches to make for easy reading. Style goes much deeper and is itself the way in which an idea is communicated to the intended audience.

Every audience has its limitations. The general audience is limited by the degree of knowledge an author can legitimately expect. The academic audience is less limited in knowledge but may be severely limited in number. Trying to approach both audiences simultaneously is normally a schizophrenic act, unlikely to please either group and likely to offend the sensitivities of both. Occasionally a work meant for scholars achieves popular success; yet not every writer can count on the good luck of Carlos Castaneda, who perhaps all along was sustained by visions of paperbacks.

All writers are beginners, only at different starting points. Well may the philosopher say, "Language is man laying his hand on time." But what happens if a teacher admits that awful truth to a freshman still trying to conjure up a topic for the research paper due next week? For who can forget the trauma of that first research paper? Perhaps whole class periods were spent in abstract discussions of choosing a topic, going to the *Reader's Guide* and other references, ferreting through the card catalogue, taking notes on index cards, observing the rules for documentation of sources. Less time may have been spent in dwelling on the sitting down to and actually writing the paper. To admit how much harder that was than all the preliminary steps might mean losing the whole game just at the point of success. The presence of the research paper in the curriculum (it is often taught in junior high, then again in the first year of high school, and again in the first year of college) might lead one to believe that carefully considered opinions would replace prejudice and that the standard of English would rise as the fund of information increased.

In the best research writing, an author does lay his hand on time, on the ideas and theories of other scholars, and on the flow of his own thoughts. All these things in his mind move faster than pen or typewriter. It is no cinch to get all the various elements into ordinary good prose. Because scholarship is known to be exacting and demanding, one sometimes hears complaints about writers who sacrifice purity to "mere success." Although it is true that some scholar-authors, knowing their academic promotion depends upon publication, have written potboilers with footnotes and bibliographies, some fine writing has been produced by sheer plod. The existence of rare and ideal forms of scholarship does not mean that every writer should try to create a new discipline, or even a new topic or question. Many authors begin by identifying critical problems which will sufficiently absorb them so that they will undertake and persevere in the effort of writing.

A scholar-author may wish to interpret a work or theory in a way that will clarify it and make it available to a larger, if still specialized, audience.

Or, finding a mistake in fact or interpretation by an earlier writer, the scholar may set out to correct the error, offering evidence for his own argument.The scholar may choose to arrange an existent body of work, giving it an order it previously lacked. Or, material from more than one discipline might be collected and merged, if only for the space of an article, into a new discipline. Or, aware that brevity is the soul of more than wit, the writer may produce a scholarly summary of works or facts in his field. In such a case, some analysis would be required, lest the work resemble those undistinguished outline series from which desperate undergraduates plagiarize their papers.

The critical problem for the scholar is how to make his concern real to the audience and to convince a publisher that the manuscript will contribute to the field. Since the readers of scholarly books and articles are most often other scholars, the publisher needs to determine whether the author's work is likely to reach its intended audience. Advice on whether to accept a manuscript is frequently sought from other authorities in the field; a wise writer might even suggest names of scholar-readers for his manuscript.

The author should consider the questions his colleagues might raise before he submits his article or book to a publisher. It is better to do this before completion of the actual work — and best — before embarking upon the necessary research. The questions: Does the manuscript represent a significant contribution to the field? Might general readers also be interested in the work? Is the work unified, so that a reader will receive a clear, imaginative impression of what is said? Is the style readable? Does the manuscript need revision? If so, how extensive? Is it too long or too short? If the work is publishable in its present form, is it likely to attract a busy publisher? What of competition in the field — are there recent publications of equal or superior merit? Are there peculiarities in the manuscript that would increase printing costs?

Such questions objectively answered are useful to the scholar-author with an idea, a work in progress, or perhaps a dissertation he thinks might provide material for publication. Some dissertations are of publishable quality and may need only minor changes. Any writer of a dissertation may believe his work is in this category; in fact, in order to persevere in the actual writing such an act of faith (in some cases amounting to an existential leap) may be necessary. But ordinarily, one's adviser and committee of dissertation readers can appraise the manuscript more objectively. Even if this small group of readers is so impressed as to encourage publication, the work still may not be quite ready, or the demand for it so limited as to put off the publisher. Naturally, if these initial readers like the dissertation, the author is encouraged and ought to explore the possibility of publication.

Universities may have particular requirements for dissertations, and these may not be synonymous with those of a publisher, even a university press. To mention a simple physical point: copy for publication must be uniformly double spaced. In dissertation style, the time honored practice is to single space long quotations, footnotes and bibliographical entries. Although the typescript then resembles a book (possibly the practice arose from wishful thinking), cramped copy cannot be edited or easily read by the typesetter. A minor matter, but when one considers the cost of time and labor in producing a book today, perhaps there is no such thing as a minor matter.

The solution would be easy if appearance were the only problem, but there is also the question of motivation. Many candidates for advanced degrees simply do not regard their theses or dissertations as the ultimate expression of their scholarly hopes. Or the author loses heart and makes compromises during a quarrel between readers in the margins of his dissertation. Or, exhausted by course work and research, the author takes neither enough time nor pains with the actual writing. Quite understandably, an author may simply want to get on with it, feeling his real contributions to the field can come later. Some papers and dissertations, however well written and worthwhile, are too limited in audience potential for publication. Such works contribute to their field and deserve to be written in publishable style, if only for the sake of the author's own craft and the delight of his colleagues. Whether or not a candidate hopes to publish, he should avoid writing "dissertation-ese," a style that like any bad habit is harder to uproot than to prevent at the outset.

It is no modest achievement whenever a dissertation is brought to light by a publisher. Criticism of published work on the grounds that it was "only a dissertation" fails to consider how few dissertations make it. A work is either of publishable quality or it isn't. Why it was written may be unimportant. How it is written makes all the difference.

The hardest thing in the world to write is the first paragraph. The first sentence is not easy, but most writers can come up with one, or at least with an opening phrase. If on some days the blank page stretches invitingly, on other days its blankness calls up Melville's horror of the white whale, or Frost's scary, inner desert places.

Writing that first paragraph means getting started, perhaps falsely. But no second paragraph can come into being without a first.

Problems arise in certain disciplines because the scholar has before him models not only of what can be said on a subject but how it can best be said.

Such stylistic excellence can inspire, but it can also paralyze an author sensitive to the difference between his own method and that which he is trying to analyze. Like Chaucer's clerk, "gladly would he learn and gladly teach." But not so gladly write.

Scholarly research leads to writing, particularly if academic survival is dependent upon publication. This pressure is not necessarily bad, but in some scholars the love of research can prove to be a fatal flaw, at once the source of greatness and possible downfall. Research itself can grow so absorbing it serves as its own end. As Samuel Johnson said, "A man will turn over half a library to make one book." The chase can be more exciting than its description, unless the author resolves to give his prose a life of its own.

Although much of what he finds through research may turn out to be intrinsically worthless or useless for his purposes, the scholar must hunt extensively. Some academic writers avoid the temptation to get lost in the lotus land of others' findings by choosing to work in an obscure territory all their own. This approach is legitimate, although sometimes a subject deserves obscurity and should be left undisturbed lest the scholar likewise sink into oblivion.

At the beginning of an academic career, one might examine lists of dissertations and monographs as well as books and articles written during a given period. Such a scrutiny will reveal not only fads in scholarly publication but — these can be especially helpful to the student — the gaps which may occur. If a scholar author is equally attracted to a popular subject and to one of equal merit but less popularity, the sensible choice is apparent.

Surprises happen. A few years ago, for example, an English professor who directs dissertations at a state university pointed out the relative absence of dissertations on Shakespeare. Of course, he added, a student entering here has a vast amount of research to uncover (which may explain the gap in the first place), but fewer young scholars were engaged in the uncovering. Most of the dissertations in the period described by the professor were concentrated in nineteenth and twentieth century American literature. Multiply that teacher by those in other universities giving their graduate students similar advice, and in a few years a situation may reverse itself and call for a new direction. On the other hand, it is possible for a dissertation director to have a hidden agenda and to attract students to his specialty for political rather that scholarly reasons.

One might like to think of scholarship as emancipated from trends, but given areas at given times show heavy competition. Scholars in the humanities, whose best contributions tend to come later in their careers, naturally spend time choosing a field of concentration. This is not to advise anyone to choose what he hates, since it is hard enough to write about what one admires, but to be careful in choosing between two loves. Scholars in the natural sciences often make their marks at an earlier age, but they also can benefit from a careful survey of potential fields and from competent advice.

Such remarks are not meant to encourage the offbeat instead of solid scholarship. To be realistic, however, the academic market can carry only so much solid scholarship at the same time and place. How many manuscripts on a limited subject can or should be published in a given year? Although trends should not determine scholarly choices, the academic writer needs to know where to expect intense competition. Getting the results of one's research together is sufficiently difficult without working against the odds.

Another sort of problem may arise if the scholar-author dissipates his ideas by discussing them before they are fully formed — with colleagues or with students. Some writers do benefit from sharing ideas with an associate who can function as a critic, but ordinarily not until after the first draft. Once a theory has been stated, even tentatively in conversation, some of the force is diminished. The actual writing needs that force.

Yet another barrier exists in unnecessary preparation. Devices like sharpening all one's pencils are obvious. More subtle is the typing up of elaborate notes, which may be a commendable effort to organize when it is not instead a method of putting off the business of writing. An author may be tempted now to read one more book, to trace one more article. One thinks of Coleridge, whose writing gives evidence that he was addicted to reading footnotes and cross references — a fact which, more than his laudanum habit, might help explain why he left so much work unfinished.

Whatever preparation is necessary to a writer should be preserved. But if a ritual invades the time that should be devoted to writing, it should be sacrificed.

"Literary is very hard work," said an unknown author. Any scholar might have said the same thing, if more gracefully. "In my beginning is my end" might serve as a more appropriate motto for the scholar to nail to his desk to urge him to write.

THE USE OF QUOTATION

Who can imagine a scholarly book or article that is without quotation or paraphrase? Scholars sometimes have the Keatsian gift of "negative capability," in which an author becomes that which he looks upon. A paper or a lecture can be a patchwork of quotations, leaving the audience wondering what the author or speaker really thought of the subject. Even the general and often unwilling reader is teased by quotations and allusions in advertising copy. In conversation, people quote themselves: "So I said to her . . ."

The reader, scholarly or general, is often inclined to skip long quoted passages in print, even if these quotations are among his own favorites. Too many quotations can be like over-abundant descriptive writing in a novel; the reader may skim or yawn through to the end, whatever the intrinsic beauties of a passage.

Direct quotations should be chosen for their force and support of the author's point. Sometimes a paraphrase would be better.

Good writers guard against simply giving a summary rather than an analysis of facts. Episodic writing laced with quotations can be boring even to the scholarly reader whose favorite five act play is the subject of the plot summary. Unless the subject is obscure, the author ought to avoid mere summary or enumeration of facts.

STYLE

Paragraphs should hold together internally. A series of short paragraphs often contains undeveloped ideas and gives the paper a choppy look. Paragraphs that are too long, on the other hand, may put off even the serious reader. The use of the active voice makes for vigorous writing, as do positive statements, tight sentences, and parallel constructions to express related ideas. Omit needless words and hackneyed expressions.

A teacher who thinks about it will probably admit the impossibility of teaching good writing and good writing manners simultaneously. Accurate punctuation and spelling are signs of literacy; yet such good manners do not make effective style any more than etiquette alone constitutes character.

A skilled editor can help an author out with mechanical errors (not that writers are advised to be careless), but style is an individual thing. An editor does not simply suggest a correct spelling, but he may offer suggestions or question an author on style. Since style is part of the author's identity, the exchange of questions and answers can be touchy, but it need not be.

The academic writer is identified as one deeply in his field, reflecting and analyzing, making his discoveries available to others in the same discipline. Like all writers the scholar reveals his identity in his work — and if his manuscript has no identifying marks, who will want to publish it? An author who begins with a general design in mind and writes clearly without interjecting his opinion at every turn, will find that his views emerge readily and naturally, with a better chance of acceptance.

Elaborate figures of speech or a breezy manner detract from academic writing — and other kinds of prose, too. Well presented material makes the audience *want* to know what it needs to know. Scholarship then achieves the grace appropriate to its nature.

A writer once said that writing is an act of faith. Perhaps in today's academic market a manuscript is an author's act of hope. Desire for tenure or promotion may run as strong as the hope to make a contribution to the field; however, if the scholar-author does not believe in the worth of his work, he is unlikely to reach his audience.

A distinguished scholar recently confided to his class of graduate students a discovery made when contributing scholars exchanged manuscripts for a book he was editing. In going over each other's work, the authors found a number of small mistakes. The errors were caught at the manuscript stage, fortunately, but the incident does show the difficulty of spotting one's own mistakes.

Many writers would catch their errors once set glaringly in type, but in the twentieth century such discoveries may be too late. In the nineteenth century, when printers' revisions were cheap, an author could make changes on the cold print, a fact which helps explain the high quality of much writing from that period. Current technology, however, calls for corrections near the beginning phases of the work. The felicitous expressions should all be in by the time the typescript is ready. Scholars, like other writers, consult Webster's for correct usage and spelling, but there are problems a dictionary cannot solve. For this reason, most manuals for academic writers include a section on mechanics.

PUNCTUATION

Period

The period goes at the end of the sentence and within quotation marks, although one sees exceptions. When citing the source of a quotation within the text, it may be less confusing to have the period last: "Then the rains came" (p. 102).

Use a period after numerals or letters in a list:

1. theological
2. moral

a. odes
b. elegies

In scholarly writing, use a period even when the urge to use an exclamation point is strong.

Question Mark

Besides the usual appearance of the question mark to express a query or doubt at the end of a sentence, there are some moot question marks.

In a sentence which includes an interrogative sentence, keep the question mark:

Who will be on the new team? was everyone's thought.

But do not use a question mark after indirect questions or after comments that only pretend to be questions:

We asked Tom whether he had been in Oslo then.

Will you please clean your room.

That last sentence could be construed to express a query or a doubt, but more often a command is meant.

Colon

To introduce a long, indented quotation use a complete sentence followed by a colon:

Notice that in this example no quotation marks are used.
The printer will set the quotation in reduced type.

The colon, weaker than a period but stronger than a semicolon, is also used to introduce lists or series. A colon with equal space on either side separates volume and page reference as well as biblical chapter and verse:

PMLA 33:16   Matt. 4:6-8

Place the colon outside parentheses and quotation marks:

I liked the poem "Found Horizon": it was
imaginative.

In current usage, that particular colon would probably be a semicolon (so much for rules); what more can be said?

Semicolon

The semicolon shows a more definite break in the sentence than does the comma. If some scholarly authors appear to be addicted to the semicolon, the probable cause is that early in their careers they read so many comma spliced papers from their students. The easiest way to correct this mistake, which consists in the inadequate division of two sentences by a comma, is to change the comma to a semicolon.

> Osbert has returned; I have remained.

The example shows perfectly adequate punctuation; yet, it can be habit forming. A semicolon normally appears before these words used in place of a conjunction: *hence, however, indeed, so, then, thus, yet.* If a compound sentence will be made more manageable use a semicolon instead of a comma. Use a semicolon before expressions like *for example or e.g.* If a semicolon will clarify items in a series, use one between items. The semicolon, like the colon, appears outside parentheses and quotation marks.

Dash

A dash might be considered as a punctuation mark between the semicolon and comma in strength, but there is more than one kind of dash. The en dash is longer than a hyphen in actual print, but, in typing, a hyphen represents the en dash. The en dash is used with numbers and in compounds:

> pp. 16-23   Oshkosh-Omaha flight

Type two hyphens to indicate an em dash, which is the most commonly used. A 2-em dash indicates missing letters, so----; a 3-em dash means a whole word omitted. This dash is also used by the printer in bibliographies to represent an author's name before his second and subsequent books in the list-

> Shapiro, Karl. In *Defense of Ignorance*
>   New York: Random House, 1960.
> ------. *Poems: 1940-1953.* New York: Random House, 1953.

A break in thought is indicated by a dash or pair of dashes:

> I want--or do I--to find the manuscript.

A dash can emphasize a point:
>   His use of quotation--and quotation
>   used sparingly--is accurate.

Sometimes dashes substitute for parentheses:
>   The work of the second generation--Byron,
>   Keats, and Shelley--was different.

A dash may also replace a semicolon before expressions such as *that is, for example,* or their abbreviated forms, *i.e., e.g.* Dashes replace quotation marks in direct discourse in French, Spanish, Italian, and Russian.

Comma

Although the comma seems to be diminishing in frequency, there remain several occasions upon which it is necessary, or at least helpful. If in doubt, read the sentence out loud.

Use a comma after elements that break the continuity of thought. Unless the clauses are short, a comma normally occurs in compound sentences before the conjunction. The main principle in the use of the comma is clarity. For example, a comma helps before a conjunction which introduces an independent clause:

> He went away, and we do not know when
> he will return to pick up his mail.

This respectable but rather loose sentence could be tightened: We do not know when he will return to pick up his mail. But effective writing means knowing when to use a tight sentence, when a loose one. Some writers achieve the delicate balance. Probably the scales are tipped unjustly in favor of loose sentences, of which a leading variety is the comma-plus-conjunction used to join independent clauses. *And,* particularly, is a weak conjunction, for it states no clear relationship between clauses. This is an age when all speak of relevance, and who promotes it? (Note the confusion created by that *and.* Does it really mean but? Or does the reader expect another sentence, telling him who it is who promotes relevance?)

If both clauses have the same subject when the connective is *and,* no comma is needed; however, use a comma if the connective is *but:*

> I love him and hate him.
> I love him, but hate him.

If the second part of a two part sentence begins with *for, or, nor, while, as* (meaning because), a comma precedes the conjunction. Remember not to use a comma as a substitute for a semicolon between independent clauses. An exception to the rule against comma splices is tolerated if the clauses are short.

> He loves me, he loves me not.

Purists might insist on a semicolon, but the comma seems adequate. On the other hand, sentences should not be broken in two by a period when a comma is enough.

Commas are necessary, most of the time, to set off parenthetical expressions. As with all simple rules, the problems arise in interpretation. If a parenthetical expression is short and does not interrupt the flow of the sentence, no commas may be needed. Under no circumstances, however, should only one comma be used in enclosing a parenthetic expression. (Note that *however* in the preceding sentence needed two commas.)

Commas are used in setting off non-restrictive clauses. A non-restrictive clause adds rather than defines:

Fresno, where Emma lives, is in California.

Restrictive clauses do not require commas. These clauses define or limit:

People who travel west should wear sunglasses.

In the second case, the clause tells which people are meant. Emma's presence in Fresno, in the first sentence, does nothing to define or limit the town, but simply adds someone to it.

The comma may or may not be used after introductory adverbial phrases. Clarity is the guide. If the adverbial phrase appears immediately before the verb, use no comma:

On the mountain stands a maiden.

A comma after mountain would violate the sentence. The case is not always clear:

After lunch, they hiked through the forest.

Since the phrase is short, the comma could easily drop out. Contemporary usage would probably favor a comma free sentence in such a case.

Introductory participial phrases, unless they occur immediately before the verb, require a comma.

Hiking along the trail was Kenneth.
Hiking along the trail, Kenneth thought deeply.

The more common error, as readers of so many unpublished papers realize, has nothing to do with the presence or absence of the comma in such a case. Too often a writer may get lost in the sentence and wander into a dangling participle:

wrong　　Hiking along the trail the thought struck Kenneth.

Commas are necessary after interjections, transitional adverbs, direct address, appositives, or whatever else needs to be excused before bursting into the sentence. In a series, a comma follows each item. If the items are in themselves long, a semicolon may prove helpful.

A comma is usually placed after the penultimate item in a series and before the conjunction:

> The material is red, blue, yellow,
> and green.

The comma after yellow might have been omitted, if the author is consistent in his resolve to omit such commas wherever they occur, or might have occurred, in his manuscript.

Parentheses

Parentheses enclose words to ease their breaking into the flow of the sentence. Words within parentheses may explain, expand, or digress. The more closely related these words are to the main sentence, the less likely the need for parentheses. In some cases, dashes or commas suffice.

A paragraph containing several parentheses (unless they are used to enclose citations of sources within the text) probably needs rewriting. A paragraph ought to hang together through the relationship of its sentences to one another. Too many breaks in the central thought may cause the paragraph to collapse.

For further information on punctuation, see Porter G. Perrin's *Writer's Guide and Index to English,* published in Chicago by Scott Foresman.

Possessives

Forming the possessive of nouns is sometimes confusing, particularly if the word ends in *s*. The general rule is to add an apostrophe plus *s*. Consider Keats's odes. Like all general rules, this one has exceptions--most notably, *Moses', Jesus', righteousness'.*

Possessive pronouns *his, hers, yours, theirs, oneself,* and *its* have no apostrophes. As teachers and readers of papers well know, *its* is particularly troublesome to some writers. *Its* is the possessive; *it's* is the contraction for it is.

Plurals

To form plurals, ordinarily add *s* or *es:*

Johns and Marys

Joneses and Hayeses

even contemporary Demostheneses

The last example, although technically correct, sounds so awkward it makes one think being right is not always enough. In such a case, rephrase.

A simple s or es is adequate in such instances:

PMLAs   SPCAs   1970s

sixes and sevens

If a period occurs in the abbreviation, or if a letter is used as a word, an apostrophe is required:

p's and q's   Ph. D.'s

As a writer should choose Webster's first choice in spelling, so he should follow the first choice for the plural form if two forms are given:

memorandums   not memoranda

appendixes   not appendices

but

symposia   not symposiums

millenia   not milleniums

SPELLING

In most cases, the dictionary settles doubts about spelling, but even such authoritative dictionaries as *Webster's Third International* or its abridged version *Seventh New Collegiate* may leave some questions unanswered. The Scylla and Charybdis of spelling is whether or not to hyphenate compounds. Sometimes words have fused and are spelled solid--*barnyard*. Other words are spelled open as separate unhyphenated words--*attorney general*. Still other words are hyphenated--*vice-president*.

Although it may appear to be begging the question, if a writer finds his manuscript contains too many hyphens between words, he might consider making minor revisions. Too many compounds, or too many nouns used as adjectives, can mean a heavy style.

Hyphens are helpful in compound numerals (twenty-six), compounds with self- (self-assured), family relationships (son-in-law); however, no absolute rule can be stated. Sometimes a hyphen or an open spelling avoids a confusion of letters: *Hell-like* or *hell like* is preferable to *helllike*.

If a writer's question on hyphenation is unanswered by the dictionary, he may take comfort in the knowledge that the tendency is away from the use of the hyphen except in formal writing. The academic writer can trust the editors of a university publishing house to know the particular publisher's rules. In doubt, the writer should type the compound closed or open without a hyphen. The editor, who has the publisher's idea of uniformity in mind, will add any hyphens deemed necessary.

DIVISION OF WORDS

To divide words correctly, consult the dictionary and trust the manuscript editor. American usage divides words according to pronunciation. Division usually occurs after a vowel, or between two consonants, unless either practice would violate pronunciation. One letter divisions are impossible; two letter divisions are legitimate but distracting. Unless the consonant before *ing* is doubled, the ending appears by itself. Avoid division of proper names and abbreviations.

CAPITALIZATION

Although the trend is down, or away from the use of capitals, sometimes capitalization is necessary. Use capitals for names of persons, for titles when used with persons' names, but not if the title appears in apposition:

               Mayor Richard J. Daley

but

               Richard J. Daley, mayor of Chicago

and

               the mayor

in similar fashion, "Yes, Aunt Marina is my aunt."

Designation of people by race, language, tribe, or religion calls for capitals, except when the designation is based simply on color or usage--*black, white, aborigine.* Place names are capitalized; their adjectives given lower case:

Orient	oriental
Middle West	middle western
or Midwest	midwestern

Capitalize titles of institutions, organizations, and companies--Chicago Symphony Orchestra *but* the orchestra. Lower case most literary and historical period designations unless a proper name is included--romantic period *but*

Victorian era. Exceptions based on tradition or clarity do employ capitals--Middle Ages.

Use capitals for archaelogical, anthropological, and geological periods--Cenozoic era, Quaternary period. Very recent time designations are lower cased--atomic age, in keeping with the trend away from capitals, perhaps.

Religion is profoundly conservative about the tradition of capitals, but even here one finds reforms. In doubt, reverently drop capitals in favor of lower case.

For titles of works, capitalize all nouns, pronouns, adjectives, verbs, adverbs, and subordinate conjunctions. Lower case articles, coordinate conjunctions, and prepositions, unless they are the first or last words in the title. For titles in scientific citations, however, ordinarily capitalize only the first word and proper names within the title.

NUMBERS

When should numbers be spelled out, when given in figures? No absolute rule exists, although in scientific writing figures are used more freely. In general writing, it is suggested that figures be used for exactwnumbers of more than one hundred. Spell out a number even in this category if it is the first or last word in the sentence. Numbers under one hundred should be spelled out--with obvious exceptions:

42 A.D.   p. 16

In the sciences the symbol % is preferred; in the humanities, the term *percent*. Spell out time designations unless the exact moment is given:

six o'clock   6:02 p.m.

A writer with further questions on style and mechanics is referred to Perrin's W*riter's Guide and Index to English,* the University of Chicago's *Manual of Style,* William Strunk and E.B. White's classic little book *The Elements of Style,* or the section devoted purely to style and composition in *The Writer's Manual.*

TWO

PREPARATION OF THE SCHOLARLY MANUSCRIPT

Once a writer knows that his article or book has been accepted, he can look forward to the pleasure of taking more pains. Preparing the manuscript for publisher and printer is chiefly the author's responsibility, although he may expect assistance from an editor. The primary virtue for the scholar-author to cultivate is clarity. A manuscript clear in matter and form is the best insurance against confusion and delay.

Paper for the typescript should be 8½ x 11 and of good quality. Avoid "erasable" and highly glazed papers. Some "erasables" work so well words can disappear under the pressure of a thumb. Lots of people touch a manuscript on its way to becoming a book; their many hands can literally make light work--or faint copy. Such paper also develops spots which will not readily take the written corrections and queries of editor and author.

Usually two copies of the manuscript are sent to the publisher, the first typescript and a carbon or machine copy. The author keeps the second carbon or copy for himself. It is best to use the same typewriter for the whole manuscript, or at least the same type size. Pica, because it is larger, is preferable to elite type but not absolutely necessary. The ribbon should be fresh and the type bars clean. A manuscript which contains many diacritical marks and symbols may call for a special typewriter. If the marks and symbols are not available, they may be written in by a scrupulously careful hand. Corrections of typographical errors should be made clearly; it is unfair to expect the editor to guess at the author's intentions. Misinterpretation can cause an infinity of delays.

Appearance counts. You can't judge a book by its cover (at this stage the cover is only a gleam in the eye of the production department), but a neat manuscript may influence a publisher's reader. Once a manuscript is accepted, clear copy keeps everyone from editors to proof-readers calm and functioning efficiently. Besides causing delays, mistakes in the manuscript can increase the cost of printing and even diminish the author's profits.

A small, unpublished scandal which occurred a few years ago in a midwestern college illustrates the importance of appearance. A beautifully typed paper on Chaucer was entered in a competition in the liberal arts division. Only the student's closest friends knew that, although the paper itself was original, the footnotes were hopelessly inaccurate, put together at the last moment to give the paper the requisite scholarly look. How could anything so tidy be so inaccurate, even a mockery of academic technique? The judges, pressed for time, checked no page numbers and awarded the paper first prize. Errors of this sort, when they might honestly (not deliberately) occur in a manuscript submitted for publication, might be caught by a careful editor; nevertheless, accuracy in documentation is the author's responsibility. A manuscript ought to have both the appearance and the reality of being correct.

Quotations in the Manuscript

The first and most general rule applying to quotations is to copy them faithfully, even to the idiosyncrasies of spelling. If he must, the scholar-author can always insert a *sic* to show that the mistake or peculiarity is not his. The bracketed term *sic* should not be overworked, especially if the scholar is dealing with a text abounding in unusual spelling or vocabulary. The reader will catch on in such instances.

When the entire quoted passage is not pertinent, use ellipsis marks . . . to indicate that parts of a quotation have been omitted. If the ellipsis occurs after a complete sentence in the quotation, type four dots instead of three . . . . One dot stands for the period.

To indicate the omission of a paragraph or more, type a full line of ellipsis marks:

. . . .

Follow the same pattern for the omission of a full line or more in poetry.

An author's interpolations within quotations are enclosed in brackets [not parentheses]. If the typewriter has no brackets, draw them in by hand.

To emphasize key words in a quotation, underline them and write in brackets [italics mine]. Or indicate at the end of the sentence in parentheses (italics mine). Or explain the situation in a footnote. Always follow whichever method is least likely to confuse the reader.

Short quotations are usually run in with the text, simply set in the same type size and enclosed in quotation marks. Longer quotations are separated from the main text, indented, and set in reduced type without quotation marks. In typing such block quotations, indent them and use no quotation marks, but double space them. In typing dissertations, theses, and papers, single spacing is the usual method for long quotations. Although a sensible plan would train scholars to prepare all manuscripts as if for publication, universities have their own requirements and a student should check and follow them.

Who can define absolutely what is a long quotation, what is a short one? If the quotation is eight to ten typed lines, then it should probably be handled as long. But if this practice would give pages a chopped up look, then long quotations can be run with the test. On the other hand, a short quotation of a few lines of poetry might be more effectively indented. Two lines of poetry run with the text are separated by a *solidus* or slash: "Here thou, great Anna, whom three realms obey,/ Dost sometimes counsel take--and sometimes tea."

Sometimes only a few quoted words or a phrase are needed to support an author's point. With skill these words can be enclosed in quotation marks and woven into the syntax of the author's own sentence: in their reading of "sometimes tea" enthusiasts of the occult claim that what "three realms obey" in the commands of "great Anna" is often based on a scrutiny of tea leaves.

Cross References

Cross references, when unavoidable in a manuscript, should be typed in (see p. 000). The page numbers cannot be given since they are unknown until the page proofs are ready. Include the page numbers of the manuscript, however, in the margin on the line which contains (see p. 000) to help the editor. Even more helpful to author and editor would be the determination of a way to avoid using a cross reference in the first place.

The Complete Manuscript

What should an author submit as a complete manuscript?   The body of the book is obviously the bulk of the text, but there are important separate pages in a scholarly manuscript.

Title page, table of contents, lists of illustrations and tables (if any), legends and captions for any illustrations, the illustrations and tables themselves, footnotes, bibliography or reference list, glossary or any other material to appear at the back of the book--except the index--all these elements should be included. Unless he makes other arrangements, the author is responsible for the index, but this section can be finished only when all the page proofs are in and page numbers in the actual book are known.

An article destined to appear in a scholarly journal is simpler than a book; yet, the author should here also remember to put in categories separate from the main text any matter calling for special treatment by the printer. Among problems printers handle separately are footnotes, tables, illustrations, and legends.

Footnotes are numbered consecutively but labled by chapter. Notes for chapter 1 may run 1-13; for chapter 2, 14-28. The footnote pages themselves are numbered according to their place at the end of the text. If the typescript of the text ends on p. 259, the notes would begin on p. 260 of the typescript. The printer will solve the problem of placing the notes at the bottom of the appropriate page. Since the finished book will differ in appearance and pagination, it is a waste of time for the author to type the footnotes at the bottom of the pages. The extra effort would result only in a nuisance for the printer. In works destined to be microfilmed rather than printed, as is often the case with dissertations, the courteous typist puts notes at the bottom of the page to spare the reader from spinning through the microfilm to check a reference.

In some publications, notes appear at the end of an article or book. In rare cases, notes may appear at the end of a chapter. Separate sheets bearing tables, which may be either typed or pasted on, are not numbered in the manuscript prepared for publication, but each page should indicate the manuscript page number to which it belongs.

Put illustrations, with their legends typed on separate sheets, in an envelope. Avoid folding, clipping, pinning, stapling, and other potential mutilations. Further protect illustrations with sheets of cardboard.

Remember to double space all copy for publication. Type nothing single space, not even indented quotations. Be generous with margins, at least an inch all around the page. Chapters should begin at least three inches from the top of a page.

Type chapter titles and subheads with initial capitals only--the first letter of each word not a preposition, article, or coordinate conjunction. Do not underline titles of chapters and subheads

If the manuscript includes a glossary or a list of abbreviations, the list should be alphabetized and typed flush left. Use no period after the term. Align all definitions, leaving about four spaces between the longest word and definition. Indent runover lines under the beginning line of the definition. Use periods after all definitions if some definitions are more than one sentence in length. The rule here, as in many mechanical matters, is consistency. The printer may do some rearranging for the sake of aesthetics.

For bibliographies or lists of references, type each entry flush left. Indent runover lines about three spaces. Do not forget to double space.

Mathematical Copy

Since it almost always requires some handwork, mathematical copy poses special difficulties and is known among printers as "penalty copy." Some type is impossible to set and actual drawings must be made. With such problems in mind, the author of a mathematical work should avoid ambiguous expressions, submit a list of special signs and symbols used, and be clear in whatever signs he writes in. A careful reading of the publisher's style sheet is recommended.

THREE

WORK IN PRODUCTION

After a manuscript is accepted, what happens to it? The production department of the publishing house needs the second copy of a book in manuscript for design and an estimate of cost. The first copy becomes the care of an editor who informs the author when he may expect edited copy.

An author, knowing the merit of his work, may grow protective of it and even resentful of another's editorial efforts. Still, the questions and corrections of a good editor are the expressed concerns of an ally who cares about the progress of the work. An editor may be more objective about whether those for whom a book is intended are likely to read it. At least, an editor can help the author determine whether his assumptions about the audience are accurate. What must be explained, what taken for granted?

An article aimed at scholars of the Middle Ages need not identify Chretien de Troyes or Marie de France. To the specialized audience familiar with these persons, introductions would be superfluous. On the other hand, the author should not presume knowledge of obscure points or material available to only a limited number of scholars.

An editor familiar with the author's field can offer sound advice on which sections of a manuscript might need tightening, which might be expanded. The rule is to take editorial questions seriously and to answer even those which might seem naive to the author. Such questions may appear in the margins of the manuscript or in a letter from the editor.

Among the marks and remarks the author may find in an edited manuscript are the traditional proofreader's signs and symbols:

Proofreaders' Marks

¶	Begin new paragraph		⋀	Insert comma
ₙₒ ¶	No new paragraph		⋀	Insert apostrophe
ℓ	Delete		" " ⋀	Insert quotation marks
ℓ	Delete space		(?)	Insert question mark
#	Insert space			
ls	Letterspace			
[	Move left		⊙	Insert period
]	Move right		:/	Insert colon
⌐	Move up		;/	Insert semicolon
⌐⌐	Move down		/=/	Insert hyphen
][	Center		N̄	Insert en dash
=	Align horizontally		M̄	Insert em dash
‖	Align vertically		cap	Capitalize
tr	Transpose		lc	Lower case
⌐	Push down type		sc	Set in small capitals
stet	Let it stand			
ital	Italicize		✕	Broken letter
rom	Set in roman		⊘	Reverse (type upside down)
bf	Set in boldface			
wf	Wrong font; set correctly			

Editors' Suggestions

In addition to these time honored marks, the author may receive suggestions to rearrange or alter parts of his book or article.

The editor, as the second person to go over the manuscript carefully (the author, it is hoped, being first) may catch errors originally missed. In states of exaltation or fatigue, and an author who has finished a manuscript may be in either state, a person may fail to spot minor flaws. It is the function of the editor not to bring the author down, but to point out any imperfections that would mar the total effect of the work. True, at times a correction may be merely pedantic. Consider a mythic editor who might look askance at "Or like stout Cortez when with eagle eyes/ He stared at the Pacific..." Such an editor might say in the margin that it was Balboa, not Cortez, who discovered the Pacific; however, in the case of Keats's sonnet "On First Looking into Chapman's Homer," poetic license and the demands of meter triumph over fact. Most of the time, though, editors can be relied upon for the right kind of help.

Author's Revisions

What about changes not suggested by the editor which occur to the author after he receives the edited copy? Good writing often means rewriting. Now is the time for any final changes in the text. Quotations should be checked at this stage, too. To wait until the galley or page proofs are in is to court delay and to increase the cost of production. Further, the more last minute changes, the greater the potential for errors in the printed work. There is some risk in making even necessary corrections, since a new error may creep in while the old one is being correctly reset.

Deadlines and Proofreading

The author, eager to see his book in print, will do well to observe the deadline for returning the edited manuscript to the publisher. If the editor's date is impossible, notification to that effect should be sent immediately. Missing this deadline can mean rescheduling the book with the printer. Meanwhile, especially in competitive areas, someone else may come out with a book or article on the same topic for the same audience. While such an event would most often not diminish the intrinsic value of the original work, a book's potential royalties might shrink. Such is the price of procrastination.

Modern technology may create a *deus ex machina* to replace current methods of checking work in production. Until that new creation, the author must learn to cope with the widespread, traditional, and unglamorous way of handling galleys and page proofs. Again, the first rule to observe pertains to all deadlines sent by publisher to author.

The author usually receives two copies of the galley proofs. These long sheets may arrive in stages, as the printer finishes parts of the book, or they may come all at once. One set of galleys bears the proofreader's corrections; the author should read carefully and add his own corrections, if any are necessary, to this set. The author keeps the second set of galleys for reference; so it is helpful to copy all corrections from the first set onto the galleys retained.

Most publishers also send the edited manuscript with the galleys. Galleys should be checked against the manuscript. For this job an author needs an alert and generous person, perhaps one who owes him a favor. One person reads aloud from the manuscript; the other follows the galley proofs. Never read from proofs to copy, since a proof may lack a line or two and still make sense to the ear. The best way to catch such an error is to hear what was omitted from the original text. The reader ought to read everything in sight, even the humble punctuation marks. Be especially careful with numbers, where the intrusion of an extra digit can make a ridiculous difference.

Many proofreaders are sharp-eyed, but none claim infallibility. Aware of this reality, the author and his reader-helper will be on the lookout for any errors the proofreaders may have missed. Such errors are corrected by the standard symbols or, if necessary, by words or phrases used economically.

Mistakes appearing in the galleys which are correct in the edited manuscript are called printer's errors. An author or editor who catches these "typos" may mark them PE. No charge is made against the author's royalties for the correction of such mistakes. Changes deemed necessary, although the printer did not err, can be costly. The contract between author and publisher usually spells out how much of the expense of these alterations the publisher will pay — and how much will come out of a book's earnings.

The author, then, should not be led into the temptation to rewrite whole chunks of his work in the margins of the galley sheets. Maybe he thinks now of a happier phrase than one in the original manuscript. After all, good writing is often a matter of unfinished business. But something must be kept for a new edition of another book. Meanwhile, the author should tell his new vision or revision to no man, least of all the editor or the typesetter, as the eleventh hour approaches. Even a minor change may mean resetting a paragraph of type. In the process of moving, things get lost or new and different errors appear. Mindful of these dire warnings, an author who must change a word will consider substituting one of about the same length. In this way, the line itself may remain unaltered.

When page proofs are ready, the author receives two sets, one of which is a corrected set to be returned to the publisher. The other set is for the author's record or use in getting the index together. Also in this package are the corrected galleys, which go back to the publisher with the page proofs.

The author checks page proofs against galleys, a task he can manage by himself if the sheets are placed side by side. (By this time any friend who helped with the edited manuscript and galleys has probably disappeared.) In this job, not every word need be read, but the author should check to see that every correction indicated in the galleys appears in the page proofs. Lines above and below corrected lines in the page proofs should be checked to make sure the corrected line got back into the right place.

If the word "reset" occurs in the galley margins, it means the printer has had to reset material not marked for correction on the galley. Perhaps the type was broken, but whatever the unknown accident, the author should make sure the line has been reset correctly, that nothing has disappeared, no new error added. Another good idea is to check the top and bottom lines of each page proof to see that no lines have been lost. Remember to check the footnotes.

Any author's alterations on the page proofs are even more expensive than changes on the galleys. This cautionary remark is not meant to encourage an author to let a previously undetected enormity remain in the text. But an additional sheet indicating a few *errata* might be less costly. In doubtful cases, the editor ought to be consulted.

It should be noted that sometimes publishers by-pass the galley stage and go straight to page proofs as a means of speeding up the publication date. This procedure requires even greater technical care on the part of the author.

Although a book is not born with the page proofs, after this phase the author is less directly involved with such matters as reproduction proofs, folded sheets, book covers. An author now can almost relax and await delivery--unless, of course, there is to be an index, which is the next complication to consider.

The Index

What kind of book requires an index? Any serious work of non-fiction, unless it is short or unless it is divided into short sections. Who has not felt relief upon finding an index at the back of a thick book, or irritation upon not finding one?

The author is in the best position to index his work, but a professional indexer well acquainted with the field might in some cases be more objective about what items to put in the index. Time itself may determine who prepares an index, if an author's schedule prevents him from undertaking this important task.

Indexes may contain entries based on subject, persons, and titles of works. Also possible is an index of first lines of poems, usually set in a separate index. Persons and subjects may be separated if an index would otherwise be too long or unwieldly.

A simple subject entry might read:
    Furniture: 16, 30, 37
With subentries:
    Furniture: armchairs, 16; lamps, 30; tables, 37
Sometimes the entry is a cross reference:
    Household goods: *See* Furniture

This entry directs the reader to the material he is looking for by telling him it is under another heading. If the reference instead contains *see also*, it means information can be found under both subjects.

Index entries are usually set in run-in style, one subentry after another without a break in lines. If the work is complicated, the index may be indented with each subentry on a separate line. In either method, all lines after the first are indented from the left.

The author who prepares his own index, and often he is the best person to do so, should know that this is one of the pressure jobs of publication. An index cannot be finished before the page proofs are back from the printer for the obvious reason that the page numbers are until then unknown. Before this time, the author can be thinking about what headings he wants in the index. By the stage of the page proofs, author and editor will have solved all technical considerations like peculiar spelling or usage, which means the author will know how a name should appear in the index. If it is *Katharine* in the text, it must be *Katharine* in the index, not *Katherine,* to offer an obvious example.

For the actual indexing, the author needs a large working surface, a good supply by three-by-five cards, an alphabetical guide for the cards, and a file box. To avoid errors in interpretation, the index cards may be typed. As the author goes through the page proofs and spots a likely item for the index, he should take a card, write a key word or subject, a phrase that indicates what aspect of the subject is discussed, the page or pages on which it occurs. Mark the page proofs with the subject or key word whenever a card is needed.

After going through the page proofs and making the index cards, retrace the steps to catch any items skipped. Such omissions will be unmarked, since the marked items show that cards were made on the first trip through the proofs. Index cards, unless prepared by one familiar with the technique and adept at doing several things at once, should be kept in the same order as the page numbers until the end of the book is reached. Then the cards should be alphabetized. Some professional indexers start working, at least partially, in alphabetical order as they go, so that page references can be added to a card with the same subject. Like all short cuts, this method can waste time for one who is in unfamiliar territory.

The real test in indexing is to edit the cards. At this stage the cards are grouped and headings and subheadings definitely established. Subentries are needed if there are many page references to a subject or main entry. (Consider the reader who may want to know only one special point under a main topic.) Arrange subentries either alphabetically or chronologically as they appear in the text. Type the index in one column. Double space. Keep the index cards.

How long should an index be for a scholarly book? Two to five percent of the length of the book is a possible answer. For a 200 page book, this means four to ten pages of index. A short index means about five references per page of text; a long index, about fifteen. The rules are approximate, not absolute.

FOUR

Footnotes

Footnotes should be as few and concise as possible. Their purpose is to cite sources which, if included in the text, would interrupt the flow of thought. Following this logic, an author may include brief references parenthetically in the text, particularly if a given source is cited frequently. The author, typesetter, and ultimately the reader will appreciate not having to drop their attention to the bottom of the page. The first time the source is used, however, the reference usually appears in full form in a footnote. In this first note the author informs his readers that the source is "hereafter cited in text."

Basically there are four kinds of footnotes: to cite the source of a quotation or specific material in the text; to comment on discussion when to do so within the text would be an interruption; to make cross references; to make acknowledgments.

Sometimes the references appear at the back of the book where they are more accurately called endnotes. Very occasionally, notes may occur at the end of chapters. For articles, the practice varies according to the publication. Wherever the notes appear in the final version, the author preparing the manuscript for a publisher submits footnotes in a separate action. The task of placement and setting of type, which differs in size from the text and requires separate treatment, belongs to the printer. This point deserves special stress for the academic writer who is accustomed to typing, or seeing typed, references at the bottom of the page in papers, theses and dissertations. Another point to remember--footnotes are double spaced in the manuscript prepared for publication.

Footnote numbers in the text are typed less than a full space above the line, preferably at the end of a sentence unless a quotation is involved, like this.[1] Use no punctuation after the footnote number in the text. In the footnote itself, the numbers are typed on the line followed by a period. Some publishers follow this practice in setting type; others raise the number in the footnote, too. Typists of dissertations or papers not intended for immediate publication ordinarily raise the number.

If a footnote refers to several sources, yoke them together with a single number:

| Don't | According to Swaine,[1] Moriarity,[2] and Sarauskas,[3] |
| Do | According to Swaine, Moriarity, and Sarauskas,[1] |

The footnote would then read:

1. Charles Swaine, *The New Hermeneutics* (Chicago: 1973), p. 27; William Moriarity, *Hurtling toward the Eschaton* (Baileys Harbor, 1972), p. 21; George Sarauskas, *Comment on Current Eschatolgical Studies* (Clusterville, 1973), p. 14.

The example above might also have included the name of the publisher as well as the place of publication. Whether or not this information is given varies according to publishers. In doubt, include the information; a reader appreciates whatever helps him locate the source of citation easily.

The full footnote citing a book requires, in this order: author's full name, title of work, editor or translator's names, name of series and volume or number, total number of volumes, number of edition if other than the first, publishing place, publisher, date, volume if needed, page number, line number if helpful. Of course, not every footnote needs to be *that* full, but such is the most formidable type.

Articles are identified by author's name, title, periodical, volume and number, date, page.

The usual punctuation after each item is the comma--unless the next item is enclosed in parentheses. No comma occurs before the first parenthesis, but a comma appears after the second or closing parenthesis.

Yet, as the French say, no general statement is true, not even this one. There are exceptions to the rules above. For many books, there is no question of a series or number of volumes, and even if a book is in a series it is necessary to mention that fact only when relevant. Sometimes, as previously indicated, it is sufficient to give the place of publication without the name of the publisher, especially when the information is provided in the bibliography. Since not every work cited in a footnote appears in the bibliography, and vice-versa, the author must be sure such a footnote includes adequate information about the book or article. In the case of unpublished material, for example, a reader needs to know the title of the document and its date, folio number or other clue, name of collection, name of depository and city.

After the first full citation, the author shortens all references to a given work. In writing for *some* scholarly journals, omit the title in second and subsequent references and give only the author's last name, followed by a comma, and the page number. If there are references to more than one work by the same author, however, a short form of the title may be necessary to avoid confusion.

In reference to a book, the second note may include only the author's or authors' last names, the shortened title of the book in italics, and page number. Facts of publication may be omitted. For an article, give the author's last name, short title of the article, and page number. Omit the name of the periodical, volume number, and date. For a manuscript collection, omit the name and place of depository, except when more than one collection having the same name appears in the references.

A word on short titles--if a full title contains only two or three words, it is silly to shorten it beyond possibly dropping "the" and "a." If the title is long, use the key words in their natural order. *A Comment upon Cultural Trends 1800-1900 by a Careful Observer* should not be altered to read *Nineteenth Century Trends* but rather *Cultural Trends 1800-1900.*

If a work is cited often in a work, then an altered and abbreviated title may be used if the author informs the reader of this use in the first full reference. If many such altered titles are planned, a list may appear either at the beginning of the book or in an appendix. For names of persons appearing frequently, initials unspaced and without periods are acceptable: EN for all references to T*he Papers of Edmund Nightengale.*

What about those time honored scholarly tools, op. cit. and ibid.? Space savers in footnotes, they may now be disappearing from some presses. The University of Chicago Press, for example, prefers the short title form. The reader is clearly briefed by a short title, whereas an op. cit. on p. 101 when the work was last seen on p. 3 is maddening. Of course op. cit., which stands for the title, and ibid., which stands for author and title, are still acceptable forms. As for idem or its abbreviation id., which means the same, this term may take the place of the author's name and is used for titles only in legal references. In recent practice when scholarly Latin phrases or abbreviations are used in footnotes, they are not italicized; so, there is no need to underscore in the typescript.

Here are some examples of simple footnotes:

1. Isabel Snarley, *The Great Hoax* (Omaha: Duchesne Press, 1956), p. 172.

If the author's full name is given in the text, then the note would read:

1. *The Great Hoax* (Omaha: Duchesne Press, 1956), p. 172.

If author and title appear in the text, the note would include only the facts of publication and the page number:

1. Omaha, Duchesne Press, 1956, p. 172.

If the title appears in the text, or to get around using op. cit., a possible note would be:

1. Isabel Snarley, p. 172.

The last two examples could be more distracting to the reader than an interruption in the actual text. Individual cases are determined by the nature of the discussion.

For more than one author:

2. James E. Miller, Jr., Karl Shapiro, and Bernice Slote, *Start with the Sun* (Lincoln: University of Nebraska Press, 1960), p. 33.

When there are more than three authors, the footnote may mention only the first followed by et al. All the authors should be named in the bibliography.

For a book without an author in which the editor's name occurs on the title page, the editor's name goes first in the footnote:

3. Agnes Donohue, ed., *Casebook on the Hawthorne Question* (New York: Crowell Co., 1963), p. 5.

The proper abbreviation for more than one editor is eds. Comp. is the abbreviation for compiler; trans. for translator.

If the author's name appears on the title page of an edited or translated work, then the author's name is first, followed by the title, then the abbreviated ed. or trans., followed by the names of editor or translator. (In this instance the abbreviations stand for *edited by* or *translated by;* so, "eds." even if there is more than one editor would be inappropriate.)

4. Antonia Shimerda, *Travels,* trans.
Gerald Pokorny (Chicago, 1939), p. 14.

If in the discussion within the text, the editor or translator is more significant than the author, as would be the case if the text is about editing or translating, then the editor or translator appears first, followed by the appropriate abbreviation, then title, then author:

5. Gerald Pokorny, trans., *Travels*
by Antonia Shimerda (Chicago, 1939), p. 14.

Titles

The correct full title of a book, pamphlet, or periodical is to be found on the title page, not necessarily as it appears on the spine. Again, the full title should be used in the first full reference, although exceptions might even here be made for unusually long titles. *Journey to Seattle after Much Meditation and Lengthy Discussion with Peers in the Summer of 1973* could, even in the first footnote, be reduced to *Journey to Seattle . . . .*

Another reminder in the preparation of a manuscript — titles are typed with initial capitals for nouns, pronouns, adjectives, verbs, adverbs, and subordinate conjunctions. Lower case is used for articles, coordinate conjunctions, and prepositions unless these are the first or last words in the title.

Underscore any titles which the printer is to set in italics. Use a colon to separate the main title from any subtitle.

Quotation marks are used to set off titles of other works contained in a title: Jeremiah Williams, *Response to "Journey to Seattle."*

For titles of articles in a periodical, chapters in a book, or unpublished works, use quotation marks. Do not underscore.

For newspapers, most often the city is included as part of the title. Underscore to indicate italics. The printer should respect authors who show awareness of which papers do not include their city as part of the title, e.g., *The Times* of London.

Series titles (a series consists in individual volumes or booklets) are capitalized like titles but are neither underscored nor enclosed in quotation marks: Gopi Krishna, *The Secret of Yoga,* Religious Perspectives, ed. Ruth Nanda Anshen (New York: Harper & Row, 1972), p. 16.

Paperback Editions

Although there are many fine paperback editions available to scholars and general readers, the careful academic writer knows from experience that the hardbound edition in the library is the one most likely to be consulted should a reader wish to trace a reference. With this possibility in mind, the author will use hardbound editions as his references. If a paperback edition is necessarily used, the fact should be noted. If the scholar is writing a textbook or other work intended primarily for students, it is helpful to mention the availability of paperback editions, whether the reference is to a hard or a paperbound book.

Facts of Publication

These facts are helpful to the reader who may try to locate the source of a quotation or other information. In a footnote the facts of publication are given in parentheses, as indicated in several previous examples. Full information consists of city, publisher, and date of publication. Again, no punctuation goes before the first parenthesis; a colon separates city from publisher. The closing parenthesis is followed by a comma, then the page number:

Author, *Title* (New York: Pure Tone Press, 1961), p. 23.

The name of the state or country is unnecessary unless the city is not well known or confusion might otherwise occur — e.g., Cambridge. When Cambridge appears alone, the usual assumption is that England is meant. The reference may read (Cambridge: at the University Press, 1949) or simply (Cambridge, 1949); England should not appear. To designate the other Cambridge, use either (Cambridge, Mass: Harvard University Press, 1950) or (Cambridge: Harvard University Press, 1950).

If no place or publisher appears on the title page, the lack of information is indicated by (n.p., 1832). If no date is given, n.d.

Exercise care in spelling and punctuating the names of publishers. In doubt, consult the appropriate list of American publishers in *Books in Print* (R.R. Bowker Co.). For publishers in Great Britain, see *British Books in Print* (J. Whitaker and Sons and R.R. Bowker).

Whether to use the publisher's name or simply the city of publication is, as discussed earlier, a moot question. A point in favor of mentioning the publisher's name is, of course, that it may help the reader. The plan also makes sense for books protected by copyright. In cases where the footnote refers to a quotation for which a publisher has granted permission, the publisher's name must appear.

Dates

Although the date of publication for a book is simply the year, for a periodical more than the year may be needed. If in a bound volume the page numbers run consecutively throughout, the volume in arabic is enough:

> 10. Jeremy Mort, "Second Assignment,"
> *Pastoral Review* 13 (1972): 130-36.

Notice that there is no "p." for page and that a colon separates volume number from page. Also acceptable:

> 11. Jeremy Mort, "Second Assignment,"
> *Pastoral Review* 13:130-36 (October 1972).

Whichever correct form appeals to the author should be observed consistently.

If there is no volume number, use month and year without parentheses:

> 12. Jeremy Mort, "Second Assignment,"
> *Pastoral Review*, October 1972, pp. 130-36.

Strictly speaking, daily newspapers and weekly publications need only day, month, and year. Page numbers may be omitted; in fact, since different editions of an issue may carry stories on different pages, page numbers can be irritating for the reader who wants to trace a story. On the other hand, it can be even more irritating to the user of microfilmed newspaper to trace a reference without the clue a page number provides. For the *New York Times* and *The Times* of London, page numbers, provided the author states which edition he used, are obviously helpful.

About page numbers whenever they are given: be specific. Avoid "f." or "ff." Consider the plight of the reader who is confronted by "p. 3 ff." in reference to a 600 page book. Where might he logically expect the reference to stop?

* * * * * *

Omit facts of publication for well known reference works, but indicate the edition cited if other than the first.

Biblical references include abbreviated book, chapter, and verse--no page numbers: Heb. 12:3 or Matt. 8:1-5.

For poems or plays, if the section, scene, line, or stanza numbers are given, the facts of publication are not essential:

Hamlet, act 2, sc. 1, lines 5-14.

or

Hamlet, 2. 1. 5-14.

If the title of the play or the poem is mentioned in the text, its repetition is unnecessary in the footnote. Even less distracting, in some instances, is the inclusion of act, scene, and line parenthetically in the text.

Classics and Law

Although it is possible to get lost in the exceptions to rules in any scholarly field, two fields themselves are exceptions in the method of citing sources--the classics and law. For the classics, the writer should consult the *Oxford Classical Dictionary* for the list of abbreviations scholars frequently use. The academic writer publishing a legal work checks the Harvard Law Review Association's *Uniform System of Citation.*

Further Exceptions

Still other exceptions arise in the citation of books and articles in the natural sciences and in the treatment of public documents. Questions occurring in these two areas will be taken up later.

By now one may have gathered that there really is no definitive work that covers all the rules and exceptions of documentation. Nor is such a publication likely. Footnotes. may be a condition chronic to serious readers and writers. If there were a universal cure, no one would be struggling with individual cases. Readers who would probe the question more deeply are referred to any or all of three excellent guides which are not always in agreement with one another: A *Manual of Style* published by the University of Chicago Press for authors, editors, and copywriters; Porter G. Perrin's *Writer's Guide and Index to English* (Chicago; Scott, Foresman); *The MLA Style Sheet* produced by the Modern Language Association with copies obtainable through the treasurer of that group at an address listed in PMLA.

FIVE

BIBLIOGRAPHY

At the end of most scholarly works there is a list of references. The list may be called *Bibliography, Works Cited,* or *References,* and it includes works the author thinks significantly related to his own work. In arranging the bibliography the author ought to think of the reader.

Ordinarily a bibliography is arranged alphabetically according to authors' surnames, but if the list is unusually long, the reader might welcome divisions by category. Or the author may help by providing brief comments on each work to guide the reader. Since the author has broken the ground, there is no need for the reader to do so. An annotated bibliography at once informs the reader and saves his time.

Within the individual bibliographical entry these facts are included: names of author, editor, translator, full title of work, series, volume number, edition if other than the first, city, publisher, date. The traditional punctuation mark after each main part is the period:

> Whitney, Anne. *Rewriting a Play.*
> Geneva: Church Press, 1973.

The author's name is inverted, there are no parentheses around the facts of publication. For a book, pages are not mentioned as they would be in the case of an article.

The bibliographical entry for an article includes: author, title of article (may be omitted in scientific references), periodical, volume number, or date, pages on which the article occurs:

> Curley, Chie. "Recovering a Lost
> Technique." *Classical Guitar Review*
> 42:485-89.

If a work has more than one author, the name of the first is always reversed. The others' names may appear in normal order, although some presses prefer to reverse all. Either of these two forms is acceptable when used consistently:

Barber, Fred, Hopwell, Igor, and Olson, Mary

or   Barber, Fred, Igor Hopwell, and Mary Olson

If the author is unknown, list the work by title only, not by "Anon." If the author uses a pseudonym, use the real name with the penname in brackets, since that is how libraries catalogue books, and anyone tracing a source will do so according to this method.

For an "institutional" author:

Ancient Language Association. *Toward Understanding a Language Spoken by Only Ten Elderly Men.* San Francisco: Sauron Co., 1948.

If the editor has served as author, introduce the entry: Plunkett, William, ed. *Early Examples of Printers' Devices.* For an editor plus author: Martin, Samuel. *Early Examples of Printers' Devices.* Edited by William Plunkett. . .

For a translator:
Verenska, Marya. *Love Letters.* Translated by Robert Knauf. . . .

For a volume in a series:

Lamb, Linda. *Expatriates.* Perspectives in Culture, edited by Mitchell Kerr, vol. 5. New York: Calgary Press, 1969.

For an edition after the first:

Egan, Bartholomew. *Studies.* 3rd rev. ed . . . .

The general rules for bibliographies apply to unpublished material, including dissertations and theses. After the title the reader should be informed of the nature of the work:

Swan, Carl. "Evaluation of Summer Programs." Master's thesis, Seattle University, 1973.

If the work has not been published but has been duplicated, indicate after the title–e.g., "Mimeographed." Manuscripts cited in the bibliography should be identified by city, depository, and collection name or number, particularly if such information would assist a serious reader.

SIX

DOCUMENTATION IN THE NATURAL SCIENCES

Considerable heat or light could be generated in a dialogue between scholars in the sciences and those in the humanities on the best ways of citing sources. To the general reader the question may have little significance, but readers blessed (or cursed) with proofreader's eye will have noticed minor stylistic differences between academic writers in the two cultures.

In the sciences footnotes are sometimes used, but more often the writer employs other methods of citing sources. The reference may simply consist in the author's last name and date of publication set in parentheses in the main text, preferably before a punctuation mark but any other place which is logical. Or, the list of references at the end of the book may be numbered and the number of the reference inserted parenthetically in the text whenever the source is cited. This procedure is less immediately clear to the reader, but that inconvenience must be weighed against the possibility of a cluttered looking page if the name and page method is used--a possibility which becomes a probability in a manuscript containing a great number of such references. If the number system is chosen, proofs need careful checking to make sure no mistakes have been made and that the right numbers appear in the text.

The reference list, arranged alphabetically, gives the authors' last names and first initials only:

Multhauf, R.P. 1966. *Origins of chemistry.*
London: Oldbourne.

Notice that the date precedes the title, a fact which makes sense to readers of scientific and technological works. Capitalization within the title resembles that of the sentence–first word only. Underscore the titles of books to indicate italics to the printer. Titles of articles are set in roman type. The scholarly author in the natural sciences may, if he consistently does so, omit the titles of articles.

The facts of publication include, for a book, the city and publisher's name in abbreviated form. (As shown in the previous example, the date appears before the title.) For an article, give the abbreviated name of the journal, underscored, volume number, and run of pages.

> McNeill, A.   Further notes on alchemy.
> *JCE* 9:13-19.

Since abbreviations appear frequently in scientific writing, the author is advised to consult *Chemical Abstracts List of Periodicals.* Any abbreviations in the manuscript which could cause confusion to the reader may be explained in a list at the back of the book.

SEVEN

A NOTE ON PUBLIC DOCUMENTS

Since the reader tracing an author's sources normally goes to a library, and since most libraries subscribe to the National Union Catalogue and the Library of Congress card service, the best plan for the scholarly author to follow is the Library of Congress method of citation for public documents.

According to this method, for "author" give country, state, city, town, or other division, followed by the appropriate legislative body, executive department, court, bureau, board, commission, committee, and any further designation. Items are separated by commas. The author should ask himself how and where the reader might find the public document cited. Everett S. Brown's *Manual of Government Publications* (New York: Appleton-Century-Crofts, 1950) may answer further questions of the author.

EIGHT

RIGHTS AND PERMISSIONS

An editor of a distinguished magazine recently faced a problem, or rather an angry author whose book had received an adverse review in the editor's magazine. The scholar-author had hoped his book would gain a large audience and felt the reviewer had jeopardized his chances. The review, agreed the editor, was unfavorable; yet, it stopped short of libel.

What course is open to an offended author? In periodicals which observe the practice, the author can write a rebuttal to the review. Although such an action may do little to promote the book, it can soothe the author's wounded pride. The sympathetic editor in the case described placated the author with a promise. If ever the reviewer were to publish a book, as he quite likely would, the offended author would enjoy the opportunity to review it in the editor's magazine. (Even Machiavelli, who once declared that a person whom one has offended should not be allowed to live, might have approved such editorial sagacity.) Perhaps it is better to be attacked than to be neglected.

The point illustrated by the story is that once an author has burst into print, his published work is not protected from attack. His properly copyrighted article or book is, however, guarded against theft.

Although it is the publisher's duty to register the copyright, the author ought to know something about the matter — if only because scholars are frequently involved in seeking permission to use copyrighted material. All that is necessary to gain statutory copyright is the publishing of a proper copyright notice. According to the provision of the law, the notice printed at the beginning of the book, on the title page or immediately following must contain the word "Copyright" or "Copr.," or the symbol ©; the copyright holder's name; the year when first published, if the work is literary, musical, or dramatic. These are the main requirements for the page on which copyright appears, for works published in the United States. To be covered under the

Universal Copyright Convention observed by most major countries the symbol © must appear.

Since 1909 the law provides that two copies of the work be deposited in the copyright office "promptly"; however, the term is loosely interpreted to mean any time after publication and before the copyright period has expired. Copyright lasts twenty-eight years and is renewable for a second term of the same length. A completed registration form and a small fee are sent along with the copies of the printed work, to Copyright Office, Library of Congress, Washington, D.C. 20559.

An author who grants the right to publish and sell his work may also give the publisher the exclusive copyright. Should the author wish to copyright the work in his own name, and if the publisher agrees, the publisher is still the one who prepares the registration certificate for the copyright office. Periodicals, unless an author specifically retains copyright, ordinarily own this right. While the author can expect every assistance from the publisher in the procedure of obtaining copyright, the author fends for himself in his own scholarly use of material copyrighted by others.

What is stolen, what legitimately borrowed? Less baldly put, when does an author need to ask permission? Or, what is fair use? These can be thorny questions for the honest scholar, nightmares for the scrupulous.

Copyright protects works from being actually copied. If one were to type or xerox several copies of a book to sell or give away, such action would obviously be literary piracy. Petty larceny is harder to determine. The unauthorized use of eight lines of a poem might violate copyright, especially if the poem is a sonnet. On the other hand, fifty words might be legitimately quoted without permission from a longer work.

The consideration here is not plagiarism, that unscholarly and dishonest use of a source without giving credit, but of the actual quotation or reproduction without permission from the copyright holder. Although some publishers have guidelines on permissible quantity and proportion of reproduction, no absolute rule exists.

In the bad old days before copyright, scholars and everyone else borrowed freely from each other. Before praising the generosity of the ancients, one ought to consider that modern techniques of printing and reproduction have more to do with the change in attitude than contemporary stinginess. Occasionally, even in the twentieth century, instances of pure altruism occur--as in J. Frank Dobie's un-notice of copyright in his *Guide to Life and Literature in the Southwest:*

Not copyright in 1942
Again not copyright in 1952
Anybody is welcome to help himself to any
of it in anyway

How does the scholar determine whether a work is protected by copyright? In a published work, if the year of copyright falls within the past fifty-six years, copyright is probably in effect. For works published in foreign countries subscribing to copyright, the protection lasts for the author's lifetime and usually fifty years after death. Strictly speaking, there is no such thing as an international copyright to guarantee absolutely that an author's work will be protected throughout the world.

Unpublished works are tricky--diaries, or letters, which are usually owned by the recipient but reprinted only with the sender's permission. Some works contain copyright notice and offer clear evidence that someone is claiming protection, but even when an unpublished work contains no such notice, it may be protected by common law copyright.

What works fall clearly outside copyright? In general, published works on which copyright has expired, ideas, plans, or theories, titles and names, obscene and immoral works, government publications. Some might argue on this basis that the best things in life, if not free, are at least in the public domain. Technically, manuscripts are not copyrightable; scholars should beware of anyone offering--for a fee--to secure copyright for their unpublished work.

The practical problem is when to seek permission, mindful that the publisher will ask whether the author has exercised care not to violate anyone else's copyright. To help scholars the Association of American University Presses passed a resolution on permissions:

1. That publications issued under our imprints may be quoted without specific prior permission in works of original scholarship for accurate citation of authority or for criticism, review, or evaluation, subject to the conditions listed below.

2. That appropriate credit be given in the case of each quotation.

3. That waiver of the requirement for specific permission does not extend to quotations that are complete units in themselves (as poems, letters, short stories, essays, journal articles, complete chapters or sections of books, maps, charts, graphs, tables, drawings,

or other illustrative materials), in whatever form they may be reproduced, nor does the waiver extend to quotation of whatever length presented as primary material for its own sake (as in anthologies or books of readings).

4.   The fact that specific permission for quoting of material may be waived under this agreement does not relieve the quoting author and publisher from the responsibility of determining fair use of such material.

Among the signers of the resolution are:

> The University of Arizona Press
> Bollingen Foundation
> The Brookings Institution
> Brown University Press
> University of California Press
> The Press of Case Western Reserve University
> The University of Chicago Press
> Columbia University Press
> Cornell University Press
> Duke University Press
> Duquesne University Press
> Fordham University Press
> The University of Georgia Press
> University of Hawaii Press
> The University of Illinois Press
> Indiana University Press
> The Iowa State University Press
> The John Hopkins Press
> The University Press of Kansas
> University of Kentucky Press
> Louisiana State University Press
> McGill University Press
> The University of Massachusetts Press
> The M.I.T. Press
> The Metropolitan Museum of Art
> University of Miami Press
> The Michigan State University Press
> University of Missouri Press
> University of Nebraska Press
> The University of New Mexico Press

New York University Press
University of North Carolina Press
Northwestern University Press
University of Notre Dame Press
Ohio University Press
Ohio State University Press
University of Pennsylvania Press
Pennsylvania State University Press
Princeton University Press
Smithsonian Institution
University of South Carolina Press
Southern Illinois University Press
Southern Methodist University Press
Stanford University Press
Syracuse University Press
University of Tennessee Press
University of Texas Press
University of Toronto Press
Vanderbilt University Press
University Press of Virginia
University of Washington Press
Wayne State University Press
The University of Wisconsin Press
Yale University Press

If part of the author's own work has been previously published, he must contact his former publisher for permission to reprint, unless the copyright is retained in the author's name. Even so, the original publication should be duly noted. In the process of writing the book, a careful author will keep on record any copyright owners whose permission he may need. Sometimes the granting of such permissions takes incredibly long; yet, a publisher wants to be sure these permissions are in before setting type.

Who pays the fees when material is charged? The author, unless his publisher says otherwise in writing. In instances of quotation for which permission is unnecessary, the author simply credits the source either in the text of his book or in a note. It is axiomatic that a writer should not misinterpret another's opinion for the sake of his own argument.

Fair Use

Though aware of all these burdens, the scholar should not lose heart. The copyright holder may have rights; so does the scholar--specifically, the right of fair use.

If the quotation is prose, not an entity in a larger work, and if using it does not diminish the value of the original, should the author seek permission? Probably not. As the University of Chicago Press Manual of Style declares: "The right of fair use is a valuable one and should not be allowed to decay through failure of scholars to employ it boldly." (12th ed., 1969, p. 93).

In doubt, the author ought to screw his courage to the sticking point. In court cases, the criteria for fair use are: type of use, amount of material and proportion, relative value, degree to which use may adversely effect sales. The burden of proof rests with the holder of the copyright, who may reason, as did Charles Schulz after the piracy of *Peanuts,* that it is better to be worth stealing from than not.

A woman whose next door neighbor had just published a book recently denied another neighbor's request to borrow: "I'll be blunt. I want her book to sell. So buy your own copy." While no one would say that borrowing a single book seriously diminishes its chances, what about wholesale borrowing made possible by photocopying techniques?

When works had to be copied by hand, there would have been more cases of writers' cramp than violations of the doctrine of fair use. But now even a churchgoer might find a photocopied hymnal in the pew, let the holy anthem rise, and violate a composer's or publisher's right.

On the other hand, fair use seems to cover a library's right to microfilm, particularly if a book is rare and might deteriorate from handling. (Who would believe the horror story of chocolate bars munched in a rare book room, if that truth were told here?) To make many copies of a book for distribution to a class would be unfair use. Such an act, however noble the ideal of sharing knowledge, substitutes for the original work and will interfere with sales.

Fair use covers quotations in review or critical articles, as well as longer works. The publisher who once complained that every Ph.D. season his firm was besieged with request to quote even the most trivial passages was giving scholars the hint to let common sense as well as honesty guide their choices. Sensitive authors need encouragement to take arms against a sea of permissions. Fair use is fair use.

When there is no help for it and the author knows it is only fair to seek permission, how may he expedite the matter? Some publishers provide their own forms. In any event, requests must be written and sent in duplicate and must include the title of the work and the page number of the desired quotation. The author should describe the work in which the material will appear. This description gives title, approximate length, form, publisher, probable date and price, and anything special about the rights requested.

Scholars who contemplate producing an anthology or a casebook may face considerable expense in the form of deductions from their royalties. Again, the publisher may share some of these costs, but prices here, as everywhere else, are rising. The anthologist is advised to use original texts, uncopyrighted, or on which the terms of copyright have expired. Perhaps for not very mysterious reasons some anthologies are relatively thin in works published during the last fifty-six years. If the book is to be a twentieth century anthology, the author may hope its popularity will more than compensate for the burden of seeking and paying for permissions.

As for the casebook, a phenomenon which has appeared during the past few years and which offers students a wide range of information on a subject in the space of a single book, permission fees may run high. The editor of a casebook on Hawthorne may freely use the original nineteenth century texts, reprinting a number of short stories without permission. Permission must be sought, however, from the holders of copyright on any critical essays which must be used if the editor wants the casebook to be up to date. The figure quoted by the editor of just such a casebook she published in 1963 was $800.00. When the same editor brought out a casebook on a twentieth century novelist in 1968 the fee was $2000.00. These facts are mentioned not to dismay potential scholarly editors, but to inform and prepare them.

NINE

SCHOLARLY REPRINTING

Many university presses regularly allow titles to go out of print, even out of copyright. Once copyright has expired, a work is in the public domain and can never be copyrighted again. Such a work may be reprinted by a scholarly reprint publisher--or publishers--since the work is no longer protected even when reprinted. To guard against this sort of duplication and competition, many scholarly reprint publishers prefer to seek permission from the original publisher to reprint titles still covered by copyright and to pay whatever royalties are due. Of course, if the title is in the original publisher's own backlist of out of print books and is within the period of copyright, the publisher may simple reissue the work.

Because university presses do not aim at the mass market, books are printed in limited numbers. Works of lasting value can become scarce or unavailable after a few years and deserve reprinting. Monographs and articles, too, may exist in such small quantities that the demand will one day exceed the supply. Scholarly reissues, in print or microfilm, are thus a boon to private scholars and university libraries. See Carol A. Nemeyer's *Scholarly Reprint Publishing in the United States* (New York: R.R. Bowker, 1972) for a comprehensive survey of an industry important to academic readers and writers. Bowker, a respected name in publishing, is also a Xerox company.

TEN

CONTRACTS

The scholar should have a general knowledge of publication agreements, in the hope that such information will assume practical meaning. If, for example, an author enters into a royalty agreement, he receives a percentage of the sales, either of the list (retail) price or of the publisher's net receipts. A sale of rights, on the other hand, is a once and for all payment to the author for turning over copyright and all other rights and interests in the work. All sales profits then go to the publisher.

Occasionally, a new publishing house offers stock option agreements. In such a profit sharing arrangement, the author is given a certain number of shares when he signs the contract and may subsequently buy more stock at reduced rates. Finally, there is the subsidy publishing agreement. The author pays the publisher to print the book and receives several hundred copies. If the book sells, the author may claim royalties up to eighty percent. Although it is true that many fine books have been printed privately and distributed by their authors, a writer considering such a course ought to remember that the trade name for firms specializing in this field is "vanity" publishing houses. The publisher risks nothing; the author bears the expenses.

There is a legitimate place for private and subsidized publishing, but it does not come under "vanity" publishing. Increasingly, the cost of publication has forced specialized publishers to ask authors to make concessions: no royalty paid on the first thousand or more copies sold; less than standard royalty; a flat amount of royalty paid. In some instances, predicated on the fact that the author is likely to receive a salary increase based on the work being published, some presses ask for financial contributions to offset the cost of publishing. The author is caught in the middle, under these circumstances. Old line commercial publishers will reject the manuscript with a statement, "We do not feel we could realize enough in sales to satisfy you or ourselves." The temptation, therefore, is strong to look to private publication.

Only the naive will resort to "vanity" publication and little will follow in taking such a step. Under the circumstances, it is well to consult with book specialists — editors and agents — who can advise what solutions are available that will serve more scholarly purposes.

The language of contracts between publisher and scholar varies, but some general observations are possible. The author gives the publisher the full exclusive right to publish and promote the book. Unless the publisher agrees to secure copyright in the author's name, the author also turns over this right. The author promises to have the finished manuscript by the deadline in a form ready for editor and typesetter; however, art work, illustrations, and, of course, the index need not be in final form at this time. The length of the manuscript should approximate that specified originally. If the author is unable to deliver the manuscript by the date set, he should notify his publisher at once.

In warranting sole ownership of the manuscript, the author assumes liability for any claim or suit brought against the publisher. This means not only that an author must observe the copyright of authors but that his work should be free of libelous material. Some limitation should be put on the author's warranty; a phrase such as "to the author's knowledge" or "so far as the author knows" will be enough. If "by reason of a final judgment" is included, the author's liability is limited to only successful suits in which there have been court decisions. Money from book sales may be withheld from an author until a court case is settled.

Sometimes the publisher asks the scholar to let the firm have his next book. In such a situation the author is obliged, if he accepts the invitation, to submit his next manuscript. The contract should provide that he is free to send his work elsewhere unless the new manuscript is accepted for publication within a reasonable and specified amount of time, say not more than ninety days.

The author may negotiate with the publisher for the date of publication, but usually the contract contains no specific date. Even if the author is given some idea of when to expect publication, the publisher decides when and how to distribute the book. Here again the publisher is the author's ally and can call upon a reserve of promotional people whose sense of timing will help the book. Also among publishers' rights are selection of paper, print, binding, and the setting of price. Before the contract is signed, the author ought to bring up any suggestions he has which he thinks may belong in the contract.

After publication, the author receives some complimentary copies and may buy further copies at a discount indicated in the contract. When the book has been out for a reasonable time and sales justify it, the publisher may ask the author to produce a revised edition. This eventuality is covered in the original contract; if the author is unable or unwilling to comply, the publisher may assign the work to another author. If, on the other hand, the supply of the book eventually exceeds the demand for copies, the publisher may decide to remainder (sell at a reduced rate) and let the book go out of print. With this possibility in mind, the author should see that the contract specifies that all rights for his out of print book return to him.

Some contracts bind the author against competing with himself and his publisher by producing a work elsewhere that would diminish the sales of the book. This provision may be qualified, but the publisher and the author need a clear understanding when they draw up the contract.

A case of misunderstanding occurred recently when a noted theologian was lecturing to the public. The lecture itself, with editing, was to appear in a periodical within the next two months. Imagine the chagrin of publisher and editor as they sat in the wings and heard the speaker grant indulgence to those in the audience he saw diving to retrieve their tape recorders. Frank discussion before can prevent such an accident.

The publisher, as bearer of the financial burden, is the prime risk taker. Even before publication, the author may receive an advance. If the advance is outright, it is a gift to the author. In an advance against royalties, the publisher makes deductions for the cost of permission fees, author's alterations, etc., from the first royalty payment. Scholarly books do not usually attract large outright advances except in the case of an established author for whom two or more publishers might be vying.

Another matter to consider, although it is ordinarily less vital in scholarly or technical books, is that of subsidiary rights. These rights may cover serialization, written condensations, book clubs, foreign editions in English, reprints by other publishers, anthologies, microfilm and microcard, advertising, movies, television, radio, and stage. Frequently publisher and author share proceeds from the sale of subsidiary rights, but these rights are negotiable. An author with an eye to future developments might retain certain subsidiary rights. Although it is unlikely that a scholarly article will be transformed into a movie, it is quite possible that the composer of an anthology or a casebook may be interested in reprinting an article or a section of a longer work.

The publisher reports book sales to the author and, under the royalty agreement, sends him a check. Since royalties have a natural fascination for authors, further information might prove useful. The amount paid the author is a percentage (often ten percent) of the list price of the book, or a percentage based on net receipts. (Before signing a net receipts contract, the author should ask about publishers discounts to booksellers.) Ten to fifteen percent of the net receipts is the usual rate for academic books. According to some contracts, the percentage increases with the sale of books.

A point to remember about royalties: if they are too high, the book and the author may be the losers. Producing and promoting a book is an expensive adventure, the cost of which must be covered by book sales.

If in the process of working on his book the author is incapacitated, he is normally free of the contract. If the publisher delays reasonably in bringing out the book, the firm may be at fault and the contract cancelled. Such a delay may well spring from circumstances beyond the publisher's control--a paper shortage or a printers' strike--for which he cannot be blamed. In any case, the author should not try to cancel a contract without first obtaining legal advice as to whether a publisher might be considered at fault.

More positively--besides responsibilities spelled out in the contract, there are other ways a scholarly author can help the cause. The publishing house has a department devoted to book sales, but the author may also provide material for advertising. Knowing better than anyone else the nature of his work and its intended audience, the author might recommend journals in which a review would help. Or he might furnish a list of names of those to whom promotional material should be sent. Most of the time publishers will welcome these suggestions, especially from a tactful author who realizes the existence of budgetary limitations in promoting a book.

The publisher may send complimentary copies to scholars in the field. If a recipient favorably reviews or endorses a work, the publisher may want to use quotations from the review or endorsement to advertise the book. The publisher must of course obtain the endorsing scholar's permission before quoting him in this way.

Authors with further questions on the legal aspects of scholarly publication should consult John C. Hogan and Saul Cohen's *Author's Guide to Scholarly Publishing and the Law* (Englewood Cliffs, N.J.: Prentice-Hall, Inc., 1965). The remarks in the sections on rights, permissions, and contracts are consistent with those found in that slim, excellent volume.

ELEVEN

A NOTE ON ARTICLES

"If only," said the weary director of dissertations, "the university would drop the dissertation requirement and instead demand three articles of publishable quality. One of the articles might *be* published." Few writers write with the intention of not being published. For academic writers publication can be crucial: university teachers may be hired to do one job but are often paid and promoted according to how they do another. A deserving and lucky scholar may live to see his dissertation published as a book. More than likely, however, his work will be preserved on microfilm in the university library.

To the recent writer of a dissertation, published or not, the thought of beginning another work of book length can be dismaying. Added to this natural and understandable reluctance may be the pressures of a new teaching job. Perhaps it is consoling to junior members of a department to think that scholars whose careers are more advanced, and whose teaching schedules may be reduced to encourage further publication, do not always have a book in mind, either. This is as it should be, since pedantry consists in the use of intellectual means where they do not fit, and such a use is the expansion of a topic to book length, when it could more appropriately be covered in an article. Even authors who are at work on a real book may during the process want--or need--to write shorter works for journals in their fields.

Scholars come to know periodicals likely to publish their works through their own research, the advice of colleagues, and lists and manuals offered by some journals. The *Publication Manual of the American Psychological Association*, for example, gives in addition to practical advice on style a descriptive list of the association's various journals.

Whether the manual or style sheet is the *Writing of American Military History or The Writing of Geography* or *The MLA Style Sheet*, the point on which all agree is the need for clarity. The opaque style practiced by some academic writers only demonstrates that need. If an article is unclear, the reader may misinterpret the author's intention.

Clear writing is a sign of sound thinking. The author of a book has time and space to clarify thought; the writer of an article lacks that leisure. To draw an analogy from the writing of fiction, a novel with its several themes differs in more than length from a short story compressed to present a single theme. In the shorter work, the first sentence leads more directly to the last.

Every scholar-author, whether as a student or a teacher, has probably made some use of a manual on research and report writing. Many of these manuals are helpful, but some are misleading in a beautifully Platonic way. For it is, or can be, misleading to think of the scholar as first having an idea, then testing it, almost at the second step removed from reality, in the laboratory or library, and finally writing it up, by now three steps removed from the reality of his original idea. Some articles and reports appear to have been written by this method; their readers feel the considerable descent from the first idea or theory to the dull plains of the final version. A charitable reader may decide the author's thinking is simply beyond him, but a critical reader--like the undreamy editor of a learned journal--may wonder whether the author's thinking was clear in the first place.

Much sound thinking is not clear in the first place and becomes so only after examination and change. A practical way to examine and perhaps change one's thought is to write it out, at least roughly, before it may seem time to begin writing. Obedience to the lock-step of idea-research, writing-up is no sub-stitute for the virtue of clarity. True, according to F.R. Leavis, "the mark of the genuine research student is that he has something he wants to do," but that something if often modified and developed during research and actual writing. Since language guides judgment a stint of writing before the research is finished encourages reflection on what one is doing. Such a plan may prove particularly helpful to the reluctant writer who confesses, "I like research but hate writing the results." If writing is regarded as a last minute chore after the amassing of all relevant, and some irrelevant, data, then the "results" suffer. So does the reader-from the writer's value language or pseudo-jargon, or from that style of technical discourse which conceals not thought but the absence of thought.

An author willing to do some writing during the time devoted to thesis-and-research can begin to test his ability to meet his colleague's arguments with reason and finesse. All along, he will have been developing the attribute of any good prose writer--knowing the minds of others. According to the British Royal Society, "An author should write, not for the half dozen people in the world specially interested in his line of work but for the hundred or so who may be interested in some aspect of it if the paper is well written."

How to attract that audience of a hundred--or more, as some scholars might hope? In his useful manual *The Writing of Geography* (Manchester University Press, 1971), T.W. Freeman says, "The prime need is to write everything down straightaway." In geography, this means actual sketches, maps, interview notes, information that at the moment may seem useless. At the same time, Freeman advises the student, a scholar should be searching for relationships and crystallizing his findings as the fieldwork proceeds. This method calls for writing on the job, then writing at leisure, setting the paper aside after it is "finished," and going back to it again. An author in scrutinizing his work asks whether the article is a real contribution to the field covered by a journal, is as clear and brief as it should be, and is in proper form for the printer.

Another practical detail which ought not to be put off is the study of the conventions of the journal for which the article is intended. Recent issues should be scanned to detect changes in editorial policy. In some periodicals acceptable articles are growing shorter: one technical journal which formerly ran articles of 7000 words now features articles of 5000 or even 3000 words. Any helpful information published inside the front cover should not be overlooked.

Readers might expect, if they do not always find, good style in journals in the humanities, especially in languages. Actually, good writing is to be expected in every field. A manual on the writing of American military history, for example, advises authors to correct ambiguity, jargon, and sentences that require two readings through the study of models like the "simple and lucid prose" of Bertrand Russell. Editors of scientific periodicals are also concerned about how articles are written, since bad scientific writing is often the outward sign of an inward confusion of thought.

According to research scholar and editor F.P. Woodford, "In the linked worlds of experimental science, scientific editing, and scientific communication many scientists are wondering just how serious an effect the bad writing in out journals will have on the future of science." The poor writer "takes what should be lively, inspiring and beautiful and, in an attempt to make it seem dignified, chokes it to death. . .buries the stiff old mummy with much pomp and circumstance in the most distinguished journal that will take it" *(Science* 156: 743–45). In the belief that most poor writing is accomplished without the author's clear perception of how bad results are achieved, editor and astronomer Paul Merrill suggests these elements of poor style: ignore the reader, be verbose, vague, pompous, and never revise *(Scientific Monthly* 64:72-74). Bad writing shuns the clarity of a statement, "Three stars are white," and prefers to say, "In three instances the stars are white in color."

The author of good articles, on the other hand, achieves clarity by thinking often of the reader, the field, the purpose of the article, what conclusions can be drawn, and the significance of these conclusions. An article intended for a journal with highly limited circulation will differ from an article for a periodical with wider circulation; the writer must be aware of how knowledgeable an audience is likely to be. Whether or not he is a teacher, a scholar has a responsibility to students in the field. As one scholar says, "How can we hope to have our students think straight if we can't send them to the most celebrated journal in the country without cautioning them about the wooly thinking they will find there?"

Whatever their field, scholarly writers might think of ways to brighten the gloomy vision described by Jacques Barzun in his *House of Intellect:* "The change which is overtaking English is not simplification and clarification but obscurity, pretension and pedantry." If there is a crisis in language, scholars can help by wasting no words.

Article writing is an opportunity to achieve a tight, coherent style. The article writer may also be remotely preparing for a future book, since constructing a shorter work serves as practice for handling the book unit or chapter. A longer article — thirty or more pages — has its own "chapters" or parts indicated by numbers, subheads, or blank spaces. In a shorter paper or review of 1500 words, the parts are simply the paragraphs, usually about a dozen.

An author's failure to link paragraphs in an article may be more noticeable than it would be in a book, since there are obviously fewer paragraphs in an article. Not that a topic sentence must inevitably be present, but some core must exist within the paragraph. It helps, too, if the last sentence of a paragraph suggests the first sentence of the next.

Articles offer fewer chances than books for the use of long quotations, and the judicious writer will weave brief quotations into his text. Accuracy in quoting a source is essential: someone once estimated that writers who do not collate their copy with its sources have a one in ten chance of making a mistake. Perhaps strangely, brighter and more perceptive writers are most likely to err. A good way to catch such slips before they appear glaringly in print is to press a friend into the service of following the typescript while the writer reads the original quotation, including the punctuation marks.

Blunders in articles may not be more serious than in books, but they can be more conspicuous.

Some errors in the typescript are likely, so likely that editors are chary of "perfect" pages which carry no written in corrections. The impression such a paper can give is that the author has failed to give his work that final careful proofreading which often turns up mistakes.

In proofreading his work the author might pretend he is a barbarian puzzling over words of a ccivilized writer. Better, the proofreading author should imagine himself as the civilized critic examining the savings of a barbarian. This is not to say the author should look upon his work with hostility or despair (after all, according to H.D.F. Kitto, the term *barbarian* in its origins carried no overtones of savagery but simply categorized people who said "bar bar" instead of speaking Greek), but that the judgment of one's own work requires a little distance, even the gift of alienation. People need all the uncritical love they can get, as Kurt Vonnegut says; but manuscripts need critical attention.

If a writer cares about his work, and it is to be hoped that he does, then only a lapse of time or an act of will can make that work seem sufficiently foreign to him to allow objectivity. An author who cannot shake the notion that what he has written is his flesh and blood (it is), might emulate Shelley who, upon looking out a window at some children playing is said to have asked, "Whose children are those?" to which his wife Mary answered, "They are your children." The proofreading and revising writer should keep asking, "Whose work is this?" Then, at the end of the proofreading and revision, when it is too late and too expensive to make further changes, the author can rediscover the work as his own and take appropriate pleasure in the recognition.

A last word about the first words of the article: the title. Although some parents pick out names before the birth of their offspring, others wait to see the child. The writer of an article ought to be equally careful in choosing a title, listing possible names as the work is in progress but waiting until the paper is finished to give it a final title. If the writer of a book is stuck, he can expect some editorial help in the choice of a name, but the editor of a scholarly journal may prove a less likely source of help. Probably a periodical editor sees many articles on the same subject and needs to be sold on the particular merits of this article; a good title is influential in the selling. Consider, too, that most readers tend to remember books they have read but more readily forget shorter works like essays and reports, especially if their reading covers a number of articles on the same subject. Any device that fixes an article in the mind of its scholarly audience--and a title is such a device-- aids the author who wants his work remembered and cited by other authors. A good title is clear and descriptive without undue length. Brevity helps, although it is not an absolute. Even great writers have trouble with titles: "Call the poem anything you like," the teacher said to the student writing an essay on the Tintern Abbey poem, "but do not call it what Wordsworth did--*Lines.*"

Once the article has been submitted, and if the journal is operating at peak efficiency, the writer may expect to hear whether his work is accepted within a reasonable time—say, two months. Articles are published according to the journal's lag, which many periodicals try to keep down to a year. Timeliness and relationship to other articles may determine the date of appearance rather than the chronological order in which articles are received.

Another bonus to the article writer is that one thing often leads to another, essential to the discipline of writing. A short paper at least means staying in practice and may even contain an idea for another work. This idea should not be immediately pursued but jotted down for preservation, unless it so overwhelms the author that *it* is the subject of the article that should have been begun in the first place. For the scientist, such a moment may occur during the writing up of an experiment that fails to go as one thought it would, for here, as Pasteur advised his students, discoveries are to be made. Whatever the field, the rare moment should be just that--and not simply an excuse for the author to avoid work at hand.

Scholars, like all writers and even doers of crossword puzzles, sooner or later get stuck. Beginning an article is no guarantee against writers' block, but it does have all the promise of a good start. The word is always in the beginning; writing is always work in progress.

AFTERWORD

Scholarly authors, it is hoped, will have found the general and specific information offered in this manual helpful. By way of final, practical recommendation, an academic writer--or scholar interested in becoming one-- might do well to examine works published by a given scholarly press or learned journal. During a professional career, a scholar may have gained such information almost by osmosis, but it may be useful to identify certain characteristics. If, for example, a periodical seems to favor articles of a certain type and length, or a scholarly press seems saturated in some areas, an author can decide where to submit his work or how to modify it.

A writer who has finished a work or has one in progress might also check whether a press or journal has its own manual, handbook, or style sheet. The University of Chicago, to cite a particular press, has published its *Manual of Style,* which the present manual gratefully acknowledges.

Yet, to examine books published by a scholarly press, to pursue the specifications of one more periodical, to locate one more style sheet--all are preliminary steps. None will substitute for the actual writing.

The Writer's Manual
Book 12

How to
Style Manuscripts
for
Articles and Books

By
Jack C. Dierks

ABOUT THE AUTHOR

Jack Dierks

a partner of the authors' agency

Porter, Gould & Dierks,

draws on a wide range of experience

In the writing of

"How to Style Manuscripts for Articles and Books"

after taking an MS at Northwestern University's Medill School of Journalism,

he has worked as a magazine editor,

in writing for the public relations and advertising fields,

as a free lance writer of articles and two books.

A consumate researcher, meticulous in his use of all writing mechanica,

his study of the Spanish-American War of 1898,

A Leap to Arms,

is a highly readable account that is both scholarly and written with elan.

CONTENTS

The quotations on pages 834, 837, 838, 842 and 849

are from A *Leap to Arms: The Cuban Campaign of 1898*

and other works in progress by Jack C. Dierks.

ONE

The Style of the Seventies

What do we mean when we talk about "style"? Most of us can probably define the word correctly --- the "face" or personal character an individual offers to the world --- yet when the term is applied to an author it comes to represent all this and something much more, too; and that something is so important to both the writer and the audience he is trying to reach, that it can be said to make up the whole essence of his work.

If we want to, we might break it down into three separate meanings. They are style as a set of personal characteristics, as a creative technique, and as that deciding factor that transforms mere words on paper into lasting literature. Almost everyone, for instance, who has read widely has learned to recognize something that stands out as clearly as the Hemingway method of writing --- the short, terse sentences, the lean dialogue, the swift-moving story line --- and when we do that what we are seeing is the personal stamp "Papa" put on his work; his own readily distinguishable nature and spirit. We needn't pass judgment on its quality at this point; whether it appeals to us or not isn't the question here; we are simply recognizing it as something highly individual. Music lovers can pick out a piece by Bach or Chopin instantly by each composer's structure, melodic form and use of the instruments at his disposal. Others can be equally certain that what they are seeing in a gallery is an El Greco or a Gauguin by the way that artist put paint to canvas. The writer, we must always remember, "signs his name" in the same way by his use of words.

Now style in this sense is not something that makes its appearance overnight. It develops and evolves and nurtures itself throughout a writer's career. It is, after all, the sum of his experience, his outlook on life, and the way that he has learned to communicate these things over the years. Anyone who has read the later works of Henry James will be aware of the increasingly elaborate and intricate modes he used to transmit his subtle ideas and emotions; to the point where he became almost a parody of himself at times. Whether or not James tried consciously to build upon and over-refine his earlier way of writing is questionable, but we might make it a rule for ourselves right now that it's not a particularly good idea. Obvious attempts to cultivate your strong points often result in the ruin of what qualities you possess through faulty emphasis and exaggeration, usually because you as the author are so often unable to analyze just what your good and bad points are. A distinctive style is far more of an unconscious outpouring than many of us realize, and for this reason it's an equally unwise idea to try to copy someone else's. For what you are aping really is that individual's way of thinking and of looking at the world. Be individual, above all, and soon you will develop your own uniqueness.

The second meaning of style --- the creative technique --- becomes more clear when we begin to make certain critical judgments about a piece of work we read. The author's ideas may be gripping enough to hold our attention, and yet there's something about the way he puts them down on paper that we feel could be improved. We are now talking about him as a craftsman (which every writer is, of course); about his use of the English language; about his acquired skills. What we read strikes us as good, or bad, or indifferent, but at any rate we are examining it as *critic*. Some have made the claim that fiction ought to be immune from this type of critical examination; if a story or poem is well conceived, it rises above the accusation of being badly written, for it is in some way sanctified by the conception and creation itself. Now I don't agree with this way of thinking, and I bring it up because it seems to be a good example of the kind of "sacred cow" attitude that many authors have about their novels, plays, and short stories, and which often keeps them from developing the expertise they might otherwise acquire. The novice writer really can't afford this way of thinking. I might summon up an inspired novel, and yet write it abominably. Do my sentences and paragraphs have the right to be considered holy and untouchable, just because I have created them? Nonsense.

What, then, are the ingredients of a good style? Anyone who has done any reading at all will be aware of how tastes change with the times. The leisurely "three-decker" novel that was in fashion a hundred years ago is certainly *outre* now, and so are many of the plot techniques and choices of word and expression that were considered fine writing at the time. Nevertheless they appealed to the audiences of the day, and their authors, old-fashioned though they may seem to us now, were in tune with their world. They are, after all, universal requirements for quality that remain unchanged. To begin with, a writer must be clear in what he is trying to say. He must put what he is attempting to get across down on paper in an easily understood way; if he makes his audience reread and puzzle over his meaning, then he has failed in his job.

It has been said that "style is perfect when communication of thought or action is perfectly accomplished." The important question is how can such a meeting of minds be brought about, and the answer is that in order to achieve clarity, a writer must put every sentence and paragraph he has written under close scrutiny. Is the meaning as clear to the reader as it is to him? "Talking level" in this way is a talent all its own. Some of the brightest people you can imagine never master it. A writer must. Ambiguity and inexactitude of phrase, of sentence, of word choice is often the result of just laziness. The author may be trying to rush through what he is saying, and this can be a form of contempt for his readership, most of whom are perfectly able to recognize bad writing when they see it.

He must keep in mind that nowadays especially the competition for audience attention --- both from printed matter and other media --- is to the death. A reader will choose the material that gives him the greatest value and pleasure for time and effort expended. Do you really suppose that your ideas are so compelling that he will take the trouble to wade through a morass of muddy language in order to glean the nugget you have hidden there? And, what is just as important, neither will a literary agent or the editors at the publishing house where you submit your material. You'll certainly have to pass their scrutiny before you ever reach that Book-of-the-Month buyer. To be simple yet clear is one of a writer's most difficult tasks. It's much easier to say something elaborately, for simplicity requires putting down the essence of each thought, and to do this a writer must understand it all perfectly before he sits down at the typewriter.

The second quality the writer must have is *force* and *emphasis,* in other words, simply to say things as strongly and decisively as possible. This has nothing to do with the continual use of exclamation points, or the adoption of a strident tone through his work, but rather the indispensable knack for saying things emphatically when emphasis is called for. Decide what impact each statement, paragraph, page, and chapter is to have on the reader. From then on it is a matter of choice and selection, which is in turn a matter of the experience which can only be gained through hard work and the continual acceptance and rejection of possibilities. It's one of the prime qualities that separates competent, effective prose from the mediocre.

Color is the third essential ingredient that differentiates between good, punchy writing and that which is merely a sea of words on a page. An author who has learned how to use the bright phrase, the striking statement, can hold a reader's attention even if the latter has no real interest in the subject matter. On the other hand, a book, article, or story that lacks this quality will bring forth reader yawns even if he is basically interested in the topic discussed. Color comes largely from word choice. Don't be afraid of the offbeat and the unusual, as long as your meaning comes through. Vary the structure of your writing, too. Mix short sentences in with lengthy ones, brief paragraphs with longer; break up the pace and keep up the interest.

Above all, flee the monotonous as you would the plague. The dull author is often a lazy one; a workman who falls into the habit of saying things in a mechanical way because it is easier. And let's face it, being dull is much, much easier. One question should be continually running through your mind, until the asking of it becomes second nature: Can I say this better than I have? More colorfully, more forcefully, more originally? Explore all the possibilities. Write and then rewrite. No author worth his royalty check can ever afford to assume that the first draft that comes out of his typewriter is the best he can do. There are people who publish prolifically who appear to write this way, but that doesn't disprove the point; if they rewrote, they would probably turn out an even better product. Use variety and select words and phrases carefully that are bouncy and energetic, and which relay the impression you want the reader to take away. *Don't* try to add color by throwing in adjectives and adverbs. It must come from within the material; not from something extra painted on.

If we have seen how style can first of all be described as a display of a writer's personal characteristics, and secondly as his basic writing technique, we must combine the two to produce the third definition --- style as literature in its highest form. The latter is a quality that rises above the personal, yet needs that individuality in order to manifest itself. As J. Middleton Murry in *The Problem of Style* puts it: "Style, in this absolute sense, is a complete fusion of the personal and the universal. A great writer is never more intensely and recognizably himself than in his greatest passages; to use a vaguely metaphysical phrase, absolute style is the absolute realization of a universal significance in a personal and particular expression."

To the novice author, all this may sound a bit intimidating. Perhaps all he wants to do is to turn out good, marketable material. He may -- though we hope not -- even believe he has had his fill of *belles lettres,* especially if the classics have been presented to him as ineffectually as they sometimes are in English literature courses. But as mentioned earlier, the deliberate striving for a "great" style, for "deathless" prose can be self-defeating. It is when the writer tries to do the best job possible with his descriptive matter, his expositions, his arguments, his dialogue, plumbing the depths of his own experience and personality to bring out the best that is in him, that he had the greatest chance of creative success.

And who knows? A piece of real literature may emerge in the process.

TWO

TYPES OF WRITING

It may seem strange to suggest that something like style might be divided into rough general designations (since it would seem that something so broad might encompass anybody who ever wrote, and anything these myriad individuals had to say) yet it can be done, and the deciding factor here is the audience to which written matter is to be directed. Several authorities have divided written English into categories which have been designated as General, Formal, Informal, and Non-Standard, and there's no reason why we can't do so as well, since these terms define the differences as well as any.

General English is the most commonly seen, and would include what we normally write in our letters, and read in our newspapers, magazines, and books which are aimed at a wide audience. General English usually employs a vocabulary which is familiar to almost anyone who is at all educated, and its words refer to people, places, things, events, and actions rather than to abstract matter. It employs relatively short sentences, and lends itself especially well to the narrative form dealing with personal experience, with people, with action, either in fiction or non-fiction:

> The south face of the mountain was the worst climb, but the only passable one at that particular season. Conditions weren't good for any of the routes, of course, because of the high winds that blew almost continually at the altitude where we would be climbing. The cold was particularly fierce when combined with these gales. Much of the face was quite steep, especially when one was burdened with oxygen equipment.

Formal English, on the other hand, is usually found in books and articles written for specific groups -- doctors, lawyers, scientists, teachers -- and others having specialized interests and knowledge. Writing of this type uses a more formal vocabulary and sentence construction and has a definite erudite "tone" about it. Words may appear which are seldom used in ordinary speech and communication, specialized terminology is employed, or words that are general in nature but closely associated with the literary tradition. Sentences may be longer and more involved; allusions to the classics and the past may show up with regularity, as well as foreign words and phrases with which the audience may be expected to be familiar. Although it has a different impact -- deliberately fostered -- from the casual approach of General English, it is not necessarily dull or difficult to get through, but it does appeal to a more limited leadership. Concentration is needed, and it assumes a certain cultural level and interest and knowledge in rather specialized subject matter. In some scholarly and scientific writing a very specialized vocabulary is employed, and though Formal English can be confused and pedantic at times, full of official jargon, it is often the best way to communicate certain information, incomprehensible as it may seem to the ordinary reader:

It seems obvious that very significant changes had taken place in the armor of this period, which caused it to be quite different in appearance from that which preceded it. The substantial pauldrons, flamboyant coudieres, and overall angularity which was so characteristic of the later Tabard period had rather abruptly evolved into a smoother, more rounded style, while at the same time losing that classic form which, however it was distorted by exhibitionistic details, contributed so much to the character of Gothic armor.

Informal English, though it is at the opposite pole in style, also presupposes a close and continuing relationship between the writer and the reader, and it is the type of writing most often found in the newspaper column, the sports page, much humorous material, etc. It uses very familiar and up-to-date terminology, slang, colloquialisms, words in current use at the moment, informal designations for common things and happenings. It may include local allusions and shop talk peculiar to certain occupations or activities. Since the writer and the reader have a good deal in common -- once again specialized knowledge and interest -- the former can operate in a confidential or "chatty" style:

It doesn't take a chauvinist of the old school like myself to come to the conclusion that the female nervous system is a mass of complex internal wires that are forever becoming crossed and getting out of whack. They sure don't operate any more smoothly in an athletic contest. When two lady tennis players of equal ability face a must-win point in a critical match, then they're both going to choke, and the one who chokes the least is going to win the point. Put her in there against a man and you'll see what happens! My money's on Bobby. He's been around forever and he knows the angles like the back of his hand. King over Riggs? No way!

The final category of English -- Non-Standard -- makes up the common everyday speech of many people who are basically unschooled and unfamiliar with the traditions of the printed page. It looks and sounds different; words and constructions are not the same as the other types. Nevertheless it is the vehicle by which millions of people carry on their daily lives and occupations, and everyone may run across it in films, plays, television programs, novels, and short stories. It often looks strange in print, since spellings are sometimes changed to give it a more realistic phonetic sound.

Kipling presents us with a colorful example:

Mulvaney continued: "Whin I was full awake the palanquin was set down in a street, I suspicioned, for I cud hear people passin' and talkin'. But I knew well I was far from home. There is a queer smell upon our cantonments -- a smell av dried earth and brick-kilns wid whiffs av cavalry stable-litter. This place smelt marigold flowers an' bad wather, an' wanst somethin' alive came an' blew heavy with his muzzle at the chink av the shutter. 'It's in a village I am,' thinks I to mysilf, 'an' the parochial buffalo is investigatin' the palanquin.' But anyways I had no desire to move. Only lie still whin you're in foreign parts, an' the standin' luck of the British army will carry ye through. That is an epigram. I made ut."

All these varieties of English are used by various writers, or the same writer in different situations, because of the differing effect they have on readers and the thoughts and information they can communicate. Young writers who are only interested in "self-expression" or who deliberately try to be innovative to the point of confusion will probably not conform to any of them. Gertrude Stein and James Joyce didn't, not do some of the modern poets. The following rule is an old one, but worth mentioning again here: As far as writing furthers an author's intention, it is good; as far is it fails in this attempt it is bad, no matter how technically "correct" it may seem.

The style that an author employs must always be suited to the subject matter and his reading audience. Humor will differ greatly from a serious scholarly treatise or from an impassioned argument. Slang and raw terminology may be effective -- even necessary -- in some instances and totally out of place in others. You wouldn't write a story for *Playboy* in the same way as you would do an article for a theological journal. Yet the dichotomy between Formal, General, and Informal English styles is not always a hard and fast thing, since it is possible to combine them to some extent for effect. Once again, it must be appropriate to the subject and readership. Note the vigor and mixed word choice in this paragraph:

> There was an ethereal aura about him, of concentration, of dedication, of a unique unwordliness, which had put a screen between himself and all those interviewers who had knocked on his door over the years. Most had overlooked the puckish cast that now suddenly showed through the glacial monastic exterior. He slapped the typewriter affectionately and it gave off a cast-iron tone. Nothing portable or Olivettish there. It's one of those old black jobs with the silver-rimmed keys, unlovely, smelling of 3-in-One oil, immovable as a Mosler safe. It takes a sculls champion's wrist just to work the space-bar, and the ashtrays dance with the spoons and saucers when the thing's in operation. A real Pat O'Brien prototype right out of *The Front Page*, with all the mystique of ancient city rooms with electric fans and flies and kicked-in spittoons and long-forgotten night-beat men sitting around with sour armpits and cracked cups of joe in tipped-back chairs and straw skimmers chewing on toothpicks.

You must adjust your material and your way of saying it to the reader, both in fiction and non-fiction. Clarity of expression, words, and terminology familiar to the persons you are communicating with is the only way to do it. Avoid errors in grammar, in spelling, and in language. Most of these come about through carelessness. Above all, satisfy your reader's expectations, and don't waste your time writing anything you wouldn't enjoy reading yourself.

THREE

THE PARAGRAPH

Although any discussion of style calls for considerable treatment of the technical aspects of writing, it is not the purpose of this chapter to reduce what is essentially a creative enterprise to an over clinical study. Such things as sentence diagramming can be somewhat tedious, and we will not go into that sort of thing here. However, it would be unwise to give short shrift to something as essential to good style as the well written paragraph; it plays too great a part in determining writing quality.

The good paragraph must take a point; it must transmit an idea or an impression. It is, after all, a group of statements related to one another that the writer sets down as a step in the development of his subject. It represents one stage in the flow of his thought, and stands by itself because of the relationship of the statements it contains.

The paragraph must have a certain continuity, and each succeeding paragraph contributes to the writer's overall subject, but develops a different aspect of it. A new paragraph, ordinarily set off from what precedes it and from who follows either by indentation or by spacing above and below is a message to the reader that the writer is shifting his thought and that he, the reader, must shift his attention correspondingly. Sometimes this alteration may be slight; sometimes it's a complete shift, in which case it may be signaled by a transition, or bridging sentence.

Each sentence within a paragraph should make its contribution to the overall focus of that paragraph, that idea which can normally be set down in a single statement or "topic sentence." The development within a paragraph is simply the method by which the reader is able to share in the process which led the writer to his own view.

There may or may not be a topic sentence as such, but it is a useful hook upon which to hang the more specific statements that emanate from and around it. Beginning writers can often improve their material by learning to distill the essence of a paragraph into topic sentences, since it is good practice in learning to dispense with irrelevant details. This is not to say that a certain amount of detail isn't necessary; the same beginner will often rely too heavily upon generalization without supporting it with the particulars needed to make his point clear and understandable. The one basic rule to remember is that the reader must be led over the same territory that the writer went through in his thinking.

If a paragraph is to make its point, it needs to be developed adequately, and whether or not this occurs depends partly — but not entirely — on length. Length should be determined by subject matter, by the importance of the idea stated, and by where the material appears. Newspaper paragraphs are usually quite brief, being generally under 100 words, with 30-50 the usual length. In the slick magazines they may run from 100-150. Books vary greatly, depending on the readership to which they are aimed, but the medium range probably runs from 150-250 words. Noticeably short paragraphs run the risk of being underdeveloped, or of featuring ideas that really shouldn't be set apart at all. Paragraphs that are longer than one double-spaced manuscript page can probably be broken up somewhere.

If we wish, we can break down the normal paragraph types, in order to make them more understandable. *Narrative* paragraphs, which deal with movement in time, are made up principally of details, but ideally they are rather vividly set down, with the reader being brought into the action in many instances. Action may be described very fully, particularly in the case of biography or autobiography, where conversations are quoted and what happens is seen through the eyes of the first-person figure.

The *descriptive* paragraph is also heavily detailed, and serves as a catalog of things seen and described by the author. The writer uses it to emphasize what he considers important.

In the *support* paragraph, which is used to make a statement to the reader, the writer will usually lead off with generalizations, which are supported by details which follow afterward. Sometimes the support paragraph leads off with a topic sentence; sometimes it will move toward the climax, which occurs at the end. The latter technique is often an effective method of sustaining reader interest. There is a certain sense of suspense that comes from withholding the concluding statement, and the reader is allowed to share in the discovery with the writer, so to speak. A writer may choose to lead his reader along by easy stages when his climax is an exciting or perhaps paradoxical one, or if his generalizing statement is complex or difficult to understand.

The *pro-and-con* paragraph usually begins with a general statement supported by details, and then examines the other side of the question, after employing some sort of bridging words like *but, however, on the other hand,* etc. This is the method used when a writer wants to elaborate on his main point or attack on opposing position, and through it the reader may be aware of conflicting arguments.

Most paragraphs fall into one of these categories, and a writer's subject matter, his purpose, and the audience whom he is addressing will determine just which one he will use at any given time. The imaginative author will mix them up for the greatest effect.

How can we determine if a paragraph we write is effective? First of all. we must remember that the reader must be led from one statement to the next, all the way through:

It was in the reign of Elizabeth, in 1583, that Sir Humphrey Gilbert had first planted the flag in Newfoundland, and in the following century things had extended themselves in a natural way through competitive give-and-take with the big league nations on the continent. British seapower won a foothold in the Caribbean and Central America to forestall Spain in the new world, and a continual stream of ships began making the stormy Atlantic passage with cargoes of settlers for the North American mainland, where British colonies might counteract French influence. In the eighteenth century the bounds were set wider, as traders, soldiers and more colonists moved into India, Ceylon, South Africa, Canada. Very little was acquired as a result of direct military conquest; it might have been more accurate to class the whole thing as a trading system, except that many territories were brought into the fold for strategic reasons. In India merchants and colonists found themselves extending their domain in order to protect their original interests. Canada and many of the Caribbean islands had been won by arms from France and Spain, but Australia was simply empty ground, colonized "on the rebound" after the loss of revolutionary America, and the aggressive African land-grab which had begun in the mid-eighties was entered into out of competitive habit -- less a matter of adding more square miles than keeping rivals from doing so.

Another thing the writer must remember is to capture reader attention. The first few sentences of a paragraph have to open up the subject, and stir his audience's interest:

Nobody really knew what to expect at Daiquiri. There was a relatively open roadstead there, very much exposed to the prevailing winds, and Shafter hoped the surf wouldn't be too high, but beyond that he and even more so the men who would make the first landing suspected that this time the American army was going to have to learn by doing; the sort of thing they were walking into wasn't in the manuals at all. Some thought they'd be meeting the dons in trenches and rifle pits on the beach, where there might be some chance for bayonet play, but the old hands, many of whom had campaigned against the Nez Perce and Geronimo, scoffed at this kind of ignorance. Why would anybody -- even a Spaniard -- make himself conspicuous on the shoreline when he could dig in along the ridges just behind the beach and sweep the whole landing area from above?

Like the first paragraph in a piece, the last one has an important function. It gives the final emphasis, rounds things out, so to speak. It should leave things the way the author intended them to be left. It should sound like a final paragraph for one thing, and should tell the reader that he has reached the end:

Finally, the search for extraterrestrial life could reap momentous rewards for mankind as a whole. We never have been really sure where we came from; today we have less idea than ever where we are headed. If we find that some kind of advanced civilization does exist somewhere, we may at least assume we are part of some grand cosmic scheme. If we can communicate with such civilizations, we may learn finally just how far the human mind and spirit can perfect themselves.

To contribute to effective writing, paragraphs should show continuity within the framework of the piece as a whole. As in the case of sentences, the connection that leads the reader from one thought or idea to another is called a transition. Words like *and, but, because* and *finally* can do the job; sometimes phrases like *for example. on the contrary, on the other hand* are employed for the purpose. Often *pointer* sentences or phrases can be used to provide an easy transition between one paragraph and another:

Some say ancient Egypt was the birthplace of the tarot, since the Egyptian words for "road" (*ta*) and "king" (*ro)* combine to form a royal road of life, which the tarot is said to be. In fact the 18th century French philologist Gebelin insisted that the tarot cards were nothing less than remnants of the primeval *Book of Thoth.*

On the other hand, some will draw a comparison between the major cards in the tarot deck and the 22 letters in the Hebrew alphabet. They would have one believe the tarot has a close connection with the ancient writings of the cabala.

All these theories, however, have their debunkers. Emile de Givry who has written *Anthologie de l'Occultisme* and other books on mysticism, scoffs at the idea that Hindus, Arabs, gypsies or others originated the cards. The tarot, he claims, has no origin at all, but is simply "a mystery, an enigma, a problem."

FOUR

THE ART OF REWRITING

Unless you happen to be one of those individuals who is as rare as the whooping crane -- one who can turn out a clear, emphatic first draft -- you are going to find yourself doing rewriting, and more than likely, a lot of it. Some of the best, most successful authors are painstakingly meticulous, writing and discarding a dozen versions of a story or chapter before they are satisfied. They make sure the finished product is just as fine as they can make it, and this ability -- the capacity for taking infinite pains -- is, of course, what makes them the best and most successful authors.

In order to revise competently, a writer must develop a powerful critical sense. Without it, you will never be able to make the correct judgments that result in the necessary improvements in your work. You must be able to look at a sentence or a paragraph and see its faults. Many writers do a very quick -- almost sketchy -- first draft. They feel it is very important to get something down on paper, even if it is hurried and amateurish in quality, simply because they realize that they must record something while the thoughts are flowing. They know that it's a relatively easy job to revise later as long as they have something to work with.

First of all you ought to be familiar with the type of expression appropriate to the basic style you have chosen for your work (General or Formal English, etc.) Doing a great deal of reading will be an invaluable help in both writing and revising your work, no matter what level of competence you are operating on. You must concentrate on how words and sentences are used. Everyone does this when he first learns to read and write; the serious writer simply continues the practice on a higher level, until transmitting ideas and emotions in an effective way is second nature to him.

Remember to proofread your manuscript carefully. It is an old story in the publishing field that a writer will more often than not miss his own mistakes in spelling, punctuation, and grammar. Train yourself to catch these, and to alter unsatisfactory sentences, words, and expressions. The English language offers many ways of saying the same thing. Choose the most effective expression for the purpose you have in mind and the audience toward whom you have directed it. Take the different methods by which you can impart this information, for instance:

> The film is amusing. I am amused by the film.
> The film amused me. I find the film amusing.
> That is an amusing film. The film seemed amusing to me.

Whether we use one or another of these versions of saying the same thing is not a matter of correctness, but of choice. Whether we use long or short sentences, simple of involved ones, punchy or liesurely ones is the same matter of style, and how well you use the possibilities at your disposal. Study other writers, and see how they have done it; then develop your own sense of fitness. Look over the following examples -- some are good and some ineffective -- and see if you can analyze what enables them to do their job well or to fail at it.

The most noticeable way in which a writer can vary his sentences is in the matter of length. The newspapers, advertising and sales material, letters, a good deal of modern fiction and most magazine articles employ the short, pithy sentence structure. At its worst this method can be jerky and choppy, monotonous and tiring for the reader, with a tendency to break ideas into fragments too small to follow readily. At best this style permits ideas to come easily and directly, as if straight from the creative mind of the writer or narrator, as in this suspenseful passage from Poe:

> *Unreal!* -- Even while I breathed there came to my nostrils the breath of the vapour of heated iron! A suffocating odor pervaded the prison! A deeper glow settled each moment in the eyes that glared at my agonies! A richer tint of crimson diffused itself over the pictured horrors of blood. I panted! I gasped for breath! There could be no doubt of the design of my tormentors -- oh, most relenting! Oh! most demoniac of men!

Other material may require a longer, more liesurely treatment, in which generalizations and details are combined. This is true of the formal style in general and often characterizes the discussion of ideas or descriptive passages. Length certainly doesn't necessarily mean dullness, however:

Of course one grew to enjoy the summers in "Tsar's Village," with its 800 acres of carefully kept lawn; admired its obelisks, its Parisian triumphal arches, its pink Turkish bath, its red and gold Chinese pagoda; and took proprietary interest in its Cossack guards, its permanent garrison of 5,000 picked infantry, its four dozen incorruptible sentries guarding the halls, the stairways, the kitchens, the cellars; the plainclothes police who stationed themselves behind every bush and tree when the Tsarina rode out in the imperial carriage; its caped, ostrich-plumed servants and equerries; its hovering footmen, scurrying lackeys, its four gigantic Ali Baba-like Negro body guards in scarlet trousers, gold embroidered jackets, curved shoes and white turbans, whose only function was to open and close the doors; and certainly the imperial kennels with their eleven prize English collies.

Both long and short sentences can have their advantages, if they are well thought-out and expressed. If they aren't, we come up with that choppiness we mentioned:

Management is much more than a science. Business is an art -- a creative one. I derive immense satisfaction from the knowledge that I am practicing an art. The boss who builds a business is as much an artist as is the painter. My sense of achievement is comparable to his.

Or else something long-drawn-out and soporific:

He was not as successful in his tales of country life in which he did his best to capture that peculiar and tragic period between the wars which subsequently was destroyed by the "generation that tolerates but does not pity," not recognizing the extent of the spiritual and economic economic revolution which had taken place, and failing to communicate it really convincingly from our viewpoint beyond the Second World War, which he prophesied but was spared from seeing.

Variety in sentence length can be a strength and can be most effective, provided it is appropriate to the material. One or two short sentences after a series of long ones can have a dramatic impact. A long sentence following a number of shorts can do a good "wrap-up" job, summarizing detailed matter.

Try to keep from making your sentences over-wordy. To communicate efficiently, you must get into the habit of saying only what you mean to say, and do all you can to cut out extra "padding" and complicated means of expression. The beginning writer might write:

"The way some pro football games are won is by the kicking of field goals. The professional will say instead:

"Some pro football games are won by kicking field goals."

I'm sure most of you remember when you had a tendency to say things this way:"

> Several of my friends who had nothing much else to do would stop by the restaurant where they would have a cup of coffee and a piece of pie.

This sentence has more words than it needs. It is easier, and just as clear to simply say:

> Several of my less busy friends would stop by the restaurant for coffee and pie.

You must learn not only to be concise, but to remain emphatic while you are doing so. You can accomplish this by the use of strong and original words. Arrange your statements within the paragraph so that they lead to the conclusion you want the reader to reach, and do the same with your paragraphs, progressing toward the desired climax.

Don't write like Queen Victoria, who believed that the more capitals, underlinings and exclamation points she used, the more emphasis she was employing. Be distinctive instead. Too many beginning writers use too many words like "extremely," "certainly," "tremendously," "highly," and their writing takes on a cast of phony and somewhat frantic emotionalism. "Fabulous," "devastating," "intriguing," "fantastic," "incredible," are all words among others than are greatly overused.

Repetition can be used at times for emphasis, but in most cases it ought to be avoided. Many authors inadvertently repeat words, means of expression and ideas, because they are simply not paying attention to what they are putting down, and because they are careless about their revision. Consider the following paragraph. How could any author let this pass beyond the first draft?

> The scenery on the island is breathtakingly beautiful. The skyline is highlighted by beautiful, wooded hills. There are also many colorful bushes and banks of flowers. Jungle trails lead one to beautiful secluded spots deep in the interior of the island. All in all, the most characteristic thing about this tropical paradise, is its overall impressiveness and beauty, all year round.

Unnecessary repetition will weaken even the best of styles. It can occasionally be useful as a stylistic device. It at least keeps the reader's attention focused, and can emphasize certain emotions effectively, but sentences such as the following do neither:

> The John Hancock building is without doubt one of the tallest buildings in the world.

> The question of abortion is among the most important, yet sensitive questions facing America today.

One of the most effective means of emphasis in speaking is the pause, which allows what has just been said to sink in, and gives an anticipatory highlight to what is to follow. In order to accomplish the same thing in writing, we usually separate what we say, in order to create the artificial pause.

> If I wear my raincoat, the sun invariably comes out. When I don't, I get soaked.

Position is an important determinant in emphasizing what you want to say; the position of words and phrases focuses reader attention in different ways. The emphatic positions are located at the beginning and at the end of a sentence. Consider the following two examples:

> There are many people who dress up just to show off.
> Many people dress up just to show off.

The second does its job more economically, without the unnecessary "there are."

FIVE

REVISING YOUR WORDS AND PHRASES

When you set about revising words and phrases in your work, keep in mind the same rules and principles you learned in the revision of sentences, and remember that the effectiveness and propriety of words depends a great deal on the context of the writing. For one thing, the choice of a word is obviously determined by the subject matter, but even then much depends on who the author is; one might use a particular word or phrase, and another might not. When choosing, a writer must strike a happy medium between his own purpose and the reader's expectations and knowledge, with of course the matter of good taste thrown in. Trite words and expressions, "big" words, vague, uncertain, and tentative words are usually the mark of the amateur. Some words that we use habitually in conversation -- "good," "bad," "interesting," "important," etc. are too inexact to be effective in most instances. A writer who can't find a better way than this to express himself is either lazy or lacking in imagination or both. Above all, be sure you are clear, and make certain you avoid ambiguities like these:

I pulled out another sheet of paper and put it in my typewriter. It rather discouraged me, but I decided I would try it again.

Trite or hackneyed expressions, or *cliches* are those that may once have shown some imagination or verve, but have become stale through overuse. The writer who continually employs them just isn't looking around hard enough for new and effective ways to say things. Consider how many times you've heard and read these:

Mother Nature, Father Time, quick as a flash, bolt from the blue, irony of fate, ugly as sin, tide of battle, watery grave, the Grim Reaper, sound as a dollar, thunderous applause, standing ovation, raining cats and dogs.

Many people try to avoid triteness by deliberately and liberally sprinkling their copy with "big" words. Now long words, or unusual ones are certainly not objectionable in themselves -- their use is almost mandatory in dealing with certain objects and ideas, especially in professional, scientific, and technical writing -- but many writers use words with just too much "horse-power" for their material, either through carelessness or as a means of creative exhibitionism. Sometimes official or academic writing seems to strive almost for deliberate obscurity in the way they express concepts or instructions. This type of writing can and does alienate a reader; he goes away wondering just what it is he's read. It's far better to steer completely away from unnatural language, and to try and use more exact wording and terminology.

It's probably easier today for the writer to be exact than it has ever been. In the past one often had to make an effort to avoid or at least to tone down more explicit subject matter. One means of doing this was the *euphemism, a* watered down word or phrase which may be used in place of the more explicit term when one is in danger of offending certain segments of the reading audience. It is often less harsh, is sometimes an abstract word or of Latin origin, and its most common use is as a substitute for certain physical or sexual functions or for unpleasant social situations. Where the user of the euphemism is concerned, people are never *drunk,* but always *intoxicated;* they don't *sweat,* but *perspire* instead; they have no *belly,* but they do have an *abdomen,* or at worst a *stomach;* there are no *stinks* or *smells,* but only *odors.* The *rich* and the *poor* are a thing of the past; now they are *affluent* and *underprivileged;* we no longer have to look forward to becoming *old* but merely *a senior citizen,* which has the connotation of a good deal more dignity, and our children, *stupid or lazy* as they may have been in the past, are no longer so, but instead *retarded or unmotivated.*

Some of these words and phrases have come into such general use that we can hardly help but employ them, but their original purpose, a certain squeamishness in the matter of expression and the desire to allow people to discuss things they would have been embarrassed to talk about while using the short Anglo-Saxon word, has largely gone by the board. There are still taboos in the media (though even these seem to be fast disappearing), but the trend now is for telling it like it is, while remaining as tasteful as possible.

There are many devices for bringing variety into an author's work, one of the most common being the *synonym,* which is, of course, simply a different, hopefully more effective and interesting way of saying the thing. One must be careful, however. A synonym will often have nearly the same meaning as the original word, but have a different connotation. Different words may be used by different groups or classes of people in different circumstances. What may be a common term in Boston or in Alabama would bring quizzical looks from a listener in Chicago. We all know that *bag* and *sack* mean virtually the same thing; yet some people will use one almost exclusively and not the other. The same with *bucket and pail, streetcar and trolley* (if indeed there are any of these outside of San Francisco,) and regional preferences like *sweet potato and yam, earthworm and angleworm.* An entire chapter could be written on American vs. British terminology preferences regarding the same object.

Ordinarily a writer searches for a synonym to allow him to express himself more exactly, and so he must be very careful of both definitions and connotations. The best book to refer to for word selection is *Roget's International Thesaurus,* which lists words by topic, words of opposite meaning, slang, regional, colloquial, and foreign terms. It is not a dictionary and does not define, but simply calls to mind those words an author is familiar with but may not recall easily. Of course one should not just select words on a hit or miss principle, but always be aware of how they are commonly used in writing and in conversation.

Figurative language is of course one of the most potent weapons in the writer's arsenal. Used in conversation as a matter of course, figures of speech do much to make expression more exact, more colorful and effective. As *The Writer's Guide and Index to English* points out: "Many words which originally had narrowly restricted senses have come to be used figuratively and have extended their reference. *Head* still has its old literal denotation as a part of the body but is also applied to the highest or foremost or principal part of a wide variety of things of a screw, nail, pin, army, the force of a stream of water, bay, news story, stalk of grain, hammer, bed, gold club, beer boil, barrel -- not to mention parts of a number of machines and the leaders of all sorts of institutions and governments and movements. Ordinary speech is full of these figures: we *play ball* when we work with others; we may *chime in* by adding our voice to others."

The most common figures of speech are the *metaphor* which makes a simple, short comparison. We may want to describe Fred as an energetic, unrelenting salesman, so instead we say: "Fred's a tiger."

The *simile* serves the same purpose as the *metaphor,* but uses the words *like* or *as* in its comparison. "The ranger was an impressive fellow. Tall, straight and thick-muscled, he looked like one of the giant firs in the forest he knew so well."

The *analogy* is a more complicated device. It still implies likeness, but notes a series of points of similarity rather than just one. For example:

"Revolution can often come upon us like a storm. At first only a series of dark, lowering clouds on the horizon, it is heralded by the rising wind of discontent, and soon the gale and the rain are upon us, sweeping everything before them, heedless of the irretrievable destruction they may cause."

Often a very effective way of getting a point across is through *overstatement, understatement* or *irony*. Overstatement or exaggeration may be used to emphasize a statement or situation and intensify the reader's impression:

"Most airports, and certainly all European ones, have been and are still operated as cattle markets. How long will it be before mankind is actually marshalled to the plane by dogs, each country patriotically displaying its preference?"

Overstatement frequently uses humor, and many funny stories and tall tales depend on this element. At the opposite end of the pole is the practice of understating, which can also be humorous, but is often used in criticism. Sometimes an idea is put down in negative terms; sometimes merely in less strong terms than expected.

Irony suggests something quite different, --sometimes just the opposite -- of what is actually written. Light irony can be humorous; severe irony is usually sarcastic or satirical. The writer should experiment with words; putting old ones to new uses, even inventing new words. Sometimes it will work and sometimes not, but experimentation of this sort is the writer's job if he is to remain effective.

Another device worth mentioning is that of *allusion*, which is a reference by the writer to matter which is not directly pertinent but which explains more clearly or emphasizes or adds interest in what he is saying. He may refer to history, literature, current events, or almost anything involving things or people and what they do. It is a stylistic practice -- a way of saying something that could be said differently. As might be expected, the different types of written English will employ different allusions. Formal English, directed to a cultivated audience may make reference to Shakespeare and the classics. General English will borrow from current expressions, advertising, slang, colloquial phrases, jokes, or proverbs. Great events in the past may be recalled, wars and personalities and historical references of all kinds. Writing found in current newspapers and magazines will generally allude to current events, and personalities in the public eye.

Figures of speech can be very effective, but they must be used with care, since they tend to stand out in a body of copy. They should be used for a purpose; don't tack them on just to make an impression with the reader.

And avoid those which have become cliches over the years -- "lap of luxury," "tired as a dog," "white as the driven snow."

All the items which we have been discussing play their part in contributing to the vigor and liveliness of writing. Accuracy is not enough; there must be force, combined with readability to draw and hold a subject's attention. The following paragraph speaks its piece, but does it really excite and involve you?

> Some say that the American way of life is not what it used to be. People today seem to feel as if they are threatened, not only by external, international problems, which seem to be always with us, but by the changes in morals, attitudes and relationships which are so disturbing to those most affected and least able to adjust to them. What can be done about these threats so permeating our society? Nothing, some say. They must merely be borne, and Americans must hope that things will come out for the best in the long run.

You as a writer must remember that one of the characteristics of present day trends in the field is the use of dynamic, image-painting words and phraseology. It is particularly true of what many have termed the "new journalism," that modern method of imaginative reportage which makes so effective a use of color, creativity, and reader involvement. Take a look at this paragraph and compare it to the previous example:

> Nicholas' childhood and youthful experiences had seeded in him a fertile germ of fatalism and the inhibiting sense of being dominated by events and personalities larger than himself. On the one hand the Kaiser's memories of his grandfather, Wilhelm I, humbling the ancient enemy at Sedan, using a Bismarck brain, a Moltke will and a Krupp steel skeleton to sculpt a German empire now dreaded throughout the world, had endowed this most recent Hohenzollern with a confidence nothing could shake. The Tsar's own grandfather had closed out his life on no such triumphal note. There was the cold, never-to-be-forgotten afternoon in 1881, with the shrieks of grief and the quiet sobbing and the ghastly crimson trail up the wide staircase of the Winter Palace in St. Petersburg to mark where the shattered, one princely body of Alexander II, his leg blown off and his stomach torn open by an anarchist's bomb, was carried and laid in a state bedroom to die. Nicholas had been there, a pale, shocked boy of twelve in a blue sailor suit, and the terrible scene still conjured itself up on occasion when he was alone in those icy, marble-columned halls which were now his own home.

Aim at expressing your own ideas with similar vigor and poetry. If you are observant when you read and listen to conversation, keeping in mind how articulate people express themselves, you will find yourself writing more effectively. It is difficult to overestimate the importance of reading. In no other way can you become more sensitive and knowledgeable to the power of words and their ability to express your thoughts and feelings.

SIX

USING WORDS

Most writers and most would be writers are admittedly fascinated with words. Anyone who tries to write will be very conscious of the need to express himself, and of the words that he knows, or needs to know to be able to do it. The English language is such a rich one that an author's potential vocabulary is for all practical purposes limitless, yet the reader himself will set the necessary limit, as he must understand what the author is attempting to communicate to him.

The exact number of English words is unknown. Unabridged dictionaries -- the ponderous ones usually found in libraries and other reference rooms -- have about half a million entries, and many of these have more than one definition. When one considers that dictionaries actually omit large groups of words which are in everyday use -- slang, local terms, specifics used by scientists and those in other specialized professions and occupations, "borrowed" foreign terms and many of the thousands of new words that appear every year but never take hold in the language -- we can see that the number of words we might use is probably more than a million.

It's difficult to measure the extent of any one's vocabulary. Some have estimated that a first grader enters school with the use of about 25,000 words and adds some 5,000 a year, so that he leaves high school with a total vocabulary of about 70-80,000 words. College students may average about twice this number, but of course we are talking about words that we recognize, not those we use in day-to-day conversation. Learning new words by themselves won't turn you into a good writer, but there is a correlation between a healthy vocabulary and the ability to express ideas clearly. The best way to increase a vocabulary is through new experiences, extensive reading and communication with others, and from participation in all fields of thought and study. An inquiring, receptive attitude and the desire to learn the subject matter at hand is a necessity. Vocabulary by itself won't do the trick; what is needed is the absorption of more useful and meaningful ideas, an extension of interests, and an increase in the powers of understanding.

The first book you should have in your library is a good dictionary. No other single source will have so much useful information on words. There are different types of dictionaries; some general, some specialized, but be sure to use an up-to-date one, since words are continually being added, deleted, used in new ways; and spellings and pronunciations will change over a period of time. If you do a lot of detailed work, you will probably find the unabridged edition best suited to your purposes, but for most writing the college size will do just as well. Here are some you might find helpful:

Funk & Wagnall's Standard College Dictionary

American College Dictionary

Webster's Seventh New Collegiate Dictionary

Thorndike-Barnhart Comprehensive Desk Dictionary

Webster's New World Dictionary of the English Language, College Edition

Too many people are unacquainted with the services a good dictionary provides. Read the explanatory material in the introductory sections, and see just what is available. Look up some words you are already familiar with, and some which are new to you. Entries are made according to the way a word is usually spelled. When more than one spelling is given, one will ordinarily use the first of the two forms. Dictionaries also show where a word ought to be hyphenated at the end of a line (such as leg-is-la-tion), and will respell words in specially designated letters to indicate their pronunciation.

A dictionary's primary job is to provide definitions. You must keep in mind that a dictionary does not pass judgment on a word but merely records uses that have already been found for it. It will give you the *denotation*, but often cannot supply you with the *connotation*. And the words of definition, in the broader sense, are not the "meaning" of the word; but are there to help you understand what it refers to in the area of objects or ideas. You will often need more information than the dictionary can supply to use a word properly, and you may have to go to an encyclopedia or some other reference work.

Dictionary words which are unlabeled can be assumed to belong to the general vocabulary; others may be labeled *foreign, obsolete, archaic, colloquial, dialectical, slang, British, United States,* or are referred to some field of activity such as law, medicine, printing, philosophy, astronomy, football, etc.

General dictionaries are supplemented by larger, more detailed or more specialized ones which require more specific material. The most up-to-date of the unabridged editions is *Webster's Third New International Dictionary of the English Language. The Oxford English Dictionary*, in ten volumes, has a great amount of information on English words, tracing forms and various connotations with the dates of the first recorded appearance and quotations from writers illustrating the uses of each. *The Dictionary of American English* in four volumes provides the histories of words as they have been used in the United States.

Consider, too, the following works that deal with specialized subjects:

> *Dictionary of Business Terms* (C.M. Alsager)
> *Illustrated Medical Dictionary* (W.A.N. Dorland)
> *Bouvier's Law Dictionary* (F. Rawle)
> *A Concise Dictionary of American History* (T.C. Cochran and W. Andrews)
> *Dictionary of Education* (C.V. Good)
> *A Comprehensive Dictionary Dictionary of Psychological and Psychoanalytical Terms* (N.B. English and A.C. English)
> *A Dictionary of Modern English Usage* (H.W. Fowler)
> *Dictionary of Gardening (*F.J. Chittenden)
> *Dictionary of Scientific Terms* (I.F. Henderson and W.D. Henderson)
> *A Dictionary of the Bible (*J.L. Hastings)
> *The Complete Dictionary of Abbreviations* (R.J. Schwartz)
> *A Dictionary of Slang and Unconventional English* (E. Partridge)
> *Webster's Biographical Dictionary*
> *Webster's Geographical Dictionary*

SAYING WHAT YOU MEAN

In conversation it's relatively simple to get your meaning across, merely by repeating a statement a different way, or changing the tone of your voice to emphasize what you are trying to say. When you write, it is the words themselves that must convey your meaning. Strictly speaking, words may be said to have meaning only insofar as they are used in certain statements, and in particular sentences -- that is, by *context*. We know what a word means when we can feel a connection between the word itself and the ideas it suggests to both the writer and the reader. If we want to communicate well, we must make sure that this suggestion, or meaning, is the same for both writer and reader.

This raises a number of problems. Words for hard-and-fast objects are easy enough to define, but when we are talking about abstract matters the chance for misunderstanding increases.

Concrete words have meanings which refer to established, recognizable objects. If a writer mentions a *bucket,* for example, we have a pretty good idea what he's talking about. It may be a big or a small bucket, or of a different shape than another of its type, but we still recognize the word *bucket* easily and have no trouble picturing it in our minds.

Relative words may be used by the writer to imply different shades of meaning, either consciously or unconsciously, depending upon his intention and his background and experiences. "Handsome," "ugly," "rich," "poor," "tall," "wicked," are subjective terms, their meaning dependent upon their relationship to some standard. The difficulty lies in the differing standard the reader may have from the writer's own, and when using these words it is important to distinguish *degree.* Any words such as the above can be used to greater advantage with qualifiers *(more, less, extremely)* or a more exact word than "pretty" or "short."

Abstract words can only be defined in reference to things which aren't specifically observable. Some refer to acts of relationship between people or objects or entities -- *robbery, citizenship, empire.* Others are collective, and stand for a number of individual items, such as *college, the administration, rock and roll, sports,* and define traits common to a number of people or things or situations. There is great danger in using many collective abstract words, of losing sight of whatever it is they stand for, and some others, like *art, morality, beauty, culture, masculinity* suggest attitudes that vary from person to person. A writer must be careful here to be exact, to translate his meaning into qualifying terms and to use specific examples as much as possible for illustration.

As is suggested by the foregoing examples, meanings may be altered to a large extent by how terminology is employed and in the context in which they appear. What we are talking about now is *connotation,* a suggestion of feelings or attitudes on the part of the author which arouse similar feelings and attitudes in the reader.

Take a look at the following words. They have essentially the same meanings, but very different connotations, and the attitudes they suggest are different as well:

If someone is liquored up we usually call him *drunk,* but if we want to be more polite or minimize the condition we can say *intoxicated or under the influence,* or we can be completely informal and call him *bombed, loaded or pie-eyed.*

Someone may be *slender or svelte* which have approving or fashionable connotations, or you may call them *thin*, or *skinny* or even *scrawny*, the most disapproving description of all.

Saliva and *spit* mean the same thing, but the former is a scientific and rather formal term and the latter is to many an unpleasant word. Similar differences can be noted between words like *average*, which is a factual term, and *mediocre*, which has become a derogatory one. *Fat* is factual, and suggests disapproval, *obese* is more formal, and *portly* tends to minimize the whole problem. If we call something *childlike*, we probably approve of it; if it is *childish or juvenile* we may not. Our grandfather is *old*, but if we want to be more polite we refer to him as *elderly* or by the now-fashionable and somewhat pretentious term *senior citizen.*

It's obvious that the connotations of these words are very important, and so is the context in which they are used. Important, too, is the social attitude toward whatever is being referred to, and the attitudes toward the individuals who generally use such terms. We make certain allowances if a child is speaking, or if a politician is referring to a political opponent. Terms change in connotation, too, becoming more or less acceptable socially. *Quaker*, which was once considered derogatory, is now simply factual. *Communist*, which once factual, has now become derogatory. The word *propaganda*, which was once defined as a dissemination of some truth or faith is now thought of as a deliberate attempt to deceive or sway opinion through the media.

The connotations of the above list of words and the many others which exist in the English language impart the quality of *suggestion* to writing. Such "loaded" or "slanted" terminology is often looked upon with suspicion, and with good reason. There is certainly no lack of it -- in newspapers, advertising, political material -- for it seems to be inevitable, and aside from scientific and scholarly treatises, can almost always be found to some extent. In fiction such suggestion gives the work its very life. It is not difficult to deceive with words; to manipulate and distort the truth intentionally through the use of words and phrases of a certain emotional "charge." Connotation is extremely important in any written material dealing with emotions. The writer must understand them as they relate to the attitudes and feelings of his audience. If he does not, he might just as well give up the idea of trying to communicate at all.

SEVEN

A FEW FUNDAMENTALS OF PUNCTUATION

Most writers know how to punctuate reasonably well; sheer repetition gives them the knack, but carelessness often rears its head in this area, and correction of errors in punctuation often becomes an important element in the final revision stage of writing. The writer ought to try to avoid being slipshod as to this kind of mistake. Errors in spelling tend to stand out like a sore thumb, and are rarely excused by the intelligent reader. Don't rely on editors to do your correcting for you; if your manuscript is "dirty," it will never reach the editing stage at a publishing house.

Punctuation is simply the relationship of words within a sentence and of the sentence within a paragraph. By itself punctuation can't make a good sentence out of a poor one, but it can make a weak one less confusing, and turn a complex one into something clearer and more meaningful.

(For further illustration of the rules of punctuating correctly, see Book 14, "A Writer's Handbook of Basic Composition.")

SELECTED

BIBLIOGRAPHY

Derrick, Christopher, *The Writing of Novels,* Boston: The Writer, Inc., 1969.

Fowler, H.W. *A Dictionary of Modern English Usage.* Revised by Sir Ernest Gowers. Oxford: Clarendon Press, 1965.

A Manual of Style. Chicago and London: The University of Chicago Press, 1969.

McGraw, Eloise Jarvis. *Techniques of Fiction Writing.* Boston: The Writer, Inc., 1959.

Perrin, Porter G. *The Writer's Guise and Index to English.* Chicago: Scott Foresman and Co., 1968.

Rockwell, F.A. *Modern Fiction Techniques.* Boston: The Writer, Inc., 1969.

Strunk, William Jr. *The Elements of Style.* New York: The MacMillan Co. 1968

Weeks, Edward. *Breaking into Print.* Boston: The Writer, Inc., 1966.

The Writer's Manual
Book 13

The Ins
and Outs of
Publishing Abroad

By
Madden Cassidy

ABOUT THE AUTHOR

Madden Cassidy

teaches creative writing in London.

Born in Ireland,

he began publishing at the age of seven

and has published poetry, articles, features and short stories

constantly ever since.

A collection of his short stories

was published in London in 1973.

A writer who cares about other writers,

he gives us a view of the problems that exist in breaking into print

in the British Isles.

THE BRITISH APPRENTICE

What pretensions have I to write this section? For a start, I was first published - in a national newspaper - at the age of seven. At sixteen I was keeping myself by my contributions to provincial Irish papers; no mean feat. I was paid three farthings (let's say one-third of one cent) per line and the competition was severe. In Ireland one gets the impression that every fifth person is contributing to some publication or another. At nineteen I had my first play produced, very successfully.

So why haven't you heard my name before? A natural question but one, I suggest, only a complete newcomer to this business would ask. And there are several answers.

Quickly, without stopping to think, make a list of the forty best-known writers alive in the U.S.A. today. It won't take long. There, you see! Most of you got nowhere forty. You ran out of names after about twenty. Now, consider please, all the books published in the U.S.A. in one year. If you don't know the number find it out. It's the sort of basic fact any professional writer ought to carry in his mind to give him a sense of proportion. To that number add an estimate of the authors of plays produced throughout the U.S.A. every year, the writers of scripts for radio, T.V. and films, the free lance contributors to all the magazines and newspapers. So. You have realized that the names of U.S.A. writers are legion. And most of them are quite reconciled to the fact that no one save their literary agent remembers their name. They do not all eat caviare. But, as we shall see presently, they do not all starve either.

Now you have at least one very good reason why you may not be familiar with my name. When I add that for over twenty years, apart from such highlights as the B.B.C. running a series of my short stories at peak listening hour or my name appearing among the prize winners in Literary Competitions, I have ploughed on laboriously, unknown but surviving by my writing, you will concede that I am perhaps qualified to write on this subject. This will be even more the case if I mention that for the past twelve years I have devoted overmuch time to teaching Creative Writing at Adult Education Institutes here in London.

You are undoubtedly familiar with those difficulties confronting the American writer newly embarked on a literary career. I propose here, in order to give you a standard of comparison, to show what are the corresponding difficulties facing your British counterpart.

Let's make another list. Go on: it won't hurt you - and there is method in my madness. Write down quickly the names of as many living British writers as you can remember. O.K. How many did you get? Twelve? Twenty? Thirty? Pretty good. Now please think again of the B.B.C. which broadcasts short stories as well as plays, of the television channels, the tons of books published yearly, the theatres up and down Britain as well as in London and Dublin, the commercial radio companies, the effluence of magazines coming out weekly, monthly, quarterly - a higher proportion of them, especially in Ireland, of a more literary flavour than is the case in the U.S.A., the numerous newspapers that publish short stories, and then let yourself estimate the thousands upon thousands of writers involved in all this output. Have you done that? Prepare yourself for a shock, dear reader. In Ireland, England, Scotland, and Wales the grand total of authors who live solely on their income as authors is exactly fifty-one. And that fifty-one includes two of the four highest paid writers in the world today. I'm not talking now of journalists but of novelists, playwrights, short story writers and, of course, poets. The remainder of all thousands, however much they feel committed to a literary career, however much they think of themselves as writers and nothing else, have to supplement their income, (that's putting it a little too delicately; in truth have to live mainly on their earnings from other sources), teaching, lecturing, book reviewing, casual labouring, what-have-you. A lady, one of the Grandes Dames of English Literature, whose output has been steady for fifty years - she was well-known before I was born - told me just a month ago that her royalties from all her books bring her in a total of £1,500 per year. That is 3,550 dollars or three-quarters of the national average wage here in the whole of England. An author who is a household name lives on the South Coast. When he needs to ring London he says openly to his friends he can only do so by reversing the charges.

How has this situation come about when forty to fifty years ago writing was a most lucrative profession here? The reasons are numerous. Firstly, the economics of the book trade mitigates against the primary producer. Secondly, the remuneration from writing has not begun to keep pace with the massive rise in the cost of living. The payment for a short story has scarcely risen at all in twenty years. In 1948 the national average wage was £4. Now it is £40. Payment for short stories here varies between £5 and £30. I sold a serial story on German radio. After translation fees and agent's fees I got just over £4.

£1 = \$2.30. In only the last four and a half years the cost of small basic food items has risen by several hundred per cent. Four years ago a London suburban house, in my own street as a typical example, was £5,000. Now it is £16,500. The great mass of the population counteracts this by means of their trade unions or professional organizations, by obtaining salary increases two or three times a year on threat of strike. A threatened strike by miners, electrical supply workers or dockers (longshoremen to you) must be met urgently. Can you see the prime minister or the populace at large viewing a possible strike by authors with the same degree of urgency? And from the writers you know can you imagine even a small roomful of them ever agreeing on any course of action? Then too, and you have this problem in the U.S.A. as well, each suburb or borough of London, Glasgow, Birmingham, etc., has four large public libraries. Every village has one. Remote country areas are served by mobile libraries. The libraries are permitted to buy books at 40% below list price. Several hundred people may read an author's book in each public library but the author does not make one penny on the deal. The public libraries, being free, do a roaring trade. It is they who attract the real readers at the general taxpayers' expense.

Without consulting one author or authors' representative the government passed a law declaring that developing countries, i.e. the forty million Nigerians, etc., should not have to pay authors' royalties. We were presented with a *fait accompli* and there is sweet damn all we have been able to do about it.

The cinema and T.V. really did cut down on the number of readers. Sixty years ago men and women doing dull jobs got their escape by reading. Today they get their escape by being entertained, vicariously, by Mia Farrow or Richard Chamberlain. Television should have been a wonderful boon to writers. It actually has been *to a few.* American mass-produced material offered on the world market after doing its job in the U.S.A. is much cheaper than home produced, newly written plays. So an inordinate proportion of our viewing time is taken up with Hollywood films of the forties, even the thirties, American serials, etc. Here in front of me as I write I have this week's programme for one T.V. channel. On this one day, (I can't be bothered to research further, take my word it's typical,) we have two American guest-singer slots where the famous introduces and chats with the not so famous, "Batman," Tarzan (an old film), "Kung Fu," a film devoted to an American family of singers called The Osmonds, a programme of MGM cartoons and a full-length James Stewart film. The day's viewing time given to work imported from the U.S.A. is just over half. That's about par for the course on any day on any channel. Since competition for viewers means aiming at the lowest common factor of public taste rather than its highest, the remainder of the fare available is a dreary family serial, a request spot, a professional programme on careers aimed at school leavers, a regular police programme (such and such an item has been stolen. "Has any of them been offered to you?"), five different programmes of pop music, something called "The Woody Wood-pecker Show" with which I am unacquainted (it's American too), two news programmes and two television parlour games. Great scope for the new writer! And that's only one channel!

Libraries report a steep rise in the borrowing of Trollope, Galsworthy & Co. on those occasions that one of the T.V. companies has invested in a prestige and expensive serialization half aimed at the American market. It is no coincidence that new paperback editions appear on all bookshelves at the same time. But the writers concerned are always dead and often long enough dead for the copyright to have run out. The prospect of becoming rich after your death has a strictly limited appeal.

You must be asking yourself why, if the outlook, financially speaking, is so bleak, anyone in Britain should ever want to take up writing at all. Therein lies the paradox. The principal reason why authors occupy such a lowly position on the income ladder is that they and their works are a drug on the market. For every book that gets published in Britain there are nine hundred other books that are written and which never get published. If that figure hasn't staggered you, it still, after all these years, has the power to stagger me. The figures I give here are accurate: they are the result of considerable research, close association with publishers and agents, and especially years of experience in coaching young, middle-aged, and old hopefuls in the arts of writing and of selling what they have written. In the United States about one out of every hundred book manuscripts get published.

Not only is it a buyers' market but, more particularly in Ireland, people are so anxious or determined to get into print that they actually part with all rights to their work free, gratis and for nothing. The temptation is greater than you might think. Not everyone has, no, I promised myself I would be truthful, damned few have the guts, the determination, the thick skin to withstand the innumerable rejection slips. That old cliche, the one about the struggling writer papering the walls of his room with rejection slips, like all cliches became a cliche because it was so true.

You have the same "snake in the grass" that is so prevalent here: the Vanity Publisher.

"Your novel is really excellent, Sir/Madam. I really cannot compliment you highly enough on . . . . It ought to be read. Yes, it just ought to be read. Unfortunately, publishing, is as you know, such a dicey business. So very much, even with such a fine novel as this, depends on luck. I know, I feel in my heart, it *ought* to be read. But I do not feel it would give an immediate return on the outlay. We just could not afford to publish this book, worthy though it be. We dare not risk our stockholders' money. Now if you were prepared, Sir/Madam, to defray the outlay . . . ."

So the book gets published, at fantastic expense to the author. That is twenty or a dozen, whatever number is considered safe to allay the suspicions of the "mug" getting published. The author gets rather more "courtesy copies" than most publishers, who are mean enough to sell their mothers to make candles, would think of offering. This is to lessen the chances of their attempting to buy copies in stores. No copies from Vanity Publishers go out for review *ever*. No distributor handles their published works and they are never to be found in the bookshops. Yet the "Vanity Publishers" wax fatter and fatter. The fly is induced into the web by all sorts of fair deal publicity: the honesty and straight talking of the advertisements would bring a lump to the throat of a Brooklyn policeman. Then comes the praise, which is fullsome. Then comes the dread expression "minority taste" but always accompanied by the most emphatic averment that it *ought* to be read, people, especially future generations, just *must* get the chance to read this work. Last of all comes the touch for money. I remember one Vanity Publisher who invited me to his house. His firm is not generally known as a Vanity Publisher. This was in 1956 when the pound still had some purchasing power. After extravagant compliments he asked me to contribute to the cost, just pay a share, say £750. Nothing doing. I work for money. He was a sticker. Do you know he kept on going down and down until he had reached £100? He just would not give up. Neither would I. It became a matter of will. Even then £100 was a drop in the bucket so far as the cost of bringing out a book was concerned. I left at the hundred pound mark. And the Literary World of London would be astonished at his name.

I have no sympathy with the people tricked by the Vanity Publishers. They are mugs, paying through the nose to see their name in print. I look on them as blacklegs (workers brought in from elsewhere to break a strike). The only trouble is that right on the heels of him or her comes another mug.

There is a marvellous variation on Vanity Publishing, quite legal and highly respectable. First get one room in an office in the best possible area. Generally you share the rent of that room with some other organization wishing to use the second desk, the heating and the prestigious address. Then you get a middle-aged dogsbody for typing, licking, sticking, parcelling: far less expensive and prepared to put up with so much more than the confident over-alert young miss. Then you come to a mutually satisfactory long-term arrangement with a printing firm over books, lowest quality paper, inferior type, etc. Lastly you find a not-totally-forgotten, elderly poet to judge the last twenty poems and lend his name to the entire project. Rightly chosen he'll come dead cheap. Now you're in business. Remember dignity must be the keyword throughout. Not only in the address, but especially in the name must the reputability be so obvious that no shadow of suspicion could enter, could even approach, an outsider. It is always the centenary of somebody's birth or death but the poet too must be chosen with circumspection. He must be both flawless, yet awesome. How about Milton? Let's call our project the Milton Memorial Poetry Trust. How does that grab you? Then in honour of Milton you announce a poetry competition through the columns of the literary papers and mags. Make sure the prizes, startingly high, get prominent mention in the ads. £500 for the winner, £250 for runner-up, £100 for third. Such sums are fortunes to any poet. Each poet knows he or she has one poem, sometimes he is not sure which one out of about three, that would sweep the board. Requests for entry forms, each containing stamped addressed envelope, flood in by the thousands into the little Mayfair office. Preparation of said entry form requires very careful consideration. The thousands of certain winners are at first slightly taken aback to learn that there is a "reading fee" of £3 for each poem entered . However optimism gains the day. But which of those three best to enter? Tastes do differ. Better be on the safe side and enter all three. There goes nine smackers to begin with. To inspire confidence, as in all competitions, *noms-de-plume* or numbers, not proper names, must accompany each poem. But there, quite large on the form, is a space for your name and address in capitals with a prominent square for you to fill in the *number* of copies of the Milton Memorial Trust edition you are ordering at £3 each. The order for the copies must accompany your entry. It takes a brave competitor not to feel, and somehow by juxtaposition and wording the feeling is engendered, that he ought to show willing and order at least two. No, since he is going to win anyway it might be nice to have a spare copy for that important friend, relative and so on. The average order is for four copies. The number of entrants always exceeds 2,000. The entry form gives the information that winners' names will be published on a date four months later and copies of The Milton Memorial Trust Edition will arrive by post in six months' time. In small print somewhere on the form is a clause whereby the entrant surrenders all copyright of each poem entered to The Milton Memorial Trust.

So the person operating the "racket" has received £42,000 in advance for books so printed and bound that they cost under £1 each to produce. Not only that but there is not even the ordinary publisher's risk since the operator knows in advance exactly how many books are sold. The profit is colossal. Just think of that £3 reading fee for each poem entered! So why don't we all jump on the bandwagon? Well, if too many got into the act the pickings would diminish proportionately. But the most wonderful thing is it is all so legal and above board. I have even known one of these organizations to apply for, and that's cheek enough, but actually to be awarded, a government grant for their contribution to the culture of the country at large. When the book does come out it contains, as promised, the three poems winning the huge sums, about twenty poems having won lesser prizes approximating to the usual payment for a poem and maybe four hundred poems free (because of that clause), many of which appear far better poems than those that were paid for. It's a bit like a lottery. But a ticket in the Irish Sweepstake is much cheaper and the prizes much higher.

You in the U.S.A. have your classic examples of best-sellers which were at first rejected by from one to thirteen publishing houses - the number depends on which particular best-seller we are talking about, and then was made into a highly successful movie. Well, believe me, we are not short of examples either. In the U.S.A., even more than here, there is a highly developed Joyce industry -- lecturing on Joyce, interpreting Joyce, annotating Joyce, writing theses on Joyce. Did you know Joyce himself spent fifteen years trying to get *Dubliners* published, earning three shillings and sixpence per hour teaching English for Berlitz the while? He spent seven years trying to get *Ulysses* published.

I don't know if he still holds the record, a few Americans may have exceeded it in recent years, but up until his death Somerset Maugham had made more money than any writer in history. In his *The Summing Up* (definitely required reading for anyone just embarking on a literary career) he tells quite frankly that he wrote six plays before getting one accepted.

I knew a highly successful writer of romantic novels who died just recently. She wrote nine of these enormous tomes before one was accepted. I have heard of similar cases but that was one I knew personally.

Richard Adams, the author of *Watership Down*, is now rolling in money, most of it I hasten to mention U.S.A. money. But he spent three years trying to get *Watership Down* accepted. The reasons publishers gave for rejection made hilarious reading -- to someone other than the writer, and after the work had been successfully launched.

That brings me to three very important points. Over the years, in my creative writing classes, I have noticed without exception success comes not to *the* most talented people but to those, usually just a shade less talented, who are really strong on persistence. The most highly talented will by his or her very nature produce unconventional, individualistic, hard-to-place work. But that same gift of unusual talent appears to render the possessor thin-skinned: one or two, at the very most three rejections and he or she becomes utterly unwilling to send off the written work. Come just a fraction lower on the talent scale or, again I must be honest, come even a fair way down in talent and the work is very conventional but the writer has every story, article or poem doing the rounds of the magazines and newspapers instead of lying in a drawer and is accordingly chalking up a formidable score of acceptance the while. Then too the highly original student is far less willing to go through the dreary chore of researching the predispositions of any given editor and modelling his work accordingly.

Depending on the individual personality, students are frustrated, hurt, infuriated by those ready-printed, polite rejection slips. "Why can't the publisher/editor just give me some reason, at least say something helpful for the future?" is the cry. And how wise the publisher/editor is! You all proclaim most earnestly that you do want criticism, constructive criticism. Like hell you do! The giving of literary criticism, however constructively intended, is the surest, fastest way to lose your friends. It's all right in the lecture room, the teacher is paid for it and well knows how seldom it is wholeheartedly accepted. As well criticize the first born's appearance to the proud mother. Because that written work is the fifty-year-old ex-colonel's baby. When the editor or publisher is unwise/kind enough to give you a page of criticism he has not looked at it with your eyes, viewed it from your perspective, he has missed the real point (which in truth only you can see though you'll never admit that) etc., etc.. Ask any writer whom you know well enough to be sure he is being honest, or view your own experiences objectively. Only with the passing of much time will you get over the reaction of anger or frustration. Then you will derive amusement from some and, let's hope, learn what you can from the others.

After nineteen years I still treasure two rejection slips. The first was for a short story about an Australian aboriginal boy. The rejection slip was from *Blackwood's Magazine* and signed by Blackwood himself. It consisted of this one sentence. *"We do not publish stories that have a native as the principal character."* Isn't it lovely to know that somewhere the Victorian age is not yet over! The same story subsequently won a prize in a short story competition and when I offered it to the B.B.C., with which I had had not the slightest previous contact, it resulted in my being asked for a series of stories which were read at peak listening hour. Then it was included in a collection of my short stories published recently.

My other favourite rejection slip is from a Dublin evening paper. It began, "We do not accept stories that contain reference to sex, divorce, religion, politics, ..." The list was endless and certainly appeared in one way or another to exclude anything I had ever written or hoped to write. But it ended on an encouraging note. "Do not be downhearted, however! Remember we publish one story every day; and we pay thirty shillings and sixpence for every story published." The reason I love it will not be so obvious to Americans unless I explain that thirty-three shillings and sixpence equals three dollars fifty cents, and that before I am satisfied with a story I usually re-write the damned thing about seven times. Payment would hardly cover the cost of paper used.

Our best market here for short stories, unless you are lucky enough to have a flair for writing the sort of over-emotional, romantic tosh most women's magazines use, is the B.B.C. sound radio. After acceptance there are the conferences on alterations to ensure your work appeals to the ear rather than the eye, lengthy conferences as the B.B.C. officials are being paid for their time although you are not. Then endless rehearsals if you are to deliver the talk or read the story yourself. You can take for granted the expenditure of a minimum of one week's fulltime work over and above the writing of the original story. All for considerably less than the national average weekly wage. But at least once they have accepted your script you get paid at once. Radio Eireann, the Irish equivalent, *pays you when they use the material* -- which may be years later. And their rates are *less than half* those of the B.B.C.

Mentioning that *Blackwood's* rejection reminds me of one other. For all sorts of reasons that do not concern us here there has been in Britain, since end of the last war, an increasing tendency to ape American ways, adopt American attitudes, even misuse American idioms and slang. Many years ago I sent *Argosy*, the English short story magazine, not the American one of the same name, an adventure story also set among Australian aborigines revealing purely incidentally how incredibly victimized they are. I had spent years among them as a teacher and found them fascinating. *Argosy* wrote back saying they liked the story very much but that it was not their policy to publish anything verging on the colour question. Later came the era of Martin Luther King, idolized by many in the U.S.A., so of course idolized in England, the students' sit-ins and all the rest of it. English media reflected the new liberal American attitude. Sympathy with people victimised because of the colour of their skin became respectable. It occurred to me that *Argosy* might now have a different editor or that no one would remember the same story after so many years. I resubmitted it. It was accepted at once. So I have a rejection slip and an acceptance slip for the same story from the same magazine without one word changed between time!

As we are selling in a buyers' market we get the dirty end of the stick. I once received from a national newspaper, *The Irish Press,* a rejection slip for a topical article exactly to the day one year after I had submitted it. Had I, in the meantime, offered the article elsewhere I would be, by the standards of every editor, dishonest. To be fair, I know cases of writers being treated nearly as badly here in England. But how Irish writers continue to exist, never mind maintain their high standards, is to me one of this world's mysteries.

Beware, I abjure thee, beware of the editor who writes complimentary things about your story or humorous article and says he would be pleased to consider it if you would kindly cut it to half, quarter or whatever, of its original length. To begin with, if you are a writer worthy of the name, you left no excess fat in the original. All its qualities including its size gave it the attractiveness you wanted it to have. No matter which method you use, pruning or re-writing from scratch, the end product will be a totally different animal, and if it has any attractions they will not be the ones that attracted your editor in the first place. The moment of illumination will be altered. Back will come a polite note saying he/she finds the result disappointing: it hasn't got the qualities of the original. You could have told him that in the beginning. Your time has been wasted. I don't know how much of this goes on in the U.S.A., but I assure you it is a common experience over here. Another variation is, "We liked this story very much and in general it is just right for our magazine. However our readers do not like stories written in the first person. Would you kindly re-write it in the third person and we shall be pleased to re-consider it?" How do they know their readers would accept nothing in the first person? Have they ever been consulted? Your reason for writing the story in the first person was not just caprice; it was an intrinsic part of the plot, atmosphere, moment of enlightenment, or overall effect. Re-written with that taken away you have a horse of a very different colour -- and a sadly castrated horse to boot. Back will come the inevitable rejection slip. Here writers really are a dime a dozen and the powers that be have no conscience whatever about abusing us. You have to protect yourself by knowing when to say, "No." Though I have an excellent education from a purely academic point of view I never had one formal lesson in creative writing as such. I had to learn by trial and error and it is the fruit of that learning I pass on to my students.

Understandably your work should be perfectly set out when you submit it. Bearing this in mind I had a three-act play professionally typed with stage directions in red, and bound. It cost me five pounds per copy. At present day charges, sixty pounds each would be cheap. I knew from experience that despite every precaution copies do tend to disappear. For me at that time the expenditure was monstrous. I was living on my shoe laces. Nevertheless when the first theater manager did not return the copy, ignored my letters, and could never be interviewed I thought to protect my investment by not only sending the copies of the play by registered post but also enclosing an enormous pre-paid registered envelope for return. And while you are writing a long play you cannot be spending whole days writing articles or doing anything else so I was at starvation point. The double registering was for me a ghastly expense. I sent play and enclosed registered envelope to a world famous director who shall be nameless. I did get that play back. Back it came to me, not in the enclosed registered envelope, but in an old envelope with the address of her Theatre Workshop crossed out, mine pencilled in and no stamps at all so I had to pay a fine. All thirteen expensively produced copies have gone the way of last fall's leaves.

Of course nowadays I would never be so foolish as to go to that sort of expense. I have been backstage in far too many theatres. Let's not think of the well-known impressarios whose names may be found in the appropriate directories. Let's not think, even, of the professional theatres either in London or the provinces. Would you believe that *amateur* theatres here in London get so many hundred unsolicited plays per month that they would have to employ someone full time just to post them back to the senders? Amateur theatres cannot afford to *employ* anyone. Do you think any of those plays get read? Imagine then what the situation must be like in the offices of the well-known theatre managers.

The television companies get over the difficulty by employing what we call "skim readers." You know them as "first readers." The larger publishing houses do the same. Theatre management companies ditto. A skim reader does not read. He or she flicks through at the rate of twenty minutes per book or play. If the work seems promising it gets more time. A skim reader winnows a given fraction - he is told in advance exactly what fraction - of the total offerings and gives that to a reader, a person who really and truly reads. He in turn winnows again and presents his pre-ordained harvest (the company is geared to four new titles in the spring, six for Christmas market) which is subjected to conference and finally decided upon. I have made it my business to get to know some skim readers. First of all please think about the job itself. Would you like to do it? Flicking through a paragraph on this page, a sentence on that one, twenty minutes per script. Would a person who could be a lecturer in literature take such a job? Would a person of very fine susceptibilities take such a job? Particularly when I add that it is very badly paid. The skim readers I have personally known, employed by companies so big that even you in the U.S.A. have heard of them, most emphatically are incapable of writing anything themselves except a note or a casual letter and are completely lacking in literary taste or knowledge of literature. I hereby most solemnly aver that every skim reader I have known would have thrown out a present day Kafka, Joyce, or Katherine Mansfield. I have not met one that, speaking as a teacher of considerable experience, I could feel confident, were he or she my student, would pass G.C.E. "O" Level (the easier English university entrance exam now given to those students who are going to specialize in Engineering or something else considered totally technical).

One highly successful publisher has a variation on the skim reading. No, that's the wrong word altogether. He has a substitute that is to him both more satisfying and infinitely cheaper. He himself reads and either rejects or passes on to his pre-conference readers every single new offering. Yes, that's quite true. He reads them himself. *He reads pages one and sixty-nine.* Still he makes most of his profit on thrillers. Correction! All of it. I suppose you could safely reject a thriller on just two pages. Imagine Faulkner getting judged that way.

The situation must be similar in the U.S.A. Here one source of a writer's income is *competition.* A highbrow newspaper or a magazine decides to boost its sales by running a short story competition with a really high sum as first, and often only, prize: the winning story to be decided by the world famous writer W.Q.. Are you really so innocent as to suppose the great W.Q. reads all the nine thousand entries? Perhaps he reads the first five, precious few more. He may employ skim readers. A television company offers a grand sum as prize for the best new play in a much publicized competition; the judges to include that successful playwright X.Z., the renowned critic T.Y., and the great actor Sir A.B.C. There are two thousand entries and to my certain knowledge X.Z., T.Y., and Sir A.B.C. divide between them the labour of reading the final dozen chosen by employees of the company. And, in all cases, W.Q., X.Z., T.Y., and Sir A.B.C. will pontificate upon the quality of the entries as a whole.

I'm playing the game a bit dirty here since I myself have almost made winning short story competitions, including one by a major U.S.A. newspaper, a habit. But when I decided to write this section I set myself the handicap of being honest whatever the consequences.

I ought to tell you about that American winning. Sixteen years ago I had a holiday in Spain. It was my kind of holiday; nothing planned, just let things happen: and they sure do. I was coming back to London -- the hard slow way, by third class rail. Once on the tedious, penniless journey through the whole of France (scenic beauty does not invariably relieve the pange of hunger) I borrowed the copy of the now late lamented New York *Herald Tribune* being read by the young couple opposite me. Even Americans end up broke if they have had a good enough holiday. The paper was running a story competition for Americans on holiday in Europe. The theme was the European attitude toward Americans. Only Americans could enter. I not only had never been in America but had rarely seen an American film. You would not be reading this if you were not the kind of person who grants every man the right to his tastes. I prefer Swedish, Polish, French, etc., films to American. So my knowledge of the U.S.A. was nil but, on the other hand, I did know Europe, on the seamy side. I thought why the hell not. I entered the competition as a citizen of the U.S.A. I won a prize, but not the top one. I sat back and waited for the money. Came a letter from the N.Y.H.T. asking for the name and address of my American bank as currency regulations then in force prevented them sending money abroad. I've talked myself out of worse than that. Back I sent a real tear-jerker. I was a student, absolutely broke, frantic to get back to my college before the commencement of the new semester and relying on their cheque to eat and pay my return ticket. To help me in my ordeal they rushed through some arrangement whereby I was enabled to collect the money from American Express in Park Lane. I was having peristalsis trouble by that time, fearful I would be required to produce a passport or proof of American citizenship. Wonderfully trustful people, the Americans! Such was not the case. Hunger is a hard taskmaster.

Don't think me patronizing when I say we learn a lot from our students. I personally feel strongly that when I stop learning I shall die. No, it is not technique we learn from them. Nor do we steal their ideas. That business of having one's ideas stolen belongs to the crass "beginner," for want of a more appropriate word. Some authorities have argued that there are seven basic plots and to prove it have enumerated them to me. Other authorities have done the same with the thirty-two plots they believe to be basic. I can show the embryo, frequently developed well beyond that stage, of all but one of Shakespeare's plays. I used to do a lot of my writing in the conducive atmosphere of a nearby reference library. At a time when my photograph appeared on the cover of a well-known magazine, which also carried an article on me inside, I was waylaid by one of the younger assistant librarians. How should he go about getting his story published? I made every helpful suggestion I could think of. He expressed himself greatly worried that submitting his story in the manner I suggested might result in someone stealing his story or ideas. I tried to reassure him on that point, but without success. I then did what I should have done right at the start. I asked a few questions about his masterpiece, its length and suitability for various publications. It was at this point he revealed to me that not one word of this masterpiece he feared might get stolen if submitted had as yet been set on paper. Throughout my career as lecturer in English at two polytechnics and two literary institutes that sort of thing, more or less, has happened to me more times than I can remember or than you would believe.

When I mention the wholesale employment of skim readers over here and of the publisher who rejects as a result of reading pages one and sixty-nine a very important question must have occurred to you. It is one my colleagues and I chase around in the staff-room or over a beer quite often. If Shakespeare were alive today, writing in today's English, running the gauntlets we run, would he be recognized as great in the sense that today we call Shakespeare great? To frame the question another way, what are the chances of a 1976 equivalent of Shakespeare, in literary ability, falling through the net of skim readers? My colleagues and I differ radically on this and I feel I'm right. Don't we all! Subject *Finnegan's Wake, Ulysses, The Sound and the Fury, The Trial, and Tristram Shandy* to that page-one, page-sixty-nine test. There! Everyone was capable of appreciating good literature, for whom reading a page of *Ulysses* would not have been a form of torture rather than a pleasure. How many *Tristam Shandys* are blushing unseen, wasting their sweetness in an attic trunk?

So far as I am concerned I have seen the proof. Over the years I think of a west of Ireland writer called Farrigal Daly, who emigrated to Canada. He wrote exquisite prose poem stories with some queer supernatural quality about them. Each and every story had an ingredient peculiarly his own. The treatment was consistently highly original. They were better than anything of the kind I have ever read, and I have been a compulsive reader getting through at least four new books a week despite my heavy schedule, since I was seven. There is a mistake there. They were not better than anything of the kind. I had never before seen the same kind. Nor have I since. They were as much a breakthrough as Katherine Mansfield's work or Dorothy Parker's external monologues. And a long time has passed now. And I have never seen any of his work in print.

Then I think of a young Englishman, very young, who had spent over half his life in Borstals (prisons for juveniles) and prisons. I was shown his work by two social worker friends of mine. He had been released temporarily into their care and allowed to go work like anyone else as one of the many current experiments to find alternatives to prison. In prison he had no typewriter, fountain nor, ball point pen. Everything had been written or drawn on stereotyped, unlined, darkish prison paper with those old nib and stick type pens. No one line was even slightly irregular, every letter perfectly shaped and proportioned. They were all children's stories, with his own ink drawings. They far excelled Hans Christian Anderson. Their strongest feature was a playful gentleness. Yet all his crimes had involved violence! I was excited. The quality of the material was so high. I planned to meet with him, but when I arrived at my friends, they did not want his name mentioned. He had let them down badly. He had ruined the experiment. He had used the time when he was supposed to be working to plan, locate accomplices, and carry out robberies involving considerable violence. He was sent back to prison with a far longer sentence. What happened to the huge stack of leaves, each a gentle story lovingly illustrated, constituting years of meticulous devotion, I shall never know.

I think of a young Bangladeshi, twenty or twenty-one, who writes as good poetry as any written in England today, with sure mature technique and startingly apt imagery. But he is trying to keep himself alive by any work he can get and at the same time study for accountancy exams.

All three people I have mentioned had, by coincidence - it must be coincidence: I can think of no other explanation - this quality in common. When I, or most people I know, write some letters are bigger and some smaller. The handwriting is irregular. The Irishman and the Bangladeshi had no access to a typewriter. In all three cases the handwriting was unnaturally perfect. Another thing: I change my mind, alter words, swop phrases around. They never did. The first time was the only time.

The young Bangladeshi and the Irishman had another odd quality. I have watched them do this. Some of my poems or stories take many years to write. They both wrote straight off, without hesitation. Someone came late to the class bearing a newspaper reporting floods in Bangladesh and a horrifying number of deaths. Straightaway, on the instant, Mahmoud produced a poem, a very fine and, for him, an unusually long poem. I have a very fine poem I started twenty five years ago and have never yet succeeded in finishing to my satisfaction.

All right. My three examples were not Shakespeares or Cervanteses. But if, within the teaching experience of one lecturer, three people who would have pushed the borders of literature one little bit further (and not so little either) could have sunk without trace then yes, I say today's equivalent of such writers might never get into print. *Ulysses* has had the greatest effect of any work on the literature of this century. Yet, no publisher would risk the money to publish it. It remained for Joyce, after seven years of trying, to find an American lady who put up the cash to enable its first edition to come into being.

Our hypothetical genius runs an even greater risk than the amphorous but often victorious obstacles to getting into print. It is deciding once you are absolutely positive of your own quality that the whole damn silly business of persuading all these other people of it is to no purpose. If you really believe in the quality of your own work, your belief is neither added to nor diminished one whit by another's attitude. In other words to some top writers the game simply isn't worth the candle. The really top artists, composers, poets, playwrights, never really needed praise. Not one of them was lacking in self-esteem. To write, paint, compose, for money if necessary, yes. But just as generalizations are both true and untrue not every great or, for sake of accuracy, potentially great artist is dying to paint. Creating to the utmost of your ability is excruciating agony. Rossini amassed a fortune by the age of thirty-seven. After *William Tell* he wrote nothing more. He was a truly great and highly popular composer. How could such a born creative artist live without composing? Very happily indeed, if you study his life. Granted, in real old age he composed, but Matinees Musicales only for his own amusement, not for money or even for public performance.

There is a greater threat still to all modern Cervantes. Not that easy common despicable obstacle we have all had to overcome that if you don't complete the work it can never be a failure: if you don't try you can't fail, but worse. What I call the *Oblomov* syndrome. All would-be writers should be compelled, by force if need be, to read Goncharov's *Oblomov*. In the novel the character, Oblomov, really has all the qualities needed for literary success. Nevertheless each time he approaches his work he is attacked by all sorts of severe and quite real illnesses. You see writing really is damned hard work. Straight creating always is. Though the need to create is devouring, the pain of doing so can cause the mind to produce very real illnesses to avoid the greater agony involved.

Throughout the whole of my teaching career, first at elementary level, then secondary, and now tertiary I felt I could not be a good writer if all of life I knew was the inside of classrooms. I worked during every single vacation except the one just finished. I have been a docker, barman, postman, hospital porter, factory unskilled labourer, gardner, sawmill carpenter. I cannot remember the rest. In every job I worked very hard. No job, without exception, left me so tired at the end of the day as does teaching. And teaching hardly begins to be tiring when compared with writing -- for the great mass of us, that is. Whatever a good teacher puts into his teaching, call it creativity, call it factor x if you like, it is exactly that same substance a writer puts into writing. After two hours teaching Creative Writing I find myself so drained of that factor x that I can produce nothing for at least twenty-four hours. My most earnest advice to you, the budding writer, is this. If circumstances compel you to earn your living somehow else while you write, let that living be earned as differently from writing as possible. It is inexpressibly easier to be a bricklayer and a writer than a teacher of English and a writer. Beware of any job such as copywriter for an advertising company. Take that on and say goodbye forever to your literary ambitions. Look for some routine boring job, preferably one like weaving or bricklaying which leaves your mind free to roam the day long and sends you home at night brim full of mental energy.

In reading through all this you, being intelligent people, naturally wondered why, with conditions for the writer so bad here, we do not try the American market more. Oh, but we do. Just as soon as a novelist has half or even quarter made his name, his agent and publisher are grovelling frantically among the U.S.A. possibilities. And once one (possibility) materializes he's made (financially) because you pay so much better over there but he's made reputationwise too because of the cachet of having been successful in the U.S.A. It was otherwise before the world war. Power and money bring their own glamour.

Seventeen years ago I was standing at the counter of the Touring Club de France in Paris. It's the sort of place you call at for information, good hotels, etc. I was being attended to. After me came in an American, sixty-odd, lean, greying but very well dressed. He began, "I'm an American and I'd like to know ... ." Forty French girls raised forty heads, gave him langorous looks, the sort I imagine American girls reserve for Rock Hudson, and signed ruefully. There was I, a hale, hearty, twenty-six year-old Irishman, handsome I had always been led to believe, yet I did not evoke even one sigh of any kind. The rue and the langorous looks were not for the inhabitant of the Cashmere overcoat. They were for the dollar, for the land where, twenty years of Hollywood products had conditioned us to accepting, even unemployed shopgirls occupied apartments of endless perspective, where every working class family runs two cars.

Writers just starting out here do not aim for the American market. They have been wisely taught that to begin with one should found one's writing on one's own personal experience. The exceptions are few and famous. Just as the most successful churner out of women's romantic novels - the only thing that safely pays here except for school text books - is a far from effeminate but wisely anonymous middle-aged gentleman, so it happens that the most prolific writer of westerns is a Yorkshireman who has never himself been west of Liverpool. Young Irish poets send their mss. straight to the U.S.A. They have no alternative. Magazines here pay poets in free copies. I teach my students that that is a form of dishonesty and that anyone submitting to it is a blackleg. They all agree with me.

From the point of view of the article or short story writer the American market is even harder to break into than the native market. Editors on both sides of the Atlantic insist, "Read our last dozen issues. Angle your story/ article to suit our requirements." Unless it is the *Nursing Monthly* or the *Presbyterian Times* you find the stories have nothing more in common than any dozen short stories picked at random from anywhere. The editor would strongly disagree but it is quite obvious that in most cases he or she picked the story of the month on pure whim. All they usually have in common is quality.

If this section has been depressing for you, my brief was to tell you, from the inside, what it's like for the young British writer starting out. If I have achieved nothing else, I have shown that the picture is rosier in the U.S.A. Is it worth it for us? The thrill of seeing what one has written in print wore off for me in childhood; but I notice it is still a thrill the first time to any student however mature. A greater thrill is the receipt of one's first cheque. On a deeper level, you do influence people and to a greater or lesser degree the world in general by the product of your writing. I don't mean you should all start off intending to be another Thomas à Kempis, Karl Marx, or Harriet Beecher Stowe. But you can put your point of view across to more people by the written word, make more people think, or make more people happy.

May I tell you about the greatest thrill I ever had in connection with my writing? All right, so it contradicts something I have said earlier! What else do you expect from a human but contradictions? They are inherent in our make up; the more so when the human in question is an Irishman. To me the loveliest experience in life is one of my children, just past the baby stage, climbing onto my knee and paying me quite naturally some unrehearsed heart-and-soul-heating compliment. Next to that, I had always thought, came looking at Rembrandt's last self portrait. But better even than Rembrandt is what I am going to tell you. There was a fashion here in London that caught on widely for a few years of intellectual coffee bars. You knew they were intellectual because there were bare boards instead of tables, benches instead of chairs, and instead of wallpaper there was bare plaster. Chess sets were also much in evidence. Conversation was "intelligent" in that self-conscious, superficial way peculiar to undergraduates. Some people at the "table" behind me were laying down the law loudly (it was *de rigueur* that all speaking be loud) on literature. One man made himself heard. He declared that the greatest short story he knew of he had not actually read. They quietened to hear the explanation. He described a story he had heard broad cast about a year before. *It was a story of mine.* A story read over the air is so emphemeral. There is no record to jolt the memory. Yet some man had thought that story of mine good enough to treasure it and recall it to his friends. Unfortunately, I heard him tell them, he did not know the writer. How many people even learn, never mind remember, the writer of any radio, film, or T.V. script. Still I had to get out of there fast. *I was blushing.*

Other people elsewhere in this book are expounding method and sales to you. And of course they will tell you what I am going to tell you now. I make no apology. It is something you can not be told too often and better you should learn it here than by an unfortunate occurrence. First: Make sure that you have in your possession a copy of every item you send out. That script is your blood, sweat, and tears. And scripts have got lost before. Second: keep a record of where every item is. Make an enormous chart with a column for the titles, a column for the date of sending out, a column for the destination, *Mademoiselle, The Atlantic Monthly,* your parish magazine or whatever, then a column for date of return and lastly a column for the fate of your offspring. Number your lines horizontally so as soon as you get an item back fill it all in again, within one day have that item out earning its keep and on the right side of the first rejection (sorry) put the new starting out number. The method is foolproof. If you lose anything you know exactly where it has been lost. I evolved that system as the result of my own misfortunes. This very day an Italian friend of mine remarked to me that he had previously read in Italian a story of mine he had just finished reading in English. I *know* that I have never been paid Italian translation rights for that story or for any other story. As if that were not bad enough, years ago exactly the same thing happened with another Italian friend and another story. You cannot subject your friends to the third degree. In any case it is easy to recognize a story, not so easy to say which year you read the same story in Italian, in what magazine, what date. Without all that information there's not a damn thing I can do. Another very good friend whom I had not seen for a long time told me happily of hearing one of my stories broadcast. I was not equally happy for I had never sold the broadcasting rights of that story. Unfortunately years had passed. He could not remember which station or broadcasting company or even for certain which year. I have strong suspicions of the explanation. Beware the agent's ad that promises too much. A long time ago, fed up with my rate of progress, I put every single thing I had written into strong envelopes and sent the lot off to such an agent. The months dragged by. Correspondence remained unanswered. The best possible address of course. But the entire business was conducted by two women in an attic at the very top of the building. The old lady assured me all my stuff had been posted back to me. She provided a date. When I asked for a copy of the letter she had sent accompanying my work she sat down at the typewriter and straight out of her head typed what she remembered having written to me so many months before. What could I do about it? Stuff does get lost no matter how many precautions you take, but with a chart such as I suggest you can keep track and cut down the losses.

Now here's a thought for new American writers. Someone said, "A prophet is not without honour save in his own country." I notice every American agent or editor or publisher wants a full list of everything I have had published or produced. One actually begins to suspect the poor souls are impressed by articles published in *The Times* or plays staged in Glasgow. Well the Atlantic can be crossed two ways. If you are prepared to take less money, your work offered here will have behind it all the glamour of the Yankee dollar as well as novelty value. Then you can approach your American editor or agent with an impressive list of acceptances by the *Cambourne Packet,* the *Skibereen Eagle* or the *New Statesman.* How about that?

The Writer's Manual
Book 14

A Writer's
Handbook of
Basic
Composition

By
Boyd B. Burnside
and
William R. Burnside

ABOUT THE AUTHOR

Boyd B. Burnside
took a PhB and master's degree at the University of Chicago
and spent seventeen years
in both teaching and administration at a number of colleges,
among them Grinnell College and the University of Tampa
where he was dean of men and director of placement.
He has had considerable experience in writing
admissions and educational promotional programs.
For eight years he has represented the authors' agency,
Porter, Gould & Dierks, covering the West Coast.

Boyd B. Burnside's son, William R.,
holds a degree from Raymond College
at the University of the Pacific.
While earning his bachelor of arts,
he worked in campus radio and a number of his scripts
have been broadcast.
He is working on a master's in broadcast communication arts.
He also assists his father in representing the authors' agency
out of a San Francisco office.

COMPOSITION HANDBOOK

Contents

COMPOSITION HANDBOOK

Contents (Continued)

INTRODUCTION

Composition is certainly not the most exciting subject you can study. But it is one of the most important subjects you as a writer must know. Within its confines lie the basic tools you must use to make yourself understandable. By crafting your writing through the proper application of the tools of composition, you will be able to express yourself clearly. Misusing a semi-colon in writing is like using a screwdriver on a nail in carpentry. Writing in sentence fragments can leave the same impression with your reader that a poorly supported roof would leave with a master carpenter. If you do not write so that your readers can understand you, there is not much point in writing at all.

In music or in art a composition is an intellectual creation depicted in some form by the composer or artist. In writing it is the artful use of the elements of language in creating the means of communication essential to a civilized society. Composition is an elastic term as it is used by text-book writers. With some it is all inclusive, covering the field of writing in every aspect. From an instructional point of view in presenting the study of English, both rhetoric and composition must be considered: Rhetoric being the art of writing effectively; composition being the study of rules and principles necessary for complete understanding and appreciation of the writer's work by the reader. Rhetoric is covered elsewhere in *The Writer's Manual.* Here the essential elements of composition are presented in a concise form designed for ready reference as well as for study. This presentation is not meant to be an exhaustive study (lest we exhaust the reader) but is intended as a meaningful survey for continuing use by the reader.

Many people, oddly enough, see little connection between composition and good writing. Good writing is not accidental. It results from a carefully planned, organized, and constructed approach; by ordering words into sentences; sentences into paragraphs until the whole is achieved. An English teacher asked to have a manuscript she had written evaluated. It had much to offer: good characterization, valid intrigue, and colorful description, but it rambled and was full of fragmented sentences. In one episode the main character saw someone she wanted to speak to in the bank across the street.

She started toward the bank, but never got there. In discussing various aspects of the work, it was suggested she might make use of several good books; among them *The Art of Plain Talk* by Rudolph Flesch and *The Elements of Style* by William Strunk, Jr. She rose to her feet, her body rigid and erect. "But I TEACH those books!", she protested. Unfortunately her writing did not reflect that.

To give you some idea of how writing is affected by composition, read the following "fragment" from a novel in process. It contains many common errors. (A revised version is given in the Appendix.) Unless you are able to find and correct all the errors, you should find the following chapters worthwhile reading.

"NOVEL FRAGMENT"

He walked slowly through the gathering evening mist, his steps punctuated by the distant tolling of the cathedral bell. Eleven o'clock. At the corner, he stops, beneath the filtered glow of the streetlamp. The address on the card in his hands reads "1130 Calle Niebla", and it was already damp as he put it back into his pocket.

Turning down the alleyway to his right, his slow, measured steps took him to a doorway marked by a faint orange light and a sign, whose legend, obscured by the accumulated grime of many years, was illegible to all but those who knew its inscription by heart. He looked briefly around, making sure he was not observed; then walked down the three worn steps, now shiny-slick with the heavy mist, to the heavy iron bound door.

Pushing it heavily open with the long, slender fingers of his left hand, he thought to himself, 'half an hour left.'

As he made his way to the bar he called out; "Cerveza, Jose, San Miguel." The bartender, a squat heavy man with a bristling black moustache turned and stared for a moment and then poured the beer and retreated to the far end of the counter. Quentin sipped at his glass and watched the slow progress of the clock on the far wall. There was no-one there he knew, except for Jose. He moved slowly down the bar and spoke softly to him. "If anyone asks, I was here tonight until 12:30." He slid a bill across the counter.

Returning to his stool, Quentin idled his way through his remaining beer. Watching the light from the dull lamp behind him strike smouldering sparks in the opal on his right forefinger. He let his mind wander ahead, to the meeting that he could not understand. That morning, when he found the card with the pencilled note on its back beneath his hotelroom door, he had been surprised: he had not expected to meet any of his contacts face to face. Now he wondered at the change in plans. His was the kind of profession where ignorance was, if not bliss, at least security. Perhaps someone was onto them; perhaps this was the only way to safely alert him to the change in plans; perhaps . . .

The clock struck 11:30. Quentin stood abruptly, took a bill and some coins from his pocket, and dropped it on the counter. Back on the damp, shrouded street he turned to his right and walked swiftly into the beckoning darkness. Two blocks on, a turn to the left, and he walked up the unsteady stairs of the third house on the right hand side. The blackness of the night was here unrelieved by even the faintest glimmer of municipal illumination, and only the most painstaking gathering of stray lamplight, escaped from behind carefully drawn shades and curtains, served to identify the number as 1130. Two knocks, pause, then three, another pause, then two again. The ritual was executed correctly, but no response came from within. After a long moment of anticipation, Quentin repeated the formula. Still no answer. Listening closely for any sign of life behind the door, he became aware of footsteps echoing distantly, then nearer. They moved steadily down the street Quentin had just left, then, quite unexpectedly, turned at the corner just as he had done moments before. Quentin's hand was on the doorknob, and before he had time to think about it, or anything else, for that matter, he stood inside a darkened, unfamiliar hall.

The door was safely closed behind him, and Quentin listened as the footsteps passed the house slowly and faded into the distance. He waited a moment to be sure they did not return, then moved cautiously down the narrow hall. The door at the far end was ajar. It opened inward to a light push.

A faint odor of burnt rope, mingled with some sort of incense or perfume, greeted Quentin as he stepped inside. His eyes were accustomed to the darkness by now, but the stillness disturbed his ears. A wall of silence hung over the room, and even his breathing seemed an intrusion. He checked the room quickly with his eyes, and once he had determined that he was alone, turned on the overhead light.

As the room takes on a ruddy warmth from the glowing tinted fixture, Quentin discovers that he was wrong in assuming his solitariness. There, slumped over the circular wooden table in the center of the deep persian carpet, is a girl dressed in embroidered jeans and white peasant blouse. The dark red stain, still spreading slowly beneath her left arm, reminds him that in the future he must be more punctual. A brief glance at his watch tells him he was only seven minutes late. 'Seven minutes,' he thinks to himself as he silently switches off the light. 'Seven minutes,' the number revolves quietly in his mind as he slips out the door, and assuring himself that he leaves as unremarked as he arrived, moves slowly down the dampening streets toward his next appointment.

ຽ ຽ ຽ

Whatever potential this piece of writing may have cannot be realized until it is put into better grammatical shape. Regardless of its literary merit, a good portion of it is not even in acceptable English. Consider your own reactions to the poor grammar and bothersome mistakes. You may begin to understand why any writer must pay close attention to composition. The matter becomes even clearer if you put yourself in the position of an editor reading such a manuscript submitted for publication.

A good knowledge of composition is an asset you cannot afford to be without. If you are at all serious about writing, it is indispensable. In writing, as in any kind of workmanship, the more mistakes you make, the less your product is worth. In the following chapters, you will find a summary of basic composition designed to help you avoid making the kinds of errors to be found in the novel fragment.

It is assumed the reader already possesses some basic knowledge of grammar. Therefore, treatment and explanations in this book tend to be concise rather than exhaustive. If you require more fundamental treatment, the bibliography contains several suggestions that will be helpful.

No book on composition should be read only once, unless you aren't serious about improving your writing skills. It's a bit like cracking a black walnut picked from the tree. First there is that bothersome hull that must be removed. If it is still green, the hull will leave stains on your hands that only time will gradually diminish for walnut juice seeps deeply into the pores of whatever skin it touches. Once through that, there is the nut itself, covered with ridges sharp enough to cut unsuspecting fingers. Cracking the nut requires a well directed blow with a hammer. If you strike the nut less than squarely, it will fly off with a force, and distance, in proportion to the hammer power you delivered. Finally, you learn the skill -- learn how to crack the nut. Undoubtedly, you will half the nut on the first blow, then half the halves on successive blows. Whatever system you devise, eventually you get out the nut-meat. The smell of the process will set the salivary glands working until you pop a piece in your mouth. It is so delicious to the taste, you reach for the next nut, and the next, and the next, content to stick with the tedious process as the pile of walnut meats grows to your satisfaction.

Walking toward good composition is not dissimilar. It is hard work, requiring your utmost concentration and all the creativity you can bring to bear. This manual is intended to be kept at hand when writing, for reference whenever you have a question about composition. Knowing how to rub words together is surely a great part of any good writing; knowing how to rub words together *accurately* is the rest of the task.

Good luck to you in the effort.

CHAPTER ONE

Punctuation

What is punctuation? Why punctuate? It is "the act, practice, or system of inserting standardized marks or signs in written matter to clarify the meaning and separate structural units." That definition is simple, concise, and to the point, but it does not tell us how and does not explain why we need to punctuate.

Rudolph Flesch, in his delightful little book *The Art of Plain Talk*, makes the point that the new writer probably thinks punctuation marks were devised by the devil. The punctuation marks we use today have become standardized over a long period of years, are fixed in the public's mind, and are the means by which the writer makes his writing understandable to the reader. The conventions or rules are simple and if you take the time to study the writing of others, you will see that without some agreed upon system of indicating the way a writer wants to be read, the reader might never understand or feel what the writer is attempting to convey.

In speaking you pause for effect; you use your voice to indicate mood, feelings. You emphasize important facts by varying the tone or the volume of your voice. You make certain your listener gets your message. In the written word you must have the same means of making sure you are understood. A good writer uses punctuation just as he does the right word or phrase as a means of conveying his whole meaning to the reader. His usage becomes a part of his style of writing.

Read the following newspaper item from which all punctuation has been removed.

Modern techniques of tapping the earths black gold with drills originated in the United States in 1859 at Titusville, Pennsylvania a retired railroad conductor Edwin Drake punched downward with a steam driven bit and struck oil at 69½ feet large reservoirs could be found he proved by pricking the earths skin an industry was born and life on this planet began changing in quantum jumps unparalleled in history crude oil welled up easily from the shallow holes of Pennsylvania and California on a hill called spindletop in east Texas a gaspropelled geyser of oil blew drill pipe high in the air in 1901 signaling a well that spurted out 100000 barrels a day before it was capped a worker turned to a newspaper reporter at the scene and drawled mister thats some gusher aint it an old word took on a new meaning of instant wealth gushers dramatic but wasteful are now usually prevented by pressure valves but the search for oil retains an excitement and challenge uniquely its own

It is impossible to grasp the full meaning of this passage without pausing at various places to be certain you understood what the writer was saying. Now read it with the punctuation restored and you suddenly discover the importance of punctuation in writing, if we are to understand its meaning.

Modern techniques of tapping the earth's black gold with drills originated in the United States. In 1859 at Titusville, Pennsylvania, a retired railroad conductor, Edwin L. Drake, punched downward with a steam-driven bit and struck oil at 69½ feet. Large reservoirs could be found, he proved, by pricking the earth's skin! An industry was born, and life on this planet began changing in quantum jumps unparalleled in history.

Crude oil welled up easily from the shallow holes of Pennsylvania and California. On a hill called Spindletop in east Texas, a gas propelled geyser of oil blew drill pipe high in the air in 1901, signaling a well that spurted out 100,000 barrels a day before it was capped.

A worker turned to a newspaper reporter at the scene and drawled, "Mister, that's some gusher, ain't it?" An old word took on a new meaning of instant wealth.

Gushers, dramatic but wasteful, are now usually prevented by pressure valves, but the search for oil remains an excitement and challenge uniquely its own.

If you had no punctuation marks to use, you would have to devise some means of indicating to readers when to pause, when to stop; some means of conveying your attitudes and other factors important to you in expressing yourself. Ground rules, acceptable to, or acknowledged by all, need to be established in order to have meaningful communication. The conventions or rules that have grown up over a long period of time may not solve every writing problem, but if punctuation is used meaningfully, according to accepted usage, the reader will better appreciate and understand what you are expressing. Some writers say they punctuate 'by ear' and to some extent this is possible. Many will observe that 'rules are made to be broken.' However, as one noted writer, Robert Graves, commented, "You must know the rules of grammar before you can presume to break them."

The ground rules that follow are given in as brief and condensed a form as possible in order to provide a ready reference as well as to present the essential principles of contemporary punctuation.

The Period

A.   The period is used after a declarative sentence.

> John came home from school
> We watched the movie on television.

B.   Use the period after an imperative sentence unless the meaning is strong enough to require an exclamation point.

> Go close the window.
> Shut off the T V and get to bed.

A question stated so that it is a polite command is regarded as imperative.

> Will you please study your lesson before you start to write.
> Please follow the directions given.

The Question Mark

A.   Use a question mark after an interrogative sentence.

> Who called?
> Where shall we go?
> Did he say it is midnight?

B.   The question mark may be used in a declarative sentence.

> You are going to the opera?

C.   Use a question mark in parentheses to indicate doubt or uncertainty as to fact, or to indicate an ironical attitude on the part of the writer.

> The story was written in 1774 (?).
> You bought your suit at the cheapest store(?).
> That is the best you can do (?).

D.   Do NOT use a question mark after an indirect question or after a polite request.

> I asked who won the game.
> Will you please eat your dinner.

The Exclamation Point

A. The exclamation point is used after an emphatic word, phrase, clause, or sentence.

>   HELP! HELP!
>   What a game!
>   Hold that gangplank!

B. Do NOT use more than one exclamation point.

>   CORRECT   :   Right on!
>   INCORRECT :   Right on!!

The Versatile Comma

The comma indicates a slight pause. It is one of the most useful and abused of the various marks of punctuation. Mastery of the comma will greatly increase your ability to punctuate, and to write effectively.

The over use of the comma is as faulty as leaving the comma out when needed. Some writers seem to have a supply of commas set aside in a desk container and as they write they throw in a few in the same way an Italian cook uses seasoning. Others never use them or use them so sparsely that one thought crowds into another and you have to back-track to get the meaning or the feel of the piece. There are sound basic rules for comma usage, but today there is more license - more freedom - for artful usage.

A. Use of the comma in forms of address, dates, and titles:
>   I live at 1496 Sacramento Avenue,
>   San Francisco, Ca 94102

>   The picnic will be July 4, 1976.
>   (Military usage omits the comma by placing the
>   day before the month: 4 July 1976)

>   John Smith, M.D.
>   Tom Jones, Ph. D.
>   Susan Ames, R.N.
>   Martha Taylor, Editor
>   J.J. O'Conner, Attorney-at-law

B. A short series of independent clauses may be separated by a comma eliminating a conjunction.

>   He swore, he raved, he ranted on and on.

C.   A comma is necessary to prevent misunderstanding in a sentence using several names or objects.

>   I sold my car to John, and his cousin then bought it from him.

D.   A comma is useful after an introductory word, phrase, or clause to clarify the meaning for the reader.

>   If we do not hurry, we will miss the train.
>   Unless John and Mary get the house they want,
>   they may never move to the city.

The use of the comma in introductory words, phrases, and clauses, often causes trouble for many writers. Much depends upon the meaning. "However," for example, is often used as an introductory word, yet it does not always take a comma after it.

>   However, she decided not to bake a cake.
>   However clear the sky looked, the weather-man
>   had predicted rain.

E.   The use of the comma to separate the various elements in a series of either words, phrases, or clauses, is currently a matter of taste. The conservatives require a comma after each; the more modern style used by many newspapers, magazines and book-publishers approves leaving the comma out entirely if the conjunction is used with each part, unless the series is very long.

>   The colors of our flag are red, white and blue.
>   A banner may be red or white or blue or a combination
>   of these colors.

Note: If et cetera, or the abbreviation "etc"., is used a comma preceeds it. If it does not end the sentence, then a comma is used after it as well.

>   He stopped at the hardware store to get a hammer,
>   nails, etc., he needed to finish his project.
>
>   He stopped at the hardware store to get a hammer,
>   nails, etc.

The use of etc., is overworked. It should be avoided as it really adds little and is best omitted in most instances.

F.   The comma in compound sentences

>   The comma is used between main clauses in a compound sentence and is placed before the coordinating conjunction.

For example:

	and	
	but	
	for	
Main clause	or	main clause
	not	
	yet	
	so	

The sun is setting, and we can not get home before dark.
I have heard him talk, but I do not think he says very much.
Uncle John was good at entertaining visitors, for he always had a good story to tell.
A good speaker should observe his audience carefully, or he may lose contact with them.
James was not a good listener, nor was he a good speaker.
He was a noted mountain climber, yet he could not scale the wall ahead of him.
We were too late for the concert, so we went back home.

Note: 1. Do **NOT** confuse comma use in a compound sentence with a simple sentence containing a compound verb.

INCORRECT The boy stopped for a moment, and then crossed the street.
CORRECT The boy stopped for a moment and then crossed the street.
(The boy stopped and crossed — therefore, no comma).

2. The comma is **NOT** used after the coordinating conjunction.

CORRECT — John enjoys playing golf, but Joe prefers to play tennis.
INCORRECT — John enjoys playing golf, but, Joe prefers to play tennis.

3. The comma splice — a common error
The comma is **NOT** used between two main clauses not joined by a coordinating conjunction.

RIGHT — Our history teacher was very interesting, and we always paid close attention.
WRONG — Our history teacher was very interesting, we always paid close attention.

This error in usage can be avoided by using a semicolon instead of a comma and the coordinating conjunction.

> Our history teacher was very interesting; we always paid close attention.

4. The comma may be omitted if the two main clauses are very short.

> Mary spoke and John listened.
> Joe ran but Don walked.
> The cat came out but the dog didn't.

G. Use of commas in a series

1. The "rule" states a comma is needed after each word, phrase, or clause in a series of three or more.

> I bought apples, peaches, bananas, and pears at the corner market.
> Jane made the beds, dusted the furniture, and vacuumed the rug.

In the second example there is a tendency today to leave out the comma before "and" if the series is only three items, as noted previously in reference to "Introductory Words, Phrases or Clauses."

> The snow is falling, the wind is blowing and snow drifts will soon block the roads.

In a series of clauses, careful writers may prefer to use the comma before "and" to avoid any misconception on the part of the reader.

2. No comma is needed when only two items are listed.

> Dave ordered a roll and coffee.

H. Commas between coordinate adjectives (of equal importance). These adjectives precede and modify the same noun or pronoun.

> He was a kind, patient man.   (Kind and patient modify man)
>
> It was a hot, humid evening.   (Hot and humid modify evening)

Note that no comma is placed before the noun or pronoun. You can test the use of coordinate adjectives by:

1.   Inserting a conjunction in place of a comma if you prefer.
>   RIGHT: It was a hot and humid evening.
>   RIGHT: It was a humid, hot evening.

2.   You can reverse the order with no serious change in meaning.
>   It was a hot, humid evening.

I.   Use of the comma in connection with restrictive and nonrestrictive words, phrases, and clauses.

1.   Commas are not used to set off restrictive items.
>   President John F. Kennedy was shot and killed in 1963.
>   (The words John F. Kennedy are needed to complete the thought of the sentence.)
>
>   A boat with a leak will sink.
>   (With a leak completes the sentence.)

2.   Commas are used to indicate nonrestrictive words, phrases, and clauses.
>   The President, John F. Kennedy, was shot and killed in 1963.
>   (John F. Kennedy is not needed to complete a logical sentence.)
>   San Francisco, where I live, is a city with many hills.
>   (Where I live does not restrict the identity of San Francisco. A nonrestrictive element modifies but does not restrict.)

J.   Use of commas to set off parenthetical words, phrases, and clauses.

1.   Parenthetical elements are words or expressions which interrupt the sentence but they are not modifiers.

>   Words most commonly used:

accordingly	however
besides	moreover
consequently	perhaps
furthermore	therefore

The need is, perhaps, too great.
The cost will be divided, therefore, between the city and the county.
It was, however, a pleasant evening.
The motion, consequently, was lost.

2.   Parenthetical phrases and clauses are set off in the same manner as nonrestrictive phrases.

    a.   A few examples of such phrases are:

in fact	on the other hand
in conclusion	of course
in reality	to be sure

    b.   Clauses

I am certain	he reported
I repeat	I think

3.   A comma is used to set off a noun used in direct address. The name or title of the person addressed may come at the beginning, at the end, or in the middle of a sentence.

    John, will you answer the telephone?

    Answer the telephone, John.

    Sir, your cab is waiting.

    Your cab, sir, is waiting.

    It was very thoughtful of you, my dear, to call.

    Pardon me, young man, this seat is taken.

4.   An interjection requires a comma.

    Ah, such a lovely day for a picnic.

    Oh, I thought Roy was coming with us.

    Well, if you do not hurry we will miss the plane.

    Dear me, I forgot to lock the door.

    My, you do look weary.

(If the interjection is strongly emotional, it requires an exclamation point. In this case, no comma is used.)

5.   Dialogue: Commas are used to indicate who is speaking.

    The president said, "We will not have a meeting next week."

    The student asked, "When is this paper due?"

    "When you come to San Francisco," my cousin said, "be sure to call me."

If you are using an indirect quote, no commas are needed.

    The president said there would be no meeting next Tuesday.

6.   Commas are used to indicate opposites or contrasts.

    This work requires a man, not a boy.

    San Francisco, not Los Angeles, is the financial center of the West.

    His painting, not his sculpture, made him famous.

The comma is the most versatile of all punctuation marks. According to today's standards, use the comma whenever it may be needed to prevent misreading. But keep the rules in mind so that you do not use the comma where none is needed. The overuse of the comma can create as much difficulty for a reader as using none at all.

The Semicolon

The semicolon is a mark of punctuation indicating a degree of separation of coordinate elements intermediate between the comma and the period. Stated another way, it indicates a greater break in thought than the comma and less of a break than the period.

Why, and when, should you use it?

A.　A semicolon is used between independent clauses when the conjunction is omitted.

> Arthur, please close the window; it is beginning to rain
> Jack will make a good captain; he has the confidence of the entire team.

Actually, the period is interchangeable with the semicolon when used between two independent clauses.

> Arthur, please close the window. It is beginning to rain.
> Jack will make a good captain. He has the confidence of the whole team.

B.　In compound sentences the semicolon separates the parts of the sentence when the clauses are connected by such conjunctive adverbs as:

consequently	in fact
hence	furthermore
however	nevertheless
so	than

> I am not feeling well; however, I must get to the meeting.
> The senator lost interest in his constituents; consequently he was defeated in the election.

C.　If any clause in a compound sentence contains one or more commas, the semicolon must be used to separate the independent clauses.

> If James is elected, he will serve; but he will not be popular.
> Bill, my nephew, is majoring in science; but his cousin, Ralph, has not declared his major yet.

D.   The semicolon is used to separate phrases and clauses when one or more of the phrases or clauses contains a comma and to separate clauses when necessary for clarity.

> The port of San Francisco has not done well since the city took it over from the state; several shipping companies, because of increased rents, moved elsewhere; maintenance costs, due to inflation, have increased.

> The jockey made a fast, clean start; kept a respectful distance behind the pacemaker; moved his horse ahead at the final turn; then took the lead in the race.

E.   The semicolon is NOT used between parts of unequal rank, such as a clause and a phrase.

> Although it was an exciting movie; I did not have time to see the ending.   (WRONG)
> Although it was an exciting movie, I did not have time to see the ending.   (RIGHT)

The Colon

Generally speaking, the colon is a mark of punctuation indicating a pause greater than a semicolon, but less than a period. However, it has several specific uses such as indicating that a list to emphasize a statement or quotation.

A.   The colon is used after the salutation in a formal letter.

> Dear Sir:
> Dear Mr. Armstrong:

A comma usually suffices in informal address.

> Dear Son,
> Dear Mary,

B.   The colon is used before a series or to introduce a list.

> The baker had three kinds of pie: lemon, cherry and apple.
> Jane made a notation that she needed several items: a thimble, needles, thread, and pins.

C.   Certain types of separation use the colon .

   1.   Use a colon when the time of day is written in figures to show hours and minutes, but no colon is necessary when minutes are not indicated.
   6:30 A.M.
   7 P.M.

   2.   Biblical reference — Psalm 22:10

D.   A formal quotation is preceded by a colon.

   In his discourse on present day colleges and universities Dr. Robert M. Hutchins said:

E.   You use a colon if you wish to emphasize a statement:

   Helen concerned herself about one thing above all others: her children's education.

F.   A colon is needed between two clauses when one explains or amplifies the preceding clause.

   He has declared his political intentions: he will not become a candidate for any office.

Do NOT permit a colon to separate a verb from its object.

   I enjoy: classical music, popular music, and Dixieland Jazz.
   (INCORRECT)
   I enjoy classical music, popular music, and Dixieland Jazz.
   (CORRECT)
   I enjoy many types of music: classical music, popular music, and Dixieland Jazz.   (CORRECT)

Likewise, do NOT let a colon come between a preposition and its object.

   Jack is involved in: hunting, fishing, and tennis.   (INCORRECT)
   Jack is involved in hunting, fishing, and tennis.   (CORRECT)

The following passage employs the use of the comma, semicolon, and colon correctly:

   Today an architect must envision all the essential components that must be woven into his plan for the whole: miles of wiring and piping; cables, heating, ventilating, and air-conditioning ducts, intakes, and outlets; as well as systems to control the building's functional needs.

Much vitality would be lost if this passage were broken into separate sentences.

The Dash

There is a tendency to overuse the dash in current writing or to use it carelessly in place of a comma or a semicolon. To some writers it seems to be an easy way to indicate a break in thought and to avoid having to decide what punctuation mark to use. The dash is not simply a substitute, and it has meaningful uses. It is used to indicate an omission.

Ms. P — began writing poetry when she was sixteen years old.

To indicate a break within a sentence, a change of thought, hesitation or to set off something parenthetical.

He was — how can I put it — a lecher.
He burst into the room — I couldn't avoid him.
Have you ever felt — well, cursed?

To emphasize

When he reached for his gun, there was no choice: he had to - die.

To set off a summarizing statement.

Morning, noon, night — it made no difference in his anguish.

The Hyphen

The Hyphen is a convenient punctuation mark, rather than a necessary one, in most of its uses. It is, perhaps, best to approach the question of its use with a negative rather than a positive set of "rules".

A.   The primary use of the hyphen is to divide a word at the end of a line when space does not permit completing the word.

   1.   Words may be divided only between syllables, and one syllable words must never be divided.

If you receive more than one copy of this brochure, please give one to an interested friend.   (CORRECT)

Your Cancelled check or your charge account billing will acknowledge receipe of your order.   (CORRECT)
The balance is due at the time of delivery and may be paid i-
n cash or by check.   (INCORRECT)

2. Do not divide contractions.

    It would be incorrect to divide can-'t, you-'re, should-n't, and like words.

3. Avoid dividing the final word on a page.

B. The hyphen is used in some compound words for the sake of clarity. In many cases only the context of the sentence will determine whether a hyphen is required.

    > He was the runner-up.
    > His aid-de-camp came in the door.
    > He felt run-down.
    > The house was in a run down condition.

C. Hyphens are used to separate prefixes from words where the meaning would not otherwise be clear.

    > She re-covered the couch.
    > The stolen automobile was recovered.

D. The hyphen is generally used after certain prefixes to simplify an otherwise confusing combination.

all-American	Pre-Renaissance
mid-Atlantic	self-confident

Quotation Marks

A. Quotation marks are required at the beginning and end of words spoken in direct conversation, but not indirect quotations.

    > Ray said, "I am ready to go."
    > Ray said he is ready to go.

B. Single quotation marks are used to enclose a quotation within a quotation.
    > "Martha, remember what your father said, 'I will meet you at the library at 5:30; no later.'"

C. Quotation marks are used to enclose words or phrases that a writer does not wish to claim as his own or desires to call to the reader's special attention.
    > It seemed like a "once in a life-time" opportunity.
    > To some Roy appeared to be too "nice" for words.

D. Colloquial expressions and slang and humor unsuited for use in formal writing should be enclosed in quotation marks. There is a temptation to "overwork" this usage.

E. Quotation marks are used to enclose the titles of short stories, essays, and articles.

> Have you read Thornton Wilder's "The Happy Journey to Trenton and Camden?" Leo N. Tolstoi's "Patriotism and Christianity" has influenced men of all ages.

The titles of books and periodicals are generally put in italics, rather than enclosed by quotation marks. In a typewritten manuscript, they should be underlined.

F. Punctuation.

Most authorities agree that the comma and the period should be placed inside quotation marks. If a question mark, semicolon or exclamation point belongs to the quotation, it goes inside the quotation marks as well. If it does not belong to the quoted portion, it is placed outside.

> The nurse said, "Call the doctor."
> The doctor answered, "Why did you call?"
> "No," said the doctor, "I can not come now."
> Did you hear the doctor say, "I can not come now"?
> He said, "Call an ambulance"; but it was too late.
> "He's dead!" the nurse exclaimed.

Some argue that these conventions are not logical usages, but are accepted for the convenience of printers. Whatever the case, it is clear such usage is deeply imbedded in writing practice.

The Apostrophe

A. The possessive of nouns and pronouns is most commonly formed by adding an apostrophe and an s.
> That man's hat has a spot on it.
> Look for him in the children's playroom.

B. In words ending in s or z it is common practice to add only an apostrophe at the end. This is especially true with Biblical, classical, and common names, and common names ending in s and z.

> Check the babies' bottles.
> Where is the ladies' room?
> That must be James' car.
> The picture portrayed Ulysses' voyage.

C. Possessive pronouns do not take the apostrophe.

> This is yours; that is theirs.
> Its failure was of no consequence.

D. An apostrophe is used to show that one or more letters have been omitted.

> It's for it is; can't for cannot:
> you're for you are; we'll for we will;
> where'er for wherever; '76 for 1976.

E. A common error is to confuse the possessive pronoun its for it's — it is. The possessive plural pronoun takes no apostrophe.

The apostrophe followed by a *d* may indicate that the word or expression is being used as a verb in the past tense.

> The clerk OK'd the shipment.

Parentheses

Parentheses, dashes, and commas all may be used to set off parenthetical material. However, there are certain usages where parentheses are deemed best.

A. Parentheses are preferred in setting off illustrative or supplemental elements.

> Samuel Clemens (Mark Twain) wrote *Tom Sawyer.*
> He decided to jump the fence (about 4 ft. high) rather than unlock the gate.
> Thomas Jefferson (1743-1826) was the third president of the United States, (1801-1809)

B. When parentheses occur in a sentence no other punctuation is used unless it is needed or required as a regular part of the sentence.

> The amount of land needed (about 10 acres) will be easy to secure.
> Unless he pays the back payments (over $500.00), the bank will foreclose on the mortgage.

C.   Parentheses are used to enclose a question mark when it is used to note uncertainty.

> Your father was born in 1906 (?).

Brackets

Do not confuse brackets with parentheses.

A.   Use brackets to enclose editorial remarks or words that are inserted in a direct quotation by someone other than the original writer.

> The historian said, "That was the year [1917] America entered the war." (The date adds clarification.)

Brackets are used to enclose stage directions in narrative as well as dramatic writing.

> [James smiling : enters from the left.]
> [Anna bowing slightly] : "I am happy to meet you."

> This allusion to the Ides of March [among the Romans a fatal or inauspicious day] was understood as a threat.

Italics

In a typewritten manuscript, Italic type is indicated by underlining.

A.   Use italics to indicate title of books, pamphlets, bulletins, newspapers and magazines.

> *Eleanor and Franklin*
> San Francisco *Chronicle* or *San Francisco Chronicle*
> *Harper's Magazine*

B.   Use italics to indicate the titles of plays, movies, musical productions, etc.

> *Lavender and Old Lace* (play)
> *The Sundown Kid* (movie)
> Bizet's *Carmen* (opera)

C.   Italics are used to indicate names of ships, trains, etc.

> *Royal Viking* (ship)
> *City of San Francisco* (train)

Abbreviations

Abbreviations and symbols are used much less in general writing than they used to be, but they are employed more than ever in technical writing of all types. In general writing we still find them in footnotes, bibliographies, tables and lists of various kinds. The present trend is strongly away from the use of periods along with many of the abbreviations which had been used formerly. Despite the obvious trend to try to get along without abbreviating at all if possible, there are still some words which a writer almost never spells out. They include such titles as Mr., Mrs. (and Ms.), and Dr. when they appear before a name, abbreviations for degrees or other affiliations after a name, like Ph.D, or M.P., and other abbreviations in common and traditional use such as A.M. and P.M., A.D. and B.C.

Names and Titles

Normally, you should not abbreviate given names:
William not *Wm.* McKinley; *George* not *Geo.* Washington

Some names have a middle initial that doesn't stand for a name at all, and some given names consist of initials only. For the sake of consistency it's a good policy to use a period with all initials which appear with a name, even though the letter doesn't stand for anything:
Example: Harry S. Truman

When people are referred to only by their initials, such as two or three well known American presidents, no periods are needed:
FDR, LBJ

When a civil or a military title is used with the surname alone the title should be spelled out.
General MacArthur, President Buchanan

When full names are used, the title is usually abbreviated:
Maj.Gen.Thomas A. Balastier

Always abbreviate social titles, whether you use them with the full name or just the surname:
Mr., Mrs., Ms., M., MM., Mlle., Mme.

The titles Reverend and Honorable are spelled out if they are preceeded by "the."

The abbreviations Jr., Sr., II, III, etc. after an individual's name are part of the name and are used in connection with any titles. Jr. and Sr. are preceeded by a comma, but the others are not.

The abbreviation Esq. is never used when any other title is given, either before or after the name:

Robert Foote, Esq. (Not Mr. Robert Foote, Esq.)
Mr., Mrs. and Dr. are also dropped if another title is used:
Arthur D. Harrison, M. D.

The following abbreviations are often used in connection with the names of business firms:

Co., Inc., Corp., Bros., Ltd.

In regular text it's a good idea to give a firm's name in its full form, but Inc. or Ltd. may be dropped. In lists, footnotes, etc. the above abbreviations may be used.

The names of government agencies, associations, broadcasting companies, fraternal and service organizations, union and other such groups are normally abbreviated. They are usually set in capitals without the use of periods:

SEC, AMA, UNESCO, CORE, AFL–CIO, CBS, YMCA, NATO, WACS, USMC.

Always spell the names of states, territories, and possessions of the United States when they stand alone in the text. When they follow the name of a city or town it is best to spell them out also, except in lists, footnotes, bibliographies, and indexes.

Addresses

In almost all forms of writing, addresses should be spelled out in full, including these words:

Street, Road, Boulevard, Avenue, Drive, Lane, Parkway, Terrace, Court, Place, Square, Building, North, South, East and West.

Abbreviations may be used in lists and tabular matter, however, as follows:

St., Rd., Blvd., Ave., Dr., La., Pkwy., Terr., Ct., Pl.,
Sq., Bldg., N., S., E., W.

Names of Countries

The names of countries are spelled out in the ordinary body of the text, with the exception of the Soviet Union, which is often abbreviated *USSR*. In tabular matter others may be abbreviated as follows:

U.S., U.K., or G.B., W. Ger., Fr., Swed., It., Can., Mex., etc.

Directions

The points of the compass should be abbreviated as follows:
N, S, E, W, and NE, NW, SE, SW
Also: NNE, ENE, ESE, SSE, etc. and N by W, NW by W, etc.

When standing by themselves the words *latitude* and *longitude* are not abbreviated. In work of a scientific or technical nature, one of two forms of abbreviations may be used:
lat. 44° 28'18" or lat. 44-28-18

Time Designations

Time of Day
The abbreviations indicating "morning" and "afternoon" are usually set in capitals:
A.M., ante meridian (before noon)
P.M., post meridian (after noon)

Days of the Week
The days of the week should be spelled out in the text, but may be appreciated when you use them in footnotes, tables, chronologies, etc:
Mon., Tues., Wed., Thurs., Fri., Sat., Sun.

Months of the Year
Always spell out the names of the months in regular text matter, whether they stand alone or are used in connection with dates. You may abbreviate them, however, in the same circumstances as the days of the week as follows:
Jan., Feb., Mar., Apr., May, June, July, Aug., Sept., Oct., Nov., Dec.

Some publications, such as *Reader's Guide to Periodical Literature*, will abbreviate them this way:
Ja,   F,   Mr,   Ap,   My,   Je,   Jl,   Ag,   S,   O,   N,   D.

Years
Abbreviations for terms used in chronology are as follows. They are normally set in small capitals by the printer:
A.D., *anno Domini* (in the year of our Lord)
B.C., before Christ

General Abbreviations

abbr.	abbreviation	Gr.	Greek
abr.	abridged	hdqrs.	headquarters
adj.	adjective	hist.	history

adv.	adverb	inst.	institution
art.	article	I.Q.	intelligence quotient
b.	born	It.	Italian
bibliog.	bibliography	l.	Left (stage)
biol.	biology	lit.	literally
comp.	compiled	m. or masc.	masculine
cont.	continued	m.	married
copr. or ©	copyright	math.	mathematics
d.	died, daughter	med.	medical, medieval, medium
dial.	dialect	mgr.	manager
dept.	department	misc.	miscellaneous
dict.	dictionary	mus.	music, museum
dist.	district	nat.	national, natural
div.	division, divorced	neg.	negative
do.	ditto	pl.	plural
doz.	dozen	pub.	publisher
ed.	edition, editor	r.	right (stage)
Eng.	English	s.	son
esp.	especially	sing.	singular
f. or fem.	feminine	sociol.	sociology
Fr.	French	Sp.	Spanish
geog.	geography	subj.	subject
geol.	geology	syn.	synonym
geom.	geometry	trans.	translated
Ger.	German	treas.	treasurer
		yr.	your, year

Measure

You probably won't use the abbreviations for the English units of measure very often unless you are writing a technical work. You certainly ought to have them to refer to, however-

in. or " inch	rd. rod
ft. or ' foot	mi. mile
yd. yard	

The system of measure is complicated greatly by there being three methods of measuring weight -- one the common method, another in use by jewelers, and a third the apothecaries' measure. The abbreviations are as follows:

gr.	grain	fl. dr.	fluid dram
dr.	dram	fl. oz.	fluid ounce
oz.	ounce	gi.	gill
lb.	pound	pt.	pint
cwt.	hundred weight	qt.	quart
pk.	peck	gal.	gallon
bu.	bushel	bbl.	barrel

There are also the abbreviations for the units of time:

sec.	second	d.	day
min.	minute	mo.	month
h. or hr.	hour	yr.	year

International Measure

It's only a matter of time before the United States adopts the system of international measurement now in use by the rest of the world. It is a system that employs three basic units — the meter for length, the gram for weight, and the liter for volume. Prefixes are used to indicate the multiples or fractions of these basic units:

milli —	1/1000)	deca — or deka — (10)
centi —	1/100)	hecto — (100)
deci —	(1/10)	kilo — (1,000)

Examples: km. kilometer; m. meter; cm. centimeter; mm. millimeter;kg. kilogram, g. gram; cg. centigram; mg. milligram; l. liter, etc.

Special Abbreviations:

acct.	account	doz.	dozen
agt.	agent	mdse.	merchandise
bal.	balance	mfg.	manufacturing
bu.	bushel	pd.	paid
COD	cash on delivery	std.	standard
cwt.	hundredweight		

Symbols:

#	number	©	copyright
/	per	£	pound sterling
%	percent	s. or /	shilling
c/o	in care of	d.	penny, pence
@	at		
$	dollar		

Capitalization

Just when and how to go about capitalizing the names of persons, places, events, official bodies, the titles of artistic and literary works etc. can be confusing even to the experienced writer. Although there is no one set of rules that can be considered universally applicable, publishers working in English -- both here and in Britain -- usually discourage the overuse of capital letters, a practice which has an old-fashioned look about it. Authors sometimes have their own reason for capitalizing terms not normally handled this way, and if editor and author can get together there is no reason why the latter can't be indulged through mutual agreement provided the reasons are sound. But many authors are unaware of inconsistencies in their work, and it is the editor's job to establish a style and eliminate these. Once again, rules for capitalization are cut and dried, but as a writer keep in mind that there is an increasing tendency towards a *down* (lowercase) style as opposed to an *up* (uppercase) style.

Personal Names

Names and initials of persons are always capitalized:

George Washington, Clare Booth Luce, W.C. Fields

Many names of foreign origin -- particularly French, Spanish, Italian, German, Dutch, and Portuguese -- include those prefixes called *particles -- de, du, la, l', della, von, van, van der, etc.* Practice in capitalization varies widely for names of this type, and some authority should be consulted in doubtful cases, but generally the surname keeps the particle when used alone:

(Wernher) von Braun
(Vivien) della Chiesa
(Martin) Van Buren
(Eamon) de Valera

Titles and Offices

Civil, military, noble, religious and professional titles are always capitalized when they immediately precede a personal name:

President Ford
General Eisenhower
Queen Wilhelmina

Titles which follow a personal name or which are used in place of a name are almost always lowercased.

Civil titles

> Theodore Roosevelt, president of the United States
> Richard M. Daley, mayor of Chicago
> Winston S. Churchill, prime minister of England
> Emperor Wilhelm II of Germany
> the president, the mayor, the prime minister, the kaiser

Titles of nobility

> Elizabeth II, Queen Elizabeth
> queen of England, the queen

Military titles

> General Ulysses S. Grant, commander-in-chief of the Union army
> Chester W. Nimitz, commander of the Pacific fleet
> Corporal Joe Doaks, a noncommissioned officer
> the commander-in-chief, the general, the admiral, the corporal

Professional titles

> Vincent Williams, president of Northwestern University
> Harry Butler, vice-president of Butler Corporation

Religious titles

> Pope Paul VI, Francis Cardinal Spellman *or* Cardinal Francis Spellman,
> the Reverend Thomas McKay, Rabbi Benjamin Fine
>
> the pope, the papacy, the cardinal, the college of cardinals, the minister,
> the rabbi
>
> Prince Philip, duke of Edinburgh; the duke;
> Viscount Montgomery of Alamein; the viscount

Titles of honor should be capitalized, however:
> Her Majesty, His Royal Highness, Your Honor, His Holiness, Your Grace.

Place Names

Parts of the World

Certain nouns and adjectives which are used to designate regions of the world, or of a continent or a country ought to be capitalized, but purely descriptive adjectives are always lowercased:

> East, Orient, Middle East, Eastern culture
> West, Far West, Middle West, western, middle western

North Atlantic, South Pacific
the equator
South Pole

In newspapers and magazines we now often see *Western Europe* and *Eastern Europe* capitalized when these terms refer to political and not merely geographical divisions of the continent. The same applies to readings on the American Civil War, where *Northern* and *Southern* are commonly capitalized for the same reason.

Political Divisions

Political divisions of the world, of states, countries, and cities are normally capitalized when they follow the name and are considered to be a part of it, such as *county, state, city, empire, kingdom, colony, territory,* etc.They are usually lowercased when they stand alone or precede the name:

British Empire, Cook County, Union of Soviet Socialist Republics, the Republic of France, Oklahoma Territory.

Names in common Use

Popular and traditional place names are usually capitalized, and quotation marks are not used in this case:

The Buckeye State, the Channel, City of Brotherly Love, Deep South, Lake District, Left Bank, the Loop, Promised Land, South Seas, the States (the U.S.), the Village (Greenwich Village), Wild West.

Topographical Names

Names of oceans, mountains, rivers, islands, etc. are capitalized, as is the generic term when used as part of the name:

Sahara Desert, Black Forest, Great Barrier Reef, Carpathian Mountains, Arctic Ocean, Mississippi River, Caribbean Sea.

When a generic term is used descriptively rather than as part of the name, or when it is used alone, it is lowercased:

The Mississippi valley, the Chinese coast, the California desert, the Australian outback.

Buildings and Public Places

Names of buildings, streets, monuments, etc. should be capitalized:

The White House, the Capitol, Statue of Liberty, the Pyramids. Such terms as *boulevard, avenue, building, bridge, hotel, church, park, fountain, square, street, room, theater* are also capitalized when used as part of an official name:

Lincoln Park, Fifth Avenue, Adler Planitarium, Empire State Building, Piccadilly Circus, Golden Gate Bridge, Pump Room.

Titles of foreign streets, structures, etc. are capitalized when they appear in the original language:

Champs—Elysses, Unter den Linden, Piazza san Marco.

Names of Organizations

Governmental and judicial organizations

Full names of all administrative, legislative and judicial offices, departments, and bureaus are usually capitalized:

Senate, Parliament, House of Commons, United Nations Security Council, Chicago Board of Education, United States Supreme Court.

Do not capitalize:

government, executive, administration, court, cabinet, legislative or judicial branch.

Political and Economic Organizations

Names of national and international organizations, movements, and political parties are capitalized, but not the words *party, movement, platform*, etc.

North Atlantic Treaty Organization, Communist party, Holy Alliance, Common Market, Tammany Hall.

Nouns and adjectives designating political and economic systems of thought are lowercased:

democracy, nazism, communism, socialism

Institutions and Companies

The titles of companies and institutions and their internal departments and divisions are capitalized:

The University of Illinois, Smithsonian Institution,. General Electric Corporation, American Airlines, Vienna Philharmonic.

Associations and Conferences

The writer should capitalize the official names of all societies and organizations:

> Young Men's Christian Association, Chicago White Sox, Girl Scouts of America, Union League Club, Ku Klux Klan.

Acts and Laws

Full titles of acts, laws, treaties, plans, policies, and other agreements and documents are generally capitalized:

> Declaration of Independence, Marshall Plan, Constitution of the United States, Magna Charta, Treaty of Versailles, Mayflower Compact. Taft-Hartley Act.

Time and Calendar Designations

You should capitalize the names of days of the week and months of the year; also religious holidays and seasons, and most other holidays and specially designated days:

> Monday, Christmas Eve, Good Friday, Lent, Passover, Yuletide, Fourth of July, Labor Day, Thanksgiving Day, Veterans Day.

Gods, Dieties and Other Religious Names

Many writers are too free in their use of capitals when it comes to religious matter, due to the custom of capitalizing a great deal which was prevalent in former times, or because of an almost unconscious desire not to treat sacred subjects "lightly". Generally speaking, a good rule to follow is to capitalize proper nouns and adjectives, and put all other words in lowercase.

To begin with, the name of God and of all other dieties is capitalized:

> Christ, the Father, the Holy Ghost, King of Kings, the Lord, Messiah, the Savior, the Supreme Being.

Pronouns referring to these were formerly invariably capitalized, but this rule no longer holds, except in cases where it is employed to avoid ambiguity:

> Put your faith in Him, God offers to man according to His will. But God in his mercy, Jesus and his followers.

Other Holy or Revered Persons

The names of apostles, saints, prophets, and the like are often capitalized:

The Blessed Virgin, the Virgin, Buddha, Our Lady, the Prophet,

Religious Groups

Names of all religions, churches and other communions, their members and adjectives derived from these are written in upper case:

Catholicism, the Church of England, Islam, Buddhist, Hinduism,

Do the same with denominations -- both Christian and non-Christian -- orders, sects, and most other religious movements:

The Presbyterian church, Gentile, Jehovah's Witnesses, Methodism, Mormon, Zen.

Also the names of smaller organized religious bodies and the places in which they meet:

Abbey of Mont Saint-Michel, Faith Evangelical Lutheran Church, Congregation Tifereth Moshe, St. Nicholas Hellenic Orthodox Church.

Capitalize names for the Bible and its versions and editions, the books of the Bible, and other sacred or highly revered works:

Authorized, or King James Version, Holy Writ, Scriptures, Vulgate, Genesis, Book of Leviticus, Psalms, the Gospel of St. Luke, Acts of the Apostles, Dead Sea Scrolls, Koran, Talmud, Upanishads.

Also: Ten Commandments, the Beatitudes, Sermon on the Mount, Gloria Patri, Hail Mary, the Litany, the Lord's Prayer, Te Deum.

Military Terms

Full titles of armies, navies, fleets, companies, regiments, battalions, corps, etc. are capitalized. But the words *army* and *navy* are not when they are used alone, in the plural, or when they are not part of an official title:

United States Marine Corps, Joint Chiefs of Staff, Pacific Fleet, Luftwaffe, the Allies, Axis Powers, Army of Northern Virginia, Rough Riders, Eighth Army, Afrika Korps, Northumberland Fusiliers.

Wars, Battles and Campaigns

The full titles of wars should be capitalized, but the words *war and battle* are not when used by themselves. All military awards and citations are capitalized as well:

World War I, the Civil War, French Revolution, Battle of El Alamein, Norman Conquest. Spanish-American War, Congressional Medal of Honor, Silver Star, Victoria Cross.

Ships and Airplanes

Names of ships, aircraft and spacecraft are italicized, but abbreviations such as S. S. or H. M. S. preceding them are capitalized:

> *Constitution,* S.S. *United States, Graf Zeppelin,* H.M.S. *Hood, Gemini VI*

Medical Terms

The names of diseases, symptoms, tests, syndromes, etc. should be lowercased, except when proper names are included in the term:

> Hodgkin's disease, Meniere's syndrome, smear test, Bright's disease,

Physical and Chemical Terms

As in the previous case, proper names attached to laws, principles, theorems, etc. are capitalized, as are the symbols of chemical elements and compounds. When the latter are written out, they should be lowercased:

> Einstein's theory of relativity, Boyle's law, Newton's first law, sodium chloride, NaCl.

Astronomical Terms

The names of stars, planets, constellations, and other heavenly bodies are capitalized:

> Jupiter, Big Dipper, North Star, Ursa Major, The Milky Way, Halley's Comet.

Popular Names of Plants and Animals

Common plant and animal names are capitalized in various ways. A good suggestion might be to adhere to a lowercase style when dealing with the names of wild plants and animals, capitalizing only the proper nouns used with them:

> black-eyed susan, rhesus monkey, Canada thistle, Virginia creeper jack-in-the-pulpit, small-mouth bass.

Follow the same procedure for domestic animals and commonly grown plants:

> Rhode Island red, Hereford cattle, English setter, golden retriever, rambler rose.

Titles of Works

Capitalize the first and last words of all titles, and also all nouns, pronouns, adjectives, adverbs and subordinate conjunctions. Articles, prepositions and coordinate conjunctions should be lowercased, unless they form the first or last word of either the title or the subtitle.

Some titles must be punctuated. A colon should be added, for example, between the main title and a subtitle. Commas should be added when a series appears:

> A Leap to Arms: The Cuban Campaign of 1898
> The Watergate Affair -- And its Aftermath

Books and Periodicals

Titles and subtitles of published books, pamphlets, collections, magazines and newspapers should appear in italics when they are included in the text. Words such as *introduction, foreward, preface, contents, index, bibliography, etc.* are lowercased when they are referred to:

> George Bernard Shaw expounds on many of his ideas in his preface to *Man and Superman.*

Plays and Poems

Titles of lengthy poems and of collections of poetry are italicized, but the titles of short poems are set in roman type and used with quotation marks:

> *The Ballad of Reading Gaol,* " The Charge of the Light Brigade"

When mentioning a series of poems, set them all down in italics.

The titles of plays are italicized, regardless of the length of the work.

> Anton Chekhov's *The Cherry Orchard* is often presented in Chicago.

Films, Television, and Radio

The titles of motion pictures are italicized, while those of television and radio programs are set in roman type with quotation marks:

> the film *Last Tango in Paris,* NBC's "Bonanza."

Paintings and Sculpture

The titles of paintings, drawings, statues and other works of art of this type should be italicized:

> Sargent's *Lord Ribblesdale,* Michaelangelo's *David,* Rodin's *The Thinker.*

Musical Works

The titles of longer musical compositions -- operas for instance -- should be italicized. Song titles and shorter works are generally used with quotation marks. When mentioning a series of titles, it is easier and less confusing just to italicize them all, regardless of length. Of course many compositions don't have titles as such, being known rather by the name of the musical form in which they are written, plus a musical key or both. These should be capitalized, but not italicized or quoted:

> Beethoven's Ninth Symphony, *H.M.S. Pinafore,* "Begin the Beguine," *William Tell* Overture.

Numbers

There is no hard and fast rule for the style usage of numbers in textual matter -- at least none that everyone is willing to follow -- yet a writer must arrive at a certain consistency, and the most common problem -- the question of when to use figures and when to spell out numbers -- has to be dealt with in some way. The following suggestions can serve as correctly as any.

In text matter which is of a non-scientific nature, exact numbers of less than one hundred should be spelled out, while numbers of a hundred or more should be expressed in figures:

> When I first joined the club there were fifty-five members:
> There are more than 170 rooms in the new hotel.

Two important exceptions to our rule are year numbers and numbers referring to parts of a book. Both are always expressed in figures:

> The Second World War broke out in 1939.
> I believe you'll find that reference on page 74 of the text we talked about.

Numbers referring to the same category within a paragraph should be treated alike. Don't spell out some and use figures for others. If the largest has three or more digits, use figures for all of them.

When dealing with round numbers remember that approximate figures in hundreds, thousands or millions should be spelled out. Remember, too, that the word *thousand* is used only with even thousands; the number 4,700, for example, is spelled *forty-seven hundred.*

Large round numbers are often set down in figures as follows:

> 1.7 million, 6.3 billion

One rule that should always be kept in mind is that at the beginning of a sentence any number that would ordinarily be written in figures is spelled out:

One hundred twenty people were on the first commuter train.

Special Rules for Special Cases

In ordinary text pages physical quantities such as areas, volumes, distances, lengths, etc. are treated according to the rules we have just set down dealing with the spelling out of numbers:

Some horses can run forty miles per hour.
The box was twelve cubic feet in size.

In scientific, technical, mathematical, and statistical usage, however, these should be expressed in figures:

50 miles, 35 pounds, 7 liters

Fractional amounts should be set down in figures:

It is best to type your manuscript on 8½ by 11-inch bond.

If abbreviations are used with units of measure, the quantity should be expressed in figures:

10 mi., 2 hrs., 120 lbs.

Decimals and percentages are usually set in figures, too:

The bank pays an interest of 6 percent on savings accounts.
In college he ran the quarter-mile in 48.6 seconds.

Time

The time of day is normally spelled out when it appears in the text:

We usually take a coffee break at half past two.
The ball game is almost always over by five.

If you want to be more exact, however, it should be handled this way:

The plane leaves at precisely 12:20.

Figures should be used when the time of day is used with A.M. or P.M.:

9 A.M., 7:30 P.M.

In the twenty-four-hour system of time which the military services use, it is not necessary to punctuate between the hours and the minutes:

Taps were always at 2200.

Dates

You may write dates in either of these two ways:

> His son was born on July 4, 1948
> > or
> On 7 April 1943 the offensive began.

Don't use *st, d and th* after the figures of dates:

> October 14, not October 14th.

Spell out centuries and decades in lowercase:

> eighteenth century, in the nineties

> but: the 1940s

Money

Amounts of money in U.S. currency follow the general ruling for either spelling out or expressing in figures:

> Tickets for the play were priced at seven dollars each.
> They say that candy bars are all going up to fifteen cents.
> The suit cost $175.

As in the case of other large numbers, sums of money that would be awkward to spell out in full or to express in figures may be set down in units of millions or billions, along with figures and a dollar sign:

> A cost of $5 million was quoted by the company treasurer.
> That nation's defense budget is nearly $20 billion.

Foreign money -- pounds, francs, marks, and other currencies of the world -- are generally handled the same way, with a unit symbol preceding the amount. The U.S. Government Printing Office publishes a pamphlet called the *Style Manual*, and if you are in doubt as to custom, refer to the section entitled "Foreign Money."

Names

Kings, emperors, popes, etc. bearing the same names are identified by numerals appearing after the name:

> George III, Louis XV, Henry VIII, Julius II.

Roman numerals are also used by families to differentiate between male members with the same names. If, for instance, William Gates Jones' son or grandson is christened with the same name, he would add "Jr." to his name. If a third member of the family is given the name he would add "III," and a fourth would add "IV" etc. When the eldest bearing the name dies, William Gates Jones, Jr. drops the "junior," William Gates Jones III (if he is a grandson) becomes William Gates Jones, Jr. and so on. If the original or one of the early bearers of the name was a famous person, however, a younger namesake often keeps using the suffix: Douglas Fairbanks, Jr., Adlai Stevenson III.

Governmental Names

Governments, dynasties, and other governing bodies which succeed one another are usually designated by a number which is spelled out and which precedes the name:

> Third Reich, Fifth Dynasty, Second Continental Congress, Fourth Republic.

Numerals of less than one hundred which designate political divisions should be spelled out:

> Fifth Naval District, Twelfth Ward, Third Precinct.

Do the same with numerals of less than one hundred which are used to designate military subdivisions:

> Sixth Army, Third Infantry Division, Thirty-third Regiment.

Organizations

Churches, religious organizations, and other houses of worship generally use numerals spelled out before the name of the church.

> First Lutheran Church, Fourth Presbytherian Church.

Addresses, Streets, Roads

Federal, interstate, and state highways are designated by arabic numerals:

> U.S. Route 66, Interstate 90.

It's usually customary to spell out the names of numbered streets, though, if the number is under one hundred:

> Fifth Avenue, Forty-Second Street

In English and American addresses, numbers are usually written in Arabic numerals before the name of the street:

154 East Erie Street, Chicago, Illinois 60611
1236 Sherman Avenue, Evanston, Illinois 60202

Numbers and Their Uses

The plurals of spelled-out numbers are formed just like the plurals of other nouns:

Some say American life was more predictable in the 1940s and 1950s.

The new magazine was slanted toward readers in their twenties and thirties.

The league bowling averages were topped by two 182s and two 180s.

In most figures of a thousand or more, commas should be used between every group of three digits:

7,842   364,000   4,000,000,000

There are exceptions to the rule. Addresses, page numbers, year numbers of four digits and decimal fractions of less than one are written in figures without commas.

Inclusive or continued numbers are always separated by a dash. You can use the following as a general rule of thumb:

If the first number is:	Write it this way:
Less than 100	4-12, 95-96
100 or a multiple of it	103-108, 509-521
More than 100 but less than 110	102-3 also 1006-7
More than 110	470-75 811-936
	also 1762-67

Examples: The war of 1914-18, the winter of 1900-1901
              A.D. 600-664

Roman Numerals

The following list of roman numerals with their arabic equivalents may help you for a quick referral, but it would be wise to learn the rather simple rules by which they are formed. A smaller letter before a larger one detracts from its value, and a small letter after a larger one adds to it. A bar over a letter multiplies its value by one thousand.

1	I	16	XVI	80	LXXX
2	II	17	XVII	90	XC
3	III	18	XVIII	100	C
4	IV	19	XIX	200	CC
5	V	20	XX	300	CCC
6	VI	21	XXI	400	CD
7	VII	22	XXII	500	D
8	VIII	23	XXIII	600	DC
9	IX	24	XIV	700	D
10	X	25	XXV	800	DCCC
11	XI	30	XXX	900	CM
12	XII	40	XL	1,000	M
13	XIII	50	L	2,000	MM
14	XIV	60	LX	3,000	MMM
15	XV	70	LXX	4,000	MI$\overline{\text{V}}$
				5,000	$\overline{\text{V}}$

In parts of speech all the words used in our language are brought together and then sorted out and labeled. Parts of Speech is the traditional term or name used for this classification system that evolved over the course of more than 400 years. The beginning of English in printed form goes back to 1475 when a printer, William Caxton [1421(?)-91] produced the first books printed in English. With the advent and advancement of printing came an ever expanding vocabulary. This necessitated a tightening of the language; the establishment of principles and procedures acceptable for general usage in order that all would know and understand the meanings of the words in use, as well as their relationship one to another.

Eight general labels are currently accepted:

Nouns	Adverbs
Pronouns	Prepositions
Verbs	Conjunctions
Adjectives	Verbals

The basis for classification depends partly upon the meaning of the word, partly on its function, and in some cases, by how the word is used in a sentence. This means you will find many words 'filed' under several labels. Also, there are several minor classifications not included under the eight major labels. These additions to the general nomenclature will be discussed at the close of this section of Parts of Speech.

The parts of speech comprise the different kinds of words that conjoin in forming all phrases, clauses, and sentences. A close look at each general classification will provide a better understanding of the meaning and function of words under each label.

A. Nouns

Nouns have several qualities and may be singular or plural. A noun names something and gives identification to persons, places, ideas, and things. Most nouns form the plural by adding *s* or *es.* Some nouns change a consonant or vowel in forming the plural while a few make no change.

boy	boys
box	boxes
leaf	leaves
hoof	hooves
man	men
deer	deer
goose	geese
sheep	sheep

There are five different classes of nouns; moreover, some nouns fit into several classes.

1. Proper nouns name a particular person, place, or thing and are capitalized.

    Adam
    Declaration of Independence
    Yosemite National Park

2. Common nouns are terms for persons, places or things; they generalize, in contrast to proper nouns which specify.

men	county
city	holiday

3. Collective nouns name a group, in a general way.

army	people
air	team
choir	

4. Concrete nouns label something we recognize through our senses.

chair	rose
cloud	sugar
music	

    (This classification could include many common nouns, e.g. *men.)*

5. Abstract nouns name an idea, a quality or a characteristic.

beauty	truth
charm	vanity

B. PRONOUNS

A pronoun tales the place of a noun or nouns. Its main use is to avoid repeating the noun. It refers back to the noun for which it substitutes. There are five kinds of pronouns.

1. Personal pronouns

I	he	she	we	they
me	him	her	us	them
you		it		

These can become possessive pronouns.

my	his	you	her	our	they
mine	its	yours	hers	ours	theirs

Personal pronouns may be linked with "——self" to indicate that the subject acted upon itself (himself, herself) or to show emphasis.

a. Action of the subject upon itself:

He forced himself to go to the dance, although he preferred not to go.

b. Emphasis:

The doctor himself took her to the hospital.

c. Other forms using -self:

myself	yourself
herself	yourselves
itself	ourselves

2. The demonstrative pronouns

this	these
that	those

These are pronouns only when they take the place of nouns

This is yours.
That is the man I was looking for.
These are the ones I want.
Those are the ones on sale.

3. Relative pronouns:
that
which
who

The relative pronoun introduces certain subordinate (dependent) clauses.

> Roy is a friend that I met in the army.

> It is the same measure which was voted down last election.

> Coolidge was a president who chose not to run for a second term.

4. Indefinite pronouns

This category covers a great assortment of pronouns that refers in general to person, places, and things.

Examples are:

anybody	few
anyone	many
each	more
either	none

5. Interrogative pronouns

These pronouns are used in questions, as the name indicates.

who	whoever	What was the football score?
which	whichever	Which seat is mine?
what	whatever	Whose coat is that?
		Who is going to the dance?
		Whatever made him fall in the creek?

C. VERBS

A verb narrates action or refers to an event or affirms a state of being. It is a word that helps to make a statement by connecting (tying) the subject to a noun, pronoun, or adjective that describes or identifies the subject. The English verbal system is extremely versatile and flexible because of the numerous additions and combinations that can be used to modify a verb. Auxiliary or 'helping' verbs make what is called a *verb phrase* containing a main verb and one or more helping verbs. For example:

> am, are, is, has, had, do, does, did can, could, may, should, shall, might, must, ought to, would have, and might have been.

Other recognized variables are known as:

1. Tense — The form of a verb that expresses distinction of time.

    a. The *present tense* noting what is happening; habitual action.

        John wakes up at the same time every day.
        He walks to work.

    b. The *past tense* noting action prior to the present or remote from the present.

        Did John wake up early yesterday?
        He walked to work last week.

    c   The *future tense* noting action which will take place.

        John will wake up earlier tomorrow.
        He will walk to work.

    d. The *present perfect* indicates action which began prior to the present time and continues to happen.

        John had walked all morning before he reached the river.

    e. The *future perfect* notes action that will have been completed some time in the future.

        John will have walked five miles before he gets to town.

2. Aspect — A means of modifying a verb indicating that the action is not permanent, using parts of *the verb to be* and adding *ing* to the simple form of the verb.

        Arthur is working on his house.
        Arthur had been working many hours before the plumber arrived.

3. Mood — The means of modifying the verb to express action as or a command or a possibility.

        Arthur can work now.
        He could finish the house by April.
        He should wear brighter colors.
        Now hear this!

4. Subjunctive mood — a variation that expresses a hypothetical condition.

        If I *were* Arthur, I would change the colors.

5. Voice — By changing the *voice* verbs can be modified to indicate

whether a subject is acting or being acted upon. If the subject acts, the *voice* is *active*. If the subject and verb indicate the subject is acted upon, the *voice* is *passive*.

> The explosion shook the house. (active)
> The house was shaken by the explosion. (passive)

6. Person — Verbs can show whether the subject is being spoken about by adding an *s* to the present tense. If a pronoun is used, the verb indicates the subject is speaking or being spoken to.

> Jack walks daily.
> I like it.
> You will like it.

7. Number — Number refers to whether the subject of the verb is singular or plural and is indicated by the use of the third person in the third person in the present tense.

> Jack comes home early.
> They come home late in the evening.
> He is walking home tonight.
> They are walking home from church.

D. AGREEMENT

It may seem redundant to say that the subject and verb must agree in number and person; that a singular subject takes a singular verb, while a plural subject takes a plural verb. However, when other words or phrases occur between the subject and the verb, many writers make errors in this area. Also, a pronoun should always agree in person and number with the noun it represents. If its antecedent is singular, the pronoun is singular; likewise the pronoun is plural if the antecedent is plural. A few illustrations clarify both problem areas.

1. A collective noun takes a singular verb if the noun concerns a group considered as one unit.

> The team was given time out by the referee.

2. If the collection noun concerns the group as individuals, it takes a plural verb.

> The team were disagreed on a plan of attack.

3. If a plural subject is used as a single unit, the verb is singular.

Fifty performances is quite a record.
The short and sweet of it is we won.

4.   A plural verb is used with a compound subject.

Salad and dessert are in the refrigerator.

5.   Do not be led astray by such expressions as *in addition to, together with*, or *as well as.*   If the subject is singular, the verb will be.

A brochure, together with other material, is enclosed. Modern as well as classical music was played at the concert.

There are other words that create problems at times. Note that these words take the singular verb form:

anyone	everyone	each	someone
anybody	everybody	one	much
nobody	no one	none	

These words are plural and take the plural verb form.

both, few, many, several

In using either. . . or and neither . . . nor, the verb agrees in number or person with the part of the subject nearest to it. Here are a few examples:

Either Bill or his roommates are at fault.
Neither his roommates nor Bill is at fault.
Either they or I am going to the police.
Neither I nor they are going to the police.

E.   ADJECTIVES

An adjective modifies the meaning of a noun by denoting how its quality, or extent makes it different from anything else. It describes or limits a noun or pronoun. A *descriptive adjective* expresses quality and is placed either before the noun it describes or after the connecting verb.

The *gray* day is not always foggy.
The first car in the parade was a *red* car.
Next year will be my *last* year here.
He said that was his *final* word on the subject.

A *limiting adjective* refers to quantity or relationship. It is almost always placed before the noun.

every year, *much* work, *several* chapters, the *fifth* house. The words *which* and *what* and the article *a, an,* and *the* often accompany limiting adjectives and serve as such.

Which road do you take? *What* city do we reach next?

F. ADVERBS

An *adverb* qualifies a verb, an adjective, or another adverb.

> They fought *savagely.* (modifies verb)
> John is *exceptionally* kind to animals. (modifies adjective)
> The narrow canyon made the river flow *very rapidly.*
> (modifies adverb)

In English the adverb almost always ends in *ly* and usually any adjective can be made into an adverb by the addition of this ending. For example: slow, slowly, swift, swiftly. However, there are exceptions such as: here, now, much, and fast.

The adverb usually specifies the time, place, cause, or manner of action expressed by the verb it modifies. When it is used to modify another adverb or an adjective, it indicates the degree expressed.

> He sometimes walks into town.
> He walks sometimes through the woods.
> He has sometimes walked around the woods.

When an adjective or adverb is modified to indicate degrees of quality quantity, or relation, their forms change. The changes expressed in a range from 'positive' to 'comparative' to 'superlative'. For the superlative they add *-est*. Long adjectives and almost all adverbs add *more* for the comparative and *most* for the superlatives.

> fast, faster, fastest (adjective)
> beautiful, more beautiful, most beautiful (adjective)
> swiftly, more swiftly, most swiftly (adverb)

A descending order of quality or quantity for both the adjective and adverb is expressed by using the words *less* and *least* before the adjective or adverb.

> complex,   less complex,   least complex (adjective)
> courtly,   less courtly,   least courtly (adverb)

There are exceptions to rules and some of the exceptions or irregular adjectives and adverbs are:

good, better, best (adjective)
bad, worse, worst (adjective)
much, more, most (adjective)
well, better, best (adverb)
little, less, least (adjective or adverb as in
        He eats little, less, least)

G. PREPOSITIONS

The *preposition* connects (relates) a noun or pronoun to other words in
a sentence. The most used are:

about	at	except	since	up
above	before	for	through	with
across	behind	from	to	without
after	beside	in	toward	
along	between	off	under	
among	by	on	until	
around	down	over	unto	

Also, certain groups of words serve as prepositions but are not
prepositional phrases as such:

apart from	instead of
along side of	on account of
in front of	together with
in spite of	by means of

A *prepositional phrase* consists of a group of words that begins
with a proposition and ends with a noun or pronoun.

behind the house	on the wing
in the valley	up a tree
of mine	

H. CONJUNCTIONS

In English there are three kinds of *conjunctions:*
coordinating, correlative, and subordinating. Conjunctions link words,
phrases, or clauses in various ways.

1. Coordinating conjunctions link elements of equal rank. The con-
    junctions used in this manner are and, but, or, for, nor, yet, so.

    Deer and *quail* abound in many parts of northern California.
    (word linkage)

The snow swirled and drifted over the highway. (phrase)
The boy riding the bicycle and *the girl who is roller skating are cousins.* (clause):

2. Correlative conjunctions are just what their name implies: two related conjunctions used together.

 These are both. . .and, either. . .or, neither. . .nor, not. . .but, and not only. . .but also. (The also of but. . .*also* is often omitted.)

 Either a curb must be put on inflation or unions will be demanding higher wages.
 Both the jockey and the horse waited patiently at the gate.
 Neither big business nor the president has a solution for inflation.
 He brought a present not only for his son but also for his wife.
 He chided not only the boys but the girls in the class.

3. Subordinating conjunctions are used to begin subordinating (dependent) clauses and are used to join dependent clauses to independent clauses. The following are examples of subordinate conjunctions:

after	although	as
as soon as	because	before
even if	if	in order that
provided that	since	than
that	though	unless
where as	while	

 A bell rings *when* the starting gate is lifted.
 The starting gate is not lifted *unless* the horses are ready.
 As soon as the starting gate lifts, everyone shouts "They're Off!".

H. VERBALS

 Verbals is a catch-all term which covers types of words derived from verbs but which do not function as verbs.

1. The *infinitive* is a verb form identical with the first person singular and is usually preceded by *to*. It may function as a noun, and adjective, or as an adverb.

John wanted to stay. (noun-direct object)
There were many letters to write. (adjective)
Dave finds it hard to obey. (adverb)

In some combinations the *to* is understood and not written.

Jack made us go.
We watched the bird land.
We heard the bird sing.

2.   The *participle* is a verb form used as an adjective. The *present participle* always has *-ing* as an ending which is joined to the verb.

The cheering crowd spurred the players to victory

The *past participle* usually ends in *-ed*. There are some irregular forms ending in *-d, -t, -n, and -en*.

stoo*d*, knel*t*, swor*n*, writt*en*

A *dented* fender ruins the beauty of a car.
The *written* word can be persuasive.
A *sworn* statement may convince the judge.
As things *stood*, we had little chance to win.

3.   The *gerund*, like the present participle, *has -ing* as an ending. It serves as a noun and is sometimes called a verbal noun.

Swimming is good exercise.
Skiing can be dangerous.
Seeing is *believing*.

The gerund phrase, as the *gerund*, may be used as a noun. It consists of an infinitive and its object plus any other modifiers of the gerund.

Ray enjoyed *running along the beach*.
Forcing a man to walk the plank was one means of execution
      when pirates roamed the seas.

I.   INTERJECTIONS

Some authorities consider the *interjection* as one of the parts of speech while others explain it as a detached element. It is an expression used to convey and emphasize feelings or to call special attention to something or someone. An interjection is usually used with a sentence but it may stand alone as a sudden outburst.

Oh, I didn't know you were here.
Hey! Watch where you are going.
Heavens!

The sentence is the basic unit in writing. But what exactly is a sentence? If you were to look up the word "sentence" in a dictionary of your choice, you would find a sentence is a unit of speech expressing an idea, containing a subject and a predicate. While this definition is technically accurate, it can be misleading. In order to be a good sentence, a group of words must do more than simply express an idea and contain both a subject and a predicate.

A good sentence must make sense. If it does not make sense, it has failed, however adequately it may fulfill a formal definition. The object of any kind of writing is communication, and in order to be effective, communication must be understandable.

Watching the light from the dull lamp behind him strike
smouldering sparks in the opal of his right forefinger.

This example (taken from the 'fragment' in the introduction) is not a sentence but a fragment, even though it contains a subject ("light") and a predicate ("strike"). It is a fragment because by itself it does not make sense. Who was watching the light strike smouldering sparks in the opal? This information, necessary to make a clear and understandable sentence, is not given. A good sentence must be able to stand by itself and reveal meaning.

SIMPLE SENTENCES

The basic sentence, the simple sentence, contains only one clause, and often only one subject and one predicate.

John ran down the hill.

John is the subject and "ran," the predicate, tells what John did. A simple sentence may also have a compound subject, and even a compound predicate, provided it retains its single clause structure.

> Both pen and paper were on the desk.
> Paula and Mary dove into the water and swam
>   to the far side of the pool.

Because it is an independent clause, the simple sentence does not rely on external information to make its internal meaning clear.

COMPOUND SENTENCES

Compound sentences are made up of two or more independent clauses joined together by coordinating conjunctions or semi-colons. The use of a coordinating conjunction (and, but, for, or, nor, so, etc.) or a semi-colon establishes that the parts of the sentence being joined are of equal rank and importance.

> The rain came late this year so the crops will not be good.
> He considered the problem carefully, but it became more and more confusing despite his best efforts to find a solution.
> There was very little George could do; Edgar had carefully sealed off the only exit to the room, and George was hardly strong enough to break through the walls.

While the individual clauses in these sentences could stand by themselves, they are joined together because they are closely related in subject matter. The clauses themselves may be as long or as short as any simple sentence. But if you find yourself joining long sentences together, with a coordinating conjunction, take care that your meaning remains clear and the whole does not become confusing. The longer the sentence, the harder it is to follow.

COMPLEX SENTENCES

The complex sentence is similar to the compound sentence. It is made up of two or more clauses, but only one of these is an independent clause. The rest are dependent clauses, and are introduced by subordinating conjunctions (after, although, as, because, before, if, since, than, though, unless, until, when, while, etc.). The subordinating conjunction indicates that the clause following it is less important than the independent clause or main clause. The dependent clauses rely on the main clause to make their meaning clear, and cannot stand alone. They are indicated in the examples below by italics.

> I saw Mary at the station *when I went to get my ticket.*
> There is no telling what Edgar may do *since he is quite uncontrollable when he becomes angry.*
> *When the show starts,* the people in front will sit down.

Compound and complex sentences may be combined to form what is known as a compound-complex sentence. Such construction tends to be long and unwieldly, but can be useful for variety.

> *If only George had not asked about Lenore,* he would not have been so abruptly interrupted, but George had always been an inquisitive man.

The dependent clause appears in italics.

FRAGMENTS

A fragment is any group of words punctuated as a sentence that is not a complete sentence. Anything from "To fall asleep." to the example quoted at the beginning of this chapter can be a fragment, and the more complex and lengthy the fragment, the harder it is to identify as such. Avoid writing in fragments until you receive your first $50,000 book advance. By that time, the urge will have passed. Fragments are poor grammar; fragments are also incomplete thoughts and rather than communicate to a reader, they will only confuse him.

> If someone said to you

> > "When George gets here."

your immediate reaction would be to ignore the point or, if it was important enough, ask questions that would clarify the comment. The person speaking to you has not really told you anything. You need to have more information before what he said will make sense:

> "When George gets here we will begin the meeting."
> "Tell me when George gets here."

If people spoke in fragments all the time, you would probably think they were sub-normal in intelligence and not very effective in communicating with you.

It is equally true of writing. If you do not write in complete thoughts, those who read what you have written will have difficulty understanding it. Most will simply not waste their time trying to put together the pieces, and if you are writing for publication, the consequences of writing in fragments are both obvious and unpleasant.

How, then, to avoid fragments in your writing? The most effective way is to consider each sentence you write separately, preferably both before and after you write it. Be sure it meets all the requirements of a good sentence.

Does it have both a subject and a predicate, and above all, does it make sense when taken by itself?

The most common kind of sentence fragments are simply dependent clauses that should be attached either to the sentence that precedes them or to the one that follows them. They may read understandably within their written context, but unless they can stand by themselves as well, they are not sentences.

> Whatever your opinion on the subject may be, there will be someone to oppose you. Although you will be challenged. Although you will be pressed hard on every point, you must learn to stand as firm as your belief.

If read aloud, this passage makes sense. But in print the second 'sentence' stands out as a fragment. The problem may be solved by adding the fragment to the sentence that follows it:

> Although you will be challenged, although you will be pressed hard on every point, you must learn to stand as firm as your belief.

Fragments can often be corrected by adding them to adjoining sentences. Where this is not possible, fragments can often be made into sentences by changing a few words. In the example, dropping the word *although* makes the fragment an acceptable sentence.

> You will be challenged.

However, this alters the style of the clause and makes changes in the following sentence advisable.

Sentence fragments are best avoided. Not only are they poor vehicles for the clear communication of ideas, they are among the cardinal grammatical sins. Except in special cases (discussed in Chapter VI), they will mark your writing as substandard and often cause it to be rejected without serious consideration of its content.

RUN—ONS

A run-on is a sentence without the good sense to know when to quit. It wanders along, slipping through 'and's and 'or's, and manages to avoid running into a period until it has become thoroughly confusing.

> George had already arrived by the time Edgar returned home, and Edgar invited him in and offered him refreshments and asked if he had a place to stay for the night.

If the example above had any concept of grammatical etiquette, it would have stopped after "Edgar invited him in" at the very latest. A much better way of expressing the same thought would be:

> George had already arrived by the time Edgar returned home. Edgar greeted him, offered him refreshment, and asked if he had a place to stay for the night.

Another kind of run-on sentence is one in which two unrelated ideas are joined together, usually with a comma. (This kind of error is also known as a comma splice.)

> The sun broke through the clouds early that morning, Jim came by at noon.

Here confusion arises because the only relationship between the two clauses is their inclusion in the same sentence. The reader finds himself looking for a relationship that was never there. Ideas that are not closely related should be placed in separate sentences:

> The sun broke through the clouds early that morning. Jim came by at noon.

The best rule to follow with respect to run-ons is, "When in doubt, break it up." (Be aware of sentence fragments when you put this into practice.) It is not always desirable to write in short sentences, but it will do less harm than letting run-ons slip by. Run-ons fall into the same class of grammatical errors as fragments, and should be scrupulously avoided.

DANGLING PARTICIPLES

Another common problem which leads to faulty sentences is the dangling participle. A dangling participle is a verbal phrase, used as a modifier, which is not clearly related to the noun it was introduced to modify. Instead it is left dangling, and often gets connected to an inappropriate but convenient noun, creating a strange image:

> *Flying by the window,* John noticed the sparrows.

The modifying phrase appears at the beginning of the sentence instead of following the noun it was meant to describe. Thus, John gets his wings.

> John noticed *the sparrows flying by the window.*
> Mary Lou, *wearing a flowered print dress and blue platform shoes,* greeted George as he came in.

While these are not as amusing as the original constructions they do convey the images they were intended to relate.

AGREEMENT

Among the easiest mistakes you can make in writing sentences, and among the hardest to discover, are mistakes in internal sentence agreement. There are also a number of easy errors you can make.

George and Edgar is having dinner.

In this instance it is obvious that the verb should be "are," since there are two subjects (George and Edgar). This illustrates an error in subject verb agreement. When the subject is plural, the predicate must also be plural.

The committee are out to lunch.

In this case the subject is plural only by implication. Although a committee is made up of a number of people, only one committee is discussed in the sentence. The verb should be singular:

The committee is out to lunch.

Other problems in numerical agreement within the sentence occur between nouns and their pronouns. Take the following example from the 'fragment' in the introduction:

Quentin stood abruptly, took a bill and some coins from his pocket, and dropped it on the counter.

The pronoun "it" stands for what was dropped on the counter, but both a bill and some coins were dropped on the counter. The pronoun should be plural:

Quentin stood abruptly, took a bill and some coins from his pocket, and dropped *them* on the counter.

Another kind of agreement which often produces problems is agreement in tense within the sentence. If you start a sentence in the past tense, then slip into the present tense, your sentence will sound odd and confusing:

The address on the card in his hands *reads* 1130 Calle Niebla, and it *was* already damp as he *put* it back into his pocket.

The verb in the first clause, "reads," places the action in the present, but the remaining verbs, "was" and "put," indicate action in the past. The result is disorienting to anyone reading the sentence. Always be consistent in tense within a sentence.

The address on the card in his hands *read* 1130 Calle Niebla, and it *was* already damp as he *put* it back into his pocket.

Because your sentences are the basis, the fundamental units of your writing. the quality of your writing will depend upon the quality of your sentences. A good sentence is complete and concise. It neither says so little nor so much that it might be confusing to anyone you expect to read it. A good sentence is internally coherent. It does not shift in tense or number. The type and length of your sentences may vary, as they should in order to avoid monotony and to add some style to your writing. But these rules always apply. By keeping the rules of the writing craft in mind, when writing and reviewing your work, you will be able to express yourself more effectively and - more importantly - with clarity.

CHAPTER FOUR

Spelling

If you are endowed with a 'photographic' memory, it is possible you have no difficulty spelling correctly. But, if you are one of the many not born with good visual memory, you will have to work at training it or compensating for it.

Make certain your writing is free of mistakes in spelling. Readers who may be careless about their own spelling will be critical of yours, particularly editors. Subjectively, editors begin to suspect your educational preparation or, at least, your writing skill. Although absolute correctness in spelling may not be possible, most mistakes can be avoided by a careful analysis of your problem areas, by having at hand a good dictionary to check yourself when in doubt, and by meticulously proofreading what you have written.

Our language does not have each letter expressed by a single sound so you can not rely on the way a word is pronounced as the way it will be spelled. Consider, for example, the various sound of a as in *fare*, *mat*, *any*, *lay*, *far*, *war*, *human;* or the *ou* variations in *bough*, *enough*, *though*, *through*. We also have many words where the sound is the same but the words are spelled differently and, of course, have different meanings: *cite, site, sight, meat, meet, mete: write, right, rite*, are a few examples. There are words with silent letters as in *k*nife, *p*sychology, r*h*yme, *w*rote, lam*b*. Therefore, it is necessary to acquaint yourself with a few of the general rules or principles governing spelling. The rules have many exceptions, however, and learning rules will not guarantee perfect spelling. The following are principles worthwhile learning for future use.

Words with *ei* and *ie:*

An old copy-book expressed the ei — ie principle this way:

'If the letter *c* you spy
Place the *e* before the *i*.
If you do not spy a *c*
Place the *i* before the *e*
But *either, neither, leisure, seize*
Are four exceptions if you please.'
                    Anonymous
(Does that sound *weird* to you?)

After *c* the *e* comes before *i, a*nd when the sound of
the *ei* represents the long *a* in some other words.

conceive	receive	sleigh	veil
deceive	receipt	weigh	vein

Some exceptions to this rule are

counterfeit	foreign	height	heir

The *i* comes before *e* when the sound to be expressed
is the long ee.

believe	grief	niece
field	lien	thiet

The exceptions to this principle can not be classified although a few take
the *e* sound as in *either, leisure, neither, seize, weird,* while others follow
no rule, for example *mischief, sieve, view.*

Forming the plural of nouns:

In forming the plural of nouns, most nouns add *s* to the singular form.

cat	cats	table	tables

Nouns ending in *a, sh, ch, x* and *z* add *es* in forming the plural.
        class, classes; mesh, meshes; church, churches;
        box, boxes; fox, foxes; fez, fezes (also fezzes).

Words ending in *y:*

Words ending in y preceded by a consonant form the plural by changing
the *y* to *i* and adding *es.*

        candy, candies; copy, copies, lady, ladies

Words ending in *y* preceded by a vowel form their plural in the usual
manner.
        boy, boys; key, keys, ray, rays

Nouns ending in *o:*

Nouns ending in *o* preceded by a vowel use the *s* in the plural.

> radio, radios; rodeo, rodeos; taboo, taboos

The rule concerning words ending in *o* preceded by a consonant, for the plural use, add *es*, but there are many exceptions providing a wide choice between *es* and *s*.

> domino, dominos, dominoes; hero, heroes; tornado, tornados, tornadoes; torpedo, torpedos, torpedoes; volcano, volcanoes, volcanoes

Musical terms:

Musical terms nearly always take only the *s*.

> contralto, contraltos; oratorio, oratorios; solo, solos,
> piano, pianos

Exceptions:

Some few nouns follow none of the rules given and either remain the plural as in the singular or use a form of their own.

> deer, deer; sheep, sheep
> child, children
> grits, grits
> tooth, teeth
> ox, oxen

Compound nouns:

Compound nouns (more than one noun used together) use the plural form of the main word

> court-martial, courts martial
> father-in-law, fathers-in-law
> trade union, trade unions

But, if the words used as compound nouns are of equal importance, the plural of both are used.

> heads of departments
> men operators

Words ending in *f* or *fe:*

While most words ending in *f* or *fe* use *s* to form the plural, some change the *f* to *v* and *s* or *es* is added.

> chef, chefs; gulf, gulfs; muff. muffs;
> safe, safes; knife, knives; leaf, leaves;
> life, lives

When a compound is one solid word and ends in *ful* the plural is formed at the end of the compound.

> basketfuls, pocketfuls, spoonfuls

A number of words in our language are confusing because they sound the same, or very similar, but the spelling and the meaning is different. Alert yourself to such problems and rely on your dictionary when in doubt. A list of such troublesome words is:

accept	except	
affect	effect	
all ready	already	
allude	elude	
ascent	assent	
capital	capitol	
censor	censure	
cite	sight	site
compliment	complement	
correspondents	correspondence	
council	counsel	consul
creditable	credible	
decent	descent	dissent
desert	dessert	
elicit	illicit	
eminent	imminent	
farther	further	
loose	lose	
past	passed	
persecute	prosecute	
principal	principle	
stationery	stationary	

There are means at your disposal by which you can improve your spelling and advance your vocabulary at the same time. There are many compilations of words most commonly misspelled. These can be helpful, but in the end you need to recognize where your weakness lies. Keep a list of the words you persistently misspell. If you make a consistent and concerted effort to list and then use these words in their correct context in practice sentences, they will cease to be a problem. It is also an excellent means of making newly acquired words a part of your oral and written vocabulary.

It costs little, but some time, to use a good dictionary. Develop the habit so it becomes a conditioned reflex. When a word doesn't look right, reach for that dictionary. If you ever get beyond the stage of needing to consult one, you will be a phenomenon. Some basic knowledge of spelling is assured when you begin to look up a word, of course. Those who were subjected to the 'permissive school' in education have their own, particular problems. As a college instructor and guidance counselor, one such instance topped all others. A college freshman was having real difficulty putting anything down on paper. She was well above average intellectually. Her choice of the spoken word was excellent, but she had great difficulty in writing intelligible sentences. I asked "Don't you have a dictionary"? "Oh, yes, I have one but I can't use it". That seemed incredible, but it was true! She had never learned the alphabet. You can understand her plight. Many times she did not know the first letter of a word and sometimes she did not know the second or the third in relation to how to look for it without going through all the *Ds,* for example in the dictionary. Because she recognized her problem and her need, she took some remedial courses and in due time was able to proceed at the college level.

The importance and significance of owning and thoroughly knowing several good dictionaries can not be over-emphasized. Good dictionaries can provide you with a treasury of helpful information about every aspect of words. They offer the various shades of meaning that enable you not only to be certain of the correct word and spelling, but also to express yourself clearly, richly, sometimes even elegantly and artfully.

CHAPTER FIVE

Expressing Yourself

It's Not Just What You Say; It's How You Say It.

The preceding chapters afford guidelines to follow in order to write acceptably and understandably. But merely writing acceptable English is by no means the whole of writing. If you aspire to anything greater than writing business reports (and if you wish to rise above simple adequacy even in that), you must add a creative touch to your writing. This is as true at the elementary level of sentence construction as it is in the writing of novels.

Expressing yourself both accurately and well, while allowing for a bit of individualism, is not an easy task. Learn to use and expand your vocabulary, to use metaphor and simile effectively, and to know how far you can bend the rules of grammar before they break. The task is not impossible, a fact attested to by the number of successful writers in print today.

USE THE RIGHT WORD

Two books you should always have at hand when writing are a good dictionary and a good thesaurus. These are the essential tools of vocabulary building and correct word usage. If you have heard a word and think it might fit in a particular application, look it up in the dictionary unless you are positive of its meaning. Don't just check to see if the word means what you have in mind; check other meanings as well. Many times the word in question will have meanings other than the one you intend. If you find that this is the case, be sure that the context in which you employ the word limits its meaning to the one you desire.

Despite their pleas, Edgar's conviction stood firm.

In the context of this sentence, Edgar could be a man of unshakeable belief or a man about to be sentenced for a crime. The word conviction can be interpreted either way. A more carefully constructed sentence would make the intended meaning clear:

> Despite their pleas, Edgar's conviction for manslaughter stood firm.

> or

> Despite their pleas, Edgar's conviction stood firm with respect to freeing George.

If you know what you want to say but cannot find the word you need, the place to look is in a thesaurus. There words are arranged by meaning rather than alphabetically. Knowing how to use a thesaurus can be a great help in building your vocabulary, and consequently making your writing more interesting and more accurate. A thesaurus is also useful as a dictionary of synonyms. As such it can help you avoid the artless repetition of words by providing you with other ways to say the same thing. Take this example from the 'fragment'.

> (He) walked down the three worn steps, now shinyslick with the heavy mist, to the heavy iron bound door. Pushing it heavily open. . .

The use of the word heavy becomes repetitious and the lines lose much of their impact because of this. Unless you are using repetition for reinforcement or satirical effect, it will detract from your writing.

The words in a thesaurus are grouped under broad topic headings (e.g. Space, Matter, Volition) with more specific classifications under each. If you know the meaning you wish to convey, it is a simple process to work your way down through the subcategories until you come to the words that most specifically express your idea.

It is a wise writer who is aware of the popular and slang meanings of words as well as their dictionary meanings. Just as a word that has two possible readings according to the dictionary can cause confusion, so can a word that has a different slang meaning than its formal definition. Probably the most obvious example is the word gay:

> The young man seemed to her both charming and gay.

Although the dictionary does not yet reflect the change, the word gay is no longer taken to mean bright or merry. Instead the young man in the example here finds himself to be a homosexual in the eyes of most readers, regardless of what the writer may have intended.

There is no way that dictionaries can be completely accurate in reflecting current usages and their meanings. Any language that is used in daily speech is constantly changing: by the time a dictionary is compiled and goes to press, it is necessarily behind the times. This means that you must keep up with popular and slang usage on your own. Most generally accepted slang expressions appear eventually in newspapers and magazines, and their meanings can usually be gleaned from their context. At the least, if you try to keep yourself abreast of current usage, you can usually avoid being misread because the word you use has acquired new meaning. Otherwise, the results can be both confusing and embarrassing.

METAPHORIC LANGUAGE

The use of metaphoric language, metaphor and simile, is colorful as well as pervasive. In fact, you could not get through a day's normal conversation without it. Whenever you describe someone as being nutty as a fruitcake or sharp as a tack, or say that someone's remark was as subtle as a spiked baseball bat, you are employing metaphoric language. But such unthinking use of methaphor and simile often yields poor results. An understanding of what metaphoric language is and how it functions will enable you to make it work for you effectively.

A simile is a comparison that likens one thing to another for the purpose of defining it more clearly or describing it more vividly. The examples used in the preceding paragraph are similes. Simile is usually distinguished by the use of the words like and as to establish the comparison:

> fresh as the first crocus of spring
> eyes glowing softly like dying embers

The comparisons here are stated openly. Metaphors, on the other hand, tend to be more subtle; likeness is implied rather than clearly enumerated:

> Harry is such a snail at work.
> Mary was quite a social butterfly in school.

Metaphors also tend to be broader comparisons than similes. All the attributes of a snail -- slowness, intertia, and uselessness -- are implied as being Harry's without the need to list them. The use of metaphor can be a very compact means of transmitting information.

Metaphoric language is effective because it creates fresh and striking images in the mind of the reader or listener, or because it makes subjective feelings and abstract concepts understandable by comparing them to something known. Unfortunately, most metaphoric language in everyday speech does neither. When a metaphor or simile drops into common use, and becomes overworked and shopworn, it loses its ability to be fresh and strikingly informative.

> Warm as toast
> snug as a bug in a rug
> razor-sharp
> poor as a churchmouse
> on the horns of a dilemma
> hard as nails

All these examples would be considered trite and would fail to communicate effectively that which they were created to describe. If anything, less communication is achieved by their use than would be had they not been used at all. They have become so familiar that most people no longer react to them; they have become cliches. If you compare the following examples with this list of cliches, you can see the difference between effective and ineffective metaphoric language.

> The light stretched out like a cry for help, gleaming across the surface of the water.

> For murder, though it have no tongue, will speak with most miraculous organ. (William Shakespeare; Hamlet, Act II, Scene II)

These metaphors work because they present unusual and expressive images. Light is visualized as an urgent plea to convey the sudden intensity of its appearance, and murder is seen as speaking to show the force of its communication.

Once you can recognize and avoid cliches, there is still another metaphoric pitfall of which you must beware. That is the mixed metaphor. Take the following example from the 'fragment' in the introduction:

> A wall of silence hung over the room

Silence is initially likened to a wall, an over-used but fairly reasonable comparison. But if you start with a wall, you must see that it continues to behave like a wall. Walls are not found hanging over rooms. The mood of the scene in which this illustration appeared was tense, and this line was intended to accentuate that mood. Instead, the metaphor conveys a ridiculous image and destroys whatever tension was possible.

Avoiding mixed metaphors requires careful attention to the imaginary picture you are painting. Think it through before you write it down to be sure it will be internally consistent, then re-examine your image once you have it in front of you on paper. Any inconsistencies will show up if you take the time to carefully go over your work.

POETIC LICENSE CAN BE REVOKED

Unfortunately, many writers see nothing wrong with bending the rules of grammar to suit their particular tastes. They have a tendency to view mixed metaphors as profound insights, and seasoning their work liberally with fragmented, questionable sentences in search of a distinctive style. The rules of composition covered here are widely used and are useful because they make written communication clear and understandable. Usually, when these rules are not followed or when they are improperly applied, confusion on the part of the reader is the result. Take particular notice of the word *usually* in the last sentence; it is there for good reason. Most of the great writers of fiction have either bent or broken the rules of composition in developing their individual styles. So, to a certain extent, the rules were made to be broken.

Those who step beyond the boundaries of proper usage in pursuit of new and more effective means of self-expression are said to have taken poetic license. But as in any form of licensing, there are guidelines to follow as well as penalties for its abuse. The most important point to remember here is that you must know the rules before you can presume to break them. It may be argued that Shakespeare used mixed metaphors (he did) or that Heminway wrote sentence fragments (he did). But unless you can equate your writing with theirs, their example is not sufficient justification for liberties you may take. Rather, each instance which seems to call for a departure from the grammatical norm must be evaluated on its own merits. When considering such a case, keep the following guidelines in mind.

1) Be sure you are not sacrificing clarity for effect.
2) Keep your intended audience in mind.

There is a great temptation to write thoughts the way you hear them in your mind's ear. Indeed, this will often give your writing a more natural flow. But writing is a visual medium, and unless you put your thoughts on paper so that anyone for whom you might be writing can understand them clearly, your writing will not be read the way you meant it to be. Take this example from the 'fragment' in the introduction:

> Two knocks, a pause, then three, another pause,
> then two again. The ritual was executed correctly but
> still no response came from within.

The first sentence has no verb and is a fragment. It could be left that way for esthetic purposes, but it is just as effective if joined to the following sentence by a semi-colon. In fact, since the fragment is closely related to that sentence, moreso than to the one which precedes it, the fragment is more clearly understood attached than by itself:

> The blackness of the night was here unrelieved by even the faintest glimmer of municipal illumination, and only the most painstaking gathering of stray lamplight. . . served to identify the number as 1130. Two knocks, a pause, then three, another pause, then two again; the ritual was executed correctly but still no response came from within.

Unless your meaning is made *less* clear by strict adherence to proper compositional form, you should not bend the rules. Otherwise your writing is likely to appear more unskilled than creative. This brings up the second guideline, for there are many situations in which even truly creative rule-bending is not acceptable. Most formal writing does not allow for the use of creative grammar, and it is usually unwise to push the boundaries of proper composition when writing for anyone whose reactions you cannot gauge in advance (such as a publisher). Many times what seems both innovative and expressive to you will appear to him as shoddy workmanship. When you have written a successful novel or are a recognized journalist, then you can argue points of composition with your publishers. Until then, they have no reason to be persuaded.

From purely a composition point of view, this revised version of the novel fragment should be studied on two levels. As the text appears, each paragraph is printed exactly as it appeared in the introduction, with errors cited in the left hand margin. For an examination of those problems, it will be easier if the revised draft of each paragraph is ignored so that you can concentrate on the internal problems of the original. Careful study of each problem will help create an awareness of such common faults.

The revised version of the novel fragment points up other writing demands, sometimes at the expense of the composition problem in question. As Roy Porter explains in his book on juvenile writing, revision can be an endless problem in itself, where good writing is the object. He draws on a question period following a public speaking engagement when a librarian asked Dorothy Aldis how long she worked on one of her poems. Mrs. Aldis' reply was, "Sometimes, so long, I don't care if I ever see it again."

Good writing is rewritten writing. Rather than print all the drafts our budding novelist worked over, we ask you to make the leap from the original to final version, bearing in mind the questions of composition at issue, as well as the cuts that must be made in sound revision work. There is something to be learned at both levels for the serious reader.

Parenthetically, the revised fragment illustrates some considerations outside the purpose of a book on composition. Once the rules of composition are understood and assimilated as part of your writing tools, each takes its place, almost unconsciously, and adds to the total effect of your writing. For example, the author of the novel fragment ultimately had to be concerned with a firmer control over tone, distracting details, expression that makes the first version sound over-stated and naive. Such demands are only incidentally involved in a study of composition. There are other writing requirements and dimensions of good writing and, along with a sound foundation in composition, are equally important. Writing techniques are covered in other books of The *Writer's Manual* and should be understood once the fundamentals of composition are learned.

⧉⧉⧉

<table>
<tr>
<td>fragment

shift in tense
(the italicized
words are in the
wrong tense)</td>
<td>He walked slowly through the gathering evening mist, his steps punctuated by the distant tolling of the cathedral bell. *Eleven o'clock.* At the corner, he *stops,* beneath the filtered glow of the streetlamp. The address on the card in his hands *reads* 1130 Calle Niebla, and it was already damp as he put it back into his pocket.</td>
</tr>
</table>

He walked slowly through the gathering evening mist, his steps punctuated by the distant tolling of the cathedral bell: eleven o'clock. At the corner he stopped beneath the filtered glow of the streetlamp. The address on the card in his hand read 1130 Calle Niebla. It felt damp as he put it back into his pocket.

<table>
<tr>
<td>unnecessary
punctuation
(awkward)

awkward
repetition
no paragraph</td>
<td>Turning down the alleyway to his right, his slow, measured steps took him to a doorway marked by a faint orange light and a sign, whose legend, obscured by the accumulated grime of many years, was illegible to all but those who knew its inscription by heart. He looked briefly around, making sure he was not observed; then walked down the three worn steps, now shiny-slick with the *heavy* mist, to the *heavy* iron bound door.

Pushing it heavily open with the long, slender fingers of of his left hand, he thought to himself, 'half an hour left.'</td>
</tr>
</table>

Turning down the alleyway to his right, his measured steps took him to a doorway marked by a faint orange light. The name, obscured by the accumulated grime of many years, was illegible to all but those who knew it by hea... He looked briefly around making sure he was not seen, then walked down the three worn steps, shiny-slick with the thick mist, to the heavy metal bound door. Pushing it slowly open he thought to himself, 'half an hour left.'

<table>
<tr>
<td>comma
-comma

run-on</td>
<td>As he made his way to the bar he called out, "Cerveza, Jose, San Miguel." The bartender, a squat heavy man with a bristling black moustache turned and stared for a moment and then poured the beer and retreated to the far end of the counter. Quentin sipped at his glass and watched the slow</td>
</tr>
</table>

progress of the clock on the far wall. There was no-one there he knew, except for Jose. *He* moved slowly down the bar and spoke softly to him. "If anyone asks, I was here tonight until 12:30." *He* slid a bill across the counter

unclear pronouns

As he made his way to the bar he called out. "Cerveza, Jose, San Miguel.." The bartender, a squat, heavy man with a bristling black moustache, turned and stared for a moment. He poured his new guest a beer and retreated to the far end of the counter. Quentin sipped at his glass and watched the slow movement of the minute hand of the clock on the far wall. There was no-one there he knew, except for Jose. Quentin moved quietly down the bar and spoke softly to him. "If anyone asks, I was here tonight until 12:30." He slid a bill across the counter.

Returning to his stool, Quentin idled his way through his remaining beer. *Watching the light from the dull lamp behind him strike smouldering sparks in the opal on his right forefinger.* He let his mind wander ahead, to the he could not understand. That morning, when he found the meeting card with the pencilled note on its back beneath his hotel room door, he had been surprised: he had not expected to meet any of his contacts face to face. Now he wonderd at the change in plans. His was the kind of profession where ignorance was, if not bliss, at least security. Perhaps someone was onto them; perhaps this was the only way to safely alert him to the change in plans, perhaps . . .

fragment

unnecessary comma

misused colon

Returning to his stool, Quentin nursed his beer, feeling the wetness of the glass on his hand. The light from the dull lamp behind him reflected in the wet opal on his right forefinger. He let his mind wander to the meeting that he could not understand. That morning, when he found the card with the pencilled note on its back beneath his hotelroom door, he had been surprised; he had not expected to meet any of his contacts face to face. He wondered about the change in plans. His was the kind of profession where ignorance was, if not bliss, at least security. Perhaps someone was onto them; perhaps this was the only way to safely alert him to the change in plans; perhaps . . .

The clock struck 11:30. Quentin stood abruptly, took a bill and some coins from his pocket, and dropped it on the counter. Back on the damp, shrouded street he turned to his right and walked swiftly into the beckoning darkness. Two blocks on, a turn to the left, and he walked up the unsteady stairs of the third house on the right hand side.

awkward repetition

fragment

fragment

no
referent
for
pronoun

The blackness of the night was here unrelieved by even the faintest glimmer of municipal illumination, and only the most painstaking gathering of stray lamplight, escaped from behind carefully drawn shades and curtains, served to identify the number as 1130. Two *knocks, a pause,* then *three, another pause, then two again.* The ritual was executed correctly, but still no response came from within. After a long moment of anticipation, Quentin repeated the formula. Still no answer. Listening closely for any sign of life behind the door, he became aware of footsteps echoing distantly, then nearer. They moved steadily down the street Quentin had just left, then quite unexpectedly, turned at the corner just as he had done moments before. Quentin's hand was on the doorknob, and before he had time to think about it, or anything else for that matter, he stood inside a darkened, unfamiliar hall.

The clock struck 11:30. He had stayed too long. He stood abruptly, took a bill and some coins from his pockets, and dropped them on the counter. Back on the damp street he turned to his right and moved swiftly into the darkness. Two blocks on, a turn to the left, and he walked up the unsteady stairs of the third house on the right. The blackness of the night was unrelieved by any glimmer of municipal illumination. He squinted to identify the number as 1130. Two knocks, a pause, then three, another pause, then two again; the ritual was executed correctly but no response came from within. After a long moment he repeated the knock. Listening closely for any sound within, he became of aware of footsteps echoing distantly, then nearer. They moved steadily down the street he had just left, then, quite unexpectedly, turned at the corner just as he had done moments before. His hand was on the doorknob, and before he had time to think about what he was doing, he stood inside a dark, unfamiliar hall.

There are no grammatical errors in this next paragraph.

The door was safely closed behind him, and Quentin listened as the footsteps passed the house slowly and faded into the distance. He waited a moment to be sure they did not return, then moved cautiously down the narrow hall. The door at the far end was ajar. It opened inward to a light push.

A faint odor of burnt rope, mingled with some sort of incense or perfume, greeted Quentin as he stepped inside. His eyes were accustomed to the darkness by now, but the

mixed
metaphor

stillness disturbed his ears. *A wall of silence hung over the room,* and even his breathing seemed an intrusion. He checked the room quickly with eyes, and once he had determined that he was alone, turned on the overhead light.

A faint odor of burnt rope mingled with incense or perfume struck him as he stepped inside. His eyes grew accustomed to the darkness, but the stillness disturbed him. Silence hung shroud-like over the room; even his breathing seemed an intrusion. He checked the room quickly, and once he was convinced he was alone, turned on the overhead light.

tense
agreement
with
preceding
paragraphs

As the room *takes* on a ruddy warmth from the glowing tinted fixture, Quentin *discovers* that he was wrong in assuming his solitariness. There, slumpled over the circular table in the center of the deep persian carpet, is a girl dressed in embroidered jeans and a white peasant blouse. The dark red stain, still spreading beneath her left arm, *reminds* him that in the future he must be punctual. A brief glance at his watch tells him he was seven minutes late. 'Seven minutes,' he thinks to himself as he silently *switches* off the light. 'Seven minutes,' the number *revolves* quietly in his mind as he *slips* out the door, and assuring himself that he leaves as remarked as he arrived, *moves* slowly down the dampening streets toward his next appointment.

Slumped over the circular table in the center of the deep persian carpet was a girl dressed in embroidered jeans and white peasant blouse. A dark red stain was still spreading slowly beneath her left arm. A glance at his watch told him that he had been* only seven minutes late.

'Seven minutes,' he thought to himself as he switched off the light. 'Seven minutes,' the number revolved quietly in his mind as he slipped out the door. Assuring himself that he left as unmarked as he arrived, he moved slowly down the damp streets toward his next appointment.

---

*Note — While it would be acceptable to leave the verb here in the imperfect (e.g. "A glance at his watch told him that he was only seven minutes late."), the fact that it appears in the past perfect in the original makes the change to the imperfect in the corrected version necessary to maintain the same relationship between this verb and the predicate of the main clause of the sentence ("told") that held in the original.

BIBLIOGRAPHY

A Manual of Style, The University of Chicago Press, Chicago, 1949

Fisher, James B., *English Composition,* Visual Education Assn., Dayton, Ohio, 1963.

Flesch, Rudolf, *The Art of Plain Talk,* Harper & Brothers, New York, 1946

Flesch, Rudolf & Lass, A.H., *A New Guide to Better Writing,* Popular Library, New York, 1949

Hodges, John C. & Whitten, Mary E., *Harbrace College Handbook,* Harcourt Brace & World, Inc., New York, 1967.

Kuehl, John, *Write and Rewrite,* Meredith Press, New York, 1967

Perrin, Porter G. & Smith, George H., *Handbook of Current English, 3rd Ed.,* Scott, Foresman and Co., Glenview, Ill., 1968

Strunk, William Jr., *The Elements of Style,* The Macmillan Co., New York, 1959.

Weaver, Richard M., *A Rhetoric and Composition Handbook,* William Morrow & Co., New York, 1967.

College textbook, promotion of, 678
Collier's, 199, 358
Collin, 546
Colon, to introduce quotation, 729; between title and subtitle, 736; 772, 796, 798, 900-902; defined, 900; in formal letters, 900; before a series or list, 900; in times of day, 901; in Biblical reference, 901; in formal quotation, 901; to emphasize statements, 901; between clauses, 901; not between verb and its object, 901; not between preposition and its object, 901
Color, in writing, 829-830
Columbia, 369
"Columbo," 599, 654
Combined Book Exhibit, 486
Comedy, 589-590
Comma, 774-776, 793, 794, 893-899; defined, 893; overuse of, 893; in forms of address, dates, and titles, 893; in place of conjunction, 893; to prevent misunderstanding, 894; after introductory words, 894; with Etc., 894; in compound sentences, 894; not after coordinating conjunction, 895; comma splice, 896; omitted with short clauses, 896; in series, 896; between coordinate adjectives, 896; with restrictive and non-restrictive words, 897; to set off parenthetical words, 898; in direct address, 898; with interjections, 898; in dialogue, 898; to indicate contrast, 898; with quotation marks, 904
Commercial copywriting, 610, 618
Commissioned writing, 654-655
Common law literary property, 117
Common measure, 537
Common metre, 537
Common particular measure, 537
Communication, 829
Company publications, 382
Compensation, 538, 540
Complex sentence, 938-939
Complimentary copies for author, 815, 816

Composition, 885, 886, 888, 889
Compound sentence, do not confuse with compound verb, 895; joined by coordinate conjunction, 895, 938; joined by semi-colon, 899, 938; defined, 938
Concentration, 207
Concrete language, 722-723
Concrete poetry, 537
Confessions of Nat Turner, The, 336
Conflict, 123; nuts and bolts of fiction, 125; 565, 567, 558-569
Congress, Library of, 267
Congreve, William, 298
Conjunction, 926; coordinating, 895, 934; correlative, 935; subordinating, 935
Connell, Evan S. Jr., 152
Connotation, 852, 854, 855
Conoco Today, 383
Conrad, Joseph, 32, 137, 143, 161, 305
Consonance, 524, 538, 541
Consumer magazines, 367; rates, 367; literary and little magazines, 367; religious magazines, 368; sports and outdoors, 369; regionals and metropolitans, 370; teen and young adult, 371; juvenile, 372; alternate and radical, 373; newspaper Sunday supplements, 373
Contests, 652
Context, use of, 853
Continuity, in paragraphing, 835, 838
Contractions, 33
Contracts, 815-816
"Convergence of the Twain, The," 511
Cooley High, 602
Cooper James Fenimore, 295
Co-operative advertising, 671
Coordinating conjunction, 895, 934
Copyright, 15, 17, 18; in the name of the publisher, 20; expiration law, 72; all about copyright 117; copyright application, 117; definition of copyright, 117; copyright owner, 117; unpublished works, 117; statutory copyright, 117, 119; copyright for unpublished work, 117; fees, 117;